Saint Thomas Aquinas

VOLUME 2

JEAN-PIERRE TORRELL, O.P.

Saint Thomas Aquinas

VOLUME 2

Spiritual Master

translated by

Robert Royal

The Catholic University of America Press

Washington, D.C.

Originally published as *Saint Thomas d'Aquin, Maître Spirituel* by
Editions Universitaires, Fribourg, Suisse, and Editions du Cerf, Paris.
Copyright © 1996 Editions Universitaires, Fribourg, Suisse.

The paper used in this publication meets the minimum requirements of
American National Standards for Information Science—Permanence of
Paper for Printed Library materials, ANSI Z39.48-1984.

∞

Library of Congress Cataloging-in-Publication Data
Torrell, Jean-Pierre.
[Initiation à Saint Thomas d'Aquin. English]
Saint Thomas Aquinas, Volume 2 : spiritual master /
Jean-Pierre Torrell ; translated by Robert Royal.
p. cm.
includes bibliographical references and indexes.
1. Thomas, Aquinas, Saint, 1225?–1274. 2. Christian saints—Italy—
Biography. 3. Theology, Doctrinal—History—Middle Ages.
600–1500. 4. Catholic Church—Doctrines—History. I. Title.
BX4700.T6T5713 2003
230´.2´092—dc20
95-42079
ISBN 0-8132-1315-0 (cloth : alk. paper)
ISBN 0-8132-1316-9 (pbk. : alk. paper)

Contents

Preface

For anyone who knows Saint Thomas Aquinas only by hearsay, it may be surprising to see him presented as a spiritual master. The author of the *Summa Theologiae* is certainly well known as a first-class intellectual, but not as a mystic. At the risk of surprising still further, we must not hesitate to say that his intellectual renown is partly misleading. The figure who at times seems to be known only for his philosophy is also first and foremost a theologian, a commentator on Sacred Scripture, an attentive student of the Fathers of the Church, and a man concerned about the spiritual and pastoral repercussions of his teaching. His disciples know this well and have long labored to facilitate access to their Master's secret garden.

The list of authors who have tried to reveal this unknown Thomas would be too long to reproduce here, but we must mention the name Louis Chardon (1595–1651), whose *La Croix de Jésus* is a stylistic masterpiece that draws on great themes from Thomas in a very personal way.[1] Closer to our own time, Father Mennessier has edited two highly successful anthologies of texts by Friar Thomas.[2] As everyone knows, forty years ago (the book has been frequently reprinted) Father Chenu did not hesitate to include Saint Thomas in the "Spiritual Masters" series.[3] More re-

---

1. Louis Chardon, *La Croix de Jésus*, in which the most beautiful truths of mystical theology and grace are set forth (Paris, 1647; new ed., 1937); translated into English as *The Cross of Jesus*, trans. Richard T. Murphy (St. Louis, Mo., 1957). For an overview of the work with some critical questions, see Yves Congar, *Les voies du Dieu vivant* (Paris, 1962); parts 1 and 2 translated into English as *The Revelation of God*, trans. A. Manson and L. C. Sheppard (New York, 1968), 116–28. Besides Chardon, there is a whole series of seventeenth-century authors worth mentioning; on this see J.-P. Torrell, *La théologie catholique* (Paris, 1994), 39–41.

2. A.-I. Mennessier, *Saint Thomas d'Aquin* (Paris, 1942, ²1957); *Saint Thomas d'Aquin: L'homme chrétien* (Paris, 1998). The first of these collections centers on the organic conditions for spiritual progress. The second pays more attention to the economy of salvation and to the condition of man as sinner. In each case, the introductions and commentaries help greatly in understanding the texts.

3. M.-D. Chenu, *Saint Thomas d'Aquin et la théologie* (Paris, 1959).

cently, the *Dictionnaire de spiritualité* devoted a long article[4] to Thomas and, shortly after that, *La Vie spirituelle* dedicated a special issue to him.[5] In writing *L'initiation à saint Thomas*, published several years ago, I myself had a chance to see how this side of the personality and doctrine of the Master from Aquino, which deserves attention, is hardly known.[6]

In the tradition of Saint John the Evangelist and the Fathers of the Church, Thomas Aquinas's theology is clearly oriented towards contemplation and is as deeply spiritual as it is doctrinal. One could say, I believe, that it is even more spiritual than rigorously doctrinal. The very clarity of his intellectual, philosophical, and theological commitments is immediately reflected in a religious attitude that has no equivalent except that of a mystic wholly consumed by love of the absolute. Thomas himself bears witness to this at the end of his life when he leaves the "straw" of words for the "grain" of definitive reality. His own personal example shows us that there is no need to add to his theology, because it already leads to piety. We only need to pursue to the full extent what the theology itself requires of us.

Anyone who has read the preliminary outline in the *Dictionnaire de spiritualité* will quickly see that many of the themes found there will also be found here. The deep, structural lines of Thomas's thought obviously have not changed and no one has contradicted that earlier presentation. I am not seeking originality at all costs in the present volume. I hope to give greater scope to certain themes too briefly considered in the first treatment. I will also address other matters that were only elliptically alluded to and, sometimes, not mentioned at all. My goal, however, is not to reconstruct a spiritual teaching that Thomas himself did not deem useful to write. Rather, I wish to draw the general outline of that spirituality and, thus, to facilitate access to those hidden riches.

In spite of that hope, I cannot treat everything and, in several instances, it will be necessary to stop short of full exploration of paths that are opened up. Those familiar with the subject will notice that I try to fol-

4. J.-P. Torrell, "Thomas d'Aquin (saint)," *DS*, vol. 15 (1991), col. 718–73; see in particular the second part: "Théologie spirituelle," col. 749–73.

5. "Saint Thomas d'Aquin, Maître Spirituel?," *La Vie spirituelle* 147 (1993).

6. J.-P. Torrell, *Initiation à saint Thomas d'Aquin, Sa personne et son oeuvre* (Paris-Fribourg, 1993). This book has been translated into Italian (1994) and German (1995), and into English as *Saint Thomas Aquinas: The Person and His Work*, trans. Robert Royal (Washington, D.C, 1996).

low closely the large doctrinal options, but without obligating myself to take up all of them in every detail or to go very far into debates with the learned and the experts. Without entirely neglecting the underpinnings of certain positions and the legitimate diversity among certain disciples, I will more often cite at length the very texts of the Master. They are not only less difficult in technical terms than is sometimes believed, but they are also often quite beautiful and testify precisely to the spirituality that I hope to help readers perceive.

Some may ask about the originality—and perhaps even the real existence—of that spirituality. We will often note the origin in John, Paul, or Augustine of various attitudes, ideas, or recommendations. But is there really a spirituality unique to Thomas? Let us leave this question open at the outset. Little by little the answer should emerge in the course of the following chapters, but I shall not try to present it in a systematic spirit. Nothing is more foreign to Thomas's spirit than ideology or apologetics. It would be odd to praise him with arguments that he would be the first to see are weak. Truth is beautiful enough; it does not need false ornaments.

It may also be helpful to add that readers should not look for edifying proposals here. I certainly want this study to be accessible to the largest number of people possible and will try to avoid useless technical subtleties. But without aiming at erudition, we cannot avoid the rigor necessary for understanding a theologian who tries to establish the true foundations for his teaching. Assembling the evidence for the spiritual dimension of the great Thomistic themes does not require the adoption of a tone more suited to a homily or meditation. I do not wish to depreciate those literary genres but rather to acknowledge my inability to use them with the proper degree of suppleness. Others, more fortunate than I am, will eventually take up this work and draw from it a more heartfelt piety for a larger public. Nothing will bring more pleasure to the disciple of Saint Thomas who does not forget the "little old woman" whom the master sometimes finds greater than the learned doctors.

Even when it bears the name of a single author, a book is never solely the work of one person. It is my pleasure to mention here Denise Bouthillier, Denis Chardonnens, and especially Gilles Emery. They provided friendly companionship throughout the writing of this book and their close and critical reading of the manuscript resulted in many valuable suggestions. I warmly thank all of them.

Abbreviations

❧

The list below explains the signs in current use and employed in the notes and bibliography. Titles of books or articles cited in an abridged form are completely spelled out in the bibliography.

AFP	Archivum fratrum praedicatorum, Rome.
AHDLMA	Archives d'histoire doctrinale et littéraire du moyen âge, Paris.
ALMA	Archivum Latinitatis medii aevi, Bruxelles.
BA	Bibliothèque augustinienne (Oeuvres de saint Augustin), Paris.
BPM	Bulletin de Philosophie Médiévale, Louvain-la-Neuve.
CCSL	Corpus Christianorum-Series Latina, Turnhout.
DCL	La Documentation Catholique, Paris.
DS	Dictionnaire de spiritualité, Paris.
DTC	Dictionnaire de théologie catholique, Paris.
ETL	Ephemerides theologicae lovanienses, Louvain.
FOTC	The Fathers of the Church: A New Translation, Washington
FZPT	Freiburger Zeitschrift für Philosophie und Theologie, Fribourg (Suisse).
JTS	The Journal of Theological Studies, London.
MM	Miscellanea mediaevalia, Berlin.
MS	Mediaeval Studies, Toronto.
MSR	Mélanges de science religieuse, Lille.
MThZ	Münchener theologische Zeitschrift, Munich.
NRT	Nouvelle revue théologique, Louvain.
NV	Nova et vetera, Genève.
PL	Patrologia Latina (J.P. Migne), Paris.
RET	Revista Espagnola de Teologia, Madrid.
RevSR	Revue des Sciences religieuses, Strasbourg.

RFNS	Rivista di filosofia neoscolastica, Milan.
RPL	Revue philosophique de Louvain, Louvain.
RSPT	Revue des sciences philosophiques et théologiques, Paris.
RT	Revue thomiste, Toulouse
RTAM	Recherches de théologie ancienne et médiévale, Louvain.
SC	Sources chrétiennes, Paris.
STGMA	Studien und Texte zur Geistesgeschichte des Mittelalters, Leiden.
VS	Vie spirituelle, Paris.

Saint Thomas Aquinas

VOLUME 2

ᶜ⬿

Theology and Spirituality

The first thing to do is examine some terms. "Spirituality" is one of the vaguest words in contemporary religious language. People think they know what they mean when they use it, but it does not necessarily convey the same meaning to each person who hears it. It is, therefore, useless to use the word without further qualification. But if we first define what we are seeking, we will discover rather quickly that, even though the modern term "spirituality" is not the same as the old Latin term *spiritualitas*,[1] we easily find in Thomas the thing itself without the word. Before turning to that, however, we must first recall what theology is for Thomas and how he practices it. This only seems to be a detour. In reality, it will take us directly to a conclusion.

Sacra doctrina

We will use the word "theology" here because it has become accepted. Still, we know that Thomas was not a professor of theology but a master in Sacred Scripture *(magister in sacra pagina)*. He himself speaks of his field as *sacra doctrina*. He knows the term *theologia* and uses it rather often, but he does not use it with the same meaning we give it.[2] We ought to add

---

1. J.-P. Torrell, "*Spiritualitas* chez S. Thomas d'Aquin. Contribution à l'histoire d'un mot," *RSPT* 73 (1989): 575–84.
2. I. Biffi, "Per una analisi semantica dei lemmi *theologia, theologus, theologizo,* in San Tommaso: un saggio metodologico nell'uso dell'Index Thomisticus," *Teologia* 3 (1978): 148–63, revised and extended in I. Biffi, "Ricerche su 'Theologia' e su 'Metaphysica' in san Tommaso," chap. 3 in *Teologia, Storia e Contemplazione in Tommaso d'Aquino,* Saggi (Milan, 1995), 129–75.

to the word "theology," therefore, the richness of meaning that he himself gives to the expression *sacra doctrina*.

The term *sacra doctrina* covers a wide scope. It would be easy to count a dozen meanings that do not exactly overlap, but that fall into two large categories. In its *objective* meaning ("what" is taught), it initially applies to Christian truth as a body of doctrine, and doctrine in a wide sense that runs from Scripture to theology. In its *active* meaning (the act of teaching), *doctrina* suggests every activity through which Christian truth comes to us: God's instruction, made known through revelation, Tradition, Church teaching (including catechesis), and, naturally, theological training.[3]

To get a better idea of the territory covered by *sacra doctrina*, it is useful to think about Thomas's work and activities. Besides the great learned works such as his writing on the *Sentences*, the syntheses of the two *Summae*, and the commentaries on Sacred Scripture and Aristotle, we should mention two special areas. On the one hand, there are his various theological consultations and brief texts written "by request." Whether the question is taking interest on a loan or the motion of the heart, the best political regime, astrology, lots, or magic, Thomas was consulted in his day about a very wide range of subjects.[4] On the other hand, we have his work as a preacher. Although he was not a master of this art, his homilies allow us to see the natural connections in his thought among the various ways of service to the Word of God.[5]

Sacra doctrina embraces all this for Saint Thomas, and he certainly did not think himself any less a theologian in the pulpit than in the University chair. But to grasp this concept in the fullest form in which Thomas practiced it, we must see in it three main dimensions. First, the "speculative" dimension, for which Thomas is rightly esteemed and which is properly called the *intellectus fidei*: reason's effort to comprehend what is held by faith. This initial aspect of his thought was the favorite of commentators such as Capreolus, Cajetan, and John of Saint Thomas, but it is far

---

3. For more detail, see Yves Congar, "Tradition et sacra doctrina chez saint Thomas, d'Aquin," in J. Betz and H. Fries, eds., *Église et Tradition* (Le Puy, 1963), 157–94; A. Patfoort, *Thomas d'Aquin. Les clefs d'une théologie* (Paris, 1983), 13–47.

4. These "little works" (sometimes quite large!) may be found in vols. 40–43 of the Leonine Edition (hereafter, Leonine).

5. I have tried to describe this in J.-P. Torrell, "La pratique pastorale d'un théologien du XIIIe siècle. Thomas d'Aquin prédicateur," *RT* 82 (1982): 213–45, reprinted in J.-P. Torrell, *Recherches thomasiennes: Études revues et augmentées* (Paris, 2000), 282–312.

from being the only one. Thomas also pursued another line that today we would call "historical-positive." The apparent anachronism exists only in the terms, because in reality it designates exactly what Thomas did. He commented on Scripture his whole life—it was the primary form through which he taught—and he never stopped collecting materials on the subject from the Church Fathers and conciliar history.[6] This dimension has been too little utilized by his followers. There was a time when it entirely disappeared from sight through an overemphasis on Thomas's philosophical apparatus. Only in our time have the riches of the scriptural commentaries been rediscovered, along with Thomas's great debt to Saint Augustine. But there is a third line that might be called "mystical," if we are careful about defining the meaning of that term, which is to be found in the "practical" character that Thomas sees in theology (what we have grown accustomed to call "moral theology").

These three primary orientations, which Thomas joined in the undivided unity of *sacra doctrina*, did not take long to become separated again after his death. Since the beginning of the fourteenth century—whatever other interest that period may have for intellectual history—a whole series of factors, which cannot detain us here, contributed to what must be called a fragmenting of theological knowledge into various fields of specialization and perhaps even to its utter breakdown. Many people have observed—some to deplore, other to celebrate—the absence and even the impossibility of a theological synthesis in our day. In fact, we are the heirs of a process of dissociation that began centuries ago.[7]

Thomas's speculative line has been sidetracked into a "science of conclusions" in which the theologian's art lies in discovering, by means of syllogisms, *new* conclusions, candidates for adoption by the magisterium by virtue of their theological certitude. That way of doing theology is so out-of-fashion today that, in disappearing, it has taken with it speculative theology itself as an attempt to understand faith. The historical-positive line, cut off from the speculative (from which it originally had emerged), has evolved more and more into highly specialized historical erudition. It is certainly the most developed branch of theology (one thinks of the progress of both exegesis and patristics). And one could only be glad if its claim to independence in its research and methods did not carry it still fur-

6. Cf. J.-P. Torrell, *Saint Thomas Aquinas*, 54–59 and 136–41.
7. I have sketched the large lines of this history in *La théologie catholique*, chap. 2.

ther from theology proper, since its labors do not make sense except within an organic theology. As for the mystical line, unappreciated by either of the other two, it has tried to set itself up as an autonomous offshoot with an understandable tendency toward anti-intellectualism. Thus, numerous works of an "ascetic and mystical" theology (some quite noteworthy) continued to appear in the first half of the twentieth century. At least they are not like the authors of the manuals who, compensating for the aridity of their theology, added pious corollaries to the demonstrations. Theology, properly understood, should respect all three dimensions. As we examine what theology is for the Thomistic school, which continues a tradition begun by Saint Augustine and Saint Anselm, this will become clearer.

A School of Theologal Life

Before all else, theology is an expression of a God-informed life, an activity in which the virtues of faith, hope, and charity are given full scope. If we speak primarily of faith in the following pages, it is to keep things brief and to emphasize the explanatory core of certain aspects of theology. But it should be clear that this faith is not a pure intellectual adhesion to the collection of truths that occupy the theologian. It is rather, in Saint Thomas as in the Bible, the living attachment of the whole person to the divine Reality to which the person is united through faith by means of the formulas that convey that Reality to us.

This linking of theology to faith is already indicated in expressions current in Thomas's time such as "understanding of the faith" (*intellectus fidei*) and "faith seeking understanding" (*fides quaerens intellectum*). As far back as we can go in history, the thinkers who have reflected on their methods have given voice to that conviction. Although the word "theology" appeared only much later, Saint Augustine already speaks of that *scientia* "which engenders, nourishes, defends, strengthens, the sovereignly salutary faith."[8] In the final prayer of his great work on the Trinity, where he repeats in the presence of God what he wished to do, Augustine beautifully explains, "Aiming my efforts according to that rule of faith, as much as I have been able . . . I have sought Thee; *I desired to see in understanding what I held by faith.*"[9] It is quite remarkable that the inventor of the formula *fides quaerens intellectum*, Saint Anselm, also expresses his theo-

---

8. *De Trinitate* XIV, 6, 3 (BA 16, 348).
9. Ibid., XV, 28, 51 (BA 16, 523): "Desideravi intellectu uidere quod credidi."

logical project in a prayer: "I desire to understand at least a little Your truth, Your truth that my heart believes and loves." And he adds something rather significant: "I do not seek to understand in order to believe, but I *believe in order to understand (credo ut intelligam)*."[10]

The origin of this expression lies in a verse from Scripture, which reads in the Septuagint version: "If you do not believe, you will not understand."[11] Augustine, too, often repeated this verse, but he did not shrink from formulating a complementary truth: "We must understand in order to believe, but we must also believe in order to understand."[12] In both Anselm and Augustine, therefore, we have at the outset faith and its obscurity, as well as intelligence and its desire to know, along with the certainty that as each spurs on the other, both will benefit from their common endeavor. That conviction remained the common property of theology throughout the centuries; contemporary theologians, like those in the past, may differ on many points, but if they wish to remain theologians, they cannot disagree on the connection of theology and faith.[13]

In the same vein as Saint Augustine and Saint Anselm, Saint Thomas's thought maintains that theology's origin is its relationship to faith, and that it would not even exist without constant dependance on faith. Theology finds in faith not merely its point of departure but also its reason for being. Without faith, not only would theology lack justification, it would have no object. This is easy to understand, because only faith allows the theologian to come into possession of his object. Perhaps a comparison with philosophy will help clarify this point. If there were no possibility within us of grasping the real, our reasoning would be nothing but pure artifice. Even if it proceeded according to the strictest logic, it would have nothing to say about reality. Faith is that added capacity in us that requires human intelligence to rise to "the height" of divine reality. It allows us to be reunited with the divine because "the act of believing does not reach completion in the formulas [of the Creed] but in [divine] reality itself."[14]

---

10. *Proslogion* I, *Opera Omnia*, ed. F. S. Schmitt, p. 100.

11. Isa. 7:9. The original Hebrew is more accurately rendered: ". . . you will not persist."

12. *Sermo* XLIII, 7, 9 (PL 38, 58).

13. To cite only one example from this century, Edward Schillebeeckx speaks of faith as "the point of departure and permanent foundation for theology," and he develops the idea that "faith intrinsically calls upon theology." Cf. *Revelation and Theology*, trans. N. D. Smith (New York, 1967), 93–99.

14. *Summa theologiae* (ST) IIa IIae q. 1 a. 2 ad 2: "Actus autem credentis non terminatur ad enuntiabile sed ad rem."

Without faith, we would have only hollow formulas, and our most beautiful constructions would be nothing more than empty shells. With faith, we can truly begin to be theologians. Thomas makes an astonishing observation about his patron saint: when he falls on his knees at the feet of the Risen Lord who shows him his wounds, the apostle Thomas, the doubter, immediately becomes a good theologian.[15]

Faith does not adhere to its object in a static fashion. Animated by an ardent desire that comes from love for divine truth, which penetrates faith in various places, from its very first stammering words, faith is something more and better than a simple acceptance in obedience to revelation. It is animated by a "certain desire of promised good,"[16] which spurs the believer to give his assent in spite of the fear that it may leave him in the darkness that surrounds divine truth. That desire, which pushes toward the still incompletely known Good, is the true motor of theological research. Saint Thomas remarks on this in a rightly celebrated passage: "Spurred by an ardent will to believe, *man loves the truth in which he believes*, contemplates it in his spirit, and embraces as many reasons as he can find."[17]

If we can love only that which we know to some degree, it is also the case that we can truly know only that which we truly love. This maxim obviously applies to interpersonal relations, and that is precisely why it finds its highest realization in theological life. If faith without love cannot be conceived of, that is because faith addresses itself not to an abstract truth but to a Person in whom the Good and the True are one. The First Truth that is the object of faith is also the Supreme Good, the object of all human desires and acts. That is why we cannot be reunited to it in its totality except through a complex movement on our part which proceeds simultaneously from the intelligence and the will, what Saint Paul called "faith acting through love" (Gal. 5:6).[18] The knowledge we can obtain of First Truth will be no more than weak and imperfect. But it is the most

---

15. *Lectura super Ioannem (In Joannem)* 20, lect. 6, n. 2562: "Statim factus est Thomas bonus theologus ueram fidem confitendo."

16. *Quaestiones disputatae De ueritate (De uer.)* q. 14 a. 2 ad 10: "quidam appetitus boni repromissi"; cf. *Super Boetium De Trinitate (Super Boet. De Trin.)* q. 3 a. 1 ad 4, where Thomas develops this at greater length.

17. *ST* IIa IIae q. 2 a. 10: "Cum enim homo habet promptam uoluntatem ad credendum, diligit ueritatem creditam, et super ea excogitat et amplectitur si quas rationes ad hoc inuenire potest."

18. *ST* IIa IIae q. 4 a. 2 ad 3: "quia ueritas prima, quae est fidei obiectum, est finis omnium desideriorum et actionum nostrarum . . . , inde est quod per dilectionem operatur" (because the first truth, which is the object of faith, is the end of all our desires and our actions

noble knowledge we can ever acquire and will give us the greatest of joys.[19]

Theology and the Vision of God

Thomas gave a technical formulation for theology's dependence on faith in what is called the theory of subalternation. Numerous detailed studies having been dedicated to this subject; it will suffice here to recall the essence of the question and to emphasize its deep meaning.[20]

His basic presupposition is the Aristotelian notion of science, which is quite different from the current meaning and calls for some clarification. Even though Thomas, as we shall see, noticeably modifies the concept by his own usage, the general outline of his approach remains Aristotle's. For Aristotle, the science of something is a sure knowledge of it thanks to reasoning that allows us to show why it is necessarily thus and not otherwise. We obtain this knowledge by relating certain *evident* truths, which are called "principles," with some other truths less well known (discovered, in fact, from the principles), which are called "conclusions." The necessary union of truth-as-conclusion with truth-as-principle makes it possible to have a "science" of something.[21] For instance, an example that Thomas frequently gives: Christ's resurrection is the truth-as-principle that allows us to explain the resurrection of Christians, which here is a truth-as-conclusion.[22]

This example, which comes spontaneously from Thomas's pen each time he needs to propose a model of theological reasoning, shows at the

---

. . . thus faith works through dilection); the openly Augustinian inspiration in this passage refers to *De Trinitate* I, 8, 17 and 10, 20 (BA 15, 130 and 142); cf. *Summa Contra Gentiles* (SCG) III 25, n. 2064: "Est igitur ultimus finis totius hominis, et omnium operationum et desideriorum eius, cognoscere primum uerum, quod est Deus."

19. Cf. SCG I 5 and I 8.

20. This brief treatment should be supplemented by J.-P. Torrell, *La théologie catholique*, chap. 3, and H.-D. Gardeil, "La méthode de la théologie," in *La Théologie* (French translation with notes and appendices of St. Thomas Aquinas, *Summa theologiae* Ia, Prooemium and q. 1) (Paris, 1968), 93–140. In a more scholarly vein, but fundamental, is M.-D. Chenu, *La théologie comme science au XIIIe siècle* (Paris, ³1957); more recently, J.-P. Torrell, "Le savoir théologique chez saint Thomas," in *Recherches thomasiennes*, 121–57.

21. *Super Boet. De Trin.* q. 2 a. 2, Leonine, vol. 50, pp. 94–97; *Expositio libri Posteriorum Analyticorum* I 2–4; Leonine, vol. I* 2, rev. ed. (1989), pp. 10–22; T. Tshibangu, "La notion de science selon Aristote," in *Théologie positive et théologie spéculative* (Louvain-Paris, 1965), 3–34.

22. *ST* Ia q. 1 a. 8; *De uer.* q. 14 a. 2 ad 9; *Scriptum super libros Sententiarum I* (*In I Sent.*) Pro., a. 5 ad 4.

same time the main difficulty in transposing the Aristotelian model of science into theology. Science starts from principles that are "evident," basic truths, axioms or postulates, which remain undemonstrated and do not need to be demonstrated because they are immediately graspable by the light of intuition. That cannot be the case in theology: it does not have and cannot have such immediate evidence for its principles. Far from being evident, Jesus' resurrection can only be the object of faith. The example Thomas proposes therefore seems to prove the contrary of what he wishes and attempts to explain the obscure by what is more obscure.

It is here that the notion of a "subalternate" science intervenes. Aristotle had foreseen the case of certain sciences that do not have immediately evident principles, but that join themselves to another science that provides the equivalent of that evidence by the certitude of its demonstrations. For instance, optics is joined to the principles that geometry provides, and music to the laws of mathematics.[23] There is no need to enter into the details of the demonstration here; it is enough to know that theology finds itself in an analogous situation. The "science" that has the evidence for the truths on which theology draws is the knowledge that God has of himself and of his plan of salvation. He communicates that knowledge first to the blessed in their heavenly homeland, those who see him face to face thanks to the light of glory. But through the light of faith he also communicates it to men who are still on the way toward their final homeland and therefore still do not see him.

Faith, then, is the spiritual space where human ignorance is fashioned into divine science. That is the deep meaning of subalternation according to Saint Thomas. This was highly contested in his day, because it clearly does not correspond to all of Aristotle's conditions for subalternation. But here we may pass over that. As he often does in using materials that he has borrowed, Thomas puts them through a radical transposition by the very fact that he uses them in an evangelical context completely unknown to pagan philosophy. It would be wrong to criticize him from either perspective. But it should be said that if theology cannot, strictly speaking, be erected as a science in the Aristotelian mode (because it can never acquire a science of its principles: it will always be obliged to believe), it is that very fact that constitutes theology's greatness. Thomas's transposition underscores the indispensability of theological faith for theological work:

23. *ST* IIa q. 1 a. 2; *In I Sent*. Pro., a. 3 q. 2; *Super Boet. De Trin*. q. 2 a. 2 ad 5.

Whoever practices a subaltern science does not truly attain to the perfection of that science except in the measure that his knowledge remains in continuity with that of the expert who practices the subalternating science. Even so, he will not possess the science of the principles that he receives, but only some conclusions that he necessarily draws from it. Thus, the believer may possess the science of what he may conclude from the articles of the faith.[24]

If we recall again the desire to see, which animates this research, we can discern the place of theology in Christian life. Theology is no stranger to the movement of the Christian in search of God; on the contrary, it takes its place precisely along the trajectory that leads from faith to the Beatific Vision. Therefore, the theologian finds himself in a completely different position than that of a scholar in some other branch of knowledge. He does not need to leave theology to find God. It is enough for him to push the demands of his science to the limit in order to be irresistibly drawn toward Him who is the final aim of the life of a believer.

The "Subject" of Theology

When he wishes to express scientifically the role that divine reality plays in the elaboration of knowledge, Thomas speaks of God as the "subject" of theology. In his enumeration of the principal characteristics of theology, beginning with the very first pages of the *Summa Theologiae*, he asks how it is to be distinguished from the other branches of knowledge, or what is its specific difference. A single word is enough, but we have to understand it well. God is the "subject" of this science: "In *sacra doctrina*, all things are considered from God's point of view: or they deal with God himself, or with things that are connected with God as their beginning or end. It follows that God is truly the subject of this science."[25]

In this response, so open and simple in appearance, Thomas takes a stance unique among his contemporaries. Peter Lombard, following Saint Augustine, saw the material of theology in the opposition between the letter of Scripture and the reality it signified (*res* and *signa*); Hugh of Saint Victor situated the material of theology in the work of the redemption; and the Franciscans, among them Saint Bonaventure, saw it as rather in Christ and the Church. Thomas concedes that theology speaks about all these things, but he refuses to see in them the subject of theology proper-

---

24. *De uer.* q. 14 a. 9 ad 3.
25. *ST* Ia q. 1 a. 7.

ly understood. These varied points of view only *describe* reality; he himself wished to *explain* that reality, something far more ambitious. But that is precisely what he proposes in making God himself the subject of this particular science. His disciples were not mistaken about this; since the first generation of Thomas's students, they have made it one of their special themes.

We have trouble understanding why this point is so important. In French, we use the word "object" where Thomas speaks of "subject." Though it may lead to a somewhat difficult analysis, we cannot rest content here with the approximate equivalence of these terms without winding up in a regrettable confusion. We need to define what the notion of "subject" means in Thomas's Aristotelian perspective—and to be aware of what happens when we forget that precise meaning. The "subject" is the reality outside the mind, which science seeks to know. In fact, a science has no other end than knowledge of its subject. But that external reality can only be known to the extent that the knower can appropriate it internally and cause it to exist in his mind. This is possible through concepts, i.e., ideas that are formed from reality. Concepts are the several ways in which intelligence grasps external reality; and these constitute the "object" of a science. Thus, Thomas defines the object of the science as all the conclusions that the science succeeds in establishing about its subject. This is easy to grasp, but this first distinction between subject and object is nonetheless fundamental. It has the advantage of reminding us that the first thing known, the object, is not the subject and therefore cannot be the end pursued in seeking knowledge. It has only an instrumental relation to that end. Nor does it express everything about the subject. In fact, concepts have to be multiplied and related to one another by a judgment about existence so that the mind may find itself in a position to say something about the subject. Finally, the knower must frequently recognize the perpetual inadequacy of the known object to the reality he seeks to know.

When we are dealing with a form of knowledge whose subject is God, these things are even clearer. A true theologian can never forget that his subject, the end he pursues, is knowledge of the living God in the history of salvation. And without playing with the meaning of the word "subject," we may here rediscover a modern equivalent. To speak of God as a "subject" is also to say that he is not reduced to an "object"—not even to a mentally schematic object that the theologian can know. A subject is a person with whom one is acquainted and whom one loves (because the person has given himself to be known and loved), and whom one invokes and meets in prayer. Theology experienced a dramatic turnaround on the day that, deceived by the definition of science as a "habitus of conclusions," and forgetful of the distinction between subject and object and of its actual significance, theologians (beginning in the fourteenth century) started to speak of the aim of their research as no longer acquaintance with the subject, but with the object. They begin to deduce as many conclusions as possible from the truths contained in the deposit of revelation. This straying from the truth has been denounced quite often and there is no need to do so again here.[26] It is enough for us to understand that Thomas's position is completely different. He certainly defines theology as a science of conclusions (as opposed to principles, of which he cannot possess the science, only the faith),[27] but that is not the end that he gives to theology. The end, beyond all possible doubt, is acquaintance with theology's subject.[28]

Therefore, this is the first thing Saint Thomas means when he says that God himself is the subject of theology. But this also means that we have to go back to God to find the explanatory key for all the other descriptive perspectives. Neither the creation nor the redemption can be explained solely in terms of the work performed. It requires recourse to the subject who took the initiative, God himself and his merciful love. Nor can the Church be explained in herself; we have to "go back" to Him who is the Head, the Christ, and even he in his humanity is only the one sent by the Father and the Trinity. In everything that concerns him, the theologian is constantly referred to the primary origin, which is Love flowing from its Trinitarian source. Thomas draws from this the concrete lesson that everything in theology, absolutely everything, must be considered in connection with God. It is from him that all things come, it is toward him that all creatures move. In the first, purely theoretical approach, this position therefore constitutes a radical demand that all theological knowledge and all human effort place God at the center of everything that can be

---

26. See for example M. J. Congar, "Théologie," *DTC*, vol. 15 (1946), col. 398 and 418–19; E. Schillebeeckx, *Revelation and Theology*, 131–36; C. Dumont, "La réflexion sur la méthode théologique," *NRT* 83 (1961): 1034–50, cf. 1037–38; and *NRT* 84 (1962): 17–35.

27. See, for instance, *In I Sent.* Pro., a. 3 sol. 2 ad 2: "In hac doctrina non acquiritur habitus fidei qui est quasi habitus principiorum; sed acquiritur habitus eorum quae ex eis deducuntur."

28. *In I Sent.* Pro., a. 4: "Subiecti cognitio principaliter intenditur in scientia."

done, said, and thought. No mystic has ever said anything stronger. For it is clear that if theology is theologically centered, so will the spirituality that flows from it.

A second point, but one far from secondary: this central thesis also explains certain qualities of theology itself. Thus, that a theologian is a contemplative is a consequence of the first thesis that God is the subject of theology. Thomas returns to this when he asks whether theology is a "practical" science. Put that way, the question might make us smile. But it really aims at determining whether theology may be extended so as to deal with the rules of human action. The answer is unequivocal: if theology is, as we have said, a kind of participation in the knowledge that God has given us of himself, then it is certainly a practical science:

> by the very same knowledge that God knows himself and accomplishes everything he does, [but, Thomas adds,] theology is nevertheless more speculative (= contemplative) than practical, for theology is more interested in divine realities than in human acts. Theology only addresses human acts in so far as through them man orients himself toward the perfect knowledge of God which constitutes beatitude.[29]

This answer puts Thomas into a class of his own in the long line of theorists about theological science. Up until his appearance, theology was of course spoken of as a contemplative science, but essentially as it was ordered to the perfect practice of charity. "This knowledge is ordered toward action," said his contemporary Robert Kilwardby. In his early commentary on the *Sentences* and after, Thomas was the first to see it as, on the contrary, oriented toward contemplation. As we have just seen, since theology is completely directed toward God, that orientation carries all others along with it. We are obviously not dealing with a reality that human action could bring into existence. God is not a human construct and we cannot dispose of him any way we wish. He can only be known and loved by us. That is what Thomas wants to take into account when he claims that theology must *primarily* be speculative.

This answer contains another key point for our present purposes. It allows us to see that Thomas does not recognize a distinction, which has become quite common among us, between moral theology and dogmatic theology. Similarly, he ignores the division of labor between positive the-

29. *ST* Ia q. 1 a. 4.

ology and reflexive theology. It is one and the same *sacra doctrina* that encompasses everything, even, as we have seen, later concepts such as "spirituality" or spiritual theology. We may readily allow the benefits brought about by the increasing specialization in various realms of theological knowledge. But we can also hope the several practitioners will discover a more acute awareness of the fundamental unity of the whole enterprise. For Thomas, that unity still manifested itself, and we shall come upon it quite early in his great theological synthesis.

A Certain Stamp of the Divine Science

Continuing with Saint Thomas, we must still explain another thesis that appears quite technical. It has, however, an undeniable spiritual dimension. In theology, faith plays the role that the *habitus* of first principles plays in our natural knowledge. To understand this we clearly need to know what a "habitus" is and what the "principles" of theology are. In Thomas's language, habitus (from the Greek *hexis*) is a key notion, which our English word "habit" not only does not translate properly but suggests almost the contrary of the true meaning. Habit is a fixed mechanism, a routine; habitus is, instead, an inventive capacity, perfecting the human faculty in which it is rooted, to which it gives perfect liberty in its exercise. A worker's know-how is a habitus; so is the skill of a doctor or the knowledge of a scientist. Midway between a nature and its action, habitus is the sign and expression of its full flowering. An entirely gratuitous divine gift, faith resides in us in the form of a habitus. It is therefore a special perfecting that superelevates our natural capacity of knowing to the heights of a new object: God himself and the world of divine things. As the precise form that grace takes in our intellects, faith is a kind of participation in the very life of God, and it actualizes between him and us a kind of connaturality that renders us capable of spontaneously grasping what God indicates. What is called the *sensus fidei* is precisely this capacity to understand "naturally," so to speak, supernatural things, the way one friend understands another—without having to speak.[30]

This explains Saint Thomas's formulation: faith is like the habitus that allows us to grasp the principles of theology,[31] principles being the first

---

30. Cf. *ST* IIIa q. 1 a. 6 ad 3, on the two ways of judging divine things; we shall return later to this subject.

31. *Super Boet. De Trin.* q. 5 a. 4 ad 8: ". . . fides, quae *est quasi habitus principiorum*

truths from which theology begins its scientific elaboration. With this sense of their essential character, Thomas identifies the principles of theology with the articles of the Creed. And by means of the play of relations between principles and conclusions that make up the scientific process, he ultimately reduces them to two absolutely primary truths: God exists and he loves us. This is no arbitrary reconstruction. Thomas finds a similar expression in the epistle to the Hebrews (11:6): "Whoever approaches God must believe that *He exists* and that *He rewards* those who seek him." These first two *credibilia* contain in sum the whole of the faith: "In God's Being can be found everything that we believe exists eternally in him: that is our beatitude; in our faith in his providence we find included everything that he has done in time for our salvation; which is the path to beatitude."[32] We immediately recognize here the ancient distinction of the Greek Fathers between *theologia*, that part of theology that interests itself directly in the intimate life of God (the Trinity of the persons), and *oikonomia*, that which he has done in time to save us, salvation history. Thomas uses a slightly more technical expression (end and means), but is very close to the letter of the New Testament in the following passage:

The realities that belong in themselves to the faith are those that in vision will delight us one day in eternal life and that in the present life lead us toward that vision. Two things will then be offered for our contemplation: the divine secret, the vision of which will render us blessed, and the mystery of Christ's humanity, through which we have access to the glorious liberty of the sons of God (Rom. 5:2). This is, moreover, in accord with the saying of Saint John (17:3) "Eternal life is to know you as the one true God and Jesus Christ whom you have sent."[33]

The link established here between the idea of articles of faith and final beatitude is quite striking, and Thomas deliberately emphasizes it: "What belongs in itself to the object of the faith is that through which man is rendered blessed."[34] The notion of a beginning irresistibly calls for the notion

---

theologiae"; cf. ibid., q. 3 a. 1 ad 4 where the parallel between the intuition of first principles in the light of reason and the apprehension by faith of supernatural truths is developed in depth. To the objection that theology is not a science because it lacks the most elementary certitude, Thomas replies that the habitus that constitutes the light of faith is more certain, not only than any other demonstration, but even than the habitus of first principles, since bodily weakness can impede the proper functioning of the latter.

32. *ST* IIa IIae q. 1 a. 7.

33. *ST* IIa IIae q. 1 a. 8. For the role this verse plays in the structure of the *Summa*, see *ST* Ia q. 2 Pro., and *ST* IIIa q. 1 Pro.

34. *ST* IIa IIae q. 2 a. 5: "fidei obiectum per se est id per quod homo beatus efficitur."

of an end. And it is here that the hermeneutic interest in the notion of an article of the faith/principle of theology unveils itself. In light of the texts mentioned and many others, it is clear that the internal intelligibility of the content of revelation is linked to its value for salvation. Every revealed truth obviously has value for salvation, but the link—and ultimately the hierarchy—that we can establish among them stems from their connection with God who is grasped as the original author and supremely beatifying end of the creature. Therefore, their pure and simple identification with that end or their greater or lesser proximity to him play an absolutely decisive role in these questions.[35]

We might thus complete what remains to be said about the idea of a science. Truth-principles and truth-conclusions are not related in an isolated fashion. The aim of the scientific process is much more ambitious. All revealed truths must be mutually related in order to reconstruct the internal intelligibility of the revealed datum.[36] Finally, it is around these first two *credibilia* that the labor of theological explication must be organized if we wish to have some chance of grasping the internal coherence of God's saving plan. God's salvific will clearly has no other cause than his entirely free and disinterested love. We do not impose on it the intelligible structures of our minds. Rather, in the conviction that God has brought forth all things "with number, weight, and measure" (Wisd. 11:20) and that he guides all things "with all wisdom and intelligence" (Eph. 1:8), the theologian applies himself to discovering the organic connection that exists among the various works of God: "God does not will that because of this, but he does will this to be because of that."[37] It is discovering these reciprocal relations and grasping them in as complete a synthesis as possible, in which they are situated according to their relative impor-

---

35. Though we cannot spend much time on this point, I might note that this view helps us understand the Second Vatican Council's recommendation about the necessity to take account of the "hierarchy of the truths of Catholic doctrine" in ecumenical practice. Cf. *Unitatis redintegratio* n. 11. On this, see Y. Congar, "On the hierarchia veritatum," *Orientalia christiana analecta* 195 (1973): 409–20; W. Henn, *The Hierarchy of Truths according to Yves Congar, O.P.* (Rome, 1987).

36. The editors of chapter 3 of *Dei Filius* at Vatican I were doubtless thinking of these views when they defined the task of speculative theology: "When reason illuminated by faith seeks with care, piety, and moderation, it reaches, by a gift of God, a very fruitful understanding of the mysteries, thanks both to the analogy with things that it knows naturally, and to the ties that bind the mysteries to one another and to man's final end."

37. *ST* Ia q. 19 a. 5: "Vult ergo [Deus] hoc esse propter hoc, sed non propter hoc uult hoc."

tance, that finally leads to a better understanding of the work of their author, God himself, the only subject of *sacra doctrina*.

Thomas expresses that ideal in a formula borrowed from the tradition
of Avicenna, but which he makes completely his own: science is nothing
more than a "reproduction in the soul of the reality that is known," since
science is said to be the assimilation of the knower to the known reality itself.[38] Or, according to another and quite telling formula, the structure of
the real is reproduced in the understanding according to a reasoned organization of concepts of existing things *(ordinata aggregatio)*.[39] The
teacher who has already done this reconstruction for himself finds himself
prepared to imprint in the understanding of his hearers a systematic view
of the reality that he wishes to communicate to them. A celebrated formula of Thomas's, sometimes misunderstood, might be explained thus:
sacra doctrina is like "a certain stamp of divine knowledge."[40] Far from
claiming an excessive privilege for theology (since every human science is
a kind of participation in divine science), this formula is merely an exact
description of the dependence of the theologian's knowledge on God's
own knowledge. The privilege here is not theology's but faith's, for it is
faith that allows us to receive the revelations given us by God himself.[41]
Connecting our knowledge with God's knowledge of himself, faith renders possible the birth and development of theological knowledge.

A "Pious" Science

The linkage of theology with faith, which is to be found at every stage
of research, allows us to appreciate two indispensable qualities of theology.
To begin with, by the very fact that it is animated by the faith, theology is a
"pious" science and it demands a living faith, which is to say a faith pene-

38. *De uer.* q. 11 a. 1 arg. 11: "Scientia nihil aliud est quam descriptio rerum in anima,
cum scientia esse dicatur assimilatio scientis ad scitum."

39. *SCG* I 56 (no. 470): "Habitus [scientiae] . . . *est ordinata aggregatio ipsarum
specierum existentium in intellectu* non secundum completum actum, sed medio modo in-
ter potentiam et actum (the habitus [of knowledge] is the reasoned organization of the
species themselves existing in the intellect, not according to a complete act, but in a way intermediate between potency and act)."

40. *ST* Ia q. 1 a. 3 ad 2: "uelut quaedam impressio diuinae scientiae."

41. Elsewhere, Thomas uses a very similar expression, when speaking about faith, *Super
Boet. De Trin.* q. 3 a. 1 ad 4: "Lumen . . . fidei . . . *est quasi quaedam sigillatio prime ueritatis in mente* (the light of faith is like a certain truth by an original stamp in the mind)
. . ."; *sigillatio* is also used as the equivalent of *impressio* in the field of natural knowledge;
cf. *De uer.* q. 2 a. 1 arg. 6 and ad 6 with reference to Algazel.

trated ("informed" as Thomas says) by charity in order to correspond fully to its definition. It may be that theology is sometimes practiced with a dead or insufficient faith, but that is an abnormal situation. Theological study demands the same faith as do Christian life and prayer. And though these are different activities, the same faith finds expression in them all. "Contemplative prayer or theological speculation are specifically different variants in their psychological manifestations; but in theological structure, they have the same object, the same beginning, the same end."[42] This is why Thomas's Prologue to the *Sentences* says that for him who practices it, theology takes on the modality of prayer *(modus oratiuus)*.[43] There is no doubt that, for him, prayer belongs to the practice of theology.

Furthermore, always in dependence on the faith that is its soul and moving force, theology has an undeniably eschatological dimension. And here, along with faith and charity we come upon hope, the third theological virtue. In Thomas's view, theology achieves a kind of anticipation of the knowledge that will blossom out in the beatific vision. He says with the utmost lucidity: "The last end of this *doctrina* is the contemplation of the primary truth in the heavenly homeland."[44] That is what is meant when we speak of theology as "speculative" knowledge; in Thomistic language, that word, so devalued today, means nothing more than "contemplative,"[45] and thus whoever does theology must be, like the subject itself, entirely turned toward the object of knowledge which is also the final end of the Christian life.

Clearly, this is only a characteristic of theology because it is first a characteristic of the faith that animates it. For it is indeed faith that gets that "foretaste" *(praelibatio quaedam)* of the divine goods that we will enjoy in the beatific vision.[46] But Thomas also applies this to the science of divine

---

42. M.-D. Chenu, *La foi dans l'intelligence* (Paris, 1964), 134.

43. *In I Sent.* Pro., a. 5 sol.

44. *In I Sent.* Pro., a. 3 sol. 1 and ad 1: "Sed quia scientia omnis principaliter pensanda est ex fine, *finis autem huius doctrinae est contemplatio primae ueritatis in patria*, ideo principaliter speculatiua est"; there are further details about this point in J.-P. Torrell, "Théologie et sainteté," *RT* 71 (1971): 205–21, cf. 205–12.

45. Cf. S. Pinckaers, "Recherche de la signification véritable du terme 'spéculatif'," *NRT* 81 (1959): 673–95.

46. *Compendium theologiae seu brevis compilatio theologiae ad fratrem Raynaldum* (*Comp. theol.*) I, 2; see also the more explicit definition in the *Summa* (*ST* IIa IIae q. 4 a. 1): "faith is a habitus of the soul which initiates eternal life in us by making our intellect adhere to realities that we do not see." This same doctrine is often repeated, cf. *De uer.* q. 14 a. 2.

things: "Through it, we can enjoy a certain participation in and assimilation to divine knowledge, even while we are still on the way, to the extent that we adhere through infused faith to the first truth itself."[47]

If theology is indeed the reality just described—and there is no doubt that for Saint Thomas it is—we can easily understand why for him there was no need to elaborate a spirituality *alongside* his theology. His theology itself is a spiritual theology, and we should always be able to recognize a Thomist theologian by the spiritual tone that he gives to even the most technical investigations. Sometimes we may have to bring out certain elements for readers not yet prepared to perceive them on their own. But such elements are nonetheless always there, at least as a seed. Meanwhile, the word "spirituality" has in our time taken on other connotations, and it is important to be aware of them in order to avoid using the term wrongly and even at cross purposes to Thomas's intentions.

Three Meanings of the Word "Spirituality"

Following Walter H. Principe,[48] the greatest expert on this question, we will use here three principal meanings of the word "spirituality." Setting aside the third,[49] the first two have clear equivalents in Saint Thomas.

In the first meaning, "spirituality" designates the reality lived by a given person. Saint Paul's language already suggests this, and in accord with its etymology *(Spiritus → spiritualitas)* spirituality means the quality of a life conducted by the movement of the Spirit: "The natural (psychic) man does not accept the things of the Spirit *(Pneuma)* of God: they are foolishness to him and he cannot understand them, for they must be judged *spiritually*. But the *spiritual (pneumatikos)* man judges all things and is judged by no one."[50] The first appearances in Latin of *spiritualitas*—in the

47. *Super Boet. De Trin* .q. 2 a. 2.

48. W. H. Principe, "Toward Defining Spirituality," *Studies in Religion/Sciences Religieuses* 12 (1983): 127–41, cf. 153–57; *Thomas Aquinas' Spirituality* (Toronto, 1984), 3–5; "Spirituality, Christian," *The New Dictionary of Catholic Spirituality*, ed. M. Downey (Collegeville, Minn., 1993), 931–38. In French, see the synthesis in the entry "Spiritualité," *DS*, vol. 14 (1990), col. 1142–73, in which two authors have divided up the subject: "I: Le mot et l'histoire" (A. Solignac) and "II. La notion de spiritualité" (M. Dupuy).

49. According to Principe, spirituality is in this case a kind of taught knowledge, a scientific discipline; it can be studied in specialized institutions from different points of view: theological, historical, the phenomenology of religions, etc. We leave aside this third meaning, which has no special interest for us here.

50. 1 Cor. 2:14–15. For the meaning of *pneumatikos* in Saint Paul, see as well Rom. 1:11,

fifth and sixth centuries[51]—retain this meaning, as does Saint Thomas.

The word itself is not very common (some seventy uses) and is most often opposed to *corporeitas* (the spirit as distinguished from the body) referring to a life of grace under the action of the Holy Spirit. "It is in the man Christ that from the outset is found a perfect spirituality," and it is also "from him that spirituality derives in all human beings."[52] If Christ is the source of all spirituality, clearly it is because he received the Holy Spirit fully, but as a consequence all those born in the Spirit (John 3:7) are spiritual; and we may recognize them by their deeds: "The characteristics of the Holy Spirit may be seen in the spiritual person. (We recognize it in various individuals, particularly in their words): in hearing them, we perceive their spirituality."[53] But this is also a life entirely lived in charity and the other virtues received from the Spirit of love: "The spiritual life comes from charity *(spiritualitas autem uita per caritatem est).*"[54] This first meaning of "spirituality" then is very close to the one we are familiar with: the grace of the Spirit at work in a person who experiences its radiance. In that sense, there is no doubt that Saint Thomas had a personal spirituality. We can see it in several traits of the portrait that we have put forward.[55]

7:14, 15:27; 1 Cor. 3:1, 9:11, 10:3–4, 12:1, 14:1, 14:37, 15:44, 15:46; Gal. 6:1; Eph. 1:3, 5:19; Col. 1:9, 3:16.

51. The first mention of *spiritualitas* is in the seventh letter of pseudo-Jerome (in reality, Pelagius): "Age ut in spiritualitate proficias. Cave ne quod accepisti bonum, incautus et negligens custos amittas" (PL 30, 114D–115A). The second use comes a century later in the fourteenth letter of Saint Avit addressed to his brother: "Minus enim procul dubio salva observatione apparet affectus, sed ostendistis quanta spiritualitate vos exercere delectet quod praeterisse sic doluit" (MGH, *Auctores antiquissimi* VI/2, ed. R. Peiper [Berlin, 1883], 47). For further details, see J. Leclerq, "Spiritualitas," *Studi medievali*, Serie terza 3 (1961): 279–96, particularly 280–82; A. Solignac, "L'apparition du mot *spiritualitas* au moyen âge," ALMA 44–45 (1985): 185–206, especially 186–89.

52. ST IIIa q. 34 a. 1 ad 1; *Super primam ad Corinthios (In I ad Cor.)* 15, lect. 7, ed. Marietti, nn. 994, 991, and 1004; cf. J.-P. Torrell, "Spiritualitas," 582–83.

53. *Super Evangelium S. Ioannis lectura (In Ioannem)* III, lect. 1, ed. Marietti, n. 456: "In *viro spirituali* sunt proprietates Spiritus Sancti. . . . Eius indicium sumis per vocem verborum suorum, quam dum audis, cognoscis eius *spiritualitatem.*"

54. *In III Sent.* d. 38 q. 1 a. 4 sol.; *Quodlibet (Quodl.)* VII, a. 17 ad 5: "*Vita spiritualis* a nullo potest conseruari nisi per actus uirtutum"; ST Ia IIae q. 65 a. 2 s. c.: "Per uirtutes perficitur uita spiritualis"; cf. ST IIIa q. 59 a. 3 arg. 2; etc. The word *spiritualis* is found about 7,000 times in Thomas's work; only an exhaustive study would allow us to make sense of all that, but to extrapolate from the results of a survey of 500 of these cases, I can estimate that the expression *uita spiritualis* may be found there 280 times with the precise meaning that we are seeking: a life in charity and the exercise of the evangelical virtues, which are obtained through baptism and maintained by the Eucharist and the other sacraments.

55. Cf. my *Saint Thomas Aquinas*, chap. 14.

The second meaning of the word "spirituality" refers to a spiritual doctrine. Taught by a person remarkable for his own personal spirituality, this doctrine is most often a formulation of his own lived experience, sometimes barely distinguishable from its most immediately personal traits. We might think here about the writing of the saints, Teresa of Avila or John of the Cross, or the practical recommendations of Saint Ignatius. But we might just as well consider the rule of saints who have founded orders, such as Saint Benedict or Saint Francis. They taught the art of living the Gospel and thus gave birth to spiritualities—Benedictine, Franciscan, etc. In these instances, we can see quite well that the "theory" depends on practice and the teachings stem less from a science arrived at intellectually than from knowledge acquired through a long apprenticeship under the guidance of the Spirit. This is not always the case, but sometimes it is the best explanation: we may call them spiritual doctrine and even spiritual theology, as much as spirituality.

And it is here that we may hope to rediscover Saint Thomas. Jacques Maritain once proposed a useful distinction between two levels of spiritual doctrines.[56] First, comes the plane of the *practically practical*, where the writings of the saints that have just been mentioned are situated. By proposing concrete rules of action according to a certain spirit, their aim is to stimulate a renewal of the original spirit or at the very least the appearance of a similar experience. Born of experience, such teaching refers to experience and directly aims at concrete moral action here and now. Except in homilies—which are sometimes very close to the ordinary Christian experience—Thomas Aquinas never proposes any doctrine practically practical in this sense.

It is quite different on the plane of *speculatively practical* knowledge, which is the plane of moral philosophy or theology. That knowledge is practical because of its directive finality over action; it remains speculative because it studies the rules of action in their generality, leaving for another occasion how to direct action in its concrete singularity. Following the received formula, moral theology is a reflexive knowledge that becomes practical only by extension. If moral theology were to propose immediate solutions to all the problems of daily life, it would quickly change into casuistry—with all the complex paths that we know from history. By

56. J. Maritain, "Saint John of the Cross, Practitioner of Contemplation," chap. 8 in *Distinguish to Unite or the Three Degrees of Knowledge,* trans. under the supervision of Gerard Phelan (Notre Dame, Ind., 1995).

contrast, if we assume that there is a reflexive level for theology where it brings forward the basic laws that command human action and Christian life in this world and before God—as Saint Thomas does—then we shall quickly discover that this reflection is pregnant with a spiritual doctrine.[57]

Let us put a question at this point: if this doctrine is indeed found in Saint Thomas, why did he not explicitly distinguish it from the rest of his thought, so that it would not go unappreciated? The answer is quite simple: spirituality of the Thomist sort remains unnoticed only by those who do not read Thomas deeply (the same happens with the more explicit spiritual masters if we are satisfied with studying them only superficially). Those who study Thomas in depth know what is to be found in him, even if they usually feel no need to emphasize it. If Saint Thomas himself did not write that explicit work on spirituality that we seek, spirituality nonetheless finds a place in the *Summa Theologiae*. As Gilson once magnificently put it, "[t]hus his *Summa Theologiae*, with its abstract clarity, its impersonal transparency, crystallizes before our very eyes and for all eternity [Aquinas's] very interior life."[58]

This may be a surprising assertion, and we shall try to justify it. But it is beyond doubt true. Thomas's spiritual doctrine is an implicit and necessary dimension of his theology. In that sense, we might say that he is not only a thinker and a master of thinking, but a master of living. In both cases, he is not like the ideologue who imposes his system. Rather, like a true master, he teaches his disciples to think and to live on their own.[59] To put it slightly differently, his teaching and his life are laden with values that may easily inspire people to behave in a special way both as human beings and as Christians. And that we can quite rightly call "spirituality."

57. Those wishing to go further in reflecting on what simultaneously unites and distinguishes moral theology and spiritual theology, should look at the highly illuminating study by M.-M. Labourdette, "Qu'est-ce que la théologie spirituelle?," *RT* 92 (1992): 355–72: a moral theologian without equal who is attentive to the experience of saints and mystics, P. Labourdette elaborates on the reflection initiated by J. Maritain.

58. É. Gilson, *Le Thomisme* (Paris, ⁶1987), 457. The fifth edition has been translated into English as *The Christian Philosophy of St. Thomas Aquinas*, trans. L. K. Shook (New York, 1956), 376.

59. See the instrumental conception of the teacher's role in *De ueritate* q. 11.

PART I

A Trinitarian Spirituality

༂

CHAPTER II

He Who Is Beyond All Things

The primacy that Saint Thomas gives to God in the organization of theological knowledge appears as soon as we glance at the structure of the *Summa Theologiae*. Whether it is a question of the divine essence itself, or of the distinction among the persons in the Trinity, or even of how we are to understand Creation, it is always the Triune God who is considered, in himself or in his work. It is impossible for a Christian theologian to deal with God in his unity or his Creation, or to turn his three-personed life into an abstraction, without mutilating the mystery. The Christian knows only the God of revelation, and that light illumines his whole effort to understand the faith.

Thomas approaches his subject in a way that is a bit disconcerting for the unprepared reader. His approach helps us to grasp his intentions more clearly: "We must first ask if *God exists*; then how he is or *how he is not*; we must then inquire into *his operation*: his knowledge, will, and power."[1] Thus, we must first establish God's existence. This had already been clearly stated in the *Summa contra Gentiles*:

Among all the things that we must study concerning God in himself, we must put first, for it is the necessary foundation of the whole work, the demonstration of God's existence. If that is not achieved, then the entire study of divine realities fatally collapses.[2]

We should not, though, be deceived about the reason for this approach. It is not a matter of pretending that God does not exist, of acting

1. *ST* Ia q. 2 Pro.
2. *SCG* I 9.

"as if" God did not exist. Thomas has no doubt, not even a methodological one, on this score. In his faith, he welcomes the truth of God's existence as the first truth that he confesses in the Credo. And he constantly refers to revealed Scripture. It is quite significant, for example, that in the article where he develops the "five ways" for the proof of God's existence, he takes as his starting point the theophany of the Burning Bush: "I am He who is."[3] We would do a great injustice to the inspiration behind his research if we were to look only to his philosophical framework. He wants to reassure us through reason of what he holds through faith, and, as a theologian, to work out the content of the revelation to Moses. Contrary to what we might think, his approach is less directed against atheism than against those who maintain that God's existence is evident, that there is no need to establish it. To those persons Thomas replies: "*In itself* God's existence is evident, but not *for us*."[4] The proof of this is that there are many non-believers. But if the theologian must at least show that belief is not unreasonable, it is perhaps still more important that he himself be aware of what the first article of the confession of faith implies.

Without repeating here Thomas's approach, which continues to engage the wisdom of interpreters,[5] it is helpful to disengage its structure and meaning. Thomas does not start with religious subjectivity but rather with observation of the exterior world. That is why the proof from motion comes first. Motion here does not mean pure physical movement but metaphysical movement, which allows us to make inferences and is found in the passing of every potency to act. Now, to avoid infinite regress, this passing from potency to act, observable in the whole created world, must result in the conclusion that a First Mover exists, who has no need to be moved by another, because he is pure act. This is what everyone understands to be meant when we speak of God. The four other ways ex-

3. *ST* Ia q. 2 a. 3 s. c.; it is no less significant that at the end of this first section dedicated to the study of God, Thomas returns to an examination of this name to ask if "He who is" is God's proper name. Cf. the argument in the following pages.

4. *ST* Ia q. 2 a. 1.

5. The five ways Thomas employs to establish God's existence have been the subject of a vast literature. I refer here simply to two classics: É. Gilson, *The Christian Philosophy of St. Thomas Aquinas*, 59–83; J. Maritain, *Approaches to God*, trans. Peter O'Reilly (London, 1955). Since these two figures are philosophers, it is worth mentioning a theologian who makes indispensable further contributions: G. Lafont, *Structures et méthode dans la Somme théologique de saint Thomas d'Aquin* (Paris, 1961, reprinted 1996), especially chapter 1, "La lumière de Dieu," pp. 35–100.

plore the different aspects under which God's universal causality is proven in Creation—efficient cause, possibility and necessity, degrees of being, the government of the world—but the structure remains fundamentally the same. In each case, we are led to the existence of a First, who is the only explanatory cause for the world, for he is simultaneously both its First Principle and its Final End.

The religious or spiritual meaning of this approach is also quite clear. Thomas's attempt to establish the existence of God is not rationalist pretension but a confession of humility. Man cannot fully grasp God.[6] The oceans of ink that have been spilled on the first questions of the *Summa Theologiae* cannot drown out what even a "naive" reading easily allows us to confirm: Thomas not only feels obliged to demonstrate that God exists, he knows himself incapable of arriving at a final knowledge of God. He constantly repeats the same leitmotiv: we cannot know "what he is" *(quid est)*, only "what he is not" *(quid non est)*. Still, Thomas does not give up the effort; he will have to confess that *God is known as unknown.*[7] And if he dares to say something of God, it will be "like someone who stutters."[8]

Knowledge and Non-knowledge of God

At the moment in which Friar Thomas approached it, this question already had a long history, and the years immediately preceding were not the most agitated part of it. In 1241, a little more than ten years before Thomas began teaching, William of Auvergne, bishop of Paris at the time, in consultation with theologians at the university, had to condemn a general tendency that had been spreading since the beginning of the century: the belief that it was impossible, for angels as well as men, to know

6. J. Maritain once put it forcefully: ". . . to demonstrate the existence of God is neither to subject Him to our grasp, nor to define Him, nor to seize Him, nor to manipulate anything except ideas which are inadequate to such an object, nor to judge anything except our own proper and radical dependence. The procedure by which reason demonstrates that God exists, puts reason itself in an attitude of natural adoration and of intellectual admiration," *Distinguish to Unite*, 239.

7. *Super Boet. De Trin.* q. 1 a. 2 ad 1; cf. the title of J.-H. Nicolas, *Dieu connu comme inconnu* (Paris, 1966).

8. *In I Sent.* d. 22 q. 1 a. 1: "Since we know God imperfectly, thus we also name him imperfectly, as if stuttering *(quasi balbutiendo)*, says Saint Gregory. Only He understands himself perfectly, if I may put it this way, in generating the Word who is consubstantial with him."

God in his essence.[9] The bishop firmly recalled that, on the contrary, "God is seen in his essence or substance by the angels and by all the saints, and will be seen by the glorified souls."[10]

In fact, Christian thought had inherited from the Bible two apparently contradictory affirmations. Saint Paul had stated with great force that God "lives in inaccessible light [and] *no one among men has seen him nor can see him.*" Saint John is no less categorical: "*No one has ever seen God.*"[11] But he also assures us: "We will be like him, because *we will see him as he is.*"[12] Following their own genius and the different contexts in which they developed, the two Christian traditions, East and West, each put the accent on one or the other of these affirmations.

Under the inspiration of Saint Augustine, transmitted by Saint Gregory the Great, the West considers that, of course, we await the vision of God in Heaven as the extension of a life lived in grace. God is by nature invisible to our fleshly eyes, but Jesus solemnly says, "*Blessed are the pure of heart, for they shall see God*" (Matt. 5:8). We must therefore believe that it is possible. If God has been pronounced invisible, it is in order to show that he is not a body, not to forbid to pure hearts the vision of His substance.[13] For Augustine, all our Christian hope gravitates toward the future vision of God in the heavenly city. And we have seen how Thomas, in his wake, conceives of the theological enterprise as occurring in the light of faith, infused with love, that progresses toward understanding. In the Augustinian tradition, the theologians allow to the saints, even while still on earth, a certain knowledge of the divine essence, of the *quid est* of God.[14]

9. Thomas alludes to that condemnation several times; for example, *De ueritate* q. 8 a. 1; *ST* Ia q. 12 a. 1; *In Ioannem I, 18*, lect. 11, n. 212.

10. *Chartularium Universitatis Parisiensis (Chartul.)* I, n. 128, p. 170: "Deus in sua essentia vel substantia videbitur ab angelis et omnibus sanctis et videtur ab animabus glorificatis." The document is dated January 13, 1241.

11. 1 Tim. 6:16; John 1:18.

12. 1 John 3:2; see also John 17:3: "Eternal life, which is that they know you . . ."

13. Augustine, *Epistola* CXLVII, 37 and 48 (to Pauline on the vision of God) (PL 33, 613, and 618).

14. On this point see H.-F. Dondaine, "Cognoscere de Deo quid est," *RTAM* 22 (1955): 72–78, who quotes several passages from Saint Bonaventure, including the one that envisions the knowledge of the *quid est* of God as "a genus differently realized by every man.": "the *quid est* of God can be known fully and perfectly in an exhaustive fashion; in that fashion, God alone can know himself. He can also be known clearly and distinctly by the blessed in heaven, and partly and darkly in as much as God is the sovereign and first Principle of all Creation and, in that fashion, in as much as creation points to him, is knowable by everyone." *De mysterio Trinitatis*, q. 1 a. 1 ad 13, *Opera Omnia*, vol. 5, p. 51 b.

On the other side, grappling with various errors of more or less Gnostic origin, particularly the rationalism of Eunomius, who thought God could be encompassed by human reason, the Greek Fathers have a tendency to emphasize God's invisibility and ineffability. And they are careful to keep close to that view when they comment on the face-to-face vision of which the New Testament speaks. This Greek tradition entered the West by two special channels: Pseudo-Dionysius and Saint John Damascene.[15] Without going into too much detail, suffice it to say that John Scotus Erigena was the starting point for explanations that tried to hold simultaneously to the legacies of both Saint Augustine and Dionysius: God will be seen in the beatific vision, not in his essence but through his manifestations, in theophanies. This solution could not help raising protests. The objections of Hugh of Saint Victor, beginning at the end of the twelfth century, are the clearest and strongest: if God is seen only as an image, then the state is not beatitude.[16] Other theologians—the Dominicans of Saint-Jacques most notably[17]—would be more sensitive to the deep religiosity coming from the Greek tradition. And the thesis about the non-knowledge of God wound up provoking the guardians of Western theological orthodoxy into the somewhat heavy-handed 1241 reaction by the bishop of Paris.[18]

15. The penetration of the West by the "light coming from the East" has been well described by M.-D. Chenu in chap. 12, "L'entrée de la théologie grecque," and chap. 13, "Orientale Lumen," of La théologie au douzième siècle (Paris, 1957), 274–322.

16. "If we always see the image alone, then we never see the truth. For the image is not the truth, even if it is connected with it. Let them spare us therefore those imaginings through which they try to obscure the light of our minds, and let them no more interpose between God and us the idols of their inventions. For us, nothing can satisfy us but Him and we cannot rest except in Him" (PL 175, 955a); Thomas approaches the problem in ST Ia q. 12 a. 2: "To say that we see God through a similitude, that amounts to saying that we do not see the divine essence (dicere Deum per similitudinem uideri, est dicere diuinam essentiam non uidere)." On this point see my study, "La vision de Dieu per essentiam selon saint Thomas d'Aquin," Micrologus 5 (1997): 43–68, reprinted in Recherches thomasiennes, pp. 177–97.

17. This seems to have been the case for, among others, Hugh of Saint-Cher, one of the first Dominican masters in Paris (1230–35). Cf. H.-F. Dondaine, "Hugues de Saint-Cher et la condamnation de 1241," RSPT 33 (1949): 170–74; and for his confrère Guerric de Saint-Quentin (1233–42), the immediate predecessor of Saint Albert the Great, cf. H.-F. Dondaine and B.-G. Guyot, "Guerric de Saint-Quentin et la condamnation de 1241," RSPT 44 (1960): 225–42; C. Trottmann, "Psychosomatique de la vision béatifique selon Guerric de Saint-Quentin," RSPT 78 (1994): 203–26.

18. This story has been magisterially recounted by H.-F. Dondaine, "L'objet et le 'medium' de la vision béatifique chez les théologiens du XIIIe siècle," RTAM 19 (1952): 60–130. See also Simon Tugwell, Albert & Thomas, Selected Writings (New York-Mahwah, 1988),

Prepared by his master's (Saint Albert) solution of this problem, Thomas's view consists in carefully distinguishing what belongs to the earthly knowledge of God and what belongs to the knowledge of him that we will have in heaven. Thus, in 1257, when Thomas encounters the greatest authorities in the Greek tradition, Dionysius and John Damascene, according to whom we cannot know the *quid est* of God, he responds serenely in the *De ueritate*:

We must understand this of the vision from this earth through which the intellect sees God through a certain [intelligible] form. Since that form cannot be adequate to the representation of the divine essence, we cannot see the divine essence through it. We know only that God lies beyond what is presented about him to the intellect and that what is presented follows from "what has remained hidden"; and there lies the highest modality of our knowing here below. This is why we do not see of God "what he is," but only "what he is not." [It will be entirely different in heaven, for according to Saint Albert's solution, which Thomas reproduces and refines, we will not have any need there for a created form in order to see God. It is He who will unite himself directly with the soul of the seer as his beatitude.] The divine essence makes itself sufficiently present in itself. That is why when God himself will be the form of the intellect we will see not only "what he is not," but also "what he is."[19]

As has forcefully been said, "this transposition from the Scriptures into Aristotelian categories of the *sicuti est* (as he is) and *uidere per speciem* (to see through a form) will become standard references among Saint Thomas's disciples. But in 1257, it led the young master to a remarkable decision, the significance of which only appears when we compare it with those of his great contemporaries."[20] Bonaventure, less of an Aristotelian, sees no problem in maintaining that a certain vision of the *"quid est"* is possible on this earth. As for Saint Albert, he thought it possible to concede a certain confused knowledge of the essence or being of God "as he is" *(ut est)* without there being for all that a knowledge of his *"quid est."*[21]

39–95, and the summary by the same author, "La crisi della teologia negativa nel sec. XIII," *Studi* n.s. 1 (1994): 241–42.

19. *De uer.* q. 8 a. 1 ad 8.

20. H.-F. Dondaine, "Cognoscere de Deo quid est," 72.

21. Cf. H.-F. Dondaine, ibid., 72–75. This passage from Albert may have been in Thomas's mind: "We must distinguish between seeing God 'as He is' *(ut est)* and seeing the *quid est* of God, just as we distinguish between seeing something 'as it is' *(ut est)* and seeing the *quid est* of that thing. To see a thing 'as it is,' is to see the being or the essence of that thing; to see the *quid est* of that thing is to see its proper definition including all its data

Thomas tried to reply to this in the passage of *De ueritate* quoted above: to know the essence of something is to know its "*quid est.*"

The dilemma therefore consisted in fully receiving the orientation of the Latin tradition, expressed in the 1241 condemnation, allowing a certain knowledge of the divine essence, without falling into the naive illusion of exhaustive knowledge. At the same time, Thomas had to accept the Greek legacy, a deep religious respect for mystery and transcendence, without renouncing the hope, nourished by Scripture, of a truly face-to-face vision. On the one hand lay the risk of a blasphemous pretension to subordinate the secret of God to the grasp of man. On the other hand, the risk was to succumb to agnosticism before an impersonal and unattainable transcendence and to deprive Christian existence of the stimulus of the final Encounter, where Hope will find the fulfillment of its infinite desire.

The Negative Path

In order to arrive at a knowledge of God that simultaneously takes into account the demands of these two divergent inspirations, Thomas uses an approach that will definitely require all of reason's resources. It consists more in denying than in affirming, in successively discarding "everything that is not God" rather than trying to define what he is. This is the "negative path" *(uia remotionis)* inherited from Pseudo-Dionysius, and we find a good illustration of it in what constitutes the preface, so to speak, of the *Summa contra Gentiles*. In this first great work of his maturity, Thomas was not driven by the (perhaps excessive) desire to be concise that characterizes the *Summa Theologiae*. We therefore often find in the earlier *Summa* fuller explanations that help us to follow the text more easily. In both works, God's existence is taken as a given ("there exists a First Being to whom we give the name God"). It remains to be examined what he is in himself:

In the study of the divine substance, the *negative path* is required above all else. The divine substance surpasses in its immensity all the forms that our intellect can hold, and thus we cannot grasp it by knowing "what it is" *(quid est)*. We can, however, get a kind of knowledge about it in understanding "what it is not" *(quid*

(Rem enim videre, ut est, est enim videre esse rei sive essentiam rei; videre autem, quid est res, est videre propriam diffinitionem includentem omnes terminos rei)"; De resurrectione, tract. 4 q. 1 a. 9, *Opera Omnia*, vol. 26 (1958), p. 328 b.

non est). And we will draw nearer to that knowledge as we can discard, through our understanding, more things from God.[22]

At the risk of a trivial comparison, we might say that Thomas uses a rather simple idea here, similar to the party game in which you try to guess the person or thing that your partner is thinking about. The simplest way to proceed is by a process of elimination. Is it a thing or is it alive? An animal or a person? Male or female? . . . Before long you can make a guess. Things are, however, less simple when we are dealing with God:

> We know a thing better the more that we can grasp the differences that distinguish it from other things. Every thing possesses a being of its own that distinguishes it from all others. That is why we begin by putting things in a *genus* consisting of things whose definition we know. That gives us a certain common knowledge about them. Then we add the *differences* that separate things from one another. And in this way we build up a complete knowledge of something.

For anyone unfamiliar with this mode of reasoning, a simple example will suffice. According to this method, things are first defined by their most general traits *(genus)*; characteristic traits (the *specific differences*) are added. So when we consider a human being as a "rational animal," the term "animal" places him in the genus of animated beings. The term distinguishes him from vegetable life and from minerals. The term "rational" formulates the specific difference that characterizes man among all the other animals. We do not imagine, however, that "rational animal" enables us to know everything about man or any specific man. This knowledge about the universal "man" is only abstract knowledge that includes many of the most general traits, but cannot arrive at knowledge of a specific man (Peter or Paul, which requires a completely different kind of approach). And even this knowledge, as meager as it is, is impossible when we are dealing with God:

> But in the study of the divine substance, since we cannot grasp "the what" *(quid)* and take it as a genus, and since we also cannot grasp its distinctiveness from other things by means of *positive* differences, we are obliged to grasp it through *negative* differences.

We have a positive difference when we add "rational" to "animal" in defining man. But since this mode of definition does not work for God,

22. SCG I 14.

we have to say instead: He's not a thing, an animal, or rational. . . . And he can be understood only by analogy:

Just as in the field of positive differences, one difference leads to another and helps us to get a better grip on the definition of something in marking out a greater number of traits that distinguish it from other things, *so a negative difference leads to others and marks out a larger number of distinctive traits.* If we affirm, for example, that God is not an accident, we distinguish him in that negation from all accidents. If we add further that he is not a body, we distinguish him from a certain number of substances. *And thus progressively, thanks to negations of this kind, we distinguish him from everything that is not him.* There will be a proper consideration of the divine substance when *God will be known as distinct from everything.* But there will be no perfect knowledge of Him, for we remain ignorant of "what he is in himself" (quid in se sit).

In spite of its length and difficulty, we had to quote this passage, for it is quite clear, both in itself and as regards Saint Thomas's purposes. He is animated by the deep conviction that it is nothing insignificant to know what God is not. Each of the negative differences specifies with increasing precision the preceding difference, and better depicts the contours of the object: "And thus, proceeding in order and distinguishing God from everything that he is not through negations of this kind, we come to a knowledge, *not positive, but true,* of his substance, since we know him as distinct from everything else."[23] The comparison with the party game, mentioned earlier, here shows its limits. The parallel does not hold entirely. Suppose that I have identified the person or thing; I find myself in known territory and there is no further mystery for me. The same is not true when the subject is God. I may affirm his existence in a positive judgment, but I cannot form an idea of that existence for myself, a concept that would express his proper mystery. "There is no definition that would enable us to know him except for his distance from everything that is not him. What he is, then, is not known but affirmed, which is to say posited by a judgment."[24] Negative theology is by no means a theology of negation.

In addition to its intellectual relevance, this passage is also quite re-

---

23. É. Gilson, *The Christian Philosophy of St. Thomas Aquinas,* 87.

24. T.-D. Humbrecht, "La théologie négative chez saint Thomas d'Aquin," *RT* 93 (1993): 535–66; *RT* 94 (1994): 71–99, in particular p. 81. This study, the most recent on the subject, is also one of the most far-seeing.

vealing about what I would call the implicit spiritual method of the Master from Aquino. We need to be very attentive to the rigor of this negative dialectic. In itself, it is an unusually demanding asceticism. If a theologian tries to practice it in the spiritual state that we tried to describe in the opening pages of this book, he cannot help but see the stages of his progress as degrees of ascent on the way that leads to God. Like every believer, he must abandon idols and turn toward the living God (Acts 14:14). He must also renounce the constructions of his own mind, personal idols that have no less a hold. In his way, Thomas invites us to this when he distinguishes the contemplation of the philosophers from Christian contemplation. The former is always tempted to stop with the pleasure of knowledge in itself and, in the end, proceeds from self-love. The latter, the contemplation of the saints, completely inspired by love for the divine Truth, ends in the object itself.[25] Completely objective, in the sense that the object itself determines its development, this ascent requires of the subject that he empty himself to the same degree that plenitude will fill him up. The practice of this theology shows itself to be an education in the spiritual life.

God Known as Unknown

Negative theology retains a constant meaning as it passes from the *Summa contra Gentiles* to the *Summa Theologiae*. But its actual practice is rather different. In the earlier work, Thomas takes his starting point from the fact that God is unchangeable. This is neither a philosophical postulate nor a conclusion, but a datum received from revelation. In three different places, the Bible repeats the same affirmation: "God is not a man

---

25. Cf. *In III Sent.* d. 35 q. 1 a. 2 sol. 1: Thomas inquires about the position of the will (affectivity) in the contemplative life and underscores that even though contemplation is the work of the intellect, the intellect is moved and accompanied by the will: "Thus the contemplative life resides in an act of the power of knowing set in motion by the will. But the operation is found, so to speak, midway between the subject and the object; it is a perfection for the subject who knows and it receives its quality from the object that specifies it. It follows, then, that the operation of the power of knowing can be qualified by affectivity (*affectari*) in a twofold way. On the one hand, *in so far as it is the perfection of the knower*, and in this case the affective quality of the operation of knowing proceeds from self-love; *affectivity worked like this in the contemplative life of the philosophers*. On the other hand, *in so far as it finds its end in the object*, and in this case the desire of contemplation proceeds from love of the object, for where love is found there too is found the vision. . . . *Affectivity works like this in the contemplative life of the saints of which we are speaking . . . and it requires charity*." See further ST IIa IIae q. 180 a. 1 and 7.

who changes," as we already read in the book of Numbers (23:19). And the same idea echoes in the prophet Malachi (3:6): "I am God, I do not change." And the apostle James (1:17) writes: "In him there is no change." Starting from that, Thomas establishes that if he is unmoved, God is also eternal, and therefore it is absolutely impossible for him to be in potentiality in any way with respect to whatever he may be. As a consequence, neither is there matter in him—since matter is defined as being in potentiality—and this leads us to discard from our conceptions of him all composition. And if he is not combined with anything else, we must then hold it as certain that God is his own essence, that he is his own Being. We cannot hope to follow the details of these developments to their conclusion. They reach the affirmation of the divine simplicity and then set out again examining God's other perfections.

In the *Summa Theologiae*, the author adopts the inverse order and takes the divine simplicity as his point of departure. He does not, however, deny his earlier intuitions. Indeed, he deepens them, as may be seen by reading the text that corresponds to the text quoted from the *Summa contra Gentiles*:

When we know the existence of some reality, it remains to be asked how it exists, in order to know what it is. But since *we cannot know what God is, but only what he is not*, we also cannot consider how he is, but rather how he is not. We must first examine *how he is not*, then how he is *known* by us, and finally how he is *named*. We can show how God is not by discarding what we know does not accord with him, such as being a compound, in motion, or several other similar things. That is why we inquire first about his simplicity, by which we discard from him all composition. But since in the material order simple things are imperfect and fragmentary, we will have to inquire next about God's perfection, his infinity, his immutability, and his unity.[26]

In starting with the divine simplicity, Thomas centers his exposition on the plenitude of God's Being and on the identification within him of Essence and Existence. God is his very existence. This supports the consideration of the divine attributes that follow. Each of them deserves careful consideration, but it will be enough for us to emphasize what springs forth most clearly from the Thomistic approach. Far from being a way by which man exerts a dominating hold over the divine mystery, this ap-

---

26. *ST* Ia q. 3 Pro.; this statement prefigures questions 4 through 11.

proach awakens in him a keen sense of the mystery that eludes his grasp. Negative theology is the intellectual form of our respect and adoration in confrontation with God's mystery.[27]

Thomas appears here, to a certain extent, as an authentic heir of the Greek tradition. This may be traced from the beginning of his career, when he encountered for the first time in this context the prestigious names who stand behind his apophatic theology.[28] We need to inquire whether the expression used in the Vulgate, when God makes himself known to Moses as "He who is" (Qui est), truly means "what God is" (his quid est) or only, as Saint John Damascene says "a certain infinite ocean of substance."[29] If Damascene is right, the objector says, given that the infinite is not comprehensible (in the sense of an exhaustive knowledge), it will not be "nameable" either. It will therefore be impossible to speak about God and he will remain unknown. For Thomas, there's no doubt; among all other names "Qui est" offers indisputable advantages for speaking of God, since it is revealed, but it doesn't follow, for all that, that we have plumbed the depths of the mystery:

All other names speak of a determined and specific being, as "wise" speaks of a certain being; but the name "qui est" says absolute being, not determined by something added; and that is why Damascene says that it does not signify what God is, but "a certain infinite ocean of substance, not determined." That is why, when we proceed to the knowledge of God by the path of negation, we deny immediately that he has corporeal traits, and then we even deny the intellectual traits as they are found in creatures, such as goodness and wisdom; and thus there only remains in our understanding his existence (quia est) and nothing else, and our intellect then finds itself in a certain confusion. Finally, being itself, such as it is found in creatures, is also denied him and he thus remains in a certain darkness of ignorance (et tunc remanet in quadam tenebra ignorantiae), ignorance through

---

27. It is worth rereading É. Gilson, Le Thomisme, 6th ed., p. 99: "This negative way of thinking about God will come to seem to us more and more characteristic of the knowledge that we have of Him. God is simple. Now, what is simple escapes us. The divine nature eludes our grasp. Human knowledge of such a God can therefore only be a negative theology. To know the divine being is to accept that we do not know it."

28. "Apophatic" (From the Greek, apophasis = negation) is sometimes used as the equivalent of "negative theology" (theologia apophatikê), which is Pseudo-Dionysius' own term.

29. De fide orthodoxa I, 9, 2: PG 94, 836. Burgundionis versio, ed. E. M. Buytaert (Louvain, 1955), 49: "Totum enim in seipso comprehendens habet esse, velut quoddam pelagus substantiae infinitum et indeterminatum."

which we are united to God in the best way, at least in the present life; as Diony-sius says, this ignorance is a kind of cloud in which God is said to dwell.[30]

This passage from the *Commentary on the Sentences*, which has been called "the most apophatic in Thomas's whole work,"[31] is not the only one of its kind, however, and it is quite remarkable that we find similar state-ments at every point in Thomas's intellectual evolution. Ten years after the commentary on the *Sentences*, the *Summa contra Gentiles* takes up the same question in an even more explicit passage:

The separated substance knows by its own power that God exists *(quia est)*, that he is the cause of everything, above everything *(eminentem)*, separate *(remotum)* not only from everything that is but from everything that a created intelligence can conceive of. We can ourselves obtain something of this knowledge of God: through his effects, we know that God exists *(quia est)* and that he is the cause of beings, above and separate from them *(supereminens et remotus)*. This is the sum-mit of our knowledge of God in this life, as Dionysius says *(Mystical Theology* I, 3): *we are united to God as to an unknown.* That comes from the fact that we know of him "what he is not," *(quid non sit)*, "what he is" *(quid est)* remaining com-pletely unknown *(penitus ignotum)*. That is why, to signify our ignorance of that sublime knowledge, it says of Moses that *he approached the dark cloud in which God dwells* (Exod. 20:21).[32]

Thomas defines these matters in the context of a parallel with angelic knowledge. Even though he does not dream of eliminating the mystery, he points out that we are not totally helpless before it. These same two ori-entations are found to a greater or lesser extent in various passages, and it would be easy to multiply examples. Without trying to be exhaustive, we

---

30. *In I Sent.* d. 8 q. 1 a. 1 ad 4; the texts from Pseudo-Dionysius that will recur fre-quently in this context are the following: *De diuinis nominibus* VII 3 (PG 3, 869–72); *De mystica theologia* 1–2 (PG 3, 997–1000); *Epistola V, Ad Dorothaeum* (PG 3, 1074). We should also consult in this context: Saint Albertus Magnus, *Super Dionysii Mysticam The-ologiam et Epistulas (Super Dion. Myst. Theol.)*, *Opera Omnia*, ed. Col., vol. 37 (1951).

31. T.-D. Humbrecht, *RT* (1994): 78 ff.; this text has often been commented on. See es-pecially Joseph Owens, "Aquinas 'Darkness of Ignorance' in the Most Refined Notion of God," *The Southwestern Journal of Philosophy* 5 (1974): 93–110.

32. SCG III 39, n. 2270; in addition to Dionysius, this passage also shows the influence of Proclus, since it is from him that Thomas takes the *penitus ignotum*. Cf. *Super librum De causis*, prop. 6, ed. H.-D. Saffrey (Fribourg-Louvain, 1954), 43; C. D'Ancona Costa, *Tommaso d'Aquino, Commento al "Libro delle Cause"* (Milan, 1986), 229 ff.; A. Pegis has commented on the passage from the *Contra Gentiles*, "Penitus manet ignotum," *MS* 27 (1965): 212–26.

might note that, if we leave aside the learned works to see how Thomas addresses the faithful, the preacher in him expresses himself no differently than does the theologian:

No path is as fruitful for the knowledge of God as that which proceeds by separation *(per remotionem)*. *We know that God is perfectly known when we become aware that he is still beyond everything that we can think about him.* That is why it is said of Moses—who was as intimate *(familiarissimus)* with God as we can be in this life—that he approached God in the cloud and in darkness, which is to say that he came to the knowledge of God by learning "what God is not." It is this way of separation that indicates what the name "holy" means [the thrice-holy of the Seraphim in Isaiah 6:2].[33]

Almost like a litany, this series of passages, to which it would be easy to add,[34] testifies impressively that this initial modesty is never lost from view and that it is repeated every time the occasion presents itself. But at the same time—and also as often as necessary—the theologian refuses to abdicate. God has given him the intellect as his most precious gift and he believes that the highest homage we may render to God consists precisely in using its powers to probe the mystery. Numerous studies have been dedicated to Saint Thomas's apophatic way, but we cannot use this term about Thomas without adding some necessary nuances. The repeated references to Dionysius are in this context like a ritual refrain, and they doubtless signify the considerable authority that he had for medieval thinkers. But as usual—whether he's dealing with Aristotle or someone else—Thomas does not follow Dionysius without serious modifications.

The most obvious of these modifications was rightly noted a long time ago. Contrary to what he found in the available translations, Thomas does not say, as does Dionysius, that God remains *completely* unknown *("omnino" ignoto)*, but he simply says that we attain to him *as* unknown *("tanquam" ignotum; "quasi" ignoto)*.[35] Furthermore, while Dionysius puts God beyond being and believes in his absolute unknownness, Thomas puts God above *"being such as it is found in creatures,"*[36] meaning by this

---

33. Sermon *Seraphim stabant* (unpublished), in J.-P. Torrell, "La pratique pastorale," p. 241, note 141.

34. Cf. *In III Sent.* d. 35 q. 2 a. 2 sol. 2; *Super Boet. De Trin.* q. 2 a. 2 ad 1; *De uer.* q. 2 a. 1 ad 9; *Quaestiones disputatae De potentia (De pot.)* q. 7 a. 5 ad 14; *In Col. 1*, lect. 4, n. 30.

35. Cf. P. Marc's note on *SCG* III 39, n. 2270 and T.-D. Humbrecht, "La théologie négative," *RT* (1994), note 92, p. 91.

36. Cf. the passage from *In I Sent.* d. 8 q. 2 a. 2 ad 4 quoted above.

that there is no conception of being that is common to God and to creatures. But that is not to say that the name "Qui est" may not be applied to God in any way.[37] Thomas does not see God as only the cause of being. God is much more than that. Though the way of causation allows him to state something indispensable about God, he wants to go still further.

We see in particular how he simultaneously repeats, extends, and modifies the triple way that the celebrated Areopagite proposed for approaching God.[38] The basic change in the very order of the three ways shows clearly that Thomas does not share Dionysius's absolute apophatic stance, and that negation does not eliminate the need for affirmation.[39] As Thomas remarks of Maimonides, it is not enough to say that God is alive because he does not possess being as an inanimate body does. By that method, we might say that God is a lion because he does not possess being as a bird does:

The meaning of the negation is itself founded upon a certain affirmation. . . . That is why *if the human intellect could not know anything about God affirmatively, it would not be able to deny anything about him either.* Because if nothing the intellect tells us about God is affirmatively true, it would possess no knowledge of him. That is why, following Dionysius, we must state that these names [of perfections] signify [in reality] the divine substance, although in a defective and imperfect way.[40]

---

37. On this point see É. Gilson, *The Christian Philosophy of St. Thomas Aquinas*, 139–40, who believes that Thomas's modifications of the way of approaching God proposed by Dionysius result in a reversal. It is true that Thomas completely subverts Dionysius's doctrine, but things are not quite that simple. Though Thomas does not think it useful to be content once and for all with proposing Dionysius's three ways, it is not from lack of attention or arbitrariness, but rather it depends on the context, as M. B. Ewbank has demonstrated (see the following note).

38. M. B. Ewbank, "Diverse Orderings of Dionysius's *Triplex Via* by St. Thomas Aquinas," *MS* 52 (1990): 82–109.

39. T.-D. Humbrecht is invaluable on this point because he shows that negative theology cannot function without a prior positive theology.

40. *De pot.* q. 7 a. 5: "Intellectus negationis semper fundatur in aliqua affirmatione . . . *Unde nisi intellectus humanus aliquid de Deo affirmatiue cognosceret, nihil de Deo posset negare.* Non autem cognosceret si nihil quod de Deo dicit uerificaretur affirmatiue. Et ideo . . . dicendum est quod huiusmodi nomina significant diuinam substantiam, quamuis deficienter et imperfecte." G. Emery has pointed out the similarity of Thomas's position to that of his teacher Albertus Magnus, who wrote: "Omnis negatio fundatur supra aliquam affirmationem; unde ubi non est uere affirmatio, neque erit etiam uere negatio" (*Super Dion. Myst. Theol.; Opera Omnia*, vol. 5, p. 475).

A Threefold Path to God

It is important for our purposes to pause briefly on this new aspect of the question. It is true that Thomas expects his disciples to practice a profound intellectual renunciation, but that is something quite different from a more or less disguised resignation. The theologian must show a deep intellectual magnanimity in order to make use of all his mental resources with the same degree of rigor. We especially observe this in the methodical progression in developing the three paths. To go over this material in a general way, let us look at one of Thomas's most explicit treatments, his commentary on a verse from Romans 1:20: "Since the creation of the world, the invisible things of God have been understood through his works." This scriptural commonplace is on Paul's lips in his discourse to the Athenians (Acts 17:24–28) and in the Book of Wisdom 13:5: "The greatness and beauty of creatures leads us by analogy to the contemplation of their author." These passages call for further elaboration:

We should understand, however, that for man in this life something about God remains completely unknown, namely *what he is (quid est Deus)*. . . . The reason for this is that human knowledge finds its starting point in realities that are connatural to us, bodily creatures, which are not suited to representing the divine essence. Nevertheless, as Dionysius says in the *Divine Names* (7:4), it is possible for man to know God from his creatures in a triplex way.

The first is through [the way of] causality. Given that creatures are defective and changing, it is necessary to lead them back [*reducere*: to return as an explanation for their existence] to an unchangeable and perfect principle. In this path, we touch upon the existence of God *(cognoscitur de Deo an est)*.[41]

In itself, this first way is insufficient and, strictly speaking, misleading, for the concept of cause does not have the same meaning when used about God as it does when used about man. In technical terms (that we will have to explain but which are indispensable), cause is here an analogous and not a univocal term.[42] We speak of a term as univocal when it applies equally to two or more different realities: applied to a dog or cat the term "animal" has the same meaning. An analogous term, on the contrary, designates a certain resemblance within a difference. This is true of all the names or qualities that we can apply to God. None of our perfec-

---

41. *In ad Romanos I*, lect. 6, nn. 114–15.
42. Cf. *ST* Ia q. 13 a. 5.

tions, even the most elevated things that we may dream of, are suited to God in the same way they are suited to us. If we take, for instance, the notion of cause as applied to God or man, we cannot simply say: God has a role with respect to creation similar to the one a human artisan has with respect to what he creates. In order not to fall into error, this first approximation must immediately be corrected. The creation of the universe does not refer to its author in the same way that the existence of a painting enables us to infer the existence of a painter. For God does not act on pre-existing material (before the creation nothing existed) and we have to leave the order of created things in order to find creation's reason for being. That is why Thomas adds:

> The second way is the way of *eminence* (here: *excellentiae*). Creatures are not led back to the first principle as to their proper and univocal cause (such as occurs when a man engenders another man), but to a transcendent and universal cause. We understand in this way that God is above everything (*super omnia*).

We might think that the process is over the moment we characterize God as a transcendent cause, the cause above all causes. This would be to misunderstand the intellectual and spiritual demands of the Master from Aquino:

> In saying that God is alive, we have in the mind something else than that he is the cause of our life or that he is different from inanimate bodies. . . . Similarly, when we say: God is good, the meaning is not: God is the cause of goodness, or that God is not bad; rather, what we call goodness in creatures preexists in God—and, in truth, according to a superior mode.[43] It does not follow, then, that it belongs to God to be good because he is the cause of goodness. Rather, it's the reverse: because he is good, he pours out goodness into things. In the words of Saint Augustine: It is because he is good that we exist.[44]

If we only see in God the cause of all goodness or all wisdom in this world, he would be conceived of on the basis of this world. God would be being, or good, or wise as human beings are. And thus univocity threatens the truth. We must therefore take a final step:

---

43. Thomas has already explained this matter in *ST* Ia q. 4 aa. 2–3.

44. *ST* Ia q. 13 a. 2 with a reference to Augustine's *De Doctrina christiana* I, 32, 35 (BA 11, 224). Thomas returns to this subject in article 6 of the same question: "The names attributed to God do not aim only at his causality; they also aim at his essence. For when we say God is good, or wise, *we mean not only that God is the cause of wisdom or goodness, we mean that in him these qualities pre-exist in a supereminent way.*"

The third way is the way of negation. If God is a transcendent cause, nothing of that which we find in creatures can be attributed to him. . . . That is why we say of God that He is in-finite, un-changing, and so forth.

This final step in the development of the argument therefore consists in denying that what we call being, goodness, wisdom exist in God in the way that we know them in this life. God is the source of all because everything pre-exists in him; but he is not alive, wise, or good in the way that human beings are. While entirely affirming the existence of his perfections, Thomas denies that we can know the divine way of realizing perfections.[45] We know, therefore, that God possesses in an eminent way everything that is a good in our world, but the way in which he possesses it absolutely escapes us. The essence (the *ratio* or the *res significata* in the usual terminology) of these perfections is in him, but our way of knowing and speaking *(modus significandi)* is not proportioned to the way in which they exist, which remains inaccessible to us.

He Who Is

The final account, however, is not entirely negative. At the end of the long question in which he examines the knowledge of God that we may try to achieve in this life, Thomas concludes:

Therefore we know God's relationship to his creatures, namely that he is the cause of them all; we know what differentiates him from these creatures, which is to say that he is himself nothing of that of which he is the cause. Finally, we know that, whatever we discard in thinking of him, we discard to indicate not some lack, but rather an excess.[46]

If we keep in mind that this threefold certitude underlies all Thomas's efforts, we may understand that even the most "negative" texts may end with a decisive affirmation:

We can say that at the end of our argument, *we know God as unknown*, because the mind discovers that it has reached the highest point of its knowledge when it knows that the *divine essence is above everything that it may grasp in our present state of life*; and although *what God is* remains unknown to the mind, it knows nonetheless *that he is.*[47]

45. T.-D. Humbrecht observes this in 'La théologie négative," *RT* (1994): 92, with an interesting reference to Claude Geffré, "Théologie naturelle et révélation dans la connaissance de Dieu un," in *L'existence de Dieu* (Paris-Tournai, 1961), 297–317.

46. *ST* Ia q. 12 a. 13.   47. *Super Boet. De Trin.* q. 2 a. 2 ad 1.

Knowledge through divine grace can only reinforce this certitude, but it does not fundamentally change anything about the structure of our knowledge as long as we are on earth. It allows us to know God through his most far-reaching effects and reveals to us knowledge to which reason alone could not attain. But it cannot approach further, to the *quid est* of God. The question that arises then is whether, in spite of everything, it is possible to speak about God other than by hyperbole or poetic metaphor. How are we going to "name" God, because "we name beings according to what we know about them"?[48] As a theologian and preacher, Thomas could not refuse this challenge without allowing the mission of the Dominican Order and his own mission to be put in question.

Consistent with everything that he had already said, Thomas concedes as a first move that "if we can name God from creatures, it is not in such a way that allows us to express the divine essence as it is in itself." We can say with Dionysius: "God has no name or he is above every attempt at naming."[49] However it would be a serious misunderstanding of Thomas to think that he is content with that: his apophatic way is not agnosticism. Like Jacob wrestling with the angel and demanding to know his name, he does not intend to let go before he receives a blessing. He patiently examines the possibility of saying something about God, starting with his effects in creation and from certain conditions. He allows that the names metaphorically applied to God (rock, fortress) belong first to creatures; but things are a bit different for the names of perfections (wisdom or goodness). Since the latter are first in God and only later in creatures, we cannot properly deny their existence in God. Dionysius's remark that these names are more truthfully denied than affirmed of God means something: "the reality signified by the name does not fit God in the same fashion that the name expresses, but in a more excellent way."[50] The distinction between the reality signified and its properly divine mode of realization thus reveals its usefulness. Thomas does not in any way wish to close God into a concept, but he very much wants to say something about him.

Two special names should be considered here. The name "God" itself, hallowed by long use, has its advantages. Although the word has been used of beings other than God himself, that appears to have been done only "according to opinion." The divine nature is not communicable to

---

48. *ST* Ia q. 13: "On the Divine Names."   49. *ST* Ia q. 13 a. 1 and ad 1.
50. *ST* Ia q. 13 a. 3 ad 2.

several individuals, as is human nature. No more than any other name does it give us knowledge of the divine nature, but it crowns the ascending dialectic of eminence, causality, and negation, because "it is precisely destined to designate a being who is above everything, who is the principle behind everything, and distinct from everything. That is exactly what all people understand when they name God."[51]

The second name that supremely suits God is the one by which he revealed himself to Moses (Exod. 3:14): "He who is." Thomas had already had several chances to comment on this phrase.[52] But when he takes it up again in the *Summa Theologiae*, he points out three reasons that seem to him to justify its eminence. First, "because of its *meaning*, because it does not designate a particular form of existence, but existence itself." Since God is the only instance of a thing whose being is his essence, no other word names him with greater appropriateness, for every being is named according to its form. Second, this name fits God because of its *universality*, for whatever is determined and limited does not suit him, since what is absolute and general is better applied to him. That is why John Damascene holds "He who is" as the principal name of God because it contains all things, like an infinite and unlimited ocean of substance. While every other name determines a certain mode of a thing's substance, the name "Qui est" determines no particular mode of being. It fits in an indeterminate way with everything. Finally, because of what it includes in its meaning *(consignificatio)*; this name signifies *present* being, which supremely suits God, whose being does not admit of past and future.

When we read this passage, the answer appears definitive: no other name is known that would be better suited to designate God. Nevertheless, the point is nuanced, and another competing point of view, so to speak, adduces the two principal names that have just been examined:

The name "Qui est" names God with greater propriety than the name "God" itself if we look to the origin of that name *(id a quo imponitur)*, which is to say "be-

---

51. *ST* Ia q. 13 a. 8 ad 2; it is striking to find here the conclusion of the treatment of each of the five ways in *ST* Ia q. 2 a. 3.

52. É. Zum Brunn, "La 'métaphysique de l'Exode' selon Thomas d'Aquin," in *Dieu et l'être. Exégèses d'Exode 3, 14 et de Coran 20, 11–24* (Paris, 1978), 245–69, has identified about twenty texts in which Thomas comments on this verse. In his first writings, Thomas reproduces the formula *Qui est*; but beginning with the *Summa theologiae* he seems to prefer the more complete *Ego sum qui sum*. The division is not absolute: *ST* Ia q. 2. a. 3 s. c. has the longer version, but *Qui est* appears at *ST* Ia q. 13 a. 11.

ing," and to its way of signifying and to "co-signify." Yet if one considers what it is intended to mean *(id ad quod imponitur nomen)*, the name "God" is more fitting because it is used to signify the divine nature.

The name "God" says nothing about the divine essence but it has the advantage of designating it as if a universal name were being applied to a particular individual in a way that is fitting to him, as if a term like "man" were applicable exclusively to someone named Peter. On the other hand, the name "Qui est," which designates God by means of a perfection found in all existing things, does not have the same advantages of incommunicability. The theologian does not reject the vocabulary of being so long as, by subjecting it to the revelation of the "Qui est," he has confirmation of its validity: "Thus, we have two names: 'God,' which expresses the divine nature but in a purely indicative fashion, and 'being,' which expresses God's supereminent perfection from the starting point of creatures. That is why 'God' affirms the way of signifying without involving the way of being, and 'Qui est' states and signifies the way of being. *Neither encloses the divine essence, and in the final analysis, Thomas's 'Qui est' designates God as ineffable."*[53]

The Name Above Every Name

After all this, we might think that Thomas finally has what he was looking for. But he knows otherwise. In this very reply, where he compares the two names, it is curious that he also adds something like literary repentance: *"Even more fitting is the Tetragrammaton, which is used to signify the very substance of God, according to which that substance is incommunicable and singular, so to speak."*[54]

The Tetragrammaton is the name by which God calls himself in the revelation of the Burning Bush. The name has four letters (YHWH), and out of reverent fear Jews avoid pronouncing it. They have even lost its exact meaning and the true pronunciation, which has given rise to innumerable explanations.[55] This name was not unknown in the Latin theological tradition, but Thomas seems to have discovered its importance in his reading of Maimonides, who devotes long passages to the

---

53. T.-D. Humbrecht, "La théologie négative" *RT* (1994): 93, emphasis added.
54. *ST* Ia q. 13 a. 11 ad 1.
55. For the *status quaestionis*, see A. Caquot, "Les énigmes d'un hémistiche biblique," and A. Cazelles, "Pour une exégèse de Ex. 3,14," in *Dieu et l'être*, pp. 17–26 and 27–44.

question and thinks the Tetragrammaton is a different name than the "Qui est."[56]

Thomas does not share Maimonides' equivocations or extreme apophatic position,[57] but it is worth noting this lineage because it confirms Thomas in his choice of a negative theology. In any event, it was the exegesis of this Jewish scholar that enabled Thomas to maintain that the Tetragrammaton is a name even more suited to God than the "Qui est." He states as much in the immediately preceding article in the *Summa* when he inquires into the propriety of the name "God": "If a certain name was given to God to signify him not as to his nature but as subject, as *such a being*, that name would be absolutely incommunicable. This is *perhaps* the case with the Tetragrammaton among the Hebrews."[58] The "perhaps" in this passage may convey a certain perplexity about the true meaning of this name. But it is more important to note that while he already mentioned it in the *Summa contra Gentiles*,[59] it is only in the *Summa Theologiae* that he makes this topical use of it. This is a serious shift, because Thomas situates himself not only in the perspective of the name's origin, but in the reality that the name was meant to signify. The name revealed to the believer is preferred to the name arrived at by the philosopher. Entirely singular, this is truly the name above every other name, and it refers only to God.

Having arrived at this point, a man seeking God's intelligibility, it would appear, cannot go any further. This would be true if Thomas were reasoning simply as a philosopher, but that was never the case in this context. Even though he seems to use only the resources of natural reason, as a theologian he had already prepared the ground explicitly and he appeals to the more elevated knowledge received through grace:

> In spite of the revelation of grace, it remains true that so long as we are in this life we do not know the Divine essence (his *quid est*) and that we are in this way united *as if to an unknown*; however, we know him more fully to the extent that he is

56. A. Maurer, "St. Thomas on the Sacred Name 'Tetragrammaton,'" *MS* 34 (1972): 274–86, reprinted in the author's collection of essays, *Being and Knowing: Studies in Thomas Aquinas and the Later Medieval Philosophers* (Toronto, 1990), 59–70. The author emphasizes that the distinction between the *Qui est* and the Tetragrammaton appeared prior to Maimonides in Saint Jerome and even in Philo.

57. Cf. A. Wohlmann, *Thomas d'Aquin et Maïmonide, Un dialogue exemplaire* (Paris, 1988), especially pp.105–64.

58. *ST* Ia q. 13 a. 9.

59. As T.-D. Humbrecht has noticed, cf. *SCG* IV 7, n. 3408.

accessible to us through his most numerous and excellent effects and because *divine revelation allows us to attribute to him qualities that natural reason could not apprehend, such as the fact that God is both one and triune.*[60]

Thomas does not immediately pursue this avenue, but he returns to it later when he again takes up the question of divine names in the midst of the treatise on the Trinity. There he inquires into the personal names properly attributed to each of the divine persons: the Father, who has no other proper name; the Son, who also has as proper names both "Word" and "Image"; the Holy Spirit, to whom are personally fitting the names "Gift" and "Love."[61] This new way of envisaging matters takes nothing away from the impossibility of knowing in this life God's *"quid est"* or from the structure of knowledge of God obtained from his effects. But we see in this text that Thomas does not lose sight of the new perspectives that open up to reason by means of revelation.

The revelation of the *"Qui est,"* however, already authorizes theology to take the lead and to penetrate the mystery of God beyond his unity, a unity which philosophical reason does not feel it has the right to go beyond. With a sureness of intuition that does honor to their profound knowledge of the Bible, the medieval theologians were not afraid to build on the *"Qui est"* of Exodus and to see in it a rough outline of the mystery of the Trinity. They felt themselves authorized by the whole tradition that found expression in art and liturgy, which the *Gloss* reflects: "This true being is that of the living God, the Trinity; what *is*, in the true sense, is the Father with the Son and the Holy Spirit. That is why we say God lives, for the divine essence lives a life that death does not affect."[62] By relating the Exodus text to all the New Testament passages in which Jesus speaks of himself by affirming his existence in absolute terms ("I Am"), numerous writers, both Franciscan and Dominican, are able to provide a Christological exegesis of the name revealed to Moses.

Thomas is therefore not alone when he follows this tradition by recalling, along with the *Gloss*, that we appropriate the divine name for the person of the Son "not in virtue of its proper significance, but because of the context: which is to say insofar as the Word God addressed to Moses pre-

60. *ST* Ia q. 12 a. 13 ad 1.
61. Cf. *ST* Ia qq. 33–38.
62. On this point, see the rich study by É. H. Wéber, "L'herméneutique christologique d'Exode 3,14 chez quelques maîtres parisiens du XIIIe siècle," *in Celui qui est* (Paris, 1986), 47–101, from which I have borrowed this reference to the *Gloss* (cf. p. 54).

figured the liberation of the human race later achieved by the Son."[63] The texts collected in the *Catena aurea* show to what extent Thomas shares the general feeling of the Fathers that the theophanies of the Old Testament were veiled sayings of the Word, prefigurations of the Incarnation.[64] But among the theologians of his own age, Thomas better keeps his eye on negative theology.[65] Without going into all the texts here, we can read the most explicit of them in order to grasp how much revelation overturns a purely rational approach:

So far as concerns what we must believe about him, Christ teaches three things: first, the majesty of his divinity, then his origin in the Father, and finally his indissoluble union with the Father.

He teaches the majesty of his divinity when he says: *I Am;* which is to say, I have within me God's nature, and *I am the very same one who spoke to Moses* saying: *I am he who is.*

In order not to exclude the distinction of the persons he then teaches the Jews faith in his origin in the Father because subsistent being pertains to the whole Trinity, saying: *Of myself I do nothing, but what the Father has taught me, that I say.* Because from the beginning he did works and taught, Jesus shows his origin in the Father on the one hand, in what he does: *Of myself I do nothing. . . .* On the other hand, he shows it by what he teaches: *but as the Father has taught me,* which is to say has given me knowledge by begetting me in knowledge. Given that the nature of truth is simple, for the Son, to know is to be. Thus, in the same way that the Father by begetting him has given being to the Son, so God has given him to know: *My teaching is not my own.*

And in order that we not understand that he has been sent from the Father as if he had been separated from him, he teaches us in the third place to believe in his indissoluble union with the Father, saying: *he who has sent me,* which is to say the Father, *is with me:* on the one hand, by unity of essence: *I am in the Father and the Father in me;* on the other hand, in a union of love: *the Father loves the Son and shows him everything he does.* Thus the Father has sent the Son in such a way that he has not departed from him: *he has not left me alone,* because his love envelops me. But though the two are inseparable, one is sent *(missus)* and the other sends, for the Incarnation is a sending, and it pertains only to the Son and not to the Father.[66]

63. *ST* Ia q. 39 a. 8.
64. Cf. Wéber, "L'herméneutique christologique," 92.
65. É. Wéber has nicely formulated this: "Albert and Thomas are too-little-followed exponents of the apophatic doctrine inherited from Dionysius and explained by John Scotus Erigena" (ibid., 88).
66. *In Ioannem VIII,* 28, lect. 3, n. 1192.

What follows in the texts deserves to be better known, but would take us too far afield. We should at least feel some astonishment at not finding the Holy Spirit here, an absence which we also feel elsewhere. Thomas takes care to warn readers: "If the Holy spirit is not mentioned here, we should understand that *wherever it is a question of the Father and the Son*, and especially when it's a question of the divine majesty, *the Holy Spirit* is understood [literally, is "co-understood"], *because he is the link that unites Father and Son*."[67] There is almost no need to point out the breadth of the new fields open for reflection here. Thomas takes back nothing of what he has said about the unknowableness of the divine essence. He simply knows that the revelation to Moses of the divine simplicity in the theophany of the Burning Bush expands with the revelation of the Trinitarian unity. And he receives in the humility of Christian faith the revelation of what is absolutely beyond anything to which reason can lay claim. Jesus came to give an answer to the question about God which man would never have dreamed of.

The God No One Has Ever Seen

Thomas returned to this question one last time at the very end of his life, in his lessons on Saint John, the most finished of his scriptural commentaries.[68] The prologue to the fourth evangelist ends, we recall, with an affirmation with which we began the present chapter: "No one has ever seen God; only the Son who is in the bosom of the Father, has made him known" (John 1:18). But Thomas comments that we are not lacking for texts that speak of the possibility of seeing God; how then are we to understand Saint John's assertion? Thomas launches into his most detailed exposition of this question. We shall leave aside the highly technical points unnecessary for our present purposes. But let us look at the greater part of the main themes:

We have to understand that there is a threefold way of "seeing God." First, by means of a creature substituted for God and offered to our bodily eye; it is thus that Abraham is believed to have seen God when he saw three men but adored only one of them (cf. Gen. 18).

Then, by way of an imaginary representation; in this way Isaiah saw the Lord sitting on a high throne (cf. Isa. 6). We find in Scripture several similar visions.

---

67. *In Ioannem XVII*, 3, lect. 1, n. 2187.
68. Cf. J.-P. Torrell, *Saint Thomas Aquinas*, 198–201.

Finally, we may see God by an intelligible form *(speciem intelligibilem)* abstracted from sensible realities. That is the case for those who, contemplating the greatness of creatures, grasp in the understanding the greatness of the creator (cf. Wisd. 13:5, Rom. 1:20).

God is also seen in another way through a certain light infused by God into the mind during contemplation. This was how Jacob saw God face to face (cf. Gen. 28:10–19), according to Saint Gregory, in a vision resulting from Jacob's deep contemplation.

However, we cannot arrive by any of these visions at the vision of the divine essence . . . for no created form *(creata species)* can represent the divine essence, since nothing finite can represent the infinite. . . . That is why the knowledge in which God is seen by means of creatures is not the vision of his essence but only a vision from afar, in a darkened mirror (cf. 1 Cor. 13:12) . . . for these ways of knowing do not tell us what God is, but only what he is not or that he exists. According to Dionysius, that is the highest knowledge of God we can expect in this life, and it is achieved only through the negations of all creatures and of everything that we can understand.

Some people have maintained that the divine essence will never be seen by created intelligence and that it is seen neither by the angels nor by the blessed in heaven. [We come here to the proposition condemned in 1241; Thomas pronounces it false and heretical for three reasons, the last of which was of extreme importance for him, and we shall return to it:] To take from men the possibility of seeing the divine essence is to deprive them of beatitude itself. The vision of the divine essence is therefore necessary for the beatitude of the created intelligence: *Blessed are the pure of heart for they shall see God* (Matt. 5:8).

In matters of the divine essence, we must pay attention to three things. First, the divine essence will never be seen by the bodily eye, nor perceived by the senses or imagination, because we can only perceive sensible things through the senses, and God is not a body. . . .

Next, so long as the human intelligence is linked to the body, it cannot see God, for it is weighed down by the corruptible flesh so that it cannot achieve the summit of contemplation. The more the soul is purified from its bodily passions and liberated from earthly affections, the more it is raised to the contemplation of truth and *tastes how good is the Lord* (Ps. 33:9). Now, the highest degree of contemplation is to see God in his essence. And that is why so long as man lives in this body, subject by necessity to multiple passions, he cannot see God in his essence: *No man can see me and live* (Exod. 33:20). For the human intelligence to see the divine essence it is therefore necessary that it leave this body completely, either through death (cf. 2 Cor. 5:8) or in ecstasy (cf. 2 Cor. 12:3).

We must finally remember that *no created intellect*, no matter how fully separated from the body as we may imagine, whether by death or rapture, *can totally understand the divine essence* by seeing it. Thus it is often said that, although the blessed see all of the divine essence *(tota)*, since it is perfectly simple and does not have parts, they do not see it totally *(totaliter)*, for that would be to "comprehend" it. When I say "totally," I refer to a certain mode of vision. Now, in God every mode is identical with his essence; that is why he who does not see him totally does not "comprehend" him. Properly speaking, we say that someone "comprehends" a reality when he understands it as much as it is understandable in itself; otherwise, although he understands it, he does not "comprehend" it. [This type of exhaustive understanding is not possible except with regard to knowledge of created things. When we are dealing with the uncreated and infinite God, it is impossible for the finite and created intellect to arrive at that comprehensive understanding.] God alone comprehends himself, because his power in the act of knowing is as vast as his existence in the act of being . . .

Given the preceding, we see that we must understand Saint John's expression, "No one has ever seen God," in a threefold way: (1) No one, which is to say no mortal, has ever seen God, which is to say the divine essence, through bodily or imaginative vision. (2) No one in this mortal life has seen the divine essence itself. (3) No one, man or angel, has seen God with comprehensive vision.[69]

This long passage might serve as an outline for the present chapter; ending with it gives us the advantage of collecting the essential points in a vision of the whole that would otherwise be quite difficult to express. We cannot help but be struck by Thomas's constant commitment from the outset of his career to preserve the emphasis of the Latin tradition: man will never be truly happy unless he arrives at the vision of the divine essence. But at the same time we have to note his equally firm intention not to lose the mystery that the Greek tradition so strongly emphasized. That vision of the divine essence will never be complete knowledge, even in heaven. We can never fault Thomas regarding this point:

The blessed soul of Christ himself did not have that comprehensive understanding; the only Son of God alone, who is in the bosom of the Father, could enjoy that. That is why the Lord says (11:27): "No one knows the Father but the Son and those to whom the Son wishes to reveal him." The evangelist seems to speak here of that understanding of comprehension. No one really comprehends the divine essence except God alone, Father, Son, and Holy Spirit.[70]

69. *In Ioannem I, 18,* lect. 11, nn. 208–21.
70. *In Ioannem I, 18,* lect. 11, n. 219.

A widely diffused hagiographical account represents Saint Thomas as, while still a child, tirelessly asking his family the same question: "What is God?" The story is apocryphal, but the legend expresses the truth more deeply than strict historical accuracy. We can now see from the evidence that the full-fledged theologian made this supposedly child's question the central occupation of his adult life. Following his method and the progressive deepening of his thought, Thomas's disciples too are led to put God beyond all things.

☞

CHAPTER III

God and the World

From a theology that puts God at the center of its concern, a number of important consequences follow. The most immediate involves the very organization of the theological material. The synthesis of knowledge about God must be presented in a way that stresses the sovereign primacy owed to the unique subject of that knowledge. The solution to this organizational problem is found in Thomas's plan for the *Summa Theologiae*. The pedagogical aspect of that plan, however, should not lead us into error, for along with its uses as a classroom tool, it introduces us to the whole of Friar Thomas's teachings, most notably to his views on Creation, man as the image of God, God's presence in the world, and the world's presence to God. These are large theological questions as well as major themes in the spirituality of every age.

Tha Alpha and the Omega

After a little more than a decade of teaching various audiences, Thomas recognized limitations in the way that theological faculties in his day typically sought to instruct students. Commentaries, whether on the book of *Sentences* or on Sacred Scripture, condemned professors to presenting their thinking in a scattered and fragmentary way, whenever the text permitted. The grouping of points into Disputed Questions allowed a focus on certain subjects. But these still remained in a dispersed state and students had no comprehensive view of the theological material. Thomas speaks of this situation in the famous Prologue to the *Summa:*

We have observed that the beginners in this subject are quite hampered by using the writings of different authors, whether by the unnecessary multiplication of questions, articles, and arguments, or because what they ought to learn is not dealt with according to the demands of the subject itself *(secundum ordinem disciplinae)* but rather as a commentary on books requires or on the occasion of Disputed Questions; or finally because the frequent repetition of the same things engenders weariness and confusion in the minds of the listeners.[1]

People often wonder about the intellectual level of the students Thomas is aiming at, because today even experienced specialists have a hard time reading the book he offers them. But the same question applies to Saint Albert or Saint Bonaventure, who are no easier to approach. Thomas was not overestimating the capacities of his listeners; he was thinking less about the difficulty of the subjects treated than about the way he might put them together into an organized body of doctrine. Instead of proposing a simple series of questions to be followed without close links to one another, he offers a synthesis that already generates knowledge by its very emphasis on interconnections and internal coherence. The great originality of the *Summa* lies not in its content—to a very large degree, Thomas is happy to reproduce traditional Christian teaching, and his dependence on numerous philosophers and theologians shows as much—but in its organization. He calls it the "order of knowing" *(ordo disciplinae)*, and he enunciates it with characteristic moderation at the beginning of the next question:

Given that the object of *sacra doctrina* is to transmit knowledge of God, not only as it is in itself, but also as the *beginning and end of all things*, particularly of the rational creature . . . we must treat first of God *(Prima Pars)*, then of the rational creature's movement toward God *(Secunda Pars)*, and finally of Christ, who in his humanity is for us the way that leads to God *(Tertia Pars)*.[2]

The great simplicity of this passage obviously does not convey everything and we will have to look further into various points at the proper time. For the moment, the essential matter is to note the consequences of what we have identified as the subject of theology: "God as the beginning

---

1. *ST* Ia q. 1 Pro.; I cannot emphasize enough the harshness of this criticism: "unnecessary multiplication of problems, distinctions, and arguments; absurd and haphazard order of exposition; repetition of the same things. And the result: teaching unsuited to learning and doctrinally disastrous, which increases mental confusion, tires students, and paralyzes instruction" (M. Hubert, "L'humour de saint Thomas d'Aquin en face de la scolastique," in *1274—Année charnière—Mutations et continuités* (Paris, 1977), 729). Thomas's abandonment of his habitual restraint suggests just how strong the indictment was.

2. *ST* Ia q. 2 Pro.

and end of all things." Thomas's commentary on the *Sentences* already took the same view, though the vocabulary was slightly different: "The theologian considers creatures as they come from the First Principle and as they return to their end, which is God himself."[3] In the time-honored expression of the theologians, the "exit-return" *(exitus-reditus)* scheme underlies the plan of the *Summa*. I have treated the question at length elsewhere (along with interpretations of it proposed by today's disciples of the Master).[4] Therefore, there is no need to repeat here detailed explanations, but there is much to say about the implications of Thomas's position.

The Neoplatonic origin of Thomas's scheme has often been noted. But this is only true in a way that must be more carefully understood in order to avoid serious misunderstanding. When Thomas, following his sources, uses the word *exitus* (or *egressus*) to say that creatures "come forth" from God, he clearly does not mean to adopt a doctrine of emanation, eternal and necessary, in the Neoplatonic mode.[5] A thinker in the Judeo-Christian tradition, Thomas could only conceive of that "coming forth" as a free creation, inaugurating time and the history of salvation. And perhaps to signify this more clearly, he uses the standard vocabulary less often as he proceeds from the *Sentences* to the *Summa*. Instead of speaking about the "coming forth" of creatures, he will henceforth speak rather of how they "proceed" from God by the Creator's act.[6]

This changes nothing, however, in the central intuition: the connec-

---

3. *In II Sent.*, Pro.

4. See my *Saint Thomas Aquinas*, chapter 8; to the bibliography there I would add I. Biffi's much more detailed inquiry into the subject, "Il piano della Summa Theologiae e la teologia come scienza e come storia," chap. 6 in *Teologia, Storia, e Contemplazione*, 223–312.

5. Besides his contemporaries Bonaventure and Albert (cf. G. Emery, below), I ought to mention in particular the *Liber de Causis* and Pseudo-Dionysius among the sources in which Thomas could have found this doctrine. See the constantly convincing work by M. Seckler, *Le salut et l'histoire: la pensée de saint Thomas d'Aquin sur la théologie de l'histoire* (Paris, 1967), in particular chapter 3: "Saint Thomas et le néoplatonisme," which demonstrates Thomas's double correction to the Plotinian necessitarianism through the Christian idea of creation: the liberty of the divine initiative and the beginning of creation in time.

6. In the Latin of the Vulgate, the term *procedere* is used by Jesus to say that he has "proceeded *(processi)* from God" (John 8:42). The same is true of the Holy Spirit "who proceeds *(procedit)* from the Father" (John 15:26). The technical use of "proceed" and "procession" in speaking of the Trinity comes from these passages. Thomas uses the same word, "procession," to describe the "coming forth" of creatures from God in the creation, cf. *ST* Ia q. 44 Pro. in particular. Still, I should not overstate this development: the vocabulary of procession is already present in the commentary on the *Sentences*.

tion of the universe to God in a circular movement of creatures who have come forth from him and are led back toward their origin, now viewed as their final end. If it were not so long ago, we might honor Thomas for having eliminated the cycle on behalf of a new linear conception of time.[7] Today, we are more aware that the linear conception—quite true, since the history of salvation moves toward a goal—is built into the great movement of "exit-return." Thomas makes it the structure of his work only because it discloses its presence in the whole universe:

It is when it makes a return to its beginning that an effect is sovereignly perfect. Thus, a circle, of all the geometric figures, and circular motion, of all motions, are sovereignly perfect because in them is found the return to the beginning. And thus for the created universe to reach its ultimate perfection, it is necessary for creatures to return to their beginning. Now, all creatures, together and individually, return to their beginning insofar as they bear within themselves a resemblance to it in their very being and nature, which constitute for them a certain perfection.[8]

The seeming simplicity of the point of departure here should not lead us to think that this is a naive, imaginary representation. The philosophical formulation can be much more precise:

Everything found in us comes from God and is linked with him as to its efficient cause and its exemplary cause: he is the efficient cause, since through God's active power everything is accomplished in us; he is the exemplary cause, because everything in us which is of God imitates God in a certain way.[9]

Thomas misses no opportunity to emphasize this circular movement as a whole, and he aims at reproducing it in the plan of the *Summa*. Thus, after the part that speaks of the one true and three-personed God of Christian revelation (qq. 2–43), more than half of the *Prima Pars* deals primarily with the procession of creatures from God and the way in which God is concerned with them (qq. 44–119). After that begins the description of the return movement of creatures toward God, which takes up the whole of

7. Thus É. Gilson, *The Spirit of Mediaeval Philosophy*, trans. A. H. C. Downes (New York, 1940), 388.

8. SCG II 46, n. 1230.

9. SCG IV 21, n. 3576. This dimension of things is becoming better recognized, cf. J.-P. Torrell, *Saint Thomas Aquinas*, 153–56; J. Aertsen, "The Circulation-Motive and Man in the Thought of Thomas Aquinas," in *L'homme et son univers au Moyen Age*, ed. Chr. Wenin, vol. 1 (Louvain-la-Neuve, 1986), 432–39; J. Aertsen, *Nature and Creature: Thomas Aquinas's Way of Thought* (Leiden, 1988).

the *Secunda Pars* and the *Tertia Pars*. We have to emphasize the "and," because another misconception often follows the first. Certain readers, applying too rigidly the notion of movement of exit to the First Part and movement of return to the Second Part, are then unable to place the Third Part correctly. Such readers have set themselves up to be surprised, because they believe that Thomas speaks of Christ only as a kind of addition.

It is rather implausible that as rigorously Christian an author as Thomas would have "forgotten" Christ in laying out his plan. If he put Christ in the Third Part, he wanted it that way. And we shall soon see why. But it is already clear that this error in reading is hardly to be explained through the prior and false identification of the "exit-return" scheme with Plotinus's emanationism. Careful and extensive reading of Thomas's works will correct this misunderstanding. Though the vocabulary is Neo-platonic, the reality to which it is applied is biblical. It is not only a question of structure, supposedly reflecting the timeless myth of the eternal return, but indeed of a history that unfolds according to salvation time. Thus the creature's return toward God does not end with the description of the contemplative life at the end of the *Secunda Pars*. It only ends with the real entry into beatitude at the time of Christ's return, when he will come to take the saved into his Glory. Death prevented Thomas from bringing this work to completion, but that is the place to which he wanted to guide his readers. The prologue to the Third Part is very clear on this:

Our Savior, the Lord Jesus . . . showed himself to us as the way of truth, by which it is now possible for us to be resurrected and to come to the blessedness of eternal life.

These words repeat almost literally the first words of the *Summa*, which described the subject of the Third Part as "Christ, who in his humanity is for us the way that leads to God." Whatever reasons led Thomas to choose this way of exposition, there is no doubt that the circular motion he describes is not completed except *through Christ*. The God we speak of is not the impersonal First Principle of some form of Deism, but the Creator and Redeemer of the Bible. This can also be seen in the prologue to the Second Part, which begins by reminding us of the first page of Genesis on man as the image of God. This key passage, deliberately placed at the *Summa's* center of gravity, at the very point where, having described the "exit," Thomas begins the movement of "return," leaves no doubt about the biblical inspiration of the whole work. We will return to this shortly.

Trinity and Creation

We do not entirely understand the circular scheme of the *Summa* until we see that Thomas also envisions a trinitarian plan in the connection of the world with its creator. This vision of a theologically unified world — which he basically shares with his great contemporaries Albert and Bonaventure — was present at the very start of his theological reflection.[10] Thomas's youthful writings, however, are often invaluable in clarifying his mature work, but they are not well known. At the beginning of his career, Thomas was often more explicit than he would be later on. This is a familiar phenomenon. The first time that a writer recognizes an important idea, he tries to explore it fully and to show all its facets. Later, he remains content with quickly recalling it and assuming that it is known to his readers from his first treatment. That is how Thomas's comments develop on the relationship between the creation and the Trinity. Even though the lines devoted to this subject in the commentary on the *Sentences* are very dense, we find in them a more full-bodied statement than in the *Summa*:

> In the exit of creatures from the First Principle, we observe a kind of circular movement (*quaedam circulatio uel regiratio*) owing to the fact that all things return as to their end to that from which they came forth as their Beginning. That is why the return to their end must be accomplished by the same causes that led to their emergence from their Beginning. Now, as we have already said, since the procession of persons is the explicative reason [*ratio*: this very rich term has several simultaneous meanings: cause, model, reason, motif, etc.] for the production of creatures by the First Principle, this same procession is therefore also the *ratio* for their return to their end.[11]

Though the conciseness of this passage gives it a slightly enigmatic character, it may be easily understood if we look at the passage to which the

---

10. This was magisterially established by G. Emery, *La Trinité créatrice: Trinité et création dans les commentaires aux Sentences de Thomas d'Aquin et de ses précurseurs Albert le Grand et Bonaventure* (Paris, 1995). The same author presents this argument in shortened form in his article, "Trinité et Création. Le principe trinitaire de la création dans les Commentaires d'Albert le Grand, de Bonaventure et de Thomas d'Aquin sur les Sentences," *RSPT* 79 (1995): 405–30.

11. *In I Sent.* d. 14 q. 2 a. 2.

author refers.[12] A few pages earlier, he had explained that the procession of creatures, which is to say the creation, cannot be well understood from the standpoint of the creator, unless we take into account two points of view. On the one hand, we have the divine *nature*, whose fullness and perfection explain the perfection of the creature, since that divine nature is both the realizing cause and the model. On the other hand, the *will* that does all these things gives freely, out of love, not out of a sort of natural necessity. Now, as we hold by faith that there is a procession of persons in God, in the interior unity of the divine essence, we may conclude from this that this intra-Trinitarian procession, which is perfect, must also be the cause and explanatory reason for the procession of creatures as well.

From the point of view of nature, the perfection of creatures represents the perfection of the divine nature only very imperfectly. This is quite clear, but we must nonetheless trace their perfection back to its explanatory principle in the Son, who contains all the perfection of the divine nature, since he is the perfect image of the Father. In this way, the procession of the Son is the model, the exemplar, and the reason for the procession of creatures in the natural order, where they imitate and reproduce something of the divine nature.

From a second point of view, according to which the procession of creatures results from the divine will, we must trace the procession back to a principle that explains all the gifts that will distributes. The first principle in this order can only be love, since it is only because of love that all things are freely granted existence by the divine will. Love, then, is their explanatory reason. Thus, inasmuch as the procession of creatures results from divine liberality, it is traced to the person of the Holy Spirit, who proceeds by way of love.

This teaching, already present in many other passages of this same book of the *Sentences*,[13] is identical to what we find very clearly represented in the *Summa*:

To create belongs to God by reason of his being, and his being is identical to his essence, which in turn is common to the three Persons. We thus see that to create

12. Thomas refers to the absolutely decisive passage in *In I Sent.* d. 10 q. 1 a. 1. Its density defies translation, but I paraphrase it in the text above.

13. See, for example, *In I Sent.* d. 14 q. 1 a. 1, which also deals with the intra-Trinitarian processions and their connections to creation. See also *In I Sent.* d. 27 q. 2 a. 3 ad 6: "non tantum essentia [diuina] habet ordinem ad creaturam, *sed etiam processio personalis, quae est ratio processionis creaturarum.*"

is not only fitting to one of the Persons, but is common to the whole Trinity. Nonetheless, the divine Persons, by reason of their very procession, possess a causality that touches on the creation of things. Indeed . . . God is the cause of things, through his intelligence and will, as an artisan produces through his art. Now, the artisan works according to the word in his intelligence and the love that his will bears toward his work. *Thus God the Father has produced the creation through his Word, who is the Son, and through his Love, which is the Holy Spirit. It is in this way that the processions of the Persons are the reason for the procession of the creatures in the same measure as they include the essential attributes of knowledge and will.*[14]

Having thus established what is directly involved in the *production* of creatures, we may now return to the text of the *Sentences* on which we are commenting. It continues with observations on the *return* of creatures to God, which it similarly places in connection with the procession of the Son and the Holy Spirit:

Just as we have been created by the Son and the Holy Spirit, so are we united by them to our final end. This was already Augustine's thinking when he evoked *the Beginning to which we return*, which is to say the Father; *the Model which we follow*, namely the Son; and *the Grace that reconciles us* [the Holy Spirit]. In the same fashion, Saint Hilary speaks of the *unique non-beginning and the beginning of everything to which all things are linked through the Son.*[15]

Among its many other uses, this passage develops the doctrine about the procession of creatures through the addition of the divine "missions." Mission is spoken of, as we know, to suggest the Father's sending (Latin: *missio*) of the Son, or the Father and Son's sending of the Holy Spirit, mediating the gift of grace to rational creatures. We will deal more fully with this in the following chapter. Suffice it to say here that the Spirit's operation in the creature's heart allows the return of the work to its Artisan. We meet here for the first time a crucial decision of Thomas's, which we shall frequently encounter elsewhere, and which translates with great precision his vision of the world: Despite the differing levels of the gift of being and

14. *ST* Ia q. 45 a. 6.
15. *In I Sent.* d. 14 q. 2 a. 2. The quotation from Augustine is taken from the *De uera religione* c. 55, n. 113 (BA 8, 188–91); the quotation from Saint Hilary is from *De Synodis* 59, XXVI (PL 10, 521). G. Emery's fine examination of these issues is very helpful, "Le Père et l'oeuvre trinitaire de la création selon le Commentaire des Sentences de S. Thomas d'Aquin," in *Ordo sapientiae et amoris: Image et message de saint Thomas d'Aquin à travers les récentes études historiques, hermeneutiques et doctrinales*, ed. C.-J. Pinto de Oliveira (Fribourg, 1993), 85–117.

the gift of grace, Thomas finds no gap between them. It is the same God who takes the initiative in both kinds of gift in the unity of his plan of salvation for the world:

There are two ways to consider the procession of persons in creatures. First, we have the reason for their coming forth from the Beginning, and it is this procession that we observe in the natural gifts in which we subsist; thus Dionysius can state in his *Divine Names* that the divine wisdom and goodness proceed into creatures.

"Natural gifts" here correspond to what we already named the level of nature. Man shares the state of existing with everything that is, but in his case he is invested with a unique nobility because he has been endowed with a soul that is both intelligent and free. That is truly a divine gift, but it is not enough to allow the rational creature's return to God, nor does it allow an explanation of that process. Thus Thomas continues:

This procession can also be observed according as it is the reason for returning to the end, but only in those gifts that unite us closely to the ultimate End, which is to say to God, sanctifying grace [in this life] and glory [in the life to come].

To help us understand this, Thomas uses a comparison with natural generation. We cannot say that a baby is united with its father in the possession of the same human species from the moment of conception; that is not true until the end of the generative act, when the child has become a human person. Similarly, among our various known participations in the divine goodness, there is no immediate union with God through his initial gifts (which is to say, in the fact of subsisting in natural being). That union occurs only through the ultimate gifts that allow us to adhere to him as our end. That is why we say that the Holy Spirit is not given immediately with the being of nature, but only with the sanctifying gifts that bring about our birth in the being of grace.[16]

The passages that speak directly about creation rightly emphasize the exemplary role of the Image and the central efficacy of the First Principle. These allow us to see more fully the role of the Incarnate Word. But we now turn to texts in which the Spirit clearly comes to the fore, because it is through him and his gifts that the creature is truly enabled to rejoin the Exemplar. In other words, in continuing his consideration of the Trinity

16. This last paragraph is a paraphrase of the concluding portion of *In I Sent.* d. 14 q. 2 a. 2.

as Creator, Thomas speaks to us of the Trinity as divinizing agent. At the very heart of his theology, the Trinity is explicitly related to the doctrines of both creation and of salvation. Thomas is fond of that connection and he repeats it in a revealing passage of the *Summa:*

> Knowledge of the divine persons was necessary for us for two reasons. The first is to make us think rightly about the creation of things. Indeed, to affirm that God made everything through his Word, which is to reject the error that God produced things by natural necessity, and to posit in him the procession of Love, which shows that God produced creatures, not because he had to, nor for any other reason exterior to him: it was through love of His goodness.[17]

We recognize here a warning about potential confusion over the origins of the circular schema. But we also note that Thomas's idea of God is not narrow. He knows by experience that in our world no being acts except toward some end, whether to acquire something or achieve a result—in other words, in a self-interested way. But He-Who-Is-Beyond-Everything clearly does not act to acquire something that he lacks. We must therefore conclude that God's creation of the world has no other motive than the communicating of his own goodness, his proper perfection. Since he lacks absolutely nothing, God can only act in a perfectly disinterested way.[18] We see here how mistaken it would be to overvalue Thomas's use of a Neoplatonic vocabulary. If there are similarities, they are at most superficial. The underlying thought is fully Christian. The secret weakness of the emanationist schema is here corrected in a radical way. If God creates through his Logos, his Word (John 1:3), it is an act of reflexive thought, not a natural emanation. It is "the act of an Artist not the proliferation of Substance."[19]

In a first phase, the revelation of the Trinity allows us to understand correctly the "why" of creation. Thomas, however, recognizes another motive that, in his eyes, is even more important: "The second, and main,

---

17. *ST* Ia q. 32 a. 1 sol. 3.

18. Cf. *ST* Ia q. 44 a. 4: "Every agent acts for the sake of some end . . . and every imperfect agent . . . hopes to acquire something by his act. But the first agent . . . does not act to achieve some end; he does not propose something to himself except to communicate his perfection, which is to say his own goodness. For its part, each creature hopes to obtain its proper perfection, which is to achieve a resemblance to the divine perfection and goodness, the divine goodness which is the end of all things." See also *ST* Ia q. 44 a. 4 ad. 1; *De pot.* q. 3 a. 7 ad 2; etc.

19. H.-F. Dondaine, annotation 85 in *La Trinité* (French translation with notes and appendices of St. Thomas Aquinas, *Summa theologiae* Ia qq. 27–43), vol. 1 (Paris, 1950), 200.

reason was to give us a true notion of the salvation of the human race, a salvation achieved through the Incarnation of the Son and the gift of the Holy Spirit." This relating of creation to salvation, of the world's origin to its fulfillment in blessedness—in which we recognize the plan of the *Summa*—shows to what extent, in this perspective, the whole course of time is immersed, so to speak, in the Trinity. Exit-creation and return-divinization are embraced in the eternal cycle of the divine processions. To repeat a striking expression of one of the best commentators, "the concrete revelation of the mystery of the Trinity is robed in the revelation of the economy of salvation and of the origins of the world."[20]

The Divine Artist

This teaching about creation is filled with all kinds of doctrinal and spiritual implications, which are scattered, little by little, in the pages that follow in St. Thomas. The first point that arises for meditation is God as artisan, and even artist, who imprints upon his work a trace of his beauty.[21] This was a commonplace in medieval thought, which found expression even in painting. We have, for instance, a miniature of the school of Chartres in which the creator, compass in hand, is busy making a perfectly spherical earth. We should not say that art imitates nature here, since before the creation there was *nothing*. The divine Creator must, therefore, have taken himself as the model. We also know the general principle whereby the effect resembles the cause and, more precisely, the work its author. We are therefore obliged to conclude that the creation resembles the creator:

God is the first, exemplary cause of all things. We will be convinced of this if we recall that a model is necessary to produce something when the effect is to receive a determined form. Indeed, because the artisan follows a model he produces a determined form in the material, whether the model is exterior to him or interior to him, and conceived of by his mind. Now, it is clear that the things produced by nature receive a determined form. This determination of forms must be referred, as to its first principle, to the divine wisdom which has elaborated the order of the universe, which consists in the differentiated disposition of things. And that is why we must say that the divine wisdom contains the notions of all things, which ear-

20. H.-F. Dondaine, ibid.; for a fuller treatment, see É. Bailleux, "La création, oeuvre de la Trinité, selon saint Thomas," *RT* 62 (1962): 27–50.
21. Cf. R. Imbach, "*Dieu comme artiste*: Méditation historique sur les liens de nos conceptions de Dieu et du Beau," in *Les Échos de Saint-Maurice* n.s. 15 (1985): 5–19.

lier we have called the "ideas," that is, the exemplary forms existing in the divine intelligence.[22] Although these are many according to their relations with various realities, they are not really distinct from the divine essence, since diverse beings may participate in various ways in their resemblance to that origin. Thus God himself is the first model of all.[23]

Though the image is only approximate, the comparison of the divine Artist with an earthly artisan in the midst of creation is highly evocative, more than we might first think. For the Trinity is the origin of that work of art which is the world, and we have seen that each Person participates in this, as is appropriate, following the order of processions.[24] If this is the way things are, another conclusion follows: we will of necessity find a resemblance, a "trace" (vestigium) of the Trinity in all creatures and not only in man. Basing his position on Saint Augustine, Thomas is not afraid to affirm as much, but he distinguishes two ways in which an effect can resemble its cause: as vestige or as image.

We will return to the image in the next chapter. But the doctrine of a vestige is already quite rich. We speak of a vestige or trace when the effect represents the causality of the agent that has produced it, but does not represent its form. Thus smoke or ash evoke the image of fire, but do not reproduce it: "The trace clearly shows that someone has passed by, but it does not tell us who." Still, this is something, significant enough for Thomas to assert:

in all creatures there is a representation of the Trinity in a vestigial mode, in the sense that we find in each of them something that we must necessarily refer to the divine persons as its cause. . . . Indeed, insofar as it is a substance, a creature represents its cause and principle and thus manifests the Father, Beginning without beginning. Inasmuch as it has a certain form and species, the creature represents

22. On this see the important study by L. B. Geiger, "Les idées divines dans l'oeuvre de S. Thomas," in A. Maurer, ed., St. Thomas Aquinas 1274–1974: Commemorative Studies, vol. 1 (Toronto, 1974), 175–209.

23. ST Ia q. 44 a. 3. These ideas are common in Thomas, cf. De uer. q. 2 a. 5 and the commentary of S.-Th. Bonino Thomas d'Aquin: De la vérité, question 2 (La science en Dieu) (Fribourg, 1996), note 38, p. 448; F. J. Kovach, "Divine Art in Saint Thomas," in Arts libéraux et Philosophie au Moyen Age (Montreal-Paris, 1969), 663–71; and the still fuller treatment by H. Merle, "Ars," BPM 28 (1986): 95–133.

24. We should not underrate the philosophical development that leads us back from the effect to the cause. It is equally important not to overestimate in this regard the Trinitarian traces in creation. Only the revelation of the Trinity allows us to read them as such. Recall the severe warnings against pretensions to "prove" the Trinity of divine Persons through natural reason, cf. ST Ia q. 32 a. 1.

the Word, for the form of the work comes from the artisan who conceived it. Finally, insofar as it is ordered to other realities, the creature represents the Holy Spirit as love, for the orientation of one thing to another is the effect of the creative will.[25]

In support of these examples, which find their inspiration in Augustine,[26] Thomas again refers to the celebrated triad in the Book of Wisdom (11:21) according to which God has brought forth all things according to "weight, measure, and number": "measure connecting the substance of a limited thing with its proper elements, number leads to species, and weight to order." According to Thomas, we might easily add to this triad many explanations by different thinkers. But he is careful not to push this systematizing spirit too far, to the point of wanting to see it everywhere. It is enough for one or another of these elements to be present so that, the Trinity being known through faith, we may go on to these kinds of connections.

Saint Thomas often explained the crucial distinction between image and vestige.[27] Without lingering on this point here, we should note in passing the spiritual importance of this teaching. That God is recognizable in the traces he left in creation is evidently the starting point for the ways to demonstrate God's existence.[28] But we might also take "recognize" here in the sense of "confessing." And that opens the way to praise and wonder. Like the Psalmist, Thomas knows quite well that "the heavens are filled with the glory of God," and he is neither the first nor the only one to do so. Augustine in particular, to whom Thomas refers, holds that "creatures are like words that express the unique divine Word."[29]

---

25. *ST* Ia q. 45 a. 7. Cf. *SCG* III 26, n. 3633, where Thomas underscores that we speak in similar cases of vestige and not image because the resemblance in non-rational beings is only distant and dark *(propter remotam repraesentationem et obscuram in irrationabilibus rebus)*.

26. See *De Trinitate* VI, 10, 11–12 (BA 15, 496–501), and the fuller texts in Books X–XI; see BA 15, 589–91, with the relevant note 45: "L'homme à l'image."

27. Notably in *In I Sent.* d. 3 q. 2 a. 2; *De pot.* q. 9 a. 9; and especially *ST* Ia q. 93 a. 6, to which we shall soon turn. For a reflective development of what the notion of vestige entails, the reader is directed to B. Montagnes, "La Parole de Dieu dans la création," *RT* 54 (1954): 213–41. It is worth noting that the text from which he begins is not one of the authentic sermons by Thomas.

28. Cf. *ST* Ia q. 2 a. 3; *Expositio super Iob ad litteram (In Iob)* XI, lines 112–14, Leonine, vol. 26, p. 76: "The vestiges are like signs of God in creatures from which God can be known in a certain way." It should be noted that this points to an "ascending" movement as opposed to the "descending" treatment in the *Summa* in the text on which I am commenting.

29. *In I Sent.* d. 27 q. 2 a. 2 qc. 2 ad 3: "Creation cannot be called 'word' properly

Though Thomas does not have the style of an Augustine or the lyricism of a Saint John of the Cross, he makes use of this conception[30] and expresses it with the sobriety proper to his own vocation: "The whole world is nothing other than a vast representation of the divine Wisdom in the mind of the Father."[31] Thomas's legitimate and necessary preoccupation with precisely defining the status of the knowledge of God we derive from the creation has sometimes relegated to secondary importance among Thomas's disciples the ecstatic feeling of wonder that grips the believer when he sees all these signs of the Trinity. But nothing prevents us from reading the Master himself in that way.[32]

The Presence of the Trinity in the World

Thomas's teaching on a Trinity wholly engaged in creative and restorative action brings us again to the root of the doctrine of the presence of God in the world, which Thomas shares with the great mystics. But he expresses it with an unexpected force and gives the reasons for it with his customary care and precision. He relates it all directly to a verse at the opening of John's Gospel (1:3). Thomas knew at least six different exegeses

---

speaking, it is rather the 'voice of the word' (vox verbi), just as the voice manifests the thought (verbum) so creation manifests the divine art. Thus, the Fathers assert that by his only Word, God has spoken the whole creation. Creatures are thus like words expressing the unique divine Word (Unde creaturae sunt quasi uoces exprimentes unum Verbum diuinum). That is why Saint Augustine can say: Omnia clamant, Deus fecit. But he can only say this by way of metaphor." Recall the unforgettable passage in Confessiones X, 6, 9 (BA 14, 154–59): to the question of the person who is seeking God, the beauty of creatures replies, "It is he who made us."

30. Without attempting to make John of the Cross into a Thomist, which has sometimes been tried, I might still remark that a Thomist inspiration may easily be discerned in the Spiritual Canticle, couplet 5: "Pouring out a thousand graces, / He passed these groves in haste; / And having looked at them, / With His image alone, / Clothed them in beauty." The commentary of the mystic thus surprisingly meets the expressions of the theologians: "God created all things with remarkable ease and brevity, and in them he left some trace of Who He is, not only in giving all things being from nothing, but even by endowing them with innumerable graces and qualities . . . creatures are like a trace of God's passing. Through them one can track down His grandeur, might, wisdom, and other divine attributes," John of the Cross, The Collected Works of St. John of the Cross, trans. Kieran Kavanaugh and Otilio Rodriguez, rev. ed., with revisions and introductions by Kieran Kavanaugh (Washington, D.C., 1991), 434.

31. In Ioannem I, 10, lect. 5, n. 136.

32. Despite the dryness of the reports (simple course notes), we may glimpse some idea of this in the commentaries on the Psalms (Postilla super Psalmos), for example, In Ps. VIII, n. 3; In Ps. XVIII, nn. 1–3, passim; ed. Vivès, vol. 18, pp. 266; 326–28.

of this passage, which he reads, following Saint Augustine, as saying: "Whatever was made was life in Him."[33] He sees not only spiritual creatures but the whole creation as pre-existing in God: "If we consider things as they are in the Word, they are not only alive, but they are the Life. For their ideas, which exist spiritually in God's wisdom and by which things have been made by the Word himself, are life."[34]

Artistic creation provides another illustration here. Before its creation, the work is not non-existent, properly speaking, since it already exists in the artist's thought. But such work is not life pure and simple, because the artist's intelligence is not one with his being. In God, by contrast, there is nothing that is not God, and his intelligence is at one with his life and his essence: "This is why everything in God not only *lives*, but *is* life itself . . . and that is why the creature in God is one with the creating essence *(creatura in Deo est creatrix essentia)*. Considered thus, as they are in the Word, things are life." This is Thomas's constant position, which he always supports by recourse to John's prologue: "Things are pre-existent in God according to the mode of the Word himself. That mode consists in being one, simple, immaterial, *to be* not only *alive but Life itself,* since the Word is his being."[35]

Thus, there is a presence of creation in God, but the contrary is no less true: there is an "existence of God in things."[36] This is a key passage for grasping how taking a position that seems purely philosophical immediately calls for a theological translation and mystical development. Thomas takes as starting point one of his clearest oppositions: "God alone

33. "Quod factum est in ipso vita erat." Besides Augustine, Thomas cites Origen, Hillary, Chysostom, the Manichaeans, and an anonymous homily. Today's exegetes, however, read this passage as saying, "Without him nothing was. He was the life of every being." But we do not have to get into that debate here. It's enough for us to highlight Thomas's starting point.

34. *In Ioannem I,* lect. 2, n. 91; we know that the mystics often repeat this language. Cf., for example, Angelus Silesius, *Cherubinischer Wandersmann,* in *Sämtliche poetische Werke,* vol 3 (Munich, 1952): "Before being anything else, I was the life of God. That is why he has also given himself to me entirely."

35. *SCG* IV 13, n. 3494. Cf. *De pot.* q. 3 a. 16 ad 24; *ST* Ia q. 39 a. 8; q. 4 a. 2: "Since God is the first efficient cause of things, the perfections of all things must pre-exist in God in a superior mode." Thomas comes close to Saint Augustine here, *De Genesi ad litteram* V, 15, 33 (BA 48, 419–20); *In Evangelium Iohannis tractatus (In Ev. Ioh. tract.)* 37, 8 (BA 73A, 231–35), and perhaps even closer to Saint Anselm, *Monologion* 36, *Opera Omnia,* vol. 1, p. 55. For the metaphysical problems posed here, see J.-H. Nicolas, *Synthèse dogmatique, Complément: De l'univers à la Trinité* (Fribourg-Paris, 1993), 34–42.

36. Cf. *ST* Ia q. 8, which is entirely devoted to this subject.

is being in his essence and his very being *(Ipsum esse subsistens)*. And it therefore follows that, for every other existing thing, its being can be created and received only from God, who produces it as his proper effect, just as to burn is the proper effect of fire." This dependence of all things on God for their being is found not only in their creation, at the moment when they begin to exist. It lasts as long as they subsist. A telling comparison will help us to understand: Daytime lasts only as long as the sunlight illuminates the air. When the sun disappears, there is no more light or day. The parallel with the God who gives being leads to some further truths:

So long, therefore, as a thing possesses being, *God must be present in it,* and in conformity with the way in which it possesses being. Now, being in each thing is the most intimate and deepest thing it possesses, since being plays a role in everything that is in it, the role of form, of the determining principle. . . . We must, therefore, necessarily conclude from this that *God is in all things in the most intimate way.*[37]

Thomas insists on this point with a vehemence that is a little surprising.[38] But we are in the realms of paradoxes. Contrary to what happens with a material thing, God's presence in things is not an imprisonment. Things do not contain God. The opposite is true: "spiritual things contain whatever they are in, as the soul contains the body. God therefore is in things also, and contains things."[39] That having been established, Thomas does not fear to go even further: "God is in all things and entirely in each of them, just as the soul is entirely in each part of the body."[40] This first af-

---

37. *ST* Ia q. 8 a. 1: "*Oportet quod Deus sit in omnibus rebus, et intime.*" On this, see *ST* Ia q. 3: "On God's Simplicity," especially article 4, for confirmation that in God essence is identical with his act of being *(esse).* As to the fact that *esse* is the form of every existing thing, Thomas gives a very strong formulation: "being is the actuality of every thing and of the forms themselves" *(ipsum esse est actualitas omnium rerum et etiam ipsarum formarum),* *ST* Ia q. 4 a. 1 ad 3; cf. *De pot.* q. 7 a. 2 ad 9: *esse est actualitas omnium actuum et propter hoc est perfectio omnium perfectionum* (being is the actuality of every act and because of this it is the perfection of every perfection). É. Gilson labored to give this notion the highest importance, notably in *The Christian Philosophy of St. Thomas Aquinas,* chapter 4, pp. 84–95.

38. Thomas goes so far as to concede that God may be found even in demons, at least in so far as they are existing realities *(ST* Ia q. 8 a. 1 ad 4). There is even more reason for him to be in the sinner, whose sinful act has no other physical reality than what God gives it at each moment.

39. *ST* Ia q. 8 a. 1 ad 2.

40. *ST* Ia q. 8 a. 2 ad 3.

firmation is subsequently made richer and more precise. Given that the known is found in the knower and the loved in the lover, it follows that, with regard to intelligence and will, "things are in God much more than God is in things."[41]

It is thus only by analogy with the corporeal world that we say God is found in all things. These comparisons always require delicate manipulation, and Thomas knows it. After having encountered pantheism,[42] he discarded the ancient Stoic tradition of seeing God as the soul of the world. That relatively crude anthropomorphism is not only insufficient to account satisfactorily for God's immanence in his creation, but it wholly fails to preserve his transcendence.[43] Now Thomas believed in both simultaneously; furthermore, he uses them to explicate the deeply differentiated modes in which God is present in his creation, opening up inexhaustible perspectives for contemplation.

In a famous passage written while he was still a young theologian, Thomas distinguishes three ways in which we may say that God exists in creation.[44] The first is found in the whole creation, living and non-living; the second, by contrast, is present only in spiritual beings capable of receiving grace and, therefore, of approaching God in a personal way; as to the third, it occurs only in Jesus Christ, whose hypostatic union puts him at the height of the creation:

The first [way of being present] is found through simple similarity, which is to say in the degree to which we find in the creature a resemblance to the divine goodness [this corresponds to what we earlier characterized as a "vestige"], without reaching God in his substance. This way of connection [between God and his creature] occurs in every creature in whom God may be found in his essence, presence, and power.

The theologians speak here of a "presence of immensity." Thomas explains it quite clearly in the *Summa*.[45] But he is even more explicit in a passage written toward the end of his life:

41. *ST* Ia q. 8 a. 3 ad 3: "Magis res sunt in Deo quam Deus in rebus."
42. *ST* Ia q. 3 a 8.
43. Cf. J.-H. Nicolas, "Transcendance et immanence de Dieu," *ST* 10 (1981): 337–49.
44. *In I Sent.* d. 37 q. 1 a. 2.
45. *ST* Ia q. 8. a. 3: "God is in everything by his power, because everything is subject to him; he is in everything by his presence, because everything is open and, so to speak, naked to his gaze; he is in everything by his essence, because he is present to everything as the universal cause of being." We must also see in this article how these three words refute an

It is often said that God is in every thing by His essence, presence, and power. To understand this, we must grasp that someone is said to be in everything which is subject to him by his *power*, just as the king is said to be in the whole kingdom which is subject to him, without really being there in his presence and essence. Through his *presence*, someone is said to be in all realities that are under his gaze, as the king is said to be through his presence in his palace. But someone is said to be in realities through his *essence*, which is His substance, as the king is [in his own individuality] in a single, determined place.

We say that God is everywhere in the world by his *power*, because everything is subject to Him—*If I ascend to the heavens, you are there . . . if I take the wings of the dawn and dwell in the utmost ends of the sea, there too your hand shall guide me and your right hand shall hold me fast* (Ps. 138:8). God is also everywhere by his *presence*, for *everything in the world is naked and open to his sight* (Heb. 4:13). Finally, God is everywhere by his *essence*, for its essence is what is most intimate in every reality. . . . Now God created and preserves all things according to the act of being in each reality. And since the act of being is what is most intimate in each reality, it is manifest that God is in all realities by his essence, through which he creates them.[46]

Unfortunately, we do not have Thomas's commentary on Psalm 138, but what we know of his reflections on the Book of Job shows that, far from seeing God who has all things under his gaze and searches hearts as the pitiless judge to which he is sometimes reduced, Thomas sees God also as the one who leads man "on the way to eternity."[47] Indeed there is a second way that God makes himself present in his creature. The second way is found

when the creature touches God himself considered in his substance and not in a simple similarity, and that by his operation. That takes place when someone adheres through faith to the First Truth itself and, in charity, to the Sovereign Good. Such is then the second mode, according to which *God is specially in the saints through grace.*

---

equal number of opposing errors. *Power* aims at refuting the error of the Manichaeans who tried to remove material and visible things from the influence of the Good God in order to submit them to the Evil God who, in their system, ruled over them. *Presence* seeks to displace the error of Averroes and others who, while admitting that everything is subject to the divine power, maintained that that same power does not care about simple, material realities (cf. ST Ia q. 22. a. 2). *Essence* corrects the view of Avicenna, who, while admitting divine providence over all things, denies that creation could have been achieved without intermediaries (cf. ST Ia q. 45 a. 5).

46. *In Ioannem I*, lect. 5, n. 134.

47. Ps. 139:24. See the additional comments in J.-P. Torrell, *Dieu qui es-tu?* (Paris, 1974), 170–75.

In this bare form, Thomas here evokes the doctrine of the divine indwelling, which has drawn forth learned commentaries. In Thomas, however, it retains a Johannine simplicity: "If any among you loves me . . . we will come to him and we will make our dwelling within him" (John 14:23). The context here is clear enough. We are not dealing with canonized saints but with all Christians who live according to the theological virtues. That qualification is enough to bring out the immeasurable difference between the presence of the immensity of God the Creator in all things, even material ones, and the presence that he reserves for those who love him, because he loved them first: "Apart from grace, there is no perfection superadded to the substance which God introduces into a being as a known and beloved object. Grace alone grounds a special mode of God's being in things."[48]

As to the third way of God's presence in the world, Thomas mentions it rather briefly here: "There is, however, another special way of God's existence in man, *by union*." This simple word has something a bit enigmatic about it, but Thomas has explained it in a passage of the *Sentences*, that will serve as a guide:

The creature touches God himself not only by the mode of operation, but also in his being proper. This must be understood to be not the act that constitutes the divine essence—for the creature cannot be changed into the divine nature—but from the act that constitutes the hypostasis, or the person in union with whom the creature is elevated. That is the last mode [of presence], by which God is in Christ by the [hypostatic] union.

Put more simply, it is, therefore, the coming of the Word made Flesh which realizes this third way of presence in the creation. And we return here to the notorious question among theologians about the reason for the Incarnation: Why did God become man? . . . Starting with the good principle that this sort of question can be answered only from Scripture, Thomas responds by saying that God probably would not have become incarnate if man had not sinned. But he recognizes that there is a variety of opinions on this point:

Some say that even if man had not sinned, the son of God would have been incarnated. Others assert the opposite. It seems preferable to agree with the latter.

---

48. *ST* Ia q. 8 a. 3 ad 4; for more details on this passage, see the exhaustive study by J. Prades, "*Deus specialiter est in sanctis per gratiam*," *El misterio de la inhabitación de la Trinidad en los escritos de santo Tomás* (Rome, 1993).

For things that depend solely on the divine will and to which the creature has no right can be known to us only in the measure that God wishes to show them to us and transmits them to us through Sacred Scripture. Now the reason that Sacred Scripture everywhere gives for the Incarnation is the sin of the first man. It thus appears *more likely (conuenientius)* that this mystery was willed by God as a remedy for sin, so that without sin the Incarnation would not have taken place. *However we must recognize that the power of God is not thus limited and that, even without the sin, God might have become incarnate.*[49]

The passionate controversy with the Scotists led the Thomists to harden their Master's position somewhat. His moderation is not sufficiently noted ("The latter seems preferable"), nor is the fact that he was only underscoring what seemed more appropriate,[50] leaving open other possibilities. In fact, when he delves more fully into the appropriateness of the Incarnation, he highlights a metaphysical reason and, following Dionysius, explains:

God's nature is goodness. . . . It follows that everything essential to the good is fitting to God. Now, it is the essence of the good to communicate itself. . . . It therefore belongs to the Sovereign Good to communicate himself sovereignly to the creature. And that sovereign communication takes place when God unites himself to a created nature in such a way as to form a single person from three realities: the Word, the soul, and the flesh, and, as Saint Augustine put it . . . the *appropriateness* of the Incarnation thus appears manifest."[51]

---

49. *ST* IIIa q. 1 a. 3. The parallel passage in *In III Sent.* d. 1 q. 1 a. 3 seems more favorable to this final opinion: "Others say that, granted what is produced by the incarnation of the Son of God is not only liberation from sin, but also the glorification *(exaltatio)* of human nature and the coronation *(consummatio)* of the whole universe, the incarnation could have occurred for these reasons, even without sin. *And this may be held as probable.*" See also *In I ad Tim.* I, 15, lect. 4, n. 40. On this question, once hotly debated, we have the study by H. Bouëssé, *Le Sauveur du Monde, 1: La place du Christ dans le plan de Dieu* (Chambéry-Leysse, 1951). Very good, but misleading in some details, is M. Corbin, "La Parole devenue chair. Lecture de la première question de la *Tertia Pars* de la Somme théologique de Thomas d'Aquin," *RSPT* 67 (1978): 5–40, reproduced in *L'inouï de Dieu, Six études christologiques* (Paris, 1980), 109–58. (On page 112 the author omits a "not" which is found in the text of the commentary on Timothy. We must rather read "this question *is not* of great importance.")

50. On the significance of the argument about appropriateness, see the important study by G. Narcisse, *Les raisons de Dieu: Argument de convenance et esthétique théologique selon saint Thomas d'Aquin et Hans Urs von Balthasar* (Fribourg, 1997). We also have Narcisse's enlightening preliminary study, "Les enjeux épistémologiques de l'argument de convenance selon saint Thomas d'Aquin," in *Ordo sapientiae et amoris*, 143–67.

51. *ST* IIIa q. 1 a. 1.

In this way, the coming of the Word into the flesh is no longer caused solely by the *felix culpa*—which is sometimes hard to separate from a certain anthropocentrism—but Christ also appears as the summit and crowning of a universe entirely ruled by the communication of the Divine Being and the Good, according to the three large modalities that we have recalled.[52] This is the only way to see the wonderful gradation that brings Thomas to the presence of God in the world. But it is quite obvious that the second and third modes of presence are not in natural continuity with the first. If the first must exist in order that grace might be "grafted" onto it, there is between them a radical difference of nature, reduced to its possibilities, and of grace that is the effect of the pure divine liberality. And this is why we cannot conceive of them in a rigorously symmetrical way.[53] The descending order of natural gifts does not allow any intermediary between God's action and the creature when He is communicating being. But the ascending order, which is the return of the creature toward God, not only tolerates certain mediations but necessarily demands them, such as the humanity of Christ and the gift of the Holy Spirit's grace. Christ is found, in fact, at the perfect intersection of the two orders of mediation, descending and ascending. And that is why—as Thomas explains in commenting on a slightly obscure verse from the Book of Sirach (about "the rivers that return to their source," Sir. 1:7)—circularity finds in Christ its most perfect and beautiful expression:

It is the mystery of the Incarnation that is signified by this return of rivers to their source. . . . These rivers are the natural goods with which God has filled his creatures—being, life, intelligence . . . and the source from which they come is God. . . . Although they are in a state of dispersal throughout the creation, these

52. Although it deals with the question without any special connection to our subject here, it is worth looking at the fuller study by Th. R. Potvin, *The Theology of the Primacy of Christ According to St. Thomas Aquinas and its Scriptural Foundations* (Fribourg, 1973).

53. Thomas explains this precisely with regard to the hypostatic union (*ST* IIIa q. 6 a. 1): "We can envisage a double connection between God and the creature. The first stems from the fact that creatures are caused by God and depend on him as the principle of their being. From that point of view, in virtue of his infinite power, God touches all things immediately in causing and preserving them. In this way God is immediately in all things by his essence, presence, and power. The second connection stems from the fact that things are led toward God as their end; from that point of view, we find intermediaries between the creature and God, for the lower creatures are led toward God by the higher ones, as Dionysius teaches in the *Celestial Hierarchies* (4, 3). It is to this connection and order that the assumption of human nature by the Word of God belongs, God being the end of that assumption. The Word is thus united to the flesh by the soul."

goods are brought together in man, for he is like the horizon, the limit where the corporeal nature and the spiritual nature are rejoined. Standing in the middle, he participates in both spiritual and temporal goods. . . . That is why when human nature was reunited with God by the mystery of the Incarnation, all the rivers of natural goods returned to their source.[54]

God Who Loves the World

If we are guided by these texts, the cogency of the circular diagram carries us irresistibly with Christ toward the Father. In any event, before examining more fully the movement of return in the following chapters, we must still look a bit further into the movement of going forth. To grasp how the Christian should act in this world, it is fundamental to understand the way in which God himself acts, if we may put it that way, with respect to the world.

We might begin with a simple observation. As we know, Thomas often turned to the Bible, and with special frequency to the wisdom literature.[55] Now, among the numerous quotations from the Book of Wisdom that come from his pen, this is one of the most common: "*You love all things and you hold in disdain nothing of what you have made, for if you hated something, you would not have made it. How could something exist if you had not willed it? How would it remain in being if you had not called upon it?*"[56] Thomas like to quote these words when he asks himself: Does God love everything? He replies without hesitation:

God loves everything that exists. In effect, everything that exists is good by the single fact that it exists, for being is in itself a good like any perfection that it may possess. Since God's will is the cause of everything, therefore no thing has being or perfection except to the extent that it is willed by God. God wishes some good for every thing, therefore, and since to love someone is nothing other that to wish him well, it is clear that God loves every thing that is.

But his love is not like our love. . . . The love by which we wish well to some-

---

54. *In III Sent.* Pro. For a similar argument, SCG IV 55, n. 3937; "Given that man is in a sense the culmination of creatures, since he presupposes them all in the natural order of his generation, it was wholly appropriate that he would be united to the first principle *in order that the perfection of the universe would be attained by a kind of circle.*"

55. Cf. J.-P. Torrell and D. Bouthillier, "Quand saint Thomas méditait sur le prophète Isaïe," *RT* 90 (1990): 5–47, cf. p. 9.

56. Wisd. 11:25–26, Vulgate text quoted in *ST* Ia q. 20 a. 2 s.c.. There are at least 18 uses of verse 25 and 4 of verse 26 in a dozen or so of Thomas's works, with the two *Summas* (10 uses) predominating.

one is not the cause of his goodness. On the contrary, it is that person's goodness, real or supposed, that elicits the love by which we wish to preserve the good that he has and even to increase it, and makes us work toward that end. *By contrast, God's love is the cause that spreads and creates goodness among things.*[57]

It is impossible to put more simply and strongly the difference between God's love and ours. What the wildest love shows itself powerless to do for the highly beloved, God does for each one of us. Like a sun that could make a flower bloom even without seed or water, so God's love makes being arise from nothingness—at every instant. For the creation is not an act without sequel. God does not lose interest in this world he has made. Faith and reason alike cause us to admit that creatures are preserved in being by God. "The being of creatures depends so much on God that they would not be able to subsist for an instant and would return to nothing if they were not preserved in being by the operation of the divine power."[58] We can easily explain this if we remember that God is not only the cause of the *coming into existence* of each being, but in the most intimate and direct fashion, of *being* itself.[59] The conclusion naturally follows, but there is no need to imagine a new divine intervention: "The preservation of things by God does not suppose a new act on his part, but only that he continues to give being."[60]

This point may be obvious by now, but it is necessary to add that we encounter in this context of divine government of the world (or Providence—the terms are almost synonymous) the three Divine Persons at work as they were in the creation of things. When Thomas reads these words of Christ in John's Gospel (5:17): "My Father is at work until now, and I too am at work," he comments boldly:

---

57. *ST* Ia q. 20 a. 2: *"Sed amor Dei est perfundens et creans bonitatem in rebus."*

58. *ST* Ia q. 104 a. 1.

59. Thomas repeats here his favorite comparison (ibid.): "The situation of every creature with respect to God is the same as that of the atmosphere to the sun that illuminates it. . . . God alone is being in his essence, because his essence is his existence; by contrast, every creature is being by participation, for it is not its essence to exist."

60. We could, if we wished, speak here of continued creation, but on condition that we understand clearly that it is only in connection with us that this occurs in time. From God's point of view, "that action [is performed] outside of motion and time," *ST* Ia q. 104 a. 1 ad 4. See Ch.-V. Héris's notes on this passage in *Le gouvernement divin* (French translation with notes and appendices of St. Thomas Aquinas, *Summa theologiae* Ia qq. 103–9), vol. 1 (Paris, 1959), 253 ff.

Therefore, *my Father*, in founding nature in the beginning, *is at work until now*, in maintaining and preserving it in the very same operation, *and I too am at work*, for I am the Word of the Father by which he achieves all things. . . . Thus, just as it is by his Word that he has achieved the original foundation of things, so too their preservation. . . . *I too am at work*, because I am the Word of the Father through whom all things were made and are preserved.[61]

Thomas seems to miss no chance to emphasize the constant action of the Word. Thus when he explains Jesus' words "I am leaving this world and going to the Father," he does not think it necessary to remark that this is not a physical departure nor an abandonment of the world by his withdrawal. "The providence of his government . . . *is always in harmony with the Father who governs the world*, and he is always with his own people through the help of his grace."[62] The same goes for the Holy Spirit. When Thomas speaks of the way in which "the divine persons, by reason of their own procession, possess a causality involving the creation of things," and of what properly belongs to each of them, he also describes the role of the Holy Spirit: "to govern as master and to enliven what is created by the Father and the Son." That role belongs to the Spirit "because goodness is attributed to him, who leads things to their proper ends by ruling over them, and life-giving power is attributed to him because life consists in a kind of internal motion and the first mover of things is both their goal and their goodness."[63] This passage very accurately echoes another key passage in the *Summa contra Gentiles* to which we will have to return when we look at the Holy Spirit:

Since the government of the world is assimilable to a certain motion by which God rules and directs all things to their proper ends, and if it is true that the impulse and motion come from the Holy Spirit insofar as he is love, then it is entirely appropriate to attribute government of the universe and propagation to the Holy Spirit.[64]

This position on the creation and on the permanent presence of the Word "who sustains the universe through his powerful word,"[65] brings Thomas to examine in passing one of those impossible suppositions that historians often find in the mystics: "If God were to withdraw his power

---

61. *In Ioannem V*, 17, lect. 2, n. 740.   62. *In Ioannem XVI*, 28, n. 2163.
63. *ST* Ia q. 45 a. 6 ad 2.   64. *SCG* IV 20, n. 3572.
65. Heb. 1:3. See Thomas's lovely commentary on this passage: *In ad Hebraeos I*, lect. 2, nn. 30–37.

from things for a single instant, they would all fall back into nothingness and would cease to exist." Thomas attributes to Origen (though it may more properly come from John Scotus Erigena) a suggestive comparison: when we stop speaking, there is no longer any voice. Similarly, if God stopped speaking his Word, the Word's effects would cease immediately and there would no longer be a created universe.[66]

Thomas does not shy away from this notion, but addresses it in greater detail. We have to admit that God could reduce the beings that he has made to nothing, *for he has not created by natural necessity.* Since everything depends on his free will, we must admit that nothing obliges him to create. Nor would he have any need for new action; he only would have to stop acting.[67] But here the impossible character of this idea reasserts itself. And indeed, Thomas rectifies the point swiftly: "*Absolutely nothing is reduced to nothingness,*" for such an annihilation would not serve as a manifestation of God's power. Rather, it would oppose itself to that idea because it is in the preservation of beings that the power and goodness of God appear at their maximum.[68]

It has sometimes been suggested that Thomas taught a version of divine immutability that would have made God a being indifferent to his creation. He says "[although] creatures are in a real relation with God . . . there is no real relation of God with respect to his creature."[69] We have to note the mistake that would result from a poor reading of this sentence. We should not understand it in a purely psychological sense, since it states an indisputable metaphysical assertion. Simply, it means that "God is outside of the whole order of created things (*Cum . . . Deus sit extra totum ordinem creaturae*)." He gives creation its constancy, but the opposite is not true. The relation is necessarily asymmetrical. Imagination can see nothing here. And if we really wish to implicate God in his creation (to make him share our sufferings, for example, as many theologians try to do today), we would only be making an unnecessary idol, nothing more.[70] That god would not be God.

---

66. *In Ioannem I*, lect. 5, n. 135; *De pot.* q. 4 a. 2 ad 8 and 14.
67. Cf. *ST* Ia q. 104 a. 3. 68. Cf. *ST* Ia q. 104 a. 4 and ad 1.
69. *ST* Ia q. 13 a. 7. Cf., on this point, H. Seidl, "De l'immutabilité de Dieu dans l'acte de la création et dans la relation avec les hommes," *RT* 87 (1987): 615–29. More accessible, but very enlightening is M. Gervais, "Incarnation et immuabilité divine," *RevSR* 50 (1976): 215–43, which shows convincingly the groundlessness of the criticisms of Thomas by several contemporary theologians.
70. On this, see J.-H. Nicolas, "Aimante et bienheureuse Trinité," *RT* 78 (1978): 271–92,

Far from being a stranger to his creation, Thomas's God is personally present to each being in a more intimate way than that being is present to itself. More than once the insightful reader will think of Saint Augustine, to whom Thomas owes so much: "But you, you are deeper than my inmost being, and higher than my own heights."[71] Thomas does not have Augustine's literary genius. He says nothing different than Augustine, however, and a reading of his pages on God's active presence in his creation will guide us toward the admiring adoration that results from the experience of that presence.

That experience can only intensify when we fully realize to what extent Thomas's God has nothing in common with the impersonal principle of deism, which is unconcerned with the world. The Trinitarian God of the Bible is actively involved in his creation. Not only is he its absolute origin and constant support, but he loves it with the same love that he loves himself:

It is not only his Son that the Father loves through the Holy Spirit, *but also himself and us*; for . . . to love, in the notional sense, does not only evoke the production of a divine Person, it evokes the Person produced by way of love, and the love expresses a connection with the thing loved. That is why, just as the Father expresses himself and every creature through the Word that he begets since the Word he begets suffices to represent the Father and every creature, so too, *the Father loves himself and every creature through the Holy Spirit*, for the Holy Spirit proceeds as love of that first Good by reason of which the Father loves himself *as well as every creature*. From this, there may also be found as a second feature, in the Word and the proceeding Love, a connection with the creature, for divine truth and goodness are the origins of the knowledge and love that God has for creatures.[72]

○ which offers a fine tuning of J. Moltmann's book, *Crucified God: The Cross of Christ as the Foundation and Criticism of Christian Theology*, trans. R. A. Wilson and John Bowden (New York, 1974). Moltmann cites many sources. It is worth noticing that Jacques Maritain, in "Réflexions sur le savoir théologique," *RT* 69 (1969): 5–27, avoids the psychologizing wrong turn when he tries to speak of God's compassion: "the concept and the word sorrow cannot be used about God except metaphorically. . . . we must, however, seek in an *unnamed* divine perfection the eternal example of what is sorrow in us with its nobility" (p. 314).

71. *Confessiones* III, 6, 11: "Tu autem eras interior intimo meo et superior summo meo." The commentary in the *Bibliothèque augustinienne* (13, 383) sees in this brief "definition" of God the perfect expression of both his immanence and his transcendence: "thus God is at the same time intimately at the heart of man, even if he is a sinner, and completely other than man in his holiness."

72. *ST* Ia q. 37 a. 2 ad 3. Similar indications, developed to greater and lesser degrees, are

And it is not surprising that we find a similar position in Thomas about the person of the Son. Saint Thomas presents it in his commentary on Saint Paul's expression in Ephesians (1:6), "The grace that he granted us in the beloved Son":

We must note that certain people are loved in themselves and others because of another. Indeed, when I truly love someone, I love him along with all he loves. Thus when we are loved by God, it is not [directly] because of ourselves; *we are loved because of Him who is the beloved of the Father.* That is why the Apostle adds *in his beloved Son,* on account of whom he loves us in the measure that we resemble him. Love is effectively founded on that resemblance. . . . Now the son is by nature similar to the Father, and that is why he is loved by him in the first place. He is *by nature* and in the most excellent manner the Beloved of the Father. As to us, we are sons *by adoption* in the degree to which we are in conformity with the Son [by nature]; that is why we have a certain participation in God's love.[73]

The texts gathered together in this chapter should suffice to show the coherence of Thomas's vision of the world and of the God who emerges from it. Thomas cannot speak of creation without showing the three Persons at work, any more than he can speak of the presence of God in his creation without showing its crowning point in Christ. Furthermore, he cannot speak of the creation in a human being without speaking of salvation, which is to say re-creation in love. This constancy and insistence are not without their reasons, and the links between them are everywhere assumed, even when they are not explicitly pronounced. Given that they enter structurally into the very synthesis of the *Summa,* we *cannot* overlook them.

---

not lacking elsewhere. For example, *De uer.* q. 22 a. 1 ad 11: "Ex hoc enim quod Deus se ipso fruitur alia in se dirigit." Cf. *De pot.* q. 3 a. 15 ad 14; *In I Sent.* d. 32 q. 1 a. 3.

73. *In ad Eph. I, 6,* lect. 2, n. 16.

⌇

CHAPTER IV

Image and Beatitude

How to bring together the two terms in the above title is a task imposed on the reader from the very first pages of the *Summa*. When he asks himself about the possibility of a creature resembling God, Thomas answers with two scriptural texts. The first has been given a fair amount of attention: "We have made man in our own image and likeness" (Gen. 1:26). But the second is rather unexpected: "When He comes, we shall be like Him, because we shall see Him as He is" (1 John 3:2).[1] Therefore, this provocative summary puts side by side creation and the second coming. Or better expressed, it recalls in biblical terms the final destination of the image and clearly suggests the whole path that it must traverse to reach its goal. The connection is not mere chance: when Thomas comes to speak of beatitude, he will again quote the same verse from Saint John: "We shall see Him as He is," taking it a bit further with another passage from the same evangelist, "Eternal life is to know You alone as true God."[2]

The Beginning and the End

This approach, typical of Saint Thomas, constantly places before his disciple the end Thomas proposes, or perhaps it is better to say the end

---

1. *ST* Ia q. 4 a. 3 s. c.. On the connection between these terms, see the excellent study by C. E. O'Neill, "L'homme ouvert à Dieu *(Capax Dei),*" in N. A. Luyten, ed., *L'anthropologie de saint Thomas* (Fribourg, 1974), 54–74, especially pp. 61–62, reprinted in P. Bühler, ed., *Humain à l'image de Dieu* (Geneva, 1989), 241–60. The General Prologue to the commentary on the *Sentences* also makes multiple connections between protology and eschatology. G. Emery, to whom I owe this reference, rightly sees in all this a characteristic intuition of Thomas's.

2. *ST* Ia q. 12 a. 1 s. c. and a. 4 s. c..

that God proposes. The prologue to the Second Part, as we shall soon see, is regularly cited in this context. But in reality the first question of the *Summa* already speaks of the matter:

Man is ordered to God as to a certain end that surpasses reason's grasp since, according to the prophet Isaiah (64:4), "eye has not seen, besides you O God, what you have prepared for those who love you." Now, it is necessary that the end be known in advance so that man may direct his desires and acts toward it. It was therefore necessary to man's salvation that certain things surpassing reason would be divinely revealed to him.[3]

We are irresistibly reminded of the popular saying, "He who wills the end must will the means." But Thomas gives straightaway its most fully elaborated form, placing the creature in front of the final end, in relation to which everything else is ordered. "Everything else" is not thereby reduced to pure means—that would be to sell far too cheaply real values that are, in their own way, true ends. But this does suggest that those values themselves only receive their full significance in connection with their final end. Though the last to be attained, the end must first be known, and everything else must be adjusted to it. Therefore, if we want to have some chance of understanding it, we must try to grasp the divine initiative where it appears with the greatest clarity—right at the beginning and at the end of salvation history. This is exactly what Thomas does by beginning his description of the return movement with a reminder linking man, as the image of God, and the end placed before him:

Man being made in the image of God—and by this we must understand, according to John Damascene, that he is endowed with intelligence, free will, and power for autonomous action—having dealt with the Exemplar, who is God, . . . we must now address what pertains to his image, which is to say man, since he is also the principle for his own acts because he possesses free will and command over his action.

This text serves as prologue to the Second Part and is quickly completed with some additional reflections that leave no doubt as to the author's intentions. This man, of whom he is going to speak, is not considered in a static way, like inanimate matter. But, if it can be put this way, he is a being in the process of becoming:

---

3. *ST* Ia q. 1 a. 1.

[In the creature's movement toward God], the first thing that presents itself for our consideration is the final end of human life. We will have to ask later about the ways in which man achieves his end or deviates from it, because it is from the end that we have to derive the idea of what leads to that end. And since it is admitted that the *final end of human life is beatitude*, we must first treat of the final end in general, and then of beatitude.[4]

This second text is perhaps better known than the earlier one. In fact it provides a key as to how to read what follows, and we will frequently return to it. But reading these two crucial texts together allows us to see something important. In passing from one part of the *Summa* to another, the theologian does not abandon God as a subject in favor of man. The subject of *sacra doctrina* always remains God. But now he will not be directly considered in himself, nor as the absolute beginning of man and the universe, but rather as its culmination—its end, equally absolute, final—which attracts all things to itself by the radiation of its supreme goodness and raises, in response and in a special way, the rational creature's free action. All spiritual life finds its birth here, and it is in the field of attraction thus created that it must develop.

In the first few lines, we do not yet have the idea of the finality that lies ahead, but the idea of the exemplary. If the human being has God as its end, it is because man has been made by God "in his image and likeness" (Gen. 1:26). The result is an irresistible attraction inscribed in man's very nature to become like God in the way that an image resembles the model on which it is made. The human person will find his fulfillment in striving more and more to imitate that model. That is why Thomas devotes much attention in the First Part (q. 93) to the theme of the image of God when he speaks of man's creation and his nature. And he spontaneously recalls the theme of image when he speaks of human action. And thus the theme of the image of God organically links the First and Second Parts.[5]

These two linked factors allow Thomas to pass from God to man (from

4. *ST* Ia IIae q. 1 Pro.

5. This has been rightly underscored by G. Lafont, *Structures et méthode dans la Somme théologique de saint Thomas d'Aquin* (Paris, 1961), 265–98. He may, however, have exaggerated the *material* presence of the image theme in the Second and Third Parts, according to several scholars: H. D. Gardeil, A. Solignac, and D. J. Merriell (see the following footnotes). By contrast, the structural importance of the theme in the *Summa* is supported by S. Pinckaers, "Le thème de l'image de Dieu en l'homme et l'anthropologie," in *Humain à l'image de Dieu*, 147–63.

dogmatic theology to moral theology, as it used to be said not long ago), to unite in the same theology contemplative concerns with the wish to direct Christian life by evangelical truth. Thomas puts all his thinking about human action under simultaneous considerations: image to be restored and end to be attained (image being restored when the end is rejoined). Thomas proposes a life program under the aegis of self-fulfillment, since the creature finds itself in finding its end. His is a morality of happiness, therefore, but a happiness that is obtained only through imitation of the Exemplar, in whose likeness we are made. This leads us to a remark of Saint Paul's: "As God's favored children, be like Him" (Eph. 5:1). And we find in the Sermon on the Mount: "Be perfect as your Father in heaven is perfect" (Matt. 5:48).

It is no accident that the professor of Sacred Scripture—which Thomas was—gives so high a profile to the theme of the image of God. With him, we are invited to draw on the fountain that is always springing from the Word of God. A theologian concerned about spirituality cannot overlook this turn to the Bible. The time has happily passed when terms like beginners and advanced, or stages in the interior life, were thought to be distinguishable solely in terms of religious psychology. But it is not idle to remember that it was also a main concern of the Fathers of the Church. Saint John Damascene bears witness to that.[6] He is a kind of crossroads for the Fathers of the East. Through him Thomas finds himself reconnected to that whole tradition. And Thomas was probably more attentive to that tradition than were any of the theologians of his time (the *Catena aurea* is eloquent testimony to that). In line with this patristic heritage, it is certainly not improper to speak of a morality of divinization. This may be little known, but it is quite real nonetheless.

The Image of the Trinity

The reader of the *Summa* cannot help noticing that Thomas divided what he had to say about man into two sections. Questions 75–89 deal with man's *nature*; questions 90–102 speak of man's *creation (de productione prima hominis)*. Usually, if the reader is a philosopher and in a bit of

---

6. It is too little recognized that the text from the Damascene is quoted in the context of the study of the image of God (*ST* Ia q. 93 a. 5 arg. 2). See also D. Mongillo, "La Concezione dell'Uomo nel Prologo della Ia IIae," in *De Homine: Studia hodiernae anthropologiae, Acta VII Congressus thomistici internationalis*, vol. 2 (Rome, 1972), 227–31.

a hurry, he will limit his attention to the first part and leave the second to the theologians. This is a fatal mistake that will keep him from understanding Thomas, because Thomas has made it clear that it is as a theologian that he expects to examine man's nature.[7] Leaving the study of the body to the medical doctors, he will primarily speak of the soul and the relationship that it entertains with the body. At the same stroke he firmly announces that his study of man will not be finished until he has spoken of the image of God. For it is as the *End* that God puts himself forward in creating man.[8] A philosopher has expressed this beautifully: Thomas understood the theme of image "as giving the final cause for the production of man. The human being has been created or produced *in order to* be in the image of God. If the words *end* or *term* have meaning, we must say that the human being is, has been created, and thus willed and finally conceived by its Creator, not to be a thinking substance, for example, or a rational animal, but *in order to* be in His image."[9] In other words, in his exegesis of Genesis 1:26, the Master from Aquino sees efficient and final causes simultaneously at work: God in the act of creating man is moved by the intention to communicate to him His likeness.

Saint Thomas spoke several times about the image of God at the most decisive points in his theological speculations.[10] But it also seems that,

7. Cf. *ST* Ia q. 75 Pro.: "It pertains to the theologian *(theologus)* to consider human nature from the point of view of the soul, not the body [this belongs to the 'physicist'], at least when it is not the relation of the soul and the body that is under consideration."

8. We know that this is the very name of the question on the image of God (*ST* Ia q. 93): *De fine sive termino productionis hominis prout dicitur factus ad imaginem et similitudinem Dei.*

9. L. B. Geiger, "L'homme image de Dieu. A propos de *Summa theologiae*, Ia 93, 4," *RFNS* 66 (1974): 511–32, cf. pp. 515–16. The author continues with an observation that we shall consider later in the present chapter: "The end for which a being is created must therefore be part of its definition, if the definition of that being is perfect. The end helps us understand the nature of a being. . . . Now the end of the production of the human being is to be suited to knowing and loving God as he knows and loves himself. Man is created by God so that, in accord with the nature produced by God, he is suited to loving and knowing God as he knows and loves himself, an aptitude that is actualized by the gift of grace, imperfectly, and perfectly by the gift of glory. It is furthermore because of that, as will be shown, in the Second Part of the *Summa*, that man's beatitude can only consist in that end. The end of the production of man helps us understand what he is, in indicating that for which he is made. That must therefore figure in the definition [of man], if that definition is to be perfect" (pp. 518–19).

10. In addition to some isolated, important points, the principal locations are found in *In I Sent.* d. 3 qq. 2–5; *In II Sent.* d. 16; *De uer.* q. 10 especially aa. 1, 3, 7; *SCG* II 26, nn. 3631–33; *De pot.* q. 9 a. 9. Among the numerous studies on this subject, I should mention

while always maintaining a common basis in his first researches, Thomas made constant progress over his early self, thanks to the renewed attention with which he re-read Saint Augustine's work.[11]

Though he deals with the theme of image *ex professo* only toward the end of the First Part, it is also found in the first pages of the *Summa*.[12] And it is with reference to that theme that Thomas already specifies the type of likeness that the creature may have to his creator.[13] These references, coming so early in the *Summa*, are a significant sign that this theme is present in Thomas's thought even when he is not speaking specifically about it. And in any case, it should not surprise us that it is when he deals with the Trinity and Creation that Thomas begins to deal with some fundamental definitions.[14] When he explains why Scripture uses the term

---

M.-J. S. de Laugier de Beaurecueil, "L'homme image de Dieu selon saint Thomas d'Aquin," *Études et Recherches* 8 (1952): 45–82; *Études et Recherches* 9 (1955): 37–96, according to which Thomas progressively departed from Augustine in favor of Aristotle and Pseudo-Dionysius. But D. J. Merriell's interpretations are preferable in *To the Image of the Trinity: A Study in the Development of Aquinas's Teaching* (Toronto, 1990), which shows that, on the contrary, Thomas's progress is connected to a profound rereading of Augustine's *De Trinitate* (his up-to-date bibliography is worth consulting). See also H. D. Gardeil, Appendix II, "L'image de Dieu," in *Les origines de l'homme* (French translation with notes and appendices of St. Thomas Aquinas, *Summa theologiae* Ia qq. 90–102) (Paris, 1963), 380–421 (which is similar in bearing to Beaurecueil); A. Solignac, "Image et ressemblance," *DS*, vol. 7 (1971), col. 1446–51. (The latter is a more synthesizing article with a good bibliography. The author errs, however, when he thinks that the relative unobtrusiveness of the image theme, as he reads Saint Thomas, is linked to a withdrawing from the trinitarian foundation of creation, cf. chapter 2 of this book.). J. Pelikan, "*Imago Dei*: An Explanation of *Summa Theologiae* Part I, Question 93," in A. Parel, ed., *Calgary Aquinas Study* (Toronto, 1978), 29–48, also emphasizes the dominant Augustinian influence.

11. This emerges clearly in the meticulous study devoted to the question in D. J. Merriell, *To the Image*.

12. Cf. *ST* Ia q. 3 a. 1 ad 2: "Man is said to be in the image of God, not according to his being a body, but according to the way in which he surpasses all other animals . . . which is to say through reason and intelligence. It is therefore by intellect and reason, which are incorporeal, that man is in the image of God."

13. *ST* Ia q. 4 a. 3. Very cautious here, Thomas seems especially worried to avoid the naïve error that, from the fact that the creature resembles the creator, would draw the opposite conclusion: "in a certain sense, the creature resembles God, but God does not resemble the creature" (ad 4). Since God is outside of every genus, his action takes place without there being a communication of genus or species; creatures are only likened to him by a kind of analogy that allows them to be reducible to the universal principle of all being: *illa quae sunt a Deo assimilantur ei in quantum sunt entia ut primo et universali principio totius esse.*

14. It is rather remarkable that when Thomas says "image of God," he means at the

"image" only to speak of the Son and how some object to the word's application to man, Thomas replies with this initial distinction:

The image of someone is found in another in two ways: either in a being of the same specific nature, as the image of the king may appear in his son, or in a being of a different nature, as the image of a king may appear on a coin. Now, it is in the first way that the Son is the Image of the Father, and only in the second way that man is in the image of God. *Thus, to show the imperfection of this latter image in man's case, we do not say without nuance that he is the image of God, but he is "in the image," and thus is signified the attempt to tend toward perfection.* About the Son of God, on the contrary, we cannot say that he is "in the image": he is the perfect Image of the Father.[15]

Supposing for the moment that it is necessary to seek reasons that explain why Thomas gives such emphasis to the notion of image (for him the fact that it was a revealed datum was sufficient), the nuance it introduces here is especially helpful. The idea of a reality that is not given in a finished state, but is viewed as called upon to progress, corresponds deeply to his conception of nature as, of course, possessing a stable basis that is given, but also as fertile with the possibilities of a culmination yet to come. Man is fully himself only when he is under cultivation; similarly, the image of God in him will be fully itself only in the perfected stage of its spiritual activity.

Quite naturally, we find the image throughout the unfolding *Summa*, when Thomas inquires into the resemblance of the creation to its Creator, about the trace that the divine Artist left upon his work. The latter occasion gives him a chance to refine his view on the vestiges of the Trinity in creation.[16] In any event, it is here that a decisive step occurs. If man too participates, along with all creation, in this similarity through the vestiges in his bodily state, he also has the being of an image, properly speak-

---

same time "image of the Trinity." He is aware of the similarity of the human person to the divine nature, even if he does not usually give it great prominence.

15. *ST* Ia q. 35 a. 2 ad 3. In its simplicity, this explanation does not mince words about the ontological abyss that separates the created from the uncreated. Therefore it is this that we should be aware of in speaking of an analogical similarity, and not of an identity. Thomas will return to explaining this verbal construction "in the image" to deny that man may be said to be "in the image of the Image," which is to say solely of the Son. He believes that man is more truthfully in the image *of the Trinity*. That is why we must see in the *ad imaginem* the idea of the exemplary cause, image here being taken as a "model." (*ST* Ia q. 93 a. 5 ad 4).

16. Cf. *ST* Ia q. 45 a. 7 and chapter 2 above.

ing, of the Trinity, for he is endowed with will and intelligence, and therefore we can find in him a conceived word and a love that proceeds. There is here much more than a simple, exterior resemblance; the locus of the image is situated at the level of the *mens*, that which is the most spiritual thing in man:

> Given that the uncreated Trinity is distinguished according to the procession of the Word from the One who offers it and the procession of Love from both the one and the other . . . we may then state that in the rational creature, in whom are found the procession of the Word in the intelligence and the procession of Love in the will, there is an image of the uncreated Trinity which extends into specific traits.[17]

Since the body has no similarity other than as a vestige, it is thus at the level of the spiritual soul that the image is found,[18] because the soul alone is like God himself, capable of bearing the image. This is a basic datum found in every human being by the very fact of his creation and this soul lies at the base of the analogy of proportionality proper that Thomas de-

---

17. *ST* Ia q. 93 a. 6. Other passages are even more explicit, such as *ST* Ia q. 45 a. 7: "The processions of the divine persons occur according to the acts of intelligence and will. . . . The Son proceeds like a Word from the intelligence and the Holy Spirit like love from the will. As a result, in creatures endowed with reason, who have will and intelligence, we discover a word conceived and a love that proceeds, we also discover a representation of the Trinity by way of image."

18. That is why Thomas remarks (*ST* Ia q. 93 a. 4 ad 1): "if we consider the intellectual nature in which the image *principally* resides, the quality of image of God is found equally in man and woman." This response refutes a very negative view about women denying that they can be the image of God. But Thomas does not entirely escape the limitations of his time. In order to do justice to Saint Paul's teaching, Thomas quickly adds, referring to I Corinthians 11:7–9: "from a secondary point of view, the image of God is found in man in a way that it is not found in woman. For man is the beginning and end of woman, as God is beginning and end of all creation." Today, we know that the statement in Genesis 1:27b ? "male and female he created them," has nothing to do with the "image of God" properly speaking. It only evokes the fact of human sexual reproduction. We cannot then base on it an egalitarian anthropology any more than we can sexual inequality. Cf. Phillis A. Bird's article, in K. K. Børresen, ed., *Image of God and Gender Models in Judaeo-Christian Tradition* (Oslo, 1991). To avoid a misogynist interpretation of the image of God (which has numerous representatives in the Christian tradition), some authors (for example, Rosemary Radford Ruether in the same volume) propose a four-square rejection of an anthropology in the image of God. It is hardly necessary to point out that nothing is gained by this. Instead of going further into the question here, cf. the balanced approach of C. Capelle, *Thomas d'Aquin féministe?* (Paris, 1982) and the study by C. J. Pinto de Oliveira, "Homme et femmes dans l'anthropologie de Thomas d'Aquin," in *Humain à l'image de Dieu*, 165–190.

velops in the text above. But this is only the point of departure. Thomas never stops trying to go beyond the static conception of this brute fact and to highlight the progressive and dynamic character of the image. It is a reality in the process of becoming, present in human nature like a divine call. That is why, to suggest the evolving character of the image—another analogy of proportionality that rests on an indestructible ontological given—Thomas utilizes the notion of a gradually ascending approach that opens the way to boundless growth:

The image of God in man can therefore be found according to three degrees. First, in that man has a *natural aptitude* to know and love God, an aptitude that resides in the very nature of the spiritual soul, which is common to all men. Second, in that man *knows and loves God actually or habitually*, even though imperfectly; the image is in conformity to grace. Third, in that man *knows and loves God actually and perfectly*; here we have the image in its resemblance to glory. Also, we read in Psalm 4: "The light of your face is upon us o Lord." The Gloss distinguished three types of image: those of the creation, of the new creation, and of resemblance. The first of these images is found in all men; the second only in the just; and the third only among the blessed.[19]

As has been very rightly said, "these three aspects of the image are intimately linked, one to the other, as the three moments in a single spiritual journey."[20] If Thomas seems not to have gone from the first attempt to the definitive formulation, he at least constantly proposed degrees in his way of understanding the image, one supposing the other and completing it in a higher degree.[21] This well demonstrates that it is in the image's dynamism that its interest for spiritual theology resides: "There are two ways

19. *ST* Ia q. 93 a. 4. It is worth noting the emphasis on the words "know" and "love" God in act. It is only there that we find the image at its highest level. This is in the Augustinian tradition, and Thomas is well aware of it (cf. *De uer.* q. 10 a. 3). As has been well demonstrated, Augustine only uses substantive terms *memoria, intellectus, dilectio,* when it's a matter of a lower degree of the image (*memoria sui [hominis]*). When it's a case of the activity that has God for its object, he always uses verbs: *meminit, intellegit, diligit.* See the enlightening work of W. H. Principe, "The Dynamism of Augustine's Terms for Describing the Highest Trinitarian Image in the Human Person," ed. E. A. Livingstone (Oxford and New York, 1982), 1291–99.

20. A. Solignac, "Image et ressemblance," col. 1448, who quotes several enlightening texts and emphasizes how "the three moments of the image also correspond to the three lights of the spirit," namely *lumen naturale, gratiae, gloriae.*

21. G. Lafont, *Structures et méthode,* 271, finds an early example in the *De pot.* 9, 9, which begins with the vestige of the Creator recognizable in the triad "substance-form-order," rising from there to the particular image, which is the spiritual creature, exercising

to be in conformity [to the image of the heavenly man, the Christ, cf. 1 Cor. 15:49], one the way of grace, and the other the way of glory, the former being a path to the latter *(uia ad aliam)*, for without the way of grace, we never reach the way of glory."[22] As a recent commentator has beautifully observed, the man-image does not reflect the God-Trinity like a mirror, but in the way an actor imitates a real person, whom he represents by entering more and more deeply into the life of the character.[23]

---

his knowledge and love *of self*, and ending with the creature touched by grace and rendered conformable to God in knowledge and love *of God*. Elsewhere (*ST* IIIa q. 23 a. 3, *In III Sent.* d. 10 q. 2 a. 2 qc. 1) Thomas proposes the same type of gradation, but in terms of adoptive filiation (since the Word is simultaneously Image and Son, bringing them together is not a gratuitous exercise). We have, then, the external assimilation of every created being to God (which is still not true filiation), the specific assimilation of the spiritual creature, which is a kind of filiation at the level of nature, and finally the unitive assimilation through charity and grace. It is only in the last case that we can properly speak of adoptive filiation because it gives us a right to our inheritance as sons of God: beatitude. As for the third way of presenting this gradation, it is the one that brings into play the degrees of knowledge and love in themselves (as we find in the text of the *Summa* analyzed above).

22. *In I ad Cor.* XV, 49, lect. 7, n. 998. Elsewhere, but always in the neighborhood of the image of God—using the words of Saint Paul: "[reflecting] as in a mirror the glory of the Lord, we are transformed into that same image ever more glorious,"—Thomas explains this as being progress in the order of knowledge (and love): "*Reflecting (speculantes)* is not understood here as of a *specula* (observation post), but of a *speculum* (mirror). That means we know God himself in his glory through the mirror of reason in which there is imprinted a certain image of him. And it is he whom we reflect when, from the consideration of ourselves, we elevate ourselves to a certain knowledge of God, which transfigures us. In effect, since all knowledge is produced by assimilation of the knowing subject to the object known, it must be that those who see God are in a certain way transformed into God. If they see him to perfection, they are perfectly transfigured, as the blessed in heaven through the union of fruition. . . . If they only see him imperfectly, their transformation is imperfect, as here below through faith . . . [Saint Paul] distinguishes three degrees of knowledge in Christ's disciples. The first allows us to pass from the clarity of natural knowledge to the knowledge provided by faith. The second leads us from the clarity of the knowledge of the Ancient Covenant to the clarity of the knowledge of grace of the New Covenant. The third elevates us from the clarity of natural knowledge and that of the Old and New Covenants to the clarity of the eternal vision," *In II ad Cor.* III, 18, lect. 3, nn. 114–15.

23. D. J. Merriell, *To the Image*, p. 245: "Through Thomas' study of Augustine's *De Trinitate* he came to realize that man reflects the divine Trinity not merely as a mirror reflects a thing set to some distance from it, but as an actor who imitates the character he plays by entering into his character's life." Is there any need to explain that the word "mirror" in this context is not to be taken in entirely the same sense as the metaphor of the mirror in Saint Paul (see previous note)? As to the "actor," there is nothing unseemly here since it is a question of an interior imitation. Saint Thomas puts us on the road to bringing it together when he explains the way in which we can say that grace itself is image of God, *In II Sent.* d. 26 q. 1 a. 2 ad 5: "Image and likeness of God are said of the soul and of grace

All this is quite true, but to be fully faithful to Friar Thomas's central intuition, we have to go further. If the doctrine about the image has such importance, it is because it allows us to understand how the *exitus* and the *reditus* happen in the creature. In effect, if the former, the image of creation, is the term of the "going out," the second, the image of re-creation or according to grace, is that [term] by which the "return' begins, inaugurating the movement that will be completed in heaven along with the third, the image of glory, that is finally perfect resemblance. Only thus do we restore full force to the internal thrust of the image by placing it in the vast dynamism of the infinite circular movement that leads the whole creation toward God.

The whole creation—and specifically the human persons who consciously participate in this development—thus finds itself held and led forward in the movement of the trinitarian relations. As we see in the icon of the Trinity by Andre Roublev (in the form of a rectangle at the base of the altar, symbolizing the created universe),[24] creation is not external to, but at the heart of the Trinitarian communion. The iconographer's genius reaches the theologian's intuition and renders visible something of the *circulatio* that passes from the Father through the Son and returns toward him, through and in the Spirit, in drawing the universe into his love.

Image and Indwelling

To do justice to the whole dynamic of the great passage in the *Summa* on the image's three degrees of conformity to its model, we must in any event go back a little and try to think more precisely about the resemblance through grace of the *imago recreationis*: it attains its full flowering when it comes to the greatest splendor permitted on earth by the dwelling of the Trinity in the soul. As is his wont, Thomas deepens his thought by successive approaches. It is not enough for him to establish the Trinitarian resemblance at the level of powers, he also wants it to appear at the level of action. But even so, this does not mean just any action:

If we wish to find the image of the Trinity in the soul, we must grasp it primarily from what approaches it most closely, as much as possible, in the specific repre-

---

in different ways: the soul is called image in so far as it imitates God, grace is called image as that through which the soul imitates God." One also thinks of Saint Paul, whom we shall soon encounter: "To imitate God like well-loved children."

24. Cf. Cosmas Indicopleustès, *Topographie chrétienne* IV 7 (Paris, 1968), 544–45.

sentation of the divine Persons. Now the divine Persons are distinguished accord-ing to the procession of the Word from Him who offers it and the procession of the Love that unites one to the other. In addition, as Saint Augustine says, the Word cannot exist in our soul "without actual thought." That is why it is at the level of action that the image of God in the soul is grasped first and in its princi-pal way, *inasmuch as, starting from the knowledge we possess, we form, by thinking, a word and, springing from that, our love.*[25]

The whole context of the question allows us to understand that this is a case of the knowledge and love *of God,* and it is thus that we may under-stand the term Saint Thomas uses. In line with the etymology, he quite of-ten uses the verb *prorumpere* to express an irresistible pressure within; "*to throw oneself* into pleasures," "*to let out a torrent* of insults," "*to melt into* tears," or, more nobly, "*to burst* with thanksgiving." To take proper note of these nuances and the subject, we ought to translate as follows: *Pro-rumpimus in amorem,* as "we melt into love" [for God thus known]. In any case, we have here a strong suggestion of how Thomas conceives of love as a living force that spurs the lover toward the beloved (we shall return to this later). According to the classic formulation handed down from Pseudo-Dionysius, love provokes a going out of the self *(amor facit ex-tasim).*[26] It tears whoever loves out of his everyday routine and lands him in an adventure from which he will not emerge unscathed. It is even more important to note that the word *prorumpere* is found with the same meaning in only one other context:[27]

Grace renders man conformable to God. Since one of the divine Persons has been sent to the soul by grace, *it is necessary that the soul be conformed or assimi-lated to that Person* through some gift of grace. Now, the Holy Spirit is Love: it is therefore *the gift of charity that assimilates the soul to the Holy Spirit,* because it is in terms of charity that we speak of the coming of the Holy Spirit. The Son, for his part, is the Word—and not just any word, but He who breathes Love: "The Word that we try to make known, says Augustine, is a complete understanding of love" *(De Trin.* IX 10:15). The Son is not sent for just any perfecting of the intel-lect, but only where the intellect is instructed *in such a way that it melts in the af-*

---

25. *ST* Ia q. 93 a. 7: "springing from that, our love," does not entirely render the mean-ing of the original, for which the subject is the person who thinks: "cogitando interius uer-bum formamus, *et ex hoc in amorem prorumpimus.*"

26. Cf., for example, *ST* Ia q. 20 a. 2 ad 1; *ST* Ia IIae q. 28 a. 3; *ST* IIa IIae q. 175 a. 2; etc.

27. D. J. Merriell notices this in *To the Image,* p. 231, and has further ascertained that the word does not come from Saint Augustine. Merriell quite rightly translates *prorumpere* as "to burst forth into love."

fection of love (quo prorumpat in affectum amoris), as is written in the Gospel of John (6:45): "Whoever has heard the Father and accepted his teaching comes to me"; or in Psalm 38:4: "In my meditation a fire will be kindled." Augustine, too, uses some important terms: "The Son is sent when he is known and perceived" (*De Trin.* IV 20:28); the word *perception* means *a certain knowledge through experience*. This is, properly speaking, the "wisdom" or "savory knowledge" according to the words of Sirach (6:23): "Wisdom about the teaching justifies his name."[28]

The fact that Saint Thomas uses the verb *prorumpere* in only two places is a clear reason to look at them carefully. Certain readers may wish that he had developed these points more, but his way is more allusive. As a perspicacious commentator has seen, "Everything occurs as if a certain spiritual modesty prevented the Angelic Doctor from following up his exposition of the theology of the image and from going into detail about a spiritual theology that we would have liked to see him develop."[29] No question. But this is precisely one of those cases in which it is entirely praiseworthy for the commentator to show what the Master himself either could not or would not develop because of the plan he was following. The teaching about the indwelling of the Trinity is the crowning achievement of the teaching about the image of God.[30] Suffice it to recall how he presents this teaching of the indwelling in strict connection with the teaching on the sending of the divine Persons, or rather as its consequence:

It is said that a divine Person is *sent* insofar as he exists in someone in a new way; that he is *given* insofar as he is possessed by someone. Now, neither the one nor the other takes place except because of sanctifying grace. God has a common way of existing in all things in his essence, his power, and his presence; he is there, thus, as the cause in its effects, which participate in his goodness. But above and beyond this common mode, *there is a special mode which is proper to the rational creature: in this mode, we say that God exists as the known in the knower and the loved in the lover*. And because, in the knowing and the loving, *the rational creature attains through his action to God himself*, we say that through this special mode, not only is God in the rational creature, but also he lives in him as in his temple.[31]

---

28. *ST* Ia q. 43 a. 5 ad 2: in this text and others quoted earlier, we cannot help noticing the insistence on the conformity to God that grace realizes in us, or on the assimilation to the Holy Spirit which produces charity. We will have to return to this subject.

29. G. Lafont, *Structures et méthodes*, 288.

30. I am a bit surprised that Merriell, *To the Image*, pp. 226–35, shows great hesitation on this point, though he is more positive in his conclusions (p. 242). Several developments in this direction may be found in F. L. B. Cunningham, *St. Thomas' Doctrine on the Divine Indwelling in the Light of Scholastic Tradition* (Dubuque, Iowa, 1955), 339–49.

31. *ST* Ia q. 43 a. 3: the teaching on the divine missions and the indwelling is a subject

This "special mode of presence," to be sure, is not a simple "being there," like two persons physically being found in the same place. This special presence redoubles, so to speak, the intensity of God's presence since, in the act through which he gives being and from which the presence of immensity results, there is added the action by which he gives grace.[32] And in the same moment, he gives to the human person the capacity to reach the level of that new presence. There are not two different acts here: for God, to give grace is to give oneself to knowledge and love. As Thomas puts it, describing what will occur in the beatific vision but has already begun to be realized in this world: "if there existed a reality that would simultaneously be the source of our capacity to see and the reality seen itself, whoever sees would have to receive from that reality both the capacity to see and the 'form' through which the seeing is realized."[33] Taking into account that here below, "we walk in faith and not by sight," this is exactly what occurs in this special presence: God does not only come for an encounter with man, He gives Himself also and at the very same moment the possibility of encountering Him.

This is what makes possible the gift of sanctifying grace; it is only through the act of the theological virtues of faith (knowing) and charity (love) that God is thus reached in himself. But what is really remarkable for our purposes is that Thomas describes God's indwelling in the soul as resulting from the same acts that obtain for the image the conformity of grace to the new creation. This leads us to emphasize the continuity between the two teachings. The dynamism implied in the idea of the image of God finds its highest achievement here below in what is also the peak of human adventure, union with God, whom the soul enjoys like an object of love freely possessed. To follow Thomas on this question would take us very far. This becomes apparent in the way he explains why we can attribute the title "Gift" *(donum Dei* as it appears in the *Veni Creator)* to the Holy Spirit:

We possess whatever we can use freely or enjoy at will. In this sense, a divine Person can be *possessed* only by a rational creature united to God. The other crea-

---

much worked upon and always timely. There is a convenient and trustworthy summary in J.-H. Nicolas, *Synthèse dogmatique*, vol. 1: *De la Trinité à la Trinité* (Fribourg-Paris, 1985), 227–65. For an exhaustive study, see J. Prades, "*Deus Specialiter est.*"

32. And Thomas employs his favorite image here: "grace is caused in man by the presence of the divinity, just as light in the atmosphere results from the presence of the sun" (*ST* IIIa q. 7 a. 13).

33. *ST* Ia q. 12 a. 2.

tures can of course be moved by a divine Person; but that does not confer upon them the power to enjoy that divine Person or to use Him for their purposes. *But the rational creature sometimes obtains this privilege, when it becomes a participant in the Divine Word and the Love that proceeds to the point of enabling him freely to know God in truth and to love Him perfectly.* Only the rational creature, therefore, can possess a divine Person. As to realizing this possession, the creature cannot achieve it by his own powers; it must be *given* him from above—since what we have from elsewhere we call *given* to us.[34]

The Experience of God

This is already a strong statement, but in an attempt at stating more precisely what is at stake here, Thomas does not hesitate to resort to a still more suggestive vocabulary: in the passage where he speaks of "melting in the affection of love" at the earthly summit of the resemblance of the image, he also speaks of an "experiential knowledge" of God. This expression has brought more than one commentator up short, and they have undertaken to emphasize that the Master speaks of a "*quasi* experiential" knowledge, assigning to "quasi" the effect of softening the statement somewhat. This amounts to saying "so to speak," or "in some sense" experiential. Since Father Albert Patfoort's studies of this point,[35] hesitation is no longer in order; he has reminded us that there are other passages in which Thomas speaks without qualification of an experiential knowledge of God.[36] And even when he uses the "quasi" he continues in the same passage with a "properly." Since Thomas would certainly not contradict himself within a matter of two lines, we have to conclude that the "quasi" does not have the meaning of an experience that costs little, but that he wishes to distinguish it from another kind of knowing that is merely intel-

---

34. *ST* Ia q. 38 a. 1.

35. A. Patfoort, "*Cognitio ista est quasi experimentalis* (1 Sent., d. 14, q. 2, a. 2, ad 3)," *Angelicum* 63 (1986): 3–13; working in a similar vein, cf. H. R. G. Perez Robles, *The Experimental Cognition of the Indwelling Trinity in the Just Soul: The Thought of Fr. Ambroise Gardeil in the Line of Saint Thomas*, Diss. P.U.S.T. (Rome, 1987).

36. Such as *In I Sent.* d. 15 q. 2 ad 5: "Although the knowledge is appropriated to the Son, the gift by which this experiential knowledge (*experimentalis cognitio*) is assumed, necessary for there to be a mission, is not, however, necessarily appropriated to the Son, but it could be appropriated to the Holy Spirit, in so far as he is love"; *In I Sent.* d. 16 a. 2: "In the invisible mission of the Holy Spirit, grace bursts into the soul by virtue of the fullness of the divine love. And through that effect of grace, the experiential knowledge of this divine person is received by anyone to whom this mission is made (*cognitio illius personae diuinae experimentalis ab ipso cui fit missio*)."

lectual. That is why, commenting on Saint Augustine, he can write: "Each of them (Son or Spirit) is sent when he is *known.*" We must understand this as *not only speculative* knowing, but a knowing that also has a [frankly] experiential side *(quodammodo experimentalis).* This is underscored by what follows: "'(known) and *perceived,*' which means an experience properly speaking *(proprie experientiam)* in the gift received."[37]

These texts have given rise to various, not to say opposing, interpretations. Some have wanted to reduce the experience Thomas speaks of here to the meaning the term had in his predecessors and contemporaries, which is to say a strongly emotional sense.[38] Others, in lively reply to this thesis, and sometimes not without justification, maintain that, on the contrary, Saint Thomas frees himself from the received sense of the term and gives it a certain intellectual scope.[39] Without trying to go into this debate here, which would take us far from our purposes, it seems hard to reduce Thomas's views to either alternative. We certainly cannot eliminate intellectual knowing, properly speaking, from this experience, but it is impossible for the experience not to have simultaneously a no less firm affective dimension. It would be quite strange if, having come to the highest point of its encounter with God on earth, the soul were engaged through only one of its powers.

There are various passages little used or not used at all in these studies because they do not belong to the immediate context that has provoked the scholarly disputes. But these might clarify a great deal. Basically, the word *experience,* borrowing from the vocabulary of the senses,[40] suggests

37. *In I Sent.* d. 15, *expositio secundae partis textus:* "Hoc intelligendum est non tantum de cognitione speculativa, sed quae est etiam *quodammodo experimentalis;* quod ostendit hoc quod sequitur: 'atque percipitur' quod *proprie experientiam* in dono percepto demonstrat."

38. This, greatly simplified, is the thesis of J. F. Dedek, *Experimental Knowledge of the Indwelling Trinity: An Historical Study of the Doctrine of S. Thomas* (Mundelein, Ill., 1958); cf. also the same author's article: *"Quasi experimentalis cognitio:* A Historical Approach of the Meaning of St. Thomas," *JTS* 22 (1961): 357–90.

39. This is A. Combes's position, "Le P. John F. Dedek et la connaissance quasi expérimentale des Personnes divines selon saint Thomas d'Aquin," *Divinitas* 7 (1963): 3–82, accepted with further nuances by A. Patfoort, "Missions divines et expérience des Personnes divines selon S. Thomas," *Angelicum* 63 (1986): 545–59.

40. Cf. *ST* Ia q. 54 a. 5 ad 2: "We have experience when we know specific beings by means of the senses." The most extensive text occurs in *In Iob XII,* 11–14, Leonine, vol. 26, p. 81, lines 163–226. The sensible origin of experience in hearing and taste *(auditus* and *gustus)* serves as a paradigm for what occurs in the understanding, contemplative or practical. For a full and careful study of what experimental knowledge means in its different levels,

something of direct contact with reality transposed into the realm of divine things:

> Experience of a thing comes through the senses. . . . Now God is not removed from us, nor outside of us, he is in us. . . . That is why experience of the divine goodness is called "taste" (gustatio). . . . The effect of that experience is twofold: first, certitude of knowledge, second, the sureness of affectivity.[41]

The immediacy of divine reality thus experienced, therefore, certainly bursts into the understanding as well as into the will, and confirms them in their proper order. Clearly Thomas is following here common usage in which the term "experience" designates something other that a purely intellectual knowledge. He allows it a certain emotional content:

> There are two ways of knowing the goodness or will of God. One is speculative, and from that point of view, we are allowed neither to doubt the divine goodness nor to put it to the test [the passage speaks of "tempting" God]. The other is an affective or experimental knowing (affectiua seu experimentalis) of the divine goodness or will, when one personally experiences (dum quis experitur in seipso) the taste of the divine sweetness and the benevolence of his will, after the fashion of Hierotheos, whom Dionysius says "learned divine things through feeling them." In this point of view we are invited to experience the divine will and taste its sweetness.[42]

There is, therefore, a knowledge of divine things that is not acquired solely by study. This admission carries further weight because Thomas had already referred in the Summa to the same quotation from Pseudo-Dionysius with regard to theological wisdom. Without denying the importance of clear knowledge, in that passage he gives first place to knowledge by connaturality, which is the result of the gift of wisdom infused by the Holy Spirit.[43] The appeal to experience thus suggests something about the ineffable nature of the encounter with the divine Persons:

---

see F. Elisondo Aragón, "Conocer por experiencia: Un estudio de sus modos y valoración en la Summa theologica de Tomás de Aquino," RET 52 (1992): 5–50; 189–229.

41. In Ps. XXXIII, n. 9: ed. Vivès, vol. 18, p. 419.

42. ST IIa IIae q. 97 a. 2 ad 2; cf. ST Ia q. 64 a. 1: "There is a two-fold knowledge of truth: one kind of knowing is obtained through grace, the other through nature. What is obtained through grace is itself two-fold: one part is purely speculative, as when someone receives knowledge of the divine secrets through revelation; the other part is affective and produces love of God, and this latter is a gift of the Holy Spirit."

43. ST Ia q. 1 a. 6 ad 3. Knowledge by connaturality has evoked numerous studies: see I. Biffi, "Il giudizio 'per quandam connaturalitatem' o 'per modum inclinationis' secondo san

Come and see, says Christ in Saint John. In its mystical meaning, this signifies that the *indwelling,* whether of glory or of grace, can only be now by experience, because it cannot be explained in words. *Come,* believing and acting, and *see,* experiencing and understanding. We must remark that one achieves this knowledge in four ways: through doing good works . . . by stillness of soul . . . through taste of the divine sweetness . . . through the works of devotion.[44]

This is why another language is required and the vocabulary of experience needs to be completed with that of *fruition* of divine realities. This language, beloved by mystics, originates with Saint Augustine and his distinction between realities we may make use of *(uti)* and those we can only enjoy *(frui)*. The language has been transmitted, among other ways, in a highly classical form by Peter Lombard in his *Sentences,* which is why it finds a prominent place starting in the earliest pages of Thomas's commentary.[45] It is Peter, too, who spontaneously appears when Thomas speaks about beatitude, not only in its final state but in its beginnings, the indwelling of the divine Persons. The passage above concludes thus:

Outside of sanctifying grace there is nothing that could be the reason for a new mode of the presence of the divine Person in the rational creature. And it is solely by reason of sanctifying grace that there is a mission and temporal procession of the divine Person.—In the same way, we say that we "possess" something only when we are free to use *or enjoy* it. Now, we have no power to *enjoy a divine Person* except through sanctifying grace. However, in the very gift of sanctifying grace it is the Holy Spirit whom we possess and who dwells in man. From this the Holy Spirit himself is given and sent. [Thomas continues on a bit further responding to several points.] The gift of sanctifying grace perfects the rational creature, putting him in a state not only of freely using the created gift but also of *enjoying the divine Person himself.* There is an invisible sending through the gift of sanctifying grace, but *it is the divine Person himself who is given to us.*[46]

Grace does not therefore only permit the faithful to lead a Christian life, it already equips them for the highest mystical experience, the enjoyment of the divine Persons. "The state of grace," as is said, is the "habitual pos-

---

Tommaso: Analisi e prospettive," chap. 2 in *Teologia, Storia,* 87–127, especially the bibliography, note 20, p. 90.

44. *In Ioannem I,* 39, lect. 15, nn. 292–93; cf. also *In Ioannem XVII,* 23, lect. 5, n. 2250.

45. *In I Sent.* d. 1; see also *ST* Ia IIae q. 11. Though departing from Lombard, who did not establish the existence of a habitus for created grace, Thomas retains his teaching—and with a good deal of firmness—that it is truly the *Spirit in person* who gives himself.

46. *ST* Ia q. 43 a. 3 ad 1.

sibility of living such a fruition, a habitual possibility of living an experiential knowledge of the divine Persons."[47] This has nothing to do with intellectual resources, and Thomas sees it to be perfectly realizable for people otherwise deprived of all learned knowledge because *this knowledge from which love springs* is found abundantly among those who are fervent in their love of God, because they know the divine goodness as the final end, spreading over them its benefits." On the other side, "this knowledge cannot be perfect in persons who are not inflamed by this love."[48]

These passages in Thomas are little known, but they are not isolated thoughts. Brought together with the passages that we have already quoted on the experience of the divine Persons, which goes beyond the clear knowledge that we can grasp, they find there in some degree exemplary formulation in these other passages, where Thomas boldly gives in no uncertain terms his preference for a "little old lady" *(uetula)* burning with love of God over the scholar full of his own superiority.[49] Though this is evident to a Christian, the comparison takes on added weight coming from the pen of such a high-flying intellectual. Only Pascal can say with a certain degree of credibility that "all of philosophy is not worth an hour of trouble."

The Image in Glory

We have moved away, it seems, from the notion of the image. But this only appears so, because, we may see well now, if the soul becomes similar to its divine model in the graced activity of its knowledge and love for God, it is through the same activity that God comes to dwell in the soul and it receives, to an unimaginable degree, an experience of His nearness and sweetness. As aware as he is of the necessity for theological wisdom, which alone allows the experience to be correctly expressed, Thomas, without denying that wisdom, utilizes the vocabulary of experience that alone seemed appropriate to him for suggesting something of that fulfilling totality where affectivity is necessarily joined with understanding. For God is not solely grasped as true, but also as good.

The end of the process is not entirely reached except when the image in conformity with grace is replaced by the image in conformity with glo-

---

47. A. Patfoort, "Missions divines," 552.
48. *In I Sent.* d. 15 q. 4 a. 2 arg. 4 and ad 4.
49. Cf. J.-P. Torrell, "La pratique pastorale," 242.

ry. Thomas sees this as called for by the very definition that he gives to the image:

The image implies a resemblance that develops to the point of representing in some way the specific traits [of the model]. It necessarily follows that in the image of the Trinity in the soul would be present something that represents the divine Persons in a specific way, as much as is possible in a creature. Now, the divine Persons are distinguished by the procession of the Word from Him who offers it, and the procession of Love from both. In another way the Word of God is born of God through the knowledge that he has of himself, and Love proceeds from God according to the love that he has for himself. Now, it is manifest that the diversity of objects entails a specific diversity in word and in love. Basically, the word conceived in the heart of man with respect to stone or horse is not of the same kind, no more than is love. It follows that the divine image in man is taken from the word which is conceived from the knowledge of God and the loves that derives from it. And thus the image of God is present in the soul as it bears itself or is capable of being borne toward God. [And if it is objected that any kind of knowledge of temporal objects gives rise to this activity of knowledge and love, Thomas replies]: To verify the notion of image, we must not say that there is solely a procession of one thing from another, but we must see also what thing proceeds and from what. We must find a word about God proceeding from a knowledge of God.[50]

In this perspective, it is obvious that man then exercises to the highest possible degree of knowledge and love *of God*. Even more, however, the condition Thomas poses concerning the origin of this procession finds here an unexpected realization. Given that, in beatitude, knowledge of God will occur without any mediation of any created similarity, we are led to say that at that moment it is God Himself who will be immediately at the origin and culmination of that act of knowledge and beatifying love. To repeat here a felicitous formulation: "The actual conjunction between God and the soul-image does not admit of intermediaries. It is God himself who proceeds from God through human acts."[51]

⟶

50. *ST* Ia q. 93 a. 8 and ad 1.

51. G. Lafont, *Structure et méthodes*, 270. We should cite here Chardon's great observation, in which he beautifully expresses what happens when the eternal procession of a divine Person continues in temporal procession (= mission), and which concludes: "The eternal production is the origin of the second production; or rather the second is only an extension of the first. Or even better: the eternal and the temporal procession are but one single production. The condition of time adds nothing new to God, who is immutable and

If we may be allowed to end this chapter with a kind of homage, we would like to reproduce here some lines from an author whose services to the Thomist cause are immense. With a terseness and precision worthy of the Master, they felicitously bring together the central point of what we have tried to say here:

> The return of the rational creature is achieved in the union of knowledge and love with God, our Object. Thus the whole cycle of temporal processions is completed; it is the goal of the whole history of the world: to show to rational creatures the intimate glory of the divine Persons. This union of the soul to the Triune God is begun, at least, on the level of *habitus*, at the very first infusion of grace, with the dowry of virtues and gifts that equip the soul for acts proportionate to the divine object. This union is realized gradually in imperfect acts of grasping God in the life of the Christian here below. It expands finally into the fulfilled vision in the beatific vision, which is a perfect and unchangeable act. All during this process, God gives himself in his three Persons, makes himself present to the soul, in a real and substantial presence, which bears the name Indwelling; presence of an Object to be grasped by experience . . . of whom the definitive possession and enjoyment are fully operative only in the blessed vision, but of whom the progressive appropriations roughly attempted here below respond fully to the invisible missions of the Son and the Holy Spirit.[52]

---

the plenitude of all perfection; it affects only the creature who is made a partaker, through the change that is effected in it, of that which God is from all eternity; that is to say, *God begins to produce in the holy soul the Persons who are in His bosom, before all time," The Cross of Jesus*, trans. Richard T. Murphy, vol. 2, 35.

52. H.-F. Dondaine, *La Trinité*, vol. 2, pp. 437–38. In addition to numerous works and a very beautiful commentary in two volumes of Questions on the Trinity, from which I have drawn this passage, P. Dondaine has edited with distinction four volumes of Thomas's *opuscula*: the Leonine volumes 40–43.

⳹

CHAPTER V

The Way, the Truth, and the Life

It was easy to understand from the examination of Thomas's views in the preceding chapter that the path of the man-image toward beatitude and his entry into glory presuppose a way to be traversed, just as acquiring perfect resemblance implies a model to be imitated. The second Person of the Trinity, whom we have already spoken of as the Father's Art and perfect Image and through whom we come forth from the Father and return to Him, represents a model that is as entirely inaccessible in his uncreated perfection as the Father himself. But in his Incarnation as the Word, he wished to become one of us, and in Jesus, the Anointed, we have both the way and the model that we were seeking, and more still, the homeland to which we aspire.

Saint Thomas proposes a clear and full position on all this, and he gives some very solid indications about his views at some of the neuralgic points in the *Summa:* "In his humanity, Christ is for us the way that leads to God." Strong, if brief, this affirmation is more fully developed at the beginning of the Third Part:

Since Our Savior, the Lord Jesus, "in delivering his people from their sins" (Matt. 1:21) has shown us in his own person *the way* of *truth* by which we can pass in rising from the dead to the beatitude of immortal *life*, it is necessary for the completion of our theological enterprise, that after treating the ultimate end of human life, its virtues and vices, we now turn to consider the Savior of all in himself and the benefits he has bestowed on the human race.[1]

---

1. *ST* Ia q. 2 Pro.

A little marvel of composition, this text recalls in large lines the part of the journey already covered and announces what remains to be done with Jesus' very own words in John's Gospel (14:6): "I am the *way*, the *truth*, and the *life*." Once again, the Dominican master shows himself attentive to Scripture, which he inserts into the passage without disrupting the continuity, combining in a single sentence the "negative" dimension of Christ's work, the deliverance from sin, with its "positive" dimension, the return to the Father, the path that Christ incarnates in person: "No one goes to the Father except through me." After this, we understand better that he may be speaking of the *completion* of the theological enterprise: the whole *Summa* moves toward Christ.

Meanwhile, this unusual situation of Christ at the conclusion of the work presented theologians with a question. And it continued as a question until the deep reasons for it were noticed. We must, therefore, dispel a misunderstanding that we have already encountered and try to understand why Thomas chose to speak of Christ solely in the Third Part. The reasons for this, which are of both a theological and a pedagogical order, may best be seen in the way that they articulate morals and Christology within a vision of the whole. We will thus be able to continue pursuing our purpose, because it is clear that consideration of Christ is necessary in order to complete the theological effort, for the even stronger reason that Christian life which seeks inspiration from Jesus will find it here in a definitive way. Friar Thomas speaks about this in some very beautiful passages that leave no doubt about the place that Christ occupies in the Christian life and Thomas's own life.

The Way That Leads to God

At the moment when Thomas was thinking about synthesizing theological learning in his own way, he already had two large assemblies of moral questions in Peter Lombard's *Sentences*.[2] The first is found in the Second Book of that work (distinctions 24–44): Lombard had grouped together, after Creation and the sin of the first man, various considerations on grace and free will, original sin and its transmission, good and evil in human acts, etc. His treatment of the remaining material comes in the

---

2. Cf. L.-B. Gillon, "L'imitation du Christ et la morale de saint Thomas," *Angelicum* 36 (1959): 263–86. This study has been reproduced in Italian: *Cristo e la teologia morale* (Rome, 1961), and in English: *Christ and Moral Theology* (Staten Island, 1967).

Third Book (distinctions 23–40), after the Christology. There he speaks of the theological and moral virtues, the gifts of the Holy Spirit, states of life, commandments. Those who are familiar with the *Summa* will recognize easily in these two groupings the two large poles around which were assembled the material of the *Prima Secundae* and the *Secunda Secundae*. Those subjects are considerably enriched and reorganized by Thomas in line with a plan that owes little to Lombard. But it is in Thomas's predecessor that we find its first outline.

Two options were therefore possible. The first would have meant grouping the whole of moral theology after the Christology (the second pole of the *Sentences*). Thomas would have been able to organize his whole moral teaching in dependence upon Christ. This decision would have had the advantage of putting the figure of Christ at the highest position in the organization of Thomas's moral theology, as he is in the Christian life. By his very title as Son of God, Christ is essentially "the absolute Model that all creatures imitate in their own way, for he is the true and perfect image of the Father."[3] That decision would on the other hand have had the disadvantage of not integrating *sacra doctrina* well in the complete vision. Its absolute theocentrism stems from the fact that God alone is a sufficiently explanatory principle to be the keystone of all theological knowledge. Theological synthesis aims at discovering order and coherence in the divine plan, without attempting to impose on it a logic foreign to its nature. Thus it necessarily follows that the Trinity would be first in explanation as it is in reality. This is true of the work of creation; it is also true of the work of re-creation. The theologian cannot forget the mediating role of the humanity of Christ, but he is invited to go through that to the source of grace and salvation, God himself.

Thomas, therefore, chose a different strategy, which meant dealing with moral theology after speaking of creation and the divine government (Lombard's first pole). Instead of centering moral theology on Christ, he connects it to the Trinity indirectly through the biblical teaching about man as the image of God. For it is that man's return to the Creator he wished to describe (after having described his exit from God). He does not completely lose the advantages of the first approach, however, because he can integrate them with this approach without difficulty. To

---

3. *In I ad Cor. XI, 1*, n. 583: "Primordiale exemplar quod omnes creaturae imitantur tanquam ueram et perfectam imaginem Patris." Later we shall see the centrality of the passage.

speak of man as the image of God is to be led into invoking the Exemplar on which he is made and whom he must resemble. The Prologue to the Second Part expresses that: "Having spoken of the *Exemplar*, which is to say *God* . . . it remains to speak of his *image*, which is to say *man*. . . ." But that final aim cannot be attained except through Christ. For the image can only find its similarity to the model "through conformity of grace."[4] That grace can only be obtained by the model's mediation, for he is "as if the source of grace."[5] Christ will therefore be structurally present everywhere there is grace, and the same is true of the Holy Spirit: "United through Christ, moved through the Holy Spirit. . . . That is why whatever is achieved through the Holy Spirit is also done through Christ."[6]

It is quite true then that the person of Christ does not by itself play the central role either in the construction of the *Summa* or in the organization of Thomas's moral teaching. This is meant in no way to diminish Christ's status, but is the natural consequence of an earlier decision to invoke the whole Trinity. We do not do justice to Thomas if we do not recognize to what an extent that decision is in line with the biblical data. Not only is it prescribed by the story of Genesis, but it also is brought home to us in the Sermon on the Mount: "Be perfect as your Father in heaven is perfect" (Matt. 5:48). Saint Paul speaks in similar terms: "Seek to imitate God like beloved children" (Eph. 5:1).

The fruitfulness of this approach will quickly reveal itself. But we first must understand the rationale behind the plan of the *Summa*. In addition to the basic theological decision based upon Scripture, which we have just looked at, there was also an important pedagogical reason. Thomas could not give the example of Christ at the beginning of his moral exposition. He first had to describe the essential structure of human action. This structure is universal enough to be applied to the humanity of Christ himself, since that humanity remained unchanged in its most inward nature despite its assumption by the Word. Reading carefully what the *Tertia Pars* says about Christ's human acts (liberty, merit, passions, virtues), we are constantly referred back to the material in the *Prima Secundae*. Without question, this absolutely unique humanity calls for some particularities that belong solely to Christ, but much of what is said here also relates to our own condition in all things "except sin." It is clear that all this is true

---

4. Cf. *ST* Ia q. 97 a. 4 and chapter IV of the present work, "Image and beatitude."
5. *In Ioannem I, 16*, lect. 10, n. 201: "quasi auctori gratiae."
6. *In ad Eph. II, 18*, lect. 5, n. 121.

also for Christ, but Thomas could not have spoken of him first without then being led to numerous repetitions. Though the discussion here is more technical than in the earlier treatment, the approach was nevertheless dictated by the subject.

This does not mean, however, that the structures of general morality *(Prima Secundae)* are developed outside of all reference to Christ and his grace. Despite all the borrowing from the ancient world, the treatise on the virtues is full of specifically Christian notions. An explication of the gifts of the Holy Spirit as well as a commentary on the Sermon on the Mount follow, which show that Christ is enlightening the subject even before he is explicitly spoken of.[7] The same is true of the treatise on the ancient law, in which the author strongly emphasizes the prefiguring of the mystery of Christ.[8] And when he deals with the new law, the central point is the grace of the Holy Spirit, which is obtained by way of faith in Christ.[9] The whole is crowned by the treatment of grace, properly speaking, which repeats and brings to completion everything which has been said up to that point about human acts and virtues.[10] All this should warn us not to misunderstand Thomas's intentions: Christ's place in the Third Part of the *Summa* does not mean we inexplicably bracket what is specifically Christian. Instead, it is a deliberate decision to reclaim Christ's role in the creature's movement of return toward God and in the fulfillment of the history of salvation.

The new presence realized by grace and the divine missions, which we have found in the numerous passages examined earlier, enrich the idea of the simple presence of God in the world in a way that the creature alone would not have expected. By situating Christ at the summit of this universe, Thomas introduces all the dynamism of a *return*, guided by the Good News. This comes about not solely through the Word, but by the Word *Incarnate* who continues to send us his Spirit. As the only mediator through whom we receive grace from the Trinity, he is also the supreme guide who takes the lead in our return toward God: "It was fitting that, wishing to lead a large number of his children to Glory, He through whom and for whom all things are, was made perfect through suffering, *the Prince who was to lead them into their salvation*" (Heb. 2:10).

---

7. Cf. *ST* Ia IIae qq. 68–70.   8. Cf. *ST* Ia IIae qq. 98–105.
9. Cf. *ST* Ia IIae qq. 106–8.   10. Cf. *ST* Ia IIae qq. 109–14.

A New Way

The preceding explanations may have the appearance of an arid technical detour. But they provide help in understanding what is at stake. We may now re-read some of the passages where Thomas speaks of Christ. He is justly renowned as someone who has best presented the metaphysical problems involved in the hypostatic union. But that is only one aspect of his thought. Following this initial examination, let us uncover another facet of his approach to the mystery. We shall not reproduce here the whole of his argument. It will be more enlightening if we continue with the question that the theologians were asking themselves for a long time: *Cur Deus homo?* Why did God become man?

We have already looked at the best-known part of Friar Thomas's answer.[11] But we have to look exhaustively at what he says on this subject. Since he refuses to invoke necessity pure and simple—since we cannot put limits on God's omnipotence or deny that he could have saved us in another way[12]—he seeks instead fitting reasons that may help us grasp something about the incomprehensible love that pushed God to such an extreme measure.[13] Following Saint Augustine, Saint Anselm, and many others whom Scripture turned in this direction, Thomas naturally invokes the need for the healing of the wound cause by sin *(remedium peccati)*, for restoration *(reparatio)* of humanity to friendship with God, for satisfaction for sin, all of which appear as the most far-reaching motives.[14] Thus, the theme of satisfaction, present in the *Sentences*, and formulated perfectly in the *Compendium Theologiae*, also appears in the *Summa Theologiae*:

The Incarnation frees man from slavery to sin. As Saint Augustine says, "it was necessary for the demon to be vanquished by the justice of the man Jesus Christ." And that was produced by Christ's satisfaction for us. Man, simple man, *was not able* to make satisfaction for the whole human race. God in Himself *was not obliged to do it*; it was therefore necessary Jesus Christ be simultaneously God and man *(Homo autem purus satisfacere non poterat, Deus autem satisfacere non debebat)*. [The balancing of these two formulations is enough to show their origin—

11. Cf. above chap. 3, "God and the World."
12. *ST* IIIa q. 1 a. 2.
13. Cf. above chap. 3, note 51.
14. Cf. Anselm of Canterbury, *Cur Deus Homo* (SC 91 [Paris, 1963]); for a comparison of the two authors, see J. Bracken, "Thomas Aquinas and Anselm's Satisfaction Theory," *Angelicum* 62 (1985); 501–30, although his opposition of the two authors tends to be overly systematic.

Anselm was only an intermediary. Thomas does not hide the fact and, having quoted Augustine, he continues, according to Pope Leo the great]: "Strength is clothed in weakness, majesty in humility; for to heal us, we needed *a single mediator between God and men* (1 Tim. 2:5) who might die, on the one hand, and rise from the dead, on the other. True God, he brought the remedy; true man, he gave us the example."[15]

Despite the relevance and persistence of this question, the theme of restored equilibrium, lost by sin, is always in danger of falling into an anthropocentric view of things: sin seeming to force on God a finality he has not foreseen. Seeking a fresh approach, Thomas appears to have found one in the *Summa contra Gentiles*. Without rejecting the tradition, he frees himself somewhat from the confining views of recognized authorities, and elaborates a position of his own.[16] He proposes an argument that, at least in this form, seems never to have been applied to the subject. It was convenient that God became man to give man the possibility of seeing God:

If we contemplate the mystery of the Incarnation carefully and reverently, we find there such depth of wisdom that human knowledge is overwhelmed by it. The Apostle rightly says (1 Cor. 1:25): *The foolishness of God is wiser than the wisdom of men.* That is why to those who consider things reverently the reasons for this mystery appear ever more marvelous.[17]

These few words introduce a long chapter from which we will select here certain elements. But we cannot help feeling the restrained passion that inspires them. In spite of the theologian's sobriety, we cannot help remembering that he is the same man whose biography displays great love for Jesus Christ.[18] This is the same emotion that underlies the strict rigor in the following reasoning:

---

15. *ST* IIIa q. 1 a. 2; cf. *In III Sent.* d.1 q. 1 a. 2; *Comp. theol.* I, 200 (Leonine, vol. 42, p. 158). Among the recent works on this subject, see R. Cessario, *The Godly Image: Christ and Salvation in Catholic Thought from St. Anselm to Aquinas* (Petersham, Mass., 1990). Also, A. Patfoort, "Le vrai visage de la satisfaction du Christ selon St. Thomas: Une étude de la Somme théologique," in *Ordo sapientiae et amoris*, 247–65. One might hesitate slightly at the way that these authors give satisfaction such a central place.

16. The change of perspective had been noted by M. Corbin, "La Parole devenue chair," but he seems to treat it in too isolated a fashion. Other perspectives, however, are not ruled out.

17. *SCG* IV 54, n. 3922; cf. *De rationibus fidei ad Cantorem Antiochenum* (*De rat. Fidei*) 7, Leonine, vol. 40, p. B 66.

18. Cf. my *Saint Thomas Aquinas*, 283–89.

First of all, the Incarnation brings to man on the way to beatitude *(ad beatitudinem tendenti)* an efficacious help in the highest degree. As we have already said (cf. SCG III 48 ff.) the perfect blessedness of man consists in the immediate vision of God. Because of the immense distance between their natures, it might seem impossible for man to reach such a state when the human intellect is united to the divine essence itself in an immediate way, as the intellect to the intelligible. *Paralyzed by despair, man would then give up his quest for beatitude.*[19] But the fact that God wished to unite himself in person with human nature demonstrates to men that it is possible to be immediately united with God through the intellect, in seeing him without intermediary. It is fitting, therefore, in the highest degree that God would assume human nature in order to reanimate man's hope in beatitude. Also, after the Incarnation of Christ, men began to aspire more ardently to heavenly beatitude, as He himself said (John 10:10): *"I am come that they may have life and that they may have it more abundantly."*[20]

What immediately follows this passage takes into consideration another argument drawn from the dignity of man, which is dazzlingly manifested in the Incarnation. We shall return to this later. But to read the preceding lines as they should be read, we need to avoid giving excessive importance to the "intellectual" dimension. What follows reminds us that beatitude is not an abstract thing, where reason alone is engaged. It takes hold of the whole man with all his powers of loving:

Since man finds his perfect beatitude in the enjoyment *(fruitio)* of God, it is necessary that his affections be prepared for the desire of that divine fruition, a natural desire for beatitude whose existence in man can be verified. Now, it is love for something that awakens the desire to enjoy it. It is necessary, then, that man, on the way to perfect beatitude, would be led to love God. But nothing moves us to love someone so much as the experience of his love for us. Men cannot, therefore, get a more effective proof of God's love for them than seeing God unite himself to man personally, since the distinguishing feature of love is to unite as far as possible the lover and the beloved. It was thus a requirement for man on the way to beatitude that God would become Incarnate.[21]

---

19. Would it be psychologizing too much to see in this sentence an echo of the famous passage in which Thomas commiserates with "the anguish of these great minds" *(quantam angustiam patiebantur . . . eorum praeclara ingenia,* i.e., Alexander of Aphrodisias, Averroes, Aristotle), who did not know where to put man's beatitude because they lacked knowledge of the soul's immortality? Cf. SCG III 48, n. 2261.

20. SCG IV 54, n. 3923.

21. SCG IV 54, n. 3926.

It is hardly necessary to go further in order to recognize numerous themes that have nourished our meditations to this point. We find here immediately the man hungering for beatitude, for it is of him that Friar Thomas speaks from one end to the other of his moral reflections. But the theme of love, which he has just recalled with a glancing reference to Pseudo-Dionysius, seems to have brought to mind—and it is far from being an accident—the way Aristotle speaks of friendship:

> Since friendship consists in a certain equality, it is not possible for beings who are too different from another to be united in friendship. In order, therefore, for friendship between God and man to be more intimate, it was necessary for God to become man, since man is a natural friend to man. So that *knowing God under a visible form, we might be enraptured by him into love of the invisible.*[22]

Though the reference to Aristotle here is true enough, it should not obscure the explicit quotation from the Christmas preface that ends the passage, from which Thomas probably took his initial inspiration: *Dum uisibiliter Deum cognoscimus, in inuisibilium amorem rapiamur.* The Christmas liturgical celebration, under the aegis of the divine love for man and its manifestation in the coming of the Word in the flesh, was well suited to helping Thomas deepen his meditations on the appropriateness of the Incarnation.[23] When we find it in the *Contra Gentiles*, this theme is long since familiar to Thomas for we met with it in the commentary on the *Sentences:*

> In order for there to be an easy way to ascend to God, it was convenient that man might set out *(consurgeret)* as much by intelligence as by will, starting with what was known to him. And because it is connatural to man in the current miserable condition to draw knowledge from visible realities and fix upon them, it was therefore convenient *(congruenter)* that God become visible by taking on human nature. So that beginning from visible realities we would be carried *into the love and knowledge of invisible realities.*[24]

---

22. SCG IV 54, n. 3927; cf. Aristotle, *Nicomachean Ethics* VIII: 1,3 (1155a) and 5,5 (1157b).

23. Yves Congar once published a wonderful study (largely based on the Church Fathers) on this theme: *"Dum visibiliter Deum cognoscimus. . . .* Méditation théologique," *La Maison-Dieu* 59 (1959): 132–61, reprinted in the same author's *The Revelation of God,* 67–96.

24. *In III Sent.* d. 1 q. 1 a. 2. This theme of a progressive adaptation to divine realities beginning with what the human being can experience is common in Thomas. We find it in the *De rat. fidei,* one chapter of which is dedicated to themes concerning the Incarnation

This theme reappears one last time, without the liturgical reference, in the *Summa Theologiae*. There it certainly has a little less prominence because Thomas's desire to synthesize, which animates that whole work, leads him to assemble two imposing series of complementary convenient reasons for the Incarnation, in which he seems determined to omit nothing that can be said on the subject. With a sightly different emphasis, the theme nonetheless remains present, calling on the reader to give it its full richness starting with what he knows from other works:

> The fifth reason leads to our full participation in the divine, which is man's *beatitude and the very goal of human life*. And that has been granted us through the humanity of Christ. Again, it is Augustine who has said: "God became man so that man might become God" *(Factus est Deus homo, ut homo fieret Deus)*.[25]

Though the ending of this passage was a commonplace of the Patristic literature and our author shows nothing original here, we might note that the reference to beatitude is for him a much more personal theme in this context. Compared to an overly anthropocentric view that the Incarnation occurred because of man's sin, Thomas's view differs greatly in the emphasis on a desire to see God, which is the emptiness left in man by his Creator. The love God bears toward man is not limited to reestablishing in strict justice the equilibrium destroyed by sin. He wishes in addition to complete his plan of salvation. Thus, the Incarnation is viewed as a *manuductio*,[26] a taking of man by the hand to lead him along the path to God. This is the "new and living way" that the Epistle to the Hebrews speaks of (10:20):

(c. 5, n. 976, Leonine, vol. 40, p. B 62): "Given that man has an intellect and affectivity immersed in matter, he could not easily have raised himself to realities above. It is easy for the human being to know and love another human being, but it is not given to all to contemplate the divine height and to be carried toward it by a due affection of love. Only those turned from corporeal things to raise themselves toward spiritual ones by God's help, great labor, and commitment, can arrive there. Therefore in order to open for us all an easy way to God, God wanted to become man, *so that even the little ones might contemplate and love someone who, so to speak, would be like them*, and so, by what they are able to grasp they progress, little by little, toward what is perfect."

25. *ST* IIIa q. 1 a. 2. But this is from a spurious text attributed to Augustine (cf. *Sermo* CXXVIII [PL 39, 1997]). The four reasons given before this in the series, and dealing with "our progress in goodness," successively envisage the profit that comes from it for our *faith*, our *hope*, our *charity*, and our practice of the *virtues*. Beatitude thus appears as the end of a road traversed according to all the virtues of the Christian life.

26. *ST* IIa IIae q. 82 a. 3 ad 2: the humanity of Christ is a kind of pedagogy supremely adapted to lead to his divinity.

[The Apostle] shows how we can have the confidence to approach, because Christ, through his blood, has *initiated (initiauit)*, which is to say, he has begun *(inchoauit) for us a new path. . . .* This is the path that leads to heaven. It is *new* because, before Christ, no one had found it: "No one ascends to heaven except for the one who descends from heaven" (John 3:13). That is why he who wishes to ascend must be united to the one who descends like a limb to the body. . . . [This way] is *living*, which is to say that it endures forever, because of the fact that it manifests the fecundity *(uirtus)* of the deity who lives forever. What that path is, the Apostle makes clearer when he continues: "beyond the veil, which is to say the flesh." Just as the high priest enters into the Holy of Holies beyond the veil, so if we want to enter into the sanctuary of glory, we must pass through the body of Christ, which was the veil for his divinity. "You are truly a hidden God!" (Isa. 45:15). It is not enough to believe in God if we do not believe in the Incarnation.[27]

The explicit thematic of the way manifests once again its importance here, though we have not ever really left the subject, for it blossoms in a number of the above-cited texts. Like the desire for beatitude, it appears throughout Thomas's work. Better yet, we find in this context the circular movement whose fertility we have already seen. We have already quoted the following passage in part. But it is worth repeating, because it develops the essential nature of the intuition:

[Through the Incarnation] man receives a remarkable example of that fortunate union by which the created intellect will be united through its intelligence to the uncreated intellect. *Since God united himself to man by assuming his nature, it is no longer beyond belief that the created intellect can be united to God by seeing His essence.* It is thus that the whole work of God is in some way completed, when man, created last, returns to his beginning in a kind of circle, by being united to the very beginning of all things through the work of the Incarnation.[28]

This little assembly of related passages could be considerably expanded. It will have to suffice to dispel the worries raised by Christ's placement at the end in the *Summa*'s plan. Friar Thomas's theocentrism does not cast Christ out to the periphery. He is exactly where he should be: at the perfect center of our history, the junction between God and man. Not like a static midpoint, but as the way that ascends toward our heavenly home, "the head of our faith and he who brings it to perfection" (Heb.

27. *In ad Heb. X, 20,* lect. 2, n. 502.
28. *Comp. theol.* I, 201.

12:2), who draws us after him with the irresistible force which enlivens his own humanity toward the Father.[29]

Imitating God by Imitating Christ

The evening of the Last Supper, "knowing that he had come from God and was returning to God," Jesus gives a final sign of what he expects of his followers by the washing of the feet (John 13:3). Thomas had no further need of emphasizing in his commentary the perfect "circularity" expressed in these verses. Instead, he labors to highlight what results from Christ's attitude:

[This scene illustrates several things]; the fourth regards Christ's sanctity, because *he was going to God*. It is in this that the sanctity of man consists: to go to God. That is why he [Jesus] will immediately say: since he himself goes to God, it is his role to lead others to God. He achieves this in a special way through humility and charity, and that is why he gives this example of humility and charity.[30]

There is no better way to proceed toward our present subject. When Thomas speaks of Christ's example, he is not thinking of a motionless reproduction of a fixed model; but, as is fitting to the image on its way toward imitation, he conceives of it as a pathway: to imitate Christ is to walk after him. After this, we will find these two attitudes constantly interrelated, but with a third as well: to follow Christ is to learn to follow the Father.

All this is dispersed and inextricably mixed into a large number of passages. And the difficulty here is to select among them and put them into a useful order.[31] This is in itself significant since it shows the pervasiveness of these ideas in Aquinas's work. The passages drawn from the commentaries on the New Testament are naturally more numerous and explicit, but we will make use of them only to amplify what the large syntheses

29. On this point, we have the commentary on John. 6:44: "No one comes to me unless the Father calls him," where Thomas explains that "those who follow Christ . . . are drawn by the Father," without violence, for this is the fulfillment of their desire, *In Ioannem VI*, 44, nn. 935 ff. Cf. R. Lafontaine, "La personne du Père dans la pensée de saint Thomas," in R. Lafontaine, et al., *L'Écriture âme de la théologie* (Brussels, 1990), 81–108.

30. *In Ioannem XIII*, 3, lect. 1, n. 1743.

31. A whole set of these passages presented according to the works in which they appear may be found in A. Valsecchi, "L'imitazione di Cristo in san Tommaso d'Aquino," in G. Colombo, A. Rimoldi, A. Valsecchi, eds., *Miscellanea Carlo Figini* (Venegono Inferiore, 1964), 175–203. The author is rightly surprised that it has been believed that Thomas was not familiar with the theme of the imitation of Christ.

teach us. It is extremely important to see how the appeal to Christ's example does not arise solely from moral exhortation. It is deeply woven into
the very structure of Thomas's theology, and there are two quite distinct
ways of demonstrating its foundations.

After everything we have said, it will not be very surprising that it is,
again, with regard to the propriety of the Incarnation that the first way of
establishing Christ's exemplariness is presented. In the *Summa contra
Gentiles*, after explaining how the Word become flesh responds to the
need to open up access to blessedness for us, Thomas adds the following
relevant observation:

Blessedness . . . is virtue's recompense. It is therefore necessary that those who
strive for blessedness form themselves in virtue, to which we are aroused by word
and example. Now, a person's example and word lead us all the more effectively
to the practice of virtue the more we have a firmly rooted opinion about that person's goodness. But no man, simply as man, can give us a sense of infallible
virtue, because the holiest of men have their failings. For man to be confirmed in
virtue, *it was thus necessary to receive from a God become man instruction and examples of virtue*. Behold why the Lord Himself affirms in John's Gospel (13:15): *I
have given you the example so that you may do as I have done for you.*[32]

We find the same line presented more briefly, but quite lucidly, in the
Summa Theologiae. But there is a new accent in that work, because the
author combines the imitation of the Father with that of Jesus Christ:

[As we already know, we can adduce several reasons for the Incarnation] from the
point of view of our progress in goodness. . . . The fourth is that *it gives us a model for practicing virtue*. This is why, as Saint Augustine says: "The man we were
able to see, we were not supposed to imitate. It was necessary to imitate the God
whom we cannot see. It is, then, so as to offer to man an example that he might
see and imitate that God became man."[33]

These two passages illustrate the first way in which Thomas establishes
the value of the example of Christ's humanity. The second passage, however, already directs us toward another, decidedly deeper way of establishing it, for it refers us directly to the doctrine of the Trinity and its connections with the world. In order to understand this fully and to situate it into

32. SCG IV 54, n. 3928.
33. *ST* IIIa q. 1 a. 2, with quotation from Augustine's *Sermo* CCCLXXI, 2 (PL 39, 1024).
The theme is repeated, but more allusively, in the *Comp. theol.* I, 201: Leonine, vol. 42, p.
158.

the whole development of Thomas's thinking, we have to link it with a key passage in the *Prima Secundae*. There we shall see better that Thomas never loses sight of the fact that the Father is the ultimate model of perfection. He is also concerned to indicate the means for us to arrive at that model, even before he speaks explicitly of the role Christ plays. This passage is rather typical, for the author links the authority of Scripture to his authoritative authors: Augustine and even Aristotle. It is worth noting this because it is characteristic of his method, which seeks to profit from the wisdom of the ancients as much as from the will to combine inseparably man's quest with God's kindness toward him:

As Saint Augustine says, "the soul must follow a model in order that virtue can be formed within it; that model is God; if we follow him, we will live well." *It is therefore evident that the model for human virtue pre-exists in God, as the reasons for all things also pre-exist in him.* . . . It belongs to man to draw as close to the divine as he can, as even the Philosopher says and as is recommended to us in Sacred Scripture in various ways: *Be perfect as your Father in heaven is perfect* (Matt. 5:48).[34]

This final reference to the Father is powerfully brought forward; there is no question that He remains the first ranked.[35] But we ought to notice how much this article also looks to the future. Contrary to the idea of the Golden Mean (by which we try to characterize virtue) as mediocrity, Thomas distinguishes between human and divine virtues "*as one distinguishes between a motion and its end*":

That is to say that certain virtues are those of people on the way and tending toward resemblance to the divine. And these virtues we call "purifying." . . . On the other hand, there are the virtues of people who have already achieved some resemblance to the divine. These we call the virtues of the already purified soul. They are such that prudence looks only upon the divine; temperance no longer knows anything of earthly desires; fortitude ignores the passions; justice constantly is linked with the divine intelligence through its attempt to imitate it. We say that these virtues are those of the blessed, or of those who, in this life, are far advanced in perfection.

34. *ST* Ia IIae q. 61 a. 5: with a quotation from St. Augustine, *De moribus ecclesiae*, c. 6, nn. 9–10.

35. Cf. *In ad Eph.* V, 1, lect. 1, n. 267: "Human nature only finds its perfection in union with God. . . . It is therefore necessary to imitate Him as much as we can, for it is the son's role to imitate the father (*ad filium pertinet patrem imitari*). . . . We are his *sons*, for He is our Father through Creation . . . *beloved sons*, for He has chosen us to participate in His very life (literally: 'to participate in Him,' *ad participationem sui ipsius*)."

In its repetitiveness and insistence, this passage reveals some burning passion that goes far beyond technical precision. It reconnects us to subjects explored in the examination of the Creation, the image of God and the progress toward him that dominate Thomas's reflections. But it is also driven by an ardent desire of the Good that is beyond all goods. But its immediate interest for us lies in the referring back to the Divine Exemplar of all things, which we have found in the First Part. Thomas sees in Christ the exemplary realization of all the virtues because he is the Word Incarnate, who, in his eternity, already presides over the creation of all things. Another crucial passage, whose structural similarity to this one is striking, develops this with precision and the greatest clarity:

The first principle of the whole procession of things is the Son of God: "Through him, all things were made" (John 1:3). That is why he is also the original Model *(primordiale exemplar)* that all creatures imitate, as the true and perfect Image of the Father. Whence the expression in Colossians (1:15): "He is the Image of the invisible God, the First Born of all creation, for in him have been created all things." In a special way he is also the model *(exemplar)* of all the spiritual graces that shine in spiritual creatures, as is said to the Son in the Psalm (109:3): "In holy splendor before the morning star, like the dew I begot you." Since he has been begotten before all creatures through resplendent grace, he has in himself in an exemplary fashion *(exemplariter)* the splendor of all holiness. However that divine model was far from us. . . . That is why he wished to become man, to offer to men a human model.[36]

The commentator continues with several examples of practical applications that we can leave aside for the moment. It is more important to notice that beginning with a passage like this, we can pursue a twofold path of meditation and contemplation. The first, because it takes things from God's point of view, fits in all respects into the immediate development of many of the texts we have already read, and is the way of *ontological exemplarity.* In more scriptural terms, let's say that the accent falls here on the creature, newly made by God in the image of the Image. It utilizes Saint Paul's frequent teachings about how we are modeled within, "re-formed" in the image of the well-beloved Son by grace, of which he is mediator: "Those he foreknew, he also predestined to be conformed to the image of His Son, so that he might be the first-born among many

36. *In I ad Cor. XI,* 1, n. 563; the same argument is found, notably, in *De rat. fidei* 5, n. 973 (Leonine, vol. 40, p. B 61): since all things were created through the Word, it was fitting that they would also be restored by Him: see also the commentary on John 13:15 below.

brothers" (Rom. 8:29). This relatively complex theme, which is much used and quite prolific in Thomas's work, will be dealt with in the next chapter.

The way of *moral exemplarity* is more immediately evident; but it is, in reality, second in importance to the other way. It also follows the impulse prepared in many places already mentioned: the Incarnation of the Word offers to man-the-image an accessible model which teaches him to conform himself to the original, inaccessible model which presided over his creation. The emphasis is on Christ, the living incarnation of the gospel virtues, and on man's effort to collaborate with God through the grace that he receives from Him. This theme, which is somewhat homiletic, is abundantly present in Thomas's commentaries on Scripture, but it is far from being absent in the other works.

"I Have Given You the Example . . ."

The fact that Christ represents the absolute model of Christian life is sufficient to explain Thomas's insistence on the point, but we will better understand his reasoning if we return to the reading of his meditation on the washing of the feet. Like a true spiritual master, Thomas has no qualms about emphasizing the practical:

[Christ Jesus] therefore said: I have done this to give you an example, that is why you must wash each other's feet, for this was my intention in acting thus. Indeed, in human action, examples are more effective than words *(plus mouent exempla quam verba)*. Man acts and chooses according to what seems good; that is why from the very fact that he chooses this or that, he shows that it appears good to him, far more than if he said that he had to choose it. It follows that if someone says something but does something else, what he does persuades others much more that what he says. That is why it is of the highest necessity to join example to words.

But a man's example, simply as man, is not enough for imitation by the whole human race, whether because human reason is unable to conceive of everything [from life or the good], or because reason is deceived in the consideration of things themselves. That is why the example of the Son of God is given to us, who cannot be deceived and who is more than sufficient in every domain. Saint Augustine teaches that "pride cannot be cured except by divine humility." The same is true of avarice and the other vices.

Properly understood, it was highly "fitting" that the Son of God would be given us as an example of all virtues. He is in effect the Art of the Father and, therefore, *just as he was the first example of the creation, he is also the first example of holiness* (1 Pet. 2:21: "Christ suffered for us, leaving you an example so that you may walk in his footsteps").[37]

Plus movent exempla quam verba. The tone is a given. This formulation from the *Lectura super Ioannem* had long been known to Thomas; we can already find it among the themes on the Incarnation in the *Contra Gentiles*.[38] He reproduces the same text in the *Summa Theologiae* with a significant appeal to common experience.[39] Doubtless, this is a commonplace of human wisdom, but it would not be going too far to think of Thomas's Dominican heritage in this context, since it was often said about Saint Dominic that he preached by example as much as by word *(uerbo et exemplo).*[40]

Christ's exemplariness in act for the whole of the Christian life is found in various works, notably in the opuscula Thomas wrote in defense of the religious life. But we will also come across it in another context when we look at following Christ in the religious life. We could select from the Second Part of the *Summa* a group of texts demonstrating that Thomas never loses sight of the point. But this work having already been done,[41] it will be more fruitful to trace the development of the Third Part in order to draw from it some repeated indications of the virtues illustrated by Christ and proposed for imitation by his followers. Thus, in continuing to

37. *In Ioannem XIII*, 15, lect. 3, n. 1781.

38. SCG IV 55, nn. 3950–51: "It is not unfitting to say that Christ wished to suffer death on the cross to give us an example of humility [this being a case, doubtless, of a virtue that does not pertain to God, but which the Word, in his humanity, can assume]. Although men have been formed to humility by the divine teachings . . . deeds stimulate action more than do words *(ad agendum magis prouocant facta quam uerba)* and more effectively the better confirmed is the reputation for virtue of the one who acts. Thus, although we find numerous examples of humility in other men, the example of the Man-God, whom we know could not be mistaken and whose humility is all the more admirable since his majesty is so sublime, is extremely well-suited to spurring us on in this way." See also the notes by P. Marc (Marietti edition of the SCG) on this passage, which indicate its classical and patristic roots.

39. *ST* Ia IIae q. 34 a. 1: "In the domain of human actions and passions, where the experience of the largest number counts for a great deal, *magis mouent exempla quam uerba.*"

40. Cf. M.-H. Vicaire, *Saint Dominic and His Times*, trans. Kathleen Pond (New York, 1964), 135.

41. Cf. A Valsecchi, *L'imitazione di Cristo*, 194–98. The same author has placed Thomas's position in the broader context of the scriptural and patristic traditions in an illuminating article: "Gesù Cristo nostra legge," *La Scuola Cattolica* 88 (1960): 81–110; 161–90, where he also shows that many of these ideas, belonging to the common basis of Christian thought, are also found in other authors of Thomas's day, notably Saint Bonaventure.

adduce reasons for the Incarnation, Thomas explains that it was necessary for Christ to assume a body that could suffer, "to give us an example of patience in supporting human suffering and limitation with courage."[42] On the other hand, Jesus did not want to assume sinfulness, for he would not have been able to give an example of it for humanity—for sin does not belong to the definition of human nature—nor as an example of virtue, since sin is contrary to virtue.[43] By contrast, when he wanted to pray, that was to invite us to confident and frequent prayer.[44] When he submitted to circumcision and other precepts of the law, it was to give us a living example of humility and obedience.[45] In the same way, his baptism should stimulate us by its example to receive baptism ourselves.[46]

Each event in Jesus' life (fasting, temptations, life in the midst of the crowd) provides an opportunity for similar remarks. Thus, Thomas can sum up: "By the manner in which he lived (conuersatio), the Lord gave everyone the example of perfection in everything that refers in itself to salvation."[47] Better still is this striking formulation: "Christ's action was our instruction (Christi actio fuit nostra instructio)."[48] In slightly differing form, depending on the context, this axiom (which Thomas got from Cassiodorus by way of Peter Lombard) recurs seventeen times in his work.[49] Although Thomas carefully emphasizes that things are not exactly the same in Christ's case and our own, we ought to read this assertion in the light of the true faith to understand it properly. Thomas never disputes the fundamental truth of the formula. And its frequent appearance gives full testimony to his desire to take very seriously Christ's concrete acts as much as his explicit teachings.

This exemplary value of Christ's activity culminates in the final days of

---

42. ST IIIa q. 14 a. 1: "propter exemplum patientiae quod nobis exhibet passiones et defectus humanos fortiter tolerando."

43. ST IIIa q. 15 a. 1.   44. ST IIIa q. 21 a. 3.

45. ST IIIa q. 37 a. 4.

46. ST IIIa q. 39 a. 2 ad 1; cf. a. 1 and a. 3 ad 3: Christus proponebatur hominibus in exemplum omnium.

47. ST IIIa q. 40 a. 2 ad 1.   48. ST IIIa q. 40 a. 1 ad 3.

49. On this see the precise and stimulating study by R. Schenk, "Omnis Christi actio nostra est instructio, The Deeds and Sayings of Jesus as Revelation in the View of Thomas Aquinas," in Leo Elders, ed. La doctrine de la révélation divine (Vatican City, 1990), 103–31. The formula is more frequently used in the commentary on the Sentences than in the Summa (the only instance is quoted above), but it is found in several other places (cf. Schenk, note 51, p. 111). In the sermon Puer Iesus (Busa, vol. 6, p. 33a) an equivalent appears: Cuncta quae Dominus fecit uel in carne passus est, documenta et exempla sunt salutaria.

his earthly life. To the question of whether there was a more appropriate means than the Passion for liberating the human race, Thomas replies as is his custom with an entire series of things that made it suitable. First and significantly, the Passion shows man "how much God loves him, thus evoking in return man's own love [toward God], in which the perfection of salvation consists." But second, Christ has given us in His Passion "an example of obedience, humility, constancy, justice and other virtues now manifest, which are also necessary for man's salvation. That is why Saint Peter writes (1 Pet. 2:21): *Christ suffered for us, leaving us an example so that we might follow in his footsteps.*"[50]

These brief citations from the *Summa* are sufficient to assure us that Christ's exemplarity is unceasingly present in Master Thomas's reflections, but they scarcely convey the emotion that can animate him when he speaks about the subject in his courses or his preaching. Let us read one of these pages and add to the commentary on the washing of the feet, which emphasizes Christ's humility, speaking of the love that inspired His obedience:

Observing the commandments is one effect of the divine charity. Not only of the divine charity through which we love, but that by which (Jesus) has loved us. By the very fact that he loves us, he calls upon us and helps us to observe his commandments, which can come about only through grace. *His love consists in this: it is not we who have loved God, it is He who loved us first* (1 John 4:10).

To this he adds an example by saying: *Keep my Father's commandments as I myself have kept them.* In effect, just as the love by which the Father loves him is the example of the love by which he loves us, so he wished that his obedience would be an example for ours. Christ thus shows that he remains in the love of the Father through the fact that he keeps his commandments in all things. For he went even to death (Phil. 2:8): *He was obedient even until death, death on a cross;* he refrained from sin (1 Pet. 2:22): *He did not commit sin and no deceit was on his lips.* We must understand this of Christ in his humanity (John 8:29): *He never leaves me alone, for I always do what is pleasing to him.* That is why he can say: I remain in His love, for there is nothing in me (always in terms of his humanity) that would be contrary to His love.[51]

As can easily be understood, texts like this one are of the highest significance in illustrating a theology that wants to be an inspiration for the whole of the Christian life. Without dwelling further on the point, we will

50. *ST* IIIa q. 46 a. 3; similar passages occur in ibid., a. 4; q. 50 a. 1; q. 51 a. 1; etc.
51. *In Ioannem XV*, 10, lect. 2, nn. 2002–3.

conclude this section with a passage taken from the commentary on the Credo, where we find this lovely meditation on the meaning of the Cross:

As blessed Augustine says, Christ's Passion is enough to instruct us fully about our way of life. Whoever wants to lead a perfect life has nothing more to do than spurn what Christ spurned on the Cross and to desire what he desired.

Indeed, there is not a single example of virtue that the Cross does not give us. Do you seek an example of charity? "There is no greater love than to give up one's life for those whom we love." And Christ did it on the Cross. . . .

Are you looking for an example of patience? The most perfect patience is found on the Cross. . . . An example of humility? Look upon the Crucified One. An example of obedience? Follow him who made himself obedient to the Father even unto death. . . . An example of scorn for earthly things? Walk after him who is the King of Kings and Lord of Lords, in whom are found all the treasures of wisdom and who, nonetheless, appears naked on the Cross, an object of mockery, spit upon, beaten, crowned with thorns, offered gall and vinegar, put to death.[52]

We have to say that these passionate accents rarely show up in scholarly works. It is all the more unfortunate that the other works are so little known, because we discover in them another facet of Friar Thomas's genius. But at least some of his readers have noticed them, and such a figure as Louis Chardon has profited from using these passages where the Dominican friar's love of the Cross shows through.[53] We will have to return a little later to this subject when we speak of the ways to God that Thomas sets before his disciples.

Thomas does not stop here in his consideration of the mystery of Christ. After his Passion and death on the Cross follow the resurrection, ascension, and position at the right hand of the Father. The approach will be different, as we will soon see, but we should already note that Thomas leaves out nothing from Christ's Passover. In this, he is faithful to the plan that is traced in his study: to take into account everything that Christ did and suffered for us (acta et passa Christi in carne).[54]

---

52. *Expositio in Symbolum* (*In Symb.*) 4, nn. 919–24. This passage may be distantly inspired by Saint Augustine, *Enarratio in Ps. LXI*, 22 (PL 36, 745–46). But this way of formulating it seems Thomas's own. See also *Enarratio in Ps. XLVIII*, ser. 1, 11 (PL 35, 551). But while the Augustinian inspiration of Thomas's commentary on John is clear, I have not been able to find a parallel to this passionate outpouring.

53. Cf. F. Florand, "Introduction," to L. Chardon, *La croix de Jésus*, rev. ed. (Paris, 1937), pp. xcvi–cv. See also D. Bouthillier, "Le Christ en son mystère dans les *collationes* du *super Isaiam* de saint Thomas d'Aquin," in *Ordo sapientiae et amoris*, 37–64.

54. Cf. *ST* IIIa Pro.; q. 27 Pro.; q. 48 a. 6: "*omnes actiones et passiones* Christi instrumentaliter operantur in uirtute diuinitatis ad salutem humanam."

The Way and Our Home

Since this chapter is, in the first place, dedicated to "the way," let us conclude with a reading of Thomas's exposition of the Gospel of John, who speaks of Christ as the gate, then as the way through which we must pass to return to the Father. Some paraphrasing and ample quotation will allow us to gain a fuller idea of Thomas's style as commentator on Scripture. The *Lectura super Ioannem*, which dates from the end of Thomas's life,[55] offers some of the most developed examples of his theological exegesis.[56]

Concerning the gate which leads into the sheepfold (John 10), Thomas recalls with a certain complacency, in a first attempt, Saint John Chrysostom's exegesis, which states that this gate is the Sacred Scriptures. Through them, we have our first access to God. Then, just as the gate protects those who are inside, the Scriptures preserve the lives of the faithful. Finally, the gate does not let the wolf in, just as the Scriptures put the faithful in safety, sheltered from the evil that heretics might bring upon them. We do not enter, therefore, through the good gate if we try to teach the faithful something other than through Sacred Scripture.[57] Thomas does not say so here, but his concerns as a theologian lead him to mention it often elsewhere: when we are speaking of God, we cannot lightly neglect the words of Sacred Scripture.[58]

Against this exegesis of Chrysostom's, we have Jesus' explicit affirmation: *I am the gate for the sheep.* Chrysostom certainly is aware of this, and Thomas, following him, remarks that Christ also calls himself not only the gate but the gatekeeper and even the shepherd. If then he speaks of it in so different a way, nothing prevents the word "gate" from having two different applications: after Christ, there is no more just application of the term than to Sacred Scripture itself.[59] But Thomas knows still another way of exegesis on this point:

According to Saint Augustine,[60] however, the word "gate" is applied first to Christ, because in the Apocalypse (4:1, "A gate was opened to Heaven") it is through him

---

55. Probably 1270–72; cf. my *Saint Thomas Aquinas*, 198–201.
56. See the Preface by M.-D. Philippe in *Saint Thomas d'Aquin Commentaire sur l'Evangile de saint Jean*, vol. 1 (Versailles-Buxy, ²1981), 7–49.
57. *In Ioannem X*, lect 1, n. 1366.
58. Cf. *Contra errores Graecorum (Contra err. Graec.)* I, Leonine, vol. 40, p. A 72.
59. Ibid., n. 1367.
60. Cf. *In Ev. Ioh. tract.* 45, 5 and 15 (BA 73B, 55 and 83–85).

that we enter. Whoever wishes, therefore, to enter into the sheepfold must enter by the gate, Christ, and not by another opening. We must note, though, that it is both the sheep and the shepherd who enter into the sheepfold: the sheep to be sheltered there, the shepherd to watch them there. If, therefore, you wish to enter as a sheep to be protected, or as a shepherd to protect the sheep, you must pass through the Christ-gate and not by another way. [Thomas gives a rather long exposition here of the characteristics of the bad shepherds, then concludes:] We must know that just as it is impossible to be a protected sheep without entering the gate, so it is impossible for the shepherd to protect without entering through the same gate, Christ. . . . The bad shepherds pass not through this gate, but instead through the gate of ambition, of secular power and simony; they are thieves and brigands. . . . Given that Christ, that gate, made himself little in humility, they alone can enter who imitate Christ's humility. Those who did not enter through him, but by another way, are the proud, who do not recognize his humility and do not imitate him who, though God, became man.[61]

Christ's indispensable character emerges clearly enough in this passage and there is no need to emphasize it further. But we should note in passing, perhaps, the tone the author uses here. Moral exhortation is combined with dogmatic and exegetical exposition without breaking the continuity. As in the passages cited earlier, what we have here is not preaching, but it is quite close to it. We expect as much from the Master writing a commentary on the Bible: he must also bring out the spiritual meaning of Scripture.[62] We see here how regrettable it is that this part of Thomas's work is so widely unknown. To have some chance of knowing him as a master of the Christian life requires us to become familiar with these texts. The passage that follows will make this still clearer:

If Christ is the gate, it follows that to enter into the sheepfold we pass through him. That is clear. But it is also what specially belongs to Christ. Indeed, no one can pass through the gate that leads to beatitude if that is not the truth, for beatitude is nothing more than the joy of truth (gaudium de ueritate). Now, Christ in his divinity is identified with truth; that is why in his humanity he enters by way of himself, that is, through the truth that he is in his being God. By contrast, we are not the truth, we are only children of light through our participation in the true, uncreated light; that is why we must pass through the truth that is Christ.[63]

61. *Contra err. Graec.*, n. 1368.

62. Cf. my *Saint Thomas Aquinas*, 55–59.

63. *Contra err. Graec.*, n. 1369. Cf. J. C. Smith, "Christ as 'Pastor,' 'Ostium,' et 'Agnus' in St. Thomas Aquinas," *Angelicum* 56 (1979): 93–118.

In the same vein, but even more fully developed, is the exposition of Jesus' declaration: *I am the Way, the Truth, and the Life. No one comes to the Father except through me* (John 14:6). It provides Friar Thomas with a chance to write a stunning section:

Christ had already taught many things to his followers about the Father and the Son. But they did not know that Christ was going to the Father and that the Son was the route by which he would go. Indeed, it is difficult to go to the Father. It is not surprising that they did not know it! For if Christ in his humanity was well known to them, they did not know his divinity except in a very imperfect way. . . .

I am the Way, the Truth, and the Life, says Jesus. With a single stroke, he unveils to them the way and the goal of the way. . . . *The way*, as we have seen, is Christ. We understand this because *it is through him that we have access to the Father* (Eph. 2:18). . . . But this way is not distant from the goal, the one touches the other; that is why Christ adds: *the Truth and the Life*. He is simultaneously the one and the other: the way, according to his humanity; the goal according to his divinity. . . .

The goal of this way is the culmination of all human desires. Indeed, man desires two things above all: one that is proper to his nature: to know the truth. The other he shares with everything that is: to remain in being. Now, Christ is the way to arrive at the truth since he is the Truth. . . . He is also the way to arrive at life since he himself is Life. . . . Therefore, Christ is designated in himself as the way and the goal. He is the goal because *he is in himself everything that can be the object of desire: the Truth and the Life*.

If, then, you seek your way, pass by way of Christ: He is the Way. Isaiah prophesies (30:21): "This is the way, follow it." Saint Augustine says: "Pass by way of man to arrive at God." "It is better to limp on the way than to stride firmly, but lost, on the byway." Even if we do not advance quickly, whoever hobbles along on the right path approaches the destination; he who walks off the path distances himself farther from the goal the more quickly he runs.

If you wish to know where to go, adhere to Christ: he is the Truth that all of us wish to attain. . . . If you wish to find a place to rest, adhere to Christ, for he is the Life. . . . Adhere to Christ, then, if you want to be sure; you cannot deviate for he is the way. Those who adhere to him do not walk through the desert, but along a well-marked path. . . . So too, you will not be able to go astray, because he is the truth and teaches all truth. . . . No more will you able to be shaken, for he is the Life and gives life. . . . As Saint Augustine mentions several times, when the Lord says: I am the Way, the Truth, and the Life, it is as if he were saying: By what route do you want to go? I am the Way. Where do you wish to go? I am the Truth. Where do you wish to dwell? I am the Life.[64]

64. *In Ioannem XIV*, 6, lect. 2–3, nn. 1865–70. Cf. P. de Cointet, "'Attache-toi au

For anyone familiar with Saint Thomas, the lyricism of this passage is somewhat surprising. He may suspect a strong Augustinian inspiration behind these words, perhaps even explicit quotations not identified in current editions of Thomas's text. If we check this, the Augustinian influence is quite real, but there are few literal quotations.[65] In particular, while the constant opposition between the way and the goal, to which Augustine returned quite often, is certainly one of Thomas's debts to this predecessor, we do not find in Augustine the repeated exhortation "Adhere to Christ," any more than one finds explicitly in Saint Thomas—though the idea, again, is there—the contrast dear to the Bishop of Hippo between the *Heavenly Home* and *the Way.*[66] There are thus several memories of Augustine that come spontaneously to Friar Thomas's mind, but he is so imbued with Augustine that these traces transform his own usual style. The man whom we know only in the sober and chaste style of the great philosophical and theological works is caught in the act of teaching. In fact, the commentary on Saint John has come down to us in the notes *(reportationes)* of Reginald of Piperno, who heard Thomas's lectures. And we seem to grasp Thomas's oral style from these notes. The insistent repetition of the exhortation *Adhaere Christo* might, thus, reveal something about the Friar Preacher's soul. And that is one of the more precious things that we might draw from this research.

Christ!', L'imitation du Christ dans la vie spirituelle selon S. Thomas d'Aquin," *Sources* 12 (1989): 64–74.

65. The closest parallel is *Sermo* CXLI 4, 4 (PL 38, 777–78), from which two literal quotations are drawn: "Ambula per hominem, et peruenis ad Deum"; "Melius est enim in uia claudicare, quam praeter uiam fortiter ambulare." See also *Tractatus in Iam Ioannis* X, 1 (SC 75, 408–10); *Enarratio in Ps.* LXVI, 3, 5 (PL 36, 807), M.-F. Berrouard, "Saint Augustin et le mystère du Christ Chemin, Vérité et Vie. La méditation théologique du *Tractatus 69 in Iohannis Euangelium* sur Io. 14 6a," in *Collectanea Augustiniana, Mélanges T. J. Van Bavel,* vol. 2 (Louvain, 1991), 431–49.

66. Following the beautiful title of G. Madec's book, *La patrie et la voie: Le Christ dans la vie et la pensée de saint Augustin* (Paris, 1989); cf. Augustine, *Sermo* XCII, 3, 3: "Ipse est patria quo imus, ipse uia qua imus" (PL 38, 573); *Sermo* CXXIII, 3, 3: "Deus Christus patria est quo imus: homo Christus uia est qua imus" (PL 38, 685).

⌖

CHAPTER VI

The Image of the First-Born Son

Looking at things from the human point of view, Christ's moral example is the first thing that presents itself for the theologian's consideration. In the Christian life, the imitation of Christ is the way to salvation. But when we examine this idea further, the usual approach shows itself to be inadequate. The slide from moral philosophy to moralism is easy and frequent, and it risks making Christ into the model of a man among other great men. Great men, of course, bring honor to the human race, but for a Christian, Christ is something entirely different from a mere man.

In the *Summa Theologiae*, Saint Thomas invites us instead to consider things from God's point of view. In this way, a vast perspective opens up to the eyes of the theologian. For the imitation of Christ only becomes possible by the grace he gives us and which has already conformed us to him. At the north portal of the Cathedral of Chartres, we see God creating the first man, His eyes fixed on the New Adam. And it is in accord with the latter image that he fashions man. The accent is placed from the very beginning not on human effort, but on God working in man.

In order to express this, we must call upon some technical considerations that run the risk of making this chapter more difficult to read. But we should not avoid these difficulties. As we said in the opening pages of the present work, it is in its very rigor that the theology of the Master from Aquino generates the spiritual life. So we should not allow ourselves to be put off when we meet expressions such as agent or instrument, efficient or dispositive cause, for the first time. They are necessary to the exact expression of what we are concerned with here, because they lead to a rich and deep reflection that it would be a shame to ignore.

As will become quickly apparent—and this will help in the reading of the present chapter—our reflections here will be guided by a saying of Saint Paul's that we have already met with, but that we have to explore further: "All those who from the first were known to him [the Father], he has also *predestined to be molded into the image of his Son*, so that he may be the eldest-born among many brethren."[1] The theologians express this in more technical language when they say that grace is a "Christ-molding" reality. This word speaks for itself and the doctrine is as simple as it is beautiful. It puts to work two great data: God alone is the source of grace, but it comes to us through Christ's mediation and it bears his imprint.

Only God Deifies

The basic principle, then, is that God alone gives grace. The reason for this is evident. While the second letter of Peter (1:4) gives a description of grace as a "participation in the divine nature," clearly only God can communicate that participation. Friar Thomas explains this with greater precision, but says nothing more:

The gift of grace is beyond the forces of all created nature, for it is nothing but a certain *participation in the divine nature* which transcends every creature. It is impossible, therefore, that any creature whatever can cause grace. It is, then, *necessary that God alone deifies (deificet)*, communicating a share in *(consortium)* the divine nature in the form of a certain participation by way of assimilation. . . .[2]

Beyond the principal conclusion, which is evident and requires no further emphasis, we should note in this passage the use of the verb "deify." The Western theological tradition is sometimes criticized for not paying attention to the teachings of the Greek Fathers, who understood the Christian life as a kind of "divinization." We will not go into the rather sterile polemics on this question here, but we might say in passing that the criticism is entirely without foundation in the case of Saint Thomas. For him, grace is a deiform structure, which is why God alone can give it to us. Thomas uses the terms "deify" and "deiform" so often as to leave no doubt on the subject.[3] There is no mystery in this. The *Catena aurea*

1. Rom. 8:29, according to the TOB translation, which is closer to the Greek original than it is to the Latin text that was available to Thomas.
2. *ST* Ia IIae q. 112 a. 1. *De uer.* q. 27 a. 3, without using the term *deifico*, arrives at a similarly strong conclusion.
3. The *Index thomisticus* shows 34 appearances of *deifico*, 10 of which occur in the commentary on Dionysius' *Divine Names*, in the sense of participation/union with God, and 17

draws on the work of fifty-seven Greek authors as opposed to only twenty-two Latin authors. We can well understand, then, that Thomas regarded himself as the legitimate heir of the Greek Fathers. And naturally the names of Gregory Nazianzen, Pseudo-Dionysius, and John Damascene come regularly from Thomas's pen with their special vocabulary in this context.[4]

Though he feels no need to show off his erudition, he does not hesitate to use this language in a personal way. Thomas speaks of saints as "deified" by the grace of adoption,[5] or through glorious knowledge of God in heaven.[6] In this last context, he also talks about the saints who have become "deiform" through the face-to-face[7] vision of God. But he also uses the term for the saints still on the way, on earth. Grace and charity, as well as the gift of wisdom,[8] make us deiform;[9] but in fact, Christians are deiform from the moment of their baptism, for the Holy Spirit is the main agent.[10] These data, which strictly speaking concern only these two specific words, should be supplemented with a full examination of everything that Thomas says about created grace as participation in the divine nature. This is so great a matter for him that he sees the gift of grace as a kind of new creation that surpasses the old one,[11] because grace is a good greater than the entire universe;[12] it even exceeds the nobility of Christ's

---

others in a Christological context. Christ is the deified man par excellence. The term *deiformitas* is found 51 times, the majority (28) of them in connection with the angels; it has a rather strong intellectual connotation that *deifico* seems not to have.

4. Cf. J.-P. Torrell, *Saint Thomas Aquinas*, 136–41. Recent studies show increasingly to what an unsuspected extent Thomas follows the Church Fathers, both by way of reference and in his method. Cf. G. Emery, "Le photinisme et ses précurseurs chez saint Thomas. Cérinthe, les Ebionites, Paul de Samosate et Photin," *RT* 95 (1995): 371–98.

5. *Comp. theol.* I, 202 (Leonine, vol. 42, p. 138). The context concerns the errors that have been made about the hypostatic union and Thomas repeats that Christ was neither a *homo per gratiam deificatus*, nor *per gratiam adoptionis deificatus*.

6. *In Ioannem XIII*, 32, n. 1830.

7. *ST* Ia q. 12 a. 6; *In librum beati Dionysii De divinis nominibus expositio (In De div. nom.)* I, 2, n. 70; cf. also the "deiformity" of glorified bodies, *In ad Thess. IV*, 16, n. 103.

8. *In III Sent.*, d. 35 q. 2 a. 1 qc. 1 ad 1.

9. *In II Sent.* d. 26 q. 1 a. 4 ad 3: "Grace confers a perfection on the soul in a certain divine being, not solely in the order of action, but also in that *those who have grace are constituted as deiform*, and that is why, as sons, they are pleasing to God."; *In III Sent.* d. 27 q. 2 a. 1 ad 9: "To the extent that men are *made deiform through charity*, they are above the human condition and their *conuersatio* is in heaven. They are found with God and the angels to the extent that they are like them, as the Lord says (Matt. 5:48): *Be perfect as your Father in heaven is perfect.*"

10. *In IV Sent.* d. 3 a. 3 qc. 1 ad 2.

11. *In II ad Cor. V*, 17, n. 192.

12. *ST* Ia IIae q. 113 a. 9 and ad 2.

soul,[13] because what God is as a substance is realized as an accident in the soul which participates in the divine goodness.[14]

Agent and Instrument

The preceding quotations, which have been chosen from among many other possibilities, do not need to be multiplied for the moment because we will have many other opportunities to find grace at work in our lives. Here, it suffices to have recalled that for Thomas grace is the principle of our divinization.[15] We must now add that this divinization is realized by Christ's mediation, because, in the technical language often used in Thomas's work, Christ is "the instrument" of divinization:

As Saint John Damascene says, Christ's humanity is like *"the instrument of his divinity."* Now, the instrument does not produce the act of the principal agent by virtue of its own effectiveness, but only through the motion of that principal agent. That is why the humanity of Christ does not cause grace by itself, but only through the divinity to which it is united and that makes its acts to be salutary.[16]

These initial qualifications are easy to understand; whether we are speaking of a hammer or a pen, the instrument does nothing by itself. Someone must use it. It is particularly important to notice the quotation from Saint John Damascene. This entirely fundamental doctrine, that might be thought to be a pure product of Western scholasticism, was also received from the Greek Fathers. Thomas will push it to a degree of precision that his predecessors clearly never reached, particularly as applied to Christ. The fecundity of his intuition, however, makes it worth the trouble to go into it more deeply.

13. *De uer.* q. 27 a. 1 ad 6.
14. *ST* Ia IIae q. 110 a. 2 ad 2.
15. To complete the texts cited, see the passages assembled by H.-T. Conus in the entry, "Divinisation," *DS*, vol. 3 (1957), col. 1426–32: "Saint Thomas."
16. *ST* Ia IIae q. 112 a. 1 ad 1; cf. St. John Damascene, *De fide orthodoxa*, ed. Buytaert, cap. 59, p. 239, and cap. 63, p. 258 (PG 94, 1060 and 1080). Thomas did not immediately come to this view. Following Saint Augustine, he speaks in the commentary on the *Sentences* (*In III Sent.* d. 13 q. 2 a. 1) only of a *dispositive* or *ministerial* grace in Christ's humanity: God producing grace *on the occasion* of Christ's action. The passage to a true instrumental cause in his thinking only happens between question 27 and 29 of the *De ueritate*; from that point on in Thomas's work, Christ's humanity concurs in reality with the production of grace and leaves its mark upon it. Thus, in all the later work, grace is not only divine, it is "Christian." Cf. J. R. Geiselmann, "Christus und die Kirche nach Thomas von Aquin," *Theologische Quartalschrift* 107 (1926): 198–222; 108 (1927): 233–55, which closely examines this evolution.

We find it in the opening pages of the *Tertia Pars*, specifically in a refutation of the heresy attributed to Nestorius. According to Saint Cyril, Nestorius stated that the Word had assumed his humanity, not by way of personal union, but only in the way we might make use of an instrument. In that view, the man Christ was not truly God but only his *organon*, his instrument. Saint Cyril simply rejects that way of speaking about this subject. But Saint John Damascene, following Saint Athanasius among others, recognizes a portion of truth in Nestorius. Thomas adheres to that position and explains it by remarking that we can speak of an instrument in two different ways. We have a *separate* instrument that might be a tool or some weapon, a saw or a sword. But we may also have an instrument *joined* to or inseparable from the person, such as his body or hand. It is in the second way that Christ's humanity acts as an "instrument" inseparably united to the person of the Son of God.[17]

Clearly, this way of understanding the instrument as strictly and inseparably joined to the person, notably modifies the basic analogy and purifies it of any overly material echoes. Even as rectified, as we shall see, Thomas softens the analogy still further when he uses it with respect to Christ's humanity, because this instrument is not merely joined but also *animated and free*. But before we look more carefully into this analogy, a special way Thomas uses it will allow us to identify its exact position in the process of the production of grace. Thomas asks himself if the sacraments of the New Law draw their effectiveness from Christ's Passion:

A sacrament works to produce grace as does an instrument. . . . But there are two kinds of instruments: one separate, like a staff; the other joined, like a hand. It is through the intermediary of the joined instrument that the separate instrument is set in motion, such as the staff by the hand. Now, the main efficient cause of grace is God himself, for whom Christ's humanity is a joined instrument and the sacrament a separate instrument. That is why it is necessary that the salvific efficacy *(uirtus)* of Christ's divinity pass through his humanity in the sacraments. . . . It is clear then that the Church's sacraments receive their specific efficacy from Christ's Passion and that receiving the sacraments puts us in communication with the salutary virtue of Christ's Passion. The water and blood flowing from the side of Christ hanging on the cross symbolize this truth; water speaks of baptism and blood of the Eucharist, for they are the most important sacraments.[18]

17. *ST* IIIa q. 2 a. 6 ad 4.
18. *ST* IIIa q. 62 a. 5. The treatise on the sacraments is the proper place for these kinds of points. Cf. *ST* IIIa q. 64 a. 3 and 4. But Thomas already say this in the question on the

This passage opens up some questions about the Church. For Thomas, we must remember, Christian existence cannot be merely an ecclesial existence. But what concerns us directly here is the exact hierarchy by which the causes at work in the production of grace are organized. Between God, who is the primary source, and the sacraments, which are the final stages by which he meets us again, there is Christ, the obligatory transition point. Here, the idea of instrumentality reveals a new virtuality. In the constant teaching of the Master of Aquino, the instrument "modifies" the action of the main cause:

> The instrument has a twofold action: an instrumental action in which it works, not by its own virtue, but by virtue of the main agent, as well as an action proper to it which belongs to it by virtue of its own form. Thus, because of its edge, the axe is able to cut, but as an instrument used by an artisan, it is able to produce a piece of furniture. In any event, it only carries out its instrumental action in working its own proper action; it produces a piece of furniture by cutting.[19]

The simple example that Thomas borrows from the world of his everyday experience allows him to state a position as simple as it is central for our present purposes. We may decide not to use an instrument, but if we use it, it will leave its mark on the effect it produces. True, an instrument does nothing by itself, but it does something, and the final result bears its traces. Think of the world of music: a violin is only an instrument in the hands of a virtuoso, but depending on whether it is a Stradivarius or broken-down fiddle the sound will change completely. Putting this point in an eminent and entirely unique form, it applies equally to Christ's humanity and his action:

> [Since each of Christ's two natures has its own proper operation, says Thomas, the action of his humanity is not eliminated through its union with the divine nature in the person of the Word] furthermore the divine nature makes use of the operation of the human nature, in the way that the main agent makes use of the operation of his instrument. . . . The action of the instrument as instrument is not different from the action of the main agent, but this does not stop it from having its own operation. Since, in Christ, the operation of the human nature, insofar as it is an instrument of his divinity, does not differ from the divine operation; our

---

cause of grace (cf. *ST* Ia IIae q. 112 a. 1 ad 2). For more details, see A.-M. Roguet's comments in *Les sacrements* (French translation with notes and appendices of St. Thomas Aquinas, *Summa theologiae* IIIa qq. 60–65) (Paris, 1999).

19. *ST* IIIa q. 62 a. 1 ad 2. The same point is made in *ST* Ia q. 45 a. 5 and even more explicitly in *SCG* IV 41, nn. 3798–800.

salvation is the single work of the humanity and divinity of Christ. But Christ's human nature, as such, has a different operation from that of the divine nature.[20]

To translate this into terms that will immediately make it clear and allow us to see the field to which it may be applied, we can say that, without losing its divine dimension, grace also has a Christological character.

The Mysteries of Christ's Life

Even casual readers of the *Summa* know that its Third Part is dedicated to the study of the mystery of Christ (qq. 1–59), but many do not know that the author did not limit himself to investigating the ontology and psychology of the God-Man (qq. 2–26). An important part of his exposition takes into account what we might call, somewhat improperly, the Life of Jesus (qq. 27–59).[21] Using the circular scheme that was very familiar to Thomas,[22] as we now know, he examines in thirty-three questions—as many as the years of Christ's earthly life—all the significant deeds that marked Christ's existence and he probes their meaning for salvation. Far from restricting Christ's work of salvation to his last days and death on the cross, Thomas thinks that nothing is without meaning for salvation which the Incarnate Word lived. On the contrary, everything finds an echo in today's Christian life.

To give this undertaking its proper name, Thomas tried to create a "theology of the mysteries" of Jesus' life. We will understand what this is all about if we recall that the *mysterion* in Saint Paul encompasses both the divine plan of salvation and the way that plan is fulfilled in Jesus.[23] So

20. *ST* IIIa q. 19 a. 1 and ad 2. This question is too long to be quoted in full, but it is the key text on the subject. Thomas had not always so firmly maintained the application of instrumentality in the line of efficient causality (cf. note 16 above). In *In III Sent.* d. 18 a. 6 sol. 1, he still speaks of it in the line of meritorious causality. With almost a single exception (*ST* IIIa q. 1 a. 2 ad 2) linked with Anselm's notion of satisfaction, this language is not what we find in the *Summa*.

21. Some additional details on this topic appear in my *Saint Thomas Aquinas*, p. 261–66.

22. The circular scheme is developed in the first three parts: 1) entrance *(ingressus)* of the Son of God into the world, which coincides with the mystery of the incarnation (qq. 27–39); 2) unfolding *(progressus)* of his earthly life by way of all its major incidents (qq. 40–45); 3) exit *(exitus)* from the world, which is to say, passion and death (qq. 46–52); the fourth part (qq. 53–59), the heavenly life of the glorified Jesus *(exaltatio)*, without entering directly into the circular movement, describes its goal and presents it in all its fullness. This last consideration in particular shows the impropriety of using the expression "the Life of Jesus" to describe this treatment.

23. See, for example, Eph. 3:1–14, with the notes in the Jerusalem Bible.

if Christ's whole life is itself the mystery of God's love which is revealed and acts in history, each of his acts is also a "mystery" in the sense that it signifies and realizes the total "mystery."

This view is deeply traditional; it has very old antecedents in the Fathers of the Church.[24] But the scholastics had somewhat lost sight of it. At least in this form, it represents something of a novelty introduced by Thomas in the treatment of Christological matters.[25] In the theologians earlier than or contemporaneous with Thomas, the consideration of the mysteries of the life of Christ generally took place either in the study of the articles of the Creed or in the commentary on the Christological question in Peter Lombard's *Sentences*. They are also found treated separately or mixed in with other questions.[26] By grouping them into an organic whole, Thomas shows the importance he gives both to the concrete life of Christ in the organization of his Christology and to the New Testament and the Fathers in his own reflections. Though long neglected, this part of the *Summa* is starting to receive the attention it deserves.[27] And rightly so, for it is exemplary of Thomas's theological method. This is also certainly the place where we can best see the repercussions of one of Thomas's crucial theological decisions in the spiritual realm, because here he decisively puts to work his doctrine concerning the instrumentality of Christ's humanity.

Significantly, Thomas insists on the salvific efficacy that proceeded instrumentally from all that Christ did and suffered. He does not express this in a general, merely abstract way. He means to say that each and every act that Christ performed in his humanity has been and continues to be the bearer of a salvific efficacy. The *locus classicus* for this, which we must give its full importance, since it is crucial for the establishment of this doctrine, is found in a question about the Resurrection:

24. Cf. A. Grillmeier, "Généralités historiques sur les mystères de Jésus," in *Mysterium salutis*, vol. 11 (Paris, 1975), 333–57.

25. On this see the important study by L. Scheffczyk, "Die Stellung des Thomas von Aquin in der Entwicklung der Lehre von den Mysteria Vitae Christi," in M. Gerwing and G. Ruppert, eds., *Renovatio et Reformatio: wider das Bild vom "finsteren" Mittelalter: Festschrift für Ludwig Hödl zum 60. Geburtstag* (Münster, 1986), 44–70.

26. In Thomas's own work, Christ's resurrection is treated a first time in itself in *In III Sent.* d. 21 q. 2 and a second time for its effect on the resurrection of the dead, *In IV Sent.* d. 43 q. 1 a. 2.

27. See R. Lafontaine, *La résurrection et l'exaltation du Christ chez Thomas d'Aquin, Analyse comparative de S. Th. IIIa q. 53 à 59*, Excerpta ex Diss. P.U.G. (Rome, 1983) (the original, more complete thesis of the same title, is also worth consulting); L. Scheffczyk,

[According to Aristotle] "whatever is first in a given genus is the cause of all that is part of it."[28] Now, in the order of our resurrection, what is first is the Resurrection of Christ. It necessarily follows that Christ's Resurrection is the cause of ours. And further, as the Apostle rightly says: *Christ has risen from the dead, the first-fruits of all those who have fallen asleep; a man had brought us death, and a man should bring us resurrection from the dead.*[29]

We should not be disconcerted about the quotation from Aristotle at the beginning of this article. Clearly, the Philosopher is invoked here to relate the explanation that follows with a known form of reasoning. The real point of departure is faith in Christ's Resurrection as Saint Paul proclaims it. But precisely that assertion needs explaining. That is why Thomas asks a little further on about the kind of causality that would be "first" in so unusual a genus:

Properly speaking, Christ's Resurrection is not the meritorious cause of our resurrection. [Merit is essentially connected with time in earthly life; the risen Christ goes beyond the conditions of this life and, thus, he can no longer gain merit. On the contrary, he possesses what he had merited.] But the Resurrection is the efficient cause and exemplary cause of our resurrection. It is, first, the efficient cause; *Christ's humanity, in which he was resurrected, is in a certain way the instrument of his divinity and acts according to his virtue,* as has already been said [cf. 3a q. 13 a. 2; q. 19 a. 1; q. 43 a. 2]. Here are the reasons why, *everything that Christ suffered or did in his humanity being salutary by "virtue" of his divinity,* as has already been established [cf. 3a q. 48 a. 6], *Christ's Resurrection is also the efficient cause of our resurrection* by the divine "virtue," whose particular quality is to give life to the dead. *That virtue touches through its presence all times and places, and this "virtu-*

"Die Bedeutung der Mysterien des Lebens Jesu für Glauben und Leben des Christen," in the same author's edited volume, *Die Mysterien des Lebens Jesu und die christliche Existenz* (Aschaffenburg, 1984), 17–34. I. Biffi, *I misteri di Cristo in Tommaso d'Aquino,* vol. 1 (Milan, 1994), has started to assemble a series of studies that show the ominpresence of this theme and its fecundity in all Thomas's works. In a Rahnerian vein, see G. Lohaus, *Die Geheimnisse des Lebens Jesu in der Summa Theologiae des hl. Thomas von Aquin* (Freiburg im Breisgau, 1985).

28. We recognize here an application of the principle of the *maxime tale,* which Thomas uses often and in a quite personal way (since he inverts the Aristotelian sense of the origin): "whatever is first in a given genus is the principle and cause with respect to the other elements in the same genus." See the decisive work by V. de Couesnongle, "La causalité du maximum: L'utilisation par saint Thomas d'un passage d'Aristote," and "La causalité du maximum: Pourquoi saint Thomas a-t-il mal cité Aristote?," *RSPT* 38 (1954): 433–44; 658–80, complemented by L. Somme, *Fils adoptifs de Dieu par Jésus Christ: La filiation divine par adoption dans la théologie de saint Thomas d'Aquin* (Paris, 1997), 336–40.

29. *ST* IIIa q. 56 a. 1 (the quotation is from 1 Cor. 15:20).

al" contact is enough for it to have a true effectiveness. Furthermore, as we have just said [cf. 3a q. 56 a. 1 ad 2], the primordial cause of the resurrection of men is divine justice, by virtue of which Christ has the power to judge, in his role as Son of Man (cf. John 5:27), and the efficient "virtue" of his Resurrection is extended not only to the good, but also to the wicked, who are under his judgment.[30]

It is striking to read in this passage the many references the author makes to having already spoken about one or another aspect of this doctrine. Clearly, this is a strategic turning point in his thinking. We see the exemplary dimension of this causality, but we restrict ourselves for the moment to considering the efficacy of the Resurrection. The passage is often referred to, because it is the most explicit statement, but it is hardly the only such passage. Thomas speaks similarly about Christ's Passion: "(The Passion operates) by way of efficacy; to the extent that the flesh, in which Christ suffered his Passion, is the instrument of his divinity. . ."[31] The same is said about the death and even about the dead body of Christ, "for the body was the instrument of the divinity that was united with it; acting through divine virtue, even in death."[32] For those surprised by this assertion, Thomas continues that in the state of death, Christ's body certainly could no longer be an instrument of merit, but that it could very well be an instrument of efficacy because of the divinity that would have remained united to it (thus joining the most certain dogmatic points: the person of the Word did not abandon his body during the *triduum mortis*). The same explanation is presented about the Ascension: "Christ's Ascension is cause of our salvation, not by way of merit, but by way of efficacy, as the Resurrection showed."[33]

It would be wrong to conclude from the fact that only the great moments of the Paschal mystery are mentioned here that Thomas restricts his teaching on this point to only these subjects. In fact, he extends it to everything Christ did and suffered:

30. *ST* IIIa q. 56 a. 1; Thomas has earlier explained (*ST* IIIa q. 53 a. 1) that Christ's resurrection was a work of the divine justice, for it was fitting to exalt him who had been humbled. According to Luke 1:52, which he quotes on this point, we might call this the logic of the Magnificat: "He casts down the powerful and raises up the lowly." As to the work that pertains to the Son of Man, see the commentary *In Ioannem V*, 21, lect. 4, n. 761.

31. *ST* IIIa q. 49 a. 1; cf. *ST* IIIa q. 48 a. 6 ad 2: "Christ's passion, although of the flesh, has, however, a spiritual virtue by reason of its union with his divinity; it gets its efficacy through spiritual contact, which is to say through faith and the sacraments of the faith. . . ."

32. *ST* IIIa q. 50 a. 6 ad 3. Here we can best confirm that Thomas is not thinking solely about the strictly voluntary acts of Christ's humanity.

33. *ST* IIIa q. 57 a. 6 ad 1.

There is a double efficacy: principal and instrumental. The principal efficacy of salvation in the life of men is God, but given that the humanity of Christ is the instrument of his divinity . . . it follows that *every act and suffering of Christ acts instrumentally in virtue of his divinity for man's salvation*. In this way, the Passion of Christ causes man's salvation in an efficient way.[34]

Memory or Presence?

Thomas held this position from the time of his earlier writings, and we find it in his scriptural commentaries. His affirmation, then, is as constant as it is clear, but there is disagreement among Thomists on the way of explaining it. Without spending too much time on what are sometimes quite subtle discussions, we must enter into some details that are of capital importance for the spiritual theology. The question that arises is whether we should understand these passages as if they spoke of the Resurrection or of various "mysteries" as realities already come to us (*in facto esse*, following the language of the specialists) or rather as a developing reality (*in fieri*). In simpler terms, does the *resurrected* Christ save us today or is it the *resurrecting* Christ? To keep this short, we will reason starting with the Resurrection, but it certainly applies to the other mysteries as well.

Until recently, certain writers still thought that the traditional position was a matter of the Resurrection in its completed state.[35] In their view, the resurrection has current efficacy only because it became eternal in Christ's glorious humanity. During his life here below, Christ "memorialized" in his humanity, so to speak, the divinizing virtue that attached itself to each of his earthly acts in order only to exercise it in his glorified state. "The Risen Christ is so in his humanity, because his humanity passed through all those states and feelings of which it keeps an eternal 'memory,' the interior fruit, virtue, the spirit. . . . It is the glorified humanity of Christ that is the instrumental cause of grace, but *in quantum modificata per mysteria vitae hujus terrestris* (inasmuch as it is "modified" by the mysteries of that earthly life)."[36]

---

34. *ST* IIIa q. 48 a. 6: "omnes actiones et passiones Christi instrumentaliter operantur in uirtute diuinitatis ad salutem humanam."

35. Cf. J. Gaillard, "Chronique de liturgie. La théologie des mystères," *RT* 57 (1957): 510–51; the author reviews the main positions through various publications. For the so-called "traditional" position, see p. 538. For Thomas's true view, see pp. 539–40, and the extension of it by certain writers through an appeal to the beatific vision that Christ enjoys, according to Thomas, pp. 540–42.

36. M.-J. Nicolas, "Les mystères de la vie cachée," in H. Bouëssé and J.-J. Latour, eds.,

This interpretation is based on the Epistle to the Hebrews (7:24–25) which speaks of the intercession of Christ's glorious humanity, which always bears traces of his Passion. Thomas admits this, of course; but he does not give special instrumental efficacy to these glorious wounds.[37] Though the reasoning can be understood when it is a matter of the scars that Christ retains eternally in his humanity, what of the other mysteries that left no visible trace (those of the hidden life in Nazareth, for example) and that continue to work out our salvation, since it is Christ's whole life, beginning with the Incarnation, that was salvific?[38]

Christ's glorified humanity continues to exert its instrumental mediation in every age. Thomas did not mean that, however, in speaking of the Resurrection's efficacy (or that of every other mystery). Indeed, he is very clear on this subject: it is *Christ in the act of Resurrection* who saves us. His position is already settled in the *Sentences*: "Since he is God and man rising from the dead *(homo resurgens)* Christ is the near and, so to speak, univocal, cause of our resurrection."[39] We also find this in the commentaries on the Epistle to the Romans and on the Book of Job, where Thomas always speaks of the resurrection as in the process of occurring,[40] and naturally in the *Summa*, where, alongside the passage quoted above, we find this:

The efficacy of Christ's Resurrection comes to souls [the spiritual resurrection is treated here, which is to say the soul's return to the life of grace which sin had

---

Problèmes actuels de christologie (Paris, 1965), 81–100, cf. 84–85. A similar work by the same author is: "La théologie des mystères selon saint Thomas d'Aquin," in *Mens concordet voci* (*Mélanges, A.-G. Martimort*) (Paris, 1983), 489–96. The work of J. Lécuyer points in the same direction: "La pérennité des mystères du Christ," VS 87 (1952): 451–64; and "La causalité efficiente des mystères du Christ selon saint Thomas," DC 6 (1953): 91–120.

37. Cf. *ST* IIIa q. 54 a. 4.

38. Those who hold this theory are mistaken in thinking that it was traditional among Thomas's followers. Ch. Journet, *La Messe, présence de la croix* (Paris, 1957), 110, has shown that it really comes from Suarez. Cajetan's position is unclear. On the one hand, in his commentary *In IIIam q. 56 a. 1 n. II*, he heads in the same direction as Suarez in interpreting the efficacy of the resurrection; on the other, in order to take into account the efficacy of Christ's dead body, he perfectly reproduces Thomas's view, cf. *In IIIam q. 50 a. 6 n. II*.

39. *In IV Sent.* d. 43 q. 1 a. 2 sol. 1; cf. ad 3: *mediante Christo homine resurgente*.

40. *In ad Rom. VI*, 10–11, n. 490: "uita quam *Christus resurgens* acquisiuit"; n. 491: "ut (fidelis) conformetur uitae *Christi resurgentis*"; *In Iob XIX, 25*, Leonine, vol. 26, p. 116, lines 268–70: "Vita *Christi resurgentis* ad omnes homines diffundetur in resurrectione communi"; for a reading of Thomas's commentary on this verse, see D. Chardonnens, "L'espérance de la résurrection selon Thomas d'Aquin, commentateur du Livre de Job," in *Ordo sapientiae et amoris*, 65–83.

killed, so to speak] not through the virtue of the *rising body* in itself, but through the virtue of the divinity to which he is personally united.[41]

These passages leave hardly any doubt about Thomas's true position, and many writers on Thomas, though with various and notable nuances, hold the same.[42] But can it be that the acts of Christ's life, being acts historically in the past, may continue to act today? Unless we envisage—as Odo Casel once proposed[43]—a kind of historical perennialness of the mysteries, which remain present in the Church's liturgy, it seems that we are obliged to admit that it is Christ's glorious humanity itself that acts, and we then would return to an explanation involving "memorialized" mysteries.

Following Saint Thomas it is easy to reply, that it is not past action in itself that always endures. As such it has entirely ceased to exist. It is its instrumental influx that remains efficacious under the divine motion. The actual efficiency of past mysteries of Christ's life comes to them from the divine power which reaches all times and places. And this "virtual" contact, which is to say according to the *uirtus*, efficacity, is enough to account for this efficiency.[44]

Like an Invisible Star

It is sometimes objected against this position that an instrumental efficient cause would not be able to produce its effect without coexisting with

41. *ST* IIIa q. 56 a. 2 ad 2.

42. Besides Journet and Gaillard, who were mentioned above: H. Bouëssé, "La causalité efficiente instrumentale de l'humanité du Christ et des sacrements chrétiens," *RT* 39 (1934): 370–93; "La causalité efficiente et la causalité méritoire de l'humanité du Christ," *RT* 43 (1938): 265–98. T. Tschipke, *Die Menschheit Christi als Heilsorgan der Gottheit unter besonderer Berücksichtigung der Lehre des hl. Thomas von Aquin* (Freiburg im Breisgau, 1940); F. Holtz, "La valeur sotériologique de la résurrection du Christ selon Saint Thomas," *ETL* 29 (1953): 609–45; Cl.-J. Geffré, critical review of J. Lécuyer and F. Holtz's article cited above, in *BT* 9 (1954–56): nos. 1569–71, pp. 812–17 (in my opinion, this study best conveys Saint Thomas's thought on the question). More recently, see M. G. Neels, *La résurrection de Jésus sacrement de salut. La causalité salvifique de la résurrection du Christ dans la sotériologie de St. Thomas*, Diss. P.U.G. (Rome, 1973); R. Lafontaine, *La résurrection* (thesis), 267–78.

43. Cf., especially, O. Casel, *The Mystery of Christian Worship, and Other Writings*, ed. Burkhard Neunheuser, with a preface by Charles Davis (Westminster, Md., 1962); and cf. Th. Filthaut, *La Théologie des Mystères. Exposé de la controverse* (Paris-Tournai, 1954).

44. This is the Latin text of the passage cited above from *ST* IIIa q. 56 a. 1 ad 3: "*Virtus diuina praesentialiter attingit omnia loca et tempora. Et talis contactus uirtualis sufficit ad rationem efficientiae.*"

it. This difficulty is only one of those that deal with a causal contact in the physical order, but it is not thus that Thomas envisages the causality of the resurrection. This "virtual" contact is an eminently spiritual reality. As he explains quite well, the instrument is moved to produce its effect by the pricipal cause, and it is married to its conditions, including temporal ones. Inasmuch as it operates *in uirtute diuina*, the act posed by Christ is not subject to time, for God has the privilege in his eternity of touching beings which for us are past or future, as if they were present. He will therefore be able to unite the efficiency of an instrument with its recipient when the latter comes into existence, without the proper operation of the instrument itself touching it.[45] In other words, Christ's Resurrrection will truly produce its immediate effect in each of its beneficiaries at the moment chosen by God:

The effect is produced by instrumental causes according to the conditions of the principal cause. And that is why, given that God is the principal cause of our resurrection and that the Resurrection of Christ is its instrumental cause, it follows that *our own resurrection will be produced by Christ's Resurrection according to how the divine disposition has foreseen that it should take place in a given time.*[46]

The same doctrine recurs in the following passage, which is even more interesting because Thomas dialogues with an interlocutor who opposes him exactly on the impossibility of an effect differing over time:

The common cause for our resurrection is Christ's Resurrection. If you say: "It has already taken place. Why then has its effect not been produced?" I would reply that it is the cause of our resurrection *inasmuch as it operates according to the divine virtue.* Now, God acts according to the disposition of his divine wisdom. Therefore, *our resurrection will be produced according to how the divine design has foreseen it.*[47]

If we can make somewhat tangible a spiritual reality that essentially escapes all materialization, we might illustrate this with an example once

45. This response has been subjected to a harsh critique by J.-H. Nicolas, "Réactualisation des mystères rédempteurs dans et par les sacrements," *RT* 58 (1958) 20–54, without the author suspecting, it seems, that it is the very position of Saint Thomas in the texts that we will be citing.

46. *In I ad Cor. XV*, 12, lect. 2, n. 915.

47. *In I ad Thess. IV*, lect. 2, n. 98. The same response appears in *ST* IIIa q. 56 a. 1 ad 1: "*Non oportet quod statim sequatur effectus, sed secundum dispositionem Verbi Dei.*" This explanation had appeared in Thomas's work as early as *In IV Sent.* d. 43 q. 1 a. 2 ad 1 and ad 2.

proposed by Charles Journet and brought to perfection by Humbert Bouëssé: "The current influence of this past event is a little like (there are no wholly adequate images) the light of a star that currently exists but is invisible [clearly, the glorious humanity of Christ] which will reach me today through the refracted rays from a planet that is no longer [the acts of his terrestrial life]."[48]

Whatever might be the appropriateness of the comparison or even of the differences in explanation among the specialists, their technical aspect should not hide the deep simplicity of this doctrine and its spiritual implications, which give it an undeniable allure. Without retreating in the slightest from the profoundly Trinitarian character of the Thomistic inspiration, it brings to bear with incomparable force the presence of Christ the Savior at the heart of the Christian life. It is not only God-Trinity who is present to each man in the state of grace in a constant and universal manner. It is also Christ in his humanity, and not only as a presence of memory or an intentional presence by way of knowledge and love, but as a wholly efficacious presence of grace. The historical Christ, today glorified, touches us by each of the acts of his earthly life, which is thus the bearer of a divinizing life and energy.[49]

As to the concrete manner in which everything that the Savior did and suffered in the flesh reaches us even today, it suffices to reply with Thomas: "*spiritually* through faith and *bodily* through the sacraments, for Christ's humanity is simultaneously spirit and body in order that we might be able to receive into ourselves [we who are spirit and body] the effect of the sanctification that comes to us through Christ."[50] For Thomas, as for Saint Paul, the grace of baptism mysteriously makes us participants in Christ's death and Resurrection. The same is true of the Eucharist and the other sacraments.[51]

---

48. H. Bouëssé, "De la causalité de l'humanité du Christ," in *Problèmes actuels de christologie*, 175.

49. We cannot overemphasize the importance of this doctrine, but we should be careful not to reduce our author's teaching about the mysteries of Christ's life to this doctrine alone; questions 27 through 59 of the *Tertia Pars* possess an exceptional richness and nothing can take the place of reading them in their original form.

50. *De uer.* q. 27 a. 4 *(in fine)*; cf. *ST* IIIa q. 49 a. 3 ad 1: "Christ's passion obtains its effect in those to whom it is applied *by faith and charity and the sacraments of faith*"; ibid., a. 1 ad 4 and ad 5; q. 48 a. 6 ad 2; "Christ's Passion exerts its efficacy though a spiritual contact, which is to say, *by faith and the sacraments of faith*."

51. Though this is a vast and delicate question, we might ask ourselves if these saving acts can touch the just pagans who did not have access to the sacraments. We have to

Someone may ask, perhaps, what there is in the mysteries of Christ's hidden life that is not explicitly reproduced in the sacraments and has this salvific efficacy as well. Even though not sacramental in the broad sense, we might certainly think of their liturgical commemoration, for it is one of the privileged places where the faith is expressed and nourished. It is enough to have participated in the celebration of the Christmas or Easter office in a monastic community or in a devout environment to understand that there is in them an actualization of the mystery being celebrated whose effect is interiorized by prayer. The theology of the memorial, sometimes restricted to the Eucharist, allows this extension beyond all doubt: *today* Christ is born . . . *today* He is risen . . . *today* he ascends to heaven. . . . What is true in an eminent way of public prayer is also true of personal prayer. It suffices here to imagine the meditation on the scenes of Christ's life beloved by Saint Ignatius and others.[52] But one would be wrong to restrict this to explicitly religious acts. Fraternal service or charitable acts are also places where Jesus, true God and true man, continues the efficacious action of grace that his physical presence was for his contemporaries.[53]

Conformity to Christ

If we now ask ourselves about what the mysteries achieve in us by virtue of their instrumental efficacy, we must take up again one of the expositions familiar to the Master of Aquino, in which he boldly transposed a principle he got from Aristotle to put it at the service of a reality that the Greek could not even imagine. It deals with the great law according to which the efficient agent can only produce something similar to himself

---

answer positively without hesitation: there is no other grace than Christ's and it flows for them as for us from the Savior's Passion-Resurrection. Faith and the sacraments of faith normally go together, but they may be accidentally separated and the economy of salvation knows of some substitute functions proper to each situation. We might say, therefore, that *spiritualiter* the just pagans can participate in the grace of Jesus' death and resurrection through a faith that does not know itself yet as explicitly Christian; *corporaliter*, through certain mediations that are proper to them and that God alone knows.

52. Though the meaning he gave to this meditation is rather different from what we have tried to express by "mysteries," following Saint Thomas. Cf. the entry by H. J. Sieben, "Mystères de la vie du Christ, I: Étude historique," *DS*, vol. 10 (1980), col. 1874–80.

53. We might think here of what Vatican II said of religious: ". . . through them, to believers and non-believers alike, the Church truly wishes to give an increasingly clearer revelation of Christ. Through them Christ should be contemplating on the mountain, or announcing God's kingdom to the multitude, healing the sick and the maimed, and turning sinners to wholesome fruit, blessing children, doing good to all, and always obeying the will of the Father who sent Him" (*Lumen Gentium*, 46).

in such a way that there is in every action a certain assimilation of the effect to its cause. To put it in clear terms, this means here that the mysteries are the realizers of an assimilation first to Jesus and, through him, to God himself. Or more exactly: God the Father, acting in us through the grace that he accords us by the mediation of Christ thus conforms us to the image of his first-born Son. Our grace is the grace of adoptive sons, but also a grace of suffering, death, Resurrection, and Ascension, through him, with him, and in him. We are here at the heart of the ontological exemplarism and of the mystery of Christ-conforming grace.

The concrete importance of this theme fully emerges from some figures that we take as a point of departure. Vocabulary related to *conformitas* recurs with impressive regularity.[54] We can count a total of 435 occurrences of *conformitas* and related words. A little over half (236) concern the creature's conformity to God or to His will. It may be understood in the light of all that we have already said: Thomas never loses sight of the theme of the image and of its ultimate model. For Christ, 199 uses of the term occur, of which 102 aim at conformity to Christ in general, 32 address conformity to His Passion, 11 to His death, 47 to His Resurrection, 7 to other aspects of his life and his virtues.

These figures clearly need to be carefully weighed—if only because we also have terms such as *configuratio*, used less frequently, that suggest analogous subjects.[55] Nevertheless, they allow us to acknowledge at the outset the importance of this motif. If we look more closely, it is found especially in passages that deal with the great mysteries of salvation. Given the pilgrim character of the Christian life, there is a preference, perhaps, for conformation to Christ in his Passion, but, it should also be noted, it is never envisaged by itself, apart from the Resurrection:

Christ's satisfaction works its effects in us inasmuch as we are incorporated with Him, as the members with their head, as stated above. . . . Now the members must be conformed to their head. Consequently, as Christ first had grace in his soul with bodily passibility, and through the Passion attained to the glory of immortality, so we likewise, who are His members, are freed by His Passion from all

---

54. Cf. J.-P. Torrell, "Imiter Dieu comme des enfants bien-aimés. La conformité à Dieu et au Christ dans l'oeuvre de saint Thomas," in *Novitas et veritas vitae: Aux sources du renouveau de la morale chrétienne*, ed. C.-J Pinto de Oliveira (Fribourg, 1991), 53–65.

55. There are 57 occurrences: 10 for configuration to God, 15 for Christ generally, 12 for his passion, 10 for his death and burial, 6 for his resurrection, 4 for other aspects of the mystery (priesthood or sanctity).

debt of punishment, yet so that we first receive in our souls *the spirit of adoption of sons* (Rom. 8:15), whereby our names are written down for the inheritance of immortal glory, while we yet have a passible and mortal body; but afterwards, *being conformed* to the sufferings and death of Christ (Phil. 3:10), we are brought into immortal glory, according to the saying of the Apostle (Rom. 8:17): *And if sons, heirs also: heirs indeed of God, and joint heirs with Christ, if only we suffer with Him, that we may also be glorified with Him.*[56]

That conformity to Christ in his Passion generally plays out in a specific way for the other mysteries—in particular, for his death:

Just as we are *configured to his* [i.e., Christ's] *death* to the extent that we die to sin, so he himself died to mortal life, in which there is a similarity to sin, though he himself had nothing of sin. Thus all of us who have been baptized are dead to sin.[57]

We might expect less here, though Thomas is only following Saint Paul and the unfolding of the Paschal mystery, but the same holds for the mystery of Christ's burial: "Through baptism men are buried in Christ *(sepeliuntur Christo)* which is to say *conformed to his burial*."[58] For a quite stronger reason, this holds for the resurrection as well: "After dying Christ rose; it is 'convenient' then that those who have been *conformed to Christ in his death* through baptism would be *conformed also to his Resurrection* through the innocence of their lives."[59] The treatise on the sacraments is particularly rich in observations of this kind, for if "by baptism man is incorporated in Christ and is made His member, . . . *it is fitting* that what takes place in the Head should take place also in the member who is incorporated into Him."[60]

---

56. *ST* IIIa q. 49 a. 3 ad 3. In exactly the same sense, we can also cite *ST* IIIa q. 56 a. 1 ad 1: "It is necessary that first of all we be conformed to the suffering and dying Christ in this suffering and mortal life; and afterwards may come to share in the likeness of His Resurrection." Cf. *ST* Ia IIae q. 85 a. 5 ad 2; *ST* IIIa q. 66 a. 2; *SCG* IV 55 n. 3944 *(in fine)*; *In ad Rom.* VIII, lect. 3 and 4, nn. 651–53. Cf. J.-P. Torrell, *Inutile sainteté?* (Paris, 1971), 49–64

57. *In ad Rom.* VI, 3, lect. 1, n. 473.

58. Ibid., n. 474. The passage continues by emphasizing that, if there is a triple immersion in baptism, it is not only because of the Trinity, *sed ad repraesentandum triduum sepulturae Christi.*

59. Ibid., n. 477.

60. *ST* IIIa q. 69 a. 3; cf. a. 7 ad 1: "Baptism opens the gates of the heavenly kingdom to the baptized in so far as it *incorporates them in the Passion of Christ,* by applying its 'power' to man." See also q. 73 a. 3 ad 3: "Baptism is the sacrament of Christ's death and Passion,

For someone to be efficaciously freed from [temporal] pains, it is necessary that he become a participant in the Passion of Christ, which occurs in two ways. First, through the sacrament of the Passion, baptism, by which [the baptized person] is entombed with Christ in death, according to Romans 6:4, and in which the divine virtue works, which does not admit of inefficacy. That is why such pains are removed at baptism. Second, *someone becomes a participant in Christ's Passion through real conformity to Him, which is to say when we suffer with the suffering Christ.* This happens through penitence. The latter conformity comes about by our own operation and that is why it can be perfect or imperfect. . . .[61]

We cannot quote here all the relevant passages. If it had not already long been apparent, this would be the place to emphasize the profoundly Pauline inspirations for this doctrine. Nowhere does Thomas the theologian reveal himself more attentive to Scripture than when he deals with Christ, and the careful reader cannot help but be impressed by the ease with which the most rigorous technique is made to serve a deep life of faith. Clearly the verse that we have made the leitmotif of this chapter is the immediate background for this doctrine:

Those whom he first knew, he also predestined to be conformed to the image of His Son. . . . [Against "those" who maintain that God's foreknowledge of the future merits of a person is the reason for his predestination and who wish to understand Saint Paul in this way: "Those whom he knew in advance would be conformed to the image of His Son, God has predestined . . . ," Thomas replies:] We could say this in a well-grounded way if predestination aimed only at eternal life, which is a response to merit. But it is really to every salutary benefit for man foreseen through all eternity that predestination refers. Thus all the benefits that we are granted in time have been prepared from all eternity. To say that some merit on our part is presupposed, which would be the reason for predestination, amounts to saying that grace is given by virtue of our merits, that we are the source of our good works, and that only their completion relates to God.

We should rather read this passage thus: "Those whom he foreknew are those that he predestined to be conformed to the image of his Son." *That conformity is not the reason for predestination, but its term, its effect.* The Apostle also says (Eph. 1:5): "He has predestined us to be adopted sons." *The adoption is nothing else than this conformity. Whoever is adopted as son of God is conformed to his true Son.*

according as a man is born anew in Christ in virtue of His Passion; but the Eucharist is the sacrament of Christ's Passion according as a man is made perfect in union with Christ Who suffered."

61. *In III Sent.* d. 19 q. 1 a. 3 sol. 2.

[That occurs] first through the right to participate in the inheritance, as he had said earlier (Rom. 8:17): "Sons and heirs, heirs of God, co-inheritors of Christ." Then, through a participation in his glory. Indeed, he was engendered by the Father as the "splendor of his glory" (Heb. 1:3). Thus, *by the very fact that he enlightens the saints with the light of his wisdom and his grace, he renders them conformed to him.* That is why Psalm 109:3 says: "From the womb of the dawn I begot you, before the light in the splendor of the saints," which is to say, in diffusing the splendor of the saints. . . .

As to the consequences of this predestination, Paul adds: "In order that he would be the eldest of many brothers." Just as God wanted to communicate his nature to others in making them participate in likeness to his goodness, so that he is not only Good, but the author of goods, so too the Son of God wanted to communicate the conformity of his filiation, so that he would not be an only child but the Firstborn of the sons. Thus, he who is unique in his eternal generation, according to John (1:18) "The only Son who is in the bosom of the Father," becomes through the communication of grace "the Firstborn of many sons": "He who is the Firstborn among the dead, the Prince of the kings of the earth" (Apoc. 1:5).

We are thus the brothers of Christ, as much by the fact that he has communicated to us the likeness of his filiation, as we say here, as by the fact that he assumed similarity to our nature, according to the epistle to the Hebrews (2:17): "He had to become like his brothers in all things."[62]

Besides the Pauline inspiration, we can grasp in a glance how the whole doctrine is articulated. Its way of presenting the Incarnate Word, simultaneously the *exemplar* for how we have been created and recreated and the *exemplum* that we must imitate by our acts, allows Thomas forcefully to emphasize Christ's place in our Christian life and to adhere, at the same time, to a fully Trinitarian spiritual life.[63] The doctrine of the Christ model is indeed one of his great spiritual themes; but through the theme of the image which undergirds these developments, we discover without any interruption the final Exemplar: "Given that it is through his equality in essence that the Son resembles the Father, *it is necessary, if man has been made in the likeness of the Son, that he has also been made in the image of the Father.*"[64] The very same passage continues, as we already know, by saying that in fact it is the image of the whole Trinity to which we are conformed. Without further delaying on this point, to

---

62. *In ad Rom. VIII*, lect. 6, nn. 703–6. There is also the passage in Romans 8:29 that holds the *Summa's* reflections about predestination, cf. *ST* Ia q. 23, in particular a. 5.

63. Cf. G. Re, *Il cristocentrismo della vita cristiana* (Brescia, 1968).

64. *ST* Ia q. 93 a. 5 ad 4. Cf. É. Bailleux, *Á l'image du Fils premier-né*, 192–203.

which we will soon return, this offers us a chance to recall the Holy Spirit's role. Far from being absent from this process of conformation to Christ and to God, he is the agent by which it occurs:

We read in Sacred Scripture that *we are configured to the Son by the mediation of the Holy Spirit.* Witness this passage from Letter to the Romans 8:15: "You have received a Spirit that makes you adopted sons," and this passage from the Letter to the Galatians 4:6: "Because you are his sons, God has sent into your hearts the Spirit of His Son." Now, nothing is conformed to a model except by means of its own seal. We see this in created natures, where what makes them similar to the model proceeds from the model itself; thus, human seed which proceeds from a man makes something similar to the man. Consequently, we say of Christ: "He has stamped us with his seal, with his unction, he has given us in pawn the Holy Spirit present in our hearts."[65]

The First-Born of All Creatures

We might illustrate the Christological coloration of grace through the beautiful image of Louis Chardon: it is like the water of a spring that conserves all the properties of the minerals that it has passed over.[66] But as in the analogy of an instrument, we should not be fooled by the image's material implications. Christ is a lot more to us than a simple instrument. He is the head of his Mystical Body, the Church. This causes Saint Thomas to say that grace was given to Christ to make Him the first and universal principle that imparts grace in all those connected with Him.[67] Much more refined, this metaphysical principle allows us to emphasize that *Christ is not merely a relayer, but is indeed a cause of grace.* The Master from Aquino soon felt the limits of the analogy of the instrument and, without rejecting it—since it allowed for some definite advance—he moved toward a deepening of the Pauline contribution about the Body of Christ:

65. *De pot.* q. 10 a. 4.

66. L. Chardon, *The Cross of Jesus,* vol. 1, 92: "Waters which flow through certain minerals retain some of their qualities and properties and produce certain effects in those who drink those waters. In like manner, grace flows from the soul of Jesus as from its fountain-head, and as it there produced a weight which drew Him toward His passion, it must necessarily produce this inclination in those to whom a share in His cross has been given. 'The charity of Christ presseth us,' wrote St. Paul, for 'if one died for all, then all were dead' (2 Cor. 5:14). If Christ's capital grace called for His death and filled Him with so powerful an inclination toward the cross, the same urgent love will appear in His chosen souls."

67. *ST* IIIa q. 7 a. 9: "tanquam cuidam universali principio in genere habentium gratiam." We can recognize here the application of the principle *maxime tale.*

According to Saint John Damascene, Christ's humanity was like the instrument of his divinity, and that is why his actions could be salutary for us. [This Thomas accepted and he will never abandon the position, but adds this qualification:] Given that Christ's humanity was a special instrument of the divinity, it thus had to have a special connection to his divinity.

According to Dionysius . . . each being participates more in God's goodness the more closely it approaches him. It follows that the humanity of Christ, by the very fact that it is united to the divinity in the closest way and more specially than any other creature, participates in the most excellent way in the divine goodness. *It had to have not only the capacity for grace, but also the capacity for transmitting it*, a little like the way that brilliant bodies transmit to others the light of the sun. And since Christ communicates grace to all rational creatures, it follows that, in his humanity, *Christ is in some way the principle of all grace, as God is the principle of all being*. Also, just as all perfection of being has a similarity to God, so all plenitude of grace is found in Christ; he can not only act by himself in the order of grace, but also lead others to grace, and it is in this way that he is rightly the head.

Now we do not only find in the head of a natural body the sensitive power that allows it to see, hear, touch, and so forth; *but we also find in the head as in its root that from which the senses flow into the other members*. Thus, in Christ, the same habitual grace is called "grace of *union*" as is fitting to a nature united to divinity, "*capital* grace" as it pours forth on others for their salvation, and "*personal* grace" as it enables his humanity to do meritorious actions.[68]

We can see several differences between this youthful passage and the more finished formulations in the *Summa*. Christ appears here as Head because of his spreading of grace. A little later, it will be the inverse formulation that he retains: the spreading of grace to the members of the Church will be seen as the consequence of attributing the title of Head to Christ. Similarly, in the *Summa*, Thomas will distinguish much more clearly the grace of union from the two other kinds of grace. The uncreated Gift that the Person of the Word makes of himself to the humanity that He assumes[69] is not commensurable with either personal grace or capital grace. We will consider for a few moments the way in which things are organized in the synthesis—effectively, because he is the very Son of God, Christ is also "full of grace and truth,"[70] and he may thus cause grace with

---

68. *De uer.*, q. 29 a. 5. See the commentary by É. Bailleux, "Le Christ et son Esprit," *RT* 73 (1973): 386–89.

69. Cf. *ST* IIIa q. 2 a. 10; q. 6 a. 6; q. 7 a. 11; etc.

70. John 1:14, cited in *De uer.* q. 29 a. 5 ad 1.

a much greater authority than an instrument can, even if it is joined. The formula in the passage quoted above will have been noticed: "Christ is in a certain way the principle of all grace, as God is the principle of all being" (*principium quodammodo omnis gratiae, sicut Deus est principium omnis esse*). Thomas could say nothing stronger, and that is why he adds a little further on: "Christ has achieved our salvation *quasi ex propria uirtute*."[71]

The teaching on the Body of Christ reveals itself to be decisive for fully understanding the conformation of the Christian to Christ through grace. Spiritually, there is no gap between Christ and His members, for he forms with them "a single mystical person."[72] And therefore, "merit" or "satisfaction" belong to everything he does "as the actions of a man constituted in grace belong to his whole person."[73] That is why Christ's active and spreading omnipresence in the Christian life according to Saint Thomas finds its best expression in the teaching on the Mystical Body. For it is grace that flows from Christ the Head to the members with the special qualities that are his, so as to conform them to himself. In a passage that contemporary exegetes would doubtless find odd, he explains how, in his view, the unique subject of Paul's epistles is the grace of Christ considered in its connections to His ecclesial body:

> The Apostle wrote fourteen epistles. . . . This teaching bears entirely on Christ's grace, which can be considered under a threefold modality. First, as it is in the Head himself, Christ, and that is how we find it in the Epistle to the Hebrews. Then as it is in the principal members of the Mystical Body, and that is how we find it in the [Pastoral] epistles addressed to prelates. Finally, as it is in the Mystical Body itself, and that is how we find it in the epistles addressed to the Gentiles.[74]

The accuracy of this reconstruction is not much at issue here. It at least clarifies the idea that Thomas was developing of the Church, in which he places at the forefront, with an unequaled power, the interior dimension of the ecclesial communion. Following Paul and Augustine in particular, but going beyond the latter thanks to Damascene,[75] Thomas sees the

---

71. *De uer.* q. 29 a. 5 ad 3.   72. *ST* IIIa q. 48 a. 2 ad 1.
73. *ST* IIIa q. 48 a. 1.
74. General prologue to the Epistles, n. 11. This text is translated more fully in my *Saint Thomas Aquinas*, 255–56.
75. On this point, see Yves Congar, "Saint Augustin et le traité scolastique *De gratia capitis*," *Augustinianum* 20 (1980): 79–93, which recalls that the teaching of the instrumen-

Church as before all else an organism of grace in total dependence on her head, Christ:[76]

Christ possessed grace not only as an individual, but in his quality as Head of the Church, to whom all are united as the bodily members to their head, such as to constitute mystically with Him a single person. It follows that Christ's merit also extends to others insofar as they are His members; just as in an ordinary man the head's action belongs in a certain way to all his members, for the head does not act for itself alone, but for all its members.[77]

Because he recapitulates in himself all who are in his grace, Christ can therefore communicate to them the infinite merit that he obtained by his loving obedience to the Father's will. And it is in the measure to which they are linked to him that they can receive the Holy Spirit:

If the Apostle adds *in Jesus Christ* (Rom. 8:2) it is because the Spirit is given only to those who are in Christ Jesus. As the life-giving natural breath does not reach the member that is not connected to its head, in the same way the Holy Spirit does not reach the member who is not connected with his head, Christ.[78]

This does not exclude what we were just saying about the Spirit as the agent of our conformation to Christ. Because of the primary trinitarian origin and the circumincession of the divine Persons, there is a reciprocal condition of their action and, according to the point of view, the priority will differ in each case. Thus, if the Spirit is given only to those who are in Christ, the Spirit is also the one who constitutes Christ as the *primogenitus*, "the eldest of many brothers." For the Spirit has been given to Him "without limit" (John 3:34). But the Father is also implicated, for it is in the manner through which the Son has been begotten that he is also found to be the Firstborn of all creation:

God does not know the creation in a way other than He knows himself, but he knows all things in his essence as in the first efficient cause. Now, the Son is God's intellectual conception, according as he knows himself [thus knowing] as a

---

tality of Christ's humanity in producing grace was unknown to Saint Augustine, who did not conceive of His action except as a dispositive causality (cf. note 16 above).

76. Cf. *ST* IIIa q. 8 a. 1 and 5; q. 7 a. 1 and 9.

77. *ST* IIIa q. 19 a. 4; cf. q. 48 a. 2 ad 1: "The head and the members form as it were a single mystical person *(quasi una persona mystica).*" Cf. notes 55–56 above. For the various aspects of Christ's primacy, see Th. R. Potvin, *The Theology of the Primacy of Christ*, pp. 27–35 and 226–249 in particular.

78. *In ad Rom. VIII*, 2, lect. 1, n. 606.

consequence every creature. Insofar as he is begotten, he is then the Word who represents every creature and is himself the principle of every creature. *If he was not begotten in that way, he would be the Firstborn of the Father, but not the First of every creature.* [Now, Wisdom says of herself] "Come forth from the mouth of the Most High, I am firstborn of all creatures" (Sir. 24:5 in the Vulgate).[79]

A Priestly, Royal, and Prophetic Body

Once more, then, we have to return to the intratrinitarian processions to understand how the Incarnate Word acts with respect to man. We remember the parallelism between the way in which God communicates his goodness to creatures and the way in which the "Son of God wished to communicate to others the conformity of his filiation, such that he is not only the Son, but the first of the sons."[80] We might develop this further by underscoring that he also communicates to them in the Spirit the unction which has made of Him the Anointed par excellence, which is to say the Messiah, thus making of them other Christs, possessing as he does the triple quality—priestly, royal, and prophetic. This threefold appellation, honored again in the twentieth century,[81] was well known to the Dominican master:

Under the old covenant, priests and kings were anointed, as was the case for David (1 Sam. 16) and Solomon (1 Kings 1). And the prophets, too, were anointed, as was the case for Elisha, who was anointed by Elijah (1 Kings 19). These three (anointings) were suited to Christ, who was king: "He will reign over the house of David forever" (Luke 1:33). He was also a priest and offered himself to God in sacrifice (Eph. 5:2). He was similarly a prophet and proclaimed the way of salvation: "The Lord will raise up a prophet among the sons of Israel" (Deut. 18:15). How was he anointed? Not with a visible oil, for "his kingdom is not of this world" (John 18:36). And since he did not occupy a material priesthood he was not anointed with a material oil, but with the oil of the Holy Spirit . . .[82]

79. *In ad Colossenses I*, 15, lect. 4, n. 35.   80. Cf. above pp. 143–44.

81. Yves Congar's role in this is well known. See his *Lay People in the Church: A Study for a Theology of Laity*, trans. Donald Attwater (London, 1957). It is also worth recalling P. Dabin, *Le sacerdoce royal des fidèles dans la tradition ancienne et moderne* (Brussels-Paris, 1950), who has assembled a rich file of 650 pages on the priestly, kingly, and prophetic quality of the People of God, from the beginning down to our own day. See also, the more recent and excellent synthesis by J. Alfaro, "Les fonctions salvifiques du Christ comme prophète, roi et prêtre," *Mysterium salutis* 11 (Paris, 1975), 241–325; Yves Congar, "Sur la trilogie Prophète-Roi-Prêtre," *RSPT* 67 (1983): 97–116.

82. *In Ps. XLIV*, 5 (ed. Vivès, vol. 18, p. 508); cf. *Lectura super Matthaeum* (*In Matt.*) *I*,

The formulation is at times different according to the context. But though it does not always appear exactly in the fixed formula that it later acquired, the messianic trilogy is truly operative:

Other men possess certain special graces, but Christ, as head of all men, possesses all graces perfectly. That is why, as regards other men, one is a lawgiver, another a priest, still another a king; *in Christ, on the contrary, all this is joined together as in the source of all graces.* This is why it is said in Isaiah (33:22): "The Lord is our judge, the Lord is our lawgiver, the Lord is our king. He will come to us and save us."[83]

As we might well have expected after everything that has been previously said, since the Church-Body of Christ is an expression of his capital grace, all who are linked to him through baptism become kings, priests, and prophets with him:

[After recalling the meaning of anointing and the meaning of the word *Christ*, Thomas continues:] Christ is Himself king. . . . He is also priest. . . . He was equally a prophet. . . . It was fitting then for him to be anointed with the oil of sanctification and gladness [the Holy Spirit in Thomas's exegesis]. It is from Him that the sacraments come, which are the instruments of grace. . . . *But that anointing is equally fitting for Christians.* They are in effect kings and priests: "You are a chosen race, a royal priesthood" (1 Pet. 2:9), "You have made of us a kingdom and priests for our God" (Rev. 5:10). They equally possess the Holy Spirit, who is the Spirit of prophecy: "I will pour out my Spirit on all flesh" (Joel 2:28, cf. Acts 2:17). And that is why all are anointed with an invisible anointing: "The one who confirms us with you in Christ and who anointed us is God" (2 Cor. 1:21); "But you have the anointing that comes from the holy one and you have all knowledge" (1 John 2:20). But what is the relation between the anointed Christ and Christians anointed like Him? It is this: He has anointing by principal and

---

1, lect. 1, nn. 19–20: "There were three anointings in the old law. Aaron received the anointing of priests . . . Saul received from Samuel the anointing of kings . . . Elisha received the anointing of prophets. . . . Since Christ was a true priest . . . and king and prophet, he is thus properly called *the Christ* [i.e., the anointed one], by reason of the three functions he carried out. . . . Since Christ was a king, priest, and prophet, he is thus rightly called son [of Abraham and David]." *In ad Rom. I, 1,* lect. 1, n. 20: "*Christ* means *Anointed One.* . . . By this, Christ's dignity is manifested as to holiness, since priests were anointed . . . as to power, since kings were also anointed . . . and as to knowledge, since prophets equally were anointed."

83. *ST* IIIa q. 22 a. 1 ad 3. We find "lawgiver" here where we would expect "prophet," but the general context indicates rather that the difference should not be exaggerated. Cf. q. 31 a. 2: "Christ was to be king, prophet, and priest"; *Expositio super Isaiam ad litteram* (*In Isaiam*) *LXI,* 1 (Leonine, vol. 28, p. 240, lines 65 ff.); *In Matt. XXVIII,* 19, nn. 2462–64.

primary right, we and others have received it from him. . . . That is why the others are called saints, but he is the Holy One of the saints. He is the source of all holiness.[84]

We have omitted some of the quotations from Scripture for the sake of brevity. But enough remain to grasp the deeply biblical inspiration of this teaching. Doubtless, this is one of the reasons why Thomas's position so naturally concurs with Vatican II, which made the messianic trilogy the backbone of the dogmatic constitution *Lumen gentium*. The Council did not borrow this from Saint Thomas, but it is of interest to note in passing that what, at the time of the Council, might have seemed a novelty was in reality well anchored in a Tradition to which the Council itself witnessed.

There is perhaps no need to end this chapter with the usual conclusion repeating its main points. Clearly, from here on, Christ's humanity plays a structural role in Thomas Aquinas's synthesis, and this has repercussions in the Christian's lived experience, beginning with Thomas's own. He thought of himself as taking part in the Christian "we," which recurs so often in his works. Certain things even allow us to perceive something of his attitude about the humanity of Jesus Christ and his limitless confidence in his intercession:

(The Apostle shows that Christ can neither accuse nor condemn those for whom he shed his blood [cf. Romans 8: 31–39]); on the contrary, he accords to the saints great benefits both through his humanity and his divinity. According to his humanity, Paul mentions four benefits: (1) His death for our salvation . . . ; (2) His Resurrection, by which he gives us life: spiritual life on this earth, bodily life in the world to come. . . . He even emphasizes the Resurrection ("What else do I say? He who is resurrected"), for at the present moment it is rather the power of the Resurrection that we must remember rather than the weakness of the Passion; (3) His own exaltation by the Father, when he says "Who is at the right hand of God," which is to say in a position of equality with God the Father according to His divine nature and possessing the highest goods according to human nature. And that redounds to our own glory, for as the Apostle says (Eph. 2:6): "He has raised us up and seated us in the heavens with Christ Jesus." Since we are his members, we sit with him in God the Father himself . . . ; (4) His intercession for us, because he says, "He intercedes for us," as if he was our advocate. "We have an advocate with the Father, Jesus Christ" (1 John 2:1). It belongs to an advocate nei-

---

84. *In ad Heb. I*, 9, lect. 4, n. 64–66.

ther to accuse nor to condemn, but on the contrary to repel accusations and prevent condemnation. He intercedes for us in a twofold way. First, by praying for us . . . and his prayer for us is his will for our salvation: "I desire that where I am, they may also be with me" (John 17:24). *The other way he intercedes for us is to present to the Father's sight the humanity that he assumed for us and the mysteries that he celebrated in that humanity:* "He entered Heaven itself in order now to appear before the face of God on our behalf."[85]

A few lines later, in a passage strongly influenced by Saint John Chrysostom (but reformulated by Thomas for his own purposes), Thomas recalls how lovers behave: they never stop talking, to those near or far, about the object of their passion. He goes into raptures on Saint Paul, "that eminent lover of Christ" *(eximius amator Christi)*, who found such beautiful touches in speaking about the object of his love.[86] Thomas himself rarely waxes lyrical, but what he says of Christ allows us to imagine his sentiments quite well.[87]

85. *In ad Rom.* VIII, 33–34, lect. 7, nn. 719–20.
86. Ibid., n. 728. Cf. Saint John Chrysostom, *Ad Demetrium De compunctione* I, 8 (PL 47, 406).
87. Nota bene: We should inform the reader, as a complement to chapters 5 and 6, that we have dealt with these themes much more fully in a work that appeared only after the French edition of the present work had been published: *Le Christ en ses mystères. La vie et l'oevre de Jésus selon saint Thomas d'Aquin,* Jésus et Jésus-Christ 78 et 79 (Paris, Desclée, 1999), 2 vols.

CHAPTER VII

To Speak of the Holy Spirit

Ever since ecumenical dialogue put Latin theologians back in touch with their Orthodox colleagues, we have often heard the complaint that the Holy Spirit is absent from our Western theology and spirituality.[1] Without arguing here the possible merits of the charges or of the responses to them, we will discover quite quickly that, at least as far as Saint Thomas is concerned, these complaints are wide of the mark. For him, the Holy Spirit is neither absent nor unknown. He is as present everywhere in Thomas's theology as Christ himself is, and thus, in Thomas's spirituality as well. It is worthwhile, however, not to ignore the charge and to try and see where the misunderstanding lies.

The Holy Spirit in Thomas Aquinas's Works

The misunderstanding of Christ's position, we recall, came from his placement in the *Summa*'s plan. The mistake about the Holy Spirit seems better supported, because outside of the treatise on the Trinity, where it was impossible not to address the subject, the Holy Spirit seems to have no place at all. Casual readers search in vain in the *Summa*'s Table of Contents for places where the question of the Holy Spirit is addressed in itself. Dedicated readers of monographs, whether scholarly or not, which

---

1. Yves Congar has summarized these complaints and demonstrated that they are somewhat excessive: "Pneumatologie ou 'christomonisme' dans la tradition latine?," in *Ecclesia a Spiritu Sancto edocta. Mélanges théologique offerts à Mgr. Gérard Philips* (Gembloux, 1970), 42–63; by the same author, "La pneumatologie dans la théologie catholique," *RSPT* 51 (1967): 250–58; see also his beautiful books, *I Believe in the Holy Spirit*, trans. David Smith, 3 vols. (New York, 1983), where a much fuller documentation may be found.

deal with all aspects of a single subject, are disconcerted at not finding the equivalent in Saint Thomas.

In addressing the matter, we must state clearly that this is not a good reading. And without offering an apology *a priori*, we may say with certainty that, if we do not find the Holy Spirit here or there in Thomas Aquinas's work, it is because, in truth, he is everywhere. Worthy researchers have devoted themselves to detailed accounts which show indisputably the high statistical presence of the Holy Spirit in the *Summa*.[2] But rather than focus on statistics, which all too often remain at a purely material level, it would perhaps be more useful here to go quickly over the main places where we encounter more or less long developments dealing with the Holy Spirit. This portrait will be neither complete nor detailed, since there are several things to which we will return in the following pages. But if a reader would like to examine these quotations on his own in a fuller context, he may be helped by several suggestions we shall make here.

First, obviously, we have the treatise on the Trinity. In the *Summa Theologiae*, following the first part, in which Thomas situates the three Persons in themselves beginning with the processions and relations (Ia qq. 27–38), there is a second part in which they are conceptualized in their various connections (qq. 39–43). The details of the internal organization of each part are less important for us than the striking progression by which each Person is specially dealt with. One question is enough to speak of the Father (q. 33). Two are needed for the Son in his titles as Word and Image (qq. 34–35). Three are necessary for the Holy Spirit: Spirit, Love, and Gift (qq. 36–38). This progression is too smooth to be the result of chance, especially since we know from other sources that Thomas was aware of number symbolism.[3] Without lingering more on

2. Cf. A. Calvis Ramirez, "El Espíritu Santo en la Suma teológica de santo Tomás," in *Tommaso d'Aquino nel suo settimo centenario, Atti del Congresso internazionale*, vol. 4 (Naples, 1976), 92–104. The author identified 70 articles in the *Prima Pars*, 45 in the the the *Prima Secundae*, 108 in the *Secunda Secundae*, 138 in the *Tertia Pars* which concern the Holy Spirit. These numbers, which were obtained without using the *Index thomisticus*, only available later, could be further refined or nuanced today. But the conclusions to which they lead would only be strengthened, because they are merely an indication of a "deep, fundamental presence, which enlivens every part, each treatise, giving them their harmony and unity" (p. 94).

3. Cf. J. Tonneau, *La loi nouvelle* (French translation with notes and appendices of St. Thomas Aquinas, *Summa theologiae* Ia IIae qq. 106–8) (Paris, 1981), 98–99.

this subject, we can say in passing that all this is at least a sign that the Holy Spirit is considered at the same level of importance as the two other persons.[4]

Leaving aside the scattered references to the Holy Spirit that are found, as they are required, throughout the *Summa*,[5] we find at the end of the *Prima Secundae* what an attentive observer has proposed to call several "zones of great pneumatological concentration."[6] A group of three questions (Ia IIae qq. 68–70) makes up the first of these zones; they are dedicated specially to the gifts, the beatitudes, and the fruits of the Holy Spirit (mentioned 94 times). This way of connecting gifts, beatitudes, and fruits is an original contribution by the Master of Aquino; but we will have to come back to this.[7] A second section is found a little further on in a group of three questions on the law of the Gospel or the "new law" (Ia IIae q. 106–108). Though already a familiar theme from the other scholastic philosophers, it receives a very personal treatment from Thomas, and the way he speaks of the Holy Spirit (34 occurrences) is not at all accidental, since it plays a main role in the Gospel.[8] As to the third large development, if there was any doubt, it comes in the treatise on grace (Ia IIae qq. 109–114), which Thomas regularly calls the "grace of the Holy Spirit" *(gratia Spiritus Sancti)*—with the two possible meanings of the Latin expression: the grace that is the Holy Spirit or the grace given by the Holy Spirit.[9] Though even these three groups of questions do not express everything

---

4. Though with the proper nuances, each of these questions was equally dealt with in the commentary on the *Sentences*; the parallel passages can easily be identified by consulting a good edition of the *Summa*.

5. They are more frequent, as we might expect, in the *Secunda Secundae* in the discussion of the virtues—the theological virtues in particular—and in the *Tertia Pars* in the discussion of Christ and the sacraments, to which the Holy Spirit imparts efficacy.

6. Cf. A. Patfoort, "Morale et pneumatologie. Une observation de la Ia IIae," in *Les Clés*, 71–102. We will take up many of Patfoort's conclusions in what follows.

7. Cf. S. Th. Pinckaers, "La loi évangélique, vie selon l'Esprit, et le Sermon sur la montagne," NV (1985): 217–28; and chap. 7 in the same author's *Sources of Christian Ethics*, translated from the third edition by Sr. Mary Thomas Noble, O.P. (Washington, D.C., 1995), 168–90.

8. Cf. U. Kühn, *Via Caritatis. Theologie des Gesetzes bei Thomas von Aquin* (Göttingen, 1965), 218–23. The author provides a detailed study of the theme as it appears in works prior to Thomas, pp. 49–120 (French summary and discussion in M. Froidure, "La théologie protestante de la loi nouvelle peut-elle se réclamer de saint Thomas?," RSPT 51 [1967], 53–61); for a more concise treatment, see J. Tonneau, *La loi nouvelle*, 196–203.

9. Cf. J. Tonneau, *La loi nouvelle*, 226–33. The treatise on grace clearly has parallels in the commentary on the *Sentences* (*In III Sent.* dd. 26–29) and the *De ueritate* (qq. 27–29),

on the Holy Spirit, they are rich in insights and various suggestions as to his presence and action in the life of the Christian.

Another whole section in the *Summa contra Gentiles* is also important. We know that the purpose and structure of that work are rather different from those of the *Summa Theologiae*, and we find a treatment of the Trinity only in Book IV, dedicated to the "truths inaccessible to reason."[10] After a Prologue, in which he presents the general contents of the Book, the author begins with the generation of the Word (2–14), continues with questions raised by the procession of the Holy Spirit (15–25), and ends with a chapter in which he shows that there are only three Persons in God (26). As will be seen by reading them, these pages offer a remarkable example of the Master of Aquino's theological method, and in particular of the way in which he attends to Scripture and the Church Fathers. We find most notably three chapters that provide a kind of great fresco of the Holy Spirit's role in Creation, in the history of salvation, and in the return of the creature to God. A beautiful sampling from a successful symbiosis between biblical theology and reflexive theology, they offer inexhaustible perspectives for meditation.[11]

In addition to these more elaborate expositions in the large works, we have to add the developments in the biblical commentaries. In the "Reading" on the fourth evangelist, the main points are found in connection with Jesus' conversation with Nicodemus. The Johannine expressions, "to be reborn of water and the Spirit," or "The Spirit blows where it will," afford the commentator some easy starting points.[12] The promise of rivers of water allows him to specify that this gushing stream is the Holy Spirit himself.[13] The chapters that report the *logia* of Jesus on the Paraclete are also the object of an enjoyable exegesis whose spiritual notes captivate the reader.[14] But the commentary on Paul's letters is no less rich: the exposition on chapter 8 of Romans probably reaches one of the sum-

---

but we should notice that Thomas changed his view on this point when he discovered semi-Pelagianism. Cf. H. Bouillard, *Conversion et grâce chez S. Thomas d'Aquin, Étude historique* (Paris, 1944), 92–122.

10. Cf. introductory note in my *Saint Thomas Aquinas*, chapter 6, especially pp. 107–16.

11. *SCG* IV 20–22. Well-annotated editions provide helpful references to the Scriptures and Fathers.

12. *In Ioannem III*, lect. 1 and 2, nn. 449–56 in particular.

13. *In Ioannem VII*, lect. 5, nn. 1091–96.

14. *In Ioannem XIV*, lect. 4 and 6, nn. 1907–20 and 1952–60; cap. 15, lect. 5, nn. 2058–67, cap. 16, lect. 2–4, nn. 2082–115.

mits of this type of work.[15] But the commentary on First Corinthians, regarding Paul's teaching on the charisms (chapter 12), is also of great interest,[16] as is the commentary on Galatians 5 on the liberty of the spirit, which is indeed one of Thomas's favorite themes.[17]

This list could of course be easily lengthened, but we are not trying to exhaust the subject here.[18] We simply want to draw attention to these numerous and rich texts to allow easier access to whoever so desires. Despite the multiplication of high-quality studies in the past thirty years, the teaching on the Holy Spirit in Saint Thomas is far from having received the attention it deserves.[19] This brief list at least will allow us to understand that it would be unjust to attribute to the Master the future negligence of his disciples.

Common Nouns and Proper Names: The Trinitarian Appropriation

What we have just done, however, will remain inadequate until we enter into the texts themselves and we discover what Thomas says about the Holy Spirit—and how he says it. But to do that we must be willing to confront the mystery of the Trinity and to ask ourselves how we can be enti-

---

15. *In ad Rom. VIII*, lect. 1–7, nn. 595–731.

16. *In I ad Cor. XII*, lect. 1–2, nn. 709–30.

17. *In ad Gal. V*, lect. 6–7, nn. 327–41.

18. We might mention, however, a beautiful commentary on the articles of the Creed dealing with the Holy Spirit and the Church (*In Symb.* nn. 958–98), and the *collatio* 19 of the *In Isaiam*, along with the previously mentioned commentary: J.-P. Torrell and D. Bouthillier, "Quand saint Thomas méditait," 35–37.

19. In addition to the works already mentioned or still to appear, here are some additional studies. A series by G. Ferraro, "Lo spirito Santo nel commento di San Tommaso ai capitoli XIV–XVI *del quarto vangelo*," in *Tommaso d'Aquino nel suo Settimo Centenario*, vol. 4, pp. 79–91; "Aspetti di pneumatologia nell'esegesi di S. Tommaso d'Aquino all'Epistola agli Ebrei (Annotazioni di dottrina e di esegesi tomista," *ST* 13 (1981): 172–88; "Aspetti di pneumatologia nell'esegesi di S. Tommaso d'Aquino dell'Epistola ai Romani," *Euntes Docete* 36 (1983): 51–78; "La pneumatologia di San Tommaso d'Aquino nel suo commento al quarto Vangelo," *Angelicum* 66 (1989): 193–263; and "Interpretazione dei testi pneumatologici biblici nel trattato trinitario della 'Summa theologiae' di san Tommaso d'Aquino (*Ia qq.* 27–43)," *ST* 45 (1992): 53–65. Among studies by other authors: L. Elders, "Le Saint-Esprit et la Lex Nova dans les commentaires bibliques de S. Thomas d'Aquin," in *Credo in Spiritum Sanctum*, vol. 2 (Vatican City, 1983), 1195–205; S. Zedda, "Cristo e lo Spirito Santo nell'adozione a figli secondo il commento di S. Tommaso alla lettera ai romani," in *Tommaso d'Aquino nel suo Settimo Centenario*, vol. 4, pp. 105–12. For more exhaustive research, see A. Pedrini, *Bibliografia tomistica sulla pneumatologia* (Rome, 1994), which includes the titles from 1870 to 1993.

tled to say anything on the subject of the particularities of the divine Persons. The theologian has to find here a way of speaking that is simultaneously subjectively *meaningful* to our intelligence and *faithful* to the unity of the divine essence. For this task, he must navigate so as to avoid shipwreck on two reefs long mapped in Christian thought: on the one hand, tri-theism, which, by accentuating the differences among the Persons, winds up by making three gods of them, and thus would divert Christian monotheism into a polytheistic idolatry; on the other hand lies modalism, which falls into the opposite danger and does not want to see in the names Son and Spirit anything more than modalities of appearance or of designation for a single divine person, risking a return to a pre-Trinitarian monotheism.

Between these two reefs, the first great attempt at dogmatic clarification undertaken by the Church was completed at the councils of Nicea (325) and Constantinople (381) with the clear affirmation of Trinity in unity. But it was still necessary to *think* that truth, to try "understanding with the intelligence what was held through faith." In our Latin tradition, Saint Augustine's effort, furthered by Saint Anselm and taken up again by Saint Thomas and the great thirteenth-century theologians, was taken by them—at least insofar as concerns the Trinity—to a level of development not easily surpassed. The theology of the distinction of the persons through their relation of origin is one of the most remarkable examples of that development. There is a second development that is quite important to understand because it is one of our rare chances to mumble something about the unsayable. It is what is called "appropriation."[20]

By its very definition, the process of appropriation consists in "bringing a common noun to do the job of a proper name" *(trahere commune ad proprium)*. We might take for an example the well-known practice in the ancient Roman world by which the word city *(urbs)*, having been used for dozens of agglomerations of people, was applied to the city *par excellence*, the capital of the Empire. Rome was "the" City by appropriation. Some-

---

20. This subject is as vast as it is great and beautiful. For many things that we cannot include here, see H. de Lavalette, *La notion d'appropriation dans la théologie trinitaire de S. Thomas d'Aquin* (Rome, 1959), and H.-F. Dondaine, *La Trinité*, vol. 2, pp. 409–23, to whom the treatment in this chapter owes a great deal. See also J.-H. Nicolas, *Les Profondeurs de la grâce* (Paris, 1966), 110–26; B. Montagnes, "La Parole de Dieu dans la création," *RT* 54 (1954): 213–41 (on appropriation, pp. 222–30); Thomas's main texts on the subject are: ST Ia q. 39 aa. 7–8; q. 45 aa. 6–7 with their parallels.

thing analogous happens when we attribute to one of the Persons of the Trinity a quality common in reality to all three Persons, because it belongs to the divine essence itself (which is why we speak of *essential* attributes, while we speak of *properties* for the Persons). This also happens when we use "Wisdom" to speak of the Son, of "Goodness" to speak of the Holy Spirit. It suffices to pay attention to this to notice that the process is very common, but also that we must understand it properly:

> To clarify this mystery of the faith, *it is fitting to appropriate the essential attributes to the Persons.* Indeed, as we have said, it is impossible to prove the Trinity by demonstration, properly speaking; *it is fitting however for clarifying the mystery in the midst of things more within the reach of our reason.* Now, the essential attributes are more accessible to us through reason than are the properties of the Persons. For, by beginning from creatures, the sources of our knowledge, we can arrive at knowing with certainty God's essential attributes, but not His personal properties. Just as, therefore, we resort to analogies of vestige and image, discovered in creatures, to explain the doctrine of the divine persons, so too we resort to the essential attributes. *To manifest thus the Persons in the midst of the essential attributes is what we call "appropriation."*[21]

  This brief text deserves inclusion in an anthology. We may grasp several decisive points about Thomas's method with great clarity here: the progressive character of the process (from more to less well known); the meaning of the mystery (impossibility of demonstrating the Trinity) and nonetheless the desire to penetrate it as much as possible through fitting reasons (it is fitting to clarify the mystery). Appropriation, indeed, depends on this development through convenience, typical of theology, which cannot lay claim to any necessary conclusion, but that nonetheless brings some light to bear on a realm where, without it, there would reign even greater darkness.

  In truth, the development is not only theological. Augustine and, following him, Thomas had already been able to find the process in the New Testament. The name "God" is typically reserved there for the Father, the "Lord" for the Son, and the "Spirit" for the third Person of the Trinity (cf. Eph. 2:18). Elsewhere Saint Paul attributes charisms to the Spirit, the ministries to the Lord, the "operations" to God (1 Cor. 12:4–6). This way of speaking continues in the Creed: creation is there attributed to the Fa-

---

21. *ST* Ia q. 39 a. 7.

ther, our salvation to the Son, sanctification and enlivening to the Spirit. Each case is presented the way it is either because "essential" nouns are convenient to the three Persons simultaneously or because it deals with operations whose only common author is the Trinity. Linked with the revelation of the economy of salvation, ratified by the dogmatic expression of the faith, this language must then also have its legitimacy in theology. The only problem consists in the bases for and the limits to its use.

The text above declares what might be called its "subjective" foundation: the trinitarian appropriation gains a first justification in the benefit that the theologian draws from it, a certain understanding of the mystery.[22] This legitimate procedure can open the door to many imaginary "appropriations" having no more worth than the fantasies of their inventors. It is therefore important to determine what, on the part of the object, justifies the process. Now, here the Master from Aquino is very clear: "The only and primary foundation of the appropriation is its similarity to the Property":[23]

Though the essential attributes may be common to the Three, a given attribute considered in its formal reason has greater similarity with the Property of a given Person than with that of another; it may as a consequence fittingly *(conuenienter)* be appropriated to that Person. For example, power evokes a principle: it is also appropriated to the Father, who is the Beginning without a Beginning; wisdom is appropriated to the Son, who proceeds as the Word; goodness to the Holy Spirit, who proceeds as Love having the Good for its object. Thus, on the side of the object, it is the similarity of the appropriated attribute to the property of the Person that supports the fittingness of the appropriation, a fittingness that subsists independently of ourselves.[24]

22. Clearly, this is far from negligible: in the related passages of the commentary on the *Sentences* (*In I Sent.* d. 31 q. 1 a. 2), Thomas speaks of the "usefulness" that we get from this procedure: though through the essential attributes we cannot adequately arrive at the properties of the Persons, we see nonetheless in these appropriated attributes some semblance of the Persons, and that gives us a certain, though imperfect, "manifestation" of the faith; similar to this beginning from images and vestiges of the Trinity that we find in creation, we can propose a certain approach *(uia persuasiua)* to the Persons.

23. *In I Sent.* d. 31 q. 2 a. 1 ad 1; in *ST* Ia q. 39 a. 7, the resemblance also takes first place: Wisdom attributed to the Word by reason of his procession by way of the intellect; in the next place, Thomas also mentions *dissimilarity*: the Power attributed to the Father by contrast to the weakness of human fathers in old age; but we fall here into a more subjective vision of things and it does not appear that Thomas would have pursued this path further.

24. *In I Sent.* d. 31 q. 1 a. 2, slightly modified from Dondaine's translation.

Father Dondaine, who drew our attention to this passage, emphasizes that the resemblance of the attribute can bear either on "the origin in the Person, as is the case for 'power,' or on the characteristic mode of origin, as is the case for 'wisdom' and 'goodness.'. . . It is clear that *Saint Thomas fully and without limit exploits the appropriation of the things of the intellect to the Son, and the things of the will to the Holy Spirit*: this is the powerful framework that organizes and build the whole structure of appropriations in the trinitarian theology that issued from Saint Augustine and Saint Anselm."[25] This scholar's remarks are quite valuable for understanding the Master from Aquino's intentions, in which we discover, with admiration, the fulness of the kingdom, truly limitless, attributed to the Holy Spirit.

Thus, between those who see in appropriation little more than a play on words, a verbal appropriation that does not concern reality itself, and those who would make it say too much in claiming that the appropriated attribute would *only* be convenient or simply *more* so for the Person benefitting from the operation, Thomas, more modestly, sees the foundation of appropriation in "a real affinity between the attribute and the property, prior to the activity of our minds," which are satisfied with recognizing the affinity. Surely, this is little enough, and we are less surprised that theologians who cannot make appropriation say more have a tendency to neglect what it does say and often refuse to have it say anything whatever, reducing it to a play on words. But as Dondaine has remarked, if this may seem a little curt with respect to reason, is it not a sign that reason has reached one of its limits?[26] Thomas remains face-to-face with the Mystery and does not give up struggling to grasp and express it; however modest its results, appropriation remains well-founded and the theologian, in his effort to say the unsayable, may allow it an unquestionably limited but real scope.[27]

25. H.-F. Dondaine, *La Trinité*, vol. 2, note, p. 418 (emphasis added); Dondaine also remarks that Thomas goes much farther on this than Bonaventure, for whom only the appropriations that connote the order of origin are really well-founded.

26. Ibid., pp. 416–20; Dondaine includes a rather remarkable admission of Cajetan's: "In this matter, words themselves fail us; we must, however, indeed *conceive of and work our way into the properties of the Persons* by starting from appropriations" (*In Iam q. 36 a. 4 n. 8*).

27. Thomas never loses sight of the fact that appropriation does not admit any exclusivity; among many others, here is a text that quite clearly confirms P. Dondaine's remark on the distribution of appropriations between those that depend on the will and those that

The Creator Spirit

After the preceding considerations, which seem a little theoretical but whose necessity may be a little better seen now, we are ready to read one of the texts whose existence we have mentioned. It is one of the main passages in the *Summa contra Gentiles* where the principle of appropriation is fully utilized to speak of the Holy Spirit. In line with our usual method, we will quote at length the texts themselves; we will thus see the concrete importance that Thomas gives the Holy Spirit.[28]

In a first chapter, the Master of Aquino labors to bring out the effects that Scripture attributes to the Holy Spirit in connection with the whole creation. From the first, there is the creation itself and we already know why:

The love wherewith God loves His own goodness is the cause of the creation of things. . . . Now the Holy Spirit proceeds through love, the love with which God loves Himself. *Therefore the Holy Spirit is the principle of the creation of things*; and this is said in Psalm 103:30: *Send forth thy spirit and they shall be created.*"[29]

Next, Thomas has to attribute the movement of things to the Holy Spirit; the explanation of this appropriation must also be sought in his mode of procession:

Again, the Holy Spirit proceeds through love, and love is provided with a certain force of impulsion and movement. *The movement that God communicates to*

depend on the intellect: "It is true that all gifts, as gifts, are appropriated to the Holy Spirit, because that person, as Love, has the character of First Gift. *However certain gifts, considered as to their proper and specific bearing, are attributed by appropriation to the Son: precisely those that refer to the intellect.* And in terms of these particular gifts, we speak of a mission of the Son. Thus, Saint Augustine says that the Son is 'invisibly sent to each person when we know and perceive him' (*De Trinitate* IV, 20)," *ST* Ia q. 43 a. 5 ad 1; cf. *De uer.* q. 7 a. 3 ad 3.

28. Notably in SCG IV 20–22, of which an eminent exegete has said that it contains a "resolute and fervent explanation of this 'need' for appropriation in the realm of divine causality" (A. Patfoort, "Morale et pneumatologie," in *Les Clés*, note 6, p. 95, where there is also a welcome sketch of the theory of appropriation); in "Mission divines," note 30, p. 557, the same author rightly emphasizes that there is no reason to be surprised at not finding certain points of trinitarian theology there, but enough are present for our purposes.

29. SCG IV 20, n. 3570. Without delving further into this, we can confirm what I just said about the non-exclusive character of appropriations, for there is no scarcity of places where Thomas attributes the creation to the Father, cf. G. Emery, "Le Père et l'oeuvre trinitaire," in *Ordo sapientiae et amoris*, 85–117, cf. 105 ff.

things must then be properly attributed to the Holy Spirit [This is what is signified in Genesis 1:2, where we see the Spirit 'hovering' over the waters.] Saint Augustine wants us to see in the "waters" the primordial matter over which the Spirit of the Lord is said to hover, not as subject but as principle of movement.[30]

It is because of this fundamental quality of the Holy Spirit that Thomas also attributes to him mastery over the activity of the created universe:

[Indeed], the governance of things by God must be understood as a certain motion by which God directs and puts in motion all beings toward their proper ends. If then impulsion and movement are, by reason of love, the work of the Holy Spirit, *the governance and development of things, is fittingly* (convenienter) *attributed to him.* This is why it says in the Book of Job (33:4): "It is the Spirit that has made me," and in Psalm 142:10, "Your good Spirit leads me on a level path." And since the governance of subjects is the proper activity of a lord, lordship is fittingly *(convenienter)* attributed to the Holy Spirit. "The Spirit is Lord," says the Apostle (2 Cor. 3:17); so too in the Creed: "The Holy Spirit is Lord."[31]

The regular recurrence of the adverb *convenienter* in these passages should be noted. This corresponds exactly with the very thing that allows us to speak of the process of appropriation. To create beings, to give them the power of self-movement, to direct them toward their end are divine prerogatives pure and simple; Thomas does not deny it, but in seeking the *secret* power (he speaks readily of the Spirit's *hidden* origin) which may provide a rationale for all this, he cannot find anything better than Love with which to identify the Holy Spirit. He returns to it when he goes back from movement to the life that it expresses:

It is movement above all that manifests life. . . . If then, because of love, impulsion and movement belong to the Holy Spirit, it is *appropriate* to attribute life to Him. "The Spirit gives life," says Saint John (6:64); so too Ezekiel 37:6: "I will give you the Spirit and you will live." And in the Creed we profess our belief in the Spirit "the giver of life." In addition, in line with the very name Spirit (*Spiritus* = "breath"), it is the vital breath spread from the first in all the members that assures the bodily life of living things.[32]

30. SCG IV 20, n. 3571. 31. Ibid., nn. 3572–73.
32. Ibid., n. 3574.

Life in the Spirit

Up to this point, Thomas has kept to describing the "natural" effects of the Spirit in the work of creation, whether animate or inanimate. It is only in a second chapter that he comes to the rational creature, which he describes, with a wealth of detail and a profusion of scriptural citations much in his usual method, with reference to what is attributable to the Holy Spirit in our connections with God. Using a vocabulary that has now become familiar to us, it might be said that, after having seen what relates to the presence of immensity, we come here to a new mode of presence realized through grace:

Given that the Holy Spirit proceeds by way of love, the love with which God loves Himself . . . , and from the fact that in loving God we are made like that Love, we say that the Holy Spirit is given us by God. That is why the Apostle states: "God's love has been poured into our hearts through the Holy Spirit which has been given to us" (Rom. 5:5).[33]

We can only note once again Thomas's constant return to his point of departure, the procession of the Spirit as Love, which objectively undergirds the appropriations that he is preparing to develop.[34] He first recalls that the divine action does not limit itself to creating what it calls into existence. That certainly supposes that God is everywhere present as the agent is present in his effect:

Wherever there is God's work, He Himself must be found as the author. Given that the charity with which we love God is found in us by the act of the Holy Spirit, it is necessary that the Holy Spirit Himself dwell in us as long as we have charity. That is why the Apostle asks (1 Cor. 3:16): "Do you not know that your are the temple of God and that the Holy Spirit lives in you?" [This first finding implies an immediate corollary:] Given that it is by the Holy Spirit that we becomes friends

---

33. SCG IV 21, n. 3575.

34. But Thomas feels the need here to spell things out further, "for it must be known that everything that is of God in us is related to Him as to its efficient cause and its exemplary cause." God is *efficient cause*, it goes without saying, for nothing that exists comes into being except by His power; *exemplary cause*, as is also quite clear, for every perfection reflects a certain imitation of His essence. That holds equally for the three Persons; it would then be through appropriation that the word of wisdom through which we know God would be attributed to the Son, for He is specially representative of that. "So too, *the love with which we love God is specially representative of the Holy Spirit. That is why we say that charity is specially in us through the Holy Spirit*, even though it is an effect [common] to Father, Son, and Holy Spirit" (n. 3576).

of God and that the beloved being, justly in its status of being loved, is present in him who loves it, it is necessary that the Father and the Son also live in us through the Holy Spirit. The Lord says in John's Gospel (14:23): "We will come to him and we will make our dwelling with him"; similarly (1 John 3:16): "We know that he dwells in us thanks to the Spirit which he has given us."[35]

The first effect in us of the presence of God's gift, which is charity, is then the presence of the Giver Himself, the Holy Spirit, and, along with Him, the whole Trinity which comes to dwell in the soul of the just. When we inquire into the doctrine on grace or the Holy Spirit, it is striking to see how, with Thomas, we open up immediately to the truth, at once elementary and sublime, that the mystics of every age have placed highest in their experience. But Thomas does not stop there, and he forcefully emphasizes a complementary truth:

It is manifest that God loves to the highest degree those whom he has made his friends by the Holy Spirit; only so great a love could confer such a good. . . . Now, *since every beloved being lives in him who loves it, it is therefore necessary that through the Holy Spirit not only does God live in us, but we too live in God.* As Saint John says (1 John 4:16): "He who lives in charity lives in God and God in him," and "it is in this that we know that we live in Him and He in us, thanks to the Spirit that He has given to us."[36]

We will have to return to this text shortly when we deal with the communion of saints and the "affective circumincession" which link all members of the Church. The learned term, with which theology designates the mutual presence of the three Persons in the unutterable unity of the Trinity, may also be used to signify that the ecclesial union realizes at a created level something of the ineffable intra-Trinitarian exchange. In truth, this is the very definition of friendship that Thomas borrows from Aristotle and puts to work in his conception of charity, which allows him to think about this mystery. It is this very same register of charity-friendship that is deeply exploited in order to better grasp everything that this way of seeing things entails:

It belongs to friendship that one friend reveals his secrets to another. Since friendship creates a community of affection and makes, so to speak, one heart from two, what one confides to a friend seems not to leave one's own heart. That is why the

35. SCG IV 21, n. 3576.
36. Ibid., n. 3577.

Lord was able to say to his disciples (John 15:15): "I no longer call you servants, but friends, for everything I have heard from my Father I have made known to you." *Since it is the Holy Spirit that makes us friends of God, it is appropriate to attribute to Him the revelation of the divine mysteries to men.* As the Apostle says (1 Cor. 2:9): "Eye has not seen, nor ear heard, nor has it entered in the heart of man what God has prepared for those who love Him. God has revealed it to us through the Holy Spirit." And since it is beginning with what he knows that man can speak, *it is appropriate then to attribute to the Holy Spirit [the fact that] man can speak of the divine mysteries.* . . . As the Creed says with reference to the Holy Spirit, "He has spoken through the prophets."[37]

In employing little by little all the appropriate elements that go along with the friendship that God maintains with us through the Holy Spirit, we have thus passed from the revelation of divine intimacy to its transmission to the greatest number possible. Indeed, Thomas can quote several passages from the Bible that attribute the inspiration of the prophets and the sacred writers to the Spirit, and it is one of the main features of his teachings on prophecy that the prophetic message must necessarily be preceded by an inward experience in which the prophet receives the revelation of what he must transmit.[38]

This last fact expresses a sort of general law that is applied to every declaration of the Word, whoever the speaker may be: "The preacher must leave the secrecy of contemplation for the public work of preaching. Indeed, he must first draw from contemplation what he must later pour forth in preaching." This brief excerpt, drawn from one of Friar Thomas's homilies, faithfully reflects one of his chief approaches, which we also find in the well-known passage from the *Summa* where he described his ideal of the Dominican friar-preacher:

The active life which derives from the fulness of contemplation, as is the case in teaching and preaching . . . is preferable to contemplation alone. Just as it is better to illuminate than solely to shine, thus is it preferable to transmit to others what has been contemplated instead of merely contemplating.[39]

37. Ibid., n. 3578.
38. Cf. ST IIa IIae qq. 171–74 (especially q. 171 aa. 1–2 and q. 173 a. 2), with the studies by J.-P. Torrell, "Le traité de la prophétie de S. Thomas d'Aquin et la théologie de la révélation," *ST* 37 (1990): 171–95, reprinted in *Recherches sur la théorie de la prophétie au Moyen Age*, 205–29, and, in a less technical vein, "Révélation et expérience (bis)," *FZPT* 27 (1980): 383–400, reprinted in the same volume, 101–18.
39. ST IIa IIae q. 188 a. 6. The preceding quotation is taken from the sermon *Exiit qui seminat*. For a commentary on this sermon, see J.-P. Torrell, "Le semeur est sorti pour

We cannot tarry longer on these texts without departing too much from the *Contra Gentiles*, but it was important to see how, here and there, we meet with a constant movement, whose origin lies in an intimate communion of life with the Holy Spirit. If we return now to our reading, we must restate how Thomas develops his appeal to our experience of friendship: for him, it is impossible for it to remain at the level of mutual confidences, "kind words," we might dare to say:

> Friendship does not have as its sole property making its secrets known to the friend because of the unity of affection *(propter unitatem affectus)*; that same unity demands that we communicate to the friend what we possess. Since the friend is to a man "another self," it is necessary to come to his aid as to oneself in giving him everything one has. Whence this definition of friendship: "To will and to realize the good of his friend," which is found in 1 John 3:17: "But if anyone has the world's goods and sees his brother in need, yet closes his heart to all compassion, how does God's love abide in him?" This is proven to the highest degree in God, for whom to will is to do; and that is why *it is appropriate to say that all the gifts of God are given us by the Holy Spirit.*[40]

We noted in passing some of the characteristic expressions of Aristotle's doctrine,[41] which Friar Thomas eagerly adopts when he speaks of God's love for us. We will encounter this again in his teaching on the communion of saints. When he begins to go into detail about the goods proper to God, which he must communicate to us because of the frienship he has for us, Thomas mentions without hesitation and in the first instance "the beatitude of divine fruition, proper to God by his nature":

> For man to come to beatitude, he first needs to make himself conform to God thanks to certain spiritual qualities, that he must then act in accord with it, and it is thus that he arrives at beatitude. *Now the spiritual gifts come to us through the Holy Spirit; it is through Him that we are first configured to God, through Him again we are rendered ready to act well, and through Him the way to beatitude is always open to us.* The three stages evoked by the Apostle (2 Cor. 1:21–22): "It is God

---

semer. L'image du Christ prêcheur chez frère Thomas d'Aquin," *La Vie spirituelle* 147 (1993): 657–70.

40. *SCG* IV 21, n. 3579.

41. Cf. *Nicomachean Ethics* IX, 4 (1166a), and "Among brothers and friends, everything is common," ibid., VIII, 11 (1159b32), which Thomas comments on thus: "We see that among brothers and friends thus joined, all things are common: house, table, etc. . . . From this point of view, certain friendships are greater than others, according as the friends more or less hold things in common," *Sententia libri Ethicorum* (*In Ethic.*) VIII, lect. 9, Leonine, vol. 47, 2, pp. 472–73.

who has given us *unction*, who has stamped us with his *seal*, and has put in our hearts the *pledge* of his Spirit"; thus also Ephesians (1:13): "You have been marked with the *seal* of the Holy Spirit, *pledge* of our inheritance. The seal *(signatio)* is connected, it would appear, to the resemblance in configuration; unction *(unctio)* with man's aptitude with respect to the works of perfection; the pledge *(pignus)* with the hope that orients us toward the heavenly heritage, perfect beatitude.[42]

Every gift comes to us from the Spirit. We can generalize this quite honestly, for nothing is left outside his influence: through him we are configured, through him we are also made able, through him the way is always open to us. The emphasis is too insistent not to be deeply meaningful. If we also recall the way in which the Master of Aquino speaks of beatitude as the spiritual place where the man-image reaches his perfect similarity to the divine Exemplar, and if we remind ourselves further of the role that he gives to the final end in human life and in the organization of his whole theology, we see immediately that he could not have said anything stronger about the presence of the Holy Spirit in the Christian life. Many other examples will confirm this.

Besides this definite and perfect good of beatitude, that will not be allowed us, however, until the end of our earthly journey, the good will that God bears us has spurred him to adopt us as sons, in such a way as to guarantee us, so to speak, the certainty of his inheritance. This too is attributable to the Holy Spirit since, according to Romans 8:15, we have received "the Spirit of adoption which cries out in us: Abba."[43] Though brief, this note is repeated elsewhere with a meaningful precision for the trinitarian appropriation: "Though adoption is common to the whole Trinity, it is however appropriated to the Father as to its author, to the Son as to its example, *to the Holy Spirit as to the one who impresses upon us the resemblance to that example.*"[44]

Among the gifts that we receive from the Spirit, Thomas mentions in

---

42. *SCG* IV 21, n. 3580.
43. Ibid., n. 3581.
44. *ST* IIIa q. 23 a. 2 ad 3. See on this passage some pages by É. Bailleux, "Le cycle des missions trinitaires d'après saint Thomas," *RT* 63 (1963): 166–92, cf. 186–92. This theme of adoption, evoked here in passing, occupies an important place in Thomas's work, as has been well demonstrated by L. Somme, *Fils adoptifs de Dieu par Jésus Christ: La filiation divine par adoption dans la théologie de saint Thomas d'Aquin* (Paris, 1997); cf. C. Bermudez, "Hijos de Dios por la gracia en los comentarios de Santo Tomás a las cartas paulinas," *ST* 45 (1992): 78–89.

the last place the remission of sins—rather curiously, for that seems to us a preliminary. But the reason for this is the same as for everything that went before: by the very fact that there is friendship between two beings, every offense that might bring him harm is discarded: "Love covers all faults" (Prov. 10:12):

> Since it is the Holy Spirit that constitutes us as friends of God, it is normal then that it would be through Him that God forgives our sins. That is why the Lord said to his disciples: "Receive the Holy Spirit; whose sins you shall forgive will be forgiven them." And in Saint Matthew (12:31), pardon for sins is denied to those who blaspheme against the Holy Spirit, for they do not have in them that by which man can obtain pardon for his sins. From this it also comes that we say of the Holy Spirit that he renews us, that he purifies us, that he washes us. . . .[45]

We might believe that this enumeration reviews all the gifts that we receive from the Holy Spirit. That is not Thomas's opinion. In fact, he has only arranged—as he himself says at the beginning of the next chapter—some texts concerning the role that Scripture has the Holy Spirit play in the re-creating action of God toward us. It remains for us to see now with him how the Holy Spirit leads us in our return toward God.

Come to the Father

We will have to point out more than once the outlines of spiritual itineraries that Thomas proposes here and there. They remain in outline form because the purpose of the *Summa Theologiae*—and even more strongly that of other less important works—does not allow him to linger over them; nevertheless they are present.[46] Another chapter of the *Summa contra Gentiles* proposes things of interest in that it further develops the presence of the Holy Spirit. We will speak shortly about the Holy Spirit as a structural presence in the movement of return of the creature to God; as a preliminary, here is a fine illustration:

> In friendship, it is most fitting to live in intimacy with one's friend. Now, man's friendship with God occurs in the contemplation of God, as the Apostle says to the Philippians (3:20): "Our city is found in the heavens." *Given that it is the Holy Spirit who renders us friends of God, it is normal that it would be he who constitutes us as contemplators of God.* That is why the Apostle also says (2 Cor. 3:18) "As for us, all of us who contemplate with unveiled face the glory of God, are being

45. SCG IV 21, n. 3582.
46. Cf. my chapter 14, "The Way to God."

changed from light to light into that very image, as through the Spirit of the Lord."[47]

We easily understand the primary place of contemplation at the beginning of the spiritual itinerary. Though beatitude is the ultimate end, it is important to have our eyes fixed on it from the outset to be sure to guide ourselves in the right direction. It is only thus, besides, that something of the fundamental requirement of friendship will take place: to live with the Friend, for truly the contemplative life is meant to be an anticipation here below of the intimacy that will be perfect only in beatitude, but that even in the fragile and threatening conditions of this earth is already rich in spiritual joy:

It is characteristic of friendship to rejoice in the presence of the friend, to find joy in his words and gestures, to seek comfort in him in all disturbances; in moments of sadness, too, we seek a refuge and consolation especially among friends. Now, as we have just said, *it is the Holy Spirit who makes us friends of God and makes him dwell in us and we in him; it is normal then that it would be through the Holy Spirit that God's joy and consolation come to us before every earthly adversity and assault.* Furthermore, the Psalm (50:14) says: "Give me the joy of your salvation and let your generous Spirit strengthen me." Saint Paul (Rom. 14:17) states that "the Kingdom of God is justice, peace, and joy in the Holy Spirit." . . . And the Lord speaks of the Holy Spirit as being the "Paraclete," which is to say the Comforter (John 14:26).[48]

We clearly come here upon a realm that goes far beyond the psychological level where our joys, even spiritual joys, remain sometimes impure and self-interested and frequently mixed with sadness and various troubles. Thomas is thinking without a doubt of that "peace of God," which Saint Paul speaks of, which "surpasses all understanding" (Phil. 4:7). But it is still quite striking to see the constancy with which he returns to the theme of friendship to explain the action of the Spirit in the believer. So far as we can guess, Thomas did not have a merely bookish acquaintance with friendship, and his expressions allow us to sense a direct experience and a heart able to commiserate.[49] Nor would it be going too far to see in the rich way he describes the Spirit's role an echo of his own lived experience. Not only is it the Spirit who gives us the possibility of living in God's

47. SCG IV 22, n. 3585.
48. Ibid., n. 3586.
49. Cf. my Saint Thomas Aquinas, p. 283.

presence loved above everything, but we also owe to the Spirit the joy that friends find in this mutual presence. However, in the case of friendship with God, we also find man's sense of a creature's absolute dependence on his creator, which will translate conformity of wills into loving obedience:

Another property of friendship is to harmonize the will with that of a friend. Now, God's will is manifested to us through his commandments. It pertains then to the love we have for God to follow his commandments: "If you love me, keep my commandments" (John 14:15). *Since it is the Holy Spirit who makes us friends of God, it is also he who spurs us, so to speak, to follow God's commandments*, according to the saying of the Apostle (Rom. 8:14): "They are sons of God who are moved by the Spirit of God."[50]

Given that the harmony of wills cannot occur concretely except by a submission of man's will to God's and that, therefore, it goes in one direction, Thomas also is careful to prevent any possible equivocation: This submission has nothing in common with that of a slave:

We must, however, remark that the sons of God are not moved by the Holy Spirit as slaves are, but indeed as free men. Given that the free man is "he who is master of himself" (Aristotle), we freely do what we achieve on our own, which is to say, through our will. What we might do against our will is not done freely, but slavishly executed [whatever might be the way in which the will is constrained]. *The Holy Spirit, in making us friends of God, inclines us to act in such a way that our action is voluntary. Sons of God that we are, the Holy Spirit gives us the means to act freely, out of love, and not slavishly, out of fear.* Furthermore, as the Apostle well says (Rom. 8:15): "It is not a spirit of servitude that you have received, to live again in fear, but the Spirit of adoption as sons."[51]

This text powerfully expresses one of Thomas's master ideas; he must have meditated for a long time on chapter 8 of the Epistle to the Romans, and his commentary is one of the most beautiful in all his work about the Holy Spirit. But we find the same thing in his preaching.[52] Without ques-

---

50. Ibid., n. 3587.
51. Ibid., n. 3588.
52. We will see more in the sermon *Emitte Spiritum*, but I might quote here the preaching on the commandments: "Between the law of fear and the law of love there is a two-fold difference. The first is that the law of fear makes slaves of those who observe it, while the law of love makes them free men; indeed, whoever acts only out of fear acts like a slave, but he who acts out of love acts like a son. That is why the apostle says: 'Where there is the Spirit of the Lord, there is liberty'." *Collationes in decem preceptis (De decem preceptis)* I, ed.

tion, in an age when servitude was a still living, sociological reality, Friar Thomas did not see in it, as Saint Paul did, a good analogy to bring out something of the greatness of Christ's faithful, free in the glorious liberty of the children of God.

In itself, the will is turned toward what is truly good. If it is turned away by passion, bad habit, or disposition from what is the true good, to consider the natural order of the will, one acts in servile fashion if one is pushed by an external agent. If, on the contrary, we look at the act of the will, of the will as inclined toward an apparent good, a man acts freely in following a passion or bad habit; he would act slavishly, on the contrary, if in the same disposition of the will, he abstained from doing what he wished out of fear of a law that forbids it. *The Holy Spirit inclines our will through love toward the true good to which the will is naturally oriented; he also delivers us as much from the slavery that makes us act, as slaves of passion and followers of sin, against the orientation of our will, as from the slavishness that makes us act according to law, against the movement of our will, not indeed as friends but as slaves.* "Where there is the Spirit of the Lord, there is liberty" (2 Cor. 3:17); "If you are under the guidance of the Spirit, you are no longer under the law" (Gal. 5:18). This is why we still say of the Holy Spirit that he mortifies the works of the flesh: *through His love, the Holy Spirit orients us toward the true good from which the passions of the flesh turn us.* According to the saying of Romans 8:13: "If, by the Spirit, you mortify the deeds of the flesh, you will live."[53]

Our reading of the *Summa contra Gentiles* ends provisionally with this point of rest, or better this opening, this renewed invitation to choose life. Seeking to "prove" the fecundity of the theory of appropriation, we have been able to show that it allows us to justify and organize what we learn in Scripture about the Third Person of the Trinity into a theological construct. Thomas's teaching on this subject does not stop here, but we already know enough of it to understand to what extent the Spirit is universally present and at work in our history. To appropriate to the Holy Spirit the government of beings and their vivification—"that is, in brief . . . the whole history of the world and the Church"—is to acknowledge in the Spirit "the privilege of appearing as the divine Person closest to the Creation, especially to those who feel drawn by the movement of charity."[54]

J.-P. Torrell, *RSPT* 69 (1985): p. 25, lines 28–52; cf. *De decem preceptis* III, p. 29, line 43: *Caritas facit liberum et amicum.*

53. SCG IV 22, nn. 3589–90.

54. A. Patfoort, *Les Clés*, 96.

Preaching the Holy Spirit

Although it is already perfectly accessible, this teaching on the Holy Spirit was not a mere theological thesis topic; Thomas speaks about it quite volubly in his preaching. We already used in passing his homelies on the Credo. But to better grasp the concrete form that this could take, we also have a beautiful sermon that gives a more precise echo.

This text, preached on a Pentecost, is a precious witness of the rare cases in which, besides the morning preaching, we have the second part, given at Vespers;[55] which is to say that it gives us a rather full account. Unfortunately, it is still unpublished. We have to content ourselves, therefore, with a brief summary.[56] It will be enough to recognize here many themes already encountered in this chapter and, in spite of the difference in genres, a deep family resemblance.

The exordium sets the tone: "We must speak today of him without whom no one can speak properly, but who gives and can give eloquent speech to anyone."[57] Thomas then presents the Spirit as the source of all life, all movement, all sanctity. The parallel with Acts 17:28 comes to mind: *in Him, we have life, movement, and being*. Thomas adds sanctity here for, he explains, in giving all this, the Spirit cannot help moving toward the hidden source from which he proceeds, God himself. But to speak of the Creator Spirit is not merely to evoke the first production of things in their being in nature. We must also think about re-creation in the order of grace. This work of re-creation bears a fourfold aspect: the grace of charity which gives life to the soul; the wisdom of the knowledge that inclines the heart to assent and the carrying out of what it has understood; the peaceful harmony through which the subject lives in harmony with himself, others, and God; the constant firmness that excludes all fear or cowardice in the Christian struggle.

The Spirit is equally a renewer. Here, too, the effects of this renewal can be seen from a fourfold perspective: through grace, which purifies the soul from the old decay of sin and deeply renews it; through progress in

---

55. For details about Saint Thomas's preaching, see my *Saint Thomas Aquinas*, 69–74, and more fully, "La pratique pastorale," 213–45.

56. The sermon is entitled *Emitte Spiritum*, which P. Bataillon is preparing for the Leonine edition. He has kindly provided me with the text.

57. "Loquendum est de eo sine quo nullus recte loqui potest et qui omnes habundanter loqui potest facere uel facit."

justice, because instead of succumbing to weariness in daily struggles, man finds new powers in the testimony of his conscience; through illuminating wisdom, for the more he knows God, the more the Christian finds himself renewed; Christ is the New Man, for his conception, birth, Passion, Resurrection, and Ascension are new; and the fourth renewal is, finally, that of achieved glory, when our body will be wholly freed from the "old things" of sin and suffering. The Holy Spirit is the pledge of that achievement and he leads us into the heavenly inheritance.

This brief summary does not contain the biblical quotations or allusions strewn throughout the argument. No doubt, the reader will have recognized them, but we should point out a final trait: this part of Thomas's discourse very much lends itself to perceiving the orator's art. Thus, when he states that grace liberates from the old decay of sin, he ask his audience, whence comes this novelty? The response suggests itself: from the Holy Spirit. Then he continues: grace also allows progress in justice. Who then is the author of this progress? The Holy Spirit. This proceeding by question and answer is found no fewer than seven times in the sermon. We might think it affected, but it is nothing of the sort. On the contrary, it introduces a very interesting element and shows itself wholly suited to suggesting to the hearers the omnipresence of the Spirit in the Christian life.[58]

As a further proof of this universal and constant presence of the Spirit, we might add here a very beautiful homily for All Saint's Day, which situates the believer in the heart of the ecclesial communion. But it will be better to save it for its proper place in the next chapter. Nothing, obviously, can replace the reading of the texts themselves and, still less, listening to the spoken words. The echoes of both that we have reproduced here at least give us a basic idea of what they may have been like. It still remains for us to discover how the theologian takes into account in his teaching on the Church what his discourse as preacher implies.

---

58. My purpose here is not to analyze Thomas's oratorical art, but perhaps it will be of use to the reader to have this from someone who knows the matter deeply: "The authentic sermons of Saint Thomas are of uneven value; some do not exceed the average, otherwise decent enough, of the preaching in the period; others are of high quality and, without ranking their author among the great preachers of the century, assure him an entirely honorable place with them, and are not unworthy of his genius," L.-J. Bataillon, "Un sermon de saint Thomas sur la parabole du festin," *RSPT* 58 (1974): 451–56, cf. 451.

⁓

CHAPTER VIII

The Heart of the Church

The preceding chapter allowed us to meet with the Holy Sprit in his presence "on a textual level," if one may put it that way. Like primroses in spring, he arises everywhere in every possible situation. At each step, he is called forth as the One who responds completely. But at that level, Thomas does little more than put in order what he learned from the Bible, and that is only a part of his task as theologian. If we wish to grasp in greater depth the reason for the Spirit's universal and constant presence, we must return with Thomas to the central intuitions that govern his theological synthesis. We then discover that it is in the "definition" of the Holy Spirit as Love, and in His specific position at the heart of the Trinitarian communion, that we find the explanation of the role that He plays in the whole of Creation—and in its return "within the Church" toward the Divine Source whence it came forth.

Loved with the Love with Which God Is Loved

Once again the concept of procession will be particularly relevant. We recall that Thomas gets this technical term from the Trinitarian theology of the New Testament itself: "The Spirit of truth that *proceeds* from the Father."[1] In itself, he explains, "the procession of the divine persons only expresses, properly speaking, the coming forth from the first principle," and it says nothing as to the terminus of the movement of the Person who proceeds. But in the case of the Holy Spirit, given the particular way that

---

1. Cf. John 15:26: "Spiritum ueritatis qui a Patre *procedit.*"

He proceeds, which is to say as Love, the procession cannot help implying its end. Indeed, we cannot conceive of a love without a beloved object. *The procession of the Holy Spirit thus has its own particularity in that it tends toward another as toward its object, which is to say toward the beloved being.* That established, Thomas can complete the parallel between the Son and the Spirit in light of a principle that he recalls rather often:

> *The eternal processions of the persons are the cause and reason for the entire production of creatures.* Thus the generation of the Son is the reason for the entire production of the creatures, as the Father is said to have done all things through His Son. In the same way, it is necessary that the Father's Love directed toward the Son as to its object, would be the reason by which God bestows each of love's effects on the creature. *That is why the Holy Spirit, who is the Love by which the Father loves the Son, is also the Love by which He loves the creature and imparts to it His perfection.*[2]

For anyone who can recognize the weight of these words, this statement possesses something disconcerting, even dizzying, and we must be cautious not to weaken it through a misguided commentary. But if we reflect with Thomas on the mystery of God and His Creation, it states something indisputable. It is not we who have loved God, it is He who has loved us first. Since nothing outside Him can cause Him to create the world or to take an interest in it, that motivation must be found within God Himself: the Love alone with which the Father loves the Son and the Son the Father, can then account for this "exit" of God from Himself; we are loved with the love with which God loves Himself.

We cannot exhaustively examine this truth in a few words,[3] but it is already clear that it was impossible for Thomas not to speak in strong terms about the Holy Spirit and his place in the world and the Faith. We are once more in the heart of Trinitarian theology and, while it is necessary to explain the terms, the doctrine is too beautiful and deep not to be worth the effort. For we find that this way of understanding the Holy Spirit will allow us to speak of God in a new way, in fact in various new ways. To

---

2. *In I Sent.* d. 14 q. 1 a. 1.

3. Thomas repeats this point in *ST* Ia q. 37 a. 2; see also *In I Sent.* d. 32 q. 1 a. 3; *De pot.* q. 9 a. 9 ad 13; he also explains it with the help of everyday experience: "*The first gift that we grant to a beloved person is the love itself that makes us wish him well.* Thus love constitutes the first gift by virtue of which are given all the other gifts that we offer him. *Thus, since the Holy Spirit proceeds as Love, He proceeds in His capacity as first Gift*" (*ST* Ia q. 38 a. 2).

grasp this, it is enough to expound more deeply what is implied in the idea of the procession of love:

We can then consider the procession of that Love in two ways: either as it tends toward an eternal object and thus concerns *eternal procession*; or as it proceeds as Love toward a created object, inasmuch as through this Love God grants something to the creature and we then speak of *temporal procession*. Through the newness of what is granted, indeed, a new relation of the creature to God arises, and it is by way of that new relation that God can be named with a new name.[4]

This final remark also holds in a general way for everything that is said of God temporally. God is Father, Son, and Holy Spirit from all eternity by very virtue of the supereminent fertility of the intra-divine life. "Creator," however, can only be in connection to a creation. Similarly, it is in connection with us that we say of the Son that He is "Savior," or of the Holy Spirit that He is "Lord and Giver of life" (to use the words of the Creed). What then is the temporal effect of God's activity, and more particularly of the Holy Spirit, beginning with the new relationship of the creature to the Creator that arises? It is clearly grace that, in Thomas's eyes, establishes a connection so direct and special with the Holy Spirit that he calls it almost constantly "the grace *of the Holy Spirit*."[5]

Since it is by grace that the Spirit acts in the world, it is also then in grace that the final reason is found for his structural presence in Friar Thomas's theology. To grasp this, it is sufficient to return once more to the great passage in the *Commentary on the Sentences* from which we have taken our cue. We recall the governing idea: "Since all things return, as to their end, to the Principle from which they issued, we must expect that this return toward the end reaches completion according to the same

---

4. *In I Sent.* d. 14 q. 1 a. 1; the formulation there, which is slightly abstract, becomes more concrete in the *In Ioannem XV*, 26, lect. 7, n. 2061: "Third, [John] speaks of the two-fold procession of the Holy Spirit, first of his *temporal procession* when he says: 'The Paraclete whom I will send to you from the Father.' We must understand that when we say of the Holy Spirit that He is sent, this does not mean as in a change of place, since he 'fills the whole universe' (Wisd. 1:7), *but it is because He begins to live in a new way in those whom He makes the Temple of God.*"

5. According to the *Index thomisticus*, the expression *gratia Spiritus Sancti* appears 158 times in Thomas's works. It is enough to quote here the most celebrated passage: "What is most important in the new law, the thing in which its whole force consists, is the grace of the Holy Spirit given through Faith in Christ. The new law consists thus principally in the grace itself of the Holy Spirit granted to the faithful in Christ" (*ST* Ia IIae q. 106 a. 1). We will return more fully to this text in the following chapter.

causes as its exit from the Principle." In this vast fresco of the circular movement that Thomas loves to put before our eyes, Thomas states something that is for him a matter of fact: *"Just as we have been created through the Son and through the Holy Spirit, just so is it through them that we are united to our final end."* This principle is no less operative when it is a matter of the Holy Spirit than it was in the case of the Incarnate Word. The reason is as beautiful as it is deep: Since it is in the Holy Spirit and through Him that the Father and the Son love each other and love creatures, it is also in Him and through Him that their movement of return toward the Father is completed. In more technical terms, the Spirit is the *ratio* according to which God grants creatures all the effects of His love, the *ratio*, that is to say, at once the model and the cause, and thus too the explanatory reason. The creature's movement of return toward the Father begins only with the gift of sanctifying grace, through the gift of the Holy Spirit, and it clearly reaches its end under the Spirit's guidance.[6] In fact, we can say with complete certitude, nothing in the universe of nature or of grace escapes Him: absolutely unique, He fills all things.[7] That this is by appropriation takes nothing away from the force of this conclusion, but we must try to deepen still further what it brings to the Christian life.

The Grace of the Holy Spirit

When Saint Thomas states that we are loved with the Love with which God loves Himself, he is echoing a theological tradition originating in Saint Augustine.[8] But the Master of the *Sentences* had mixed in a personal interpretation with which the thirteenth century philosophers are at variance, and Thomas with them. It is worth the trouble to see where the debate lies, for it is far from being a mere academic exercise. Peter Lombard taught that since the Holy Spirit is the Love of the Father and Son, "it is through that love that they love one another and that they love us." Thomas has no trouble accepting this teaching and he will hold firmly to it throughout his career. But he does have some difficulties in admitting what follows in Lombard: *"and it is also He* [i.e., the Holy Spirit] *who is the love poured forth into our hearts so that we may love God and neigh-*

---

6. *In I Sent.* d. 14 q. 2 a. 2.

7. *In III Sent.* , d. 13 q. 2 a. 2 qc. 2 ad 1: "Unus numero omnes replet": it is difficult not to be reminded of the ancient liturgy for Pentecost: *Spiritus Domini repleuit orbem terrarum* (Wisd. 1:7) which Thomas cites: *In II Sent.* Pro.; SCG IV 17.

8. Cf. *De Trinitate* VIII, 7, 10 and XV, 19, 37 (BA 16, 58–60 and 522–24).

bor."[9] For Peter Lombard, charity is thus an uncreated reality, the very person of the Holy Spirit in us who moves our free will to love and act well.

At first sight, the thesis is grandiose: what is more simple and beautiful than that direct and multiform action of the Holy Spirit in the heart of believers? Thomas is not satisfied with this position, however, and he labors to distinguish between charity in its source, which is indeed the Holy Spirit, the absolutely first and uncreated Gift, and charity in us, a gift that we receive from the Spirit, and which is a created reality.[10] He will soon after say the same about grace and, each time he comes upon the question again, he will put grace before charity and will not cease reaffirming the created character of the one and the other.[11]

How, then, does Thomas establish the created character of grace? In the simplest way possible, by drawing a parallel between the knowledge that God has of beings and the love that He bears toward them on the one hand, and the knowledge and love that we have toward them on the other. In our case, it is already existing things that we know and that lie at the origins of our knowing; in God's case, we have the contrary: He does not know things because they are, but they are because he knows them. God's knowing is a realizing power, it brings things into existence. In the case not only of knowledge, but of love, we need a similar mode of reasoning: our love for something that exists is caused by its goodness (real or supposed, we love only what seems to us lovable). For God, it is again the contrary: it is His love that creates the goodness of beings and things. Thus, when we say that God loves a being, this means that in what He loves he causes an effect derivative from Divine Love Itself.

If we now turn to the gift of grace, we certainly mean that God is at work, and more precisely the Holy Spirit, uncreated reality. But when a

---

9. Peter Lombard, *Sententiae* d. 17 c. 6 (ed. I. Brady, vol. 1, p. 148): ". . . Spiritus Sanctus caritas est Patris et Filii, qua se invicem diligunt et nos, *et ipse idem est caritas quae diffunditur in cordibus nostris ad diligendum Deum et proximum*", the same thesis is restated in *Sententiae* d. 27 c. 5 (ibid., p. 484): *caritas est Spiritus Sanctus.*

10. *In I Sent.* d. 17 q. 1 a. 1.

11. Cf., for example, *In II Sent.* d. 26 q. 1 a. 1; *De uer.* q. 27 aa. 1–2 (grace and charity); ST Ia IIae q. 110 a. 1 (grace); ST IIa IIae q. 23 a. 2 (charity). Beginning with the *De ueritate*, Thomas, master of his order of exposition (which was not the case in the commentary on the *Sentences*) speaks of grace before speaking of charity. This is understandable since grace qualifies the soul in its essence, in making of it a radical principle of action in this supernatural realm—after the way of our nature in the natural realm (entitative habitus in his language)—while charity qualifies the will as a power of the soul—(operative habitus in the scholastic language).

person receives the gift of grace which he did not have earlier, this does not mean that it occurs through a change in the Holy Spirit himself. Rather, the person himself changes under the effect of the Spirit's action. When we say, then, that the Holy Spirit is given to someone, it means that this creature received the gift of God's love that he did not previously have. This gift is necessarily a created reality freely given by God.

We will understand the necessarily created character of this gift even better if we remember the saying of Saint John that underlies the reasoning: "God first loved us."[12] God's love for us is, thus, not the result of our own lovableness. Thomas simply adds: God, who has first loved us, also gives us what enables us to love Him. Here we come to the heart of his thesis as well as of the problem to be resolved. It is necessary that the creature be made proportionate to the end to which God calls him. That end, as we know, is blessedness, the enjoyment of God in a perfect communion of knowledge and love. By definition, this happiness is entirely disproportionate to man's powers; it is co-natural only to God. It is necessary thus that God give man not only something by which he will be able *to act* with this end in view and have his desire inclined toward it, but also something by which the *nature* of man itself will be elevated to the level of this end.[13]

For a creature thus superelevated to the very life of God, beatitude will become co-natural, so to speak. It is quite exactly for this that grace is given: to put the creature at the level of his supernatural end, to make of him a supernaturalized creature who will able to be a principle of action in this new realm. To that henceforth "divinized" nature, God also grants the gift of charity and the other theological virtues which enable man, through his intelligence and will thus supernaturalized, to act effectively in this order, which would remain inaccessible to him without this primordial gift. We cannot conclude from this, however, that Thomas rejects the partial truth that Peter Lombard's thesis contains. Quite the opposite!

It is necessary that there should be in us a habitus of charity that may be the formal principle of the act of charity. *However, this does not exclude that the Holy*

---

12. Cf. 1 John 4:10 and 19. Thomas eagerly returns to these verses, as for example in the *In Ioannem XIV*, 15, lect. 4, n. 1909: "No one can love God without having the Holy Spirit: we do not anticipate God's grace, it is grace that precedes us: 'He loved us first.' Thus, the apostles received the Holy Spirit a first time in order to love God and obey His commandments. But for them to receive it in much greater fullness, it was necessary for them to use to their profit in love and obedience this first gift received from Him."

13. Thomas explains this very clearly in *De uer.* q. 27 a. 2; cf. *ST* Ia IIae q. 110 a. 3.

Spirit, who is uncreated charity, may be present in the man who possesses charity. It is He who moves the soul to the act of charity, in the way in which God moves all things to their act, to which they are meanwhile inclined by virtue of their proper form. From this it follows that "He disposes all things with sweetness" (*suaviter*, Wis. 8:1) for He gives to all things the forms and virtues that incline them toward that to which He moves them, such that *they tend there not by force, but spontaneously.*[14]

We must remember this passage when in the following chapter we encounter the question about the connections between law and liberty. For Thomas, there is no problem, because the man in whom the Holy Spirit dwells cannot help freely loving what he understands to be the will of God. But before turning to that, we must look further into another aspect of the discussion raised by Peter Lombard's thesis. Far from being a curiosity of intellectual history, on the contrary, it is ever-living in orthodox theology.[15]

In this same context, Thomas indeed emphasizes another point, sometimes poorly understood: in connection with man's nature, grace qualifies the soul in the manner of an accidental quality.[16] Though at first sight this thesis is surprising, it is nonetheless of capital importance. It does not mean that it is accidental for a person to have grace—in the economy of salvation there is no success possible without it—but it does say quite simply that grace does not enter into the definition of humanity. Otherwise, in losing grace we would cease to be human. Or anyone who did not have grace would not really be a human being. If we try to think otherwise, saying that God just does not refuse to give grace, it would be enough to remember that, under these conditions, God Himself would be *obligated* to act in that way, and that then grace itself would no longer be freely given.

This way of speaking of grace as an accident allows us another important qualification. The accident is not properly speaking created, because it has no existence by itself; it borrows its being from the reality that it qualifies. There are white walls or men, but whiteness in itself does not exist. It is not then the accident that appears in existence, but a substance modified by the accident of whiteness which begins to exist according to this new determination. Grace lends itself to the same observation; out-

14. *Quaestiones disputatae De virtutibus; Quaestio diputata De caritate* (q. 2) a. 1.

15. Cf. J. Meyendorff, *Introduction à l'étude de Grégoire Palamas* (Paris 1959), and the important discussion by Charles Journet, "Palamisme et thomisme," *RT* 60 (1960): 429–62.

16. Cf. *ST* Ia IIae q. 110 a. 2, and parallels elsewhere.

side of its source, God, it does not exist in a separate state. What exists are persons who have received this gift that we call grace and who live thereafter according to that new quality. That is why to speak of grace as a created reality is to use a shorthand that may be deceiving. Thomas, who does not hesitate to use the expression, does so only after having recalled the way in which an accident exists in a subject, and then he adds a central qualification that he links directly with Saint Paul's thought:

Grace can be said to be created by the fact that men, relative to it, are created, that is *constituted in new being*; and they are so *ex nihilo* ["out of nothing," in the received and proper formula for qualifying the first creation], which is to say without any merit on their part, as is said in Ephesians (2:10): "Created in Christ Jesus for good works."[17]

The somewhat technical nature of this discussion should not lead us into error; we are here at the heart of several absolutely central theses of Thomas's thought, and of Christian thought, to put it bluntly. Thomas rejects Lombard's solution because, first, it leads to an absurdity. For the Holy Spirit to perform our act of charity in us, it would be necessary for our will to be united to his in the same way that Christ's human will was united to the divine will of the Word. In other words, we would need to be united to him with a union according to the person, a hypostatic union.[18]

Thomas does not say as much here, but the point is clear in this perspective: if it is the Holy Spirit who acts in our place, it is no longer we who act; the human subject is telescoped. We would not have mastery over our acts of charity, nor their liberty, nor their merit.[19] In fact, we would be excluded from the act of love of God and neighbor; we would only be the theater in which they occurred. For us to truly take part in it, for us to be in our modest way the free and meritorious cause, it is necessary that God give us its possibility, which is to say that He grants us a principle of action connatural with us and our powers of knowing, doing, and loving. Created grace and the virtues that accompany it respond to that.

---

17. *ST* Ia IIae q. 110 a. 2 ad 3: in other words, we could say that grace is created in the *moral sense*, which is to say that it is given without anything preceding in its order, but not in the strict *metaphysical sense*, where only subsistents are created, not their accidents. This distinction allows, among other things, justifying the instrumentality of Christ's humanity and the sacraments in the production of grace, for the strict notion of creation does not allow for intermediaries: creating belongs to God alone.

18. Cf. *In I Sent.* d. 17 q. 1 a. 1.

19. Cf. *ST* Ia IIae q. 114.

Without going further into this here, for we will have to return to the point at greater length, this position on the created character of grace will have immediate and profound repercussions when we have to speak of the Christian's engagement with the world. The mediation of created grace is, so to speak, the means God found for respecting the autonomy of our nature and the consistency of the things of this world. Indeed, the "accidental" character of grace does not modify the structure of reality in its own order; the realities of this world remain what they were and keep their own finality. Nevertheless, grace is not merely "plated" (like fine gold on some other type of material) onto the rational creature; it is incarnated in him. Like an accident in its subject of inhesion, it transforms and superelevates it. Thus, in men and women transformed by grace, the new World is born in which Christ's humanity is the entry, and that we call the Church. Thus also, in the intentions of those men and women who use the things of this earth, the world acquires a new finality, and the creation, which sin had turned away, is reoriented toward God.[20] Thomas would have loved this deep saying by Clement of Alexandria: "Just as God's will is a finished work, which bears the name 'world,' so too His will is man's salvation, and that is called 'the Church.'"[21] The ecclesial communion is really a specific work of the Holy Spirit, for he guarantees its unity in historical time, a little like the mutual love of the Father and the Son in the eternity of the Trinitarian communion.

The Bond of Love

Following Saint Augustine, who did innovative work on this and marked the whole Latin reflection on the Trinity with his genius — in contrast to the Greek tradition which made use of a wholly different path — the theologians of the Middle Ages in the West liked to speak of the Holy Spirit as the mutual love with which the Father and Son love each other. For Augustine, the Holy Spirit is "the unity of the two other Persons, either their sanctity or their love." And this is so personally, for "since it is their unity because it is their love, and their love because it is their sanctity, it is clear that it is not one of the two first Persons, in whom their mutual union is at work." And there is no better way to name this than to begin with the task that it accomplishes:

20. Cf. Rom. 8:19–21.
21. Clement of Alexandria, *Paedagogus*, I, 6, 27, 2 (SC 70, 161).

If the charity with which the Father loves the Son and with which the Son loves the Father reveals to us the ineffable communion of the one with the other, is it not entirely appropriate to attribute the name of Charity to the common Spirit of the Father and of the Son?[22]

Thomas does not break from this common agreement and in his first work he develops the theme with a certain complacency:

Given that the Holy Spirit proceeds as love, it belongs to Him to be the union of the Father and the Son (unio Patris et Filii) by reason of that specific way of procession. Indeed, we can consider the Father and the Son either as they share the same essence, and are thus united in essence, or as they are personally distinct, and are then united through the convergence of love (per consonatiam amoris); if we supposed against all possibility that they were not united in essence, it would then be necessary to admit between then a union of love so that their joy would be perfect.[23]

In this perspective, the Spirit is thus an act of subsisting love, which the Father and the Son emit in common, the act through which they reciprocally love each other and that unites them in the tendential and ecstatic way in which love unites the lover to the beloved. The deep beauty of this vision of things explains the seductive power that it has exercised and continues to exercise over minds. But it has the disadvantage of superimposing the "notional" act of love, which is to say the spiration of the Holy Spirit by the Father and the Son, upon the "personal" act of love, which the Holy Spirit is in Himself, the mutual love of the two first Persons.[24] Beyond problems of language and the risk of anthropomorphism, this representation of the Spirit as a "medium" in which and through which the

22. De Trinitate XV,19, 37 (BA 16, 523); cf. ibid., VI, 5, 7 (BA 16, 206–7): "The Holy Spirit is, therefore, something common, whatever it is, between the Father and the Son. But this communion itself is consubstantial and co-eternal, and if this communion itself can be appropriately designated as 'friendship,' let it be so called, but it is more aptly called 'love'" (cf. BA 15, 485; with note 40, pp. 587–88: "L'Esprit amour et lien"). A good reading of this may be found in M.-A. Vannier, Saint Augustin et le mystère trinitaire (Paris, 1993), who translates the main texts and provides an enlightening introduction to them.

23. In I Sent. d. 10 q. 1 a. 3: this teaching is repeated in the various solutions within the same article. Cf. ibid., a. 5 ad 1: procedere per modum uoluntatis conuenit Spiritui sancto, qui procedit a duobus, uniens eos, inquantum sunt distinctae personae (to proceed by way of love "is convenient" for the Holy Spirit, who proceeds from the two others uniting them, in as much as they are distinct persons).

24. These things are very clear in In I Sent. d. 10 q. 1 a. 1 ad 4; see also In I Sent. d. 32 q. 1 a. 1, where this explanation is in the foreground.

Father and Son are reunited, raises a difficulty for its origin, since it is through its relation of origin that it is convenient to grasp the Divine Person who proceeds.[25] That is why, aware of the relative insufficiency of this way of viewing things, Thomas turns little by little toward another explanation that he will bring to the fore in his great synthesizing works, the *Contra Gentiles* and the *Summa*. To do justice to all the demands of a rigorous theology, henceforth it is on the basis of the love with which God loves his own goodness that Thomas introduces the mystery of the Third Person. Just as God, in knowing himself, produces His Word, so in loving Himself he produces or "breathes" His Spirit. Indeed, in the very act of love, Thomas discerns the presence of a loving "affection" or "impression" through which the beloved is found in the lover. In the absence of a more precise term to describe this attraction of love or affectionate impression that emanates in the one who loves, we give it the name love,[26] and it is convenient thus to grasp the procession of the Holy Spirit in God who loves Himself.

We can easily see the advantage of this way of explaining things. It allows us, on the one hand, to bring together around a single object—the divine goodness—the love common to the three persons (the "essential" love) and the love through which the Father and the Son breathe forth the Holy Spirit (the "notional" love); on the other hand, it rigorously shows that relation that constitutes the person of the Holy Spirit, proceeding by way of love.[27] Saint Augustine's intuition, however, is not forgotten, for on this basis Thomas has no trouble repeating and integrating it:

25. Thomas is very careful to respect the principle he received from Saint Anselm which was to be taken up again later by the Council of Florence: "Omnia in Deo sunt unum et idem *ubi non obuiat relationis oppositio* (Everything in God is one and the same *except where an opposition of relation intervenes*)." Cf. Saint Anselm of Canterbury, *De processione Spiritus sancti*, cap. I, *Opera Omnia*, vol. 2, p. 181. The Son has everything that the Father has, except for being the Father, for he has his origin from Him; the Spirit in turn has everything that the Father and the Son do, except for being the Father and the Son, since he has his origin from them. This is, further, the reason why the Son must also be at the source of the Holy Spirit (*Filioque*), for if this were not the case, there would be no possibility of distinguishing between the Son and the Holy Spirit.

26. Thomas raises the question, however, of the mysterious character of that procession of love for which we do not have words and that we can only describe by means of circumlocutions. Cf. *ST* Ia 37 a. 1.

27. Problems connected to the conception of the Holy Spirit as a subsisting act of love are superseded after this. See the clarifications of H.-F. Dondaine, *La Trinité*, vol. 2, pp. 393–409.

We must say that the Holy Spirit is the link *(nexus)* between the Father and the Son, insofar as He is Love. Indeed, it is through a unique lovingkindness that the Father loves both Himself and the Son—and vice versa; it follows that, insofar as He is Love, the Holy Spirit evokes a reciprocal connection between the Father and the Son, a connection of lover to beloved. But by the same fact that Father and Son love each other, it is necessary that their mutual love, otherwise known as the Holy Spirit, proceed from the one and the other. *If we then consider the origin, the Holy Spirit is not in the middle: he is the Third Person of the Trinity. But if we consider the mutual connection of which we have just spoken, then, yes, he is between the two other persons as the link who unites them, proceeding from each of them.*[28]

This is a crucial passage, and we see clearly where the discrete but decisive rectification is situated. Without rejecting Saint Augustine's brilliant intuition, whose spiritual implications are so rich, Thomas introduces it in a second phase of his explanation, after establishing it on a more solid metaphysical and conceptual basis: the love that God has for his own goodness. It is through this single and unique affection that God has for his own goodness that the Father and the Son reciprocally love one another, and that is why the Holy Spirit, as Love, implies that reciprocal connection between the lover and beloved. And it is again this same Love that extends itself to all creation.[29]

But we must clearly underline that if this theme of the Spirit, Bond of Love, comes only in a second phase of Thomas's exposition, it is far from being abandoned. On the contrary, it recurs with a meaningful constancy in the Commentaries on Saint Paul's epistles, even if most often it is only mentioned in passing, as is done with a well-known and taken-for-granted doctrine.[30] It is all the more interesting to find it sometimes with a serious amplification that allows us to glimpse to what extent that quality of the Spirit is inseparable from his very definition. In one of his Disputed Ques-

---

28. *ST* Ia q. 37 a.1 ad 3.

29. The details of this approach may be found in *ST* Ia q. 37 a. 2.

30. Thus in the commentaries on Scripture where, with respect to the passages in which Saint Paul greets his correspondents mentioning only the Father and the Son, Thomas regularly adds: "The person of the Holy Spirit is not expressly mentioned, for it is understood *(intelligitur)* in his gifts, which are grace and peace, or he is understood in the two persons of the Father and the Son *of whom he is the union and the link (intelligitur in duabus personis Patris et Filii, quarum est unio et nexus)" In ad Rom. I,* lect. 4, n. 73; cf. *In I ad Cor. I,* lect. 1, n. 10; *In II ad Cor. I,* lect. 1, n. 10 (!); *In ad Gal. I,* lect. 1, n. 7; *In ad Eph. I,* lect. 1, n. 4.

tions, Thomas comes upon a somewhat specious objection, which tries to dissociate the concept of *communio* from the procession of the Holy Spirit. At the same time, it attempts to show that we can think of the procession of the Holy Spirit without considering the communion and the *Filioque* (implied in the communion). This argument, simple enough in appearance, causes us to observe that it is conceptually possible to distinguish between the anterior and the posterior, and that we may deny what is posterior without putting what is anterior in question. Thus, even without the communion, we might think about the divine persons without infringing on their plurality, given that we would not touch on the processions of origin that undergird that plurality. To this, Saint Thomas replies:

> It is conceptually *(per intellectum)* true, the procession is first connected with communion, as that which is common comes before that which is particular. However *this* procession *(talis processio)* which is to say that of the Holy Spirit, *who proceeds as love and communion and bond of the love of the Father and the Son*, is not, [even] conceptually, prior with respect to communion. [It follows that if we withdraw communion, there would no longer be procession of the Holy Spirit, for, in reality, we are dealing with the same thing. An example will make this easily understood: conceptually, "animal" comes before "man," but this is not the case if we are dealing with the "rational animal," for that is the very definition of man].[31]

Though the discussion may seem a little subtle to those not familiar with this language, something significant is at stake. The objection resulted from a confusion between the general meaning of "procession," as it is applied indifferently to the Son or to the Spirit, and the *special* meaning of the same word when it designates the procession of the Holy Spirit *(talis processio)*.[32] Now, *for the Holy Spirit to proceed is none other than to proceed as Love or Communion of the Father and the Son*. If we suppress in our minds this communion of the Father and the Son, we also suppress the procession of the Holy Spirit, for these two realities are interdepend-

---

31. *De pot.* q. 10 a. 5 ad 11: "Licet processio sit prius per intellectum quam communio, sicut commune quam proprium; *tamen talis processio, scilicet Spiritus sancti, qui procedit quasi amor et communio et nexus Patris et Filii, non est prius secundum intellectum quam communio;* unde non oportet quod remota communione remaneat processio; sicut animal est prius secundum rationem quam homo, non autem animal rationale." I am indebted to Gilles Emery for valuable clarification on the meaning of this passage as well as for other suggestions on Trinitarian theology in this chapter.

32. Cf. *In I Sent.* d. 13 q. 1 a. 3.

ent. We can, then, neither think of the distinction of the Third Person,[33] nor take into account the work that he achieves in ecclesial communion.[34]

The Link of Charity

It is not unimportant, as may be easily understood, that Saint Augustine—and all those who claim affinity with him—discovered an expression for speaking of the Holy Spirit quite close to the language of Saint Paul, who, at least twice, speaks of the *koinonia* of the Holy Spirit.[35] Saint Thomas, who found in the Vulgate *societas* or *communicatio* as translations for *koinonia* (communion), probably did not suspect that the same Greek word lay behind them. But he grasped perfectly the ecclesial repercussions of the Trinitarian doctrine.[36] To sum up everything in a word, the Holy Spirit plays a role of unification in love at the heart of the Church, which makes us think about the role that he carries out in the heart of the Trinity, and he thus creates from the assembly of the baptized a communion of love in the image of its Trinitarian source.[37]

As we know, Thomas's ecclesial doctrine is very specifically a theology

33. Cf. note 25 above.

34. This is not the place to go further into technical theological details; whoever would like to be better informed on this doctrine of the Spirit as mutual Love of the Father and the Son and on its repercussions for the Church, should consult the specialist on this subject: F. Bourassa, *Questions de théologie trinitaire* (Rome, 1970), 59–189; and by the same author, "L'Esprit-Saint 'communion' du Père et du Fil," *Science et Esprit* 29 (1977): 251–81; 30 (1978): 5–37; as well as "Dans la communion de l'Esprit-Saint," *Science et Esprit* 34 (1982): 31–56; 135–49; 239–68; these studies, both historical and systematic, for the most part deal with Saint Thomas.

35. 2 Cor.13:13 and Philip. 2:1. By translating them as "communion of the Holy Spirit" or "communion in the Holy Spirit," the ecumenical translation of the Bible emphasizes the Trinitarian character of the passages where we find this expression.

36. On this point see B.-D. de La Soujeole, "'Société' et 'communion' chez saint Thomas d'Aquin. Étude d'ecclésiologie," *RT* 90 (1990): 587–622, especially the second part, for the use and meaning of *communio* and *communicatio*.

37. As will be noticed, the parallel between Trinitarian communion and ecclesial communion is especially enlightening, but we should be careful not to push it too far. In the Trinitarian communion, the Holy Spirit is not the *principle* of Love or union; he is the one who proceeds as Love or as Bond (recall the image of the "tree blossoming *with flowers*," evoked by Thomas: the flowers are not the principle of flowering, the tree is). While in the ecclesial communion, as will be said, the Holy Spirit is properly the *principle* (exemplary and efficient cause) of the love-charity that animates the Body of Christ and gathers it into unity.

of the Body of Christ.[38] Faithful to what he learned from Saint Paul, he sees the Body as the result of the outpouring of grace that comes to it from the Head: "The soul of Christ received grace to the maximum in his eminence; and therefore because of this pre-eminence it is from Him that this grace is bestowed on others. This belongs to his very nature as Head."[39] In this context, the role of the Holy Spirit is precisely to establish the "continuity" between Christ the Head and the faithful members, for he has the property of remaining numerically *one and the same* in the Head and in the members. Thomas, who repeats this formula[40] rather often, scarcely explains it at greater length except for the following passage:

In the natural body, the faculties distributed in all the members differ numerically according to their essence, but they are joined in their root, which is numerically one [which is to say the soul, as the form of the living being, whose seat is either the heart or the head in Thomas's physical anthropology] and, further, they possess a single final form [which is to say the soul again, but here as the transcendent principle that gives to the body thus formed the being of a human per-

38. Among the numerous studies, a perceptive treatment may be found in Yves Congar, "The Idea of the Church in St. Thomas Aquinas," *Thomist* 1 (1939): 331–59; cf. also "'Ecclesia' et 'populus (fidelis)' dans l'ecclésiologie de saint Thomas," in *Commemorative Studies I*, 159–74, also treated in the same author's *Thomas d'Aquin: Sa vision de la théologie et de l'Église* (London, 1984), or in his *Église et Papauté: Regards historiques* (Paris, 1994). Cf. J.-P. Torrell, "Yves Congar et l'ecclesiologie de saint Thomas d'Aquin," *RSPT* 82 (1998): 201–42.

39. *ST* IIIa q. 8 a. 5; cf. a. 1; this position passed into the Church's teaching; thus Pius XII, with some weightiness, in *Mystici Corporis* (ed. S. Tromp, section 78): "All gifts, all virtues, all the charisms that are found eminently, abundantly, and effectively in the head, pass into the members of the Church. . . ." More recently, Vatican II affirmed in *Lumen Gentium* I, 7: "In that body, the life of Christ is poured into the believers. . . ."

40. *De uer.* q. 29 a. 4: "Est etiam in Ecclesia continuitas quaedam ratione Spiritus sancti, qui *unus et idem numero* totam Ecclesiam replet et unit"; cf. *In Symb.* a. 9, n. 971: "The catholic Church is a single body that possesses different members; the soul that enlivens this body is the Holy Spirit"; this way of speaking recurs around fifteen times (cf. Vauthier, below) but usually very succinctly. We find an exception in this passage from the *In Ioannem I*, 16, lect. 10, n. 202: "Although the habitual gifts may be different in us and in Christ, nonetheless the Holy Spirit who is in Christ, *one and the same*, fills all the saints. In this sense, Christ's plenitude is the Holy Spirit who proceeds from Him, being in Him consubstantial by nature, power, and majesty. Indeed, although the habitual gifts are different in the soul of Christ and in us, it is however *one and the same Spirit* who is in Him and who fills all those who are to be sanctified. 'One and the same Spirit produces all these gifts' [1 Cor. 12:11]; 'I will pour out My spirit on all flesh' [Joel 3:1; Acts 2:17]; 'Anyone who does not have the Spirit of Christ does not belong to Him,' [Romans 8:9]. For the unity of the Spirit creates the unity of the Church."

son]. Similarly, all the members of the Mystical Body have as their final perfection (*pro ultimo complemento*) the Holy Spirit who is numerically one in all [the Spirit thus assumes the role of the soul in the ecclesial body]. And charity itself, spread among them by the Holy Spirit, though different according to essence in the diversity of persons, is nonetheless united in its root and numerically one, for the specific root of an operation is the object itself from which it receives its specification. And that is why, as all believe in and love one and the same object, the faith and charity of all are united in one and the same root, not only in their initial root, which is the Holy Spirit, but also in their near root, which is their proper object.[41]

Detailed exegesis of this passage, lovely but difficult, has given rise to diverse interpretations,[42] but we need not enter very much here into the subtleties to understand its meaning. It suffices to stick to the essentials. The Holy Spirit thus assumes in the ecclesial body the role of the soul in the human body: entirely in the Whole and entirely in each of its parts, it is indeed present in the Head and in the Body and in each of the members. Not only is it the principle of unity for the Whole, to which it communicates supernatural life, but it is also the source of holiness, the cause of its supernatural activity and the reason for its fecundity. Omnipresent in the Church, the Spirit is its interior Guest, as it also is in the just soul. But in the case of the Holy Spirit, it is clearly the entire Trinity that also resides in the Church, since, in accordance with the principle that Thomas immediately recalls, where one of the Persons is at work, the other two other cannot fail to be present. "If anyone loves me," said Christ, "he will keep my word, and my Father will love him; we will come to him and we will make our dwelling with him" (John 14:23).

To this commonplace of Christian thought inherited from Saint Augustine,[43] the passage adds, however, a slightly more detailed teaching

---

41. *In III Sent.* d. 13 q. 2 a. 2 qc. 2 ad 1.

42. Cf. E. Vauthier, "Le Saint-Esprit principe d'unité de l'Église d'après S. Thomas d'Aquin. Corps mystique et inhabitation du Saint-Esprit," *MSR* 5 (1948): 175–96; 6 (1949): 57–80, with the discussion by Yves Congar, *Sainte Église. Études et approches ecclésiologiques* (Paris, 1963), 647–49. See also S. Dockx, "Esprit Saint, âme de l'Église," in *Ecclesia a Spiritu Sancto edocta*, 65–80.

43. We should re-read this beautiful passage: "Our spirit, through which man lives, is called the soul. . . . And you can see what the soul does in the body. It enlivens all the members. It sees through the eyes, hears through the ears. . . . It is present at the same time in all the members to make them live; it gives life to all, and its role to each. It is not the eye that hears nor the ear that sees, nor the eye or ear that speak. And meanwhile, they live: the ear lives, the tongue lives; the functions are different, the life is common. Such is the

when it speaks of *another* principle of unity: the members of the Church are united by faith and charity, or, more precisely, by the fact that they believe and love one and the same reality. Thomas expresses this in more learned terms when he remarks that it is the object that gives specification to the act. This is a simple translation of a fact of experience easily confirmed on the natural level: several different persons will find themselves gathered together for the simple reason of all wishing the same thing; that thing thus plays the role of a common end, a unifying principle for this group. What then is the known and loved end which plays the role of unifying principle for the ecclesial body? Though Thomas does not go into detail here and seems to let it be understood that it is the Holy Spirit by saying that it is simultaneously "primary root" (the soul) and "near root" (the known and loved object), this evidently can only be God Himself, the Trinity.[44] It is this end that is the perfect blessedness of the whole Church as it is of the soul of each chosen person, as it already is in an initial form in the soul of every just person beginning in this life, since everywhere that faith and charity are found, there also is found the end that they allow us to attain, God Himself.

The addition of this detail to the common doctrine allows us to come to a full understanding of that doctrine. We are immediately taken, of course, with the beauty of the assertion, but if we examine more precisely what we might be saying in speaking of the Holy Spirit as the soul of the Church, this mode of discourse says too much or too little. It says too much because body and soul, in the natural reality that we know, interpenetrate one another tightly to the point that it is impossible to disentangle them; this is what is meant in speaking of the soul that "informs" the body, it gives the body "life, movement, and being"; only the violence of death can put an end to this unity. But it is quite impossible to say this about the Holy Spirit: how can the *uncreated* Spirit enter into composition with the *created* persons who are the members of the Church? We come here upon a metaphysical impossibility.

The closest and strongest example we can use, the instance of the In-

---

Church of God. In certain saints, she does miracles, through others she teaches the truth, through still others, she preserves virginity . . . some this, others that. Each fulfills the law proper to him, and all live equally. *What the soul is for the human body, the Holy Spirit is for the Body of Christ, the Church. The Holy Spirit does in the whole Church what the soul does in all the members of a single body.*" (*Sermo* CCLXVII, n. 4 [PL 38, 1231]).

44. Yves Congar is right here in his discussion of Vauthier's study.

carnation, entails no composition between the Word and his humanity. We recall the Council of Chalcedon: the union occurs "without confusion or mixture." If there had been confusion or mixture, the union would have approached being a hybrid, neither God nor man. And yet we can say of the Incarnate Word that His humanity is united with Him in His person (a union according to hypostasis, to use the technical term). We cannot say the same of the Holy Spirit, for if we did it would be the whole of those belonging to the Church who would be thus united to the Spirit. This is an absurdity which the Fourth Lateran Council viewed as less a "heresy" than sheer "insanity," which could only spring up in the mind of a madman. Must we, then, empty this expression "soul of the Church" of all real meaning and see it only as a metaphor? That would be to say too little.

It is precisely Saint Thomas's introduction of faith and charity into this context that will allow us to understand how the Holy Spirit can be said to be "in a certain sense" the soul of the Church, without leading us into any absurdity, but at the same time without failing to give the expression its proper truth. Grace in the soul, like faith and charity in the faculties of intelligence and will, are beyond question gifts of the Holy Spirit. They are given to us to elevate us to the divine life that we are called to share in the case of grace, to allow us to act at the level of sons and daughters of God in the case of faith and charity. To understand as much as possible what happens when God is thus known and loved, we might employ an analogy to the experience of knowledge and love in our daily world. Although present at my side, the person whom I love is not *physically* present in my mind; he is present only by means of the view that I take of him and the representation that I fashion, thanks to which I internalize that presence in my heart such that I can keep that interior presence by means of memory when the physical presence ends. This is an "intentional" presence in knowledge and love,[45] as the specialists say, but quite a real presence nonetheless: the beloved lives spiritually in the lover as the lover in the beloved.

Freed from all limits connected with our fleshly existence, this purely human representation gives us exactly the analogy we need. God is present to us even more intimately than any other object of human knowl-

---

45. "Intentions" means here precisely those substitutes for reality that are the representations that we make for ourselves in order to internalize them through knowledge and love.

edge and love, as we have already seen. But even in the case of grace, we are still dealing with a presence of this type. Through His grace, we get from Him a new presence, for He is thereafter present to us as a person supernaturally known and loved. Here we come by another path to that which we discovered above in speaking of God's presence in His creature. Beyond the presence of immensity common to all things,

there is this special mode which is proper to the rational creature: in it, we say that God exists *as the known in the knower and the beloved in the lover.* And because in knowing and loving the rational creature attains through its operation to God Himself, we say that, through this special mode, not only is God in the rational creature, but also that *He dwells in it as in His temple.*[46]

We possess here the exact truth of the expression "soul of the Church" applied to the Holy Spirit. To avoid the absurdity just indicated above, it is necessary for us to distinguish between the Holy Spirit and his gifts. The Holy Spirit cannot directly fulfill the role of a soul, but he indirectly fulfills it through his gifts. To put things slightly differently, in words closer to Scripture, we might sketch what happens thus. Not only does God love us first (cf. 1 John 4:10 and 19), but He gives us what we need to love Him "because the love of God has been poured into our hearts through the Holy Spirit that has been given to us" (Rom. 5:5); and finally He comes into us who love him (John 14:23). He can then be said with all truthfulness to be the Guest of our souls and of the Church. This entire process is attributed preferentially to the Holy Spirit for reasons that we mentioned at the outset: Bond of love between the Father and the Son, it belongs to Him in a special way to realize in the Body of believers their coming together in charity.[47]

---

46. *ST* Ia q. 43 a. 3 and chapters 3 and 4 of the present volume.

47. Astute readers will doubtless have noticed that I have not used the disputed vocabulary of the distinction between the uncreated soul (the Holy Spirit) and the created soul (grace) of the Church. This has been done only to avoid a discussion inappropriate in the context, since, abstracting from words that might be judged unfortunate (but which words would be better?), the necessity of the distinction is, to my mind, beyond doubt. Little dealt with in current theology, it is treated quite directly by the two greatest ecclesiologists of our time: Ch. Journet, *L'Église du Verbe incarné*, vol. 2 (Paris 1951), 510–80; Yves Congar agrees in passing with Journet's views (*Sainte Église*, 643 and 647–49), but he had already defended a similar position on his own in *Divided Christendom: A Catholic Study of the Problem of Reunion* (London, 1939), 52 and 56–58. S. Dockx's critique (see note 42 above), does not take into account the fact that the Church is a mystical "person," or, if one wishes, a whole, mystically personal. Without going into this new subject here, I refer again to the two

Heart of the Church

Besides a few nuances, the Master of Aquino offers nothing very original in speaking of the Holy Spirit as the soul of the Church. But he is the only one in his age[48] to make the Spirit play the role of the Church's "heart": "The heart exercises a certain hidden influence [on the exterior members]. That is why it is compared to the Holy Spirit who animates and invisibly unites the Church."[49] If in the Church-Body it is fitting for Christ to be the Head, for he manifested Himself in quite visible fashion, the efficaciousness of the heart, invisible but no less indispensable, thus belongs by preference to the Holy Spirit.[50] Given the symbolic value of the heart, this is merely another way of saying that love is the highest cause of life and of the Church's unity.

The metaphor calls forth another. In our physical bodies, all the members are irrigated by the circulation of the same blood which leaves the heart; in the Mystical Body, that vital current is charity. Through charity, the Holy Spirit establishes among all the members an organic connection that makes them interdependent in the same communion:

As in a natural body the operation of one member serves to benefit the whole body, so in the spiritual body which is the Church. And as all the faithful form a single body, the good of the one is communicated to the other. "We are all members of one another" (Rom. 12:5). That is why, among the articles of the Faith that the apostles have transmitted to us, there is one about the communion of goods (communio bonorum) in the Church; that is what is called the communion of saints (communio sanctorum).[51]

As far back as we go in the history of the Apostles' Creed, the Holy Spirit, the Church, and the communion of saints always appear together.

---

theologians in whom we find the essential positions in the debate: Ch. Journet, "La sainteté de l'Église. Le livre de Jacques Maritain," Nova et Vetera 46 (1971): 1–33 (a presentation and discussion of Jacques Maritain, De l'Église du Christ [Paris, 1970]); Yves Congar, "La personne de l'Église," RT 71 (1971): 613–40.

48. According to M. Grabmann, Die Lehre des heiligen Thomas von Aquin von der Kirche als Gotteswerk (Regensburg, 1903), 184–93.

49. ST IIIa q. 8 a. 1 ad 3.

50. "By preference" alone, because the attribution seems to have nothing exclusive about it in Thomas's hands; in a parallel passage of the De ueritate q. 29 a. 4 ad 7, he notes: "The heart is a hidden organ. . . . That is why the heart can signify either the divinity of Christ or the Holy Spirit."

51. In Symb. a. 10, n. 987.

And not merely juxtaposed, but indeed as strictly linked realities: "I believe in the Holy Spirit, in the Holy Catholic Church, the communion of
saints."[52] The communion of saints does not add here to the Church;
rather it is only an explanation of the Church. But it draws on a previous
remark. Situated between grammar and theology, that remark is more
than a simple grammatical curiosity. As some may know, the formula
"communion of saints" can bear a double meaning. When *sanctorum* is
the genitive plural of *sancti*, it means "communion of saints," which is to
say of the faithful, of those who have faith. But *sanctorum* can also be the
genitive plural of *sancta*, which means holy things, the goods that the
faithful possess in common and that gather them together; sacraments,
faith, charity, God Himself. Historically, the two meanings are both well
attested and it seems impossible to determine which of the two appeared
first. Theologically, however, there is no possible doubt; it is the communion with sacred realities and, through them, the sacred Trinity itself,
which undergirds the communion of the faithful among themselves.

Now, the expression "*communio bonorum*," used here by Thomas,
lends itself to the same kinds of observations: *bonorum* can be understood
as of the *boni*, the good, which is to say once again the faithful, but it can
also be understood in connection with *bona*, the goods that are common
to them, and the Dominican Master allows no doubt to hang over the
question of what he puts first:

> But among the members of the Church, the main member is Christ, because he
> is its head. "God gave him to be head over the whole Church, which is His body"
> (Eph. 1:22–23). *Christ's good is thus communicated to all Christians, as the head's
> virtue is communicated to all the members;* and this communication is effected
> through the Church's sacraments, in which works the virtue of Christ's Passion,
> which efficaciously gives grace for the remission of sins.[53]

Thomas then quickly reviews the seven sacraments and their effects;
only after that does he come to the second meaning of the communion of
saints, the one which doubtless comes to mind most naturally:

---

52. We know that this is a case of the authentic form of the Apostles' Creed such as can
be found in one of the earliest witnesses, Saint Hippolytus of Rome around 200AD. Cf. P.
Nautin, *Je crois à l'Esprit-Saint dans la sainte Église pour la résurrection de la chair, Étude
sur l'histoire et la théologie du Symbole* (Paris, 1947).
53. *In Symb.* a. 10, n. 988.

We should furthermore know that it is not only the efficaciousness of Christ's Passion that is communicated to us, but also the merit of his life. And all the good that all the saints do is communicated to those who live in charity, for all are one: "I am companion of all who fear you" (Ps. 118:63). That is why he *who lives in charity enters into participation with all the good that is done in the whole world.*[54]

Clearly, we must take note of the italicized phrase; it returns like a refrain in all the passages where our author speaks on this subject.[55] We will allow ourselves to reproduce here a rarely quoted passage, which comes from a work little known by the majority of Saint Thomas's readers:

[Two reasons can explain the efficaciousness of one person's prayer for another; we must clearly wish to pray for that person, but that is not the first thing:] *it is the unity of charity, given that all those who live in charity form as it were a single body.* Such that the good of one flows upon all, in the way that the hand or some other member is at the service of the whole body. It is thus that all good achieved by one is of value for each of those who live in charity, according to the expression in the Psalm (118:63): "I am the companion of whoever fears you and keeps your commandments."[56]

Clearly, we have to note the place charity occupies in these passages because we are dealing with the communion *of saints,* and there is no sanctity outside of charity. But if we want to understand why charity has this mysterious fecundity, we must remember the special link that exists between charity and the Holy Spirit. Only the Spirit's presence in the body of which it is the soul allows us to understand how that mysterious reversibility of spiritual good occurs which we call the communion of saints. Charles Journet used a striking comparison about this. To give eyes to someone who does not have them would certainly be to give a *finite* perfection, those precise organs that are the eyes of the *flesh;* but this would also be to introduce him, at the same time, *spiritually* to the whole *infinity* of the horizon. To give him the capacity of seeing would be to offer him the chance to appropriate in the order of intentionality the immensity of the exterior world, to allow him to commune with it in a new way.

Charity, too, has these two facets. Inasmuch as it is a created gift, an effect produced in me by the Holy Spirit, it perfects my spiritual being, but

---

54. *In Symb.* a. 10, n. 997.
55. See for instance: *In IV Sent.* d. 45 q. 2 a. 4 qc. 1 (= Suppl. q. 71 a. 12); *Quodl.* VIII q. 5 a. 2 [12].
56. *Quodl.* II, q. 7 a. 2 [14].

it is necessarily limited to my own person. In this sense, it does not explain that mutual communion of which we seek to render an account. But if we consider that this *finite* charity allows me to enter into communication with the *infinite* charity which is the Holy Spirit, to have it dwell in me as a form spiritually present, then everything changes. For Charity in its origin puts me in communication with the world of all other persons in which it is present, since it is nothing other than the uncreated Love who, one and the same, fills the whole Church and makes of it a unity. Present in the Whole of the ecclesial Body and in each of its members, Charity realizes in those places a reciprocal indwelling of all those in the state of grace, a "mutual affective circumincession of the members of the Church, one in another" (Journet). If the Spirit of love dwells in me and if I dwell in the Spirit, in the same way all those in whom the Spirit dwells and who dwell in the Spirit, dwell also in me and I in them. We must go to this point to render an account of the mystery of the communion of saints. My charity does not simply end at my brother, it is his, and his is also mine. They communicate the resources and fecundity to each other reciprocally, which they have from the Spirit, such that the charity of the weakest member is elevated by that of the one who is most spirited, and the charity of both is held within the infallible charity of the whole Church, for it is the charity of uncreated Love, indivisible and omnipresent, that all possess in common.[57] If "every pious and holy work of a single person belongs to all,"[58] that is because of their common root, charity, itself the fruit of [the Church's] Heart, the Holy Spirit.[59]

≋

57. We notice here the exalted transposition into the Christian realm of the doctrine about friendship that we encountered in the previous chapter; Saint Thomas got it from Aristotle, but Aristotle himself received it from Plato, who was himself quite soon repeated and christianized by the first Christian thinkers in the way that I have just explained. Thus, for example, Clement of Alexandria: "And if 'the goods of friends are common' (Plato, *Phaedrus*, 279C; *Laws* V, 739C), and man is beloved of God (for he is indeed dear to God, through the mediation of the Logos), then all things become man's, because all things belong to God, and are common to both friends, God and man" (*Protreptikos* XII, 122, 3, trans. G. W. Butterworth, Loeb ed. [1939], 260–63).

58. The expression is from the Roman Catechism, sometimes called the Catechism of the Council of Trent, but it corresponds to some of the passages in Saint Thomas that we have just recalled; cf. *Catechismus Romanus. . . .* , ed. P. Rodriguez (Vatican, 1989), Pars Ia, cap. 10, p. 119. Clearly, this has been repeated in the *Catechism of the Catholic Church* (Vatican City, 1997), nos. 946–53, pp. 247–48.

59. Cf. *In IV Sent.*, d. 45 a. 2 q. 1 sol. 1: "propter communicantiam in radice operis quae est caritas." The doctrine about the communion of saints is clearly much more vast than

Among the few homilies by Saint Thomas that have been preserved, there is one for All Saints' Day,[60] in which we find the majority of the themes that we have just touched on in this chapter. It will be illuminating to see once again how the friar echoes his most elaborate theological teaching in his preaching.

This homily is based quite openly on the idea of the *congregatio fidelium*, which is probably Thomas's favorite definition of the Church. It puts the accent firmly on the communion of persons.[61] That posited, the text starts rather abruptly: no one among those who think rightly does not know that the *societas* among God, the angels, and men is unique. This statement is supported with two quotations from Scripture, each of which mentions the communion (*societas* in the Vulgate) to which God calls men in his Son Jesus Christ.[62] Thomas explains this communion here by the fact that there is a *communicatio* of angels and men in their common end, beatitude. While God possesses this beatitude by His essence, however, angels and men have access to it only through participation. Communion does not stop there: between all those who participate in the common end, there must also be a *communicatio* of works, such that those who have not yet attained the end, men still on earth (*viatores* in traditional terminology), are led toward it through the word and example of those who already possess it. This is why we celebrate the feasts of the saints, those who have already obtained beatitude: helped by their prayers, edified by their examples, stimulated by their reward, we arrive at it in our turn.

The direct consequence of this fundamental view is that Thomas does not conceive of the effort of the Christian or of the end point of that effort in individualistic terms. He reminds us that the person can rely on the community to which he belongs; even if we are not always quick to par-

---

the brief mention above. It can be fully examined in Ch. Journet, *L'Église du Verbe incarné*, vol. 2, pp. 548–61 and 662–67 in particular; see, too, the fine article by J.-M. R. Tillard, "La communion des saints," *La Vie spirituelle* 113 (1965): 249–74; and Yves Congar, "Aspects of the Communion of Saints," in *Faith and Spiritual Life*, trans. A. Manson and L. C. Sheppard (New York, 1969), 122–31; *I Believe in the Holy Spirit*, trans. David Smith, vol. 2 (New York, 1983), 59–64 (with a full bibliography).

60. The sermon *Beati qui habitant* in Th. Käppeli, "Una raccolta di prediche attribuite a S. Tommaso d'Aquino," *AFP* 13 (1943): 59–94, cf. 88–94.

61. Cf. *In Symb.* a. 9, n. 972: "We must understand that 'Church' means 'community' (*congregatio*); that is why 'Holy Church' is the same thing as 'community of the faithful' (*congregatio fidelium*) and every Christian is a member of that Church."

62. Cf. 1 Cor. 1:9 and 1 John 1:7.

don, we can say the Our Father without lying, for the sinner does not only pray on his own behalf *(in persona sui)*, but also in the name of the Church *(in persona ecclesiae)*, which does not lie.[63] Furthermore, we ought to emphasize about this insertion into the ecclesial communion that Christ teaches us to say the Our Father, not merely "Father."[64] The communion of saints thus finally appears as it really is: the mystery of our supernatural solidarity in the organism of grace which is the Body of Christ, who is the New Adam.[65]

---

63. *In orationem dominicam expositio* VI, n. 1090.

64. *In orationem dominicam expositio*, Pro., n. 1024: "To suggest the love of God, we call him 'Father'; to suggest love of neighbor, we pray in a communitarian way and for all by saying 'Our Father' and 'forgive *us our* trespasses,' which encourages in us love of neighbor."

65. Pelagianism was once characterized as "Christianity minus two mysteries, both of which are in great part mysteries of solidarity . . . in evil and in death . . . in good and in life," E. Mersch, *The Whole Christ: the Historical Development of the Doctrine of the Mystical Body in Scripture and Tradition*, trans. John R. Kelley (Milwaukee, Wis., 1938), 400; the doctrine of the communion of saints is found at the polar opposite of this deviation.

~

CHAPTER IX

The Master of the Interior Life

Though it is sometimes difficult for specialists to agree about exactly what to put under the term "spirituality," there is at least one point on which history and theology allow them to meet. When we have to define what we understand by a person—man or woman—who is "spiritual," it always involves "someone who allows himself to be led by the Spirit." Saint Thomas is clearly no exception; he even insists on this dimension: "The 'spiritual man' *(homo spiritualis)* is not merely taught what he must do by the Holy Spirit, his heart itself is moved by the Holy Spirit."[1] He explains the point with reference to the scriptural verse concerning Jesus' conversation with Nicodemus (John 3:8). The "spiritual man" *(uir spiritualis)* has the very properties of the Spirit:

"The wind blows where it will, and you hear its voice, but you do not know whence it comes nor where it goes. *Thus it is for whoever is born of the Spirit.*" Quite clearly this refers to the Holy Spirit. And there is nothing astonishing in this, for as [Jesus] had said: "He who is born of the Spirit is spirit," because *the properties of the Spirit are found in the spiritual man, as the properties of fire are found in a burning coal.*

Now in him who is born of the Holy Spirit there are the four properties of the Holy Spirit that we have just enumerated.[2] In the first place, he enjoys liberty: "Where there is the Spirit of the Lord, there is freedom" (2 Cor. 3:17), for the Spir-

1. *In ad Rom.* VIII, 14, lect. 3, n. 635.
2. Cf. *In Ioannem III*, 8, lect. 2, nn. 451–54: the Lord suggests to Nicodemus four qualities of the Spirit: "First is His power . . . for given the power of his free will, he inspires 'when he will and where he will' by illuminating hearts . . . ; the second is the sign of this, 'you hear his voice,' [which can be understood in two senses]: the voice through which he speaks interiorly to the human heart and that only the just and the saints hear . . . , and the

it leads to uprightness: "Your Good Spirit leads me on the path of righteousness" (Ps. 142:10), and frees us from slavery to sin and the law: "The law of the Spirit who gives life in Christ has freed me" (Rom. 8:2).

We detect immediately after his words [the presence of the Holy Spirit], for *in hearing we recognized his spirituality*: "The mouth speaks from the fulness of the heart" (Matt. 12:34). Finally his *origin* and his *end* are themselves hidden, for no one can judge the spiritual man: "The spiritual man judges all things, and he himself is not judged by anyone" (1 Cor. 2:15), unless he fails to understand the "you do not know whence it comes" of the beginning of his spiritual birth, which is the grace of baptism, and the "nor where it goes" of eternal life, which is still hidden from us.[3]

Where There Is the Spirit of the Lord, There Is Freedom

We often encounter the latter three qualities of the spiritual person, but notably the first quality is mentioned almost everywhere.[4] It is a meaningful sign that Thomas regularly places John 3:8 ("He who is born of the Spirit is spirit") in relation to 2 Cor. 3:17: "The Lord is Spirit, and where there is the Spirit of the Lord, there is freedom." And except for what the immediate context requires, Thomas gives practically the same exegesis of the point:

In one sense, "Spirit" [may be understood in a personal way, and must be understood as] the Holy Spirit, who is the author of the Law, is the Lord, which is to say that he acts as it pleases his freedom: "The Spirit blows where he wills" (John 3:8); "He divides up his gifts as he chooses" (1 Cor. 12:11). When Paul adds, "Where there is the Spirit of the Lord, there is freedom," it is as if he were saying: Since the Spirit is Lord, he can give us freedom to use the Scriptures of the Old Testament freely and without veils.[5] Those who do not have the Holy Spirit cannot do this.

---

voice through which he speaks in the Scriptures or by means of preachers . . . which is heard even by infidels and sinners; the third is his hidden origin: though you hear his voice, 'you do not know whence it comes,' for he comes from the Father and the Son . . . who dwell in 'inapprochable light'; the fourth quality is his end, which is equally hidden, 'you do not know where it goes'; we must therefore understand: for he leads to an end that escapes us, eternal beatitude. . . ."

3. *In Ioannem*, ibid., n. 456.

4. As in the *In Ioannem XV*, 26, lect. 5, n. 2058: "Four points concerning the Holy Spirit are recalled here: *his freedom*, his sweetness, his procession, his action. . . ."

5. The veil is clearly what 2 Cor. 2:12–18 speaks of: the one Moses wore and that, according to Saint Paul, is still found over the heart of the Jews, hindering them from recognizing Jesus as the Messiah, while it has fallen from the heart of Christians on the day of their conversion.

In another sense, we can understand "Lord" to refer to Christ Himself; we can then read the passage thus: *the Lord, which is to say Christ, is spiritual, which is to say a spirit of power (spiritus potestatis), which is why "where there is the Spirit of the Lord," there is the law of Christ understood in the Spirit (spiritualiter intellecta), not through written words only but infused into our hearts through faith, and there is also then freedom, without any obstacle by way of a veil.*[6]

The Holy Spirit is thus freedom and his first gift is liberty in the believer's soul. Thomas's close readers will not be able to help thinking here about his teaching on the new law, a point too central not to reappear often. But those who are less familiar with the *Summa* run the risk of passing over it without seeing it, because as often happens in scholastic theology, the question that introduces the point seems banal: Is the new law a written law? In fact, however, this is an expression of the newness of the Gospel in relation to the Old Law:

According to Aristotle in Book IX of the *Ethics*, "every thing is defined by what is most important in it." Now, what is most important in the New Law, in which all its power resides, is the grace of the Holy Spirit given through faith in Christ. The New Law consists thus principally in the very grace of the Holy Spirit granted to the faithful in Christ . . . Which causes Saint Augustine to say in his work *On the Spirit and the Letter* (xxi 36): "What then are these divine laws written by God Himself in the heart if not the very presence of the Holy Spirit?" . . . We must conclude from this that primarily, the New Law is an interior law, but that secondarily, it is a written law.[7]

This article, rightly celebrated, has been commented on often and quite well;[8] though not new at every point (Thomas does not hide what he owes to Saint Augustine), originality is not so important in this context as the strong and well-grounded affirmation in both Scripture and Tradition

6. *In II ad Cor. III*, 17, lect. 3, n. 111; contemporary exegesis understands Saint Paul's expression to refer to Christ, and would thus prefer the second interpretation. But the passage remains disputed and we can see that Thomas was already aware of it.

7. *ST* Ia IIae q. 106 a. 1. See the aforementioned excellent commentary by J. Tonneau, *La loi nouvelle*, from which the present translation is drawn.

8. Besides J. Tonneau, see especially S. Pinckaers, "La loi de l'Evangile ou Loi nouvelle selon saint Thomas," in *Loi et Évangile* (Geneva, 1981), 57–80; *Sources of Christian Ethics*, chap. 7, pp. 168–90. Also worth consulting is J. Étienne, "Loi et grâce. Le concept de loi nouvelle dans la Somme théologique de S. Thomas d'Aquin," *RTL* 16 (1985): 5–22 (summary) and the whole of the collected studies in L. J. Elders and K. Hedwig, *Lex et Libertas, Freedom and Law according to St. Thomas* (Rome, 1987). For the contribution of Saint Augustine on this, see I. Biffi, "La legge nuova. Agostino e Tommaso," chap. 4, in *Teologia, Storia*, 177–213.

of the centrality of the Holy Spirit and his grace. As a result, everything else is radically relativized, because it is subordinated to the rank of a simple instrumental value compared with the singular greatness that possesses the value of an end.

This does not amount, however, to a profession of some kind of anarchist refusal of all law, since the text quickly adds that there are secondary elements in the service of this unique law of the Gospel.[9] It is indeed quite remarkable that, like Saint Paul, Thomas worries about a bad understanding of this teaching, which would blithely go from liberty to license. This presents not only a chance to put people on guard, but the occasion for a useful clarification as to the reason why the Holy Spirit is thus the source of Christian liberty:

We must understand that certain people, basing themselves on these words, "Where there is the Spirit of the Lord, there is freedom," as well as on the following words: "For the just there is no law" (1 Tim. 1:9) have falsely taught that spiritual men are not under the precepts of the divine law. This is false because God's commandments are the rule of human action. . . .

What is said about the "just for whom there is no law" must be understood thus: it is not for the just, who are moved from the inside to do the things that the Law of God prescribes, that the law has been promulgated, but for the unjust, without therefore meaning that the just are no longer held to it.

Similarly, "Where there is the Spirit of the Lord, there is freedom," must be understood thus: that person is free who disposes of himself *(liber qui est causa sui)* while the serf *(servus)* depends on his lord. The one who acts on his own, therefore, acts freely, but whoever acts at the prompting of another does not act freely. *Thus, whoever avoids evil not because it is evil, but because of God's commandment, is not free. Now, it is the person who realizes the Holy Spirit, who perfects the inward spirit of man, by a good habitus, so that he does out of love what the divine law prescribes. He is thus called free, not because he submits to the divine law, but because he is moved by his good habitus to do the very thing the divine law orders.*[10]

---

9. U. Kühn, *Via caritatis*, 201, rightly points out: "The new law, to the extent that it is a written law, is, like all written law, intended to take care of and cure the real, or at least possible, obscuring of the *lex indita*. Thomas clearly sees the reality here: while man lives in this world, perpetually besieged by sin, this information is necessary, despite the law of the Spirit, to set man, in some way, on the right path and to keep him there."

10. *In II ad Cor. III*, 17, lect. 3, n. 112; the commentary on 1 Tim.1:9 (no. 23) clearly points in the same direction: "The law is not imposed on the just as a burden, for their interior habitus inclines them to accomplish the law; it is not a weight for them, for 'they are a law unto themselves' (Rom. 2:14). We can understand this to mean: 'The law is not given

Friar Thomas's formulas are emphatic, bordering on provocative, and perhaps even incomprehensible for the legalistic mentality that has been ours for centuries. In such a mentality, an act is weighed according to its conformity with laws or social norms. Beneath a seeming neglect of law, Thomas shows himself demanding in a different way and thus agrees with Saint Paul all the more securely: "Whatever does not proceed from a conviction of faith is sin."[11] There is no disdain for or deprecation of law in this, but the conscious affirmation of man's grandeur: "*Man's highest dignity is to be borne toward the good by himself and not to be driven there by other people.*"[12]

This consciousness of the absolute necessity of the internal origin of the free act raises a question when Thomas comes upon another, no less decisive, verse in Saint Paul (Rom. 8:14): "All who are led by the Spirit of God *(Spiritu Dei aguntur)* are children of God." How should we understand this?

"Those who are led by the Spirit" are "guided" by him as one is "led" by a guide or driver; the Spirit does that within us when he illumines us interiorly about what we ought to do: "Your good Spirit will guide me" (Ps. 142:10). *But since whoever is thus "guided" does not act on his own, the spiritual person is not merely instructed by the Holy Spirit, his heart is also moved by him.* We must then give a stronger meaning to the expression "those who are led by the Spirit of God." We are saying in fact that beings who are "led" are led by a superior instinct. Thus we say of animals that they do not guide themselves but that they are led, which is to say that they are moved by their nature and not from their own movement to do certain actions. So too, it is not in the first instance through his own will but through an *instinct of the Holy Spirit* that the spiritual man is impelled to do something, as Isaiah says (59:19): "For he will come like a pent-up stream that the

---

for the just, but for the unjust', *for if there were only the just, there would be no need of law; all would be their own law.*" For a similar argument, see *ST* Ia IIae q. 93 a. 6 ad 1: "Spiritual persons are not under the law because, through the charity that the Holy Spirit infuses in their *hearts*, they spontaneously do what is enjoined by the law."

11. Rom. 14:23. We will return to this verse when we deal with the role of conscience in moral action.

12. *In ad Rom. II*, 14, lect. 3, n. 217. This is a commentary on the verse: "They are a law unto themselves," which Thomas quotes often to put forth the spontaneous character that must preside over good action; in addition to the passages assembled and quoted above, cf. *In III Sent.* d. 37 a. 1 ad 5; *ST* Ia IIae q. 96 a. 5 ad 1. The importance of this verse in Thomas's work has been beautifully developed in the remarkable study by B. Montagnes, "Autonomie et dignité de l'homme," *Angelicum* 51 (1974): 186–211. We will have occasion to return to this.

breath of the Lord drives on." Or as Luke (4:1) says of Christ, he was "led into the desert by the Spirit." *This does not exclude, however, that spiritual persons act through their will and free choice, for it is the Holy Spirit who causes in them the very movement of their will and of their free choice,* as the letter to the Philippians (2:13) says: "For it is God who is at work in us, our will and our action."[13]

Friar Thomas is fond of this expression of Saint Paul's and it comes to him spontaneously in his commentary on Galatians. Those who are led by the Spirit cannot do anything contrary to the virtuous works prescribed by the law, for the Spirit teaches them to accomplish them. And this happens without constraint: "the new law produces a feeling of love that arises from freedom, for whoever loves is moved freely."[14] If we live from the Spirit, we will be led by him in all things. There is also here a meaningful equivalent: "If someone does not have the Spirit of Christ, he does not belong to Him," says Saint Paul (Rom. 8:9); and Thomas continues: "Thus those who are led by the Spirit belong to Christ."[15]

By making the reciprocal connection between the Spirit and Christ very conspicuous, Thomas is only following the language of the New Testament, and he is happy to find it explicitly in Saint Paul: "The Law of the Spirit of life in Christ Jesus has freed me from sin and death" (Rom. 8:2):

In one sense, this law is the Holy Spirit himself, such that by "the law of the Spirit," we should understand: *the law that is the Spirit.* The specific nature of law in fact is to arouse man to do good. According to Aristotle . . . the intention of the lawmaker is to create good citizens; now, human law cannot do that except by making known the good that must be done. *The Holy Spirit, the one who dwells in the soul, not only teaches what must be done by enlightening the intelligence, but he also inclines the feelings to act rightly.* "The Paraclete, the Holy Spirit whom the Father will send in my name, he will teach you all things—hence the first dimension—and will suggest everything—hence the second dimension—that I will tell him for you."

In a second sense, "the law of the Spirit" can be understood as the proper ef-

---

13. *In ad Rom. II,* 14, lect. 3, n. 635; the commentary on the epistle to the Hebrews 8:10 can be quoted in support of the same argument: "The new Covenant has been given through an inner inspiration, for it consists in the infusion of the Holy Spirit who interiorly teaches. However, it is not enough merely to know, we must also act; and thus *if the Holy Spirit first enlightens the mind to understanding. . . . he is also 'imprinted' on the heart to incline its affections toward acting well"* (lect. 2, n. 404).

14. *In ad Gal. IV,* 24, lect. 8, n. 260: *lex nova generat affectum amoris qui pertinet ad libertatem, nam qui amat ex se mouetur.*

15. *In ad Gal. V,* 24–25, lect. 7, n. 338, but see also numbers 336–40.

fect of the Holy Spirit, which is to say of the faith that works through charity. It too teaches inwardly what should be done, as Saint John (1 John 2:27) says: "His anointing will teach you all things"; in the same way, it inclines our feelings to act, according to Saint Paul (2 Cor. 5:14): "For love of Christ urges us on." This law is thus called the new law, whether because it is identified with the Holy Spirit, or because the Spirit himself works in us. . . . And if the Apostle adds "in Jesus Christ," it is because this Spirit is not given except to those who are in Christ Jesus. *As the living, natural breath does not come to the member who is not connected with the head, so the Holy Spirit does not come to the member who is not connected with his head, Christ.*[16]

It is hardly necessary to insist that we recognize in a passage like this one—the experience is easily repeatable in a large number of other passages—the reciprocal connection of the two temporal missions of the Divine Persons, the Son and the Spirit. The history of salvation, whose marks Thomas valuably assembles in his commentaries on Scripture, reflects the mutual interiority of the Trinitarian communion.[17] Without spending time demonstrating what needs no demonstration, we would do better to follow Thomas in his explanations of the way in which the Spirit works in us. For in the *Summa* he elaborates the theory of what we have read in his lessons on Scripture.

The Instinct of the Holy Spirit

What we have just seen Thomas attribute to the Holy Spirit: the illumination of the intelligence so that it may see the good to be done and the movement of the will so that it will accomplish it, is only the most evident part—the most conspicuous, so to speak—of the work of the Spirit in us. It is enough to be clear on the basic data that dominate God's omnipresence to his creature and the way in which he sustains the creature in being and acting to understand without difficulty that the action of the

16. *In ad Rom. VIII*, 2, lect. 1, nn. 602–3 and 605.

17. This trinitarian mark of the history of salvation is strongly emphasized in the *ST* Ia IIae q. 106 a. 4 ad 3: "The old law was not only the law of the Father but also the law of the Son who was prefigured in it, according to the word of the Lord: 'If you believed Moses, you would believe in me also because he wrote about me' (John 5:46). The new law, for its part, is not only the law of Christ, but also the law of the Holy Spirit, according to Romans 8:2: 'The law of the Spirit of life in Christ Jesus.' We must not then expect another law that would be that of the Holy Spirit." The tenor of this response, as the content of the whole of article 4, is naturally addressed against Joachim of Flora and his disciples. Cf. J. Tonneau, *La loi nouvelle*, note 28, pp. 129–31. See also some of the indications on this topic in B. T. Viviano, *Le Royaume de Dieu dans l'histoire* (Paris, 1992), 98–107.

Holy Spirit intervening through his grace, espouses the same laws. In one case as in the other, God cannot violate the action of his creature without denying himself. But Thomas seems to concentrate here on another object: he also wants to make us feel the intimacy of this divine action and to make us savor its sweetness. It is this to which his teaching on the gifts of the Holy Spirit corresponds.

The gifts of the Holy Spirit occupy a high place in Thomas's teaching and it is important to see their role in the spiritual life of the Christian. We can indeed inquire into their necessity, since they intervene in an organism already endowed with grace in the deepest reaches of the soul, and also equipped with virtues that enable it to know and to love in the supernatural realm.[18] In fact, the theological virtues are no less divine gifts than are the gifts of the Holy Spirit. The virtues too perfect the person by putting him in a condition of acting according to God. That is why theologians are not lacking, before and after Saint Thomas, who strongly doubt not only the necessity for distinguishing between gifts and virtues, but even the very existence of the gifts.[19] All incertitude disappears for our author because Scripture clearly speaks of the seven gifts of the Holy Spirit.[20] He thus appeals to Scripture to explain where the difference lies. This is one of the places in his work, as we have already seen several times, that is particularly enlightening about his theological method. For while reason intervenes in its proper place, because it is a question of understanding, Scripture remains the norm here:

If we want to distinguish carefully the gifts from the virtues, *we must follow Scripture's ways of speaking,* in which they are revealed to us not only under the name of "gifts," but also under the name "spirits" *(spirituum).* Thus, Isaiah says (11:2): "The spirit of wisdom and understanding will rest upon him," etc. Such words clearly give us to understand that seven (realities) are enumerated there inasmuch

18. Cf. the distinction between grace and virtues, entitative and operative habitus, dealt with in the previous chapter.

19. See the enlightening treatment by O. Lottin, *Morale fondamentale* (Tournai, 1954), 414–34. Lottin places himself in line with those authors who reject the distinction, and he thinks Thomas would not have adopted it except to be in step with the formulations of his day. One might be allowed to doubt this, given the role that Thomas has them play.

20. See Isaiah 11:2, as presented in the Septuagint and the Vulgate, both of which add piety to the list in the Hebrew text. The Hebrew only recognizes six gifts: wisdom, discernment, council, fortitude (or strength), knowledge, and fear. Thomas engages in a rather extended development of this text in treating the gifts. See *In Isaiam XI,* Leonine, vol. 28, pp. 79–80, lines 126–212.

as they are in us by divine inspiration. *Now, inspiration signifies a certain motion coming from outside.* We must indeed consider that there are two principles of movement in man: one within, which is reason, the other outside, which is God. . . .[21]

[But this assumes a certain aptitude of the person who is moved to place himself under the action of the agent, who must make him advance. Thus, a student will have to absorb a number of things before being ready to enroll in a famous teacher's school]. This is why, insofar as we are dealing with being moved by reason, human virtues are sufficient to perfect man in his internal or external action. *But when we are dealing with being moved by God, it is necessary that there be in man higher perfections that dispose him to be divinely moved.*

These perfections are called gifts, not only because they are infused by God, but because, thanks to them, man becomes perfectly disposed (prompte mobilis) to divine inspiration, as is said in Isaiah (50:5): "The Lord has opened my ear and I have not resisted; I have not turned back." The *Philosopher also* says that *those who are moved by a divine instinct do not need to deliberate according to human reason; they only have to follow the interior instinct, for they are moved by a better principle than human reason.*[22]

Borrowed from a significantly different context, Aristotle's expression undergoes a rather strong transposition.[23] But we can pass over that and focus on the aim. While virtue, even when infused by God, still remains at the disposition of the person, who can use it more or less generously, the gift puts the beneficiary in a position of perfect docility with respect to the action of the Holy Spirit. It is in such a state, simultaneously of dependence and of spontaneity, in obedience to the divine operation within him, that he no longer has to concern himself with the judgment of reason. He is moved by a higher instinct which assures him that he is in the true and the good—even in the most foolish things. The lives of the saints are full of these decisions made contrary to all human wisdom, and despite the warnings of followers. Without seeking very far, Thomas could remember Saint Dominic, who, at the risk of destroying his recent founding of the Order of Preachers, immediately sent the few friars that he had

---

21. The mere mention of God is sufficient to understand that this "exteriority" has nothing exteriorizing, nothing material. Rather, we are dealing with an otherness: what God does *in me* is not reducible to what is *from me*.

22. *ST* Ia IIae q. 68 a. 1: "*prompte mobilis* ab inspiratione divina"; the same expression as in *ST* IIa IIae q. 121 a. 1. But we find more frequently "*bene mobilis* a Spiritu Sancto (or: per Spiritum Sanctum)." Cf. *ST* Ia IIae q. 111 a. 4 ad 4; *ST* IIa IIae q. 8 a. 5; q. 19 a. 9; q. 52 a. 1.

23. Cf. *Eudemian Ethics* VII, 14 (1248a32).

gathered together at Toulouse to the four corners of Christendom: "Do not oppose me. I know quite well what I am doing."[24] The originality of the vocabulary used and, even more, of Thomas's ideas in the passage above has rightly been noted.[25] First of all, there is the word *"spiritus,"* which it would be well to translate as "breath" here, but particularly the presence of the word "instinct" and the idea it suggests.[26] Simply from the statistical point of view, the figures are rather impressive in themselves: the expression "instinct of the Holy Spirit" *(instinctus Spiritus Sancti)* recurs more than fifty times, and the mention of a divine instinct recurs some thirty times, particularly with regard to prophecy, but not solely. In the majority of cases, it is a matter of moral life and of the discernment between good and evil or of the connection to the law, or, more deeply, of what happens when someone comes to faith, in the experience of conversion. Thomas thus distinguished the exterior call, which may sound in the ears of someone who hears preaching for example, from the interior call, which is addressed to him by God and is nothing other than "a certain interior instinct *(per quemdam instinctum interiorem)* by means of which God touches man's heart through grace so that he will turn to Him. He thus calls us from the bad road to the good, and this *through grace, not through our merits."*[27]

We must emphasize the movement of grace in this last passage, intervening without previous merits in whoever is converted. In his early writings, Thomas followed without apparent difficulty the common opinion, unconsciously semi-Pelagian, that man can prepare himself for grace through his own powers.[28] A deeper reading of Saint Augustine led him to

24. *Processus canonizationis S. Dominici apud Bononiam,* n. 26. On this episode, see M.-H. Vicaire, "Relecture des origines dominicaines," *Mémoire dominicaine* 3 (1993): 159–71.

25. See the brief but very valuable study by S. Pinckaers, "L'instinct et l'Esprit au coeur de l'éthique chrétienne," in *Novitas et veritas vitae,* 213–23, to which I am indebted for several suggestions.

26. S. Pinckaers, ibid., p. 217: "what we call the gifts are breaths, inspirations received from the Holy Spirit"; cf. p. 215 for the figures quoted above.

27. *In ad Gal. I,* 15, lect. 4, n. 42; cf. *In ad Rom. VIII,* 30, lect. 6, n. 707: "This interior vocation is nothing other than a certain instinct of the mind *(quidam mentis instinctus)* by which man's heart is moved by God to adhere to the faith or to virtue. . . . This interior call is necessary, because our heart could not turn itself to God, if God himself had not attracted us."

28. As in *In II Sent.* d. 28 q. 1 a. 4: "In agreement with the other authors *(aliis consentiendo),* we say then that man can prepare himself to receive sanctifying grace through his

abandon that position and to underscore with no possible equivocation that, even here and especially here, "God works in us, ennabling us to will and to do" (Phil. 2:13). Some astute interpreters have drawn attention to the fact that this ever clearer awareness that nothing in the Christian life escapes grace should be placed alongside a growing frequency of references to the instinct of the Holy Spirit in Thomas's work. Significantly, it is during this same period that Thomas's quotations from Aristotle about the superior instinct pop up as illustrative of what the arrival of the Spirit really does in the being who wholly delivers himself over to its influence.[29]

Possessing this key notion for the spiritual life, Thomas ever after calls upon it in describing the interior movement, whether of the Spirit or of God, and he gives a lovely illustration of it in his commentary on Jesus' saying in Saint John: "No one can come to me unless drawn by the Father who sent me":[30]

We come to Christ through faith . . . since to come to Him and to believe in Him is the same thing. Now, since we cannot believe without willing, and to say "attraction" *(tractio)* supposes a certain violence, he who comes to Christ is thus constrained [to do so] in being "drawn" *(tractus)*.

I reply to this that the Father's attraction implies no constraint, for *everything that attracts does not necessarily do violence.* Thus the Father has many ways of attracting us to Christ without doing violence to man. We can indeed attract someone either by persuading him through reason . . . or by attracting him with charm. . . . Thus the Father attracts those who are taken with His majesty; but they are also attracted through the Son by reason of a marvelous delight and love of truth, which is none other than Himself. If as Saint Augustine says, "each per-

---

free will alone"; Thomas expresses himself thus again in *De ueritate* q. 24 a. 15. It is only a little later, during his stay in Orvieto, that he recognizes that God anticipates by his grace every human movement toward the Good (see for example SCG III 149). As H. Bouillard has well demonstrated in *Conversion et grâce,* 92–122, it is his fullest reading of Saint Augustine's late writings on grace, *De predestinatione sanctorum* and *De dono perseuerantiae,* which Thomas had earlier known only through passages in anthologies, that made him aware of the semi-Pelagian error (which he continues calling "Pelagian").

29. Cf. M. Seckler, *Instinkt und Glaubenswille nach Thomas von Aquin* (Mainz, 1961) (along with the important discussion by E. Schillebeeckx, "L'instinct de la foi selon S. Thomas d'Aquin," *RSPT* 48 [1964], 377–408, see in particular p. 382); J. H. Walgrave, "Instinctus Spiritus Sancti. Een prove tot Thomas-interpretatie," *ETL* 45 (1969): 417–31 (French summary).

30. John 6:44. To understand the passage that follows, we must remember that the words "attracts" and "attraction," that for us presume a certain consent on the part of the person attracted, read *tractus, tractio* in Thomas's Latin, and they imply much more clearly than in modern languages a "drawing" against the will of the person thus "drawn."

son is drawn by his delight,"[31] how much more will a man be drawn toward Christ if he finds his joy in truth, beatitude, justice, eternal life, since Christ is all this. If then it is through him that we must be drawn, let us be drawn by the joy that obtains the truth . . .

But since external revelation and the object [in which one believes] are not merely the capacity to attract in this way, and since the internal instinct which pushes and moves us to believe has that capacity equally, *the Father attracts many to the Son by the instinct of that divine operation which, from within, moves the heart of man so that he believes:* "God Himself is the One who works in us, enabling us to will and to do" (Phil. 2:13); "I lead them with cords of human kindness, / with bands of love" (Hos. 11:4); "The king's heart is in the hands of the Lord; / he turns it wherever he will" (Prov. 21:1).[32]

The Gifts of the Holy Spirit

The three quotations from Scripture that support this teaching all suggest not only the intimacy of the divine action in the depths of the being in whom it works, but also the sweetness and the delight that result. We clearly meet up here with Saint Paul's teaching on those who allow themselves to be guided by the Holy Spirit. Though Thomas developed this teaching further in connection with the beginnings of faith *(initium fidei)*, it is only at this point that we can grasp more clearly the freedom of the divine initiative in collaboration with human freedom: "The very act of believing is the result of an intelligence that adheres to the divine truth *under the impulse of a human will moved by grace*: it is thus a question of an act of free will ordered to God."[33] In fact, it is the law of irresistible sweetness, which is that of the Holy Spirit at work in us through his grace, simultaneously a light that illumines the intelligence so that it only bows to the evidence, as well as a movement over the will which freely chooses because it sees there its good.[34]

31. *Trahit sua quemque uoluptas:* Virgil, *Bucolics* II, l. 65, quoted by Augustine, *In Ev. Ioh. tract.*, 26, 4 (BA 72, 491–93).

32. *In Ioannem VI, 44*, lect. 5, n. 935: "Sed quia non solum reuelatio, uel obiectum, uirtutem attrahendi habet, sed etiam *interior instinctus impellens et mouens ad credendum, ideo trahit multos Pater ad Filium per instinctum diuinae operationis mouentis interius cor hominis ad credendum.*"

33. Cf. *ST* IIa IIae q. 2 a. 9. We also find this instinct in the ad 3 of the same article: "Whoever has faith has a sufficient motive for belief; he is moved to it through the divine authority confirmed in the miracles, *and what is more, through an interior instinct of God that invites him there (interiori instinctu Dei inuitantis).*"

34. For the place of the affections in the movement of faith, M.-M. Labourdette's study

Characteristically going to the heart of things, Thomas reviews each of the seven gifts of the Holy Spirit to determine to which power and virtue to connect them. The enterprise is not lacking in subtlety, but we must believe that the author gave it no little importance, because he came back to it with different nuances on the way from the *Sentences* to the *Summa*, precisely with the intention of grasping the reality as closely as possible.[35] We will not look into every detail here, but it will be enough for us to see that this is nothing more nor less than a demonstration of the extent to which the spiritual life is under the total and constant motion of the Spirit.[36] Far from giving the impression, as was done in other periods, that the gifts are reserved for certain "elite souls," Thomas thinks that they are not only given to all with charity itself, but also that they are given all at once, in an enlightening parallel with what occurs in the case of the virtue of prudence:

The moral virtues dispose our appetitive faculties to be governed by reason; similarly, the gifts dispose all the powers of our soul toward the motion of the Holy Spirit. Now, if the Holy Spirit dwells in us, it is through charity: "The love of God has been poured into our hearts through the Holy Spirit that has been given to us" (Rom. 5:5); so too it is through the virtue of prudence that our reason is perfected. It follows that, in the way that the moral virtues are linked among themselves in prudence, so the gifts of the Holy Spirit are linked among themselves in charity. *Thus, whoever has charity possesses all the gifts of the Holy Spirit, but without charity we do not possess any of them.*[37]

---

can be read with profit, "La vie théologale selon saint Thomas. L'affection dans la foi," *RT* 60 (1960): 364–80, which recalls, among others, the beautiful passage from *De ueritate* q. 14 a. 2 ad 10: "As to its end, [faith] finds its culmination in affectivity, for from charity it obtains meritoriousness of its end. But its beginning is also found in affectivity, to the extent that the will convinces the intelligence to adhere to the things of faith."

35. In addition to *In III Sent.* d. 34 q. 1 a. 2, see *ST* Ia IIae q. 68 a. 4 and various places in the *Secunda Secundae* where Thomas deals with each gift according to a specific virtue: understanding and knowledge in relation to faith (qq. 8–9); fear, which corresponds to hope (q. 19); wisdom to charity (q. 45); counsel to prudence (q. 52); piety to justice (q. 121); the gift of fortitude to the virtue of the same name (q. 139).

36. I refer to the study by M. M. Labourdette, "Saint Thomas et la théologie thomiste," in the entry "Les dons du Saint-Esprit," *DS*, vol. 3 (1957), col. 1610–35; cf. M.-J. Nicolas, "Les dons du Saint-Esprit," *RT* 92 (1992): 141–52. See also J. M. Muñoz Cuenca, "Doctrina de santo Tomás sobre los dones del Espíritu Santo en la Suma teológica," *Ephemerides carmeliticae* 25 (1974): 157–243. Though I have not used it here for an obvious methodological reason—we want Saint Thomas to speak for himself—I refer the reader to the classic study by John of Saint Thomas, *The Gifts of the Holy Spirit*, trans. Dominic Hughes (New York, 1951), which largely depends on the Master, including his commentaries on Scripture.

37. *ST* Ia IIae q. 68, a. 5. Absolutely central, this teaching on the connection of all the virtues in prudence and charity will be more fully dealt with in a later chapter.

This is at first glance incomprehensible for whoever imagines in his mediocrity that he can be good without being just or chaste. But this position properly translates the great thesis of the connection of the virtues that, according to the Master of Aquino, rule the Christian life. We must emphasize how far this position is from all elitism. Life under the regime of the gifts is not a game preserve restricted to a small number of people. Nothing could be further from Thomas's thinking, since he affirms with the greatest clarity that the gifts are necessary to salvation. The assertion might appear too strong in its generality if Thomas had not justified it in advance. The gifts are as entirely necessary to salvation as are charity and the other theological virtues without which it is impossible to achieve communion with God. And that is why the gifts are given together with the virtues. It will be enlightening to follow Thomas's reasoning on this point, which shows a deep knowledge of the laws governing the life according to the Spirit. The general idea remains the same: though reason suffices for attaining a purely human end, reason is radically insufficient to a supernatural end. And that is why God gives us grace and the virtues. But the virtues themselves remain at our disposal, and we can make of them only a timid use, too ungenerous, fearful and without flair; and it is precisely here that the Holy Spirit takes up the baton:

In the order of supernatural ends, reason moves us only to the extent that it is transformed, to a small degree and *imperfectly*, by the theological virtues; *its movement does not suffice if the instinct and motion of the Holy Spirit do not intervene from above*; as Saint Paul says, "Those who are led by the Spirit of God, they are the sons of God; if they are sons, they are also heirs"; the Psalm (142:10) says the same: "Your good Spirit will guide me on the path of righteousness." We must understand that *no one can obtain the heritage of that land of the blessed if he is not moved and attracted by the Holy Spirit*. This is why, to obtain that end, it is necessary for man to have the gift of the Holy Spirit.[38]

The necessity of the gifts of the Holy Spirit for salvation is understood to mean, it goes without saying, the gifts that arise from sanctifying grace, properly speaking. There are other gifts of the Spirit (those that are called in the scholastic language graces *gratis datae*, which correspond to what we today call "charisms"). Given as needed for the use of the community, they do not partake of the same kind of necessity, and Thomas explains this very clearly:

38. *ST* Ia IIae q. 68 a. 2.

Some gifts of the Holy Spirit are necessary to salvation; they are common to all the saints and always dwell in us, as is the case for charity "which never ends" (1 Cor. 13:8) and remains in the future life. Others are not necessary to salvation and are given to the faithful as a manifestation of the Spirit: "To each is given the manifestation of the Spirit for service" (1 Cor. 12:7). . . . As to the second type of gift, it is reserved to Christ to have the Holy Spirit always with him.[39] [Remarkably, however, concerning the great passage in which Saint Paul speaks of the charisms, Thomas says decisively:] In the Church, there is no one who does not have his share of the graces of the Holy Spirit (nullus est in Ecclesia qui non aliquid de gratiis Spiritus Sancti participet).[40]

When one speaks of the necessity of the gifts and their connection to the virtues, one should not therefore imagine that it means going beyond the virtues. On the contrary, according to a formula that Thomas often repeats, the gifts are granted "to help the virtues (in adiutorium uirtutum)"[41] to attain their final goal, despite our timidities, lukewarmness, pettiness. Certainly nothing goes beyond faith or charity, but our reason, which hesitates and calculates, does not always allow them a free path. God then intervenes and takes us by the hand, so to speak, in order to make us advance more surely on his pathways:

Not everything is known by human reason, not even everything that is possible for it, whether we take it in the perfection of its natural development, or we take it in the perfection that the theological virtues give to it. From this it comes that reason cannot ward off foolishness on every point or the other ills of the same kind [of which Saint Gregory speaks in the objection]. But God, with the knowledge and power of someone to whom everything is subordinated, through his intervention places us in safety from all foolishness, ignorance, spiritual sloth, hardness of heart, and other similar things. That is why we say that the gifts, which make us docilely follow the instinct of the Holy Spirit, are granted against these kinds of defects.[42]

One can only admire the penetration of these remarks. What the gifts of the Holy Spirit allow us to pass beyond are not acts manifestly contrary

39. In Ioannem XIV, 17, lect. 4, n. 1915. Cf., in particular, ST Ia IIae q.111 a. 1.
40. In I ad Cor. XII, 7, lect. 2, n. 725.
41. This is the formulation in the In Isaiam XI, Leonine, vol. 28, p. 79, line 127. This matches a similar expression in ST IIIa q. 7 a. 5 ad 1: "The virtues perfect the powers of the soul in as much as they are guided by reason; perfect as they are, they still need to be helped by the gifts that perfect the powers of the soul in as much as they are moved by the Holy Spirit."
42. ST Ia IIae q. 68 a. 2 ad 3.

to grace; that is taken for granted in whoever lives under the regime of the new law. Nor do we go beyond the theological virtues, which remain superior to the gifts since they are their roots. But it is the *human modality* of realization, what we are accustomed to call imperfections, which are so many limits and shackles to the glorious liberty of the children of God, that we surpass. So the being who is most docile to the Spirit's action will also be the freest. In that being, all action depends on grace, but grace itself not only respects, but supports the free character of his movement.[43]

The Fruits of the Spirit

Having spoken of the gifts, Thomas adds two additional questions, truly rather surprising to those who might expect from him nothing but a simple description of mental structures. But they are not intended to surprise us, since we know that Thomas is a fervent reader of Scripture. Fully aware of the fact that "the Sermon on the Mount contains the complete program for the Christian life,"[44] he asks himself, therefore, about the beatitudes, which the Lord speaks of in the Gospels (Matt. 5:3–12, Luke 6:20–26), and Saint Paul (Gal. 5:22–23) calls the fruits of the Spirit.[45] The

43. *ST* Ia IIae q. 111 a. 2 ad 2: "God does not justify us without us, for when we are justified *we adhere by our free will* to God's justice. That adhesion, however, is not the cause of grace, it is grace's effect. Everything depends, therefore, on grace *(Unde tota operatio pertinet ad gratiam)*." This is the general theory, so to speak; when he deals specifically with the action of the gifts, Thomas speaks thus about the gift of counsel (*ST* IIa IIae q. 52 a. 1 ad 3): "The children of God are moved by the Holy Spirit in their own proper way, which is to say, in respect of their free will *(secundum modum eorum, saluato scilicet libero arbitrio)*."

44. *ST* Ia IIae q. 108 a. 3: "*Sermo quem Dominus in Monte proposuit, totam informationem christianae uitae continet.*" In the *Dedicatory Letter to Urban IV* which accompanies the *Catena Aurea* on Saint Matthew, Thomas had declared similarly: "In the Gospel we are offered the essentials of the catholic faith *(forma fidei catholicae)* and the rule of all Christian life *(totius uitae regula christianae)*." The Augustinian inspiration behind this is evident; cf. S. Pinckaers, "Le commentaire du sermon sur la montagne par S. Augustin et la morale de S. Thomas," in *La Teologia morale nella storia e nella problematica attuale. Miscellanea L.-B. Gillon* (Rome, 1982), 105–26.

45. *ST* Ia IIae qq. 69–70. See also the most ample parallel passage from the commentary on Galatians 5:22–23, lesson 6, nos. 327–34. In the *In III Sent.* d. 34 q. 1 a. 6 and following Saint Augustine, Thomas had added in this context a consideration of the seven petitions of the Our Father. We should also look at *In Matt.* V, nn. 396–443 on this point, and, along with the article mentioned in the preceding note, the commentary by S. Pinckaers, "La voie spirituelle du bonheur selon saint Thomas," in *Ordo sapientiae et amoris*, 267–84, in particular pp. 276 ff., where the writer speaks of the "astonishing dialogue begun by Saint Thomas between Aristotle's philosophy and the theology that takes its origin in faith in the cross of Christ" (p. 284). See also, by the same author, *Sources of Christian Ethics*, 188–90. On this subject, one may also consult A. Gardeil, "Fruits du Saint-Esprit," *DTC*, vol. 6

proximity is not arbitrary, for there is more than one point in common between the fruits and the beatitudes, and the link with the Holy Spirit is evident from the moment we perceive that all this is rooted in the Spirit as its source. These two questions are too little read because of a tendency to regard them as secondary in the overall movement of the *Summa*,[46] but they are much appreciated by the best contemporary moral theologians.[47] These scholars enthusiastically see there "a program of life and spiritual progress," and they are inspired by it "to trace a portrait of the spiritual man."[48]

The list of the beatitudes without doubt does not need to be restated here, but perhaps it will be of use to recall the list of the fruits of the Holy Spirit as Thomas found it in the Latin of the Vulgate: charity, joy, peace, patience, benignity, goodness, long-suffering, gentleness, faith, modesty, continence, chastity.[49] To understand what all this is about, we must see that, in comparison with the virtues and the gifts, the beatitudes and fruits do not represent new categories of *habitus*, but quite simply the acts that come forth from them:

The name fruit has been transposed from corporeal things to spiritual. Now, in corporeal realities, we call something a fruit that is the product of a plant when it has arrived at ripeness and has a certain flavor. There is a fruit simultaneously with respect both to the tree that produced it and the man who picks it. Accordingly, with this example, when we are speaking of spiritual realities, we can take the word fruit in two senses: in the first meaning, we speak of the fruit of a man to designate what is *produced* by him; in the second meaning, the fruit of the man will be what is *picked* by him.[50]

(1920), col. 944–49; Ch.-A. Bernard, "Fruits du Saint-Esprit," *DS*, vol. 5 (1964), col. 1569–1575.

46. Cajetan notes that these two questions "require frequent re-reading and constant meditation, but they do not need commentary (*lectione frequenti, meditationeque iugi egent, non expositione*," in his Commentary on the passage).

47. See D. Mongillo's fine studies, "Les béatitudes et la béatitude. Le dynamique de la Somme de théologie de Thomas d'Aquin: une lecture de la Ia–IIae q. 69," *RSPT* 78 (1994): 373–88, and "La fin dernière de la personne humaine," *RT* 92 (1992): 123–40.

48. R. Bernard, note 137 to *La Vertu* (French translation with notes and appendices of St. Thomas Aquinas, *Summa theologiae* Ia IIae qq. 61–70), vol. 2 (Paris, 1935), 382. The whole of this penetrating commentary may be read with profit.

49. The Greek of the New Testament has only nine of these, not the full list.

50. *ST* Ia IIae q. 70 a. 1. Without saying so, Thomas distinguishes himself here from Bonaventure (*In III Sent.* d. 34 p. 1 a. 1 q. 1; *Opera Omnia*, vol. 3, pp. 737–38), who sees in the beatitudes not acts, but habitus. Cf. E. Longpré, "Bonaventure," *DS*, vol.1 (1937), col. 1789–90.

This simple ordering of the vocabulary permits a first clarification. If we think about what is *produced* by man, it is clear that it is human acts that receive the name "fruits." If they are such according to the capacity of reason, they are then fruits of reason; but if they are products according to a higher virtue, that of the Holy Spirit at work in the virtues and the gifts, then we say that the action of man is the fruit of the Holy Spirit, *as proceeding from a divine sowing.*"[51]

If we think, however, of fruit as what is *picked* by man, then a perspective of unsuspected dimensions is opened to our gaze. The fruit of man, as the fruit of the earth, is not only this or that isolated product, but the entire income that planting renders. Transposed to the field of human action, the *picked* fruit will be the final end which man will enjoy. "It follows that our works, in their quality as the effects of the Holy Spirit working in us, present themselves as fruits, but to the extent that they are ordered to their end, which is eternal life, they present themselves rather as flowers."[52] Thomas, whose rigorous language is quite praiseworthy, does not draw back at times from metaphor, but the one used here is especially welcome: from the sowing that the Holy Spirit performs in the soul to the fruit of beatitude, passing through the flowers of our good works, there is indeed an entire program.

But if, following Saint Paul, he speaks more readily of fruits than flowers, it is because virtuous acts bear in themselves their own delight and even, in a way, their own reward.[53] It is here, then, that we encounter the beatitudes. As the "fruits," the "beatitudes" are also acts that have the virtues and the gifts as their origin, but they are distinguished from the fruits in that they are even better acts: "We demand more of the idea of beatitude than of fruits. . . . We use the word beatitudes *only to designate perfect works*; that is why we otherwise attribute works to the gifts rather than to the virtues."[54] In particular, from the fact that they bear the same name as the fruit ultimately *picked*, the beatitudes convey even better

51. *ST* Ia IIae q. 70 a. 1. The image of the sowing by the Holy Spirit is familiar to Thomas: it is notably found in the parallel passage from the *In ad Gal.* V, 22–23, lect. 6, n. 330: "We speak of the fruit of the spirit for he 'sprouts' in the soul beginning with the spiritual sowing of grace *(ex semine spiritualis gratiae)*." See also *ST* Ia IIae q. 114 a. 3 ad 3 (cf. note 63 below).

52. *ST* Ia IIae q. 70 a. 1 ad 1.

53. *In ad Gal.* V, 22, lect. 6, n. 322: "the works of the virtues and of the Spirit are an ultimate reality *(quid ultimum)* in us."

54. *ST* Ia IIae q. 70 a. 2.

than the image of fruit, that they are only the beginning of a fulfillment yet to come.

Between Saint Ambrose, who reserves the beatitudes to the future life, and Saint Augustine, who understands them to be of the present life, or even Saint John Chrysostom, who divides them into two categories, Thomas had to find his own way.[55] His solution then is all the more interesting:

We should note that hope of future happiness may be in us in two ways. First, by reason of our having a preparation for, or a disposition, to future happiness, and this is by way of merit; *secondly, by a kind of imperfect beginning of future happiness in holy men, even in this life.* For it is one thing to hope that the tree will bear fruit when we see only the leaves, another when we see the first fruits begin to appear.

Accordingly, those things which are set down as merits in the beatitudes are a kind of preparation for, or disposition to, happiness, either perfect or inchoate: while those that are assigned as rewards may be either perfect happiness, and so refer to the future life, *or some beginning of happiness, such as is found in those who have attained perfection, in which case they refer to the present life.* When a man begins to make progress in the acts of the virtues and the gifts, it is to be hoped that he will arrive at perfection, both as a wayfarer, and as a citizen of the heavenly kingdom.[56]

These reflections convey beyond all doubt an echo of a spiritual experience, if not necessarily the author's—though we might believe so—at least that of the saints who have illustrated the beatitudes in their own way. It is quite true, as Thomas explains with respect to the gift of tears, that the saints are consoled beginning in this life because they have a share in the consoling Spirit. Similarly, those who hunger for justice are also satisfied because their food, as was Jesus', is to do the will of the Father. As to the pure of heart, it is equally true that they see God in a certain way through the gift of understanding.[57] But the echo of this spiritual experience is sensed perhaps even better when Thomas examines how the fruits are at once linked with one another and distinct:

Since, however, a fruit is something that proceeds from a source as from a seed or root, the difference between these fruits must be gathered from the various ways that the Holy Spirit produces "sprouts" *(processus)* in us: which process consists in

55. Cf. D. Buzy, "Béatitudes," *DS*, vol. 1 (1937), col. 1306–7.
56. *ST* Ia IIae q. 69 a. 2.
57. *ST* Ia IIae q. 69 a. 2 ad 3.

this, that the mind of man *(mens hominis)*[58] is set in order, first of all, in regard to itself; secondly, in regard to things that are near it; thirdly, in regard to things that are below it.

Accordingly man's mind is well disposed in regard to itself when it is in possession of itself in good times and bad. Now, the first disposition of the human mind toward the good is effected by love, which is the first of our emotions and the root of them all, as stated above (cf. Ia IIae q. 27 a. 4). Wherefore, *among the fruits of the Holy Spirit, we reckon charity first,* for the Holy Spirit is given in a special manner, as in His own likeness, since He Himself is love: "The charity of God is poured forth in our hearts by the Holy Spirit, who is given to us" (Rom. 5:5).

The necessary result of the love of charity is joy: because every lover rejoices at being united to the beloved. Now charity is always in the presence of the One it loves: "He that lives in charity, lives in God, and God in him" (1 John 4:16). Wherefore the consequence of charity is joy.

But the perfection of joy is peace, in two respects: First as regards freedom from outward disturbance; for it is impossible to rejoice perfectly in the beloved good, if one is disturbed in that enjoyment by something else; and conversely, whoever has a heart perfectly set at peace in one object, cannot be disquieted by any other, since everything else is indifferent to him: "Much peace have they that love thy Name; and for them there is no trouble" (Ps. 118:165). In fact, external things do not disturb them to the point of not being able to enjoy God. Secondly, as regards the calming of the restless desire: for he does not perfectly rejoice, who is not satisfied with the object of his joy. Now, peace demands these two conditions: that we be not disturbed by external things, and that our desires rest altogether in one object. Wherefore, after charity and joy, peace is given in the third place.[59]

Thomas continues by connecting "patience" and "long-suffering" with that good internal ordering of oneself in adversity. In what concerns uprightness of our connections with others, he will similarly situate "goodness," "benignity," "gentleness" (or equity of soul), "faith" (which takes the form of fidelity toward men and the demotion of self in the submission of the mind to God). The list finishes with the right ordering with regard to things that are below us, and it is here that "modesty," "continence," and "chastity" enter. Without needing to follow this in detailed exposition, the long quotation just cited is sufficient to show the place of

---

58. R. Bernard interprets this text a bit when he translates, here and later on, *"mens hominis"* (the mind of man), as *"the spiritual man"*: this is certainly not unjustified, but that reading could lead some to believe (contrary to the intention of its author) that Thomas is thinking about a special category of Christians, when his proposition is applicable to everyone.

59. ST Ia IIae q. 70 a. 3.

the fruits of the Holy Spirit and of the beatitudes in the construction of the spiritual organism. In fact, everything is present, here as elsewhere, and even if Saint Paul probably was not thinking of providing a systematic description, the theologian's effort to understand how things are linked, one to another, is not only not out of place, but is profoundly enlightening both about the skill of Thomist analyses and for whoever desires to distill from his reading the elements of a spiritual teaching.

More than this, however, we should note that Thomas puts the whole of the spiritual life under the banner of hope of eschatological fulfillment.[60] The play of the "already there" and the "not yet come," which the twentieth century rediscovered reading the Bible, runs through all the Master of Aquino's determinations. We have already seen this rather well with respect to his conception of theology[61] as well as in how he speaks of the sacrament of the Eucharist.[62] We will meet in another place, and with a significant emphasis, all spiritual life as placed under the sign of the way and its stages between that "unfinished beginning," which is grace at work in our lives, and the future fulfillment that will be the end of this effort:

The grace of the Holy Spirit, as we possess it in the present life, is not equal to that achieved (in actu) glory, but it is in germ (in uirtute): as the seed of the tree that contains within it the whole tree. Similarly, through grace the Holy Spirit dwells in us, who is the sufficient cause of eternal life; that is why the Apostle calls it "the down payment of our inheritance" (2 Cor. 1:22).[63]

60. This has been clearly seen by D. Mongillo, "Les béatitudes et la béatitude," p. 379, who speaks of it as the "most remarkable character of the Thomistic analysis of the Béatitudes." See also the different, but perfectly convergent, approach of É.-H. Wéber, "Le bonheur dès à présent, fondement de l'éthique selon Thomas d'Aquin," RSPT 78 (1994); 389–413, for whom this realized anticipation of beatitude through grace and the gifts is precisely what distinguishes Thomas from his contemporaries, who reserved beatitude to eschatology only.

61. Cf. chapter 1 of the present volume.

62. Let me refer here to my Saint Thomas Aquinas, 129–36. But we might also recall the anthem O sacrum conuiuium in which Thomas reminds us of the three dimensions of the sacrament: "In this sacred meal in which we receive the Christ as food, we celebrate the memory of His Passion, the soul is filled with grace, and a pledge of future glory is given to us (futurae gloriae nobis pignus datur)." See in particular ST IIIa q. 73 a. 4 and the commentary by A.-M. Roguet in L'Eucharistie (French translation with notes and appendices of St. Thomas Aquinas, Summa theologiae IIIa qq. 73–83), vol. 1 (Paris, 1960), 352 ff.; J.-P. Torrell, "Adoro te: La plus belle prière de saint Thomas," in Recherches thomasiennes, 367–75.

63. ST Ia IIae q. 114 a. 3 ad 3. This is not the only such treatment. When Thomas wonders elsewhere about the connection existing between the end of the world and the achievement of beatitude, he explains it by a chain of succeeding perfections: "The first perfection is the cause of the second perfection. Now, to attain beatitude, two elements are

The Interior Master

Among the qualities attributed to the Holy Spirit by Scripture, there is the fact that Saint John calls it with a certain insistence "the Spirit of truth" (John 14:17; 15:26), "who will lead us into all truth" (John 16:13). Attentive as he is to the specifically human in the search for the truth, Thomas could not fail to be interested at length in these verses. His teaching is here doubtless less psychological than in the texts that we have just read, but his more dogmatic intention has no less spiritual repercussion. It is also enlightening to encounter the circular figure familiar to Thomas in order to return and thus to conclude at our point of departure, through a kind of inclusion:

He is "Spirit of truth" for he proceeds from the Truth and speaks the Truth. . . . And he proceeds from it, he also leads to the Truth [which is to say to Christ] who says: "I am the Way, the Truth, and the Life" (John 14:6). In fact, as in us the love of truth comes from truth conceived of and meditated upon, so in God Love proceeds from the Truth conceived, who is the Son. *And in the same way that he proceeds from it, he also guides us to that Truth:* "He will glorify me, for he will have received from me" (John 16:14). That is why, as Ambrose puts it, "everything true, by whomever spoken, comes from the Holy Spirit" *(omne uerum a quocumque dicatur a Spiritu Sancto est).* "No one can call Jesus the Lord except in the Holy Spirit" (1 Cor. 12:3); "When the Comforter will come, whom I will send to you, the Spirit of Truth . . ." (John 15:26). To manifest the Truth then is a property of the Holy Spirit, for it is Love who reveals secrets: "I call you friends, for I have taught you everything I have learned from the Father (John 15:15)."[64]

The quotation attributed to Saint Ambrose—which is really from his anonymous contemporary, called Ambrosiaster by Erasmus—is familiar to Thomas. He repeats it often and in the most diverse contexts.[65] Without

---

required, nature and grace. The very perfection of beatitude will take place at the end of the world, but it will be preceded, for nature, by the first creation of things, and, for grace, by the Incarnation of Christ, since 'grace and virtue have come through Jesus Christ' (John 1:18). *Thus on the seventh day is the completion of nature; at Christ's incarnation, the fulfillment of grace; at the end of the world, the fulfillment of glory"*; see also *In ad Eph. I,* 14, lect. 5, n. 43, where Thomas develops the difference between the Holy Spirit as *pledge* and as *down payment* on our heritage.

64. *In Ioannem XIV,* 17, lect. 4., n. 1916.

65. There are 15 occurrences, the majority in the commentary on the *Sentences* (5) and in the *In Ioannem* (4). In this form, Thomas doubtless got the expression from Peter Lombard, *Collectanea in Epist. Pauli, in* 1 Co 12,3 (PL 191, col. 1651 A), but we also already find it in Ambrosiaster in a slightly different way; "quicquid enim uerum a quocumque dicitur,

stopping overly long on it (since this byway would take us too far afield) it is not without interest to note in passing that Thomas not only repeats Ambrosiaster's formula, but he amplifies it at times by emphasizing that it is not only all truth (omne uerum), but all good (omne bonum) that comes from the Holy Spirit.[66] Like the first, the second affirmation is perfectly consistent with the confidence that Thomas shows everywhere else about the deep goodness of the creation. We remain, in any case, in a trinitarian context here, quite clear in the passage from John, and which the author emphasizes with obvious eagerness.[67] To speak of the Spirit of Truth is not merely to speak of the witness that he renders to the Son, whose work he completes.[68] It is especially to restate how we are led by him to the Son

---

a sancto dicitur spiritu" (Commentarius in Epistulas paulinas, In Ep. ad Cor. I, 12,3: CSEL, vol. 81, 2, [Vindobonae,1968], p. 132 [PL 17 (1879), col. 258 B]). Beyond the commentary on Paul's text in which the source of the quotation is found (In I ad Cor. XII, 3, n. 718), it is enough to know that it is used above all where it is necessary to distinguish the action of the Holy Spirit on the natural plane from his action on the supernatural plane: "'Everything true, by whomever spoken, comes from the Holy Spirit,' in the sense that it is he who infuses the natural light and who moves the intelligence to understand and grasp the truth" (ST Ia IIae q. 109 a. 1 ad 1). We do not argue from this that the Holy Spirit dwells necessarily through grace in him who speaks the truth, whatever it may be, as the objection would have it here, but the universality of the Spirit's presence and action in this context corresponds exactly to the universality of the active presence of the Word in all things. Whatever darkness exists in this world where the Incarnate Word has brought his light, Thomas explains elsewhere, we can only say that "no mind is darkened to the point of not participating in anything of the divine light. In fact, all truth, whoever knows it, is entirely due to that 'light which shines in the darkness'; for 'every truth, whoever says it, comes from the Holy Spirit'" (In Ioannem I, 5, lect. 3, n. 103).

66. "Omne uerum et omne bonum est a Spiritu sancto"; this passage is not found in modern printed editions, but it will probably be in the future critical edition, since it has been communicated to R. Busa for the Index Thomisticus by the Leonine Commission. It can be found under the lemma "76773-a spiritus+sanctus" (Sectio II, vol. 21, p. 157), n. 02272. We meet with the same expression a little further on (n. 02275): "Omne uerum et omne bonum a quocumque fiat fit a Spiritu sancto." In both cases, it is a matter of the commentary on 1 Cor. 12:3 (RIL = Reportationes ineditae Leoninae).

67. At the end of a long polemical passage against "the Greeks," Thomas remarks that if the evangelist rightly says: "the Spirit of Truth who proceeds from the Father," he does not say that he does not proceed from the Father and from the Son, "because when he says the Spirit of Truth, which is to say of the Son, he implies that he proceeds from the Son. In fact the Son is always united to the Father, and inversely when we are dealing with the procession of the Holy Spirit."

68. The Spirit gives witness to the Son in three ways: "by instructing the disciples and giving them confidence to witness. . . , by communicating his teaching to those who believe in Christ. . . , by softening the heart of the listeners" (In Ioannem XV, 26, lect. 7, n. 2066).

and through the Son to the Father, for their temporal missions are as inseparable as their eternal processions:

Just as the mission of the Son had as its effect to lead us to the Father, so the mission of the Holy Spirit is to lead believers to the Son. Now the Son, Wisdom begotten, is the Truth itself: "I am the Way, the Truth, and the Life" (John 14:6). Thus, the effect of this mission is to make men participants in the divine Wisdom and to introduce them to the Truth. *The Son being the Word, brings us the teaching, but the Spirit makes us able to receive it.*

Thus when Jesus says: "He will teach you all things," he means this: *Whatever a man learns from outside himself, if the Spirit, from within, does not give him understanding, it is lost effort: "If the Spirit does not dwell in the heart of the hearer, in vain does the teacher speak."* "It is the breath of the Almighty who gives understanding" (Job 32:8). So much is this the case that even the Son, speaking through his humanity, is powerless if he is not moved from within by the Holy Spirit.

We must remember what he says above: "Whoever hears what comes from the Father and receives his teaching comes to me" (John 6:45). He explains here what this means, for whoever is not taught by the Spirit does not learn anything, which is to say, who receives the Holy Spirit from the Father and the Son, knows the Father and the Son and comes to them. The Spirit teaches us all things, inspiring us and directing us inwardly, and elevating us to spiritual things *(Facit autem nos scire omnia interius inspirando, dirigendo et ad spiritualia eleuando).*[69]

The Master of Aquino could not say, in commenting on Saint John, anything stronger than what he had already said elsewhere in various forms, but in repeating here his beloved circular movement, he gives another proof of what we might call the "structural" presence of the Holy Spirit in the world as he sees it and, as a consequence, in his own theological construction. The Spirit was already the one through whom and in whom all the gifts of God come to us, those of nature as well as those of grace. In clarifying now that the Spirit is also he in whom and through

---

69. *In Ioannem XIV*, 25, lect. 6, nn. 1958–59; cf. *ST* IIa IIae q. 177 a. 1 where we meet in plural form the same quotation from Saint Gregory: "If the Holy Spirit does not fill the hearts of the listeners, in vain does the voice of the teachers echo in the bodily ears," *In Evangelia* II, hom. 30, n. 3 (PL 76, 1222 A). We recognize here an echo of the teaching of the interior Master dear to Saint Augustine (*De magistro* 11, 38) that he repeated often in the *In Ev. Ioh. tract.* (on 1:7; 20:3; 26:7; 40:5) or in his homilies as well as his *Sermo* CLIII, 1: "We speak, but God instructs; we speak, but God teaches"; cf. M.-F. Berrouard, note 4: "Le Maître intérieur," in S. Augustin, *Homélies sur l'Évangile de S. Jean*, BA, vol. 71 (Paris, 1969), 839–40. We cannot assimilate Thomas's teaching on this point, however, to that of Saint Augustine, for it is rather different, as may be seen by reading the respective *De magistro's* (for Thomas, cf. *De uer.* q. 11).

whom, alone, the Word of the Son can be received and perceived, Thomas finishes the explanation of why it is also he, the Spirit, alone who can lead believers into the whole Truth:

As the Holy Spirit proceeds from the Truth, it pertains to him to teach them the Truth and to assimilate them to Him who is its Principle. Christ says, "the whole Truth," which is to say the truth of the faith that he will teach through a superior intelligence beginning in the present life, and in a full way in life eternal, where "we will know as we are known" (1 Cor. 13:12), for "his unction will teach us everything."[70]

Source of all truth and doctor who teaches it, from its most humble form to its complete manifestation; prime origin of all good in the order of nature as of grace; first initiator of our life as children of God, whom it teaches us to call Father; constant support of all our acts who leads them to their fulfillment; seed of eternity who gives us his fruit of eternal beatitude, the Holy Spirit is truly for Saint Thomas the first Gift, the Gift par excellence, He in whom and through whom the Father grants us His favor. It is again in him and through him that we are led back to the Son and through Him to the Father.[71]

70. *In Ioannem XVI*, 13, lect. 3, n. 2102.
71. It will not be an imposition on the reader, I hope, to offer again the words that form an epigraph, so to speak, to these chapters on the Holy Spirit: "Just as we have been created through the Son and the Holy Spirit, so it is through them that we are united to our final end."

PART II

Man in the World and Before God

༟

CHAPTER X

A Certain Idea of the Creation

To speak of spirituality is certainly to speak about God, as we have just done in the preceding pages. But it is also to speak about man, with whom God wished to establish a relationship in love which culminates in the saints. That, too, we have done up to this point. Or rather, it was impossible not to do so. God, himself, speaking to man through the prophets, the apostles, and Jesus himself, could only use human words. Man, too, does not know how to speak of God in a purely "detached" manner without implicating himself in the discourse. Under the pretext of arranging the themes in a series, there was no question, then, of artificially isolating the two partners in the spiritual dialogue. It remains true, however, that we must not fuse them, and that it is possible and sometimes necessary to separate them, lest we confound the image with the model, the creature with the Creator.

One of Thomas Aquinas's principal contributions to Christian thought is precisely to have taught theologians to distinguish what belongs to the structural order of the nature of things and what rises from the pure gratuitousness of the divine gift. Prior to everything we can say on the supernatural level,[1] there are basic natural data that cannot be forgotten, for they qualify the way in which the gift of grace itself can be received and lived. According to an old scholastic adage that repetition has not suc-

---

1. Though this priority should not always be understood chronologically, it is good to preserve, at least according to an order of nature. To take a simple example, I must first exist as a creature to receive the gift of grace; even supposing that grace is given at the same time as nature (as was the case for the first man, according to Thomas), it remains true that nature is that in which grace is received.

ceeded in turning into banality: "Grace does not destroy nature, but brings it to perfection."[2] There is hardly an assertion attributed to the Master of Aquino which is better known than that, but it conveys a truly fundamental decision. Nowhere does Thomas represent man or the world in the idealist way, as if man had only a life of the spirit and the world represented nothing but matter without any connection to us. He always sees them in their mutual links with each other, in the way God made them, with a nature that sin has not been able to destroy and that grace can repair without abolishing it.[3] In return, the exact appreciation of these natural data also qualifies the idea that we have of God Himself: our way of conceiving the creature has repercussions for our conception of the Creator.[4] This also leads to consequences in the spiritual realm.

If what I have just said is right, it will come as less of a surprise that the two most burning problems, which have provoked the most unrest since Thomas's second period teaching at Paris, were exactly two questions not exclusively philosophical, but profoundly rooted in pre-theological decisions. The two matters, on which Thomas's positions earned him the strongest enmity and even suspicion of heresy, were, on the one hand, his theory of creation and the eternity of the world and, on the other hand, his anthropology—or to put it more simply, his conception of

---

2. *In II Sent.* d. 9 q. 1 a. 8 arg. 3: "*Gratia non tollit naturam sed perficit*"; cf. *ST* Ia q. 1 a. 8 ad 2. This axiom is found in a more explicit form in a substantial development of even greater interest in *Super Boetium De Trinitate* q. 2 a. 3: "*Dona gratiarum hoc modo nature adduntur, quod eam non tollunt set magis perficiunt*" (Leonine, vol. 50, p. 98). The adage is also put forward under the form of ontological evidence: *Gratia praesupponit naturam*, and almost always in a given application, with respect to faith, to supernatural life, to the law, etc. Cf., e.g., *De uer.* q. 14 a. 9 ad 8; q. 27 a. 6 ad 3; *ST* Ia q. 2 a. 2 ad 1: "*sic enim fides praesupponit cognitionem naturalem, sicut gratia naturam, et ut perfectio perfectibile*"; *ST* Ia IIae q. 99 a. 2 ad 1; *ST* IIa IIae q. 10 a. 10; q. 104 a. 6; etc. The fundamental studies of this subject are already old, but still highly valuable: J. B. Beumer, "Gratia supponit naturam. Zur Geschichte eines theologischen Prinzips," *Gregorianum* 20 (1939): 381–406, 535–52; B. Stoeckle,"*Gratia supponit naturam*": *Geschichte und Analyse eines theologischen Axioms* (Rome, 1962).

3. It is precisely this that preserves the "accidental" character of grace (cf., on this point, what I said in chapter 8). As to the fact that sin did not destroy nature, Thomas is no less firm: "Sin could not make man totally cease to be a rational being, because then *he would not even be able to sin any more.* It is therefore impossible that that level of nature would be destroyed," *ST* Ia IIae q. 85 a. 2. On this, see the careful study by B. Quelquejeu, "'Naturalia manent integra.' Contribution à l'étude de la portée méthodologique et doctrinale de l'axiome théologique 'Gratia praesupponit naturam,'" *RSPT* 49 (1965): 640–55.

4. *SCG* II 3: "*Error circa creaturas redundat in falsam de Deo sententiam* (mistakes about creatures have repercussions in a false conception of God)."

man.[5] We will have to return to the latter question, but we can begin to enter into the first one here.

The debate on the creation itself was as lively as the one on the nature of man—perhaps deeper—and it divided various minds at the University of Paris around 1270. It involved the celebrated problem of the "eternity of the world," and numerous works of the period, including one by Saint Thomas, bear that title.[6] The questions arise differently for philosophers or for theologians. For the latter, the question is resolved by revelation itself. Since Genesis says quite clearly that the world began, it is not therefore eternal. The former, on the contrary, follow Aristotle and do not hesitate to reproduce his belief that the world existed from all eternity.

Uneasy about the consequences of this position, the Franciscan theologians boldly declared that it was unthinkable, and they claimed to be able to demonstrate by reason that indeed the world had a beginning. Friar Thomas, more aware of Aristotle's rigorous reasoning, taught that only faith causes us to hold that the world had a beginning, but that it is not possible to demonstrate this truth. It is the same for the creation as for the Trinity, he remarked, and we should take care not to treat as an object of science what cannot be such, out of fear of giving a pretext for the mockeries of the infidels:

That the world had a beginning, this is an object of faith; it is not an object of demonstration or science. It is useful to make this observation, lest by claiming to demonstrate the things of the faith by means of hardly conclusive proofs, [the things of faith] will be exposed to the derision of the unbelievers, giving them to think that we adhere for such reasons to the faith's teachings.[7]

5. I briefly went through the context of the two questions and the bibliography on the subject in my *Saint Thomas Aquinas*, 184–94. See the more ample treatment in É.-H. Wéber, *La Controverse de 1270 à l'université de Paris et son retentissement sur la pensée de S. Thomas d'Aquin* (Paris 1970). The cover adds a subtitle: *L'homme en discussion à l'université de Paris en 1270*. This book gave rise to several important reviews, notably C. B. Bazán, "Le dialogue philosophique entre Siger de Brabant et Thomas d'Aquin. A propos d'un ouvrage récent de É.-H. Wéber, O.P.," *RPL* 72 (1974): 53–155; W. H. Principe in *Speculum* 49 (1974): 163–67.

6. *De aeternitate mundi*, Leonine, vol. 43, pp. 85–89. This question has been the subject of numerous recent publications (see *Saint Thomas Aquinas*, 184–87, for the context and the relevant bibliography), but we still do not have in French the equivalent of what A. de Libera did with the *De unitate intellectus contra Averroistas* (*De unit. intell.*) (cf. note 17, chap. 11).

7. *ST* Ia q. 46 a. 2. The point about the mockery of the infidels is common in Thomas when he wishes to remind theologians of the humility of their state. Cf. *SCG* I 9; *ST* Ia q.

If this question had no other advantage than to bring fully to light the respective demands of faith and reason, it would already have been worth posing. But this is only the most obvious aspect of the approach to reality that deeply marks the consequences of Thomas's positions. His way of seeing the created universe and of understanding man's behavior in this world is in radical dependence on his conception of creation. We see this as much in the way that he recognizes the consistency and autonomy of created reality as in the way he appreciates its worth. The valuing is not the result of a voluntary decision—as if the theologian decided after the fact that this world created by God cannot be bad—but of an initial philosophical option itself commanded by the nature of things. Just as his conception of virtue supposes a certain idea of man, as we will quickly see, so his vision of man in the world rests on a metaphysics of creation. Despite the difficulty of the enterprise, we must try to explain this briefly, for it alone can account for certain fundamental spiritual choices in Thomas. Thomas's view of the world is not only free of all disdain or even condescension, it is highly positive.

A Certain Relation

Since our knowledge starts from experience of sensible realities, we have a natural tendency to represent the first creation of things by God on the model of artistic creation. A wooden statue that had no other existence than that of pure possibility—in the thought of the artist and in the trunk of the tree from which it is carved—exists in a new form through the action of the person who "created" it. In reality this schema is deceiving; what we describe in this way is an occurrence, a simple change. In creation properly speaking, there is no change at all, for there is no object capable of change. It suffices to reflect an instant to understand this. For something to change, it must first exist. Now, prior to the creation, there was *nothing*. Literally "no-thing."[8] Thomas thus refuses very firmly this imaginative representation: "The creation is not a change, it is *the very dependence of the created being on the principle of its being*. It pertains therefore to the category of relation."[9]

---

32 a. 1; *De rat. fidei* 2, Leonine, vol. 40 p. B 58 (ed. Marietti, n. 956); V. Serverat, "L 'irrisio fidei' chez Raymond Lulle et S. Thomas d'Aquin," *RT* 90 (1990): 436–48.

8. This is what the expression creation *ex nihilo* means. And we should keep from translating this: creation *starting* "from nothingness," or "from nothing," for "starting" would insidiously reintroduce the imaginary schema of change.

9. SCG II 18, n. 952. We find the great expositions of creation in SCG II 6–38, ST Ia qq.

This definition of the creation as a "dependence of the created being on its principle" is precisely what allows Thomas to be at ease about the eternity of the world: this dependence would hold true in fact quite as well if the world existed from all eternity; it is not necessary to have a beginning in time to be dependent. The connection of the created with its origin is not a problem of duration. But, in any case, we do not need to focus on that here. Rather we need to look at the use of the category of relation. At first sight, nothing seems more appropriate; on reflection, two large difficulties present themselves, and we cannot pass beyond them without a little further analysis.

First, to speak of "relation" is to speak also of "co-relation." A relation supposes two partners whose reciprocal connections modify them, if only in connecting them, one to the other, in a mutual dependence.[10] Now, while this is the case for the creature, it cannot be true of God. God cannot be dependent on anything or anyone. It is difficult then to speak about Him in terms of a "real" relation. If we retain the word "relation" in this case, it is because of a veritable requirement of thought, for we would hardly know how to conceive of a relation that would not be mutual; but whereas the theologians speak here of a real relation on the side of the creature, on God's side they admit only a relation "of reason," which is to say purely conceptual. This does not mean that God is disinterested in His creation—we know on the contrary that he maintains it in being in a continuous way—but that something entirely different is here than our intra-worldly relations. God is not subject to change; nothing then can happen to him; he is transcendent to His creation.[11] He is not then sub-

---

44–49; *De pot.* qq. 3–5. For fuller expositions, refer to J.-H. Nicolas, *Synthèse dogmatique, Complément*, 5–99. See also the rather technical exposition by G. Barzaghi, "La nozione di creazione in S. Tommaso d'Aquino," *Divus Thomas* (Bologna) 3 (1992): 62–81; É. Gilson, *Christian Philosophy of St. Thomas Aquinas*, 147–59; the already old book by A. D. Sertillanges, *L'idée de la création et ses retentissements en philosophie* (Paris, 1945), retains its interest, as does the short, but very suggestive article by M.-D. Chenu, "La condition de créature. Sur trois textes de saint Thomas," *AHDLMA* 37 (1970): 9–16. Contemporary research is hardly occupied with this question, cf. J. Arnould et al., "Bulletin de théologie. Théologie de la création," *RSPT* 78 (1994): 95–124.

10. This phrase is of course to be understood of real relations in their two terms, for there are also relations that do not necessarily imply modification and dependence of the two correlatives; this is the case of the relation between the knowing subject (*sciens*) and the object known (*scitum*); the fact of being known does not entail a thing's being modified or dependent with respect to the knowing subject.

11. *ST* Ia q. 27 a. 1 ad 3: "Deus [est] extra totum ordinem creaturae"; for the difficulties raised on this subject in several contemporary theological essays, I refer to the full analyses

ject to the relation of creatures toward Him; he transcends it *because He is its very cause.*

The solution to the second difficulty in using the category of relation is perhaps more difficult to grasp. But it will show itself as crucial for what follows. We have just defined the creation as entailing, on the side of the creature, a unilateral relation of total dependence with respect to its source. Nothing is more true; but for a creature to exist in relation with God it must first exist. That is very clear: no relation, unless between existing realities. But if this relation is the creation itself, then we have a paradoxical consequence: in the ontological order, in the order of existing realities, the relation that is creation comes *after* the creature.

This appears to create a difficulty but if we think a moment, we understand what is at stake. Between God, cause of the world, and the world that is beginning, there is absolutely nothing, not even the action of God—since we cannot imagine it as an intermediary between God and the world (God's action is God Himself). Nothing then is interposed, and it necessarily follows that *temporally* the world exists first in its status as a dependent thing, and the quality of being created is posterior to the created reality itself; it refers to its creator. This is the simple explanation of the creation *ex nihilo.* If the creative action is not exercised on a pre-existing matter, it is clearly not exercised on nothingness either.[12] It directly meets the very reality that it puts into being, and thus this being precedes—as much in reality as in the understanding that we form of it (*intellectu et natura,* as is said in more technical terms)—the relation with God which is established by that very fact. Thomas recalls this position each time that he returns to this subject,[13] and he even had occasion to defend it in his confrère and contemporary Peter of Tarentaise, who is reproached for spreading this same teaching:

---

already cited of H. Seidl, "De l'immutabilité de Dieu," who is interested in the philosophical aspect of the question, and of M. Gervais, "Incarnation et immuabilité divine," who pays more attention to the theological problems. The two authors rightly specify that the fact that the relation is not real on God's side does not in the slightest prevent its foundation being entirely real: God is *really* creator, lord, etc.

12. *De pot.* q. 3 a. 3 ad 1: "In creatione, non ens non se habet ut recipiens diuinam actionem, sed id quod creatum est (In the creation, non-being does not behave like the recipient of the divine action [which exists, in this case], but that which is created)."

13. *ST* Ia q. 45 a.3 ad 3: "If we understand the creation as a mutation, the creature is its end; but according to what it is in reality, a relation, the creature is then its subject, and precedes it in reality, as a subject precedes its accident"; cf. *In I Sent.* d. 1 a. 2 ad 4, which

It is true to say that, in reality, the creation puts nothing into the created except the relation to the creator from whom the creation has being, and which is a certain accident. *And this relation, considered from the point of view of the being that it has in the subject, is a certain accident posterior to the subject.* To the extent that it is the end of the divine creative action, however, it has a certain character of priority.[14]

This will perhaps be easier to grasp if we remember that it is possible to distinguish two aspects in the idea of relation. Inasmuch as it is an accident, which is to say inasmuch as it qualifies a subject already existing and complete by itself, the relation is evidently posterior to the subject. If then we speak of the creation as a relation, we cannot do anything but conceive of it as posterior to the created reality. But if we envision the relation under its formal aspect of relation, which is to say inasmuch as it is "toward the other" *(ad aliud)*, according to the connection itself that exists between two subjects, it is no longer then "inherent" in the subject, but only "joined" to it.[15] Under this new aspect, inasmuch as it results from the divine action, the relation of creation is in some way anterior to the created subject, as the divine action itself which is its proximate cause.[16]

These explanations may appear daunting, perhaps even idle, to someone who has never thought about them. We ask the reader's pardon, but we take the trouble to look into them because they are crucial. These distinctions are not mind games; they aim simply at respecting the complexity of reality and taking account of the double aspect under which it may be envisaged. The posteriority of the relation of creation to the existence of the thing whose dependence the relation emphasizes, fully brings to light the substantiality of the creature, which is to say the fact that the creature is an *in itself* with is own proper autonomy. And we shall see that, according to Thomas, the Creator respects the substantiality and the laws

---

G. Emery assures me is probably the origin of Peter of Tarentaise's thesis (see the following note).

14. *Responsio de 108 articulis*, a. 95, Leonine, vol. 42, p. 293: "Verum est quod creatio secundum rem nichil ponit in creato nisi relationem ad creatorem a quo habet esse, que est quoddam accidens. Et hec quidem relatio quantum ad illud esse quod habet in subiecto, accidens quoddam est posterius subiecto; sed in quantum est terminus actionis diuine creantis, habet quandam rationem prioritatis."

15. This is the difference between *inhaerens* and *assistens*, which allows Thomas to explain the distinction between the accidental being of the relation (its inherence) and the notion or even the concept of relation (pure connection *ad aliquid*, which does not involve inherence), cf. *De pot.* q. 7 a. 9 ad 7.

16. *De pot.* q. 3 a. 3 ad 3.

of his creation. According to the profound saying of the poet Hölderlin, "God made man as the ocean the continents—by withdrawing himself." But otherwise the fact that the substantial being thus established in its autonomy is equally constituted in a relation of total dependence with respect to its source manifests the relational character of its being and action. From its first arising, the real appears thus as being "toward" the other and, in the present case, "of" the Other. The creature finds in this very relation the reality and the truth of its condition of being finite and dependent.

"And God Saw That It Was Good"

This would be an insufficient treatment of the metaphysics of creation if we did not immediately add that in the Christian perspective, which is Thomas's and ours, the reason for the creation does not consist in the profit that God might derive from it.[17] Only our human actions can be motivated by interest, as noble as they may sometimes be; only God himself can be the motive of His own action. The marvel of creation lies precisely in the fact, that in not seeking anything other than his goodness, he communicates it to his creatures:

It is for themselves that God wills the universality of creatures and, at the same time, he wills that they exist for himself; the two things are in no way contradictory. Indeed, with an eye to his own goodness, God wills that creatures be, which is to say, so that they imitate [his goodness] and represent it in their way. They do so since it is from [that goodness] that they have their being and that they subsist in their natures. This comes then to the same thing as saying God made everything for himself (as Proverbs 16:4 well says: "The Lord has made all things for himself"), and that he made creatures so that they would exist (Wisd. 1:14: "He created all beings so that they subsist").[18]

By the very fact of their creation by God, the world and everything in it are good, beautiful, and true. Thomas, who holds this on the basis of the first page in the Bible, gains confirmation of it from the doctrine of the

---

17. *ST* Ia q. 44 a. 4: "It does not pertain to the first agent to act with a view to acquiring some end; he can have no end but the communication of his perfection, which is to say his goodness." In addition, it is for this reason that *"God alone is absolutely liberal,* for he does not act for his own advantage, but only with a view to [communicating] his goodness" (ibid., ad 1). I have already spoken amply about this subject in chapter 3, "God and the World." See that chapter for further details.

18. *De pot.* q. 5 a. 4.

convertibility of the transcendentals.[19] According to this approach to reality, the creature does not exist simply as a being pure and simple. The degree of being that comes to it is accompanied by a corresponding participation in the truth, goodness, and beauty of its creator. Friar Thomas's resolutely positive vision of the world is rooted at this depth.

As we deal with the deep goodness of things, the resemblance of the effect to its cause once again comes to the fore, but understood in a way far beyond what we normally think of. Even before coming to the specifically theological theme of man as image of God, it is already true to say on the natural plane that the creature resembles God in two ways: not only "is [the creature] good as God Himself is good," but also "[the creature] moves another creature toward the good, as God Himself is the cause of goodness in beings." It is in this double aspect that the double effect of God's government of His creation occurs: *conservation* of things in the good and their *motion* toward the good. This is merely to speak in a general way, for if we consider the effects of the divine guidance of the world from a particular point of view, then we would have to consider multitudinous effects—since God guides each creature to its perfection according to its own particular path.[20]

Leaving aside many questions that are raised about the doctrine of Providence,[21] and that have a considerable importance for concrete spiri-

---

19. The classic text is *De ueritate* q. 1 a. 1. It is too long to be reproduced here; but a good translation will be found in R. Imbach and M.-H. Méléard, *Philosophes médiévaux. Anthologie de textes philosophiques (XIIIᵉ–XIVᵉ siècles)* (Paris, 1986), 79–85. There is an echo of it in *ST* Ia q. 16 a. 3: "As the good is defined in relation to the appetite, so the true in relation to knowing. Now to the degree that something participates in being it is knowable. . . . The result of this is that since the good is convertible with being, the true is also. Nevertheless, just as the good adds to being the formal reason of attraction, so the true adds to being a relation to intelligence." This teaching continues to be studied, especially from the philosophical standpoint: S. Breton, "L'idée de transcendental et la genèse des transcendentaux chez saint Thomas d'Aquin," in *Saint Thomas d'Aquin aujourd'hui* (Paris 1963), 45–74; J. A. Aertsen, "Die Transzendentalienlehre bei Thomas von Aquin in ihren historischen Hintergründen und philosophischen Motiven," *MM* 19 (1988): 82–102. For the much more vast question of beauty and its place in the transcendental categories, see Umberto Eco, *The Aesthetics of Thomas Aquinas*, trans. Hugh Bredin (Cambridge, Mass., 1988) (presentation and critique by S.-Th. Bonin, *RT* 95 [1995]: 503–5); P. Dasseleer, "Être et beauté selon saint Thomas d'Aquin," in *Actualité de la pensée médiévale*, ed. J. Follon and J. McEvoy (Louvain-Paris, 1994), 268–86.

20. Cf. *ST* Ia q. 103 a. 4.

21. In addition to the exposition in *ST* Ia q. 22, see question 5 of the *De ueritate*, especially a. 1 ad 9 (First Series), where Thomas makes his vocabulary precise: unlike the divine

tual life, we can content ourselves here with studying the second effect: God gives creatures the capacity to be, in turn, a cause of goodness in the world. Thomas often had occasion to return to this point, but we would like to recall here—perhaps to make known—two passages where he deals with it in a special way. First, let us look at a special, little-known passage where the idea is calmly developed for the instruction of simple Christians and the consequences are approached with a certain fullness:

(Consideration of God as Creator) leads us to knowledge of the *dignity of man*. God indeed has created all things for man . . . and, after the angels, man is, of all the creatures, the one who most resembles God: *Let us make man in our image and likeness* (Gen. 1:26). This was never said of the heavens or the stars, but only about man. Not of his body, but of his incorruptible soul, endowed with free will, through which he resembles God more than any other creature does. . . . More worthy than any other creature, we must not in any way lessen this dignity by sin or disordered appetite for corporeal things that are inferior to us and destined to serve us. On the contrary, we must conduct ourselves according to the design that God had in mind in creating us. *Indeed, God created man to have dominion over all beings that are on earth and to submit himself to God. We must dominate and subordinate inferior creatures to ourselves and ourselves to God, to obey and serve him.* It is thus that we come to the enjoyment of God.[22]

This passage, taken from Thomas's preaching, reflects the exhortatory tone that we expect to find in a homily. It is not out of place here, but we would be wrong to neglect its doctrinal content, which proposes some main points of reflection on man in this world. If many of the themes have already been dealt with (image of God, for example), others deserve to be developed further: man's freedom in this world, the way he should conduct himself with respect to creation and his fellow men, the manner in which he should act as "master" in this creation that God has given him to dominate and manage, the diverse forms that the fulfillment of his personality may take. We will encounter all this in the coming chapters, and it will then become clear that spirituality has nothing disincarnate about it, that, indeed, it is imbued with a solid realism in the image of Master Thomas's anthropology. But there is another special place where he expressed himself more rigorously about what results from his positions concerning creation.

---

art that presides over the production of things, and the *dispositio* that rules over their harmony, *providence* orders them to their end.

22. *In Symb.* 1, *Opuscula theologica*, vol 2, n. 886.

Indeed, nowhere is this doctrine better developed, or with greater emphasis, than in the Third Book of the *Summa contra Gentiles*. The debate arises from positions of the Muslim theologians called *mutakalimoun* or *motecallemin*, and of the philosopher Avicebron, who has since been identified as the Jewish thinker Ibn Gebirol.[23] According to these authors, "no creature would have its own proper activity in the effects observed in nature: thus fire does not heat, but God causes heat in the presence of fire, thus too of all kinds of natural effects." To support this strange position, they adduce a whole series of reasons that lead them to conclude with the inactivity of every body, with the non-existence of every lesser cause; such that, in short, God alone is really acting in all the causes appearing in the world.[24]

Thomas has no trouble in formulating the immediate objections that common sense opposes to this curious theory: "In the hypothesis of the absolute ineffectiveness of creatures, it would be God who produces in an entirely immediate way and thus it is uselessly that he makes use of creatures in the production of his effects." This hardly resembles the idea of the divine wisdom, and we know otherwise that "if God has communicated his likeness to creatures, in giving them being in their turn, he has also communicated to them his likeness in such a way that creatures also possess a proper activity." But that is not all, and Friar Thomas understands how to show that this doctrine, which claims to exalt God by reserving to him all causality, ends up in fact in denying him respect, by offering too small an idea of him:

The perfection of an effect is the sign of the perfection of its cause; the more powerful its force, the more perfect its effect. Now, God is the most perfect of agents. It is also necessary then that he give perfection to the beings that he creates. So, too, *to subtract something from the perfection of creatures is to remove something from the perfection of the divine "virtue"* (*Detrahere ergo perfectioni creaturarum est detrahere perfectioni diuinae uirtutis*). Now, in the hypothesis of the inefficacy of every creature the perfection of the created world is greatly diminished, for it is the plenitude of perfection for a creature to be able to communicate its own per-

---

23. I cannot linger on the positions of these authors; to my knowledge, the most enlightening exposition of Thomas's discussion with them is found in É. Gilson, "Pourquoi saint Thomas a critiqué saint Augustin," *AHDLMA* 1 (1926–27): 5–127, which first deals with the error of the *motecallemin*, then with a critique of Ibn Gebirol, cf. pp. 8–35; (for this name, see p. 15: the term *calam* meaning word or discourse, the *motecallemin* are the partisans in the *calam*).

24. Cf. *SCG* III 69, nn. 2431–41.

fection to another. *This position thus detracts from the divine virtue.* [Thomas then develops other arguments against this theory, to conclude in similar terms.] God communicated his goodness to creatures in such a way that what one receives it can transmit to others. *To refuse to creatures their own proper action would thus be to detract from the divine goodness.*[25]

This passage is central to the discussion, but it does not end it. What follows is far from being peripheral and emphasizes that "if created things do not have their own proper action in the production of their effects, it would follow that the nature of no created thing could be known from its effects. And thus all our experimental science would be taken from us, since it proceeds primarily by going back from effects to their cause." It is quite strange that such a theory would have seen the light of day in the medieval Muslim milieu, where the sciences shone with a light still unknown in the West. This is no more than a secondary point for us, however. We should pay special attention to the words italicized above. Three times within a few lines, Thomas repeats that to diminish the creature is to wrong the Creator. For him there is no question of exalting God at the expense of man. In opposition to a spirituality in which the creature is only nothingness and where man must obliterate himself so that God may be glorified, Thomas is convinced that God is even greater when man is advanced.

We are here quite close to the perspective opened by the Prologue to the Second Part of the *Summa:* "Man too is the principle of his own acts because he possesses free will and mastery over his actions." With a surprising vigor, this "he, too" orients man not only toward God as a partner with his own complete role, but also in the world as a free and responsible agent on whom his dignity imposes a certain mode of behavior.

A Theology of Intermediary Realities

We can easily understand that all this is in direct connection with the metaphysics of creation that we have just recalled: not only do created natures have their "ontological thickness";[26] the Creator gives them the pow-

25. SCG III 69, nn. 2445–46.
26. Thomas would certainly not say, as did Bonaventure, that the world has no other reality than that of a shadow (". . . *totus mundus est umbra,* via, vestigium. . . . Unde creatura non est nisi sicut quoddam simulacrum sapientiae Dei et quoddam sculptile," *In Hexaemeron* XII 14, *Opera Omnia,* vol. 5, p. 386 b). The subject has given rise to an instructive exchange between S. Vanni-Rovighi ("La vision du monde chez saint Thomas et saint

er to act on their own proper level. He respects the laws that he has given them: "Author of nature, God takes away nothing from beings that is proper to their nature."[27] Thus Thomas says with tranquil assurance—in stark contrast with certain speculations in the following century that seem to identify arbitrariness and God's absolute power *(potentia Dei absoluta)*[28]—that God Himself cannot modify the nature of things: God can doubtless not create a circle, but if a circle exists it must of necessity be round.[29] In fact, it is "more appropriate to say that the impossible cannot be done, rather than to say that God cannot do it," but it is impossible that a man would be a donkey and four-footed.[30]

Contrary to what the *mutakalimoun* fear, this "is not owing to the fact that God would have been incapable of doing everything by himself, but that from an excess of goodness God wanted to communicate to creatures such a likeness to himself that not only do they exist, but also they are causes for others." This takes away nothing from God's causality, for without it nothing would be, nothing would act. But we can say with Saint Paul (Phil. 2:13) that "God works in us, enabling us to will and to do," without rejecting effective action on the created level. We should not conceive the Creator and the creature as two competing causes located on the same level; the latter is subordinated to the former such that each does everything on its own level:

It is clear that a single effect is not attributed to its natural cause and to God, as if one part was from God and the other from the natural agent; *it is completely from the one and the other (totus ab utroque)*, but differently. A little in the way in which a single effect is attributed entirely to the instrument and entirely to the principal cause.[31]

Bonaventure") and J. Châtillon ("Sacramentalité, beauté et vanité du monde chez saint Bonaventure"), in *1274—Année-charnière*, 667–78; 679–90. Though the latter argues that similar expressions do not remove any of the "ontological thickness" of the world, he recognizes that the accent is on the value of the sign.

27. SCG II 55, n. 1310: "Deus qui est institutor naturae non subtrahit rebus id quod est proprium naturis earum."

28. See several examples in L. Bianchi and E. Randi, *Vérités dissonnantes. Aristote à la fin du Moyen Âge* (Fribourg-Paris, 1993); cf. A. de Muralt, "La toute-puissance divine, le possible et la non-contradiction. Le principe de l'intelligibilité chez Occam," *RPL* 84 (1986): 345–61.

29. SCG II 55, n. 1299: "What suits a being in itself necessarily affects that being always and inseparably. Thus, 'roundness' belongs in itself to a circle, accidentally to a coin. It is therefore possible for the coin to cease to be round, but it is impossible that the circle not be round *(circulum autem non esse rotundum est impossibile)*."

30. ST Ia 25 a. 3.   31. SCG III 70, nn. 2465–66.

Many later theological discussions on the action of grace in man could have been avoided if this great principle, luminous in its simplicity, had not been somewhat lost from view.

But to stay close to our main purpose, it is clear that numerous consequences flow from this way of seeing the world. The most immediate appear in man's responsibility for created reality in its natural thickness. In truth, the field for these considerations could extend indefinitely, for it corresponds exactly to the realm opened by Thomas when he recalls the advantage of man over animal. To the objection that man is deprived of the natural protections and instinctive mechanisms perfected in the animals, he replies that, in fact, man has it much better, for "*he possesses reason and hands*, thanks to which he can get weapons, clothes, and other things necessary to life, and this in infinite ways. In Book III of the *De anima* (432 a 1), the hand is called 'the organ of organs.' This, too, well suits a nature endowed with reason, infinitely fertile in conceptions and capable of making an infinite number of instruments."[32] Thus the whole field of human action opens before us, but until other facets are explored in the following pages, let us content ourselves here with some quick points on two special sections.

Since the beginning of the twentieth century, and probably following the encouragement that successive popes have given to Christian reflection through their attention to political, economic, and social questions, we have seen the renewed reading of Thomas's oeuvre with an aim toward finding in it, if not direct answers to new problems, at least the principles that allow us to put the questions in their true light and, eventually, to discover some elements of a solution. Though already distant from us—going back before and just after the Second World War—these essays, in trying to put forward a theology of work, matter, the city, war, the Christian presence in the structures of the world, etc., indicate the fecundity of this theology of creation.[33] The social philosophy of Jacques Mari-

---

32. *ST* Ia q. 91 a. 3 ad 2; q. 76 a. 5 ad 4; cf. *ST* Ia IIae q. 95 a. 1.

33. To stick just to a single name in the French language, a whole segment of the pioneering work of P. Marie-Dominique Chenu could be noted here as an example. An authentic theologian and medievalist, he also occupied himself with various concrete investigations, inspired by Saint Thomas, into the then most current problems. Among many other titles, see his *La Parole de Dieu, II: L'Évangile dans le temps* (Paris 1964), which gathers together writings from 1937 to 1963; short notices written for this or that bulletin alternate with longer texts that are rarely very elaborate. The intuitions are of even greater interest than the detailed examination.

tain, in a politically committed work like *Integral Humanism*, is the best witness to it.[34] Though not always possessing Maritain's great originality, contemporary Thomist thought also pays considerable attention to these questions. Among Thomists this research never ceased,[35] and even now produces estimable works.[36]

We might also think of the most recent questions, such as the respect owed to the universe that God entrusted to man at the opening of Genesis (Gen. 1:28). Without attempting an apology that would be out of place here, we might say that Thomas's conception of creation is wholly suited to providing theological support for addressing the ecological worries of our time. We cannot expect to find in Thomas an answer to the problems that are specifically our own; that would be both anachronistic and useless. Nor will we find in him direct concern for the earth and animals such as we find in some of our contemporaries.[37] There is in him, though, a clear awareness that each species of creature corresponds to a special intention of the creator and contributes at its level of being to representing the goodness of God, so that what is missing in one being is supplied by another, and the whole universe represents the divine perfection more perfectly.[38]

The good that the universe represents, Thomas says, we have the duty to love in charity, including the irrational creatures, which we will desire as goods necessary to rational creatures.[39] We certainly cannot have friendship with these irrational creatures, "but we can love them by virtue of charity as among the goods that we will for others, in the measure that we will in charity that they are conserved for the glory of God and the use of man. And thus God Himself loves them in charity."[40] This affirmation is not an isolated one, and Thomas provides the reason why: "The good of the universe *(bonum universi)* also contains the rational creature, capable

34. We will return to this in chapter 13.
35. As witness the three volumes of the third Congress of the International Society Saint Thomas Aquinas: *Etica e società contemporanea*, ed. A. Lobato (Rome 1992).
36. See on this G. Cenacchi, *Il lavoro nel pensiero di Tommaso d'Aquino* (Rome, 1977).
37. Disappointed hope appears to have motivated the research of K. Bernath, "Thomas von Aquin und die Erde," and C. Hünemörder, "Thomas von Aquin und die Tiere," *MM* 19 (1988): 175–91 and 192–210.
38. Cf. *ST* Ia q. 47 a. 1; q. 44 a. 4.
39. This was well established by H. J. Werner, "Vom Umgang mit den Geschöpfen—Welches ist die ethische Einschätzung des Tieres bei Thomas von Aquin?" *MM* 19 (1987): 211–32. See especially pp. 226–27.
40. *ST* IIa IIae q. 25 a. 3. See the important parallel in *In III Sent.* d. 28 a. 2.

of beatitude, and to whom all other creatures are ordered; and according to this aspect it falls to God and to us to love in charity to the highest degree the good of the universe."[41]

We should not be surprised at the central place of human nature in this since, after God, it is the human who gives meaning to everything else.[42] As much as he wants to give maximum value to the things of this earth, Thomas would not dream for an instant of focusing his spirituality on the creation; rather he orients the creation toward its Creator. He would be happy to repeat with Saint Paul, "Everything is yours, but you are Christ's and Christ is God's" (1 Cor. 3:22).

Contempt for the World?

Having come to this point in our examination, we cannot help encountering a question—an obstacle that must be removed before proceeding further. For minds unfamiliar with Master Thomas's robust intellectual health, his position on the goodness of beings and of the universe might seem surprising. More often, medieval spirituality is spoken of as impregnated with a rather negative appraisal of created reality, and we must recognize that numerous medieval authors drew on what we would today call a spirituality of *contemptus mundi*, contempt for the world.[43] We might rightly ask if Friar Thomas had the same mentality. If so, that would lead us to review our presentation of these matters. The question deserves to be asked, if only to remove doubt, but it calls for a nuanced answer.

The theological positions indicated up to this point are too clear for anyone to doubt that they represent a conscious choice on our author's part. We cannot make him contradict himself on this level. On the con-

---

41. *De caritate* a. 7 ad 5: "competit Deo et nobis bonum uniuersi maxime ex caritate diligere."

42. Cf., in particular, *ST* Ia q. 65 a. 2; *SCG* III 71, n. 2474: "Res aliae, et praecipue inferiores, *ad bonum hominis ordinantur sicut ad finem*"; We will return more fully to this point in chapter 13.

43. The question is far from unambiguous. Without going into it here, I simply refer to a controversy of the 1960s, which is summarized in L.-J. Bataillon and J.-P. Jossua, "Le mépris du monde. De l'intérêt d'une discussion actuelle," *RSPT* 51 (1967): 23–38, and the list of various works on the subject in R. Bultot's enlightening article, "Spirituels et théologiens devant l'homme et devant le monde," *RT* 64 (1964): 517–48, who shows how mistaken it would be to interpret the divergences between "spirituals" and "theologians" as a simple differences of language. Numerous authors who insist on the nothingness of the creature or contempt for the world are in fact offshoots of a Platonist anthropology.

trary, an analysis of his vocabulary reveals the persistence of a spontaneous approach to things that betrays, if not an incoherence, at least a "mentality" taken from his age and place of origin, in slight disagreement with respect to that deeply positive view of reality. In itself, this would not be at all surprising; the greatest minds do not wholly escape their age, and Thomas is no exception to the rule.

The instruments that we now have allow us to verify certain matters almost instantaneously in the whole of Thomas's oeuvre.[44] In the present instance, they even provide more material than we can use. But in the absence of a complete survey, the numbers give us at least a fair idea of the right proportions. We beg the reader's pardon for this parade of data, but it bears examination. We have been able to find 446 uses of the substantives *contemptus* (438) and *contemptor* (8) in the whole of Thomas's work. In the vast majority of cases (420), these words are used in a rather unexpected way: scorn for God, his law, Christ, the sacraments, spiritual things, etc.[45] We can leave these uses aside; there are only 26 other instances relevant to our current discussion. It would take too long to review them all, but if we take them in order of decreasing frequency, we get the following list: "contempt"[46] for the world (6), for temporal things (6), for earthly things (5), for riches (5), for relatives (2), for worldly glory (1), for worldly things (1).

Among the six uses of *contemptus mundi*, we should leave out symbolic uses: the new bishop's sandals on the day of his consecration mean that he renounces the things of this world: he treads on them with his feet. We will not follow a special usage here: in a review of all the biblical books according to their main intention, Thomas follows Saint Jerome in saying that the book of Ecclesiastes teaches *contemptus mundi*. Closer to our present purposes, he three times mentions the rough habits of the religious mendicants as the sign of their "contempt" for the world. As to the

44. For example, the CD ROM *Index Thomisticus* by Roberto Busa, but I have also made use of the printed version of the *Index*, which makes it easier to define what really belongs to Thomas.

45. The way Thomas uses the verb *contemnere* is in complete harmony with his use of the substantives. Out of 576 occurrences, 520 are found in a deploring mode: contempt for God, Christ, the sacraments, the law of God, spiritual things, etc. The verb occurs 56 times in the sense of scorning something of this world: earthly goods, bodily goods, riches, honors, etc., but never about marriage.

46. Or "disdain," but we must take the context into account and remember that the first meaning of *contemnere* is "to hold as negligible."

last use of the term, it is found in the following passage, rather representative of the different contexts in which we find these kinds of expressions:

> The letter of the Gospel contains only such things as pertain to the grace of the Holy Spirit, either by disposing us thereto, or by directing us to its use. First, with regard to the intellect, the Gospel contains things about the manifestation of Christ's divinity or humanity, which dispose us by means of faith which we are given by the grace of the Holy Spirit: and then, with regard to the affections, it contains matters *touching the contempt of the world (ea quae pertinent ad contemptum mundi), which make man capable of receiving the grace of the Holy Spirit.* Indeed, *the world,* i.e., worldly men *(amatores mundi) cannot receive the Holy Spirit* (John 14:17). As to the use of spiritual grace, this consists in practicing the virtues, and the writings of the New Testament exhort men to this in diverse ways.[47]

This passage is doubly typical. By first explaining how we must understand "world," it shows that this "contempt" only bears on the evil world, in the sense that the world is rejected by Saint John and Saint Paul.[48] It does not include, then, the worth of the world created by God as such. In addition, we can grasp here the *comparative* context of the majority of the uses of the word where it is a matter of "despising" one or another of the things of the world: with respect to the love of God or the beatitude to which we are called, earthly things are *held to be negligible*. Most often, the reference to the Gospel is immediate: "If anyone wishes to come after me . . . ," or else, "If anyone loves his own more than me. . . ." Never in this context can we understand earthly things to be bad in themselves. Thomas's position is the exact opposite:

> In themselves, creatures do not turn us from God, but lead us to Him. . . . If they turn men from God, it is the fault of those who use them foolishly. Thus the words in the Book of Wisdom (14:11): "Creatures are turned into a snare to the feet of the unwise." And the very fact that they can thus withdraw us from God proves that they came from Him, for they cannot attract men except by the good found in them and that they have from Him.[49]

It is then entirely impossible to find in these few passages the expression of a general contempt or a rejection of the world and its goods, which

47. *ST* Ia IIae q. 106 a. 1 ad 1.
48. Cf. 1 John 2:15: "Do not love the world nor what is in the world. If someone loves the world, the love of the Father is not in him"; Rom. 12:2: "Do not conform yourselves to the present world."
49. *ST* Ia q. 65 a. 1 ad 3.

would permit the conclusion that Thomas saw in them something intrinsically evil.[50] Such a view would have been astonishing, for it would have meant that Thomas rejected the Aristotelian inspiration of his anthropology to adopt another of Platonic origins. Such incoherence would certainly be implausible, but it is worthwhile to be certain about the point. The general impression that emerges from these passages is rather the magnanimous or virtuous attitude as we find in Aristotle: to give generously and even to "despise" wealth spent for one's friends is to show disdain for exterior goods and much greater attachment to friends.[51] What such a man does for a friend corresponds exactly to what God Himself expects from whoever calls himself God's friend.

Religious Life and Secular Activities

Though Thomas's sporadic use of contemptus mundi does not carry any depreciation of his fully positive view of our world,[52] he does speak in a more negative way at moments. We can see this in his use of the qualifier "secular" (saecularis) and in the way he speaks about "secular activities" (negotia saecularia).[53] But his attitude is rather different depending on the two possible meanings of the word saecularis. If we are talking about the religious life, we will be obliged to conclude that it is unreconcilable with the secular; if we consider secularity as a fact, it is entirely possible to judge it more positively, even to Christianize it, and we are then at the starting point of reflection on the potential engagement of the Christian with this world.[54]

50. Bonaventure himself would vigorously protest this: "Who despises the world despises God: either this world is not made by God, or we must not despise it." He continues a little later: "mundus iste et ea quae sunt in eo, sunt amanda," In Ecclesiasten, Prooemium q. 1, s. c. 1 and 2, Opera Omnia, vol. 6, p. 6 b.

51. In Ethic. I, 9 (1169a18 and 26), Leonine, vol. 47/2, pp. 532–33 (ed. Marietti, nn. 1878 and 1881).

52. A very brief additional comparison will let us see that this vocabulary is not typical of Thomas. The Index Thomisticus takes into account several works that are not by Thomas; though statistically these works only account for around one-seventh of the whole, the use of the contemptus vocabulary is clearly greater: thus, contemptus mundi appears 16 times (as opposed to 6 in Thomas) and contemnere 1253 (as opposed to 576 in Thomas) in this much smaller corpus of writings.

53. I make use here of the remarkable inquiry by B. Montagnes, "Les activités séculières et le mépris du monde chez saint Thomas d'Aquin. Les emplois du qualicatif 'saecularis',". RSPT 55 (1971): 231–49.

54. See below chapter 13.

The first context in which we find *saecularis* arises from Saint Paul's invectives against "the wisdom of the princes of this world" (1 Cor. 2:6). Now, Thomas cannot help thinking about the wisdom transmitted by the thinkers of antiquity. He of course distinguishes that philosophical wisdom from the wisdom of the faith and from theological wisdom. But he recognizes its legitimacy and does not merely call it "secular" without several qualifications.[55] The intellectual virtue of wisdom is indeed entirely oriented by the search for the true, and in that sense it effects in us "*a certain beginning of beatitude*, which consists in the knowledge of the truth."[56] Certainly, human wisdom can turn against the wisdom of the Gospel, and Saint Paul opposes it to the folly of the Cross. Along with him, Thomas strongly affirms that "our wisdom does not lie in knowing the nature of bodies or the course of the stars or anything of that sort, but it consists in Jesus Christ alone."[57] But he knows also that knowledge is a good and beautiful thing, and that is why he does not refrain from introducing distinctions into Paul's texts:

However bad men may be, they are never entirely deprived of God's gifts, *and it is not God's gifts that must be reproved in them, but what comes from malice.* That is why [Saint Paul (1 Cor. 1:19)] does not simply say: "I will destroy their wisdom," for all wisdom comes from the Lord (cf. Isa. 29:14ff.). He says instead "I will destroy the wisdom of the wise," which is to say the wisdom that the wise of this world have erected against the true wisdom of God, and of which Saint James (3:15) states: "This wisdom does not come from above, it is worldly, animal, diabolical." . . . Because of their lack of wisdom, they have judged it impossible that God could become man and pass through death according to his human nature. Because of their lack of prudence, they have also judged it inappropriate that a man would suffer the Cross, out of scorn for disgrace (cf. Heb. 12:2).[58]

Though, with Paul, Thomas condemns the wisdom of this world, it is only to the extent that it opposes the Christian faith, and what he aims at then is at bottom only a lack of wisdom.[59] Otherwise, he is favorable to

55. The subject is too vast to be developed here; in addition to the article quoted in a previous note, see the fine study by B. Montagnes, "L'intention philosophique et la destinée de la personne," *RT* 69 (1969): 181–91; "Les deux fonctions de la sagesse: ordonner et juger," *RSPT* 53 (1969): 675–86.
56. *ST* Ia IIae q. 66 a. 3 ad 1.
57. *In ad Eph.* I, 9, n. 25; M. D. Jordan, *The Alleged Aristotelianism of Thomas Aquinas* (Toronto, 1992), 32–40 has strongly emphasized this point.
58. *In I ad Cor.* I, 19, n. 50.
59. *In I ad Cor.* I, 19, n. 49: "What is good in itself cannot appear foolish to anyone, *unless through lack of wisdom.*"

human wisdom as has been rightly underscored: "Philosophical wisdom is not depreciated, for it is not suspect as wisdom, it is only condemned in its secularity. Now, it is not secular by nature, it only becomes so by choice, exactly by the choice that places in it the ultimate meaning of human existence. The 'contempt' is not to declare it without value but to appreciate it at its just value. It is neither an illusory value from which we must turn away nor the highest value, which must be preferred to everything else. Far from sacrificing it, we must respect it as one of the intermediate ends for man that man cannot reduce to simple means and that he must not confuse with the ultimate end."[60]

Beyond the intrinsic reasons that support this judgment, there is doubtless also the fact that the practice of wisdom in Thomas's time still remained the business of clerics. It is a little different matter when he comes to speak of the properly secular tasks: the professions, commerce, the military, etc. It is not merely the good division of labor in society that requires monks and clerics to abstain from these pursuits. The use of force, even when legitimate, can degenerate into violence. And the pursuit of honest gain can, itself, decline into an unbridled seeking of profit. Even for lay people, these occupations are dangerous; all the more so are they for those who by profession ought to be peaceful and disinterested. Starting from these two examples, we feel a general mistrust coming through in many passages about secular activities.

We cannot however make a one-sided judgment here. Friar Thomas's reflections, like those of all his intellectual contemporaries, is guided by the well-known verse from Timothy (2:4): "Whoever is in God's service, should not be occupied in the world's affairs." This passage, which greatly influenced canon law about clerics, forbidding them to pursue certain occupations for the reasons we have just seen, also strongly inspired the theology of the monastic life, where this interdiction of secular occupations was understood as an incompatibility between those activities and exclusive consecration to God, and as bringing a true liberation because of an expansion of charity.

In that perspective it is undeniable that Thomas sees secular activities as being *impedimenta* for religious, i.e., obstacles. The *negotia saecularia* encompass the whole of what monks renounce by virtue of their profession: possessing goods, marrying, making one's own decisions. We recog-

60. B. Montagnes, "Les activités séculières," 240.

nize here the three evangelical counsels, deliberately connected with the three lusts denounced by Saint John (1 John 3:2), which ultimately took the form of the three religious vows: whoever accepts them is by that fact disengaged from the heart of this world's activities; those who do not embrace them, on the other hand, find themselves fully implicated in the world.[61] Thomas never condemns these three main worldly activities as illicit. He says quite clearly to the contrary that these realities, from which monks abstain, are otherwise licit.[62] If they were bad in themselves, all Christians would have to abstain from them. Not only can we do them without destroying charity, but we can live out charity without following the counsels.[63] Far from being a mark of superiority, the fact of committing oneself to the counsels is a declaration of infirmity.[64]

This appreciation of the relative value of secular activities puts us, in fact, at the heart of Thomas's theology of the religious life.[65] This is not the place to treat the subject in depth, but we can at least examine the passage on the teaching of the New Law, which clarifies the crucial difference between counsels, which are left to the choice of those to whom they are given, and precepts—essentially the twofold commandment of love—which are imposed on all as indispensable to arriving at the end, blessed eternity. It is on behalf of that unique end that everything must be appreciated:

61. Cf., e.g., *ST* IIa IIae q. 186 a. 2 ad 3; q. 184 a. 3; q. 188 a. 2 ad 2.

62. *ST* IIa IIae q. 184 a. 3 ad 3: "a rebus licitis abstinet"; q. 184 a. 5: "a rebus saecularibus abstineant quibus licite uti poterant."

63. *ST* IIa IIae q. 184 a. 3: "quae tamen caritati non contrariantur"; q. 189 a. 1 ad 5: a long response that connects observation of the counsels with the single end that is the perfection of charity.

64. *ST* IIa IIae q. 186 a. 4 ad 2. The patriarchs, such as Abraham, arrived at the perfection of charity while being married and possessing many goods, but this is a sign of their exceptional virtue. Weaker *(infirmiores)*, we must not presume about our powers and hope to be able to combine marriage, riches, and perfection. See also *ST* IIa IIae q. 188 a. 8 ad 3: only the perfect can obey the Holy Spirit directly; those still on the way toward perfection benefit greatly from obeying others. These notions recur often, particularly with regard to poverty. Cf. q. 184 a. 7 ad 1; q. 185 a. 6 and ad 1; q. 186 a. 3 ad 5. Everyone is to be detached interiorly and free with respect to those goods that can demand more than their due; this is not to require that everyone effectively practice, by a vow, poverty, celibacy, or obedience.

65. Let us refer here to the excellent studies by M.-V. Leroy, "Théologie de la vie religieuse," *RT* 92 (1992): 324–43 and by M.-M. Labourdette, "L'idéal dominicain," *RT* 92 (1992): 344–54. See also A. Motte, "La définition de la vie religieuese selon saint Thomas d'Aquin," *RT* 87 (1987): 442–53.

Man is placed between the realities of this world, where his life unfolds, and the spiritual goods, where eternal beatitude is to be found. The more he leans to one side the further he distances himself from the other, and vice versa. *To plunge completely into terrestrial realities to the point of making them the goal of our existence, the reason and rule of our acts, is to turn away totally from spiritual goods.* The commandments forbid such a disorder. However, to attain our proper end, it is not necessary to renounce the world completely, for we can arrive at eternal beatitude by using terrestrials goods, *provided that we do not make them the end of our existence.* But whoever entirely renounces the goods of this world will reach beatitude more easily. It is with a view to this that the counsels have been given.[66]

Since everything must be appreciated in light of the end, we thus find the comparative context that explains what we know of the *contemptus mundi.* The result of this enquiry becomes clear: we cannot remain unaware of Thomas's reservations about secular activities, but the reservations should not be overestimated. In the framework of a theology of the religious life, they do not call into question the positive appreciation that Thomas otherwise brings to the created universe. His reservations never let us think that terrestrial things are bad in themselves. He asserts on the contrary that we must not look down on these temporal goods, if they can help in the search for God.[67] It is also then legitimate to ask for them in prayer, "ask assistance that will help us to reach for beatitude, since our bodily life finds its sustenance in them and our virtuous activity uses them as an instrument."[68] But it is clear that to be totally detached, as the Lord asks in the beatitude about the poor in spirit, neither the counsels nor the virtues suffice. We need a special gift of the Holy Spirit:

Man is detached by virtue from temporal goods in such a way that he learns to use them with moderation; but the gift teaches him to hold them as entirely negligible *(totaliter ea contemnat).* This is why we can understand the first beatitude (Matt. 5:3) "Happy the poor in spirit," as scorn either for riches, or for honors, which is realized through humility.[69]

∿

66. *ST* Ia IIae q. 108 a. 4: this article should be read with the noteworthy commentary by J. Tonneau, *La loi nouvelle.*

67. Cf. *ST* IIa IIae q. 126 a. 1 ad 3: "Bona temporalia debent contemni, in quantum nos impediunt ab amore et timore Dei. . . . *Non autem debent contemni bona temporalia, inquantum instrumentaliter nos iuuant ad ea quae sunt diuini timoris et amoris.*"

68. *ST* IIa IIae q. 83 a. 6.

69. *ST* Ia IIae q. 69 a. 3.

In addressing doubts raised about "contempt for the world," the detour we have taken on religious or monastic life should not obscure our primary aim. Master Thomas's conception of creation, which is simultaneously that of a believing theologian and that of a philosopher, leads him to aver the autonomy and value of created reality. The creation, willed by God to show and communicate his goodness, but also for itself with its own consistency and laws, is not a pure pretext, nor a theater where Christians are merely passing figures, but properly the place where God's salvific will reflects his creating will and fulfills it with the real cooperation of man in a unique history of salvation whose salvific character does not abolish everyday reality.[70]

Much more even than the respect owed to the inanimate creation, what springs from the intrinsic value of the created universe is that human activity can give itself specific aims that, though not the final end, are still intermediate ends that are worth pursuing in themselves. To enumerate a few of them—the list could be much longer—in order of the great natural inclinations: to achieve the good everywhere we recognize it, to serve life under all its forms; to found a family; to raise children; to seek truth; to transmit knowledge by teaching; to increase it by research; to struggle for a better division of the goods of the earth; to serve one's country by political engagement, or humanity by maintaining peace among nations; not to forget the goods of friendship at the level of interpersonal relations; etc. All these objectives represent true goods that deserve to be sought out and served. Far from diverting us from our final end, they orient us toward it.[71]

---

70. Without attempting to give to the teaching explained in this chapter an external *confirmatur* which it does not need, I have been struck by the relevance of several lines by Pope Paul VI: "The central point and almost the pivot of the solution that in a prophetic and genial intuition he [Thomas] gave to the problem of the new confrontation between reason and faith, was to *reconcile the secularity of the world and the radicalism of the Gospel, escaping thus from that unnatural tendency that denies the world and its values,* without neglecting however the supreme and unavoidable demands of the supernatural order. Saint Thomas's whole doctrinal structure is indeed founded on that golden rule that he himself states beginning in the very first pages of the *Summa theologiae,* 'grace does not destroy nature, but perfects it,' and nature is subordinated to grace, reason to faith, love to charity" ("Lettre au P. Vincent de Couesnongle, Maître de l'Ordre des Frère Prêcheurs, pour le septième centenaire de la mort de saint Thomas," *RT* 75 [1975], 13–14, cf. 5–39).

71. This has been neatly demonstrated by W. H. Principe, "Aquinas' Spirituality for Christ's Faithful Living in the World," *Spirituality Today* 44 (1992): 110–31.

The Christian who is committed to similar tasks pursues the mission of the humanization of the earth, which his Creator has assigned to him (cf. Wisd. 9:2–3).[72] The is no reason, then, to do things by halves or reluctantly. On the contrary, the certainty that he must work with the future city in sight confers on man's labors a quality that labor alone cannot give: the imitation of the divine liberality that gives all the more effectively inasmuch as it is totally disinterested.

72. The way that Thomas understands the role of Adam just after the creation is deeply suggestive. Cf. *ST* Ia q. 96, and especially a. 2: "Man in a certain sense contains all things; and so according as he is master of what is within himself, in the same way he can have mastership over other things."

〜

CHAPTER XI

A Certain Idea of Man

To introduce the preceding chapter, we invoked the celebrated maxim: "grace does not destroy nature, but brings it to perfection." We are not giving in to an excessive taste for symmetry in beginning this chapter with another adage hardly less known: "Whatever is received is received according to the mode of the receiver."[1] This is true even on a material level: a liquid poured into a container takes the container's form. It is even more true of a "receiver" who is a free and intelligent being, endowed with certain qualities proper to it, but also with a special temperament and precise limits, thus capable of personal assimilation—resistance and refusal as much as reception and renewal. Let us translate our axiom freely: in the spiritual realm as elsewhere, we cannot misconstrue the laws of nature without running into defeat. It is here, following the doctrine on the creation, that we encounter the doctrine on man, the anthropology. The doctrine on man too was hotly contested by the Master of Aquino's adversaries, and it is testimony to perspicacity on their part. Among other questions of a more dogmatic type, indeed, the question about man rules over everything that can be said about the rootedness and development of the virtues in the human being. Which is to say that it directly leads into spiritual theology in Saint Thomas's school. We must then undertake a slight detour here to take more precise account of what was at stake.

1. "Quidquid recipitur ad modum recipientis recipitur (Whatever is received is received according to the mode of the receiver)." The impersonal form of the adage allows it to be used in various contexts, most often, however, in the realm of knowledge: even material things exist in us according to an immaterial mode, cf. *In III Sent.* d. 49 q. 2 a. 1; *SCG* II 79; *ST* Ia q. 75 a. 5; etc.

Man under Discussion

Consideration of man in the *Summa Theologiae* is not limited to some questions that speak of the human soul and its creation in the image of God, which come at the end of the First Part. In fact, the subject continues throughout the whole Second Part, where we find some indispensable particulars on human acts, liberty, conscience, the passions, virtues, social life and the laws that govern it, etc., without overlooking the end of human life and the means of grace that allow us to achieve it. We cannot forget this without completely misrepresenting the author's perspective. What we find in the First Part is simply the beginning of these reflections, where Thomas starts by situating man in the sheer vastness of the universe. In his own language, after having spoken of God in Himself, he turns to God in his connection with Creation. Then he wishes to explore what it means that God is the beginning and end of all things, and he must discuss how creatures proceed from God: first, there is creation in itself, as the act of God, then the various creatures who make up the created universe. He distinguishes three large categories of beings that come forth from the hand of God: angels (purely spiritual creatures), the world (a purely corporeal creature), and finally man (a creature simultaneously spiritual and corporeal).

The simple account of this division of subject matter says nothing about its content, but it at least allows us a first glimpse into the exact situation of man in this universe. Neither totally spiritual nor totally corporeal, he is both at the same time, participating through his soul in spirit and its immateriality, and through his body in matter and its corruptibility. Thomas invites the reader to marvel with him at this singular creature who appears to him as the pivotal point between two worlds at the same time that he sums up in himself the totality of the universe:

This opens up for us a marvelous perspective on the connection of things. *For it is always the case that the lowest in a genus touches the highest in the immediately lower genus.* Some of the rudimentary animals, for instance, barely surpass the life of plants; oysters, which are motionless, have only the sense of touch and are fixed to the earth like plants. That is why Blessed Dionysius can write that "divine wisdom unites the ends of higher things with the beginnings of the lower." *Among the animal organisms there exists one, the human body, endowed with a perfectly balanced make-up, which is in contact with the lowest of the higher genus, namely, the human soul, which holds the lowest rank in the genus of intellectual substances, as can be seen from its mode of understanding; so that the intellectual soul may be seen as a kind of horizon and frontier* (horizon et confinium) *of things corporeal and incorporeal, in that it is an incorporeal substance and yet the form of a body. And something composed of an intellectual substance and a body that it animates is at least as united as, and perhaps more, than a fire and its material, because the more form triumphs over matter, the greater is the unity of the composite.*[2]

This text is remarkable in several respects. First, it allows us to take into account to what extent the author presents himself here as the heir of the wisdom of the ancients, for he combines harmoniously in his synthesis not only themes, but entirely different philosophical inspirations. On the one hand, we find here, at least in the form of a strong suggestion, the ancient doctrine of man the microcosm, realizing in himself the universe "in miniature." This formula recurs no fewer than seventeen times and it would take us far afield to explore it.[3] On the other hand, we again find, especially in this passage, what has been called "the axiom of continuity," so very active in his work,[4] in which the Platonic inspiration of a metaphysics of the One and the Aristotelian addition of a philosophy of being

2. SCG II 68, n. 1453. Cf. *The Divine Names* VII, 3, *Dionysiaca* I, p. 407; cf. SCG III 61, n. 2362. The formula "horizon and confines" is frequently repeated by Thomas and comes from the *Liber de Causis*, prop. 2 (ed. H.-D. Saffrey, *Sancti Thomae de Aquino super librum De causis expositio* [Fribourg-Louvain, 1954], 10. Cf. C. D'Ancona Costa, *Tommaso d'Aquino, Commento*, 181). G. Verbeke, "Man as Frontier According to Aquinas," in G. Verbeke and D. Verhelst, eds., *Aquinas and Problems of His Time* (Leuven-The Hague, 1976), 195–223, traces the history of this expression of Platonist origin, but which is profoundly changed in meaning by Thomas. Verbeke also shows the phrase to be of particularly central importance for Thomas's conception of truth and ethics. See also F. Marty, "L'homme, horizon entre matière et esprit," in *La perfection de l'homme selon S. Thomas d'Aquin, Ses fonctions ontologiques et leur vérification dans l'ordre actuel* (Rome 1962), 163–98.

3. Instead of doing so here, let us note how, significantly, Thomas thinks of the microcosm when he tries to formulate the reasons for the Incarnation of the Word in human nature rather than in any other creature: "Given that he is constituted of a corporeal nature and a spiritual nature, man occupies, so to speak, the frontier of one and the other nature, and thus what is achieved for the salvation of man concerns the whole creation. . . . It was fitting, then, that the universal cause of all things would assume in the unity of the person [of the Word] this creature in whom it can be in the closest communion with all creatures" (SCG IV 55). See the exhaustive study by M. F. Manzanedo, "El hombre come 'Microcosmos' según santo Tomás," *Angelicum* 56 (1979): 62–92; É.-H. Wéber, *La personne humaine au XIIIe siècle* (Paris, 1991), 61–73, has labored to recover the origin and development of the term; for Thomas's anthropology, see pp. 146–198.

4. B. Montagnes, "L'axiome de continuité chez saint Thomas," *RSPT* 52 (1968): 201–21, discovered 33 passages where we find the celebrated assertion: "Semper enim inuenitur infimum supremi generis contingere supremum inferioris generis (For the lowest of the higher genus is always found to touch on the highest of the lower genus)."

flow together. The latter's empiricism corrects the risk of pseudo-universality in the former.

In Thomas's thought, this continuity is not only a matter of purely material contiguousness; it is matched by a participation on the part of the inferior thing in the perfection of the superior thing. At its highest level, the lower attains to the higher by participating in the latter's dignity through an imperfect resemblance. This principle is decisive for an anthropology that excludes all dualism from its vision of man, for there is no rupture, but rather continuity, between the biological, the sensory, and the spiritual in the human creature. The same soul is in each of them. Thomas's originality, compared with his contemporaries, appears here in its full light.

Given man's intermediate position between the world of bodies and the world of the spirit, we easily grasp that the problem put to anyone who reflects on human reality is precisely how to understand the nature of the link that holds the two disparate principles of being, spirit and matter, together. The passage we have just read presupposes a resolution of the question, for it is presented as the conclusion of a long discussion on several fronts with several interlocutors. Thomas first rejected the opinion of Plato and those who follow him, that man is really the intellectual soul.[5] The soul, in this view, makes use of a body, to which it gives movement, but not life, and in which it is only a temporary tenant.[6] To this dualist position, which has the disadvantage of attaching the soul to the body only in an accidental way, Thomas prefers Aristotle's position that the intellectual soul is not only the mover of the body, but in fact its "form." The soul gives the body life through a very intimate union that makes the two into a being that is perfectly one. But the soul is not in any way the whole of man.[7]

5. Recall the lapidary statement by Saint Augustine, In Ev. Ioh. tract. 19, n. 15 (BA 72, 207–9) "What is man? A rational soul having body." To tell the truth, this assertion represents more of a tendency than a definition per se, for Augustine also says in the same context: ". . . a soul, having body, does not make two persons, but one man. . . ."

6. Elsewhere (In II Sent. d. 1 q. 2 a. 4 ad 3) Thomas again attributes to Plato another comparison, according to which the soul is in the body like a pilot in a ship, but if this phrase became known through Aristotle and Plotinus, the image is not attributed by them to Plato. Cf. A. Mansion, "L'immortalité de l'âme et de l'intellect d'après Aristote," RPL 51 (1953): 444–72, see especially pp. 456–65.

7. This simplified summary of Thomas's thought presumes certain things to be known that cannot be pursued here. To understand his thinking, it must be followed, step by step in SCG II 56–90, or in ST Ia q. 75–83 with the notes by J. Wébert in L'âme humaine

In this perspective, "man is neither his body nor his soul," but the composite that results from the union of soul and body. And "since it is a matter of an animated body, we must not speak either of priority or posteriority; there is absolute simultaneity, since indeed the animated body coincides with the incarnate spirit."[8] The soul is doubtless the more noble part, by virtue of its spiritual nature created by God. But it is not a complete substance existing by itself. The subsisting individual, the human person, is the total reality formed by the union of soul and body. It is not the eye that sees, but the man through the eye, just as it is not the soul that feels, understands, or acts, but the man through his soul. If the body has need of the soul, the soul, for its part, has need of the body, and it can only be thought of as "unitable" to the body.[9] If its spiritual nature preserves it incorruptible and thus immortal, such that it can subsist alone after death, in the state of a separated soul, even so, "it retains in its being a natural aptness and inclination to be united to the body."[10] And Thomas declares with the greatest clarity, "Neither the definition nor the name of person are fitting to it."[11] Elsewhere, explaining that the immortality of the soul is not sufficient for beatitude, since only the resurrection of the body will fulfill the human heart's natural desire for salvation, he even

---

(French translation with notes and appendices of St. Thomas Aquinas, *Summa theologiae* Ia qq. 75–83) (Paris, 1928). It should also be studied in the important Disputed Question *De anima*, which is slightly earlier than the exposition in the *Summa*, and for which it prepares the way. See too the brief and precise exposition by L. B. Geiger, "Saint Thomas d'Aquin et le composé humain," in *L'âme et le corps* (Paris 1961), 201–20; more complete and more technical is J.-H. Nicolas, *Synthèse dogmatique, Complément*, pp. 303–47. See also the book, both simple and profound, written for a more general audience, by P.-M. Emonet, *L'âme humaine expliquée aux simples* (Chambray-lès-Tours, 1994), and M.-V. Leroy, "Chronique d'anthropologie," *RT* 75 (1975): 121–42, where the presentation is accompanied by illuminating critical remarks from an abundant literature on the subject.

8. *SCG* II 89, n. 1752. Translation by N. A. Luyten, "L'homme dans la conception de S. Thomas," in *L'anthropologie de saint Thomas*, ed. N. A. Luyten (Fribourg, 1974), 45.

9. *ST* Ia q. 75 a. 7 ad 3: "The body is not of the essence of the soul, but the soul has its very essence in being unitable to the body *(sed anima ex natura suae essentiae habet quod sit corpori unibilis)*."

10. *ST* Ia q. 76 a. 1 ad 6.

11. *ST* Ia q. 29 a. 1 ad 5: "The soul is a part of human nature; and that is why, even in a separated state, given that it retains its natural aptness for union, we cannot call it an individual substance, which is to say, a primary hypostasis or substance—no more than the hand or any other part of the human being. *Hence neither the definition nor the name person are suited to it.*" This reflection on the situation, contrary to its nature, of the soul separated from the body by death bears some valuable additions. Cf. *ST* Ia q. 89 a. 1; A. C. Pegis, "The Separated Soul and its Nature in St. Thomas," in *Commemorative Studies I*, 131–58.

uses this gripping formula: "The soul is not the whole man; *my soul is not me.*"[12]

We easily understand the importance of this opinion. Compared with all the "spiritualizing" conceptions of the human being, which risk considering the body a negligible quantity, Thomas Aquinas's solid realism leads him to affirm calmly that man is a corporeal being and that, without the body, there is no longer man. The soul is not united to the body to spiritualize it, but indeed because the soul needs the body. For without the body, the soul cannot even perform its most noble operation, understanding.[13]

This way of taking into account the mode of union of body to soul is opposed equally to two other positions successively discarded as insufficient to do justice to the complex unity of man. Among those holding the first position, we meet once again with various representatives of a Platonism enriched with numerous variations, but also with Saint Bonaventure and the Franciscans theologians who refuse to admit that the intellectual soul is the only form of the body. They agree in a common repugnance to attributing to the same soul the highest intellectual activities as well as everything that we have in common with the animals. In their view, three souls must be admitted corresponding to the three levels of life found in man: vegetative, sensitive, and intellectual.[14] Confronted with them, Thomas works resolutely to show that it is indeed the same soul that performs this triple function of animation, for each higher degree of a substantial form includes and realizes the lower degree. What can do more can also do less, we would say more colloquially. The unity of the living thing of an intellectual nature, which is man, is thus found more perfectly guaranteed, as the text above underscores.[15]

To this controversy, internal to the Christian world, a second was added, in which those who are adversaries over the first point fight side by side, because they have to confront an invading Arabism, which had already conquered a number of the philosophers of that time. These

12. In 1 ad Cor. XV, 19, lect. 2, n. 924: "*Anima* autem cum sit pars corporis hominis, *non est totus homo, et anima mea non est ego.*"
13. ST Ia q. 84 a. 4: "We cannot say that the intellective soul is united to the body for the sake of the latter. . . . *It is indeed rather the contrary that is true: the body appears especially necessary to the intelligent soul for its proper operation,* which is to understand."
14. See for example, SCG II 58; ST Ia q. 76 aa. 3–4.
15. For the whole set of these problems, see my *Saint Thomas,* 187–90: "The unicity of the substantial form."

thinkers held that there was no need for each human individual to perform for himself this noble function of understanding, since a single intellective principle, separated and common to all men, acted for the
whole of humanity. A fascinating thesis, we might say, but paradoxical.
And Thomas responds to it with a very simple question: how then would
we account for this undeniable, concrete fact: that this particular man
thinks *(hic homo singularis intelligit)?* "If someone claims that the soul is
not the form of the body, he will have to find a way to explain how the act
of thinking is the deed of this individual man. Each knows indeed by experience that it is he himself who thinks."[16] Known by the name
"monopsychism" (a single soul), this complex and multiform error is attributed to Averroes by Bonaventure and Thomas, and harshly fought by
them in certain of their contemporaries as well.[17]

It is not part of our purpose to review these controversies here in detail,
but it is important to understand what was at stake, for, beneath a purely
intellectual appearance, they bear considerable practical repercussions.
Thomas has no trouble in detecting, behind the claim of a single separate
intellect, the elimination of all individual liberty and responsibility, for
along with the intellect, the intellectual appetite — the will — is also put in
doubt: "An inadmissible conclusion, which would lead to the destruction
of all moral thought and social life."[18] As to the question of several souls
within one individual, not only does it not really take into account the
unity of the human being, but it sometimes conceals a secret depreciation
of the body and, in any case, compromises a true appreciation of the value of creation in its material dimension. Now, on all this Friar Thomas
has a clearly positive point of view. Though as a theologian he is first interested in the soul, he never forgets that it is the form of the body. The
human person is composed of soul and body; the salvation of one cannot

16. ST Ia q. 76 a. 1; cf. SCG II 59, n. 1362: "It is in the proper sense and in all truth that
we say that man thinks: *for if we can search for the true nature of the intellect, it is thanks to
the fact itself that we think*"; cf. De unit. intell.: "it is clear that this particular man thinks
(hic homo singularis intelligit); we would never try to know what the intellect is if we did
not think" (translation by de Libera, n. 61). We are here at the heart of Averroism, as it was
condemned by the bishop of Paris in 1270: "This proposition is improper and false: man
thinks" *(Chartul.* I, n. 432, prop. 2, p. 487).

17. See my *Saint Thomas Aquinas,* 191–96: "The *De unitate intellectus,"* to which
should be added A. de Libera's *Thomas d'Aquin, L'unité de l'intellect contre les averroïstes,
suivi des Textes contre Averroès antérieurs à 1270,* Latin text, with translation, introduction,
bibliography, chronology, notes, and index (Paris 1994).

18. SCG II 60, n. 1374 *in fine.*

be envisaged without the other.[19] Thomas's teaching on the passions is the place where the repercussions of this anthropology on the spiritual life most directly appear.

The Soul and Its Passions

Though it is well known that Thomas put his treatise on beatitude at the beginning of his moral reflections and that he is concerned above all about the moral and free character of human acts, it is doubtless a little less known that he goes on from that with a study of the "passions." In fact, this passage in his work has scarcely attracted the attention of moralists.[20] In accord with his deeply unified conception of man, Thomas is not content to treat the spiritual faculties—intelligence and will—and their acts—knowing and willing—which are specific to human beings. He also studies those acts that are common to men and animals, owing to their common corporeal nature and that, in man, are or at least ought to be integrated into the spirit's activities. Following an often-repeated parallel, just as our knowledge begins with sense perception, so too our first subjective reactions begin at the level of sensitive appetite (or affectivity), which is to say at the level of the natural tendency that inclines the living being toward its good (or what appears such). This natural tendency is also found, to be sure, at the intellectual level, and is then called the will that tends toward the good under its universal aspect as good. We will return to this.[21] At the level of sensitive affectivity, on the contrary, reactions

19. We must not then misunderstand the initial declaration that opens the treatise on the soul (*ST* Ia q. 75, Pro.); "After the study of the spiritual creature and the corporeal creature, we must turn to the study of man, who is composed of a spiritual substance and a corporeal substance. . . . *It pertains to the theologian to consider human nature with respect to the soul, not the body, except for the relation that the soul maintains with the body.*" This is not a declaration of incompetence, but a defining of fields; the body as such is the concern of the physician, but in its connection to the soul, it interests the theologian, as we shall quickly see.

20. See, however, É. Gilson, "Love and the Passions," chap. 2 in part 3 of *Christian Philosophy of St. Thomas Aquinas*, 271–86; M. D. Jordan, "Aquinas's Construction of a Moral Account of the Passions," *FZPT* 33 (1986): 71–97; S. Pinckaers, "Les passions et la morale," *RSPT* 74 (1990): 379–91; and above all E. Schockenhoff, *Bonum hominis. Die anthropologischen und theologischen Grundlagen der Tugendethik des Thomas von Aquin* (Mainz 1987), the purpose of which is precisely to show the anthropological roots of Thomas's moral teaching.

21. The two affective tendencies are put in place in *ST* Ia q. 80–81. See too *De ueritate* q. 25 a. 1 (translated in H.-D. Gardeil, *Introduction to the Philosophy of St. Thomas Aquinas*, trans. John A. Otto, vol. 3 (St. Louis, Mo., 1958), 248–50.

occur with respect to particular goods or evils, and it is precisely these re-actions that Thomas calls "passions," because the subject suffers them more than he is their master. They are, then, in the realm of the involun-tary. Which is to say, the word "passion" does not have for Thomas the pe-jorative connotation that it has for us, who automatically think of it as sug-gesting debauchery and excess. Passion simply designates the movement of sensibility. It begins with the lightest impression and it occurs in every affective movement, sentiment, or emotion.[22]

Without pausing here to describe their complex constitution, the fine psychological analysis of which has often been noticed, we must at least see how Thomas discerns two large divisions in the sensitive appetite. The first, which is called the "concupiscible" (or "desire") is the appetite of simple tendency that is borne toward what presents itself as sensitively good, and is turned away from everything that appears sensitively evil. In connection with this object, we observe three pairs of contrary passions: love and hate, desire and aversion, joy and sorrow. In the second place, we meet with the "irascible" (today we more typically say "aggressiveness," but the word is not neutral enough for our use here), which is the appetite of struggle, which encompasses "difficult" or "arduous" goods or evils. And it is in this respect that the appetite acts toward them. There are only two pairs of passions here—hope and despair, courage and fear—for the final quality—anger, which stems from evil that cannot be avoided—has no contrary passion.[23]

Each one of these passions may be subdivided and studied at greater length, but it is more important to notice the way they are integrated into a life properly human and, as a consequence, into the Christian life. While they are rooted in the animal nature of man, they do not remain purely in the realm of the sensory. Thus, it is right to call them passions "of the soul." Far from seeing them in the Stoic way as "maladies of the soul" (Cicero's phrase) that must necessarily be avoided as evils, Thomas

22. The fullest treatise on the passions is found at ST Ia IIae qq. 22–48. It can be read in French translation with the annotations of Albert Plé, a knowledgeable guide, in *Thomas d'Aquin, Somme théologique*, vol. 2 (Paris, 1984), 169–299; by the same author, we have *Par devoir ou par plaisir?* (Paris, 1980). See also L. Mauro, *"Umanità" della passione in S. Tom-maso* (Florence, 1974) and M. Manzanedo, *Las pasiones o emociones según santo Tomás* (Madrid, 1984).

23. In addition to the basic exposition on the concupiscible and the irascible (ST Ia q. 81 a. 2–3), see also ST Ia IIae q. 23 for the initial exposition on the whole ensemble of the pas-sions, with the enlightening table in A. Plé, op. cit., p. 181.

considers them rather as psycho-physiological data, which in themselves are neither good nor bad. But we can make good use of them if we know how to order them rightly:

The Stoics, believing that all passions are evil, had to conclude that every passion lessens the good of a human act, since the good, through its mixture with evil, is weakened or disappears entirely. And this is true indeed, if the passions are only the disordered movements of the sensitive appetite, which is to say disturbances or ailments. *But if we give the name of passion simply to all the movements of the sensitive appetite, then the perfection of the human good requires his passions to be moderated by reason.*[24]

This moderation is to be understood properly; what "moderated by reason" means is not clear at first sight.[25] In the context that Thomas uses it, as we will have other opportunities to see, the reason is not that of a man left with only his human resources. For the theologian, we are always dealing with reason enlightened by the Word of God, informed by the divine law, strengthened by grace, and putting to work all the resources of virtue at its disposal. Thus understood, as we shall see more fully with regard to conscience, reason is, so to speak, the resting place of the divine design for man. Obedience to the sensitive appetite under the rule of reason is then an entirely different thing than submission to the narrow ideal of a punctilious mediocrity that could suggest meanness of the human spirit left to itself. It is in fact an opening of the image to the likeness of its divine Exemplar. We then understand better the conviction expressed in the passage just quoted that "the perfection of the human good" passes through the rectification and integration of the passions at the level of the life of the spirit; and what follows explains why:

For since man's good is founded on reason as its root, that good will be all the more perfect according as it extends to more things pertaining to man. No one questions the fact that it matters for moral good that the actions of the outward members be controlled by the law of reason. Hence, since the sensitive appetite *can* obey reason,[26] *it belongs to the perfection of moral or human good that the passions of the soul themselves should also be controlled by reason.*

24. *ST* Ia IIae q. 24 a. 3.
25. See the attempted clarification in L. Sentis, "La lumière dont nous faisons usage. La règle de la raison et la loi divine selon Thomas d'Aquin," *RSPT* 79 (1995): 49–69.
26. Thomas refers here to a point he established earlier (cf. *ST* Ia IIae q. 17 a. 7) where he explains that the power of reason over the sensitive appetite is not "despotic" (all-powerful), but "political" (relative); We will return to this a little further on.

Accordingly just as it is better that man should both will good and really do it; *so also does it belong to the perfection of moral good that man should be moved to good, not only in respect of his will, but also in respect of his sensitive appetite,* according to Psalm lxxxiii.3: "My heart and my flesh have rejoiced in the living God," *heart* here being the intellectual appetite, and *flesh* the sensitive appetite.[27]

We cannot fail to be struck by the vehemence with which it is emphasized that moral perfection of the human being passes through the integration of the passions into the virtuous life. It goes along with the complete recognition of the fact that the human being is not only the soul, but the body as well, and then equally the sensibility. We encounter here, it is easy to see, one of the repercussions of the basic anthropological view that we mentioned at the outset of this chapter. By virtue of the unity of the substantial form in the human composite (it is the same soul that is intelligent, can will, and is sensitive), the movements of the sensibility cannot be foreign to the properly human life of the subject. They must become voluntary through participation and then will be good or evil as they are submissive or not to the higher faculties, intelligence and will. But in no way are they a negligible quantity, and the moral or spiritual life cannot ignore them. It is the whole man who must be Christianized; the human being goes toward God with all that is in him.[28]

Nature and Culture: The Virtues

Friar's Thomas's meticulous analysis does not refuse to consider man in his totality, and that is why he shows himself so careful about his carnal roots. As a creature of God even in that part of himself that brings him close to the animals, it is even in that part of himself that man must be rectified by the Good News if some day he is to achieve the divine likeness to which he is called. But the theologian would leave his task half done if he were not careful, as he explained the modalities of this process, also to propose the path of rectification. Here we meet with what is perhaps one of the most original portions of Friar Thomas's spiritual theology, his teaching on the virtues.[29]

27. *ST* Ia IIae q. 24 a. 3.
28. On this point, see the study by M.-D. Chenu, "Les passions vertueuses. L'anthropologie de saint Thomas," *RPL* 72 (1974): 11–18, who has well perceived and expressed the connection between the unity of the substantial form and the moral life: the question is one of knowing whether the soul alone is virtuous, or the body also, and thus the whole man in his unity.
29. See a highly original case for the importance of this teaching in Saint Thomas, but

To express the self-mastery that the human person must acquire over his passions, Thomas speaks freely of *imperium* (precept, command) exercised over them by reason and will. Here we have another expression to understand properly, for even understood as we shall define it, reason does not exercise absolute power over the sensitive powers. Many sensory reactions entirely escape our control and the movement of the sensitive appetite can be suddenly unleashed by an image or sensation. Even what can, theoretically, be mastered if foreseen, can in fact escape the control of reason—we frequently experience this. Thomas recalls here the phrase of Aristotle, his master in this realm: "With respect to the concupiscible and irascible, reason exercises not a 'despotic' power, the power of a master over a slave, but rather a 'political' power, the power addressed to free men not wholly subject to command."[30]

To put this in terms closer to those of modern psychology, it has been suggested that we use "reflective desire" or "desiring intelligence" to capture the twofold, interactive hold of reason and will on the passions. The *imperium* that emanates from the will is not then to be understood as a "commanding" in the sense that a legalistic morality would understand it, as sustained by the notion of Duty. It is rather a matter of harmonizing all the capacities that the human being has available. "It exerts this eminence more like an orchestra conductor than a policeman. When Saint Thomas speaks of the hold charity has on the other human capacities, he speaks about attraction (*De caritate* 3, rep. and sol. 18) or even of appeal, or invitation, or persuasion. *The dominance of the love of charity is exercised by way of a dynamic training, in order to arrive at a state where the passions are themselves attracted by a good that goes beyond them.* In any case, it is through this dominance of desire-reflection that the passions 'participate in reason' (sol 2). For however complex a man may be, he is one, and it is thus that he builds up his unity. The dominance of desire-

---

even more for the moral life itself in O. H. Pesch's "Le sommeil et les bains ou l'amour et les vertus," chap. 10 in *Thomas d'Aquin. Grandeur et limites de la théologie médiévale* (Paris 1994); the same author's basic study remains, "Die bleibende Bedeutung der thomanischen Tugendlehre. Eine theologiegeschichtliche Meditation," *FZPT* 21 (1974): 359–91 (abridged version in French: "La théologie de la vertu et les vertus théologales," *Concilium* 24 [1987]: 105–26).

30. *ST* Ia IIae q. 17 a. 7. Cf. Aristotle, *Politics* I, 5, 6 (1254b5). Far from ignoring that the passions can also resist and become obstacles, Thomas returns to the point often: besides *ST* Ia IIae q. 58 a. 2, which is the most developed passage, see *ST* Ia IIae q. 31 a. 5 ad 1; q. 34 a. 1 ad 1; q. 82 a. 4 ad 1, and the commentary on *Nicomachean Ethics* VII, 14 (1154 b 6–14), Leonine, vol. 47/2, pp. 437–38.

reflection becomes a constraint only when persuasion fails when faced with refractory passions."[31]

This passage rightly underscores the central role of charity in integrating the passions into the Christian's moral life. And we recognize here the same terms that were used in an earlier chapter to speak of the motion-allurement of the Holy Spirit. This goes straight to the root—the deepest explanation. But we will not do justice to the rich complexity of the human being or of Thomas's elaboration if we fail to make explicit that this sovereign mastery of the spirit over the passions is really the fruit of a long Christianization, accompanied with a patient humanization. That is why charity does not proceed without the other virtues, the very ones Thomas calls "habitus."

We hope to be forgiven for returning here to a small, but indispensable technical point, whose usefulness will quickly show itself. As we have already noted,[32] the Latin word habitus is the translation for the Greek hexis, and means something one has (habere = to have), a quality of body or soul, a capacity of human nature, capable of developing by the very use we make of it. We do not have a word in our modern languages to express exactly this central notion. We must thus keep habitus, but should avoid translating it as "habit," for this term suggests rather the contrary of the true meaning. Habit is a mechanism, incapable of being renewed; habitus, on the contrary, is the capacity of adaptation and extension to the ever new, which perfects the faculty in which it arises and gives it a perfect liberty, a source of true delight in action. Habitus is thus the sign and the expression of the full flowering of nature in a certain direction.

We could speak then of habitus as the know-how of an artisan or an artist, whose technical ability astounds those who do not have it, but the word is also suited to designate the qualities proper to the intellect or the will. Science is thus a habitus of the intellect, which proceeds from the capacity proper to man to learn and progressively master knowledge in a given field, so that we call a scholar someone who possesses the habitus corresponding to that field of knowledge. And he will be an even greater scholar to the extent that he possesses this habitus more perfectly, so that he may enter and make use of intellectual realms inaccessible to those who do not have the habitus.

31. A. Plé, note to ST Ia IIae q. 24, Thomas d'Aquin, Somme théologique, vol. 2, note 3, p. 182.
32. Cf. chap. 1, pp. 13.

Thomas uses precisely this category to explain what a virtue is. It is not an iron collar intended to discipline nature, in spite of itself, into following orders and precepts that cannot be anything but repugnant, but rather a supplementary perfection that moves nature in the direction of its real fulfillment. For, by reason of its creation by God, nature is already profoundly oriented toward the good. By his virtuous *habitus* the person finds himself more surely ordered toward the beatitude that is his supreme end. In applying himself to rectifying his acts, and notably in the realm of the passions, whose conflicting goals threaten to destroy him, man thus repeats in himself God's work, bringing the process of humanization of his being to as perfect completion as possible through the play of liberty. Human nature is only fully itself in the state of culture, which is obtained precisely by putting to work the good *habitus* that we call the virtues.[33]

Thus, we may better understand the definition that Thomas is quite happy to repeat: Virtue is a *good* operative *habitus*, which renders *good* whoever possesses it and also renders his work *good*.[34] This insistent repetition of the same adjective is not mere redundancy: this *habitus* directed toward action (operative) must be good, for there are bad *habitus* (the vices); it allows us to perform a work as good or beautiful as possible in its genus, for that superior facility is connected with the very notion of *habitus*. But in addition, virtue has the unique feature of making the person who exercises it good. This last characteristic is essential to distinguishing virtue from every other kind of operative *habitus*. We will best grasp this if we look at the parallel between art and the virtue of prudence. Both are virtues of the practical intellect and aim at bringing something into existence. Art is necessary to the artist who would make a beautiful work according to the norms of art; prudence is necessary to the virtuous man who would perform a beautiful act according to the norms of the Gospel. Their

---

33. There can also be bad *habitus* (vices, habitual sins) that while developing in their own way the perfecting facility implied in the notion of *habitus*, are utilized in a perverted way with respect to the final end and therefore turn from it. We can leave this question here, but perhaps we might like to know the way in which this aspect of the matter is taken into account in the *Prima Secundae:* after the passions (qq. 22–48) comes the treatise on the habitus (qq. 49–54), then the one on the virtues (qq. 55–70), and finally the treatise on the sins (qq. 71–89). These are what Thomas calls the "internal" principles of human action; he also recognizes "external" principles which are, on the one hand, God Himself, who helps us to act by instructing us through law (qq. 90–108) and sustaining us through grace (qq. 109–14), and on the other hand the devil, who pushes us toward evil through temptation, and of whom Thomas has spoken very briefly elsewhere (*ST* Ia q. 114).

34. Cf. *ST* Ia IIae q. 55 a. 3.

definitions are also similar. Art is right reason, the just rule of *the work to be made* (recta ratio *factibilium*). Prudence is right reason, the just rule of *human acts to be done* (recta ratio *agibilium*). Despite the resemblances, the difference is enormous: "Art is not necessary for the artisan to 'live well,' but only to make a good work that endures. Prudence, however, is necessary for man not only to become good but to continue to 'live well.'"[35]

The Joy of Being Saved

This distinction between doing well (making) and acting well (living) is central to the difference between *habitus* and virtues. To the simple dexterity invoked in the notion of *habitus*, the idea of virtue adds moral perfecting, and that is why only the moral virtues properly deserve the name virtues, while the intellectual virtues bear the name only in an improper fashion. It is not enough to know the good, we must also do it. And that is why "the seat of virtue properly speaking can be found only in the will or in another power insofar as it is moved by the will."[36] And it is here, we see, that we return to the treatise on the passions, for to the extent that the irascible or the concupiscible can be voluntary by participation, to that same extent they will be the seat of the virtues. Temperance will also have the task of disciplining the concupiscible through teaching it to resist everything that might distance it from the good through the practice of easy pleasures. Fortitude will have, on the contrary, the task of affirming the irascible and helping it to confront every obstacle that might divert it from the good through fear or cowardice. In both cases, the virtue strengthens the person in his attachment to the good, while giving in to the natural bent of his passions would lead him to dissolution.

We thus begin to see how virtue renders the person who exercises it good. To warn about the breakdown of the moral being and to unify it in depth even in its sensitive powers is already a great gain. But we must also mention an additional benefit so often overlooked. While a constrained act produces sadness, since it is the result of violence imposed from outside,[37] virtuous action is, on the contrary, a source of joy. This is the direct consequence of the ease with which we use virtuous *habitus*. Far from diminishing the value of the act, the pleasure with which we accomplish it

---

35. *ST* Ia IIae q. 57 a. 5 ad 1.
36. *ST* Ia IIae q. 56 a. 3.
37. Cf. *Quaestio de uirtutibus*, a. 4.

adds to it facility and merit: "The more the subject acts with pleasure given his virtuous *habitus*, the more his act will be delightful and meritorious."[38] As Thomas remarks with some insistence in commenting on Aristotle, "Actions virtuously carried out are naturally delightful. We must also add that the delight that we take belongs necessarily to virtue and enters into its definition. *We are neither good nor virtuous if we do not find joy in acting well.*"[39] We are clearly rather far here from the pious slogan so widespread not long ago: "Only that which hurts is truly meritorious." We should not necessarily conclude from this that we must not act out of duty, only pleasure. But it is certain that if we act with enough love we will find joy in it. Virtue is incompatible with sadness.[40] We should beware of inferring from the quotation from Aristotle that Thomas has no other sources on this matter. On the contrary, he gives a very beautiful commentary on a proverb quoted by Saint Paul in 1 Corinthians 9:7:

"God loves the joyful giver." Here is the reason. He who pays back, pays back someone who deserves it, which is to say only for *acts* of virtue. Now, in a virtuous act there are two things to consider: the species of the act and the way in which the agent performs it. It follows that if one of these two is not found in a given act, we will not say that it is a truly *(simpliciter)* virtuous act. Thus only he will be perfectly just according to virtue who does works of justice with joy and delight. For men who only see appearances, it is enough that the act of virtue be performed as to the proper species, but for God who searches hearts, that is not enough. *The act must also be performed in the just way, which is to say with joy and delight.* That is why God approves and pays back not "he who gives," but *he who gives "with joy" not in sadness and against his will:* "Serve the Lord with gladness" (Ps. 99); "In your offerings show joy" (Sir. 35:11); "Let him who practices mercy do so with joy" (Rom. 12:8).[41]

We can also add here what we shall soon see is far from being secondary to the main question: there is an "intelligent" use of virtue that ex-

---

38. *In III Sent.* d. 23 q. 1 a. 1 ad 4: "*Quanto delectabilius operatur propter habitum uirtutis, tanto actus eius est delectabilior et magis meritorius.*"

39. Commentary on *Nicomachean Ethics* I, 13 (1099 a 17), Leonine, vol. 47/1, p. 47, lines 85–90.

40. O. H. Pesch has rightly pointed out in his *Thomas d'Aquin* (see note 29 above) pp. 289 ff., that Thomas deals with no other passion so fully as sadness; so too Thomas treats the sin of the same name very seriously: it is called "acedia" and is opposed to the joy that comes from God. He calls "envy" the sadness that comes from the good of another (cf. *ST* IIa IIae q. 35–36).

41. *In II ad Cor.* IX, 7, lect. 1, n. 332.

cludes all stinginess. Virtue eliminates not only sadness, but niggardliness as well. Among the related virtues that Friar Thomas connects with the virtue of fortitude is one he calls magnanimity, greatness of soul. Though too little known—it certainly does not form part of current catechesis— magnanimity, which establishes "the rational standard for great honors," receives a rather extensive treatment in the *Summa*.[42] Beyond the Aristotelian inheritance (which Thomas otherwise submits to serious critique) Thomas's own social background could have lured him into thinking about this topic, if only to propose a code of social conduct for his relatives. We should not, however, exaggerate this second factor, for there is no doubt that Thomas produces an idea of man to the measure of his Creator. The greater man is, the greater God is as well. Awareness of our littleness before God does not eliminate awareness of our grandeur. That is why humility must accompany magnanimity. For the Christian, humility regulates things at every level, of course, up to the point where humility and magnanimity flow together into the notion of theological hope (what greater honor may we aspire to than sharing in the Trinitarian communion?).[43] But it remains worth noticing that virtue lies on the side of grandeur and the opposing vices are called pusillanimity and niggardliness.[44]

Perfect Virtue

Throughout this account of fortitude and temperance we have seen how Thomas shows the Christianization of man even in his primordial powers of affectivity. These observations could be pursued indefinitely. There is no field of human activity that does not lend itself to the application of new *habitus* and thus to the exercise of virtue. Fortitude and temperance are virtues of personal discipline, for they have as their object a

42. *ST* IIa IIae qq. 129–33.
43. See the masterwork by R.-A. Gauthier, *Magnanimité. L'idéal de la grandeur dans la philosophie païenne et dans la théologie chrétienne* (Paris, 1951), 295–371 and 443–65 in particular.
44. Cf. *ST* IIa IIae q. 133. *Pusillanimitas* has the same name in Latin and several modern languages. I have translated as "niggardliness" (Fr. *mesquinerie*), following several other writers, what is called *parvificentia* by Thomas. Niggardliness is really opposed to "magnificence," and not directly to magnanimity (cf. *ST* IIa IIae qq. 134–35), but we remain here within the same attitude of soul. The widow in the Gospel (Luke 21:2–4) who gives all she has acts with grandeur. The modest nature of her offering does not change anything about her gesture.

just connection of the person with his own affective reactions, his passions. But they are only the last two "cardinal" virtues.[45] The first two cardinal virtues are prudence (to which we shall return shortly) and justice, which is concerned with the objective regulation of a person's operations, no longer with respect to himself, but with respect to what he owes another, whether single persons or society. We will turn to justice in the following chapter, where we will treat more fully the social dimension of the human being.

Though these four moral virtues with their additions constitute a universally valid human datum (the reason that the exposition begins with them), the theologian knows of others besides them. If man had no other vocation than to be left to his natural powers alone, they would doubtless have been enough to assure him of personal and social success. But Christian revelation teaches us that we are called to a beatitude that surpasses man's capacities, and that God has, so to speak, adapted human nature by making it a "participant in the divine nature" (cf. 1 Pet. 1:4). At the same time, He has also given us new, virtuous *habitus* suited to this supernatural end, such that we are properly equipped to achieve it. These are the "theological" virtues, so-called for three reasons. First, because they directly have God as their object. Then, because He is the only cause of them (in technical terms, they are "infused" into us by Him alone). Finally, because we know of their existence only through divine revelation in Sacred Scripture.[46]

Our entire effort in the present book is too obviously dependent on the theological life for us to need to linger over this aspect.[47] We will say in passing, however, that if the Master of Aquino deals in detail with the theological virtues only in the *Secunda Secundae*, the simple fact that he specifies the need for them shows that his intention in the *Prima Secundae* was never simply to repeat the structure of morality inherited from pagan antiquity, as he is sometimes reproached for doing. As everywhere

45. As is well known, the adjective "cardinal" comes from the Latin *cardo* (= hinge). This means that the whole moral life hinges on these four basic virtues, which thus rule over the main realms of human and Christian life.

46. This argument is seen in *ST* Ia IIae q. 62 a. 1. In that passage, the author is content to situate the theological virtues in the complex organism of the other virtues. He returns to the subject in detail in the *Secunda Secundae*, where the treatment of Faith, Hope, and Love takes up the first 46 questions. The cardinal virtues are treated again after those questions.

47. We will return to it elsewhere in chapter 13.

else in his work, everything he owes to Aristotle or other thinkers, Stoics and the like, is radically transformed, not to say subverted from within, by the simple fact of identifying the God of Jesus Christ with the Good that all men pursue, even without knowing it.[48] That is why the reference to this end inevitably requires not only the presence of new structures, here the theological virtues, but even the transformation of existing structures.

This can be discussed along with another highly significant fact: after carefully explicating the structures of the *habitus* and the moral virtues, Thomas does not leave them to themselves. Convinced that there is no human success without grace, he wants each human virtue to be matched with an infused moral virtue, whose role is to be linked with the movement from within to lead it to all perfection attainable here below. This does not exclude the possibility that non-Christians can achieve a high state of moral worth through the repeated practice of acts that develop innate aptitudes of a humanity created by God for the good. But this means quite certainly that in Thomas's eyes—and for every theologian who has become aware of the radically disproportionate nature of man's efforts before God—"*only the infused virtues are truly perfect and should be called virtues, because they order man well for the absolutely final end.*"[49]

The Virtue of Risk

To finish this description, though it has barely been sketched, of the virtuous organism as Thomas conceives of it, we have to say a word about what, in his conception of *habitus*, is certainly one of the most original theses. We mean his teaching about prudence, which among all the virtues is accorded an exceptional place. This might be surprising, because in contemporary language, prudence suggests a timorous and even negative attitude toward action. In Thomas's perspective, on the contrary, prudence is the virtue of choice and decision, of personal responsibility, of risk consciously taken. It closes the deliberative processes by daring to prescribe action in a specific situation, singular each time, that will never repeat itself as such. Thomas has no hesitation here:

---

48. See my essay "La philosophie morale de saint Thomas d'Aquin," in M. Canto-Sperber, ed., *Dictionnaire d'éthique et de philosophie morale* (Paris, 1996), 1517–23; cf. T. F. O'Meara, "Virtues in the Theology of Thomas Aquinas," *Theological Studies* 58 (1977): 254–85.

49. *ST* Ia IIae q. 65 a. 2.

Prudence is the virtue most necessary for human life. To live well really means to act well. Now, to act well, we not only need to do something, but to do it as is required, which is to say, we must act according to an orderly choice, and not merely on impulse or from passion. But since choice relates to means in light of an end, its rectitude requires two things: a just end *(debitum finem)* and means fitted to that just end. . . . For what pertains to means, it is necessary that we be directly prepared by a *habitus* of reason, for to deliberate and to choose—operations related to means—are acts of reason. And that is why *it is necessary that there be in reason an intellectual virtue that gives it enough perfection to behave well with regard to the means to be taken. That virtue is prudence. This is why prudence is a necessary virtue to living well.*[50]

There is nothing more to explain about why virtue in general is necessary to "live well," but we must grasp what prudence adds here. First, prudence gives to the understanding its whole position in the virtuous organism. As we have said, the virtues are lived in human affectivity, with its motivations, desires, aversions, pleasures, and sorrows. That is why their seat is found in the will which has the privilege of motion, of putting into motion all the other powers of the soul. But we should not deduce from this a closed voluntarism, which would be opposed to Thomas's real thinking. He speaks incessantly of the right rule that reason must exercise over human life. The idea of reflective desire or of desiring intelligence already encountered precisely expresses this interaction of understanding and will in the conduct of human affairs. Now, with prudence, that is clearly what we find:

Moral virtue can exist without some of the intellectual virtues—viz., wisdom, science, and art—*but not without understanding*[51] and prudence. There cannot be moral virtue without prudence, because it is a habit of choosing *(electiuus)*, i.e., making good choices. Now for a choice to be good, two things are required. First, that the intention be directed to a due end; and this is the work of moral virtue, which inclines the appetitive faculty to the good that is in accord with reason, which is a due end. Secondly, that man take rightly the means which have reference to the end: and this he cannot do unless by means of a reason that knows how to *counsel, judge, and command,* which is the function of prudence and the virtues annexed to it, as stated above (q. 57 aa. 5–6). *Wherefore, there can be no moral virtue without prudence.*

---

50. *ST* Ia IIae q. 57 a. 5. Cf. C.-J. Pinto de Oliveira, "La prudence, concept-clé de la morale du P. Labourdette," *RT* 92 (1992): 267–92.

51. Understanding is here the habitus of knowledge of the true through direct intuition, also called habitus of first principles. Cf. *ST* Ia IIae q. 57 a. 2.

And consequently neither can there be without understanding. For it is by understanding that we know naturally evident principles both in the speculative and in the practical order. Consequently, just as right reason in speculative matters, in so far as it proceeds from naturally known principles, presupposes the understanding of those principles, so also does prudence, which is right reason, the just rule about things to be done *(recta ratio agibilium).*[52]

We grasp that the understanding in question here is inherent to the human spirit. The great principles it grasps are accessible to all, and are not reserved to a rational or educated elite. To the objection that there is no need to be a scholar to be virtuous and that therefore moral virtue can exist without intellectual virtue, Thomas replies with no embarrassment:

A virtuous man does not need the full use of reason in every matter, but only in the field of virtue. And this occurs for all who are virtuous. Hence even *those who seem simple, through lack of worldly cunning, may possibly be prudent* according to Matthew 10:16: "Be ye therefore wise as serpents and simple as doves."[53]

These points are less anodyne that we might think. The reference to Saint Matthew puts Thomas in the realm of the Gospel, thus distinguishing him from Socrates, for whom it is the intellectual who does what is right, to the point that our behavior depends on our knowledge.[54] But though he does not want the moral to be identified with the rule of reason, Thomas also does not want virtue to be reduced to a purely irrational inclination toward the good. That virtue might prove to be more dangerous the stronger it becomes. "Also moral virtue does not merely 'follow right reason,' in the sense that it inclines us toward what conforms with that rule, as the Platonists said, but it must also be that virtue is 'accompanied by reason,' as Aristotle meant it."[55]

Once again we have the strong vision of the substantial unity of man, which is expressed thus: no more than he is an intelligence more or less accidentally tied to the animality of his nature, is man a pure will without understanding, or vice versa. Only this illumination allows us to understand the central place that Thomas gives to prudence, which he expresses in the crucial thesis about the harmony of the virtues, or, as he says in

---

52. *ST* Ia IIae q. 58 a. 4.
53. *ST* Ia IIae q. 58 a. 4 ad 2.
54. Thomas is clearly thinking of this Socratic notion. Cf. *ST* Ia IIae q. 58 a. 2 ad 2, as well as q. 58 a. 4 ad 3.
55. *ST* Ia IIae q. 58 a. 4 ad 3.

his own terms, in their "connection" under the aegis of prudence: "There can be no moral virtue without prudence. . . . Similarly, there can be no prudence without the moral virtues." The reason for this is the same as was given earlier: if the virtues orient us rightly toward the end, it is prudence that chooses the just means in view of the end.[56]

In truth, the thesis in itself is not new, for Thomas inherits a Patristic tradition that Saint Gregory had already asserted: "The virtues cannot be perfect if they are separate, because prudence is not true prudence if it is not just, temperate, and courageous."[57] The novelty consists here in the insistence and thus also in the power of the development. We have just seen that virtue "makes good" him who possesses it; we could say that it constructs the virtuous being. But that is possible only because of the subject himself who acts through the virtues, so that far from being unaware of each other, the virtues influence one another's actions and help one another, each needing the other to attain its proper end. To repeat an image already used, each can be compared with the instruments of an orchestra, whose harmony is precisely the work of prudence. The unification of a being under the impulse of a greater virtue corresponds in fact to something that arises from experience: the passions too are linked together, "for all the passions flow from certain initial passions, for example love and hate, and terminate in others such as delight and sorrow. Similarly, all the operations that are the matter of the moral virtues are related to one another, and to the passions. Hence the whole matter of moral virtue falls under the one rule of prudence."[58]

Prudence and Charity

We cannot help remarking again that the initial conception of the substantial unity of the human being regulates this new thesis. However, after what we have just said on the theological virtues, it will be easy to guess that the connection of the moral virtues through prudence is really only an intermediate stage, and it does not occur in isolation. The definitive step in the unification of the Christian being is realized by charity, and that at a twofold level: in prudence and the infused virtues, on the one hand, to be sure, but especially in the theological virtues.

56. *ST* Ia IIae q. 65 a. 1.
57. *Moralia in Job* XXII 1, 2 (CCSL 143 A, 1092–93; PL 76, 212), quoted in *ST* Ia IIae q. 65 a. 1.
58. *ST* Ia IIae q. 65 a. 1 ad 3.

In fact, Thomas has charity play, on a higher level, the same architectonic role that he attributes to prudence on its own level. The reason for both is the same. Only charity raises man to the heights of his true end. That is why, without disputing the possibility that human virtues can exist without charity, he continues with the teaching that true virtue, as the Christian theologian understands it, cannot exist without charity. For the virtues cannot be realized without infused prudence, which itself cannot be present without charity.[59]

The inverse is also true. Charity cannot move without the moral virtues, and that is why it brings them along with it: "All the moral virtues are infused at the same time as charity."[60] This new affirmation is surprising at first sight but easily explained if we remember that God does not do things by halves. With the love of the final end, charity, he gives all at once the knowledge of that end, faith, desire, hope, and the means to reach it, the virtues. The thesis is thus not without consequences, but should not be misunderstood. It does not mean that the infused virtues relieve us of all effort or that they will be exercised without difficulty. Nothing is further from Thomas's thought than quietism: the gift of grace always calls for man's collaboration. We can have the germ of the *habitus* of a virtue and not take advantage of it, or, at least, not easily. But in Thomas's profoundly unified view of man, this means that with charity we are given the means needed and that to lose charity is to lose simultaneously all those means.

━━⌒━━

We should not pursue much further the question of the connection among the theological virtues, which Thomas begins to address following the treatment of the connection among the moral virtues. We will take it up again more fully in a later chapter. We must simply say here that the introduction of charity at the peak of the virtuous organism, and the particular beatitude that resides in communion with it at a single stroke transform the abstract notion of the final end, which he has used up until this point for convenience in a careful, brief exposition. Hereafter, it receives its most concrete content: the life in intimacy with God promised by many biblical passages. But since we are still in the treatise on the virtues, which is to say within an eschatological perspective on the way to realiza-

59. *ST* Ia IIae q. 65 a. 2.
60. *ST* Ia IIae q. 65 a. 3.

tion, we must again emphasize that Thomas also reminds us that we are dealing with a consummation still to come. From the carnal root of our point of departure to that moment when "we will be like him because we will see him as he is" (1 John 3:2), the path passes through a long struggle for victory, the spontaneity of our virtuous *habitus*.

CHAPTER XII

ॐ

Without Friends, Who Would
Want to Live?

Thomas replies to this question, which he encountered reading Aristotle, with the same conviction as the Philosopher. In every situation and at whatever age, "friendship is what is most necessary to live."[1] For both thinkers, this is a fundamental question, whose importance becomes even more apparent if we remember the further uses to which it can be put. The Latin Christian clothes it in a fulness of meaning that it could not have for the Greek thinker.

For Aristotle, the term *philia* has a much wider meaning than "friendship" has for us. As one of the best interpreters observes, "This term expresses . . . every feeling of affection or attachment for others, whether spontaneous or deliberate, owing to circumstances or to free choice: friendship properly speaking, love, benevolence, beneficence, philanthropy. In short, *altruism, sociability*. Friendship is the *social bond* par excellence, which maintains unity among the citizens of a city, or among the comrades in a group, or the associates of some business."[2] The perspectives opened up here are then quite large, since the word encompasses both friendship by choice between two people as well as the whole of social and political life.[3]

---

1. Aristotle, of course, dedicated two complete books (Books VIII and IX, 1155–72) of the *Nicomachean Ethics* to friendship, and Thomas wrote a commentary on both of them (Leonine, vol. 47/2, pp. 442–549). He also repeated numerous elements from them in his work. The quotation that heads this chapter may be found in Book VIII 1, pp. 442–44.

2. J. Tricot, *Aristote: Éthique à Nicomaque, Nouvelle traduction, avec introduction, notes et index* (Paris, 1959), 381.

3. Since we shall not return to the interpersonal relations, I refer to two studies where

For Thomas Aquinas, *philia* is translated as *amicitia*, which we would render as "friendship." The word retains for him all the resonances Aristotle gave it, but Aquinas invests it with others that come to him from the Latin tradition (particularly Cicero) as it was reread by the twelfth-century monks, Saint Bernard at their head.[4] But Thomas himself will subject the term to a veritable transformation by defining charity as a friendship between God and man. The relevant authority here is not Aristotle, but Saint John (15:15): "I call you no longer servants, but *friends*." Though the Philosopher continues to furnish the definitional structure, the elements are radically changed because the good around which the communion between God and man is established, as well as the communion among men, is the divine life communicated by grace.[5]

To set this chapter in the context of friendship, then, is to open up our reflections to a vast field that cannot be completely explored. But we must at least trace out its contours, because in man's social nature we touch upon a crucial aspect of the spiritual life, according to the Thomistic school. Thomas never thinks of man in the individualistic terms that have predominated in Western civilization since the Renaissance and Reformation. He always sees him as engaged with the community of the saved, which he calls either *ecclesia* or *populus*, a community of Christ's faithful *(congregatio fidelium)*, communion of saints *(societas sanctorum)*, or Mystical Body of Christ—to be sure, without ever abstracting it from the great human family of which it is a member by birth.

In the perspective of what we said in the chapter about the values in creation, we will continue further into the social aspect of friendship. The great principle that grace does not destroy nature, but heals it and leads it

Thomas's position is described justly and subtly: W. H. Principe, "Affectivity and the Heart in Thomas Aquinas' Spirituality," in *Spiritualities of the Heart: Approaches to Personal Wholeness in Christian Tradition*, ed. A. Callahan (New York-Mahwah, 1990), 45–63; "Loving Friendship According to Thomas Aquinas," in *The Nature and Pursuit of Love: The Philosophy of Irving Singer*, ed. D. Goicoechea (Amherst, N.Y., 1995), 128–41.

4. J. McEvoy, "Amitié, attirance et amour chez S. Thomas d'Aquin," *RPL* 91 (1993): 383–408, points out (p. 399) that neither Cicero's *De amicitia* nor Aelred de Rielvaux's work is quoted by Thomas. Thomas may not have known the latter figure owing to the shift in interest caused by the widespread introduction of Aristotle in the thirteenth century.

5. See *ST* IIa IIae q. 23 a. 1. The *Nicomachean Ethics* is quoted no fewer than five times in this article. Besides Saint John, Thomas calls on Saint Paul (1 Cor. 1:9) to borrow from him the vocabulary he needs to express the *communicatio* characteristic of charity: "The God by whom you have been called to *communion* with his Son is faithful." As is well known, *societas* in the Vulgate is the translation of the Greek term *koinônia* in Paul and Aristotle.

to perfect realization, finds its application here as well. If we want to follow Saint Thomas and be faithful to his conception of the human being in his totality, we should not make an abstraction out of the fact that the society in which the human person is called to flourish is not only the Church as the place of salvation. There are also different human communities to which the person is inextricably bound. Not only the family, about which much has already been said in spiritual theology, but even more the earthly city whose importance is not less, though it is less discussed, since its laws can facilitate a good Christian life to a great extent or, on the contrary, raise decisive obstacles to it—if only in the way it shapes attitudes.

At first, this question may appear out of place in an enquiry into spiritual theology, but it is not. Human destiny, it is true, can only be finally achieved in God alone. But it is also true that the human person does not arrive at his final end except within a community (family, society, Church). And for man there is a way of behaving within that community that is more or less in accord with his deeper nature. Christians are not all called to serve their brothers and sisters in the same way, socially or politically, but no one is excused from playing his part in the life of the city— if only in exercising the right to vote[6]—and Thomas has something to say about this subject to everyone. Like many thinkers after Augustine, Thomas sees the Christian as a member of two cities, but rather than rank them, he respects the proper finality of the earthly city and links it with man's very nature. His manner of distinguishing between temporal and spiritual even helps avoid potential conflicts from which we have suffered for centuries. In Thomas, there is a social and political ethics, as directly tied to his conception of personal morality as is his spirituality, which finds expression even in the way he sees the place of the Christian in the Church, and everyone's participation in the governing of the city. These are the themes on which we shall reflect in the following pages.

A "Political" Animal

For those who are surprised about this turn in our analysis, it should suffice to remember that Thomas himself puts us on this course in the way he speaks of the human person as a "social" being. In the theology of

6. There are obviously many cases that a Christian cannot be indifferent about, even if he lives in a monastery, from the defense of life and the struggle against laws favoring abortion, to rejection of social exclusion and help in the maintaining of peace, etc.

the religious life, one of his most characteristic expressions is often quoted, a true plea for communitarian life as opposed to the life of a hermit. Since man is "neither a beast nor a god," he must live in the company of his fellows.[7] As we know, Thomas got from Aristotle that man is "a being destined by nature to live in a city" *(physei politikon zoon)*, which is often translated today, with some risk of equivocation, as "by nature a political animal." Repeating the expression on his own, the Master of Aquino strongly underscores, in terms close to the Greek philosopher's, that it does not always turn out that way. But when it does not, such a man must either display a higher than common humanity, as did certain saints such as John the Baptist and the hermit Anthony, or be quite depraved, less than a man. Aristotle, quoting Homer, says such a man has "neither clan, nor law, nor home." And Thomas comments: he is "unsocial" because not linked in bonds of friendship, "illegal" because not submissive to the law's yoke, and "wicked" because not constrained by the rule of reason."[8]

Fidelity to Aristotle's position on these matters does not prevent Thomas from quietly correcting and even distancing himself from it. The careful reader cannot help noting a certain fluidity in the vocabulary: the author will say at times "animal *civile,*"[9] or "animal *politicum,*"[10] or even "animal politicum et *sociale.*"[11] The first two terms may be easily explained from the different Latin translations of Aristotle that Thomas had. The third term, most often used alone,[12] seems to reflect a personal choice and expresses another influence than Aristotle's. *Sociale* translates

7. *ST* IIa IIae q. 188 a. 8 ad 5. The expression is taken from Aristotle's *Politics* I, 2, 14 (1253a29). Aristotle also says in this section (1253a7) "he who is without a city is, by nature and not by chance, a being either below or above man." See Thomas's commentary, *Sententia libri Politicorum (In Polit.)* I, 1/b, Leonine, vol. 48, p. A 78–79.

8. *In Polit.* I, 1/b, Leonine, vol. 48, p. A 78. The example of John the Baptist and Anthony the hermit are also mentioned in *ST* IIa IIae q. 188 a. 8.

9. This is nearly the only language used in the commentary on the *Politics* (six out of seven uses, five of which are in chapter I 1/b, Leonine, vol. 48, pp. A 78–79); the seventh use appears in the commentary on *Nicomachean Ethics* I, 9, Leonine, vol. 47/1, p. 32.

10. This seems to be the term Thomas uses spontaneously (seven out of eleven times) when he is not commenting on Aristotle, although he uses it in his commentaries on *Nicomachean Ethics* VIII, 12 (1161b17) and IX, 10 (1169b18), Leonine, vol. 47/2, pp. 488 and 536, because the Latin translation of Aristotle's text has *politicum* at this point.

11. In *SCG* III 85, n. 2607; *ST* Ia IIae q. 72 a. 4; *Expositio libri Peryermenias* I 2, Leonine, vol. 1*1, p. 9 (and see R.-A. Gauthier's important note).

12. There are about twenty occurrences, notably in *SCG* III 117, n. 2897; 128, n. 3001; 129, n. 3013; etc.; *ST* Ia q. 96 a. 4; *ST* Ia IIae q. 95 a. 4; *ST* IIa IIae q. 109 a. 3 ad 1; q. 114 a. 2 ad 1; *ST* IIIa q. 65 a. 1; etc.

koinônikon, a term used by the Stoics to mean that man is the citizen not merely of some city, but of the *oikouménè*, the entire inhabited world of his time. We might translate this today as "citizen of the world."[13] In fact, the Aristotelian city, the *polis*, has much too narrow a horizon for a Christian—slaves and women were excluded. Thomas felt more at ease with the universalism professed by the Stoics, without turning them into Christians.

The political community is preceded by the conjugal community (because the first of all associations is between man and woman) as well as by the domestic community (because the family immediately follows from the union of man and woman). The political community thus represents a further stage of man's life in society, but is nevertheless first by nature. It subordinates the communities prior to it, but does not destroy them, because they testify, although to a lesser degree, to what has driven men to live together—language, according to Thomas, who follows Aristotle:

Indeed, we see that while certain animals have a voice or cry *(uox)*, only man has language *(locutio)*. . . . Human language serves to indicate what is useful or harmful, as well as just or unjust. Justice or injustice consists in whether certain people adapt themselves or not to questions of usefulness or harmfulness. The word, then, is proper to man for, compared with the animals, it is proper to us to have knowledge of good and evil, just and unjust, and other things of this sort that can be signified by words *(sermo)*.

Since words have thus been given to man by nature and are ordered toward allowing "communication" among men about the useful and harmful, just and unjust, and similar values, it follows—given that nature does nothing in vain—that it is natural to men to "communicate" among themselves about these things. Now, this is precisely "communication" in the values constitutive of the family and the city; man is thus by nature a domestic and political animal.[14]

"Communicate" and "communication" have been put in quotation marks here to remind us that these words have a meaning entirely different from our modern "communicate," which reduces the notion virtually

13. Cf. É. Bréhier, *Chrysippe et l'ancien stoïcisme* (Paris, 1951), 259–70: "La societé"; P.-M. Schuhl, "Préface" to *Les Stoïciens* (Paris, 1962), p. xxx: ". . . the Stoics are the first to allow a place, among the natural inclinations, for altruism, which originates in the familial inclination and that . . . extends progressively to universal society: it is the cosmopolitanism of the Stoic sage who is citizen of the world. It is not in a closed city, but in the bosom of rational humanity that man flourishes."

14. *In Polit.* I, 1/b, Leonine, vol. 48, pp. A 78–79.

to "exchange" or "inform." *Communicatio*, which Thomas found in the Latin translation of Aristotle, corresponds to the Greek's *koinônia*, which means "common possession" or "community."[15] And *koinônos* is the member who takes part in the values and goods that form this community. We thus go from simple exchange in questions of just and unjust, which seems to suggest use of the word as distinctive to man, to a convergence of all the city's members on the goods that are common to them. In these conditions, to say that man is a political animal, or even better a social animal, is not to designate in him the simple animal tendency toward a more or less gregarious instinct, but rather the capacity for virtuous development necessary to life in society. Thomas explains this a little further on: "Man is the best of the animals if he develops virtue in himself, toward which he is borne by a natural inclination; but he is the worst of the animals, if he is lacking in law or justice."[16]

The vistas that open up here could easily become the subject of a large book.[17] But we have understood enough of it for our purposes. According to Friar Thomas, the communitarian or social dimension is a fact inseparable from the human being, and he often returns to the point.[18] This is not a simple question of material convenience; even the most personal and most elevated activities require the gathering together of friends:

If we are dealing with happiness in the present life, we must say with the Philosopher that the happy man needs friends (Ethic. ix. 9), not, indeed, to make use of them, since he suffices himself; but for the purpose of a good action, viz., to have the opportunity of doing good to them; that he may delight in the good that they do; and a supplement in the good that he himself does. *Indeed, man needs the fellowship of friends to act virtuously, as much in his efforts of the active life as in the contemplative.*[19]

---

15. *Communio* and *communicatio* have been carefully studied in B.-D. de La Soujeole, "'Societé' et 'Communion' chez saint Thomas d'Aquin," *RT* 90 (1990): 587–622; see in particular pp. 602–17.

16. *In Polit.* I, 1/b, Leonine, vol. 48, p. A 79.

17. The mere translation into French of the commentary on the *Nicomachean Ethics* would be in itself very useful and would reveal many unsuspected riches. It has been translated into English; cf. *Saint Thomas Aquinas, Commentary on Aristotle's Nicomachean Ethics*, trans. C. I. Litzinger, 2 vols. (Chicago, 1964; reprint, with a foreword by Ralph McInerny, 2 vols. in 1, Notre Dame, Ind., 1993).

18. To cite only one passage until we can return to this more fully, SCG III 121, n. 3001: "Among all the things that man needs, other men are the most necessary to him."

19. *ST* Ia IIae q. 4 a. 8.

Thomas does not misrepresent the difficulties of living together, but neither does he hesitate to praise the benefits of "political communion,"[20] for it is the special space in which virtues like friendship or justice are exercised, and therefore a place for human growth. This first result is already rather remarkable, but we may feel that as long as it limits itself to the scope of the Aristotelian city, this conception of political friendship remains limited to the purely natural, human level. Aristotle states that reason is its measure, but does not say why.[21] As a faithful commentator, Thomas does not go beyond the letter of the text here, but when he speaks in his own name, he recasts things at a higher level. Following the Stoics, as handed down in particular by Saint Augustine, Thomas calls on the concept of natural law which will allow him to ground in God not only moral obligation but political friendship itself.[22]

The Natural Law and Its Main Inclinations

We have to go back to the *Prima Secundae* here. In the long, foundational exposition where the Master from Aquino reviews the principles of human action, he first mentions the interior principles that we have called, following his terminology, *habitus*.[23] But there are other principles of human action "exterior" to the person. Thomas names two: elsewhere he spoke of Satan, who spurs man to evil through temptation:[24] he dwells at much greater length in the *Prima Secundae* on the external principle that makes us do good: God Himself, who instructs through law and sustains through grace.[25] As a transcendent "external" principle, God is the origin of those virtuous *habitus* called "virtues" that perfect the creature from within and give him the ability to act in the realm of grace. Since we deal with this at length elsewhere, we do not need to linger here on the subject of grace, but this is the place to say a few words about law,[26] espe-

20. *In Polit.* III, 5, Leonine, vol. 48, p. A 201.
21. Cf. *Nicomachean Ethics* I, 2 (1095b6–7).
22. R.-A. Gauthier, *La morale d'Aristote* (Paris, 1958), 130–31, perfectly characterizes the process of going beyond Aristotle's ethic.
23. See above chapter 11, pp. 264.
24. Cf. *ST* Ia q. 114.
25. The treatise on law comes immediately after the treatise on *habitus* (*ST* Ia IIae qq. 90–108); the treatise on grace comes immediately after that (*ST* Ia IIae qq. 109–14).
26. We know that Thomas defines the law at *ST* Ia IIae q. 90 a. 4 in these terms: "a certain ordinance of reason for the common good, promulgated by him who has care of the community." Without commenting at length, I must emphasize the originality of this position: what comes first in Thomas's definition of law is not obligation, but the

cially natural law, a remarkable innovation of Thomas's ethic, thanks to which we can better perceive how the need for a further spiritual dimension is linked with man's social dimension.[27]

Like the term "nature" itself, the expression "natural law" has not received good press outside Thomist circles. We have to make an effort, then, to understand it properly. It would be a shame to lose its particular contribution.[28] To put things briefly, the eternal law is identified with the divine government of the world, with Providence; the natural law participates in the divine law in a rational creature. Indeed, if the natural law is found in all creatures which are impelled to perform acts and to pursue ends proper to them, the rational creature, for its part, is called upon freely to take up the inclination toward its end, thus becoming a kind of providence of its own for itself and others.[29] This conclusion is not reached by pure deduction; it is connected with a celebrated verse from Saint Paul: "When the pagans who do not have the law do naturally what the law orders, these men without the law are a law unto themselves; they show the reality of the law written on their hearts, witness the testimony of their conscience as well as judgments of blame or praise that they make of one another."[30] Like the new law of the Gospel, the natural law is also an "infused" law *(lex indita)*, infused by God into the human heart. The human person's ethical power is thus also seen as the reflection in him of the divine law:

connection to the common good, which is the end that it allows us to attain; that is why to establish a law and promulgate it are the responsibilities of authority, for only proper authority is in charge of the common good.

27. Of necessity, I can only present here a summary sketch; the reader is advised to see G. de Lagarde, "La sociologie thomiste," chap. 3 in *La naissance de l'esprit laïque au déclin du moyen âge*, vol. 2 (Paris, ²1958), which reviews the links among the ideas with a great deal of lucidity and emphasizes that the theory of social community is one of "Thomism's deepest and most novel reflections."

28. Since we cannot go into elucidating the term "nature" here, I refer to the detailed study by M.-J. Nicolas, "L'idée de nature dans la pensée de saint Thomas d'Aquin," *RT* 74 (1974): 533–90.

29. *ST* Ia IIae q. 91 a. 2, where Thomas quotes Psalm 4:7 to identify the light with which the Lord has blessed the creature with the natural law; in other places, the agent intellect benefits from this reading.

30. Rom. 2:14–15. See on this point B. Montagnes, "Autonomie et dignité de l'homme," who has studied in exemplary fashion Thomas's commentary on these verses and the use he makes of them in the *Summa*.

A law is in a person not only as in one who rules, but also by participation as in one who is ruled. Thus, each one is a law to himself, in the sense that he participates in the order established by the one who has posited the law. Hence St. Paul explains: "They show the reality of the law written in their hearts."[31]

This conception of the natural law goes far beyond the typical case of the pagan being a law to himself.[32] Natural law is linked with the very nature of man, placed in him by the very fact of his creation, and is constant and universal. Therefore, it does not disappear in the faithful Christian. In the words of a contemporary ethical master, it is on the contrary present in all, as the call of a dynamism inscribed in the heart of the being and simultaneously as a promise of fulfillment:

In the sense in which we take it, "natural" refers neither to the world of material nature as opposed to the world of the spirit and freedom, nor to the "historical" notion of a human state allegedly anterior to "culture." We are talking about the need to flourish proper to human nature, the nature of a personal, free being, which cannot fully become what it is except in the course of a history that it must take in hand and guide. Neither angel nor beast, he is man and must become man: that demand which, because he is free, he may fail at, is his "nature." Because man is complex, the demand of his nature is specified in his various arenas of action, calling upon him to become unified in what is most human in him. It is this internal demand that we call "natural law."[33]

There is a major passage from Thomas which shows how that internal demand diversifies into what we call the great natural inclinations. The way Thomas establishes this—through a parallel with the intellectual life—is itself richly instructive. Just as the understanding, oriented toward pure knowledge, immediately seizes the notion of being as its object, so the good is the very first notion grasped by the practical intelligence, which is oriented toward action:

31. *ST* Ia IIae q. 90 a. 3 ad 1.

32. To take only one example, it has been rightly said that this teaching provided "the most sure foundation for the rights of man, by making them flow, not from the human individual as such (the person), but from a human nature common to all human beings." J.-M. Aubert, "Permanente actualité de l'anthropologie thomiste," *DC* 45 (1992): 244–50, cf. 247, who reminds us, among others, that the path from Grotius back to Thomas passes through Vitoria.

33. M.-M. Labourdette, "La morale chrétienne et ses sources," *RT* 77 (1977): 625–42, cf. 631. For a fuller documentation, see J. Maritain, *La loi naturelle ou loi non écrite*, unpublished text, prepared by G. Brazzola (Fribourg, 1987), with the presentation by M.-M. Labourdette, "Jacques Maritain nous instruit encore," *RT* 87 (1987): 655–63.

Every agent acts for an end that has, for him, the value of a good. Consequently the first principle in the practical reason is one governed by the notion of good, viz., *good is that which all things desire. Hence this is the first precept of law: Good is to be done and pursued, and evil is to be avoided. All other precepts of the natural law are based upon this axiom and natural reason naturally envisions them as human goods.*

Since, however, the good has the nature of an end, and evil, the nature of a contrary, *hence it is that all those things to which man has a natural inclination, are naturally apprehended by reason as good, and consequently as worthy of being pursued, and their contraries as evils, to be avoided.* Wherefore the order of the precepts of the natural law derives from the order of natural inclinations.

First of all, *man feels drawn to seek the good corresponding with his nature, in which he resembles all other substances:* inasmuch as every substance seeks the preservation of its own being, according to its own nature: and by reason of this instinct, whatever assures human survival, and wards off what threatens life, which is to say death, belongs to natural law.

Secondly, *there is in man an inclination to seek certain goods more specially, according to that nature which he has in common with other animals:* and in virtue of this inclination, those things are said to belong to the natural law which natural instinct has taught to all animals, such as union of male and female, care of offspring, and so forth.

Thirdly, *we find in man an attraction to good, according to his rational nature, which is proper to him: thus man feels a natural desire to know the truth about God, and to live in society:* and in this respect, whatever pertains to this proper inclination belongs to the natural law, for instance, to shun ignorance, to avoid wronging those among whom one must live, and generally all other such things of this type.[34]

Anyone who reads this with even a minimum of care will find it astonishing. While other spiritual writers speak volubly about fighting nature so that grace may triumph, Thomas says, on the contrary, that every thing in line with nature is good in itself. Created by God, it is in itself oriented toward the good; it is sin that goes against nature.[35] The same attitude was

---

34. *ST* Ia IIae q. 94 a. 2. To complete the treatment here, see S. Pinckaers, *Sources of Christian Ethics*, 408–52, for an ample and detailed commentary on the five main inclinations.

35. One expression of this, among many others, occurs in *ST* Ia IIae q. 109 a. 2 ad 2: "To sin is nothing else than to fail in the good which belongs to any being according to its nature"; nature was made by God and oriented toward Him, so we immediately understand that, in line with Augustine's definition, often repeated by Thomas, sin is at the same time a rejection of God, *aversio a Deo*.

at work in Thomas's recognition of the natural character of the passions in themselves, which we discussed in the previous chapter. The passions are basic data that must be Christianized and not rejected, for they are the material from which our humanity is made. Even more profoundly, we again find at the source of this attitude the same positive vision already displayed in the way that Thomas spoke of the creation as God's work. But we should also note how it is common possession of human nature that inclines men to live in society; by underscoring three times that there is a *communicatio* at the base of each *inclinatio*, Thomas finds here the *koinô-nia* postulated by Aristotle at the starting point of all social amity.

Less noticeable to the untrained eye, but remarkable all the same, this passage attests yet again that Thomas regards himself as the direct heir of the wisdom of the ancients. He owes a great deal generally to Aristotle, but here he is more specifically indebted to the Stoics by way of Cicero, and it has rightly been asked if it is not in the Roman that he discovered the very idea of fundamental inclinations that first express the demands of the natural law.[36] A peevish mind might see in this a pagan intrusion into Christian morals, but we should rather see here, we believe, the renewed sign of Thomas's wish to accept the whole man and his heritage so characteristic of his concerns as a theologian. But this means that he intends to Christianize man not only in his animal nature, but indeed in everything available to man from culture.

At this level, because it is an integral part of what the Creator gave the creature along with being, the law, even participated in by man, remains divine and is prior to every positive formulation in human law. In order to reach the level that most people think of when they speak of law, it is thus necessary that the natural law, grasped at first through a kind of affective connaturality at the level of the main inclinations, be extended into positive human laws. It is not enough for law by itself to regulate the organization of human life in this world. For though nature inclines man to live in society or to practice virtue, it does not say how to do it. Many forms of

---

36. S. Pinckaers makes this observation in *Sources of Christian Ethics*, 405–7. The resemblance is indeed striking. Cf. *De officiis*, I, 4, 11–14, trans. W. Miller, Loeb ed. (1968), 12–17): ". . . Nature had endowed every species of living creature with the instinct of self-preservation . . . A common property of all creatures is also the reproductive instinct (the purpose of which is the propagation of the species). . . . Nature likewise by the power of reason associates man with man in the common bonds of speech and life; . . . Above all, the search after truth and its eager pursuit are peculiar to man. . . ."

society are possible and it is up to human beings to discover them and to regulate their proper functioning. In the same fashion, the perception of the great moral principles is one thing, the concrete practice of virtuous action is another. But the relationship with the natural law remains fundamental and decisive. There is an entirely radical decision here, and without understanding it we cannot understand the precise relationship that a human being can have with the law. What is good, right, and just precedes the law. It is not just because it is prescribed, it is prescribed because it is just. The sacred character of human life is prior to any prohibition against killing. Certain things can become unjust because they are illegal, and in fact life in societies brings with it particular applications of the great moral principles of the natural law. But legal prescription will never make good or just something that is unjust at a fundamental level.[37]

For our present purposes, we must underscore, as we just said, that for the extension of the natural law into diverse laws, man is called upon to become a kind of providence to himself. According to one of Thomas's favorite Scripture verses, "God has left man free to make his own decisions [Literally: `placed man in the hands of his own counsel']" (Sir. 15:14) to the extent that He constituted man the superintendent of his own acts."[38] This concerns the person not only in his individuality, but as a committed member of various communities. Since man is called to live in society, he must be given the means to organize it appropriately, and at the forefront of these means comes the law: "[Though] the divine law is instituted in the first instance to regulate men's connection to God (ad ordinandum homines ad Deum), human law is primarily to regulate men's connections with one another (ad ordinandum homines ad inuicem)."[39]

As a work of reason, the law has as its goal service to the good life in society, what Master Thomas calls the common good. By this we should

---

37. Thomas is absolutely categorical about this, ST Ia IIae q. 95 a. 2: "As Augustine says, 'That which is not just seems to be no law at all.' Wherefore the force of a law depends on the extent of its justice. Now in human affairs a thing is said to be just, from being right, according to the rule of reason. But the first rule of reason is the law of nature. . . . Consequently, every human law has just so much of the nature of law, as it is derived from the law of nature. But if in any point it deflects from the law of nature, it is no longer law but a perversion of law."

38. De uer. q. 5 a. 5 ad 4. The verse from Ecclesiasticus is invoked about twenty times, mostly in the Summa theologiae: ST Ia q. 22 a. 2 ad 4; q. 83 a. 1; ST Ia IIae q. 2 a. 5; q. 10 a. 4 s. c.; q. 91 a. 4 arg. 2; ST IIa IIae q. 65 a. 3 arg. 2; etc.

39. ST Ia IIae q. 99 a. 3.

understand him to mean that the dispositions of the law aim at creating an ensemble of general conditions tending to make exchanges and communications easy and, finally, friendship among members, so that each person achieves his proper fulness with respect to others, and real solidarity makes it possible to pursue a common ideal. In this view, there is no opposition between private good and common good, for "the common good is the end of each person living in community."[40] And thus:

He that seeks the common good of the many, seeks in consequence his own good, for two reasons. First, because the individual good is impossible without the common good of the family, state, or kingdom. . . . Secondly, because, man, being part of the home and the state, must consider what is good for him after what is prudent relative to the good of the many. For the good disposition of the parts depends on their relation to the whole.[41]

What Thomas says here about prudence, he repeats quite often elsewhere. Far from being an accessory, however indispensable, for the person, society is a need of his nature. And that is why the connection of person to society is a connection of part to whole, member to body: "The part [as such] is something of the whole. Now, man is in society as a part in the whole; everything he is then belongs to society."[42] It is thus that the good of the whole predominates, for it is "more divine than the good of a single individual."[43] This sentence, which has caused a lot of ink flow, has been

40. *ST* IIa IIae q. 58 a. 9 ad 3.

41. *ST* IIa IIae q. 47 a. 10 ad 2. It is rather striking to confirm again here what Thomas owed to Stoicism. Cf. Cicero, *De finibus bonorum et malorum* III, 19, trans. H. Rackham, Loeb ed. (1961), 282–84: "From this impulse is developed the sense of mutual attraction which unites human beings as such; this also is bestowed by nature. The mere fact of their common humanity requires that one man should feel another man to be akin to him. . . . It follows that we are by nature fitted to form unions, societies and states. Again they [the Stoics] hold that the universe is governed by divine will; it is a city or state of which both men and gods are members, and each one of us is a part of this universe; from which it is a natural consequence that we should prefer the common advantage to our own. For just as the laws set the safety of all above the safety of individuals, so a good, wise and law-abiding man, conscious of his duty to the state, studies the advantage of all more than that of himself or of any single individual."

42. *ST* IIa IIae q. 64 a. 5; cf. q. 64 a. 2: "every individual person is compared to the whole community as a part to the whole." Cf. *ST* Ia q. 61 a. 3; *ST* IIa IIae q. 26 a. 3; etc.

43. *In Ethic.* I, 2 (1094b10), Leonine, vol. 47/1, p. 9; cf. *ST* IIa IIae q. 99 a. 1 ad 1. On this see the fundamental studies by I. Th. Eschmann, "A Thomistic Glossary on the Principle of the Preeminence of the Common Good," *MS* 5 (1943): 123–65 (following a well-documented historical introduction, the author reprints 204 passages from Thomas that express the superiority of the common good to the private good. See the same author's "'Bonum

long understood as restricted to the natural level. When it is a case of the connection of the person to God, Thomas uses completely different language; but we already understand its bearing much better if we keep in mind his intention as a theologian who never abstracts from the final end. Even the most seemingly "sociological" passages cannot be entirely isolated from this end. Thus God appears as what he is, the true and final common good to which all other goods are subordinated:

> The particular good is ordered to the common good as its end; indeed, the being of the part exists for the being of the whole. From this comes the fact that "the good of the community is more divine than the good of an individual person." Now, it is God, the sovereign good, who is the common good [of the universe] given that the good of all depends on him. Indeed, the good by which each being is good is [simultaneously] its particular good and the good of all the others who depend on him. All things are thus oriented as to their end toward this unique good which is God.[44]

We will return to this connection of the person to the community, but we must add here that while the organization of the community requires a body of law in the service of the common good, it also requires an authority with the responsibility to promote it. This should not be understood as an unfortunate necessity following from the wickedness of men, but here too as a demand linked to human nature, and it would have occurred even if man had not sinned:

> [There are two ways of dominion *(dominium)*, Thomas explains; one with respect to slaves seen as the property of the master, the other with respect to free persons.] But a man can exercise dominion over another as a free subject, when he directs him either toward his personal good, or to the common good. Such a dominion of man over man would have existed in the state of innocence, for two reasons. First, because a man is by nature a social being, and so men in the state of inno-

---

commune melius est quam bonum unius.' Eine Studie über den Wertvorrang des Personalen bei Thomas von Aquin," *MS* 6 (1944): 62–120 (the purpose of this second study is well summarized by the contrast expressed in its title: this superiority of the common good does not lessen the primacy of the human person). A more accessible study is J. Maritain, *Person and the Common Good*, trans. John J. Fitzgerald (Notre Dame, Ind., 1966). See also J. Martinez Barrera, "Sur la finalité en politique: la question du bien commun selon saint Thomas," in J. Follon and J. McEvoy, eds., *Finalité et intentionalité: Doctrine thomiste et perspectives modernes* (Paris-Leuven, 1992), 148–61. We can go further with the same author: "De l'ordre politique chez saint Thomas d'Aquin," in *Actualité de la pensée médiévale*, 247–67.
44. SCG III 17.

cence would have lived in society. Now a social life is not possible among a number of people unless one becomes the head and promotes the common good; for the many pursue many things, whereas one pursues only one. Wherefore the Philosopher says in the beginning of the *Politics*, "Wherever many things are directed to one end, we always find one is directing and the leader."[45]

The necessity for an authority in charge of the common good is itself also one of the important principles in the Master of Aquino's "sociology," but we need not insist on it further since we will deal below with the government of man by man. We must, however, note in this last passage the care Thomas takes to preserve the liberty of persons in society. If the comparison with the whole and the part might lead us to fear lest this dimension of things be lost from view, the simple reminder of certain arguments is enough to show that the fear is nothing: a free man is not a common [vulgar] thing.

⚶

In the concrete situations with which we are familiar, the Christian is related to two large societies: the Church, to which he belongs through baptism, and the earthly city of which he is a member by birth. It is well known that Thomas Aquinas never wrote a book on the Church, nor did he devote a special treatise in the *Summa* to the Church. In the twentieth century, this is a bit astonishing. Various modern works have been written, thus, to show that he clearly did not ignore this Christian reality par excellence, and that if the Church gets no special treatment in his work, it is in truth everywhere in the movement of man's return to God.[46] We might say almost as much about the political community. Though Thomas attempted to write a *De Regno* as well as a commentary on Aristotle's *Politics*, it is noteworthy that he left both unfinished. While there are many elements for a political theory in the *Summa*, we seek in vain for a complete treatise on the subject there. However if we want to continue our reflections on man as a social being, we must try to gather together what it contains on this topic. The attempt may seem overly ambitious, but we will not attempt a full treatment: the important thing is to open up the main lines of the Master's thought.

45. *ST* Ia q. 96 a. 4; cf. q. 92 a. 1 ad 2.
46. In general terms, that is the persuasive view of Y. Congar, "The Idea of the Church." Also by the same author, see *L'Église de saint Augustin à l'époque moderne* (Paris, 1970), 232–41; and "Vision de l'Église chez Thomas d'Aquin," *RSPT* 62 (1978): 523–42.

The Church, the People of God

Beyond the laments about the lack of a *De Ecclesia* in the *Summa*, the Master of Aquino has also been accused—in a most curious and anachronistic way, if truth be told—of holding views contrary to Pius XII's in the encyclical *Mystici Corporis* (published some seven centuries later) and to have too ethereal a view of the Church, which he is alleged to have reduced to its mystical dimension at the expense of its structure and organization.[47] These discussions, born of a too-selective reading of the relevant passages, are not repeated here. They at least had the value of inviting a deeper probing into the question. Numerous valuable studies have since demonstrated the truth of the matter—notably about the place of the hierarchical ministry and the pope in particular in Thomas's thought. It would be hard today to reproach Thomas for ignoring or misunderstanding them. The truth is rather the contrary.[48]

In our research into the spiritual implications of Thomas's thought, this is the third time that we have met with the Church: first, with respect to Christ, since the Church is an outpouring of his grace, then in its connection to the Holy Spirit, which is its heart.[49] Without doubt, this theo-

47. Cf. A. Mitterer, *Gemheimnisvoller Leib Christi nach St. Thomas von Aquin und nach Papst Pius XII* (Vienna 1950): See also the refinements by Ch. Journet, in his review of the same in *BT* 8 (1947–1953): 363–73, and by Y. Congar, in *Sainte Église*, 614–15.

48. To quote just one passage in line with others that are coming, I will refer to SCG IV 76, n. 4103: "It is clear that, although the peoples are divided into various cities and regions, the Church, however, must be one: there is no second Christian people. So too for this particular people of a single Church, a single bishop must be the head of the whole people, even for the ensemble of the Christian people." We cannot conclude from reading this passage that the Pope is the single maker of Church unity. Thomas is not unaware of the role of the other bishops, nor of Scripture and Tradition, and even less, of the Eucharist. Besides the fundamental study by Y. Congar, "Aspects ecclésiologiques de la querelle entre Mendiants et Séculiers dans la deuxième moitié du XIIIe siècle et au début du XIVe siècle," *AHDLMA* 28 (1961): 34–151, I mention only two other studies among the most recent: S.-Th. Bonino, "La place du pape dans l'Église selon saint Thomas d'Aquin," *RT* 86 (1986): 392–422; C. Ryan, "The Theology of Papal Primacy in Thomas Aquinas," in C. Ryan, ed., *The Religious Roles of the Papacy: Ideals and Realities, 1150–1300* (Toronto, 1989), 193–225.

49. Cf. above chap. 6: "In the Image of the First-born Son," and chap. 9: "Heart of the Church." Those with doubts about the way Thomas holds together the "mystical" and the "sociological" aspects of the Church ought to read this passage, where Thomas connects the Pope's role in the Church with the mystery of the Trinitarian procession of the Holy Spirit: "Indeed, Christ, Son of God, consecrates his Church and puts his mark on it through the Holy Spirit, [who is] as his character and seal. . . . And similarly the Vicar of Christ, as faithful servant, watches over the Church submitted to Christ through the exercise of his primacy and governance," *Contra err. Graec.* II 32, Leonine, vol. 40, p. A 101.

logical perspective is at the forefront of Thomas's thinking and expresses itself through the appellations Body of Christ, Communion of Saints, and even "Church of the Holy Spirit."[50] Christian existence has already appeared to us as marked in its deepest interiority by its membership in the communion of grace. But there is still much to say in the new perspective of the present chapter. Without pushing the comparison beyond what it merits, we can certainly state that in a similar way to how the earthly city is the space where the natural qualities of the human being flourish, the Church is the space where man sees himself equipped for his supernatural life and where he flourishes as a son of God. Thomas does not neglect this, and he himself establishes the parallel in his commentary on the Letter to the Ephesians (2:19):

["You are no longer strangers and foreigners, but fellow citizens with the saints, and of the household of God."] To understand these words, we must know that the college of the faithful (collegium fidelium) is immediately after called in Scripture "house" [or "family" (domus), as in Timothy 3:15: "You must know how to behave in the house of God, which is the Church of God," sometimes "city" (civitas) as in Psalm 121:3: "Jerusalem which is built as a city."

Between the city that is a political college (collegium politicum) and the family that is an economic college, there is a twofold difference. Those who belong to the college of the home (collegio domus) share in common (communicant) private acts; those who belong to the college of the city (collegio civitatis) share in common public acts. Thus, those related to the college of the home are governed by a single person, the father of the family; those who belong to the college of the city are governed by a king. Thus a father of a family in his house is like a king in his kingdom.[51]

The college of the faithful has something of the city and something of the family, and the head of this college (rector collegii) is the Father, Matthew 6:9: "Our Father, who art in heaven"; Jeremiah 3:19: "You will call me Father and will follow me everywhere"; and thus this college is a family. If we consider the members, however, then it is a city, for they have in common (communicant) special acts, those of faith, hope, and love. Thus, if we pay attention to the faithful as

---

50. In Matt. XX, 25, lect. 2, n. 1668; G. Sabra, Thomas Aquinas' Vision of the Church: Fundamentals of an Ecumenical Ecclesiology (Mainz, 1987), justly emphasizes the predominance of the theological over the juridical or hierarchical elements.

51. This strongly patriarchal affirmation conflicts with a modern spirit. It is useless to deny that it bears the mark of his time—which Thomas only too clearly does not escape. But we should be careful not to make it say more than the precise comparison here suggests.

such, then it is a college of the city type; but if we regard the head of the college, then it is a college of the family type.[52]

This long text is rather difficult to translate exactly owing to the fact that *collegium* has no exact equivalent in our modern languages, but the passage is still rather clear in meaning: the Church cannot entirely be compared to any other kind of society, whether the family or the city. It has something of the city in that all its members are equal in common possession of certain goods, but it differs in that these goods, entirely special, are the theological virtues. It also resembles the city in that it has only one head, but since that head is God the Father, with whom the children can have the most intimate relationship, this society is thus transformed into a family.[53] We see at once the interest and the limits of the transposition of sociological categories to the Church,[54] and Thomas exploits the advantages, as this second passage shows:

["There is a river whose streams bring joy to God's city," Psalm 46:4.] This river is the Church, Psalm 86:3: "He has glorious predictions to make of you, city of God." Three things pertain to the definition of this city.

First, it brings together a multitude of free beings. Indeed, if there were only one person or a few, there is no city; so too, if they were slaves. Now, this is what we find in the Church, Galatians 4:31: "We are not the sons of a slave, but of a free woman."

Second, it possesses autonomy (sufficientia). When we are traveling we do not find everything that is necessary to human life, in good and bad health; but in the city we must find everything necessary for life. This autonomy occurs in the Church, for we find in her everything necessary to spiritual life, Psalm 64:5: "Fill us with the good things of your house."

Third is the unity of the citizens. It is from this, which is to say the unity of the

52. *In ad Eph.* II, 19, n. 124. I have modified the beginning of the second paragraph: we read *est* in place of *habet*, for otherwise it would have been necessary to read this as saying: "The city possesses a political college," which hardly makes sense. Or it would have become necessary to modify the meaning of the word "college" and say something like: "The city possesses a political regime," which does not seem justified by the context, where "college" has the same meaning at every point.

53. See the commentary by Y. Congar, "'Ecclesia' et 'populus (fidelis).'"

54. It is profitable to read the first part of the study by B.-D. de La Soujeole, "'Societé' et 'communion,'" 588–601, where the author develops this parallel (p. 601): "Political society is the only grouping of a social nature that may be called perfect. From this derives its analogical use for a theology of the Church as expressing the whole of the Church. Just as the city is not only an institution but also is formed by the virtuous lives of its members, so the Church as society will not solely mean 'structure' but also the 'life' which is in its breast."

citizens, that the city gets its name, since *ciuitas* is like [a contraction of] *"ciuium unitas."* This is also found in the Church, cf. John 17:21: "That they may be one as we are one." This city, then, is gladdened by the grace of the Holy Spirit which pours out in her [like a river].[55]

The main interest of this passage is not the parallel "earthly city—ec-clesial city," which was already known, but the development of the fact that the Church, like the political city, is composed of free persons *(mul-titudo liberorum)*. For anyone familiar with Saint Paul (Gal. 3:28) this may not seem entirely new, but it has been rightly emphasized:

To grasp the force of this affirmation, it is good to remember that, in the medieval city, there existed a "people above," who were the only ones really to perform acts of citizenship, and a "people below," who are often designated by expressions like *vulgus, common people,* or *popularis, populares* and did not perform them. . . . Not everyone had full use of citizenship rights in the medieval city. In the Church, Saint Thomas says, all participate in the highest activities: "ipse populus Ecclesia dicitur" [= the people themselves are called the Church"].[56]

Thus, as we saw Thomas (at the beginning of this chapter) extending Aristotle's city out to the ends of the whole world, and consequently mod-ifying some of the "political" dimensions of man into the dimensions of a "social being," we also see him decisively transforming the citizen by analogy with the dimensions of the Son of the heavenly Father. Here, he recalls that God is not a respecter of persons in his city and all are free be-fore him, which adds a distinctive new touch to the portrait of the mem-bers of the ecclesial society.

Because he never wrote a systematic treatise *De Ecclesia*, Thomas was prevented from elaborating the relevant categories at great length, but we may easily discover them in his work. And it is a shame that they are so lit-tle regarded. When the time had finally come for the theologians to write about the Church (some thirty years after Thomas's death), too many countervailing factors came into play and a "combative ecclesiology" (Congar's expression) then insisted more fully on the powers of the hier-archy rather than the equality of the baptized in their possession of a com-mon dignity. Without having misunderstood the role of clerics in the Church, Friar Thomas's ecclesiology contained the seeds of elements that did not find greater development until the documents of Vatican II.

55. *In Ps. XLV,* 5, n. 3, ed. Vivès, vol. 18, p. 515.
56. Y. Congar, "'Ecclesia' et 'populus (fidelis),'" 165–66.

We will note a somewhat analogous phenomenon in the following pages when we treat of the participation of all in the governance of the city. Though we cannot linger on the point here, it is good to recognize that, besides Christology and a theology of the Holy Spirit, the doctrine on the sacraments is a favorite place for disclosing the connection between the Church and the spiritual life. Numerous passages indeed repeat that the Church is "founded," "based," "constituted," "built" by the faith and the sacraments of the faith.[57] The very rich theme of the Church as born from the Cross can be recognized here: the water and blood gushing from Jesus' pierced side are traditionally interpreted by both East and West as the symbol of baptism and the Eucharist. Now, while for Thomas as for all theologians, baptism effects our membership in the Body of Christ, i.e., the Church, he very much emphasizes, along with Saint Augustine, that the fruit of the eucharist is not only the grace of intimacy with Christ, but indeed the unity of the ecclesial body.[58]

In addition, sacramental theology strongly emphasizes the idea of growth so greatly used in spiritual theology.[59] Thomas establishes an illuminating parallel with bodily life: "This bears a twofold perfection: one as to the person himself, the other as to the social community in which he lives, for man is by nature a social animal."[60] That is why beyond the final

57. Cf. *In IV Sent.*, d. 17 q. 3 a. 1 sol. 5; d. 18 q. 1 a. 1 sol. 1; *ST* Ia q. 92 a. 3; *ST* IIIa q. 64 a. 2 ad 3; etc.

58. From the many other passages, let me quote this quite explicit one, *ST* IIIa q. 80 a. 4: "The reality *(res)* obtained through this sacrament is two-fold: one, that it signifies and contains, namely Christ Himself; while *the other is signified but not contained, namely, Christ's mystical body, which is the communion of the saints*"; cf. *ST* IIIa q. 60 a. 3 s. c.; q. 73 a. 6. It will be remembered that in this context "signify" has the sacramental meaning of "efficacious sign." The sacrament realizes what it signifies. This topic has been thoroughly studied. Besides the commentary by A.-M. Roguet, in *L'eucharistie*, see also the fine recent study by M. Morard, "L'eucharistie clé de voûte de l'organisme sacramentel chez saint Thomas d'Aquin," *RT* 95 (1995): 217–50.

59. See chapter 14 below: "Ways to God."

60. *ST* IIIa q. 65 a, 1. Thomas seems especially interested in this analogy, for he deals with it several times before giving it definitive form. On this, see *In IV Sent.* d. 2 q. 1 a. 2, where the medical view of healing sin is dominant; *SCG* IV 58, where the parallel corporeal-spiritual makes its appearance, but is only briefly dealt with; *De articulis fidei et ecclesiae sacramentis* 2, Leonine, vol. 42, pp. 252–53, where we are already very close to the position in the *Summa*. Something worthy of interest: while the theologians of Thomas's time sought to justify the number of seven sacraments by a correspondence with the seven deadly sins (Albertus Magnus) or by the three theological virtues completed with the four cardinal virtues (Bonaventure), Thomas seems to be the only one to develop this parallel between corporeal and spiritual life, simultaneously more natural and fecund. Virtues or

fruit of the Eucharist, which is the unity of the mystical body, the connection with the whole of the community occurs in two ways. First, through the authority governing the multitude by the exercise of public functions; this corresponds in the spiritual life to the sacrament of *orders*, since according to the epistle to the Hebrews (7:27) priests do not offer the sacrifice for themselves alone, but for the whole people. Then, since this social perfecting is affected by the propagation of the species, man is also perfected here through *marriage* in his daily as well as his spiritual life, since marriage before being a sacrament is first a natural institution.

Thomas sees yet another relation between sacramental organism and ecclesial body: the sacraments are the foundation of law in the Church,[61] but we touch here on a subject much more vast than fits within our purposes.[62] On the other hand, we must still draw out some of the consequences of the temporal roots of the ecclesial community, for they lead to direct repercussions on the Christian in this world.

Spiritual and Temporal

Numerous studies have been devoted to the question of Church and State in Saint Thomas;[63] our intention here is much less ambitious. In order to link up with an earlier chapter, we will repeat a little of the examination of the term *saecularis*, whose implications we had begun to evaluate. Though its basic meaning allowed us to determine a little better Thomas's religious attitude toward the goods of this world, a second

---

vices, good works or sins, the expressions of the spiritual life do not appear in him as more or less artificially tacked on to the Christian life, but rather as manifestations of a living organism, one which can certainly be affected by illnesses and recover its health or even die, but whose growth is the usual rule and which can also, through regular exercise, firm up and consolidate itself.

61. *In IV Sent.* d. 7 q. 1 a. 1 qc. 1 ad 1: "Fundamentum cuiuslibet legis in sacramentis consistit."

62. See M. Useros Carretero, *"Statuta Ecclesiae" y "Sacramenta Ecclesiae" en la Eclesiologia de Santo Tomás* (Rome, 1962). There are various articles on the connections of law and communion in two special publications: "Pour une théologie du Droit canonique," *RSPT* 57 (1973/2); "La loi dans l'Église," *Communio*, Paris (1978/3).

63. Cf., e.g., Yves Congar, "Orientations de Bonaventure et surtout de Thomas d'Aquin dans leur vision de l'Église et celle de l'État," in 1274—*Année charnière*, 691–708. There is also a related topic suggested in the use—though relatively infrequent (sixteen appearances)—of *christianitas*; cf. A. Melloni, "Christianitas negli scritti di Tommaso d'Aquino," *Cristianesimo nella storia* 6 (1985): 45–69. Contrary to what might be expected, *christianitas* only rarely has the sociological meaning of "Christendom." Rather, it designates the quality of "the Christian being."

meaning does not in itself make any value judgments. The word is used in this sense to describe a state of fact, to signify the division of realms and different competencies between what belongs to the earthly city *(saeculum)* and to the Kingdom of God in its earthly form, the Church. The general terms temporal and spiritual,[64] or more precisely civil and ecclesial,[65] are thus distinguished and sometimes placed in opposition. This frequent usage might be illustrated with a variety of passages, as when Thomas distinguishes the type of unity proper to each society and the way each may be jeopardized through internal divisions:

Sedition differs from schism in two respects. First, because schism is opposed to the spiritual unity of the people, viz., ecclesiastical unity, whereas sedition is contrary to the temporal or secular unity of the multitude, for instance of a city or kingdom. [A second point is that schism remains on the spiritual plane, while civil sedition brings about preparation for bodily conflict.][66]

The same distinction is found when he defines how each of these two cities is ruled by a power proper to it: on the one side the power of princes, on the other that of prelates; to these it falls to order the social life of the multitude by laws suited to the common good pursued in each case:

Just as it belongs to the secular authority to promulgate laws which apply the natural law to matters of the common good in the temporal realm, so it belongs to ecclesiastical superiors to prescribe by decree those things that concern the common good of the faithful in the spiritual realm.[67]

Thus, the parallels as well as the distinctions and overlaps between the two levels are clear, but Thomas does not consider the difference absolutely neutral. In fact, he recognizes an inequality between the two realms which subjects the temporal to the spiritual:

Spiritual power is distinct from temporal. Now prelates having spiritual power sometimes interfere in matters concerning the secular power. Where does the right come from? [Thomas replies to this objection as follows]. . . . The secular power is subject to the spiritual even as the body is subject to the soul. Conse-

---

64. Thus, in *ST* IIa IIae q. 63 a. 2: *dispensatio spiritualium* is clearly distinguished from *dispensatio temporalium.*

65. Thus "secular" and "ecclesiastic" offices are distinguished (*ST* Ia IIae q. 13 a. 4 arg. 3), or "secular" judges from "ecclesiastical" judges (*ST* IIa IIae q. 33 a. 7 ad 5).

66. *ST* IIa IIae q. 42 a. 1 ad 2.

67. *ST* IIa IIae q. 147 a. 3.

quently, the spiritual prelate can intervene in those temporal matters without usurpation in the realms where the secular power is subordinate to him or which have been committed to the spiritual by the temporal authority.[68]

We can discern behind these passages the mixed situation of the medieval Church. And we remember that Thomas encountered in his youth some cases where temporal and spiritual overlapped, which led him to take strong positions.[69] Perhaps this is why, even as he emphasizes the superiority of the spiritual over the temporal, he notes no less clearly their respective competencies:

> The spiritual power and the secular power both derive from the divine power; consequently, the secular power is subordinated to the spiritual power only to the extent that it has been subjected by God, which is to say, in what concerns the salvation of souls; in this realm it is better to obey the spiritual power than the secular. *But in what concerns the political good (bonum ciuile), it is better to obey the secular power than the spiritual,* as it is said in Matthew 22:21: "Render unto Caesar the things that are Caesar's."[70]

This passage continues by reminding us of the unique case of the papal power, since the pope was then also a temporal sovereign. But this is the exception that confirms the rule. In spite of potential interference, the temporal keeps its proper autonomy and consistency, and recognition of the spiritual's superiority over the temporal cannot serve as a pretext for evading the legitimate laws of temporal rulers. This does not cease to be true even when the rulers are not Christians, for *"while the distinction between believers and unbelievers concerns the divine law that comes from grace, it does not destroy the human law which is the law of natural reason. This is why . . . the distinction does not do away with dominion and authority of unbelievers over believers."*[71] Thomas was led to reflect on this point by Saint Paul's frequent admonitions about submission to authorities, or for slaves to masters (cf. Col. 3:22, Eph. 6:5, Titus 2:9, 1 Pet. 2:18):

> Why does he [i.e., Paul] come back so often to this point? Not without reason. Indeed, a heresy had been born among the Jews that the servants of God could not

---

68. *ST* IIa IIae q. 60 a. 6 arg. 3 and ad 3.
69. See my *Saint Thomas Aquinas*, 12–15.
70. *In II Sent.* d. 44 *expositio textus*, ad 4.
71. *ST* IIa IIae q. 10 a. 10. Cf. the ad 3: "Caesar's authority pre-existed the distinction between believers and unbelievers." For a more complete examination of this question, see S. R. Castaño, "Legitima potestad de los infieles y autonomia de lo político. Exegesis tomista," *ST* 60 (1995): 266–84.

be servants of man, and it had spread among the Christian people, some saying that, having become children of God through Christ, they could not be servants of men. But Christ did not come to destroy the order of justice through faith; indeed to the contrary, it is through faith in Christ that justice is safeguarded. Now, justice means that some are subject to others, but this servitude concerns the body. Now through Christ we are freed with regard to the soul, but not from the servitude and corruption of the body; in the world to come we will be freed from bodily corruption and servitude.[72]

This bit of commentary on the epistle to Titus has an exact parallel in an article of the *Summa* that is worth the trouble to read here in order to grasp to what degree it is a constant and considered doctrine:

Faith in Christ is the principle and cause of justice, as is said in Romans 3:22: "The justice of God is obtained through faith in Christ." This faith does not therefore suppress the order founded on justice (*ordo iustitiae*). On the contrary, it affirms it. Now, the order founded on justice demands that inferiors obey their superiors; if it were otherwise, it would be the destruction of all human society. Faith in Christ does not absolve us from obedience to secular rulers.[73]

This is not the place to pursue the study of this question for itself. We will remark here that, contrary to what is still the case among his greatest contemporaries,[74] Thomas has a clearly dualist vision of the connection between Church and civil society, and he never wavers on this subject.[75] He would not have been a child of his time if he had not admitted the de

---

72. *In ad Titum* I, 9, n. 64.

73. *ST* IIa IIae q. 104 a. 6. Note, too, the ad 3, where the *ordo iustitiae* appears as the very foundation of the obedience to the prince; if the prince himself breaks his ties with that order, his subjects are free from their duty of obedience to him. See also the preceding article, q. 104 a. 5: Man owes absolute obedience to God alone.

74. Notably in Bonaventure and Albertus Magnus, who remain conduits for the equivalence between *ecclesia* and *christianitas*, which they got from the high middle ages, with the permanent and correlative risks of hierocracies and Caesaro-papism. On this, see the passages quoted in I. T. Eschmann, "St. Thomas Aquinas on the Two Powers," *MS* 20 (1958):177–205, see especially pp. 192–93.

75. Rather than Eschmann, quoted in the previous note, see here the study by L. E. Boyle, "The De Regno and the Two Powers," in the same author's *Pastoral Care: Clerical Education and Canon Law, 1200–1400* (London, 1981) and L. P. Fitzgerald, "St. Thomas Aquinas and the Two Powers," *Angelicum* 56 (1979): 515–56. For a position contrary to the one presented here, see W. J. Hankey, "'Dionysius dixit, lex divinitatis est ultima per media reducere.' Aquinas, Hierocracy and the 'Augustinisme politique,'" in *Tommaso d'Aquino. Proposte nuove di lettura*, ed. I. Tolomio (= *Medioevo* 18 [1992]) (Padua, 1992), 119–50. Despite the richness of the bibliographical documentation in this essay, many of the passages cited above seem to have escaped the attention of the author.

facto union of the two powers in the papal power, as well as the subordination of the ends of civil society to the final end of the Church. But it is quite remarkable that he also extols the distinction in principle of their proper domains and competencies, as well as their mutual subordination in their respective realms. Much ground remained to be traveled before arriving at the teaching about the connections between Church and World,[76] or about religious freedom,[77] which would appear at Vatican II. But there is hardly any doubt: we should not fail to see in Thomas's metaphysic of creation, the origins, simultaneously distant and very close, of a very clear view of these complex realities.

The Best Form of Government?

Affirmation of the autonomy of politics with respect to the religious still does not tell us anything about the notably different question of the best form of government that should be adopted in a society. To tell the truth, Thomas never spoke at great length on this topic, but we see immediately that the two questions are linked. Not only because it is a matter of one part and another of the common good of the many, but also because the basic givens that determine the choices in the two cases are the same in the end. Just as much as the demand for mutual respect in the different competencies of Church and State, the appeal to an ethic of per-

---

76. Cf., for example, Gaudium et Spes III 36: "If by the autonomy of earthly affairs we mean that created things and societies themselves enjoy their own laws and values, which must be gradually deciphered, put to use, and regulated by men, then it is entirely right to demand that autonomy. Such is not merely required by modern man, but it harmonizes also with the will of the Creator. For by the very circumstances of their having been created all things are endowed with their own stability, truth, goodness, proper laws, and order."

77. In seeking the sources of this teaching, as astute an observer as Yves Congar has noted that the principal source is found in Albertus Magnus and Thomas, who "had disengaged and established a consistency of nature independent of its condition of supernatural justice or of sin, and, consequently, a validity of the natural order independent of faith and charity. Is it not, at bottom, this line of thought that our Declaration follows [i.e., Dignitatis humanae, "On Religious Liberty"] when it establishes a right, not solely civil and relative, but natural and absolute, of the human person not to be constrained in matters of conscience, especially in religious matters? Indeed, it is on this objective reality, not on a subjective right of the erring conscience, that the Council based its teaching on religious liberty. Thus, there was no passing from an objective to a subjective order, but a new disengaging of an aspect of the objective order: the first time by Thomas and Albert, a second time by Vatican II." Yves Congar, "Avertissement," in J. Hamer and Yves Congar, eds., La liberté religieuse (Paris, 1967), 12; we will return in chapter 13 to the subject of conscience according to Thomas Aquinas.

sonal responsibility in the governing of the earthly city is inscribed in the autonomy of the human being.

We must understand, however, that we are approaching here one of the most disputed questions in the exegesis of Thomas's work. As in many other matters, and perhaps even more here, numerous interpreters have tried to find in the Master the theory that they maintain themselves. Thus, at the time of *Action Française*, a whole movement of influential theologians tried to draw Thomas's political thought toward absolute monarchy. Others placed him rather in line with a democratic current. Still others saw in him a theory of "mixed" government.[78] But it was not only a matter of the subjective dispositions of interpreters, for the differences in interpretation were not limited to French territory. English-speaking authors also held rather different positions at times.[79]

We should recognize that it is difficult enough to harmonize the Master's assertions whether we simply follow his commentary on Aristotle,[80] or his little book *De Regno* — a work specifically written for a reigning sovereign which remained incomplete[81] — or his deliberate and personal synthesis in the *Summa theologiae*. The point of view is different in each of these three cases, but things become even more complicated by the fact that *De Regno* was finished by Ptolemy of Lucca, while the commentary on the *Politics* was completed by Peter of Auvergne, and both were completed in a sense rather different from Thomas's in the *Summa*. The *De*

---

78. See the enlightening study by R. Imbach, "Démocratie ou monarchie? La discussion sur le meilleur régime politique chez quelques interprètes français de Thomas d'Aquin (1893–1928)," in *Saint Thomas au XXe siècle*, ed. S. Th. Bonino. (Paris, 1994), 335–50, which is an accurate account of these controversies and the oldest literature, which I cannot reproduce here.

79. For a convincing presentation, J. M. Blythe, "The Mixed Constitution and the Distinction between Regal and Political Power in the Work of Thomas Aquinas," *Journal of the History of Ideas* 47 (1986): 547–65, who puts forward at the beginning of his study a useful review of the relevant opinions.

80. *In Polit.*, Leonine, vol. 48 A. The work remained unfinished and stops with Book III, 6 (1280a7). See my *Saint Thomas Aquinas*, 233–34. Besides the Leonine text, all the editions of Thomas's commentary are gravely deficient, and the more or less amplified text they propose is not Thomas's, but Peter of Auvergne's, who finished it and whose views it reflects.

81. *De regno ad regem Cypri*, Leonine, vol. 42. The work is also known under the name *De Regimine principum*. The authentic part ends in the middle of chapter II 8. See my *Saint Thomas Aquinas*, 169–71. The "Letter to the Countess of Flanders" (or "to the Duchess of Brabant"), Leonine, vol. 42, pp. 360–78 also belongs to this type of literature (cf. *Saint Thomas Aquinas*, 218–20).

Regno suffered a further misadventure, since it was plundered by Giles of Rome (in his own treatise *De regimine principum*), who himself drew it in the direction of a despotic monarchical power, thus disfiguring the judiciously tempered theory of political power which seems to be Thomas's own personal view.[82] Many problems might be solved, it seems, if we posed them in a new way, more attentive to Thomas's project as a whole rather than to the immediate doctrinal tenor of certain propositions in the writings under examination. Indeed, it is important to distinguish the *De Regno* and the *Politics* from Thomas's full elaboration. We cannot give the same weight to the unfinished attempts as we do to the teachings in the *Summa*. Careful analysis of the *De Regno* in particular, whose peculiarities have long intrigued the commentators, allows us to see this. If circumstances led Thomas to begin these two works, and then abandon them so quickly, it is because at bottom the genre did not correspond to his real aims. Far from wanting to write a treatise on political philosophy, Thomas was primarily concerned with a theological vision of the Christian life, up to and including its political aspects.[83] That is why, at least in the case under consideration, it is only in the *Summa theologiae* that we find his true thinking, not in the form of an independent treatise of political theology, but scattered in fragments here and there following the demands of the project as a whole.[84]

The whole hypothesis and methodical concern in what follows here

---

82. It has been noted that Thomas's seemingly divergent positions may be reconciled if we take care to notice whether he is speaking in absolute terms (a single virtuous sovereign is the best, but Thomas sees this as an exception), or rather in the order of concrete reality (mixed government is then preferable). Cf. A. Riklin, *Die beste politische Ordnung nach Thomas von Aquin* (St. Gallen, 1991), 31–34 (I could not consult the summary of this article under the same title in *Politik und christliche Verantwortung, Festschrift für F.-M. Schmölz*, ed. G. Putz, H. Dachs, et al. [Innsbruck-Vienna, 1992], 67–90). We might ask ourselves, however, whether this kind of reading is enough. M. Jordan's proposal (below) seems to suggest a better solution.

83. We might transfer to theology what is said elsewhere about moral philosophy, in the introduction to *In Ethic.*, Leonine, vol. 47/1, p. 4: "Moral philosophy can be divided into three parts. The first, called 'monastic,' considers actions of men taken individually in so far as they are ordered to their end. The second, called 'economic,' considers the acts of the domestic group; the third is concerned with the operations of the civic multitude and is called 'political.'"

84. I summarize here the heart of the proposition (which seems truly new and relevant) of M. D. Jordan, "De Regno and the Place of Political Thinking in Saint Thomas Aquinas," *Medioevo* 18 (1992): 151–68. The proposition of J. I. Saranyana, "En busca de la

sticks to the *Summa*, a work of synthesis and the ripest fruit of Friar Thomas's genius. It is not by chance that the main passages we shall read come almost entirely from the treatises on the Old and New Law. Our author shows himself "a firm believer in law" as the guarantee of a just society.[85] For him, it is less a matter whether the best government can be assured by a single person, several, or all, than if the power-holders govern in accord with the law as itself the expression of the will of the whole people:

Properly speaking, the law first and principally aims at order in light of the common good. To establish this order in light of the common good is the business of the whole people *(totius multitudinis)* or of someone representing them *(gerentis uicem totius multitudinis)*. That is why the power of legislating belongs either to the whole people or to official figures who have that responsibility *(quae totius multitudinis curam habet)*. The reason for this is that, here as in all other realms, ordering toward the end belongs to the one who is in charge of the end.[86]

Thus, according to this passage, not only do the legislative powers belong to the people, but we must understand that only through delegation of authority does the sovereign himself have power to make laws, and Thomas says so very explicitly.[87] In these conditions, we should not be surprised that, for Thomas, the best form of government is what he calls "mixed," because it results in an equilibrium among the various forms of power described by Aristotle. All citizens being concerned, it is normally the best way to assure good order in the whole people's progress toward their end:

Two points need to be observed in the good organization of the government of a city or a nation. First, *everyone should have a part in government*, for in this, according to the second book of the *Politics*, there is a guarantee of civil peace, and everyone cherishes and supports such a state of things. The other point concerns

---

ciencia política tomasiana. Sobre el libro IV 'De regimine principum,'" *ST* 60 (1995): 256–65, who sees in Ptolemy's additions reflections of Thomas's "table-talk," seems less probable.

85. J. M. Blythe, "The Mixed Constitution," 556: "Thomas is an unswerving champion of the law."

86. *ST* Ia IIae q. 90 a. 3.

87. *ST* Ia IIae q. 97 a. 3 ad 3: "If we are dealing with a free society, able to make its own law, we must count more on the unanimous consent of the people to make them observe a disposition made manifest through custom, than on *the authority of the ruler who only has power of making laws as a representative of the people*. That is why, although individuals cannot make law, the whole people, however, can legislate."

the form of the regime or the organization of powers. We know that there are several such distinguished by Aristotle in the third book of the *Politics*, but the main ones are kingship, or the predominance of a single ruler according to virtue, and aristocracy, which is to say government by the best, or the predominance of a small number according to virtue. That is why the best organization of government for a city or kingdom is a single ruler put at the head by reason of virtue, having authority over all, while under his authority are found a certain number of subordinate heads, qualified through virtue, *and where nevertheless power thus defined belongs to the whole people, for all have the possibility of being elected or electors.* Such is the perfect regime, happily mixed *(politia bene commixta)* by combining monarchy through the pre-eminence of a single man, aristocracy through the mutiplicity of virtuous heads, and finally democracy, or popular rule by the fact that *simple citizens may be chosen as leaders, and the choice of leaders belongs to the people.*[88]

The desire for equilibrium is evident, but it is not the only justification for Thomas's preference for the mixed regime. As may be seen in what follows, Thomas is convinced from Sacred Scripture that it was precisely a mixed regime that God desired for his People:

Moses and his successors governed the people as sole and universal leaders, which is a characteristic of royalty. But the seventy-two elders were elected on the basis of merit (Deut. 1:15). . . . Here we see the aristocratic element. As to democracy, it is confirmed in that the leaders were taken from the whole of the people (cf. Exod. 18:21) . . . and the people also designated them (cf. Deut. 1:13). It is thus clear that, having been instituted by the [divine] law, this organization of powers was the best.[89]

The authority of the Fathers of the Church reinforces this Scriptural argument through a definition of law borrowed from Isidore of Seville: "Finally, there is the mixed *(commixtum)* regime, which is composed of the preceding elements, and it is the best *(optimum).*" The law is described here as "what the elders, in agreement with the people, have sanctioned," Isidore says.[90]

Thus, concern about the efficaciousness of such a government, obtained through the concentration of power in a small number of people, does not exclude insistence on the participation of all in government by

---

88. *ST* Ia IIae q. 105 a. 1. The current translations of this passage are sometimes less than accurate.
89. *ST* Ia IIae q. 105 a. 1.
90. *ST* Ia IIae q. 95 a. 4 (tertio).

means of elections and the electability of everyone. As a Dominican, Friar Thomas belonged to a religious order whose every office is filled by election. He knew quite well that the sense of personal responsibility is heightened through real engagement in the choice of those responsible for governing. As the old adage, well known in religious circles at the time, put it: "What concerns everyone should be drawn from everyone."[91] Whatever difficulties in interpretation passages in other works may present, clearly texts like this one are, at the very least, bearers of "powerful democratic elements."[92] Jacques Maritain recalled the true import of this at a sensitive moment marked by several misunderstandings.[93] Thomas's thinking here is that of someone rediscovering Greek political thought and his synthesis appears as an original combination of ancient, Patristic, and medieval thought, while his way of reading the history of Israel as that of a people under mixed government, even if a little forced, is also profoundly new.[94]

Doubtless, these passages can be read and understood in slightly different ways depending on the sensibilities, nationality, or social position of the reader. But that is quite another thing than the divergent interpretations mentioned above. Not all of these are valid. Thomas's clear choice in favor of the "mixed" regime corresponds to the way he sees man as a social being, who cannot be uninterested in the body to which he belongs. On the contrary, he must be an active and committed member. And when a man is a Christian, his faith itself forbids him to be content with an overly individualistic, "private" approach to his relationship to others.

91. Cf. Y. Congar, "Quod omnes tangit, ab omnibus tractari et approbari debet," *Revue historique de Droit français et étranger*, Series 4 (1958), 210–59. This by now old study has lost none of its value. A. Riklin, op. cit., rightly emphasizes that the medieval monarchy Thomas knew was quite often elective (even if the election only involved the great in the kingdom and was in fact often strictly limited).

92. R. Imbach's expression, "Démocratie ou monarchie?," p. 350.

93. I mention here only the most celebrated works, which in addition go well beyond a simple exegesis of Thomas's texts: *Du régime temporel et de la liberté* (Paris, 1933); "Integral Humanism," in Otto Bird, ed., Otto Bird, Joseph Evans, and Richard O'Sullivan, trans. *Integral Humanism; Freedom in the Modern World; and a Letter on Independance* (Notre Dame, Ind., 1996); *Christianity and Democracy* and *The Rights of Man and Natural Law*, trans. Doris C. Anson with an introduction by Donald Arthur Gallagher (San Francisco, 1986).

94. Cf. A. Riklin, "Die beste," 31–34; J. M. Blythe, "The Mixed Constitution," 564. See also A. Harding, "Aquinas and the Legislators," in *Théologie et Droit dans la science politique de l'État moderne* (Rome, 1991), 51–61; M. Villey, "La théologie de Thomas d'Aquin et la formation de l'État moderne," ibid., 31–49, does not have the same degree of interest.

"Spirituality" in Friar Thomas's school necessarily entails repercussions in the public realm.

﹌

What shall we conclude at the end of these lengthy developments that might appear rather distant from what is usually understood as "spiritual theology"? Our purpose in this chapter has been twofold.

First, to continue the reflections begun in the previous chapter on the idea of man. Whether Church or earthly society, the community is the spiritual organism in which Thomas's man is deeply inserted, to which he belongs entirely, even if not according to everything that is in him, which has rights over him, and whose good he must prefer to his own, outside of which he cannot live. We have not entirely exhausted these ideas, and will have to return to them in the following chapter on the way in which the human person transcends the earthly community, Church or State. But man's social character remains an established fact: the community is not simply an external benefit, a help to living better; it is inseparably linked to his nature.

Through this very fact—and this is surely the main achievement here—Thomas's subsequent approaches to man had none of the individualistic intimacy that too often dominated the spirituality of later centuries. Thomas did not write a treatise on the Church, it is true, but precisely because he wrote a *Summa theologiae*. His spirituality is no less deeply ecclesial for that, for it is not the spirituality of an isolated individual who decides by voluntary choice to associate with others—for instance, to facilitate life. Instead, his spirituality is that of a person linked since birth by his nature to a community outside of which he cannot flourish in a human manner, and linked by grace since his rebirth as an adopted child of God to the Body of Christ, of which he is a member, in a strict interdependence that finds its best expression in the communion of saints. It is only then, when all find themselves gathered around the same Supreme Common Good, that friendship, though already possible and real at the different levels we have examined in this chapter, can take on its final dimension.[95]

95. As is clear from everything preceding, I find it hard to subscribe to the opinion of O. H. Pesch, *Christian Existence According to Thomas Aquinas* (Toronto, 1989), 20–25, for whom the deep sense of the interpersonal relationship between God and man led Thomas to a certain religious individualism. There are additional reflections on this in J.-P. Torrell, "Dimension ecclésiale de l'expérience chrétienne," *FZPT* 28 (1981): 3–25.

The fact that friendship thus understood will then appear for what it is—an eschatological value that will never be fully lived except in heaven—takes nothing away from its current reality. Nor does it take anything away from the need to incarnate it more and more every day among men, for if charity is one kind of friendship, it wants love to grow even into places where it does not yet exist. But as we should better understand by now, to go to the limit of that demand, it is not enough to apply it in person-to-person relations. It is an ecclesial task. To construct a more human society it not the task of isolated Christians, it is the work of the whole Body of Christ. Thus, when the Church intervenes for the right to life, social justice, or world peace, it testifies as much to its fidelity to man in his communitarian dimension as to its fidelity to Christ's message, since the Gospel truly has political and social repercussions.

Second, we need to continue the reflections begun in an earlier chapter on the implications of the value of creation in the name of the great principle that grace does not destroy nature but leads it to perfection. Our purpose was less to develop all the implications of this axiom—which in fact underlies many other passages in the present book—than to verify its active presence in all fields of human action. According to Thomas, nature is a dynamic, not a static, reality. It is therefore not entirely itself except when it is cultivated. Natural man is not man in a brutish or savage state, but the man who is fulfilled in accord with the main inclinations of his nature in search of the true and the good in all their forms. It is in this regard that Thomas repeats numerous elements from the wisdom of the ancient Greek and Latin thinkers, notably from their personal or political moral philosophies. They are not adopted into a Christian perspective without some deep changes, but the patrimony is truly welcomed.

The doctrine of man as an eminently political and social animal is not the least precious part of this heritage. Joined with Christian influences, which may also be traced, it prevented Thomas from giving in to the facile simplifications of an excessive spiritualism that only sees in the world matter to be scorned, as well as to the temptation to reduce Christian life to the single relationship between Creator and creature. Foundational from every point of view, nonetheless, this relationship does not stop the human being from also finding himself in a world that can require service from him to others in the city. By personal choice, Thomas withdrew from the world; but he did not ignore the world. We do not have to be theologians to understand that a lay Christian can find in the pas-

sages we have just read a foundation and legitimation of active engagement in the world of his day. Without claiming to find here all the elements of a spirituality of temporal engagement, we can certainly say that,
at the very least, it provides the foundations.[96]

96. This has been well explained by W. H. Prinicipe, "Western Medieval Spirituality,"
in The New Dictionary of Catholic Spirituality, 1027–39, cf. 1031: "While Bonaventure reproduces Augustine's interiority in a masterly fashion, Aquinas lays down the foundations
for an authentic lay spirituality in reactualizing Irenaeus' theme that God is glorified to the
highest degree when each creature and all together attain the ends for which he created
them."

CHAPTER XIII

⁓

The Most Noble Thing in the World

As we have seen up to this point, according to Thomas Aquinas man seems deeply rooted in a rich carnal existence and in a community of which he is a member, and from which he is inseparable. An animal being, it is not possible for him to achieve his full development unless his bodily opacity itself is fully given over to the divinizing power of grace. A political being, there is no success possible for him outside of the various social settings to which he is indebted. Far from being viewed as a handicap, this twofold relation is, on the contrary, the basic datum received from God on the first morning of Creation. Sin has damaged but not destroyed it, and it must be Christianized.

This rootedness, however, is only the starting point. Friar Thomas is not unaware that while through an entire part of himself man is in continuity with the animal kingdom, he is also through another entire part of himself—and Thomas does not hesitate to call it the better part—in continuity with the universe of spirits. He also knows quite well that if man is a subordinate part in the social whole, man also transcends society through another whole dimension of himself.

The inexhaustible Prologue of the *Prima Secundae* accurately summarizes man's greatness: made in the image of God, the human person is endowed with free will and control over his own acts, and he is called to return to his Exemplar in sharing in His beatitude. We propose, then, to explore a twofold path in this chapter. First, however, we must take a look at some important passages for understanding Thomas's idea of the person, since the word "person" best conveys the right register in which to express the world of the soul and its spiritual operations.

The Most Noble Thing in the Universe

The classic definition of the person, derived from Boethius, already carries with it a decisive illumination because, different from every other individual of a bodily nature, the human person possesses something special as "an individual substance of a *rational nature.*"[1] The sober rigor of this definition runs the risk of obscuring its attraction, at least for those who are not very familiar with philosophical concepts, but Thomas speaks plainly: "*Person signifies what is most perfect in all of nature,* subsistence in a rational nature."[2] In fact, revelation confirms this dignity, since one of the reasons for the Incarnation was precisely to reveal this greatness to us: "God became man in order to instruct us about the dignity of human nature."[3] Among many other themes, this is one of Thomas's most cherished, and he emphasizes it whenever the occasion presents itself.[4] But even prior to its Christological use, remarkably, the development of the concept of person is first carried out as needed for the dogma of the Trinity.[5] Thus it takes on an unsuspected analogical breadth since it can be transposed to the divine "Persons" themselves:

Person signifies what is most perfect in all nature—that is, a subsistent individual of a rational nature. Now, since everything that is perfect must be attributed to

1. Cf. Boethius, *De duabus naturis,* cap. 3, PL 64, 1343; and Boethius, *Contra Eutychen et Nestorium* III, in *The Theological Tractates,* trans. H. F. Stewart, E. K. Rand, and S. J. Tester, Loeb ed. (1973), 84–86. Thomas refers very often to this definition, notably in the treatises on the Trinity and the Incarnation. Cf., e.g., *ST* Ia q. 29 a. 3 and *ST* IIIa q. 2 a. 2; cf. M. Nédoncelle, "Les variations de Boèce sur la personne," *RevSR* 29 (1995) 201–38; M. Elsässer, *Das Person-Verständis des Boethius* (Münster, 1973).

2. *ST* Ia q. 29 a. 3; cf. the ad 2: "To subsist in a rational nature is of high nobility." See several passages and S. Pinckaers's reflections thereon: "La dignité de l'homme selon S. Thomas d'Aquin," in A. Holderegger, R. Imbach, R. Suarez de Miguel, eds., *De Dignitate hominis, Mélanges offerts à Carlos Josaphat Pinto de Oliveira* (Fribourg, 1987), 89–106.

3. *ST* IIIa q. 1 a. 2. See also *ST* IIIa q. 3 a. 8., where Thomas explains that if it was preferable for the Word to be incarnated rather than the Father or the Spirit, that was because the Word is the exemplary cause of Creation, but it was also because "to achieve man's perfection *(ad consummatam hominis perfectionem),* conueniens fuit ut ipsum Verbum Dei humanae naturae personaliter uniretur."

4. *Comp. theol.* I, 201: "It was necessary for the human race that God become man *in order to show the dignity of human nature.*" Cf., also, *SCG* IV 54, n. 3924: *"This dignity of man* called to know beatitude *was manifested by God in the best way by His assuming human nature without intermediary."*

5. See several observations on this in H. Seidl, "The Concept of Person in St. Thomas Aquinas: A Contribution to Recent Discussions," *The Thomist* 51 (1987): 435–60, where the analysis also takes into account the Thomist tradition.

God, for His essence contains every perfection, this name *person* is fittingly applied to God; not, it is true, as it is applied to creatures, but in a more excellent way; as we attribute other names to God, while also giving them to creatures.[6]

The human person is thus found situated in an account of perfection where, *mutatis mutandis*, the Creator has communicated to his creatures certain of his own prerogatives. In fact, the metaphysical excellence of substance is here yoked with the Christian meaning of spirit, and the philosophical definition receives in the Christian realm a meaning unsuspected by pure reason, for it amounts to saying that it is by his soul, intelligent and free in the image of God, that man is constituted as a person. These quite clear affirmations, however, raise questions for the reader who recalls the part-whole distinction that often cropped up in characterizing man's place in society. In fact, the notion of man's connection to the social community gets a decisive addition here and an indispensable correction. To tell the truth, Thomas never loses sight of this, and he expresses it in various ways. Thus, the subordination of the part to the whole does not occur in a univocal way:

If a whole be not the last end, but ordained to a further end, then the last end of one of its parts cannot be the whole itself, but something else. Now the universe of creatures, to which man is connected as part to whole, is not the last end, but is ordained to God, as to its last end. Therefore, the last end of man is not the good of the universe, but God himself.[7]

This last ordering is clearly the reason that the rational creature is not a simple, anonymous unity lost in an undifferentiated mass; the creature becomes the object of special attention in the way God steers the universe. Thomas explains very lucidly, in what is doubtless one of his most complete and lovely expositions, the notion of providence:[8]

---

6. *ST* Ia q. 29 a. 3. Cf., again, *De pot.* q. 9 a. 3: "The nature implied in the meaning of the name person is the most worthy of all natures, since it is the intellectual nature in all its fullness *(secundum genus suum)*. So too, the mode of existence that person evokes is the most worthy of all, since it evokes a way of existing by itself. And since everything that is most noble in creatures must be attributed to God, the word 'person' can be attributed to God in 'fitting' fashion, as are other names that are properly spoken of God."

7. *ST* Ia IIae q. 2 a. 8 ad 2.

8. *SCG* III 64–163. But see also the continued reflection in the commentary on the Book of Job and the comments on it by D. Chardonnens, *L'Homme sous le regard de la Providence, Providence de Dieu et condition humaine selon l'Exposition littérale sur le Livre de Job de Thomas d'Aquin* (Paris, 1997).

It is clear that divine providence extends to all things. However, we must note that, among all other creatures, there exists a special providential governance for the intellectual and rational creatures. Indeed, they surpass the others as much by the perfection of their nature as by the dignity of their end.

By the perfection of their nature, because only the intellectual creature has mastery of its acts, determining itself through its own proper operation, while other creatures are much more moved than they move themselves. . . . By the dignity of their end, because only the intellectual creature can rejoin the final end of the universe through its operation, by knowing and loving God; while other creatures cannot come to that final end except through a certain participated similarity.[9]

This point is emphasized again in the fact that it is not only the intellectual creatures in general who are the objects of this special providence, but each single realization. Each person is its object:

Only the rational creature is led by God in his activity, not only as a species but as an individual. . . . The rational creature relates to Divine Providence as governed and worthy of attention for itself, *and not only as a species*.[10]

This naturally is found where the ordered subordination is explained by which all creatures are set into a hierarchy. Here again the rational creature receives a special position:

The less noble creatures exist for the more noble, just as the creatures who are below man are made for man. Furthermore, each and every creature exists for the perfection of the entire universe. And further still, the entire universe, with each of its parts, is ordained toward God as its end, inasmuch as *in these creatures the Divine goodness is represented through a certain likeness to the glory of God.* That does not stop rational creatures, however, from having God as their end in a special way, since *they can attain to Him by their own operations of knowing and loving*.[11]

Thomas thus situates the difference between man and the rest of the universe at one of the most active junctures in his synthesis, first in the

9. SCG III 111, n. 2855.
10. SCG III 113. The reasons for this are explained in the previous chapter of SCG III 112, nn. 2859–60: "Among the elements of the universe, the most noble are *intellectual* creatures [Thomas is thinking here also of angels, but quickly continues along the line of the merely *rational* creature]. For it is they who come closest to the divine resemblance. Intellectual natures have greater affinity to the whole than all the other natures. Each intellectual substance indeed is in a sense all things since its intelligence embraces all being, while all other substances have only a limited participation in being. It is then 'fitting' that they are ruled by God for the benefit of intellectual substances."
11. ST Ia q. 65 a. 2.

similarity of the effect to its cause, but especially in the image of God. Only the intellectual creature has this capacity of being able to know and love God, and thus of receiving Him into itself consciously:

> The universe is more perfect in goodness than the intellectual creature as regards extension and diffusion; but in intensity and concentration *the likeness of the Divine goodness is found rather in the intellectual creature, which has a capacity for the highest Good (capax summi boni).*[12]

If, then, the great law under which the good of the whole is superior to the good of a single individual remains valid, it is true only on condition that comparable things are set into order:

> The good of the universe is greater than the particular good of one, if we consider both in the same genus. *But the good of grace in one is greater than the natural good of the whole universe.*[13]

With grace, participation in the divine nature, we enter into an entirely different order, whose greatness Thomas characterizes with a rightly celebrated phrase:

> The justification of the wicked, which has as its end the eternal good of our divine participation, is a greater work than the creation of heaven and earth, for the latter only results in a perishable natural good.[14]

The context here specifies the justification of the wicked, but in fact the truth of this sentence emerges each time someone comes to grace for the first time. If the opposition between sin and participation in divine life makes the gap even wider, access to divine life still remains entirely closed to created powers alone, even without sin. It is not, therefore, simple anthropocentrism, slightly naive—man seen as the center of the universe as the world was once thought to be at the center of the cosmos—that drives this conception of the dignity of the human person, but rather the fact of his participation in divine life. Thomas could have said nothing

---

12. *ST* Ia q. 93 a. 2.

13. *ST* Ia IIae q. 113 a. 9 ad 2; cf. *ST* IIa IIae q. 152 a. 4 ad 3: "The common good is preferable to private good if it is of the same genus; but it can happen that the private good is greater in its own genus."

14. *ST* Ia IIae q. 113 a. 9. I cannot help thinking here of Pascal, *Pensées*, no. 930, ed. J. Chevalier (Paris, 1954), 1342: "From all bodies put together, we cannot make a single thought come forth: this is impossible and of a different order. From all bodies and minds, we cannot draw forth a true movement of charity: this is impossible, of a different order, supernatural."

stronger here, and it is again that which allows him to express precisely the connection of the person to the community: *"Man is not ordained to the body politic, according to all that he is and has. . . . But all that man is, and can do, and has, must be referred to God. . ."*[15]

⌒

The dignity of the human person emerges, then, from two directions: in connection with the natural universe, which he also transcends in its material aspect and social organization; and in connection with God, from whom he gets everything he is and has, and who invites him to share his own life. Following Master Thomas, we will try to grasp the preferred way of expressing this in two of its major forms: One in the realm of the moral universe, where man conducts himself as a free and responsible subject according to conscience; the other in the properly theological realm, where this highest dignity is found through the invitation to communion which God addresses to him. Through this communion, already begun in this world, the human person thus finds himself in an eschatological situation on the way to realization.

Following Conscience

Common in our age, this expression ought, at first sight, to facilitate the contemporary mind's access to Thomas Aquinas's teaching. He does not have words strong enough to affirm and repeat that we should always follow conscience—even when it is mistaken! We must, however, look at this more closely. Besides the fact that the word does not have the same meaning for him as for us, it is used in a profoundly different context. For us, conscience has a highly subjective resonance. We see it as a kind of final solicitation for which we are responsible; it is sometimes conceived of in a simplistic way, to the point of being a little naively identified with what we spontaneously think or with the reactions of our original social setting. To act according to conscience would then, in fact, amount to conducting ourselves in conformity with our surroundings.

For Thomas, things are not so simple, and he creates an elevated idea of the greatness of both man and his conscience. Conscience is certainly a solicitation that we cannot go against, but not the final solicitation. Our dignity as human persons is not a claim of absolute autonomy before

15. *ST* Ia IIae q. 21 a. 4 ad 3.

God, but acceptance of our dependence on him. If we want to understand the Master of Aquino's teaching on this, we must review things from a little higher perspective. Without doing a complete exposition or, even less, looking into contemporary disputes, we need at least to review as accurately as possible what Thomas believes, and to try to disengage from it its interest for spiritual theology.[16]

We must first recall what we said in the previous chapter about natural law, the participation of the rational creature in the eternal law, in divine Providence. This participation occurs through a proper *habitus* that Thomas calls, in a way strange to us, "synderesis." This term, which came from Saint Jerome—which he translates as "spark of conscience," and asserts was not extinguished even in Cain's heart after his crime—is the simple transliteration, probably erroneous, of a Greek term.[17] Though the designation becomes partly clear through the history of the word, its function is even more important because the whole moral life of the person depends on synderesis:

For there to be rectitude in human actions, it is necessary that there be in them a permanent principle, of an unmoveable rectitude, in the light of which all a man's acts may be examined, [and that would be] of such a kind that this perma-

16. The main places where we find the teaching on conscience, coupled with the teaching on synderesis, are the following: *In II Sent.* d. 24 q. 2 aa. 3–4; d. 39 q. 3 aa. 2–3; *De uer.* qq. 16–17; *ST* Ia q. 79 aa. 12–13; *ST* Ia IIae q. 19, aa. 5–6 (erroneous conscience); there is also *Quodlibet* III q. 12 aa. 1–2 [26–27] (erroneous conscience), and the commentaries on Scripture that I cite below. For those who would like to pursue this topic further, I note among numerous works, S. Pinckaers, *Les actes humains* (French translation with notes and appendices of St. Thomas Aquinas, *Summa theologiae* Ia IIae qq. 18–21), vol. 2 (Paris, 1966); L. Elders, "La doctrine de la conscience de saint Thomas d'Aquin," *RT* 83 (1983): 533–57, reprinted in the author's *Autour de saint Thomas d'Aquin*, vol. 2 (Paris, 1987), 63–94; T. G. Belmans, "Le paradoxe de la conscience erronée d'Abélard à Karl Rahner," *RT* 90 (1990): 570–86 (though it contains some excessive language); G. Borgonovo, *Sinderesi e coscienza nel pensiero di san Tommaso d'Aquino* (Fribourg, 1996); more accesible is S. Pinckaers, "La conception chrétienne de la conscience morale," *NV* 66 (1991): 688–99; and the same author's, "La conscience et l'erreur," *Communio* 18 (1993): 23–35.

17. Used for the first time by Saint Jerome, the word *synteresis* is perhaps a deformation of *syneidesis*, "conscience." Thomas knows this origin, but nevertheless distinguishes between conscience and synderesis. For further details on this, see the pages of Th. Deman in *La Prudence* (French translation with notes and appendices of St. Thomas Aquinas, *Summa theologiae* IIa IIae qq. 47–56) (Paris, 1949), 430–37. Further research can be done with O. Lottin's, "Syndérèse et conscience au XIIe and XIIIe siècles," in the same author's *Psychologie et Morale au XIIe et XIIIe siècles*, vol. 2 (Louvain-Gembloux, 1948), 103–350; see, too, A. Solignac's entry, "Syndérèse," *DS*, vol. 14 (1990), col. 1407–12, who, besides going over the origins of the word reviews its use in the history of mysticism.

nent principle resists everything evil and grants its assent to everything good. Such is synderesis, whose function is to reproach evil and incline toward the good; we must also allow that synderesis cannot sin.[18]

Parallel to the *intellectus*, the habitus which intuitively grasps the first principles of the intellectual life (being is, non-being is not) synderesis grasps and formulates the two great principles of the moral life that carry their proof in themselves: we need to do the good and flee from evil.[19] It is along this line, as we have seen, that the five main inclinations flow from the natural law: toward the good, continuance in being, sexual union and the education of children, knowledge of the truth, and social life.[20] However, as important as it is, the primordial intuitive grasp of moral and social life is insufficient by itself. Certain principles of natural right are accessible only after an intellectual development sometimes requiring lengthy education, as much for individuals as for humanity as a whole. To achieve a moral knowledge that may direct action, this spontaneous knowledge of final principles still requires developments and adaptations to concrete situations. Practical reason must confront this first data with everything that it knows of the natural and evangelical data which govern the realm of human and Christian action. It must also take into account the person engaged in this specific action to determine the way in which the general principles shall be applied here and now.[21]

Moral conscience intervenes precisely here. As surprising as it may seem, conscience is neither a faculty nor a *habitus*, but an act of practical reason.[22] We can, of course, accept current usage, which talks about this act beginning with the *habitus* that allows us to propose it. And at that moment synderesis itself would be that "habitual" conscience. But properly speaking, conscience is something else. It is the act by which practical reason gathers together all the available data (from synderesis, moral knowledge, experience, convictions, and various opinion, etc.) with an eye toward ending deliberation in a practical and normative decision.[23] It

18. *De uer.* q. 16 a. 2.
19. Cf. *ST* Ia 79 a. 12 and *ST* Ia IIae q. 91 a. 3.
20. It is worth rereading the passage from *ST* Ia IIae q. 94 a. 2 that I translated in chapter 12, p. 285.
21. Cf. M.-M. Labourdette, "Connaissance pratique et savoir moral," *RT* 48 (1948): 142–79.
22. Cf. *De uer.* q. 17; *ST* Ia q. 79 a. 13.
23. Cf. *ST* Ia q. 79 a. 13: "It is said that conscience attests, obliges, incites, and even accuses, reproaches, or repeats. Now, all this proceeds from the application of a certain

is practical because it aims at guiding action; however, this judgment remains in the order of knowledge. It may thus be either true or false.[24] That is why the difficult question of a conscience that errs arises, or, as it is sometimes put more briefly, of erroneous conscience. Thomas teaches that conscience binds us even when mistaken, for a fundamental reason:

The obligation to our conscience, even when mistaken, is itself of God's law *(idem est ligamen conscientiae etiam erroneae et legis Dei)*. Indeed, conscience does not order us to do this or avoid that except because it believes that something does or does not correspond to the law of God. *And truly, the law is applied to our acts only by the mediation of conscience.*[25]

We recognize in this final phrase the concise summary of what we have just read: the great moral principles find their concrete translation into moral action only through the intermediary of the judgment of conscience set forth by reason: "Conscience is in some way the dictate *(dictamen)* of reason."[26] But we must not deceive ourselves about this; if this is the case, it is because the judgment, itself in continuity with synderesis, is deemed in conformity with natural law, itself the expression in our hearts of the very law of God. We understand, then, why to go against conscience would be to sin; it would be to act against what we think is God's own law:

To know that something should be done in conscience is nothing other that to estimate that one would be acting against God if one did not do it. Now to act against God is to sin.[27] [Thomas is entirely absolute here.] If a man believes that

---

familiarity or knowledge to what we do." Cf. *In ad Rom. II*, 15, lect. 3, n. 219: "The 'witness of conscience' [of which Saint Paul speaks] is nothing other than the application of available moral knowledge to a given action, to determine whether it is good or bad." Following Aristotle *(Nicomachean Ethics VII, 5)* in a significant way, though perhaps mistaken, for it seems to introduce here a rigor that is not really present, Thomas compares the development that leads from the primary moral principles toward concrete action with a syllogism, by which we pass from premises to the conclusion (cf. *ST* Ia IIae q. 13 a. 1 ad 2; q. 76 a. 1; etc.).

24. The judgement of conscience not being final, it still remains for practical reason to "do the truth of the action," which is to say to apply its knowledge to the immediate direction of action. This role belongs to prudence, "the right reason of acts to be done" *(recta ratio agibilium)*, and it takes over at this point. But since I have already spoken of this in chapter 11, we do not need to linger further on it here.

25. *In ad Rom. XIV*, 14, lect. 2, n. 1120. This whole passage (nn. 1119–22) is one of the most important places for Thomas's teaching on conscience. See also a little further on: lect. 3, nn. 1138–40.

26. *ST* Ia IIae q. 19 a. 5.   27. *In ad Gal. V*, 53, lect. 1, n. 282.

human reason counsels something contrary to the law of God, he ought not follow his reason. In this case, in addition, reason is not entirely wrong. But when
reason deceives itself and presents something as God's order, to scorn the dictate
of reason is to scorn the order of God Himself.[28]

Conscience and Truth

Those absolute formulas that identify the voice of conscience with the
voice of God can be understood only in the proper context. Not only do
they presuppose the reason's willed effort to conform to the natural law,
and beyond that, with God himself, but besides this basic dependence,
they also presuppose a virtuous adjustment in our relations with others.
Thomas explicitly links these two attitudes in his commentary on the first
letter to Timothy (1 Tim. 1:5): "Now the end of the precept is charity out
of a pure heart, a good conscience, and faith unfeigned."

How is charity the end of the precept? . . . [We must understand that all the commandments are ordered toward promoting acts of virtue, and that the virtues
themselves are geared to one another in an organism for which charity is the sum-
mit]. The theological virtues have the final end as their object. The other virtues
have as an object what helps to gain that end. Thus, all the [other] virtues are related to the theological virtues as to their end. *Among the theological virtues, the
one that comes closest to the final end is the rule for the others: faith demonstrates
it, hope tends toward it, charity unites to it. All are thus ordered to charity, and it is
thus that charity is the end of [all] the commandments[. . . .]* The other virtues rec-
tify the person with respect to his neighbor, and from that it comes that he (the
Apostle) has a good conscience, for he does nothing to another that he would not
want done to him. . . . *What is against the neighbor is thus also against conscience.*
That is why he speaks of a "good conscience." Whoever does not have a good conscience cannot sincerely love God, for whoever does not have a good conscience
fears punishment. Now, there is no fear in love; fear drives away God rather than
uniting us to him. *Thus, the commandments by rectifying conscience dispose us to
charity.*[29]

---

28. ST Ia IIae q. 19 a. 5 ad 2.
29. *In I ad Tim. I,* 5, lect. 1, nn. 13–16. About the faith and its relationship to conscience,
Thomas also provides useful remarks in commenting on Saint Paul: "Whatever does not
proceed from a conviction of faith is sin" (Rom. 14:23). In his interpretation, he combines
two meanings of the word *fides,* in which he sees both the theological virtue of faith and
conscience itself, the only difference being the passage from a universal conviction (faith)
to a particular action done in its light (cf. *In ad Rom. XIV,* 23, lect. 3, n. 1140). He is here the
heir of two exegetical currents of the earlier theological tradition: one from the Fathers who
understood the text to refer to the faith, the other of the scholastics beginning in the XIIth

It is valuable to highlight this passage for present purposes; it gives us a rather different idea of conscience than the weak form mentioned earlier. If we assert that only the consciences of the saints are infallible, we will not be betraying Thomas's thought in the least; indeed, he says, "The infallible witness of the saints is their conscience. . . . But as it sometimes happens that conscience deceives, (Paul) adds: 'in the Holy Spirit.'"[30] The certitude of the conscience is accompanied, thus, by the clear perception of the possibility of error. Though synderesis is infallible, the same is not true of conscience, for it does not depend solely on the natural law through synderesis. It is at the mercy of many other data, among which prejudices and accepted notions, as well as a poorly formed will can irremediably falsify judgment. That is why when he deals with a conscience that deceives itself, Thomas proceeds in two phases: we must always follow conscience—the basic affirmation does not change—but that is not enough to perform a good act. For what is wrong remains wrong:

[The goodness or evil of an act does not come solely from exterior objects; a good or indifferent object in itself can become evil for the subject depending on the intention with which it is performed.] Since reason presents the thing as being evil, the will by tending thereto becomes evil . . . for it tends toward it as toward an evil and becomes itself evil because it wills the bad. [Even if what is willed is not bad in itself, it becomes so as an accident with regard to the person as a consequence of the erroneous judgement of reason. To make this better understood and at the same time to unveil the paradoxical seriousness in such a case, Thomas proposes an extreme example]: To believe in Christ is good in itself, and necessary for salvation; but the will does not tend thereto, except inasmuch as it is proposed by the reason. Consequently, if then reason presents it as something evil [for example, for a non-Christian], the will tends toward it as to something evil. . . . Every will that does not obey reason, whether right or erring, is always evil.[31]

The imperative force of the judgment of conscience is not in the least lessened, then, despite its error. And the reason for this is clear: "Though

---

century who read here the moral conscience. Cf. R. Araud, "*Quidquid non est ex fide peccatum est*. Quelques interprétations patristiques," in *L'Homme devant Dieu, Mélanges offerts au Père Henri de Lubac*, vol. 1 (Paris, 1963), 127–45; A. C. de Veer, "Rm 14,23b dans l'oeuvre de saint Augustin (*Omne quod non est ex fide peccatum est*)," *Recherches augustiniennes* 8 (1972): 149–85.

30. *In ad Rom. IX*, 1, lect. 1, n. 736; cf. *In ad Heb. XIII, 18*, lect. 3, n. 763: "The goodness of conscience comes from God alone, that is why (Paul) attributes it to the confidence he has in him."

31. *ST* Ia IIae q. 19 a. 5.

it is true that when reason is mistaken, its judgment does not derive from God, nevertheless it proposes that judgment as true, and as a result as coming from God, the source of all truth."[32] The question inevitably then arises: since we cannot disobey conscience, should we believe that we always act well in obeying it? We might think so without reflecting: I have done well because I acted according to my conscience. Thomas does not exactly say this. He resists the notion that an error of the conscience is sufficient to transform a morally evil act in itself into a morally good act. Thus, he puts the question in a different way:

Whereas the previous question is the same as inquiring "whether an erring conscience binds"; so this question is the same as inquiring "whether an erring conscience excuses [from evil]." Now this question depends on what has been said above about ignorance [and of its effect on the voluntary nature of an act]. . . . Ignorance sometimes causes an act to be involuntary, and sometimes not. And since moral good and evil consist in action in so far as it is voluntary . . . it is evident that when ignorance causes an act to be involuntary, it takes away its moral value, but not, when it does not cause the act to be involuntary . . . when ignorance is willed in any way, directly or indirectly, it does not cause the act to be involuntary. And I call that ignorance "directly" voluntary, to which the act of the will tends [I do not want to know whether this act is good or bad], and that "indirectly" voluntary, which is due to negligence, when a man does not want to know what he ought to know. . . .

If then reason or conscience err voluntarily, either directly, or through negligence, so that one errs about what one ought to know; then such an error of reason or conscience does not excuse the evil of the will that acts according to that erring reason or conscience. But if the error that causes an involuntary act arises from ignorance of some circumstance, and without any negligence, the error excuses the evil.[33]

The technical nature of this reasoning gives it perfect clarity. In conformity with his constant teaching, Thomas holds that only free acts are moral acts, and the only free acts are voluntary. If the voluntary character of the act is diminished, it's morality is as well. If then conscience obliges us even when it deceives itself, we cannot conclude that we perform a good act by following it. We would do wrong not to follow it, but it is not enough to obey it to act well. An erring conscience excuses all the more from subjective culpability to the extent that it results from invincible ig-

32. *ST* Ia IIae q. 19 a. 5 ad 3.
33. *ST* Ia IIae q. 19 a. 6.

norance. If the error has in its beginnings something voluntary, the subject would be morally responsible for an evil act. Neglectful ignorance is here grave: just as in reasoning, a false proposition at the beginning leads to a false conclusion; so in the realm of moral action an initial fault leads inevitably to others if it is not repented of, and from negligence to negligence we can come in what seems entirely good faith to a "formation of conscience," as it is sometimes ironically said, that can no longer distinguish good from evil.[34] Thomas found in Scripture a word to describe this, and with the apostle Paul he speaks of a "corrupt" (cauteriata) conscience:

The sore (cauterium) is a corruption of the flesh through [interior] fire, from which decay continually comes forth. In the same way, the conscience suffers from the fire of the perverse will, from anger, hatred, concupiscence, as from an ulcer, and there comes forth from it the false teaching of the demons; Titus 1:15; "Their spirit and conscience are soiled."[35]

We could speak as well of an "anesthetized" or "sleeping" conscience; Thomas recognizes this too and, in describing the process by which it happens, emphasizes all the ways in which conscience may recall us to order: "Men easily move away from what harms them; that is why the remorse of conscience acts like a needle, which torments whoever has a bad conscience, so that he departs from sin through a right faith and good conscience."[36]

Where today we put the problem of conscience in terms of "sincerity," Thomas remains faithful to his way and puts forward instead the search for truth and that great love which ought to attract whoever wishes to act rightly. When things are so, the person who acts according to conscience, with a concern only to assent to the truth, maintains a right intention, and in this very attention to the truth also keeps himself justly aimed at the good—even when he errs, and Thomas concedes this.[37] But he also un-

34. Thomas suggests that social conformity can play a considerable role here; In II ad Cor. I, 12, lect. 4, n. 31; Saint Paul indeed speaks of the "witness of our conscience," and not that of others, "for when it is a matter of ourselves we must always prefer the witness of our own conscience to that of the conscience of others."

35. In I ad Tim. IV, 2, lect. 1, n. 140.

36. In I ad Tim. I, 19, lect. 4, n. 51.

37. S. Pinckaers has put this well, Les actes humaines, vol. 2, p. 201: "Ignorance breaks the connection between the exterior act which is in reality evil, and the will that performs it, such that the will may remain good despite this act, for it would not have wished to do it if it had known its evilness."

derscores that the act exteriorly done is not good. Evil remains evil, and it is not enough to be mistaken to do good. That is why a man, although being entirely responsible *to* his conscience, is also responsible *for* his conscience.

The deep reason for this demanding attitude lies in the fact that conscience is not the final appeal. At its limit, a position such as would border on the most absolute individualism in its denial of all obligation toward God or our fellows. For Thomas, who does not conceive the person except in relationship with God and the human community, conscience is only an intermediary of the eternal law; it does not create obligation, but transmits it. As it is also influenced by culture, formed by many other influences that may alter its judgments, it is important to make sure of its uprightness before we believe ourselves obliged. We must not, above all, eliminate doubt or disquiet through an undeclared preference for a convenient ignorance, but must seek how to overcome these things through an ever more demanding search for the truth.[38]

This conception of conscience thus represents a formidable call to go further. And it allows us to see concretely what it means for man to be "placed in the hands of his own counsel." When he becomes his own providence, he has the grandeur of that role, and he assumes its responsibility as well. No other being in nature is comparable in this, and we understand that some non-Christian thinkers have been able to see the highest dignity of the human person. For Friar Thomas, this is, however, only one aspect of that dignity. Without opposing it in the least, a second aspect completes in on another plane, that of the theological virtues: the human person is called upon to engage with God in a new relationship, which, without removing him from time, makes him enter, so to speak, into eternity: communion with God, begun here below, will only be completed in heaven, face-to-face.

Eternal Life Already Begun

The reader will doubtless know, at least by name, the *Compendium theologiae*; we would like to render this title as "Precis of the Christian

---

38. I leave aside here the question of the perplexity of conscience often presented as the conflict of duties, since it is enough to renounce sin for the perplexity to be surmounted. Cf. *ST* Ia IIae q. 19 a. 6 ad 3; *In ad Rom. XIV*, 14, lect. 2, n. 1120; *In ad Gal. V*, 3, lect. 1, n. 282; R. Schenk, "Perplexus supposito quodam. Notizen zu einem vergessenen Schlüsselbegriff thomasischer Gewissenslehre," *RTAM* 57 (1990): 62–95.

Faith," but a more exact translation is "Summary of Theology," since it is a summing up, even if a bit scholarly. Indeed, to comply with the wish of his secretary and friend Raynald, Friar Thomas made the effort to gather together in this book the essential contents of the faith and to express them briefly in a relatively simple way. Inspired by Saint Augustine's *Enchiridion* in its structure, the exposition develops according to the three theological virtues: Faith is dealt with by following the articles of the Credo, hope in relation to the petitions of the Our Father, and charity probably would have had as its framework the Decalogue. Death prevented the author from finishing his work, but the first part is complete, and the second well begun.[39]

The plan of the work has little interest here in itself, but it conveys a certainty that the essence of Christian existence can be expressed centered around the theological virtues. In full coherence with his definition of the human person as the sole being in the universe in immediate relationship to God, Thomas puts the theological virtues at the heart of the Christian experience. They are called theological virtues because they have God directly for object, motive, and end.[40] Divine life participated in by grace, of which they are the actualization, is the anticipatory realization in time of communion with God-Trinity which will find its full completion in heaven. While there is an order of mutual priority among the virtues, the habitual way they are mentioned also has significance; not only tradition recommends this, but right reason:

Indeed, love cannot be right unless we first establish the right end of hope, and that is not possible if knowledge of the truth is lacking. You must first have faith to know the truth, then hope to put your desire on its true end, finally charity through which your love will be completely rectified.[41] [In more lapidary fashion, but still suggestively, Thomas specifies elsewhere]: "Faith shows the end, hope makes us tend toward it, charity realizes union with it."[42]

---

39. See complementary data in my *Saint Thomas Aquinas*, 164–67. The critical text is found in the Leonine edition, vol. 42.

40. Note the similarity between these two sentences from the beginning of the treatise on faith, *ST* IIa IIae q. 2 a. 3: "Only created, rational nature enjoys an immediate ordering to God (sola autem natura rationalis creata habet *immediatum ordinem ad Deum*)" and *ST* IIa IIae q. 4 a. 7: "the theological virtues whose object is the final end (necesse est *uirtutes theologicas, quarum obiectum est ultimus finis*, esse priores ceteris uirtutibus)."

41. *Comp. theol.* I, 1, Leonine, vol. 42, p. 83.

42. *In I ad Tim. I,* 5, n. 13 (this passage has been quoted more fully above for the connection of conscience to the theological virtues); the priority of faith in the order of

We will not reproduce here the whole discourse on faith,[43] but Thomas's presentation at the beginning of this *Summary of Theology* is valuable for us because it puts us immediately in the right perspective for everything we wish to say in this chapter:

Faith is a certain foretaste (*praelibatio quaedam*) of that knowledge which will be our happiness in eternal life. That is why the Apostle (Heb. 11:1) says that it is "the substance of things hoped for," as if it causes to subsist in us in inchoate fashion the realities we hope for, which is to say future beatitude. The Lord has taught that this beatifying knowledge consists in two things: the divinity of the Trinity and the humanity of Christ, when he addresses himself to the Father saying (John 17:3): "This is eternal life, to know you, the only true God, and Jesus Christ, whom you have sent." It is to the subject of these two realities, then, the divinity of the Trinity and the humanity of Christ, that the whole knowledge of the faith refers. This is not surprising, for the humanity of Christ is the way by which we come to the divinity. We must know the route, when we are on the way, in order to arrive at the end, and when we are home the action of God's graces would not suffice if men did not have knowledge of the ways by which they are saved.[44]

In this brief formulation of the contents of the faith, many things that we have already met with can be recognized, especially the first two *credibilia* around which the entire content of theology is organized.[45] However we need to pay attention here less to the content of the faith than to its definition, because it highlights with unmatched power the movement that animates it, its dynamism or élan. The verses from the letter to the Hebrews should also be noted; Thomas likes to refer to them and he enumerates their advantages elsewhere: "If we want to express this with a reg-

---

knowledge is more fully treated in *ST* IIa IIae q. 4 a. 7: "It is necessary that the final end be in the intellect before being in the will, for the will cannot bear itself toward a reality that is not first apprehended by the intellect." Cf. *ST* Ia IIae q. 62 a. 4.

43. Thomas's main exposition of the subject may be found in *ST* IIa IIae qq. 1–16, where as was the custom, he does not deal solely with the virtue of faith in itself, but also with the gifts of the Holy Spirit, which are attached to it, and with the sins opposed to it. See the notes and commentary by R. Bernard, *La Foi* (French translation with notes and appendices of St. Thomas Aquinas, *Summa theologiae* IIa IIae qq. 1–16), 2 vols. (Paris, 1940–42); M.-M. Labourdette, "La vie théologale selon saint Thomas: L'objet de la foi," *RT* 58 (1958): 597–622; "La vie théologale selon saint Thomas: L'affection dans la foi," *RT* 60 (1960): 364–80; H. Donneaud, "La surnaturalité du motif de la foi théologale chez le Père Labourdette," *RT* 92 (1992): 197–238.

44. *Comp. theol.* I, 2.

45. Cf. *ST* IIa IIae q. 1 aa. 6–7; q. 2 a. 5. See the section in chapter 1 entitled "A certain imprint of divine science."

ular definition, we can say that 'faith is a *habitus* of soul *(habitus mentis)* through which eternal life begins in us by causing our intellect to adhere to invisible realities."[46]

Already present in the *De ueritate*, the same definition was explained at length there: faith realizes in a believing subject that anticipation of eternal life through a certain similarity to the desired end. Indeed, nothing can be desired if it does not have in the person a certain proportion with respect to that end, for it is starting from that end that the desire of the end arises. For us to tend toward eternal life, it is thus necessary that there be in us a certain beginning of that end, at least in the knowledge that we get about it, and this is what faith realizes: "To the extent that there is in us a certain beginning of eternal life, which we hope for on the basis of the divine promise, faith is called 'the substance of goods that we wait for.'"[47] But by the very fact of realizing this anticipation of the end to come, faith stirs up desire for the end, for "every beginning aspires to its completion." If this is true on the natural plane, it is even more so in the realm of divine realities, where the beginning cannot help but aspire to the completion in the final end.[48] Thomas restates this in commenting on the conversation of Jesus with the Samaritan woman (John 4:14); the dynamism of a life in faith is the that of all desire: possession partly begun inflames desire for total possession:

[How could Jesus say: "He who will drink of this water will never thirst again," while Wisdom states (Sir. 24:21): "Those who drink of me will thirst again"?]. The two assertions are true simultaneously, for to drink of this water that Christ offers is at the same time to never thirst again and to desire to drink again. [We can explain this in a first meaning by comparing natural and spiritual water. Who drinks of natural water will thirst again, for that water is not perpetual and thus its effect also comes to an end]: But spiritual water has an eternal source, the Holy Spirit, who is an ever-gushing fountain of life; that is why he who drinks of this water will never thirst again, as he who has in his own heart a source of living water would never thirst.

But there is another reason that springs up for the difference between temporal and spiritual realities. Each awakens thirst, but differently. A temporal thing

46. *ST* IIa IIae q. 4 a. 1.

47. *De uer.* q. 14 a. 2. The insistent repetition of the word *inchoatio* in this article is noteworthy: faith is only a "beginning," but it is truly that. Further investigation into this point can be pursued in D. Bourgeois, "'Inchoatio vitae eternae'. La dimension eschatologique de la vertu théologale de foi chez saint Thomas d'Aquin," *Sapienza* 27 (1974): 272–314.

48. Cf. *ST* Ia IIae q. 1 a. 6.

that is obtained after being desired does not calm desire so much; the desire is always still there for something else. *By contrast, spiritual reality extinguishes the desire for something else and removes desire itself.* The reason is simple: as long as we do not possess something in this world, we regard it as fulfilling and of great price. Once possessed, it no longer appears so precious and reveals itself to be insufficient to pacify desire, which becomes enkindled by something else again. Spiritual reality on the contrary is known only when possessed, Apoc. 2:17: "No one knows it except he who receives it." That is why not to have it is not to desire it, but to have it and to know it cheers the heart and provokes desire, not of course the desire for something else, but the desire that its imperfect possession awakens—since he who receives it is imperfect—with perfect possession as its aim.

The Psalm (41:2) speaks of this thirst: "My soul thirsts for God / The source of living water." This thirst will never be totally quenched in this world, for in this life we can never perfectly grasp spiritual goods. That is why who drinks of this water will thirst again for its perfection. But he will never thirst again as he would thirst if water were lacking, for as the Psalm says (35:9): "They will be intoxicated by the abundance of your house." In the life of glory, where they drink perfectly the water of divine grace, the blessed thirst no more (Matt. 5:6): "Blessed are they who hunger and thirst for righteousness' sake" in this world "for they will be satisfied" in eternal life.[49]

If we only knew Friar Thomas's biography and personality better, this passage might offer a chance to confirm a certain correspondence with the author's spiritual life. But without dipping into psychological reconstruction that we do not have the means to verify, the passage is clear enough for our purposes. Far from being interpreted as an invitation to tranquil enjoyment, the anticipated possession of heavenly goods, in whoever benefits from it, deepens an emptiness that will be filled only by full and definite possession: "Knowledge of the faith does not pacify desire; rather it stirs it up."[50]

Like an Anchor Fixed on High

Though Thomas repeats with noteworthy insistence that this first anticipation of eternal life is truly the business of faith,[51] faith clearly is not

---

49. *In Ioannem IV*, 13–14, lect. 2, n. 586.
50. *SCG* III 40, n. 2178.
51. *De uer.* q. 14 a. 2 ad 4: "The first beginning of the things that we hope for does not occur in us by charity, but by faith"; cf. *ST* IIa IIae q. 4 a. 1: "The first beginning of the things that we hope for is realized in us through faith, for it contains in germ all other hoped-for realities."

isolated in its quest; it is strictly united to hope and charity. And to take them in order, the role of hope is forcefully recalled in the *Compendium theologiae*:

Since the human being has a natural desire to know, that desire can be quenched in the knowledge of all truth as long as it is a matter of a casual knowledge; [the truth sought] being known, the desire is calmed. But when it is a case of knowledge of the faith, the desire has no rest, because faith is an imperfect knowledge: what we believe is what we do not see. That is why the Apostle (Heb. 11:1) says that it is the "conviction of things not seen." The presence of faith thus still leaves in the soul a tendency to something else, to see perfectly the truth that we believe and to be possessed by what can introduce us to that truth. And since among the teachings of the faith we say we believe that God directs human things by providence, for this *reason he lifts up a wave of hope in the believer's heart*, to receive with the help of faith those goods that he naturally desires and that hope makes him know. That is why, after faith, hope is necessary for the perfection of Christian faith.[52]

We cannot help being struck in this passage, more than in many others, by the author's emphasis on the notion of desire: "hope presupposes desire *(spes desiderium praesupponit)*."[53] It would be mistaken to understand this term in too strictly psychological a sense, for it has a more clearly metaphysical sense. In Thomas's eyes, no creature in the universe is what it ought to be from the start; it does not reach fulfillment except at the end of an evolution and it "desires" this expansion of its whole being. This aspiration to culmination, completely fundamental and constitutive of the creature, bears the name "natural appetite," but in the case of man we speak rather of "natural desire" or of "a desire of nature." Though at first sight it is vague and indeterminate, this appetite for the more or less anonymous good will become a true desire for beatitude under the enlightenment and motion of grace, and finally identified with the only living and true God.[54]

As we shall soon see even better, apprenticeship in the spiritual life ac-

---

52. *Comp. theol.* II, 1; cf. II, 3: "ad salutem nostram post fidem etiam spes requiritur."
53. *Comp. theol.* II, 7.
54. Only a deep misunderstanding based on a very narrow consultation of the works has allowed some to suspect that Thomas "liquidated" Biblical eschatology in favor of a simple transcendental desire. Cf. J. Moltmann, "Christliche Hoffnung: Messianisch oder tranzendent? Ein theologisches Gespräch mit Joachim von Fiore und Thomas von Aquin," *MThZ* 33 (1982): 241–60; Cf. E. Schockenhoff, *Bonum hominis*, 420.

cording to the school of Thomas Aquinas gives a decisive role to the quest
for beatitude. We have already seen enough to understand that what is at
first only an irrepressible natural tendency, but little by little becomes the
face of hope in man, is taken up by the theological virtue of hope and carried to its completion.[55] Being a theological virtue, hope has God as its
object and motive: from God, we cannot expect less than God.[56] But in
his effort to compare the particular contributions of the three theological
virtues, Thomas introduces a special nuance here—achieved little by little in his intellectual evolution—to specify exactly what is the special contribution of hope. While charity makes us adhere to God because of Himself, in uniting man's spirit with God's in a feeling of love, and faith makes
man adhere to God inasmuch as he is the source of knowledge of the
truth, "hope makes us adhere to God as the principle in us of the perfect
good, inasmuch as *through hope we rely on divine help to obtain beatitude.*"[57]

Thus, the accent is on divine aid and this may be understood by reflecting on the condition of hope.[58] Hope supposes desire, for one evidently cannot hope for what one does not desire; we either fear it or scorn
it, we do not hope for it. However, desire alone is not enough; desire for
an object impossible to attain is not hope; the notion of hope adds to de-

55. It has been remarked that if Thomas's is the first extended study of the passion of human hope, it arose as a necessity in his study of the theological virtue of hope (*In III Sent.*
d. 26 q. 1), cf. S. Pinckaers, "La nature vertueuse de l'espérance," *RT* 58 (1958): 405–42;
623–42; this has been underscored by E. Schockenhoff, *Bonum hominis*, 174, who also puts
forward an excellent treatment of the passion and the virtue of hope as being for Thomas
the characteristic attitude of eschatological expectation (pp. 418–75). In French, there is
Ch.-A. Bernard, *Théologie de l'espérance selon saint Thomas d'Aquin* (Paris, 1961), valuable
for its care in showing the further spiritual applications; J.-G. Bougerol, *La théologie de l'e-
spérance au XIIe et XIIIe siècles* (Paris, 1985) (for Thomas see vol. 1, pp. 277–89). We know
that Thomas attached the gift of fear to hope. It is worthwhile to read L. Somme on this
point, "L'amour parfait chasse-t-il toute crainte? Le rôle joué par l'expression *Timor filialis*
dans l'oeuvre de saint Thomas d'Aquin," in *Ordo sapientiae et amoris*, 303–20.
   56. *ST* IIa IIae q. 17 a. 2.
   57. *ST* IIa IIae q. 17 a. 6; *Quaestio disputata De spe (De spe)*, a. 4: "The formal object of
hope, by which it is a theological virtue, is divine help . . ."; to continue using this language, I note that the "material" object is beatitude itself, the two "objects" being ordered
to one another as efficient cause to final cause.
   58. *De spe*, a. 1 summarizes with exemplary concision the four qualities of the hoped-for
object: "First, it must be a *good*; in this, hope differs from fear. Then, it must be a *future*
good; thus it differs from *joy* or *enjoyment*. Third, it mus be an *arduous* good; in this it differs from [simple] *desire*. Finally, it must concern a *possible* good; which distinguishes it
from *despair.*"

sire that we consider it *possible* to attain the desired good. But it must also be a higher good, *difficult (arduum)* to attain.[59] If it is a matter of something too easy or minimal, we rather disdain it, or if we desire to have it in hand, it is not an object of hope for the future. However, the hoped-for good may reveal itself as so difficult to attain that we cannot attain it by ourselves. We must then address ourselves to another to get it; if a man, we make a request *(petitio)* to him, if God, we offer a prayer *(oratio)*[60] to him:

> Thus what is truly the virtue of hope is not the hope we have in ourselves, nor even in another man, but only the hope we have in God. . . . That is why the realities that the Lord teaches us to request in his prayer [the Our Father] are revealed to be *desirable* and *possible, if arduous and unobtainable through human powers alone, but [only] with divine help.*[61]

It is not only his analysis that leads Thomas to confirm that hope adds to simple desire a firm confidence in its achievement, since it relies on divine help which cannot be lacking. Thomas comes upon the same idea in the image used in the Epistle to the Hebrews (6:18) which invites the faithful to "strongly hold on to the faith that is offered us (in which) we have an anchor for the soul, sure and solid, and penetrating beyond the veil":

> If man should be attached to hope as a ship to the anchor, there is, however, a difference between the anchor and hope: the anchor is fixed below; hope, on the contrary, is fixed in the highest, which is to say God. There is nothing here below that is so solid for the soul to fix itself and repose there. [Beyond the veil, where the anchor of hope is fixed, is future glory]. Our Head . . . fixed our hope there, as we say in the collect of the vigil and the day of the Ascension.[62]

---

59. As R.-A. Gauthier has neatly demonstrated, *Magnanimité*, pp. 322–27, "difficult" is not an exact synonym for "arduous," which adds to difficulty the idea of something great *(magnum)*, elevated *(altum)*, and eminent *(excellens)*.

60. As will be noticeable at several points in the following pages, when Thomas speaks of prayer, he thinks generally of prayer of petition *(oratio)*, but he situates it in a whole that encompasses all the person's religious attitudes toward God (the action of graces, devotion, adoration, in brief, all the acts of the virtue of religion, cf. *ST* IIa IIae qq. 82 ff.). But we should not put any opposition between *petitio* and *oratio* here. Thomas simply distinguishes between *simplex petitio*, which is addressed to a man, and *petitio decentium a Deo* which is *oratio*. There is *petitio* in both cases, but one is simple, and the other concerns what we can hope to obtain from God.

61. *Comp. theol.* II, 7.

62. *In ad Heb. VI*, 18, lect. 4, n. 325.

Though not rare, the allusion to the liturgy warrants attention; it is one of the indications of the climate of prayer in which Thomas practiced his research and teaching. He also does not hesitate when a text he is commenting on offers a chance to make the connection between theological explanation and Christian life. We have already often met with this trait, but it remains valuable for us:

[According to Saint Paul, Rom. 5:3–5]: "We glory in the hope of the glory of the Lord. . . . And the hope does not deceive, because the love of God has been poured forth in our hearts by the Holy Spirit who has been given to us"]. This glory that will be revealed in the future world has begun in us already through hope. [Paul shows the power of this when he emphasizes that it is born of tribulation.] Indeed, he who hopes ardently for something willingly bears with trials, even when difficult or painful. The sick person who strongly desires to get well willingly drinks the bitter medicine in order to be cured. The sign of the ardor of our hope in the name of Christ is that not only do we glory in the hope of future glory, but also in the tribulations that we bear for it. That is why (the Apostle) says: "not only do we glory" in the hope of glory, but also: "we glory in tribulations" through which we come to glory (Acts 14:21): "We must pass through many tribulations to enter in the Kingdom of Heaven." . . . It is, indeed, well known that we easily bear difficulties for what we love. If then someone bears patiently the adversities of this world to obtain eternal goods, he proves by that very fact that he loves eternal goods more than those of this world.[63]

The Interpreter of Desire

It is not a matter of indifference that this note occurs more often in the commentaries on Scripture than in the *Summa*. In Thomas's thought, the *Summa* is a manual, which contains only what is strictly necessary; though they can be quite concise, his courses on the Bible generally testify to a more ample perspective. There is a manual, however, halfway it seems between these two concerns, and that is the *Compendium theologiae*. Compared with the *Summa*, where the treatment of hope is more directly centered on the structure of the virtue, the originality of the *Compendium* is to connect a little treatise on prayer[64] with the study of the virtue. The *Summa* naturally does not ignore this dimension; its concern for conciseness leads to a quite remarkable formulation: prayer is "the in-

63. *In ad Rom. V*, 2–5, lect. 1, nn. 385–86 and 388.
64. This suggestion cannot be developed here. See S. Pinckaers, *La Prière chrétienne* (Fribourg, 1989).

terpreter of hope *(spei interpretatiua)"*[65] or "the interpreter of desire *(desiderii interpres)."*[66] Without the formulation, the *Compendium* makes a similar case and develops its exposition in relation to the different petitions in the Our Father. What might seem no more than a simple literary procedure is in fact deeply grounded in Thomas's vision of things. Indeed, in a meaningful way, Thomas sees prayer as taking place in the great providential design that guides the world:

Though [God] through his providential disposition of things watches over all creation, *he takes special care of rational creatures, who are invested with the dignity of being in his image, and who can come to him through knowledge and love, in their mastery over their acts, and in having free choice of good or evil.* [Their confidence in God is not limited thus to hope for their continuation in being from Him, but extends to hoping for his help in choosing good and avoiding evil, which is granted them in the form of grace]. *Regenerated in baptism, men have a more elevated hope, that of obtaining from God their eternal inheritance.*[67] . . . Through the spirit of adoption that we have received, we can say "Abba, Father" (Rom. 8:15); to show us that it is necessary to pray in this hope, the Lord began his prayer with the word "Father." This simple word prepares man's heart to pray with sincerity to obtain what he hopes for, for the children must behave like imitators of their parents. Thus, whoever confesses God as his Father must labor to live as an imitator of God, avoiding everything that renders him dissimilar to God and practicing everything that assimilates us to God.[68]

---

65. *ST* IIa IIae q. 17 a. 2 arg. 2: "Petitio est *spei interpretatiua*"; q. 17 a. 4 ad 3: "Petitio est *interpretatiua spei*"; the expression is not found in the *Compendium*, but it perfectly sums up its meaning.

66. *ST* IIa IIae q. 83 a. 1 ad 1 (as is well known, q. 83 is the place where Thomas deals with petitionary prayer in the framework of the virtue of religion, with all the fullness we might desire; with 17 articles it is the longest question in the *Summa*); the expression is found elsewhere as well: *In orationem dominicam*, Pro., n. 1022; *In I ad Tim. II, 1*, lect. 1, n. 58; see also the fine book by L. Maidl, *Desiderii Interpres. Genese und Grundstruktur der Gebetstheologie des Thomas von Aquin* (Paderborn, 1994); see pp. 193–204 for the link between prayer and hope.

67. Let us note in this passage the mention of the eternal inheritance; though Thomas admits that we can ask God for everything it is legitimate to desire for a good life on earth, he is however intimately convinced that beatitude is the first and main object of all prayer. Thus, when he asks, *ST* IIa IIae q. 83 a. 4: "Must we pray to God alone?," he answers without hesitation: "All our prayers must be ordered to obtaining grace and glory, which God alone is able to bestow upon us." This connection of prayer to beatitude sometimes takes on expressions that are disconcerting for us: thus, when Thomas asks himself if it is fitting for animals to pray, he responds in the negative, "for they are not participants in eternal life, which is the main request in prayer," *In IV Sent.* d. 15 q. 4 a. 6 qc. 3.

68. *Comp. theol.* II, 4.

It is rather striking to find in this passage so many of the themes we have already amply encountered in the course of our examination. Not only the dignity of the person whose destiny infinitely surpasses that of every other creature, and who can only fulfill it freely, since he has mastery over his own acts, but also—and not least important, since the latter explains the former—his status as created in the image of God. The fact that Thomas places this capacity at the source of all moral action—since it is a matter of choosing between good and evil—sufficiently shows the importance he grants it. But we also have in this passage an appeal to the imitation of God "as well-loved children" proposed as the means to perfect the resemblance in ourselves.[69] That all this is gathered here under the sign of hope shows to what extent Thomas sees in it the virtue of *homo viator*, of man on the way to beatitude.[70] In its further application, prayer too is seen as a characteristic attitude of man in this world, a free but limited being and thus dependent:

Given that the order of Divine Providence attributes to each being a way of achieving its end in conformity with its nature, man has also received his own proper way of obtaining from God what he hopes for conformable with the habitual course of the human condition. Indeed, it pertains to the human condition to ask in order to receive from another, and especially from a superior, what we hope from him. Thus, prayer has been prescribed by God for men in order for them to receive from Him what they hope for. [Not of course to let God know our needs, but to become more conscious of them ourselves. Christian prayer, however, has a special character.] When it is a matter of prayer to a man, we must have a certain familiarity with him to feel authorized to address ourselves to him. *Prayer directed to God, on the contrary, makes us enter into intimacy with him; when we adore him in spirit and truth, our spirit is raised up to him and enters into a colloquy of spiritual affection with him. In praying thus, this affectionate intimacy prepares a way to return to prayer with even greater confidence.* As the Psalm (16:6) says: "I have called," in praying with confidence, "and you have heard me, O God"; as if, the first prayer having gained for him the divine intimacy, he may continue with greater confidence. For that reason, assiduousness in prayer and frequency of petitions are not tiresome but agreeable to God (Luke 18:1): "We must pray without ceasing." The Lord himself invites us to it (Matt. 7:7): "Ask and you shall receive, seek and you will find, knock and it shall be opened unto you."

69. The quotation from Ephesians 4:1–2 is also repeated at the beginning of the following chapter: *Comp. theol.* II, 5, lines 3–4.

70. Cf. Ch.-A. Bernard, *Théologie de l'espérance*, 151; hope as a theological virtue cannot be found in the blessed, cf. *ST* Ia IIae q. 67 a. 4; *ST* IIa IIae q. 18 a. 2; *De spe*, a. 4.

In prayer addressed to men, on the contrary, insistence of petition turns into importuning.[71]

The affectionate confidence that presides over prayer is precisely the proper effect of the virtue of hope. Indeed, hope could fail only if he to whom we pray were lacking in power to grant us what we ask; now in the case of God, power is not in doubt since he made heaven and earth, and he guides with his sovereignty all things.[72] We may, then, ask everything from Him, but in fact charity regulates the order of our hope and petitions. Charity will then ask that God be loved above all things, which is what the first petition in the Our Father means: "Hallowed be thy name."[73] But the petitions—corresponding to the second petition in the Our Father—have greater interest for us here. After the glory rendered to God, "What man desires and seeks is to be himself a participant in the divine glory (*particeps diuine glorie*)."[74] Thomas thus reintroduces here what we would today call the eschatological dimension of hope. Though he does not use the word, that is what he means. We are without question already in anticipatory possession of glory since grace is nothing other than that, but we still do not possess it in its totality. We live it under the regime of hope. In a profoundly Biblical way, it is in relation to the Holy Spirit that we find the clearest exposition of this:

We are in Christ in a twofold way: through grace and through glory. Through grace, because we are anointed by the grace of the Holy Spirit and united with Christ in becoming his members. . . . *Union through glory we do not yet have in reality (in re), but we have it through a sure hope, since we have the firm hope of eternal life.* In this hope we have a twofold certitude of arriving at this union: in one we have a sign of it, in the other a pledge.

71. *Comp. theol.* II, 2. Note in this passage the theme of *familiaritas*. The man who prays becomes "familiar" to God; we are quite far here from the God of metaphysics, but quite close to Him who invites us to share his friendship through the theological virtue of charity.

72. Thomas specially insists on the confidence engendered by hope in chapters 4 and 6 of the *Compendium theologiae*.

73. Cf. *Comp. theol.* II, 8: so that God may be loved and sanctified, he must first be known, and Thomas develops here an entire, small treatise on the knowledge of God, passing from natural knowledge to the revelation of the Old, and then the New Testament, going thus from the beginning to the completion (*ut id quod inchoatum est ad consummationem perueniat*); however among the indications that manifest the sanctity of God, "the most evident is the sanctity of men sanctified by the divine indwelling."

74. *Comp. theol.* II, 9: this very long chapter (more than 500 lines, 6 large pages in the Leonine edition) is in fact a veritable little treatise on beatitude.

The sign is evident, for it is the sign of faith [baptism, which configures us to Christ]. . . . To be configured to Christ is a special and sure sign of eternal life. As to the pledge, that is the greater, for it is the Holy Spirit; that is why Paul says: "He has put into our hearts the earnest of the Holy Spirit." That, no one can attain by his own powers. But when it is a matter of a pledge (or earnest) we must consider two things: it is an advance worth at least as much as, if not more than, the reality itself. These two traits are found in the Holy Spirit. Indeed, if we consider the Holy Spirit in its reality *(substantiam Spiritus Sancti)*, it is evident that he is worth as much as eternal life, which is none other than God Himself, since eternal life is equally in the three Persons. *But if we consider the way in which we possess him, then the pledge produces hope and not possession of eternal life, for in this life we do not possess it in a perfect way.* And thus we will be perfectly blessed only when we possess it perfectly in heaven; Ephesians 1:13: "You have been marked with the seal of the Spirit [of the Promise, which constitutes the downpayment of our heritage]."[75]

Marked thus by the waiting for the completion to come while in a possession already begun, hope—and not only hope, but the entire Christian life[76]—is thus situated under the eschatological sign of the *already* and the *not yet* at its very heart, characterized by the sharing of divine beatitude. Here we have only the burden of choice, since Thomas has often spoken of beatitude, with the vision of God at its heart, as the final end of the Christian life. But before we examine this under the aegis of charity, since we have committed ourselves here to introducing the *Compendium theologiae*, we find there a long chapter in which Thomas specifies methodically and with controlled passion in what that final beatitude consists which alone can satisfy the desire of man supernaturalized by grace. Insatiable by definition and always in quest of something else, man finally reaches his goal, as we recognize, when he no longer seeks, when he is finally appeased. Only the vision of God can give that plenitude of perpetual joy which is born of the saints sharing in the joy that God has in Himself:

75. *In II ad Cor. I*, 21–22, lect. 5, nn. 44–46; the same application of this teaching on the downpayment of the Holy Spirit is repeated in *In II ad Cor. V*, 5, lect. 2, n. 161, and in the *In Symb.*, a. 8, n. 969.

76. It would take a long chapter to gather together all the elements that would allow us to sketch the broad outlines of Thomas's eschatology. If his useless polemical points are put aside, P. Künzle provides some elements toward this end, "Thomas von Aquin und die moderne Eschatologie," *FZPT* 8 (1961): 109–20; on various works, see the reflections of M.-M. Labourdette, "Espérance et histoire," *RT* 72 (1972): 455–74, especially the final pages

The plenitude of joy is taken not only from that reality in which we rejoice, but also from the disposition of the one who experiences it; when he has present before him the cause of his joy, he is carried toward it with all his love. Now, through the vision of the divine essence, the soul grasps God present in this way. This vision itself completely inflames the soul's affections in the divine love. Indeed, if, according to Dionysius, a being is lovable in the measure of its beauty and goodness, *it is impossible that God—who is the very essence of beauty and goodness—would be seen without being loved. That is why perfect vision is accompanied by perfect love. . . .* The joy that we take in the presence [of a beloved being] is the greater the more that it is loved. It follows, then, that this joy will be perfect not only by reason of the reality in which we rejoice, but also on the part of the one who experiences it, and that joy is the perfect joy of human beatitude, which caused Saint Augustine to say that beatitude is the "joy [born] of truth *(gaudium de ueritate).'"*[77]

To describe this communion with God, the true object of our hope, Thomas, ordinarily quite sober, turns lyrical and multiplies the superlatives: God is "the good of all goods" *(bonum omnis boni);* with him we obtain "the most complete repose and full security" *(plena quies et securitas),* "absolute peace" *(omnimoda pax),* "the tranquillity of a perfect peace" *(perfecta pacis tranquillitas),* etc. And in particular, he informs us that "the inquietude of desire will cease by reason of the fulfilling presence of the supreme good and the absence of all evil."

If we are tempted to read this description from a highly personal point of view, Thomas refers us to what he said several pages earlier about the first word in the Lord's Prayer: we say *"Our* Father" and not *"My* Father" to show the communitarian nature of our Christian vocation.[78] "God's love [for us] is not 'private' but 'common' and is addressed to all"; in the same way, "we do not pray 'individually' *(singulariter)* but with a single heart *(ex unanimi consensu)."* And elsewhere, "even if our hope bases itself mainly on divine help, we are also helped by our brothers to obtain more easily what we ask." In support of this communitarian nature of Christian prayer, Thomas multiplies quotations from Scriptural and Patristic authorities to conclude finally: "Since our hope is addressed to God through Christ . . . the only Son, through whom we become adoptive

relating to hope. A fuller treatment may be found particularly in M. Seckler, *Le salut et l'histoire, La pensée de saint Thomas d'Aquin sur la théologie de l'histoire* (Paris, 1967).

77. *Comp. theol.* II, 9, lines 385–409; the reference here (to *Confessiones* X, 23, 33) indicates once again how Augustine is a constant inspiration to Thomas.

78. *Comp. theol.* II, 5, from which the following quotations are drawn.

children," we cannot claim God's paternity for ourselves alone; that would be to risk usurping a title that does not belong exclusively to us. In addition, it is not only in prayer that this sense of community appears; in beatitude itself there is a place for joy in friendly communion.[79] But here, if it still needs to be said, we already come upon the third theological virtue.

It Would Have to Be That Man Is God

As we already know, the *Compedium theologiae* does not contain the third part, which was supposed to deal with charity. This is certainly regrettable because it would not have been inferior to the first two parts. But when we are dealing with charity, we only need to choose which texts to use, because Thomas speaks of it in numerous places.[80] Following Thomas, we have done likewise,[81] and we will return to charity with even greater emphasis in the following chapter. In line with what is to come, here we only intend to place in better relief the deep unity of the theological life and its accentuated eschatological dimension. Master Thomas never loses sight of these two aspects and introduces them simultaneously when he begins to speak of the connection of the virtues:

Charity signifies not only the love of God, but also a certain friendship with Him; which implies, besides love, a certain mutual return of love, together with a certain mutual communion, as stated in the *Ethics* viii. 2. That these are the condition of charity is evident from 1 John 4:16: "He that abideth in charity, abideth in God,

---

79. Cf. *ST* Ia IIae q. 4 a. 8.

80. Besides the treatise on charity (*ST* IIa IIae q. 23–46), the parallel passages in the commentary on the *Sentences* (d. 27–32) are noteworthy, as is the Disputed Question *De caritate*. The three volumes of the "Revue des Jeunes" are always useful: *La Charité* (French translation with notes and appendices of St. Thomas Aquinas, *Summa theologiae* IIa IIae qq. 23–46), 2 vols. by H.-D. Noble (Paris, ²1950, and 1967); vol. 3 by H.-D. Gardeil (Paris, 1957); I recommend, for those who have access to it, the mimeographed course by M.-M. Labourdette, *Cours de la théologie morale: La Charité, IIa IIae 23–46* (Toulouse, 1959–60). The theological history of the treatise in the twentieth century has been marked by long discussions that there is no need to enter into here; in order not to multiply references to studies, now sometimes out of date and hardly accessible, I refer simply to T.-M. Hamonic, "Dieu peut-il être légitimement convoité? Quelques aspects de la théologie thomiste de l'amour selon le P. Labourdette," *RT* 92 (1992): 239–64, where the reader will find a useful presentation of the *status quaestionis*, with a fine essay as an appendix by P. Labourdette, "Faire sa joie de la joie de Dieu."

81. For charity as friendship with God, I recommend re-reading chapters 20–22 of *SCG* IV, translated for the most part in chapter 7 of the present work. See in particular the sections entitled "Life in the Spirit," and "Come toward the Father."

and God in him," and from 1 Corinthians 1:9: "God is faithful, he by whom you are called unto communion with His Son." *Now this communion of man with God, which is a certain familiar interchange with Him, is begun here in this life by grace, but will be perfected in the future life by glory; both of these things we hold by faith and hope.* Wherefore just as we cannot have friendship with a person if we do not have confidence or the hope of sharing some fellowship or familiar interaction; so too no one can have friendship with God, which is charity, if he does not have faith, so as to believe in this communion and interchange with God, and to hope to belong himself to this communion. *Therefore, charity is quite impossible without faith and hope.*[82]

It is scarcely possible to put the unity of the theological life into greater and more powerful relief, and there is no need to emphasize it further. But we can still mine this definition of charity as a friendship. We understand it when it concerns mutual love between human persons, for then we can confirm the conditions for friendship that Thomas enumerates in following Aristotle. It must be a benevolent love between two persons who wish well to each other.[83] Benevolent love by itself is not enough, however, for friendship. There must be reciprocity *(mutua amatio)* as well: "for the friend loves in his friend someone who also loves him."[84] For that to be possible, it is necessary that there be a certain *communicatio* between them, a certain type of "communion," what Aristotle intended with the word *koinônia*, which presupposes the sharing of the same good among friends and that is expressed in a common activity, a "living together" *(conuiuere).*[85]

This last condition reveals itself to be as crucial as reciprocity. It rules out true friendship between people who cannot "commune," join with each other over values, goods that are equally dear to them, and to share them in a corresponding common life (a *conuersatio*). The stranger in the house, or in the city, cannot share in the properly familial or political

---

82. *ST* Ia IIae q. 65 a. 5; in accord with the meaning of the Greek word *koinônia*, translated as *societas* in the Vulgate, I have here translated *societas* as "communion."

83. *ST* Ia q. 20 a. 1 ad 3: "The act of love always has two objects: the good that someone wishes for another, and the person for whom this good is willed; to love someone is properly that: to wish good for him."

84. *ST* IIa IIae q. 23 a. 1: "quia amicus est amico amicus."

85. Cf. *ST* IIa IIae q. 23 a. 1 in particular. See the study by J. McEvoy, "Amitié, attirance et amour," who underscores the originality of Thomas's conception of friendship. See also M. F. Manzanedo, "La amistad según santo Tomás," *Angelicum* 71 (1994): 371–426, which is more philosophical and a little scholarly, but very complete (bibliography).

friendship, while the sharing in another common good may associate him with another kind of friendship. We need only think of Saint Paul when he is speaking of what takes place in the Church-Body of Christ (Eph. 2:20): "You are no longer strangers and sojourners, but fellow-citizens of the saints and the household of God."[86] Aristotle was thinking of the same thing when he wrote: "if one friend is too far from the other, *as for example God is distant from man*, no friendship is possible."[87] But that is also exactly the difficulty that raises one objection to the definition of charity as a friendship:

"Nothing is more fitting to friends than to live together," says the Philosopher. Now, charity is addressed to God and the angels "with whom man does not have *conuersatio*" (Dan. 2:11). Thus, charity is not a friendship.[88]

Thomas could have replied to this with an *ad hominem*, as Christ did in Saint John: "You are gods,"[89] for in fact that is what the grace of the Holy Spirit does: in making us adopted children, it puts us, so to speak, on an equal footing with God, thus rendering reciprocity possible. However, Thomas prefers to explain in a more specific way what here undergirds *communicatio*:

In man, there are two kinds of life: the first is exterior, according to our sensory and bodily nature; according to this life, there is no "communion" *(communicatio)* or "common life" *(conuersatio)* possible between man and God, or the angels. The second is the spiritual life, that of the soul, and according to it, the "common life" with God or the angels is possible for us. Certainly in an imperfect way in this life, "our *conuersatio* is found in the heavens" (Phil. 3:20); but this *conuersatio* will find its perfection in our heavenly home, when "the servants of God will see his face" (Rev. 23:3). Thus the imperfect charity here below will be perfect in heaven.[90]

---

86. We might also think of the first epistle of John (1 John 1:3–4): "What we have seen and heard, we have announced to you, so that you too may be in communion with us. As to our communion, it is with the Father and with His Son Jesus Christ." As we know, "communion," here renders the term *koinônia*, as it does a little further on (1:7), where the sharing in the Gospel message realizes fraternal *koinônia*. See also Acts 2:42 and 4:32.

87. *Nicomachean Ethics* VIII, 9 (1159a4); Thomas has perfectly grasped the meaning: "If friends are too far away from each other, as are for example men and God, the friendship of which we are speaking will no longer be possible [To desire a very large good for a friend, for example, to become king, amounts to losing him]." *In Ethic.* VIII, lect. 7., Leonine, vol. 47/2, p. 465.

88. *ST* IIa IIae q. 23 a. 1 arg. 1.

89. John 10:34–35, with a quotation from Psalm 81:6.

90. *ST* IIa IIae q. 23 a. 1 ad 1.

There is clearly nothing surprising in the fact that the communion with God occurs solely according to our soul and our spiritual powers, since only they render possible a life of knowing and love indispensable to friendly commerce.[91] We must emphasize rather the consistency added to the definition of charity-friendship by the "communication" between God and man based on the common possession of certain goods, and even more it is important to set in relief the precise good that is at the origin of this friendship: "Charity is not just any love of God, but *the love by which God is loved as object of beatitude*, and to whom faith and hope order us."[92] It is not then directly grace, as we might have thought; if Thomas were thinking here of grace, he would have spoken of a communication of the divine "nature," as he often does. Besides the common entitative possession of grace, he thus means to indicate something more, which is related to the order of operation, activity, life; that communication is quite precisely beatitude itself:

Given that *there is a certain "communication" of man with God since he "communicates" his beatitude to us*, a certain friendship must be based on this "communication." This "communication" is at play in 1 Corinthians 1:9: "God is faithful by Whom you have been called to the 'communion' with his Son." Charity is loved based on this communication; it is thus clear that charity is a certain friendship of man with God.[93]

Differently stated, God not only wants us to be happy, he wants us to be happy with the happiness with which he himself is happy, his beatitude. Charity associates us then with the good already possessed in common by the three persons of the Trinity, in their very life, their happiness, and makes us participate in their eternal exchange.

[Besides the love with which God loves all creation], there is also true love, properly speaking, similar to friendship, by which God loves his creation not as an artist might love his work, but like the communion of friendship, as a friend loves a friend, to the extent that he introduces him into the joy of communion, *so that*

---

91. *ST* Ia q. 20 a. 2 ad 3: "Friendship cannot exist except toward rational creatures, who are capable of returning love *(redamatio)* and communicating with one another *(communicatio)* in the various works of life, and who may fare well or ill, according to the changes of fortune and happiness; even as to them is benevolence properly speaking exercised. But irrational creatures cannot attain to loving God, nor to any share in the intellectual and beatific life that He lives."

92. *ST* Ia IIae q. 65 a. 5 ad 1.

93. *ST* IIa IIae q. 23 a. 1.

their glory and their beatitude are precisely the same by which God himself is hap-py. It is with this love that he loves the saints. . . ."[94]

Like faith and hope, but in its own way, charity realizes in us in an in-choate state, "in hope," under an eschatological mode, the eternal life to which we are called. With faith and hope, it relates then to the "already" and "not yet," but better than them—although not without them—it unites the person to the object of his love, the lover to the Beloved, the Lover to the beloved, for it is the nature of love to produce union.[95] A pre-carious anticipation, fragile and threatened, as is everything temporal—"We carry this treasure in earthen vessels," 2 Corinthians 4:7—but a firm and assured possession, for the good that assures us here of friendly com-munion is none other than the Good of all goods, identified with the Friend himself, and with the Friend, eternity entered into our lives.

94. *In II Sent.* d. 26 q. 1 a. 1 ad 2.
95. I ought to introduce here the entire question of the effects of love (*ST* Ia IIae q. 28); instead, I refer once again to the chapters of the *SCG* IV 20–22, which treat so beautifully the friendship with God realized by the Holy Spirit.

CHAPTER XIV

Ways to God

Spiritual masters habitually put forward a way of the soul to God. Even if they do not always do so explicitly, their disciples at least take their personalities and manner of life as a special model of sanctity. But it is not rare to find explicit propositions for advance in the spiritual life; we can discern such intentions in the *Soul's Journey into God* with Saint Bonaventure, the *Way of Perfection* with Saint Teresa of Avila, or the *Ascent of Mount Carmel* with Saint John of the Cross. There is no difficulty in further multiplying examples.[1] The question that arises for us here is whether there is something analogous to be found in Saint Thomas.

Doubtless there is, as we already know. The whole of the Second and Third Parts of the *Summa* are presented to us as a description of the *"movement* of the rational creature toward God" in following Christ, who in his humanity is for us *"the way* that leads to God."[2] It is astonishing that this clear statement is not better known or put to better use by the Master's disciples. There are of course many reasons for this. The main reason may be that there has been greater interest in the philosophical aspects of his thought than in its properly theological inspiration. It might still be objected that the "way" proposed by Thomas takes many detours (though he can scarcely be accused of truancy). The thing itself, however, is there. Massively. This way exists, and all creation follows the way of return toward God. Man is invited to traverse it in his own proper way, which is to say freely, in the footsteps of his Savior.

1. Cf. E. Berteaud, "Guides spirituels," *DS*, vol. 6 (1967), col. 1154–69.
2. *ST* Ia q. 2, Pro.

This first given, though absolutely fundamental, is still too general to respond to the demands that we have a right to expect from a spiritual itinerary. Yet it also contains a certain number of paths that Friar Thomas, without great insistence but with a more than sufficient clarity, proposes here and there. We will no doubt be surprised at the purposiveness and firmness with which they appear in different realms. He views man as a being of desire, unfulfilled so long as he has not reached the object of his love; Thomas's conception of beatitude goes beyond all that might be earnestly desired, and we must learn to distinguish it from everything that is not beatitude; his very idea of the new creature, whose growth is comparable with that of a physical organism, called to develop itself by following Christ in traversing the various degrees leading to perfect charity; all this converges toward the new commandment and with impressive force ceaselessly leads him back to the center of spiritual effort.

Man and His Desire

Here, we can only reflect the energy of so many of the passages already examined, in which we saw at play the circular movement imprinted by God on the work that came forth from his hands. Thomas's constant return to this movement underscores that he perceived its dynamism quite well and wanted to respect it at all costs. We find a definitive theological formulation of it when he asks himself about the reasons why God alone can produce grace:

Given that the beginning and the end of the universe are identical, the end [pursued through the gift] of grace itself must be proportioned to its agent cause. Thus, just as the primordial act by which creatures come to be, which is to say creation, is the act of God as first and only beginning and final end of creatures, so the gift of grace, through which the soul finds itself immediately united with the last end, comes from God alone.[3]

After everything that we have read up to this point, this passage reveals nothing new, properly speaking, but it confirms that the itinerary proposed by Thomas, and that we will try to expose following his lead, is a way of grace where man will certainly have to work out his own progress, but God always retains the primary initiative. Other equally clear passages propose several variants within this itinerary, but these particularities do not really affect the fundamental perspective.

3. De uer. q. 27 a. 3 in fine.

The theology of the image of God indisputably activates this dynamic. For if the image is capable of achieving a resemblance, it is because, from creation on, God has made his creature *for himself*, and has constituted him in such a way that he will never find proper fulfillment except in the measure that he will more and more deeply resemble God:

> By the very fact that beings tend toward their perfection, they seek their good, since every being is good to the extent of its perfection. *By the very fact that they seek their good, they tend toward resemblance to the divine:* every being resembles God in the measure of its goodness. And this or that particular good is desirable insofar as it resembles the first good; also, a being goes to its proper good by reason of the divine resemblance, and not the inverse. It is, then, evident that *all beings seek divine resemblance as their proper end.*[4]

God has thus left, at the deepest level of every being, a desire to return to him. Thomas is so strongly convinced of this that he goes so far as to say that "the *final and perfect beatitude of man can only consist in the vision of the divine essence,* (because) man cannot be perfectly happy as long as there remains something for him to desire and seek." His intellect attains its perfection only in knowing the essence of the first cause, because its object is there. Only thus will he obtain union with God in whom alone is found his true happiness. As long as he has not arrived, "there naturally remains for man an unsatisfied desire," "a *natural* desire to know that cause. He is then not perfectly happy."[5] And as he had already said rightly about beatitude: "If the rational intellect does not come to rejoin the first cause of things, a natural desire would remain in vain."[6]

After the considerations of a mystical order to which the passages on the loving experience of God[7] lend themselves, they are cut short by a more "objective" and even "rationalist" tone. In reality, these two approaches—mystical and rational—mutually support each other. The first takes on its full value as a crowning achievement of the human adventure only in the light of the second, which underscores the irrepressible char-

---

4. *SCG* III 24, n. 2051.

5. *ST* Ia IIae q. 3 a. 8: "Ultima et perfecta beatitudo non potest esse nisi in uisione diuinae essentiae. . . . Homo non est perfecte beatus quandiu restat sibi aliquid desiderandum et quaerendum. . . . Ad perfectam beatitudinem requiritur quod intellectus pertingat ad ipsam essentiam primae causae. Et sic perfectionem suam habebit per unionem ad Deum sicut ad obiectum in quo solo beatitudo hominis consistit."

6. *ST* Ia q. 12 a. 1.

7. Cf. above in chapter 4: "Image and beatitude."

acter of the desire they express. We touch here on one of the main lines of force in the Master of Aquino's thought. And we could cite dozens of texts with the same meaning:

It is impossible for a natural desire to be in vain; it would be so if the intelligence were unable to attain to the divine substance that all spirits naturally desire; and it follows that we must affirm that it is possible, both for the separated substances and for our souls, to see the divine essence."[8] [A little further on, it is equally clear:] We have earlier proven that every intelligence naturally desires the vision of the divine substance. Now a natural desire cannot be in vain. All created intelligences, then, can attain the vision of God, despite the inferiority of their nature.[9]

We can understand the rigor of this reasoning in full only if we give to the word "natural" all the force that it can have for Saint Thomas. As has been very well said, "Nothing natural can be vain: everything natural is made to attain its end. There are first principles here in their order. There would thus be an intellectual scandal if the natural desire of knowing the essence of the divine cause could be frustrated. Nature does not simultaneously realize contradictories."[10]

These passages from the Master, to which many others could be added,[11] have given a certain trouble to the commentators of the classical age of Thomism. Indeed, the whole point about the inherent possibility of realizing natural desires shapes the famous question of the "natural desire to see God"—or put differently in a shortened form that makes us feel the incongruity—"the natural desire for the supernatural." Does this not amount to saying that the supernatural, which is to say grace, is owing to nature, since God could not have put in man a desire that would have remained vain? But then what becomes of the gratuitousness of grace? Ca-

---

8. SCG III 51, n. 2284; cf. ibid., 50.

9. SCG III 57, n. 2334: ". . . omnis intellectus naturaliter desiderat diuinae substantiae uisionem. Naturale autem desiderium non potest esse inane. Quilibet intellectus creatus potest peruenire ad diuinae substantiae uisionem, non impediente inferioritate naturae."

10. A. Gardeil, *La structure de l'âme et l'expérience mystique*, vol. 1 (Paris, ³1927), 281.

11. On this point see the decisive study by J. Laporta, *La Destinée de la nature humaine selon saint Thomas d'Aquin* (Paris, 1965), with the review by M.-M. Labourdette, *RT* 66 (1966): 283–89, who gives his agreement. I support above P. Labourdette's interpretation as it may be found in his *Cours de théologie morale* I²: *La fin dernière de la vie humaine (La Béatitude)*, rev. ed (Toulouse, 1990), whose very terms I sometimes use. See also S. Pinckaers, "Le désir naturel de voir Dieu," *Nova et Vetera* 51 (1976): 256–73, which underscores that "the argument from the natural desire to see God, with the role that it plays in the question of man's happiness, is . . . a discovery attributable to Saint Thomas's genius" (p. 260).

jetan believed that he had resolved the problem by saying that this desire to see God is only *natural to the supernaturalized man*; the desire is in fact supernatural.[12]

This is to state a truism, but it is not without foundation; that supernatural desire certainly exists, since it is included in the theological virtues, and especially in hope. But another thing is at issue here. That is why Sylvester of Ferrara, another great commentator, denies Cajetan's interpretation, but labors to qualify this desire in some way (elicited, free, conditional, inefficacious), so that there is no longer the necessity that Saint Thomas attributes to a desire of nature and we then lose all the force of his argument. This desire, thus qualified, is no more than the sign that a capacity for obedience *probably* exists in man, which is to say *a pure nonrepugnance* at a supernatural elevation.[13]

We do not need to go further into this discussion, which has exercised minds for centuries.[14] What the discussion particularly witnesses to — which remained unperceived by its very protagonists — is the complete change in perspective that intervened between the thirteenth century and the epoch begun by the Renaissance and Reformation, when the word "nature" was taken in a very different sense than the one Thomas gave it.[15] It began to signify nothing more than "pure" nature, as was said, which means the nature of a man solely defined as rational animal, without the least supernatural gift, without the least vocation to share the divine condition or to see God. That nature clearly can have no aspiration to share the divine life for which it was not made; it finds itself in that regard in a state of simple non-repugnance, like the marble that certainly can become a statue under the hands of Michelangelo, but that neither asks for nor wishes it, and had no "desire" for it.

12. *In Iam q.* 12, 1, *nn.* V–X, Leonine, vol. 4, pp. 115–16 (Rome, 1888).

13. In *SCG* 51, Leonine, vol. 14, pp. 141–43 (Rome 1926); a clear and vigorous summary of the positions of the Thomist commentators can be found in A. Gardeil, *La structure de l'âme*, vol. 1, pp. 268–307; the author adheres to Sylvester of Ferrara's position.

14. Its most recent reincarnation was in the polemics raised by several publications of Henri de Lubac, *Surnaturel, Études historiques* (Paris, 1946; *Augustinianism and Modern Theology*, trans. Lancelot Sheppard (New York, 1969); and *The Mystery of the Supernatural*, trans. Rosemary Sheed (New York, 1967); cf. my review: *RT* 66 (1966): 93–107, and de Lubac's later reflections in *Mémoire sur l'occasion de mes écrits* (Namur, 1989).

15. On Cajetan, see the study by O. Boulnois, "Puissance neutre et puissance obédientielle. De l'homme à Dieu selon Duns Scot et Cajétan," in B. Pinchard and S. Ricci, eds., *Rationalisme analogique et humanisme théologique. La culture de Thomas de Vio "Il Gaetano"* (Naples, 1993), 31–69.

In Saint Thomas, human nature is completely different. It has the natural, which is to say innate, and therefore necessary, desire, to know in itself the source of all that is. This desire of nature is one with the very being of man, such that his intellect cannot stop before being filled with the knowledge in itself of the Being who is at the source of his being and every being, no more than his love can be fulfilled without attaining to the Good which is the source of all goods.[16] This is still not a question of the desire for the divine vision as such, but it is of such a nature that it extends to everything that can fill up man and that remains unsatisfied as long as he has not attained to it. That is why, far from being a pure non-repugnance to the supernatural, man's nature unconsciously aspires to it, such that, when through revelation his Good will be known to him by its true name, this necessary desire of nature will be accompanied with a free desire, comforted by grace that will finally allow him to attain his end.[17]

Capable of God

If human nature is such according to Saint Thomas, it is evidently so because it is made in the image of God. We find there the foundation and explanation of this desire, and the texts often repeat it. At the point where he establishes whether the beatific vision belonged to Christ on this earth, Thomas begins by recalling what is the case for all men:

16. Most often Thomas reasons in terms of intelligence and knowledge, for he envisages the faculty of *apprehension* of the good, which will constitute beatitude; we should beware of concluding from this that it excludes love. Passages abound that say the contrary, as *Comp. theol.* I, 109: "Man's full achievement occurs in obtaining the final end, perfect happiness or beatitude, which consists in the vision of God. . . . And the vision of God is accompanied by the repose of the intelligence and will. Of the intelligence because when it reaches the first cause, in which all things can be known, the seeking of the intellect ceases. Of the will because when it arrives at the final end in which is found the plenitude of all good, there is nothing more to desire. . . . It is thus clear that the final achievement of man is found in the repose and perfect pacification of the intelligence and the will." Notable for the play of intelligence and will in beatitude are *SCG* III 26 and *ST* Ia IIae q. 3 a. 4. If we want to take into account the difference between this conception of beatitude and the philosophical one condemned in Paris in 1277, we may read with great interest, A. de Libera, "Averroïsme éthique et philosophie mystique. De la félicité intellectuelle à la vie bienheureuse," in L. Bianchi, ed., *Filosofia e Teologia nel Trecento. Studi in ricordo di Eugenio Randi* (Louvain-la-Neuve, 1994), 33–56.

17. Thomas speaks of this conscious desire in *ST* Ia IIae q. 5 a. 8, where he distinguishes between beatitude under its common reason of good ("*Et sic necesse est quod omnis homo beatitudinem uelit*") and the beatitude according to how we know in what it consists: "*Et sic non omnes cognoscunt beatitudinem, quia nesciunt cui rei communis ratio beatitudinis conueniat.*"

Man is in potentiality to the knowledge of the blessed, which consists in the vision of God; and *he is ordained to it as to an end; since the rational creature is capable of that blessed knowledge inasmuch as he is made in the image of God.* [And
if it is objected that man is not made for the beatific vision because it is beyond
his nature, the answer is very clear]: In a certain sense, the beatific vision is *beyond* the nature of the rational soul, inasmuch as that soul cannot reach it by its
own strength; but in another way it is *in accordance with its nature, inasmuch as it
is capable of it by nature, having been made in the likeness of God.*[18]

Thus Thomas does not say that every man naturally has the explicit desire for the beatific vision, but what he certainly does say is that man's true
happiness is only found there, as he also says that man is naturally capable
of receiving the divine gift of grace, for he is made in the image of the author of all grace, and through grace he will thus be able to satisfy the natural desire that belongs to him. Among the texts that support this reflection, Thomas repeats here a passage from Saint Augustine to which he
gives added force by mentioning the very "natural" character of this possibility: "The soul is *naturally capable of grace*; as Saint Augustine puts it:
*from the fact alone that the soul is in the image of God, it is capable of God
through grace.*"[19] These are far from rare expressions,[20] and they are not
limited to the theologian in the act of reflecting. When Thomas wishes,
in his preaching, to speak of eternal life, he spontaneously turns to this
language:

[Eternal life consists] in the perfect satisfaction of man's desire. Indeed, each of
the blessed will possess in heaven a good beyond what he will have desired and
hoped for here below. The reason for this is that no one can in this life fully satisfy his desire and no created thing can fill up man's desire. God alone can satisfy it

18. *ST* IIIa q. 9 a. 2 and ad 3: "Visio seu scientia beata est quodammodo supra naturam
animae rationalis, inquantum scilicet propria uirtute ad eam peruenire non potest. *Alio
modo uero est secundum naturam ipsius, inquantum scilicet secundum naturam suam est capax eius, prout scilicet est ad imaginem Dei facta.*"

19. "*Naturaliter* anima est gratiae capax: '*eo enim quod facta est ad imaginem Dei, capax
est Dei per gratiam,*' ut Augustinus dicit," *ST* Ia IIae q. 113 a. 10, with a reference to *De Trinitate* XIV, 8,11 (BA 16, 374), where the bearing is, however, different: "Eo quippe ipso imago
ejus est, quo ejus capax est, ejusque particeps esse potest (For what makes it an image is that
it is a capacity for God, that it can participate in God. So great a good is only possible because it is the image of God)."

20. Besides the passage quoted above, *capax Dei* is found a dozen times, notably in *ST*
IIIa q. 4 a. 1 ad 2; *De uer.* q. 22 a. 2 ad 5; but there are many other equivalent expressions: *ca-
pax summi boni* (*ST* Ia q. 93 a. 2 ad 3), *capax perfecti boni, capax uisionis diuinae essentiae*
(*ST* Ia IIae q. 5 a. 1), *capax uitae aeternae* (*ST* IIa IIae q. 25 a. 3 ad 2); etc.

totally and even infinitely surpass it. That is why man finds his rest only in God, as Saint Augustine puts it: *You have made us for yourself, Lord, and our hearts are restless till they rest in You.*[21] And since the saints in heaven possess God perfectly, it is clear that their desire will be fulfilled and even surpassed through their glory.[22]

We are not surprised to find Augustine here; Thomas is much closer to him than to the later scholastics of the baroque period and their "pure" nature. His natural desire expresses in its way the immortal pàges that open the *Confessions*. To recall this does not mean annexing the great doctor from Hippo to the glory of the Master from Aquino. Rather, it is a matter of recognizing a heritage and to add, through that, to an exact understanding of what he wanted to say. What Thomas, following Aristotle, soberly summarizes under the form of the desire to know, when pushed to the limit in fact expresses the insatiable quest for the good, the true, and the beautiful found in all human hearts.

What Does Not Constitute Happiness

If Thomas is capable of bringing together in a striking summary the image (Gen. 1:26) and beatitude (1 John 3:2), he never forgets, however, the historical situation of the human being. With his usual conciseness, he recalls that it is "the very condition of man, not to be given, as is the case with angels, to attain immediately to perfection. That is why *he must traverse a longer path than that of the angels to merit beatitude.*"[23] Given this, the idea of the path to be covered is for Thomas also as entirely connatural as the idea of the circular movement. Within that schema, the spiritual itinerary is clearly located on the way of return, the *reditus*, but this is only a further detail called for by the nature of *homo viator*. It is one of the points that guides the Second Part of the *Summa*. That part begins with an investigation into the final end because man, whose destiny must unfold in time, cannot put himself on the way if he does not know toward what end he must direct his steps. Thomas thus proceeds to an analysis of final causality applied to the whole of human life and concludes from it that the absolutely final end of man is to attain God as object of knowledge and love. Beatitude thus understood is infinitely greater than the more or less vague or intense happiness that we all dream about. If the

---

21. *Confessiones* I, 1, 1 (BA 13, 273).   22. *In Symb.* 12, n. 1012.
23. *ST* Ia q. 62 a. 5 ad 1.

human being is moved by beatitude to the point that the desire he has is virtually a natural turning toward the light, it is clear that we do not have here one enterprise among others, but rather the only matter that is decisive, and that it is absolutely important not to miss.

Hence the necessity, for the theologian who tries to render an account, to discern this good with the greatest exactness. With his customary rigor—which is also the rigor of numerous contemporaries, since the scholastic method imposed itself on everyone—Thomas poses every possible question in this realm. But following a method well-known to him, he proceeds by way of a negative, ascending development.[24] To know in what this true happiness consists, we must first know *what it is not*, and then successively discard everything *"that does not constitute happiness."* Not everything is equally original in this presentation and we find here some commonplaces from ancient ethics,[25] but their regrouping in this form, and especially the movement and end of the process, clarify the whole and give it unequaled power. After the first try in the *Sentences*, where he was still constrained by the commentary form, Thomas produced two versions of it: one more explicit in the *Summa contra Gentiles*, the other more compact in the *Summa Theologiae*. The order of the latter seems more rigorous, but the meaning of the explication is identical: in both cases, it is a matter of searching for the essential.[26]

From the very outset, external goods do not make for happiness. These are not *riches:* natural or artificial, they are destined for the service of man and not the contrary; they cannot, then, be his end. To serve them is to reverse the normal order of things, to alienate oneself. Neither are *honors* happiness: honor is really a sign and witness to an excellence already found in the honored person. Honor did not create the excellence, but

24. One recognizes here the same development as in the investigation about God; from negation to negation, progressively discarding everything that is not the divine substance, we come to a proper knowledge of it when it is known as distinct from everything that it is not; to know what God is not, is not to know nothing about God.

25. Beginning with Aristotle, *Nicomachean Ethics* I, 2–3; but everything Thomas owes to his reading of Saint Augustine also shows itself. Cf. M.-A. Vannier, "Du bonheur à la béatitude d'après S. Augustin et S. Thomas," *Vie spirituelle* 698 (1992): 45–58.

26. SCG III 27–36; the same negative development appears in *Comp. theol.* II, 9 and in *ST* Ia IIae q. 2 aa. 1–7. S. Pinckaers provides a suggestive analysis and commentary in "La voie spirituelle du bonheur"; the author suggests in addition that we can read the commentary on the beatitudes as also proposing an itinerary, cf. *In Matt.* V, 1–9, nn. 396–443; we should remember, however, that from n. 444 to n. 582, current editions transmit an apocryphal text. Cf. J.-P. Torrell, *Saint Thomas Aquinas*, 339.

presupposes it. From this point of view, beatitude is the supreme excellence, but not the honor that is rendered to it. Furthermore, neither *glory* or *renown* constitute this supreme happiness. Recognition of our merits by others adds nothing to our value; it is quite different for the knowledge that God has of merits, for that is the cause of our true beatitude. Besides, honor received from men is often misleading. . . . Finally, *power* cannot be our happiness: power is really a principle of action more than an end, and in addition it is sometimes used badly. Then, it is unhappiness, not happiness.

To sum up, we must thus believe that beatitude cannot consist in the exterior goods examined to this point: first, they may be appropriate to the wicked as well as the good; second, they are not enough, because we also need holiness, wisdom, etc.; third, they can be harmful and contribute to the unhappiness of those who possess them; fourth, they depend on exterior causes, and often on chance, while an end supposes that man directs himself toward beatitude through principles that are within him, since he is oriented to beatitude by nature. The result of all this, then, is that beatitude cannot reside in these kinds of goods.

Is beatitude then found in interior goods? Thomas reproduces the same kind of negative dialectic to discard mercilessly all false pretenses. It cannot be the *goods of the body*; those serve to maintain life, health, but do not constitute a good in itself. *Life* itself is not made to be withheld, kept in good form (which would be a quite lame ideal), but to be used to attain the true end that we seek. That end cannot be *bodily enjoyments* either, pleasure as we say: first, because pleasure is linked with sense perception and results from goods that are inferior to that end; then because pleasure follows on the possession of the good being enjoyed, and thus does not constitute that good.

After this first round of elimination, we must again envision the goods of the soul. In the sense in which the word "good" has been taken up to this point, which is to say "the very *reality* that we desire as final end," the answer can only be negative: "It is impossible for the final end of man to be the soul itself or something of the soul." The reason is easy to grasp: the soul is a reality in potentiality: in potentiality to knowing or virtue, it requires a passing into act to have its perfection; now, what is in potentiality cannot have the character of a final end; it is then impossible that the soul be the final end of itself. But neither is it possible that there is some other good of the soul, for beatitude must have an absolutely perfect and fulfill-

ing character to be capable of satisfying the desire of nature. No participated good inherent to the nature of the soul can be in that position.

The word "end," however, has another meaning: instead of designating
a good pursued, it can point to the obtaining of that good, its possession or
use by the soul. And in this sense, beatitude is indeed something of the
soul. Thomas summarizes: "The very reality that is desired as end is *that
in which* beatitude consists; it is that reality that renders blessed. Beatitude
itself is the *possession* of that reality. We can thus conclude: beatitude is
something of the soul, but what it consists in is something outside the
soul."[27] At the end of this development, one last step remains to be taken,
one conclusion to be drawn:

> [Beatitude must be] *a perfect good, capable of entirely pacifying desire,* if there
> were something else to desire, it could not be a final end. Now, *the object of the
> will, the faculty of human desire, is the universal* good, just as the object of the in-
> tellect is universal truth. Whence it follows that *nothing can pacify the human
> will but the universal good,* even though it is not realized in any creature, but sole-
> ly in God. . . . Thus God alone can fill the human will, as the Psalm (102:5) says:
> *It is he who fulfills your desire.* Thus, man's beatitude consists only in God.[28]

We cannot fail to note in the conclusion of this negative dialectic a return of desire. This forbids us to read these passages in an overly detached
fashion. Natural desire is indeed the secret spring that sustains man's
whole progress in quest of beatitude. Despite the negative appearance of
all that he discards, it is this desire that makes Thomas propose a positively oriented spiritual itinerary here, an itinerary that does not oppose nature, but that on the contrary seeks its flourishing. With a spareness worthy of the Desert Fathers, Thomas leads the disciple on the royal road to
his only good.

The Royal Road

All man's acts (and not only his religious acts) are thus subject to the attraction of beatitude. But between his desire and beatitude really gained
there is a long journey toward the end. With a rare analytical fulness and
fineness that prepare unexpected new openings and sometimes outright

---

27. *ST* Ia IIae q. 2 a. 7. The same conclusion is repeated in the ad 3: "Beatitude itself,
being the perfection of the soul, is a good inherent to the soul. But that in which beatitude
consists, which is to say what makes a thing blessed, that is outside the soul."

28. *ST* Ia IIae q. 2 a. 8.

surprises for the reader, Thomas carefully studies the mechanism of the free acts that permit the choice for or against the final end, the virtues that help our progress, the vices that oppose it. We already know that these form the subject of the Second Part of the *Summa* in its two sub-parts. Our intention is not to recall all that; we have already looked into it here and there at appropriate places.[29]

To deal with the essentials, we will first pass through the *theological* virtues, so named because God is their formal *motive* and essential *object*.[30] They bear directly on the end: through faith, "eternal life is begun in us";[31] through hope, we have the audacity to hope from God nothing less than God Himself.[32] As for charity, "it attains to God Himself in such a way that it fixes itself in Him without waiting for anything else,"[33] and it is through charity that we reach perfection.[34] Each of these is analyzed with equal care in Thomas, but we will concern ourselves here with charity, for when it is a matter of the concrete path that leads to beatitude, Thomas knows none other than the one proposed by Jesus Christ: "You will love the Lord your God with your whole heart, your whole soul, and your whole mind. . . . and your neighbor as yourself."[35] He regularly adds here the energetic declarations by Saint Paul: "If I have not charity, I am nothing," "Charity is the bond of perfection."[36]

We should not be surprised that charity plays an absolutely unique role in the theology and spiritual vision of the Master of Aquino. That was already apparent in his definition of charity as a friendship.[37] Thomas certainly did not invent the application of affective categories to the relations between God and man, but he seems to have been the first to transpose

29. Useful in this regard is S. Pinckaers, *Sources of Christian Ethics*.

30. *ST* IIa IIae q. 4 a. 7: "*uirtutes theologicae quarum obiectum est ultimus finis.*" It will be recalled that I spoke more fully of faith and hope in the previous chapter.

31. *ST* IIa IIae q. 4 a. 1: "*fides est habitus mentis qua inchoatur uita eterna in nobis*"; cf. *De uer.* q. 14 a. 2, and above chapter 1: "A pious science."

32. Cf. *ST* IIa IIae q. 17 a. 2.

33. *ST* IIa IIae q. 23 a. 6.

34. *ST* IIa IIae q. 184 a. 1: "We say of something that it is perfect when it attains its proper end, which is its ultimate perfection. Now *charity unites us to God, the ultimate end of the human spirit*, for 'he who remains in charity, remains in God and God in him'. The perfection of the Christian life, then, is specially taken from charity."

35. Matt. 22:34–40, with Thomas's commentary.

36. 1 Cor. 13:2 and Col. 3:14, which must be read in the context of the *De perfectione spiritualis vitae* (*De perfect.*) 2, Leonine, vol. 41, p. B 69, which we shall soon encounter.

37. *ST* IIa IIae q. 23 a. 1; cf. above chap. 13, pp. 337ff.

into this register the notion of friendship, *koinônia* as it is found in the *Nicomachean Ethics*, thus opening up a pathway to very rich perspectives.[38] But it is not less remarkable—and will directly occupy us here—how he speaks of charity as a virtue of man on the way. Beatitude in a beginning state, charity has by its very nature an inability to remain at rest as long as it has not reach its term, and that is why charity is normally in perpetual growth:

> Here below, charity can increase. For we are called wayfarers *(uiatores)* by reason of our being on the way to God, Who is the last end of our beatitude. In this way we advance to the extent that we draw closer to God. And it is not the steps of the body that bring us closer, but the affections of our soul. Now this approach is the result of charity, since it unites our soul to God. Consequently, it is essential to the nature of charity here below that it can increase, for if it could not, the progressive path that characterizes our earthly life would not exist. Hence the Apostle calls charity the way, when he says: "I am going to show you a yet more excellent way."[39]

The increase in charity, presented here as a possibility linked to our very nature, also appears as a necessity linked to the subject who practices it. This passage reflects a sharp consciousness of the successive nature of human life; engaged in time, man has a history of the virtues even in his organs, and what follows takes this into account, thanks to an often-repeated comparison: "Spiritual growth of charity is similar in a certain way to bodily growth." The analogy is not merely mechanical and we must not understand this growth as purely quantitative, but even so, there are in nature times of latency and times of flourishing or expansion:

> Just as charity does not actually increase through whatever act of charity, but each act disposes to an increase, so also one act of charity makes man more ready to act again according to charity and, this readiness increasing, man breaks out into an act of more fervent love, which marks his effort to advance in charity. It is then that his charity increases actually.[40]

---

38. Cf. L.-B. Gillon, "Charité, Dominicains," *DS*, vol. 2 (1953), col. 580–84. Though Aristotle is called into service here, I cannot overemphasize that the authority Thomas explicitly invokes at the head of his study is none other than John 15:14–15: "I no longer call you servants. . . . I call you *friends*." Cf. *ST* IIa IIae q. 23 a. 6 s. c.; *In Ioannem*, ibid., lect. 3, nn. 2010ff.

39. *ST* IIa IIae q. 24 a. 4.

40. *ST* IIa IIae q. 24 a. 6.

Charity, as a virtue of a being in motion, tending toward its perfection, does not grow in a mathematical way. Its growth consists much more in the taking root of virtue in the subject who possesses it, in a suppleness, a promptness and growing fervor of love of God and neighbor, in "a likeness to the Holy Spirit to be more perfectly participated by the soul."[41] We may perhaps be intrigued by the Master's assertion that charity does not increase at each of its acts.[42] We can easily comprehend this, however, if we recall his teaching on the growth of the *habitus*.[43] As we have already said, the *habitus* is a qualification of our operative powers, a kind of acquired know-how that makes us capable of acting with ease and quickness in the domain that it qualifies.[44] In the spiritual life, if the virtues are *habitus*, not acquired, but infused, which is to say given by God, their exercise still remains at our disposition. I have charity only because God gave it to me, but it depends on my freedom to make use of it or not, or even possibly to lose it. Now, in the natural realm, if the *habitus* is perfected in the normal way, by the use that we make of it, it can happen that it be not used to its maximum capacity and remain underemployed. The know-how then degenerates into a repetitive routine and, instead of the artist in potentiality that he was, the artisan remains an honest tinkerer. Only creative work in search of perfection and new ways of expression could boost him to a higher level.

Analogically—for this remains in God's hands—it is a bit the same for charity. I can, without losing charity entirely, carry out only *lukewarm* acts, and charity then remains under-employed. These are certainly not sins, for the act of a virtue cannot be sinful, but, according to the standard language, they are at least imperfections.[45] I can also perform *fervent* acts and exert myself to be attentive to the demands of the love of God and neighbor; but I then do nothing extraordinary—in the sense of the Ser-

---

41. *ST* IIa IIae q. 24 a. 5 ad 3.

42. In fact, the commentaries on this article are numerous. If possible, one should read the luminous explanations by M.-M. Labourdette, *La Charité*, commentary on question 24, pp. 63–89. Failing that, see the entry, "Accroissement des vertus," *DS*, vol.1 (1937), col. 137–66, divided in two parts which successively present Saint Thomas's position (Th. Deman, O.P.), and Suarez's position (F. de Lanversin, S.J.).

43. Cf. *ST* Ia IIae q. 52.

44. Cf. above chap. 11, pp. 264ff.

45. Cf. E. Hugueny, "Imperfection," *DTC*, vol. 7 (1923), col. 1286–98; A. Solignac and B. Zomparelli, "Imperfection et imperfection morale," *DS*, vol. 7 (1971), col. 1620–30. Note, however, that, starting from a different context, these authors qualify "less fervent" acts as venial sins; in the perspective adopted here, this would be excessive.

mon on the Mount—I just keep charity in a "good state of repair," for this is its normal state. More is needed to make it grow: we must perform *more fervent* acts. God then intervenes, he who alone can give the increase in charity of which this article speaks. Everything becomes clear after that moment, and we understand simultaneously the truly formidable appeal to holiness underneath the anodyne appearance of the formulation.

We can be sure of what Thomas is thinking by continuing our reading. A bit as if he is warning about the temptation to think too quickly that we have come to the end of the way, he adds a crucial consideration:

We cannot assign a limit to the growth of charity here below. Indeed, charity itself considered in its specific nature has no limit to its increase, since it is a participation in the infinite charity which is the Holy Spirit. In like manner, considered in its efficient cause, which is infinite, i.e., God, it also cannot have a limit. Finally, on the part of the subject who carries it out, there is no limit to this increase, because whenever charity increases, there is a corresponding increased ability to receive a further increase. It is therefore evident that *it is not possible to fix any limits to the increase of charity in this life.*[46]

Here too, the formal aspect of the development allows us easily to understand the breadth of the field opened up to spiritual progress. But as if he were afraid that he had not emphasized it enough, Thomas repeats the question in another form: Is it possible to have perfect charity in this life?

The perfection of charity may be understood in two ways: first with regard to the object loved, secondly with regard to the person who loves. With regard to the object loved, charity is perfect when the object is loved as much as it is lovable. Now God is as lovable as He is good, and since His goodness is infinite, He is infinitely lovable. But no creature can love infinitely since all created power is finite. Consequently no creature's charity can be perfect in this first sense; the charity of God alone can, whereby He loves Himself.

On the part of the person who loves, charity is perfect when he loves as much as he can. This happens in three ways. First, so that a man's whole heart is always actually borne toward God: this is the perfection of the charity of heaven. It is not possible here below; by reason of human weakness. It is impossible to think continually of God, and to be moved ceaselessly by love toward Him. Secondly, charity is perfect when a man makes an earnest endeavor to give his time to God and Divine things, while leaving everything else except for what is strictly necessary to the present life. This is the perfection of charity that is possible here below; but it

46. *ST* IIa IIae q. 24 a. 7.

is not common to all who have charity. Thirdly, charity is perfect when a man gives his heart to God habitually, viz., *by neither thinking nor desiring anything contrary to the love of God;* and this perfection is common to all who have charity.[47]

Without Love I Am Nothing

We recognize in the second category in this long quotation ("to give his time to God leaving everything else") a summary description of the religious state. We do not have to linger over this. We might note, however, that the perfection of charity is not limited to this. It is proposed to all *not to will, not even to think, of anything that would be contrary to the love of God.* The contrary would be surprising, but we must not lessen this program in any way. It is no less demanding than the Sermon on the Mount: *"The lowest degree of Divine love is to love nothing more than God, or contrary to God, or equally to God. And whoever does not attain this degree of perfection fails to fulfill this precept."*[48] This is in fact how the essence of charity goes, which is to say holiness.[49] Growth in charity is at the heart of the Christian life. It cannot be stopped before it reaches its term, for its term is God, and we cannot love God too much: "The perfection of the way . . . can always increase *(semper habet quo crescat)."*[50] To wish not to progress would be fatal for it.

Thomas has nowhere better expressed himself on this matter than in his little work *The Perfection of the Spiritual Life.* It came out of his controversy with the seculars and we already know that the author does not mince words there: he nonetheless weighs his propositions, and this gives an uncommon power to his definition of the essence of the spiritual life:

[As previously we find at the starting point a comparison between bodily and spiritual life. The perfection of an animal supposes that it has attained its full stature and that it is in a condition to perform the operations that pertain to it. The rest will be rather secondary.] So too, in the spiritual life a man will be called perfect purely and simply as a function of what constitutes the essence of the spiritual

47. *ST* IIa IIae q. 24 a. 8. Slightly different are *ST* IIa IIae q. 184 a. 2, and *De perfectione spiritualis uitae* 6, quoted above on pp. 361–62.
48. *ST* IIa IIae q. 184 a. 3 ad 2.
49. This has been well examined by A. Huerga, "La perfección del *homo spiritualis,*" *ST* 42 (1991): 242–49.
50. *ST* IIa IIae q. 24 a. 8 ad 3.

life. . . . *Now the spiritual life consists principally in charity; if someone does not have it we might consider that he is nothing spiritually (quam qui non habet nihil esse spiritualiter reputatur).* That is what Saint Paul (1 Cor. 13:2) says: *"If I have not charity, I am nothing"*; and Saint John (1 John 3:15): *"He who does not love remains in death."* He then will be perfect in the spiritual life who is perfect in charity. . . . This is evident starting with Scripture since the Apostle attributes perfection principally to charity (Col. 3:14): *"And above all these put on love, which binds everything together in perfect harmony."* [We could speak about perfection a propos of many other things, of knowledge for example, but] whatever the perfection of knowledge may be as someone possesses it, *without charity it will be held as nothing (sine caritate nihil esse iudicetur)."*[51]

A text from the same period (Easter 1270) expresses itself in the same terms, but some further specifications show quite well what is at stake:

To envision the perfection of the spiritual life, we must begin with charity: he who does not have it is nothing spiritually [the obligatory references to 1 Corinthians 13:2 and Colossians 3:14 follow]. Now, love has a transforming power through which the person loving is in a way transported into the one loved. Thus Dionysius explains (*De divinis nominibus* 4): "Divine love provokes a going out from the self *(extasim)*; it does not leave the loving person to himself, but (gives him) to the one loved." Since, furthermore, totality and perfection are identified with each other (cf., Aristotle, *Physics* III 207 a 13–14), *he will have perfect charity who, through love, will be entirely transformed in God, thus sacrificing all things and himself for God.* . . . He whose soul is thus inwardly held, to the point of scorning—on God's account—himself and all that he possesses, following what the Apostle says (Phil. 3:7: "But whatever gain I had, I counted as loss for the sake of Christ"), *he is perfect, whether religious or secular, cleric or lay, and married as well.* Indeed, Abraham was married and rich, but the Lord nonetheless addressed himself to him (Gen. 17:7): "Walk before me and be perfect."[52]

Despite the context of the struggle in favor of the religious state—the state of perfection, as was said in Thomas's time—we see that is not in question here. What is described here is the Christian ideal pure and simple. It does not reside in vows—not even in the vow of poverty, Thomas will say about the intentions of the Franciscans—but in the hearty and fervent observation, without compromise, of the twofold commandment of love. Here as elsewhere, Scripture remains the principal

---

51. *De perfect.* 2, Leonine, vol. 41, p. B 69.

52. *Quodl.* III q. 6 a. 3 [17]. The example of Abraham is found in *De perfect.* 8, Leonine, vol. 41, p. B 73.

source and he takes that into account both in the justice of the intuition and in the vigorousness of the expression.

It is necessary to grasp these things in the freshness of their emergence to understand to what extent the inspiration here is purely evangelical; but it is also good to note that the theological analysis does not remain there. Besides his insistence on the fact that charity realizes the immediate union with God, Thomas expresses the absolutely central role that charity plays in Christian life in repeating that it is "the mother of all the virtues."[53] Unlike the opposed proverb ("Idleness is the mother of all the vices") here is a matter entirely different from the wisdom condensed by generations of moralists, a specific theological position: charity is the "form" of the virtues. Though faith and hope, in the logical order of their appearance, precede charity (although in reality all three are given by God simultaneously), "in the order of perfection, charity precedes faith and hope, by the fact that faith, as well as hope, is formed by charity and acquires thus its perfection as a virtue. *Charity is thus the mother of all virtues and their root, inasmuch as it is the* form *of them all.*"[54]

Indeed, in the moral order, it is the end that plays the decisive role; now, charity is precisely the virtue that connects directly with the final end; consequently it falls to charity to order all the virtues to the final end.[55] To put this in less technical terms, this means not only that charity is the summit of the virtuous organism, as a sovereign who reigns without governing but, more radically, that *without charity there is no true virtue.* This is not an a priori thesis invented to meet the needs of the case; we can well see that it directly translates Saint Paul's "without charity I am nothing." But we must also see that it is linked to Thomas's central position on the connection among the virtues. The ancient moralists had long before him discovered the architectonic role of prudence in the constitution of moral virtues, since without prudence there is no true virtue. Taking up this position in his own way, Thomas guided it to its Christian culmination in underscoring that there is no true virtue except to the extent

53. *ST* IIa IIae q. 186 a. 7 ad 1.
54. *ST* Ia IIae q. 62 a. 4; cf. *ST* IIa IIae q. 23 a. 8 ad 3: "Charity is called the end of all the virtues because it orders all the other virtues to their proper end. And since the mother is she who conceives and gives birth to another, charity is called the *mother* of the virtues, because by virtue of the appetite for the final end, *it engenders the acts of the other virtues by commanding them.*"
55. *ST* IIa IIae q. 23 a. 8.

that the virtuous movement is newly gripped and perfected by grace. To each natural virtue thus corresponds an infused virtue that leads it to full flourishing. But as is clear, grace does not proceed without charity, and it follows that to lose charity is also to lose all the other virtues.[56]

Without going into all the details of this view (we can only refer the reader to a fuller exposition),[57] we must specify that this does not mean that it is impossible to do a good act without charity; this sort of rigorism is entirely foreign to the Master of Aquino, but it certainly means that such an act will not be truly virtuous, which is to say leading to the final end, that it is animated by charity, consciously or unconsciously. This thesis, which seems rather abrupt at first sight, and as such is not accepted by all theologians, simply translates in all its demanding nature and gospel grandeur the sovereignty of the commandment of love.

The Degrees of Charity

If we follow Thomas in his analysis of charity, we will quickly see that his main positions open up at every point to concrete applications that stimulate his disciple to further reflection and depth. So it is alongside the eminently classical thesis of the degrees of charity that we find the analogy, already met with, about natural development:

The spiritual increase of charity may be compared with man's bodily growth. We can, doubtless, distinguish many different degrees, yet it has certain fixed divisions characterized by actions or pursuits corresponding to that growth. Thus infancy precedes the age of reason; another stage begins with the use of reason and speech; then comes puberty and the possibility of reproduction, and so on until full development.

In like manner the diverse degrees of charity are distinguished according to the different pursuits inspired by development itself. For at first keeping away from sin and resisting concupiscence, which lead in a direction opposed to charity, is the main concern. This concerns *beginners*, in whom charity has to be nourished or strengthened lest it be destroyed: in the next phase, the main concern is the intention of progress in the good. This is the pursuit of the *proficient*, whose aim is mainly at strengthening their charity by adding to it. Finally, there is a third pursuit, whose chief aim is union with and enjoyment of God. This belongs to the *perfect* who "depart to be with Christ." This is the very law of motion:

---

56. Cf. *ST* Ia IIae q. 65, especially a. 3. It is also worthwhile to reread what I said above in chapter 11, "The virtue of risk," and "Prudence and charity."

57. For example, M.-M. Labourdette, *La charité* (cf. above note 42), pp. 49–63.

we see the body distance itself from its point of departure, then progressively approach, and finally, at the end, find repose.[58]

Thomas knows quite well that in life things are never so simple as in this tripartite scheme. He thus concedes that we could envision many other gradations; but if we look at the matter closely, he says, we always come upon a scheme of this kind. We must however understand the meaning of these distinctions well; they are not separations. The beginners are not solely occupied with resisting sin; they too make progress, and all the more so when they feel themselves more assured. So too, we must not believe that the perfect have no further need to move forward, though it is not their main concern; what enlivens them is the constant will to attach themselves to God in the most intimate way. On the other hand, even though they too have concern about union with God, the first two categories grapple with other, more immediate preoccupations.[59]

To tell the truth, this typology of the spiritual life is not original to Thomas.[60] Given that the theme of degrees of charity was already proposed by the Master of the *Sentences* with a passage from Saint Augustine, all the commentators had to talk about it, and Thomas was no exception.[61] In what followed, this way of seeing things became a true banality in books of spirituality.[62] But it is nonetheless certain that Thomas happily reproduced this teaching and made it his own. He had already made use of it, without any scholarly constraint, in a youthful work and took it as the subject of a beautiful spiritual meditation. With a very sure theo-

---

58. *ST* IIa IIae q. 24 a. 9.

59. Ibid., replies to the arguments.

60. For his Patristic antecedents, see P. Pourrat's entry, "Commençants," *DS*, vol. 2 (1953), col. 1143–56; A. Solignac, "Voies (purgative, illuminative, unitive)," *DS*, vol.16 (1994), col. 1200–215; Pourrat remarks that the teaching on the three degrees of charity is sometimes matched by a similar teaching on three ways (purgative, illuminative, unitive) as in Saint Bonaventure who seems to be the first to bring them together (*De triplici via, Opera Omnia*, vol. 8, pp. 1–17). Thomas, who knew the vocabulary of the three ways quite well since he found it in the *Hierarchia coelestis* VII (compare, e.g., *In II Sent.* d. 9 a. 2) and who also knew Bonaventure (dating from 1259–60) does not himself bring these two currents together.

61. *In III Sent.* d. 29 a. 8 qc. 1; cf. S. Augustine, *Tractatus in Iam Ioannis*, tract.V, 4 (SC 75, 255): charity does not reach perfection from birth, "it is born to become perfect: once born, it is nourished; nourished, it becomes strong; strong, it becomes perfect."

62. One of the best, though strongly marked by its time, remains R. Garrigou-Lagrange, *The Three Ages of the Interior Life: Prelude of Life Eternal*, trans. Sr. M. Timothea Doyle (St. Louis, Mo., 1947–48), which is entirely based on this three-fold structure.

logical instinct, the man who at the time was hardly more than the assistant of Saint Albert was already placing all progress in the spiritual life under the aegis of the Holy Spirit:

The Spirit is given to *beginners* at the start of justification . . . in the path of renewal . . . in the privilege of adoption. . . . (It is also given) to those *progressing* to shape their intelligence . . . , to fortify their will . . . , to confirm their actions. . . . (It is also given) to the *perfect*: as the privilege of liberty . . . , as the bond of unity . . . , as the pledge of the inheritance. . . .[63]

A little later, when he has to defend the Dominican religious ideal against the attacks of the secular masters at the University of Paris, he engages the question even more deeply and at the same time manifests his passion for his chosen way of life and the high esteem in which he holds the Christian life. Instead of speaking of degrees of charity along an ascending path, he presents them in descending order. Charity finds its perfect realization only in God himself; only he can love himself as he deserves to be loved. The second degree finds its verification in the blessed already in heaven, since they adhere to God with their whole being. Neither of these two first realizations is accessible to us, but there remains the charity of human beings still on the way:

We love God with *our whole heart, with our whole mind, with our whole soul, with our whole strength,* if nothing is lacking in the divine charity by which we refer everything to God in a habitual or actual way *(actu uel habitu).* That is the perfection prescribed for us.

In the first place, it is necessary that man refer everything to God as his end: *Whatever therefore you eat or you drink, or whatever you do, do everything to the glory of God* (1 Cor. 10:31). This is achieved when we consecrate our lives to God's service, such that everything that we do for ourselves is virtually ordered to God, or at least they are not acts that turn from God, like sin. Thus, man loves God *with his whole heart.*

In the second place, man must submit his intellect to God by receiving in faith what is divinely revealed: *We take every thought captive for the service of Christ* (2 Cor. 10:5). Thus God is loved *with our whole mind.*

In the third place, we must love in God everything that we love, and refer all our affections to the love of God: *For if we were beside ourselves, it was for God; if we are rational, it is for you* (2 Cor. 5:13). Thus do we love God *with our whole soul.*

---

63. *In Isaiam XLIV,* 3, Leonine, vol. 28, p. 188; cf. J.-P. Torrell and D. Bouthillier, "Quand saint Thomas méditait," 35–37.

In the fourth place, we must love God in such a way that all our exterior acts, our words and deeds, derive from charity: *Let all things be done from charity* (1 Cor. 16:14). Thus, God is loved *with our whole strength*.

Here is the third degree of *perfect charity to which all are held* by the necessity of the [new] commandment.[64]

In reading this passage, we automatically think that its author is describing what he expects of religious. In reality, Thomas knows very well that "those who embrace the state of perfection do not profess to be perfect but rather to tend toward perfection."[65] He will thus speak of the state of perfection at the right time, but here he addresses himself to all Christians in the very name of the Gospel. Though we are different according to our state of life, the spiritual demand is no less for one than for another.[66] The point of his proposal is that the perfection of charity is not something facultative — of the counsels, as is said — it is an imperative prescription, a precept:

In itself and essentially, *perfection of Christian life consists in charity*, first in love of God, then in love of neighbor. . . . Now, love of God and neighbor do not fall under a precept only following a limited measure, the rest remaining merely a counsel. To be convinced of this, it suffices to take note of the very formulation of the precept that designates perfection: "You shall love the Lord thy God with your whole heart." . . . And similarly: "You shall love your neighbor as yourself." Each person loves himself to the maximum. This is understood, for "The end of such instruction is love" (1 Tim. 1:5). Now, when it is a matter of an end, it is not possible to keep to a limited measure. The doctor does not set a limit to the health that he wishes to restore, such as he does for medicine or diet that he prescribes for the sake of healing. Thus it is clear that perfection resides essentially in the precepts.[67]

64. *De perfect.* 6, Leonine, vol. 41, p. B 71; cf. *In III Sent.* d. 27 q. 3 a. 4; *ST* IIa IIae q. 44 a. 6.

65. *ST* IIa IIae q. 184, a. 5 ad 2; cf. a. 4: "Nothing stops some people from being perfect, who are not in the state of perfection, and others from being in the state of perfection, who are not perfect." All of question 184 is dedicated to this subject.

66. Thomas repeats this teaching in *ST* IIa IIae q. 184 a. 3 and in numerous other places.

67. *ST* IIa IIae q. 184 a. 3; cf. the ad 2: "*Perfectio diuinae dilectionis uniuersaliter cadit sub praecepto.*"

The Hymn to Charity

This title, often used to designate chapter 13 of 1 Corinthians, seems suited to introduce the long quotation that follows. In reading it, we will again confirm the way in which Thomas the preacher extends the work of Thomas the theologian without leaving out any of his intuitions. Indeed, he gives them a warmth that his scholarly writings sometimes lack:

Clearly, not everyone can pass time in laborious studies. Also, Christ gave us a law whose brevity renders it accessible to everyone, and that no one therefore has a right to ignore: such is the law of divine love, that "brief word that the Lord declared to the universe."[68]

Such a law, let us acknowledge, must be the rule of all human actions. The work of art follows artistic canons. So, the human act, just and virtuous when it follows the norms of charity, loses its uprightness and perfection if it departs from them. This, then, is the principle of every good: the law of love. In its train follow many other benefits.

First, it is the source of spiritual life. It is a natural and manifest fact that the loving heart is inhabited by what it loves. Whoever loves God, possesses him within. "Who dwells in charity dwells in God and God in him" (John 4:16). And such is the nature of love that it transforms whoever loves into the beloved being. If we love base and fleeting things, we become base and unstable; if we love God, we will be completely divine: "Whoever is united with the Lord becomes one spirit with him" (1 Cor. 6:17). Saint Augustine states: "God is the life of the soul, as the soul is the life of the body that it animates." . . . Without charity, the soul no longer acts: "Whoever does not love abides in death" (1 John 3:14). Even if you have all the charisms of the Holy Spirit, without charity you are dead. Whether the gift of tongues or of knowledge, the gift of faith or prophecy, all the gifts that you might wish, will not make you alive if you do not love. That death, clothed in gold and precious stones, is no less a cadaver.

Charity assures the observance of the divine precepts: "The love of God is never at rest," says Saint Gregory, "it acts and does great things. If it does not act, then it is not charity." The manifest sign of charity is its promptitude in carrying out the divine precepts. We observe the one who loves undertaking great and difficult labors for the beloved. Our Lord tells us: "Whoever loves me will keep my commandments" (John 14:23). Let us understand this well: to observe the commandment of love is to fulfill the whole law. In the case of positive precepts, charity gives a fulness to their performance that is nothing other than the love with which

68. Rom. 9:28, according to the Vulgate. Cf. J.-P. Torrell, "La pratique pastorale," 235.

a person obeys them. In the case of prohibitions, it is again charity that obeys for "it does nothing unfitting" (1 Cor. 13:4).

Charity is also protection against adversity. Whoever possesses it cannot be harmed. "All things," says Saint Paul, "work together for good for those who love God" (Rom. 8:29). Opposition and difficulty appear full of sweetness for whoever loves. Such is our experience of love.

Charity finally leads to happiness. Eternal beatitude is promised solely to the friends of God. Without charity, everything else is insufficient. . . . Though there are differences among the blessed, those differences pertain only to the degree of love and not to the other virtues. Many have been more abstinent than the apostles, but the apostles surpass all others in beatitude through the eminence of their charity. . . .

Charity leads to the forgiveness of sins. A clear experience of love: when one who has offended me comes to love me from the bottom of his heart, love will cause the offense to be forgotten. . . . The example of Mary Magdalene is highly pertinent here: "Numerous sins will be forgiven her," says the Lord. And why? "For she has loved much" (Luke 7:47). But perhaps someone will say: if charity is enough, what is the use of penitence? Be certain, no one truly loves if he does not truly repent. . . .

Then charity illumines the heart. "We are surrounded by darkness," says Job (37:19), often not knowing what to do, what even to wish for: charity teaches us everything needed for salvation, "his anointing will teach you all things" (1 John 2:27). The reason for this is that wherever there is charity, there is also the Holy Spirit, who knows all and leads us on the straight path. . . . Charity puts perfect joy within us. . . . It also gives perfect peace. . . .

Finally, it is charity that causes man's greatness. . . . Charity makes a friend out of a servant. Thus not only are we free, but we have become sons, bearing the name and being so in truth. "The Holy Spirit himself gives to our spirit the witness that we are children of God. And if we are children, we are also heirs, heirs of God and co-heir with Christ" (Rom. 8:17).

All gifts come down from the Father of lights, but none that is not surpassed by charity. We can have the other gifts without grace and the Holy Spirit, but with charity we necessarily have the Holy Spirit: "The love of God has been spread in our hearts by the Holy Spirit who has been given to us" (Rom. 5:5).[69]

Such a passage defies commentary and it might be best left to the reader's private meditation. The abyss of God's love is not less unfathomable to human intelligence than is his mystery. Without claiming to provide here

---

69. *De decem preceptis* II–IV, ed. Torrell, pp. 26–30, where there are source notes and indications of parallel passages.

what we cannot, we may perhaps be allowed to observe that these homilies on the commandment of love—for we know they were preached—allow the author's evangelical fervor to shine forth fully. That evangelical fervor, confirmed in many ways, does not appear here by chance. We have elsewhere spoken of the "double evangelism" that inspires his conception of religious life; perhaps we have not sufficiently emphasized to what extent Thomas is here in complete harmony with his religious family and its founder, Saint Dominic, *uir euangelicus*.[70] We cannot forget that, Dominicans or Franciscans, the mendicant friars deeply affected the approach to the religious life in the thirteenth century, and Friar Thomas took part in that shift.[71]

Thomas participates in it in his own way, however, with his own proper charism, so that his theological practice bears the marks of his personal commitment. For many years and with the same Dominican fervor (as a historian of the order of Preachers), Father Chenu has pointed to the evangelical roots of the mendicants' theology.[72] It is not merely a case of giving proper weight to the harmony between theory and practice *(uerbo et exemplo)* which characterizes the new Masters, but rather of emphasizing the deep renewal that the traditional biblical inspiration also underwent at their hands. As heir to the Saint-Jacques tradition, where, under Hugh of Saint-Cher's direction, revision of the Bible and the preparation of concordances had taken place simultaneously some thirty years earlier, Thomas represents the ripest fruits of that earlier work.[73]

Several times already—not to say constantly—we have met with this Biblical vein in different parts of Thomas's theology. In his spiritual approach, this translates into direct recourse to the Gospel, which he teaches as much as he meditates on.[74] He does not dream of proposing any

70. Cf. M.-H. Vicaire, *Histoire de saint Dominique*, 1: *Un homme évangélique* (Paris, 1982), pp. 10 and 218, who proposes as a translation of *uir euangelicus:* "l'homme qui s'efforce de recommencer les apôtres." The work has been translated into English as *Saint Dominic and His Times*, trans. Kathleen Pond (New York, 1964), where see pp. x and 101.

71. Cf. my *Saint Thomas Aquinas*, chapter 5, "The Defender of the mendicant religious life"; see in particular p. 90 for the "double evangelism."

72. Cf. *Introduction à l'étude de saint Thomas d'Aquin* (Paris, ²1954), 38–43: "L'évangélisme": cf., also, "Evangélisme et théologie au XIIIe siècle," in *Mélanges offerts au R. P. Ferdinand Cavallera* (Toulouse, 1948), 339–46; "Le réveil évangélique," in *La théologie au douzième siècle* (Paris, 1957), 252–73.

73. See on this point B. Smalley, *The Gospels in the Schools c. 1100–c. 1280* (London and Ronceverte, 1985), 257–79.

74. Cf. "La pratique pastorale," 231–33.

method other than the Gospel. Nor does he know another path than the one that enters by the straight gate; he contents himself with repeating: "The whole law depends on charity *(Tota lex pendet a caritate).*"[75] Nothing more. He does not offer descriptions of states of the soul on the way, as will blossom around Thomas—though fine psychological analyses are not unfamiliar to him. But whoever becomes a disciple of Thomas through frequent reading will constantly find himself referred to the words and example of the one true Master. In this, Thomas too is *uir euangelicus.*[76]

The Model of All Perfections

This chapter has led us to recognize the essential character of charity in the Christian life, with the full importance that Thomas gives to this notion. In charity we best see how eternal life has already begun and also how it is a journey with various stages; it can never turn back or pause without denying itself, because the desire for its completion belongs to charity's very nature.

This process, realized in an eminent way here, marks the totality of the Christian life. We can see this particularly in the realm of the sacramental life where, in keeping with his analogy with bodily growth, Thomas justifies there being seven sacraments by pairing each of them with the great stages of spiritual development and the major needs of the organism of grace, healing or fortifying as the case may be.[77] This intuition, familiar to today's theologians, seems to have been a personal creation of the Dominican friar in his own day. Extremely fruitful, it shows once again Thomas's attention to the Christian as a reality in the process of becoming. But this is not the place to linger on the point; it will be more enlightening to view the same ideas in light of following Christ.

If it is true that Christ is the first model for all the virtues,[78] we might

---

75. *De decem preceptis* XI, ed.Torrell, p. 227.

76. Thomas, in his humility, prevented the attribution of this title, first given to Saint Dominic, to himself, but the similarities of the two in this matter allow us to introduce a complementary remark. It has been often noted, and recently once again, that while there are several Dominican traits in spirituality, there is not, properly speaking, a "Dominican school of spirituality" (cf. Simon Tugwell, "Editorial," pages 9–12 in *Mémoire dominicaine* 2 (Spring 1993): "Courants dominicains de spiritualité"). In this sense, there is a spiritual theology in Saint Thomas; there is no "Thomist (or Thomistic) spirituality" in the strict sense.

77. *ST* IIIa q. 65 a. 1.

78. See chapter 5 above, "I have given you the example."

expect him to be presented to us as the model for perfect charity, which contains all the other virtues. Better yet, it is in Christ's charity that the necessity of following and imitating him is founded. When Thomas comes upon the Lord's declaration (John 15:13): "You are my friends if you do what I command," he comments, "Earlier, the Lord exhorted us to fraternal charity by his example; here he shows why, through the blessing granted them, his friends are *obliged to act in imitation of Christ, because Christ has taken them into his love.*"[79]

The imitation and following of Christ are striking formulations in their connection to perfection. Thus, with regard to the calling of the first apostles on the shores of the lake, who left everything to follow Christ, Thomas says:

> In the final analysis, it is not a great thing to renounce everything [many philosophers cared nothing for wealth, Thomas also observes]. Perfection consists rather in following Christ, and that is done through charity: "If I give everything to the poor. . . . If I have not charity, all that is of no use to me" (1 Cor. 13:3). Perfection does not consist in exterior things: poverty, virginity, and so forth; *they are only the means for charity.* That is why the Gospel adds: "*And they followed him.*"[80]

"*If you want to be perfect,* go, sell all you have, and give it to the poor and you will have treasure in heaven; *then, come follow me.*"[81] Jesus' invitation to the rich young man (Matt. 19:21) is obviously the ideal chance to speak about the topic again. Thomas repeats this verse in his little book, *Perfection of the Spiritual Life*; the context, social as much as Scriptural, necessarily calls for a comparison between perfection and the abandonment of riches, and we sense in the texts a friendly polemic with the Franciscans over the importance of the vow of poverty for religious life. Here, we can excerpt from it what interests us:

> *Perfection consists in following Christ,* while the abandoning of wealth is only the way. It is not enough, then, says Saint Jerome, to renounce one's goods; we must also do what Saint Peter did: *and we must follow you.* [We revisit the example of

---

79. *In Ioannem XV*, 13, lect. 3, n. 2010.

80. *In Matt. IV*, 22, lect. 2, n. 373.

81. *In Matt. XIX*, 21, n. 1593; the commentary here is a little more detailed, but no less direct: "If perfection does not reside in the renunciation of wealth, in what does it consist? We must reply: *in the perfection of charity* (Col. 3:14): 'Above all else, have charity, it is the bond of perfection. Thus love of God is perfection, renunciation of wealth is the way of perfection.' . . . He will be perfect in charity who loves God to the point of renouncing himself and his own *(usque ad contemptum sui et suorum).*"

Abraham, who had great wealth, but whom the Lord simply asked:] "Walk before me and be perfect," showing thus that his perfection consisted precisely in walking in the Lord's presence and in loving him perfectly even to the point of renouncing himself and all that was his; which he demonstrated in an eminent way by the sacrifice of his son.[82]

The accent is strongly on following Christ. It inspires Thomas to lapidary formulas. Always with respect to the "Come, follow me," he strongly emphasizes: *"Follow me. Here is the summit of perfection (finis perfectionis). There are those who follow God with all their heart and who are perfect. Follow me, which is to say imitate Christ's life."*[83] The same passage continues in a way that applies not only to the Order of Preachers,[84] but we cannot dwell on it. The formulas have a universal enough value to be applied to all Christ's disciples. When Thomas comes upon Jesus' words concerning the "good and faithful" servant whom the master will compensate by "setting him over all his goods," he understands them as an allusion to beatitude, which may be interpreted in different ways:

The third is union with Christ. In this world, *we do not reach perfection except by following the footsteps of Christ,* just as, in the other world, *eternal happiness is only obtained through union with Christ.* They will be set over all his goods, since the will is in conformity with the divine will.[85]

It is highly significant to find here, strictly linked together, following Christ on this earth and the union with Christ in beatitude. Christ remains simultaneously the way and the goal, and Thomas repeats it each time that the context lends itself to the point. Thus, with regard to the saying of Jesus in Saint John (10:27–28): "My sheep hear my voice; I know them and they follow me; I give them eternal life," Thomas comments:

82. *De perfect.* 8, Leonine, vol. 41, p. B 73; the chapter ends with the same affirmation: "Haec est ergo prima uia perueniendi ad perfectionem ut aliquis *studio sequendi Christum,* dimissis diuitiis paupertatem sequetur."

83. *In Matt. XIX,* 21, n. 1598.

84. The passages continues with these words: *Imitatio enim est in sollicitudine praedicandi, docendi, curam habendi.* This is one of those example where we see how Friar Thomas is personally committed to this debate and never loses sight of his own proper way of following Christ; cf. J.-P. Torrell, "Le semeur est sorti." This has also been noted by L. B. Porter, "*Summa Contra Gentiles III,* Chapters 131–135: A Rare Glimpse into the Heart as well as the Mind of Aquinas," *The Thomist* 58 (1994): 245–64.

85. *In Matt. XXIV,* 47, lect. 4, n. 2003; the first interpretation understands the words of the Gospel to refer to the beatitude that consists in the enjoyment of God himself since he is above all other goods; the second interpretation understands these words to refer to the recompense of good pastors in the Church.

Four things that correspond among themselves should be considered here: two depend on us, in our acts with respect to Christ, and two depend on Christ, who accomplishes them in us.

The first, which refers to us, is obedience to Christ. . . . The second, which refers to Christ, is his choice of us and the love that he bears us. . . . The third, which again depends on us, is the imitation of Christ. . . . The fourth refers again to Christ, and it is the compensation that corresponds to him: "I give them eternal life." As if he were saying: they follow me here below on the path of humility and innocence; I will see to it that they follow me also in the world beyond and that they enter into the joy of eternal life.[86]

86. *In Ioannem* X, 27–28, lect. 5, nn. 1444–49.

CHAPTER XV

Conclusion: Major Ideas and Sources

The purpose of this book has not been to offer a comprehensive inventory of everything that we can hope to find in Saint Thomas about spirituality. The reader, of course, will be right to notice that many things are still lacking here. We shall not try to enumerate them—still less to guess at them, since each person alone can know what he is looking for in such a realm, which touches on the most intimate personal matters. I would like simply to recall that total comprehensiveness was never my goal. If I have left certain things out, it was not through oversight or deliberate neglect. Numerous subjects having been dealt with through others, it would be pointless to treat them a second time.

What should be done here, rather, is to draw attention to the implicit spirituality of some of the Master of Aquino's larger decisions. We rightly celebrate him as a philosopher of major scope. He is certainly that.[1] We are just beginning to rediscover that the largest part of his work is that of a theologian. In this regard, Thomas is first of all concerned about faith and its repercussions on Christian behavior in this world. Though his work is often considered as too intellectual for the average Christian, that is only because of a dramatic misunderstanding, and because of a failure to understand how to read it with the deeply religious attitude of its author. When Thomas reasons about faith to try to understand what he believes,

---

1. It may be good to read in this connection the judgment of a true connoisseur on one of Thomas's philosophical *opuscula*, which he terms "a jewel of philosophic argumentation": "Exegesis of the *De Anima*, critique of Averroism, general theory of the soul and of thought, brief history of Peripatetism, the *De unitate intellectus contra auerroistas* is one of the major works in the history of thought," A. de Libera, trans., *L'unité de l'intellect*, 73.

it is not merely a matter of logical rigor. On the contrary, it involves the totality of his person, and he invites his disciples to do the same. Whoever
will read and re-read one or another of the beautiful pages translated here
will no longer doubt the spiritual nature of this theology. We had to
demonstrate this at least for certain subjects. But there is still much to do
on various other points. If this essay raises still other questions, its aims
will have been met and even surpassed.

   To synthesize now, two principal points deserve our attention. First, it
is important to abstract as faithfully as possible the main traits of the Master of Aquino's spiritual theology. Without repeating what has already
been said, we must summarize and set in relief some consequences that
flow from them. Then, we will have to review the sources of this spirituality. In other words, we need to place Thomas in the milieu where he orig-
inated, to recall the fertile soil where he set down roots. As Congar once
said, Saint Thomas is not Melchisedek! He has his own proper physiog-
nomy, as well as his own genealogy, and it is enlightening to recall some
of his ancestry.

Major Ideas

   A *Trinitarian spirituality.*—Though we have tried to grasp the main
lines of argument that our reading has allowed us to identify, clearly we
need to put trinitarian spirituality among the most important items.
Viewed, as it is, in the movement of the "exit" from the Trinity and the
"return" toward it, at the initiative of the Father and thanks to the conjoint
work of the Son and Holy Spirit, Christian life according to Saint Thomas
is a resolutely theological, trinitarian reality. It finds its summit in the
coming to and presence in us of the divine persons, known and loved in
an intimate and direct experience, where the soul becomes day after day
more in conformity with its divine model, until the day when, totally
transformed by grace, having finally acquired perfect similarity, it will enter in a definitive way into the very movement of the intratrinitarian exchanges.

   The person of the Father is honored here in a special way, since he is
the source from which all comes forth and the summit to which all returns. But he offers an unfathomable abyss to contemplation that we can
only anticipate here below in waiting for the blessed vision. Far from
thinking it possible to appropriate the mystery of God by way of mastery
through his concepts and reasonings, Thomas never ceases to be aware

that the mystery escapes our every grasp and he invites his disciple to prostrate himself alongside him in adoration of the Ineffable. Far, however, from conceiving of the mystery of the Wholly-Other in the fashion of the fearful and distant sacred found in the history of religions, Thomas identifies it with the Wholly-Near, with the Father of our brother and Lord, Jesus, who engenders us by his life in the image of his well-beloved Son.

In this approach to Christian reality, the person of the Son is also put in relief in a quite specific fashion. As the Word, he presides at the first creation of things; as Word Incarnate, he leads the return of humanity to God. According to the language proposed here, he is simultaneously the one after whom we are created and recreated (ontological exemplarism), but also the perfect incarnation of all virtues and therefore, as a consequence, the model offered to all those who call upon him, and whom they must freely follow and imitate (moral exemplarism). Though everything in the Aristotelian idea of science that he is thought to have drawn on should have led Thomas to neglect this particular and contingent fact, resistant to generalizations, he refused to empty it of meaning and preferred to subvert the Greek philosopher's work by giving Christ the unique and irreplaceable role that the Gospel grants him. Thomas's elaboration of this is no less rigorous than usual, but it is dominated by another idea of coherence, drawn from the history of salvation. He knew quite well that the "proprieties" he discovered in this material had nothing of logical necessity.

As to the Holy Spirit, engaged by the same right as the Son in the first creation, he is the one who, through his universal and constant action— "the grace of the Holy Spirit"—makes possible the return to the Father by allowing us to become committed to following Christ. It is only through him that our way of return to the bosom of the Father begins, and it is only thanks to him that it can end, for it is only through the grace of the Spirit of adoption that we are conformed to the image of the only Son by nature. In the name of the love that presides over the Trinity's action in this world, Thomas does not hesitate to give the Holy Spirit, by appropriation, the supreme mastery over the history of salvation, as he also gives it the primary role in the direction of the Christian's personal life as well as in the church's life. The Spirit thus appears as the hinge, so to speak, between the divine initiative and human freedom, in the ineffable communion of friendship that God himself wished to establish with his image.

This Trinitarian orientation finds structural correspondence in the

Summa. This is not the place to return to it, but, it is worth repeating: that orientation allows a transcending of the simplistic alternatives sometimes proposed. Thomas's theology is neither theocentric nor Christocentric to the detriment of one or the other divine persons. So too his spirituality is not solely filial, nor is it simply focused on Christ or the Spirit, but it is theological, trinitarian: each person is equally present and active, and the relation to the indivisible One-in-Three is truly definitive.

A *spirituality of deification.*—The word may perhaps be surprising in the context of a Western spirituality, which is regarded as foreign to this way of presenting the Christian life. There is no doubt, however, that Thomas fully adopts, here as elsewhere, the Patristic heritage: "The Son of God became man in order to make men gods and sons of God."[2] He knows the vocabulary of *deificatio* and *deiformitas,* and it is used in partic- ular in his commentaries on Pseudo-Dionysius. Nor does he refrain from making independent use of it. The very reality of divinization, more im- portant than the words, is the same reality of grace, a deiform structure that assimilates and conforms to God. In more than half of the cases where he uses the terms, the vocabulary of *imitatio* and *conformitas*— which we might naturally believe is reserved for the "following of Christ"—they are used about God himself. This is a simple consequence of the specially Trinitarian nature of Thomas's thought. But he does not fail to give it full weight. What results is that—contrary to the impression left by many manuals of spirituality—Thomas does not put the accent so much on man's moral effort, as if sanctity were to be conquered by force, but rather on the work of grace in us, by which the Father configures us "in the image of the First-born Son."

An *"objective" spirituality.*—Given God's absolute primacy—original source and final end—the fundamental attitude of the human person who encounters him is to fix his gaze on God. God, humanity's only beat- itude, is not the object of any transitive act, any "doing"; he can only be "contemplated." Thomas inserts his entire treatment of Christian action between two considerations on beatitude,[3] and thereby strongly under-

2. *Comp. theol.* I 214, Leonine, vol. 42, p. 168 (ed. Marietti, n. 429): graces flow from Christ to men, "*ita quod Filius Dei factus homo homines faceret deos et filios Dei.*" Cf. chap. 6 above, particularly the section "Only God Deifies."

3. I am referring here, of course, to the five questions that begin the *Prima Secundae,* but the consideration does not end until the questions on the contemplative life that close

scores that contemplation is first and last among man's concrete activities in quest for supreme happiness.[4] The whole person and his acts are thus focused on that supreme "object," *alpha* and *omega* of all being and act. He is then normally led to detach himself from himself and his subjective problems, but this is only a consequence. First comes the attachment to God, not the detachment from the world. It has sometimes been forgotten that "distaste for the world is not the same as the taste for God."[5]

Contrary to the procedure of the spiritual writers in a self-reflective age, Thomas does not elaborate on descriptions of states of the soul and stages on the pathway in search of God, nor on methods of prayer or mortification of the senses, etc. Without overlooking all that, Thomas speaks about it in a much more allusive way, leaving his disciples to take care of the desired adaptations. He insists a great deal more on the need to do the good; by that very fact, we are detached from evil. In his spiritual teaching, the notion of virtue—which must be practiced in joy—is above all else charity, and takes away sin. The result is a sovereign freedom with respect to everything inessential:

Clearly, all cannot pass their time in laborious studies. So Christ gave us a law that in its brevity is accessible to all, and that no one thus has the right to ignore: such is the law of divine love, that "brief word" that the Lord declares to the universe.[6]

A *"realist" spirituality.*—This word first means that the spiritual subject is not a disincarnate spirit, nor a soul that has a body, but indeed a person that is himself only in the close union of his two components, body and soul. Thomas proposes to us "a certain idea of man," from which flows a certain way of envisioning the interior life and the practice of virtue: not a "liberation" of the body, not even from "inferior" powers, but a progressive rectification, a Christianization of the whole being in direct orientation toward God.

---

the *Secunda Secundae*; and we must continue even further, to the point Thomas was not able to reach in writing the *Summa*, as far as the Second Coming of Christ, which finally introduces the new creation into the vision of God face-to-face.

4. On the notion of contemplation, we refer to the study by I. Biffi, "'Contemplatio' e 'vita contemplativa' nella *Summa theologiae* di san Tommaso," in the same author's *Teologia, Storia*, 1–85; on the "practice" of the contemplative life as Saint Thomas thought of it, see the beautiful book by J.-H. Nicolas, *Contemplation et vie contemplative en christianisme* (Fribourg-Paris, 1980).

5. Th. Deman, "Pour une vie spirituelle 'objective'," *La Vie spirituelle* 71 (1944): 100–22, cf. 101.

6. It is worthwhile to reread the complete passage in chapter 14 above: "The Hymn to Charity."

In opposition to a hasty supernaturalism that tends to overlook the proper level of nature, "realist" also evokes Thomas's theology of creation and creation's profound goodness, the autonomy of the temporal, and the validity of intermediate ends whose specific demands are neither suppressed or obscured by the gift of grace. All this constitutes the indispensable base of a spirituality for use by faithful lay persons, whatever their work in the world, who may thus be sustained and affirmed in their final orientation toward God, without being led to practice an equivocal "scorn of the world" that would make them miniature monks. Though by personal vocation Thomas himself practiced a religious spirituality, his work lays solid foundations for a theology of terrestrial things, in a respect for human values that cannot be missing from any true spirituality.

A *spirituality of human flourishing.*—Some people speak here of an "ethics of happiness,"[7] but that is only a difference in accent. Thomas certainly does not overlook the place of evil and suffering in human life (as his long meditation on the Book of Job attests),[8] but we cannot sum up his spirituality as praise of the Cross, even if he speaks beautifully about it. Nor does he merely accentuate an Epicurean pursuit of pleasure, though he invites us "to become what we are." Certainly, he understands in his own way this maxim of the ancient sage, but he does not reject it entirely. Thomas's conception of man and his freedom implies that man does not find himself unless he finds God. As sons of God called to serve him in joy and love, destined to inherit the Kingdom, there is no reason for us to conduct ourselves as slaves, in fear. The repeated appeal to the experience of friendship clarifies the place that Thomas recognizes for human values to express the mystery of our relations with God. Even if these values need to be purified and restored to full integrity, life in the Spirit according to Thomas is not found solely in renunciation or obligation, but surely in realization through love.

A *spirituality of communion.*—This qualification has a double meaning. First, because man is by nature a "social" animal, and cannot flourish

7. Cf. S. Pinckaers, "Kindliness and Spiritual Spontaneity," in *Sources of Christian Ethics*, 465–68: ". . . natural inclination to goodness, . . . which is, at the same time, the inclination to happiness (if it is true that authentic happiness consists in the fulfillment of our love for the true good, and the enjoyment it gives us. . . . the first great question of the moral life, [is] that of happiness . . ." (p. 465).

8. Cf., D. Chardonnens, *L'homme sous le regard de la Providence.* See also L. A. Perotto, "La mistica del dolore nel *Commento* di S. Tommaso al *Libro di Giobbe*," ST 60 (1995): 191–203, whose title, however, seems a little too strong.

except in relation to his fellows. Then, because his participation in differ-ent communities, civil or religious, must find a translation to the spiritual level. Here as elsewhere—and sometimes without the subject knowing it—the natural fact finds a repetition and realization on the level of grace. Now, we receive grace only through and in the Church, the Body of Christ, whose extent is simultaneously more vast and more intimate than the human eye can recognize. That is why Thomas's Christian is first and foremost a member of the ecclesial Body; through the sacraments, bap-tism and the holy eucharist especially, he receives from the Head, Christ, his whole life, and, in the Holy Spirit, the Heart of the Church, he is strictly united and bound, in the Communion of Saints, to all the other members of the Body. This communitarian dimension is not simply im-plied in the definition of the Church as Body (or as *congregatio* or *popu-lus*); prior to all theological reflection, its value in spirituality, prayer, or liturgy manifests the very nature of things. The interior life is not simply a private, individual affair; it neither withdraws nor separates the person from the All of which he is a part. It spontaneously inspires in him an at-titude of communion, of membership in the All, not a sense of being merely a fragment of it.

Sources

Father Chenu once explained why he was attached to Saint Thomas in a little book that brought him much trouble, and contained these lapidary sentences:

We are Thomists. With good reason. We might even say: by nature, born in Saint Thomas through Dominican vocation. After all, theological systems are only the expression of a spirituality. [Then reviewing the links that he believed he had es-tablished between Bonaventure's Augustinianism and Saint Francis, or between Molinism and Saint Ignatius, he continues:] A *theology worthy of the name is a spirituality that has found rational instruments adequate to its religious experience.* It is not mere historical chance that Saint Thomas joined the Order of Saint Do-minic; it is not because of incoherent grace that the Order of Saint Dominic re-ceived Saint Thomas Aquinas.[9]

It would take a large book to confirm the ins and outs of this thesis— for it is a thesis, and its simplicity should not veil either its depth or its

9. M.-D. Chenu, *Une école de théologie: Le Saulchoir*, with studies by G. Alberigo, E. Fouilloux, J. Ladrière, and J.-P. Jossua (Paris, 1985), 148–49; the book first appeared in 1937.

problematic aspects. Though it is doubtless true that Thomas's theology has something to do with his membership in the Dominican Order, we cannot understand this in too exclusive a fashion without running the risk of identifying "Thomism" and "Dominican-ness." Numerous disciples of Saint Dominic as well as of Saint Thomas are clearly not prepared to do so. This would also sell short everything that Thomas owes to other sources that go beyond specifically Dominican things alone, well into human and ecclesial experience. We certainly have to take the Dominican heritage into account among the sources of Thomas's spirituality, but we can also find many others.

Ancient wisdom.—Though the impact of the ancient pagan moralists on Thomas's spirituality is rather indirect, we should not misunderstand how much Saint Thomas owes them in his valuing of human virtue and the created world. This is not the place to go into the details of the various borrowings that we have mentioned in passing. Today, we have a tendency not to exaggerate Aristotle's contributions to Thomas—which nevertheless are real, especially through the *Nicomachean Ethics.* Every day we discover more of Thomas's debt to Stoicism by way of Saint Augustine and Cicero.[10] Through this "reception" of the philosophical and moral thought of the ancients, there is, in truth, in Thomas a will to accept the whole of man and his heritage. For Thomas, man is not brute nature, but man in a cultured state. This is one way among others to honor the truth wherever it is found and, ultimately, to render homage to God himself in whom man has his origin. Like the good, which we can achieve only under the influence (even if secret) of grace, all truth, by whomever spoken, comes from the Holy Spirit.[11] It is certain, however, that the properly Christian sources exert a much more massive influence.

Sacred Scripture.—At first sight, the Pauline strain is the most striking. When it is a matter of valuing the Christ-conforming nature of grace or the imitation of Christ, Thomas finds immediately usable material in Paul, which he most often is content to put into a theological form. Though we might think that this primacy of Paul's is only perhaps a trick of perspective—since the Pauline corpus, fully commented on, occupies a major place among Thomas's works—it would remain to be explained

---

10. See on this G. Verbeke, "S. Thomas et le stoïcisme," *MM* 1 (1962) 48–68; *The Presence of Stoicism in Medieval Thought* (Washington, 1983).

11. Cf. above chapter 9, note 65.

why Thomas had a predilection for Paul's texts. We have to see in it at least an affinity between the two authors. It is also true, however, that the commentary on Saint John is also quite prominent and, as we have seen, for the imitation of Christ, as well as for the work of the Holy Spirit, the fourth Gospel is a special source. But we cannot forget the Old Testament either; the *Collationes* on Isaiah and the preaching demonstrate a remarkable familiarity with it.

Far ahead of all other sources, philosophical or theological, the Word of God remains for Thomas the Word of life, and he finds in it his primary inspiration and standard: "Saint Thomas's whole theology is a commentary on the Bible; he does not put forward a single conclusion without justifying it through some word of Sacred Scripture, which is the Word of God."[12] This judgment, which might be excessive taken out of context, states a deep truth: Thomas expresses himself in an equally categorical way: "In cases of divine things, we cannot lightly speak otherwise than Sacred Scripture speaks of them."[13] We should not be surprised then that the firmness of this position, which is translated into a theological method through a choice to follow the literal sense,[14] found its way into the spiritual theology. Thomas could not have spoken as he did of Christ's or the Spirit's work if he had not long studied and meditated on chapter 8 of the Letter to the Romans or the Discourse after the Last Supper in the Fourth Gospel.

The Liturgy. — Some who know Thomas well may be surprised by this source. They may recall that he claimed to have missed the Holy Thursday office once in order to respond immediately to a consultation requested by the Master of the Order.[15] It has been concluded from this that

12. É. Gilson, *Les tribulations de Sophie* (Paris, 1967), 47.

13. *Contra err. Graec.* I 1, Leonine, vol. 40, p. A 72: "De diuinis non de facili debet homo aliter loqui quam sacra Scriptura loquatur"; cf. *ST* 1a q. 36 a. 2 ad 1: "We must not teach about God what is not found in Sacred Scripture, whether in its very own terms or with regard to meaning." Far from being isolated instances, these formulas express a main conviction, often recognized. Cf. B. Decker, "Schriftprinzip und Ergänzungstradition in der Theologie des hl. Thomas von Aquin," in *Schrift und Tradition, herausgegeben von der deutschen Arbeitsgemeinschaft für Mariologie* (Essen, 1962), 191–221 (cf. my presentation: *RT* 64 [1964], 114–18).

14. Cf. M. Aillet, *Lire la Bible avec S. Thomas. Le passage de la littera à la res dans la Somme théologique* (Fribourg, 1993).

15. *Responsio de 43 articulis*, Prol., Leonine, vol. 42, p. 327. Thomas had received this letter on the vigil "during the celebration of Mass." Some practices that are surprising today

work took him away from prayer.[16] This overlooks the fact that, besides his dispensation as a Master in theology, which freed him from certain obligations, he daily prayed the divine office, and we could refer to many connections between his theology and the celebration of the liturgical year.[17] He led his life as a theologian in a lived experience of the liturgy, and we find echos of it in his preaching and elsewhere, under the form *dicitur* or *cantatur*, by which he introduces into his arguments something sung in the liturgy (the formula is found thirty-three times). But beyond the mere words, one of the best examples of this correspondence between liturgy and theology is found with regard to the current efficacity of the mysteries of Christ's life, where Thomas's proposed explanation closely meets the "today" of liturgical celebration.[18] Though we are often reminded of his youthful experiences with the Benedictines, he could also rightly have said: "I owe to the liturgy, to the celebration of the Christian mysteries, half of what I have perceived in theology."[19]

The Fathers, and especially Saint Augustine. — The scholastic method of citing "authorities" obliged each medieval author to support the least assertion with reference to the testimony from the past which sustained it. The procedure rapidly degenerated and, when it did not result in arranging the earlier testimony to make it say what it did not in fact say, it sometimes became a mere formal mechanism, with no soul. We should not forget, however, that recourse to the Fathers is an integral part of what is best about the theological method. Most of the time, at least in Thomas, we see in this procedure a sign of an ecclesial orientation: the theologian does not think as an isolated being and does not seek originality at any price. He wants to echo a tradition. Thomas's composition of the *Catena aurea* witnesses to that, and the decisive influence of that work on

---

were certainly less so at that time. In the preceding century, Peter the Venerable also speaks of a letter from one of his religious which he read during the office.

16. In addition, there is another passage where Thomas speaks of compensating for missing the office with work, *De substantiis separatis*, Prol., Leonine, vol. 40, p. D 41; but we can only speculate about the reasons for this. Cf. my *Saint Thomas Aquinas*, 220–22.

17. On this, see L. G. Walsh, "Liturgy in the Theology of St. Thomas," *The Thomist* 38 (1974): 557–83.

18. Cf. above chapter 6, p. 140.

19. Y. Congar, *Une vie pour la vérité, Jean Puyo interroge le Père Congar* (Paris, 1975), 30; cf. the same author's *Tradition and Traditions: An Historical and Theological Essay* (New York, 1967), 427–35.

Thomas's subsequent labors has often been noted.[20] Though perhaps it is less original than once thought, it now appears better situated in the great Tradition of the Church.

There is still much detailed work to be done in order to appreciate everything that Thomas owes to his predecessors, Greek and Latin, but it is impossible to go through this book without noticing the omnipresence of Saint Augustine. Thomas departed from him on several crucial points, but Augustine's influence on the commentary on Saint John is evident. Similarly, the Augustinian coloration of Thomas's teaching on the Body of Christ is incontestable. Thomas reads Paul with Augustine's help. But these are not the only points where the influence may be verified. The some two thousand citations of Augustine in the *Summa theologiae* are obviously not mere decoration. They attest, rather, to an "uninterrupted dialogue" with him.[21] These partly qualify the oppositions between the two authors systematically offered not long ago. They also explain, perhaps, one side of the personal spiritual evolution of Thomas himself.[22]

The Dominican heritage.—A good part of what needs to be said under this heading has already been dealt with in my first volume. Thomas's choice of the Dominican Order over the Benedictines—and perhaps over others as well—led him to identify his personal commitment with that of a religious family, and the fieriness of the commitment is somewhat unexpected. We see it with unequaled clarity in his attitude and writings on the mendicant life, and in the way that he speaks about poverty, study, teaching, and the universal mission to preach.[23] Even allowing for the climate of rivalry and at times hostility between seculars and regulars that dominated his age, no secular master of the period could have written these pages, nor could a Franciscan master.[24]

We can best follow the presence of this Dominican inspiration in looking at the stages of the young Thomas's life and of his intellectual and religious formation. Though we cannot overlook the time he passed at Monte Cassino and Naples, we also cannot overestimate the long years of

20. Cf. L.-J. Bataillon, "Saint Thomas et les Pères: de la Catena à la *Tertia Pars*," in *Ordo sapientiae et amoris*, 15–36; G. Emery, "Le photinisme et ses précurseurs chez saint Thomas," *RT* 95 (1995): 371–98.

21. In L. Elders's felicitous phrase.

22. Cf. my *Saint Thomas Aquinas*, 244–46.

23. On this, see chapter 5 in my *Saint Thomas Aquinas: "The Defender of the Mendicant Religious Life"*; see also chapter 14 of the present work, p. 365.

24. The different conception of poverty in the two orders alone makes this easy to grasp.

formation in the company of Saint Albert. After that he simultaneously set off down the twofold path of respect for ancient wisdom (Aristotle) and of reverence toward the transcendent mystery of God (Dionysius). But he also owes to the Master of Cologne, among other things, several of the main intuitions in his Trinitarian theology of creation.

We can only guess, at times, what Thomas obtained from the atmosphere at Saint-Jacques, and we still need to understand this more precisely. Besides the religious fervor of a still-young foundation, what human riches and what scholarly resources did he not find in that special place, linked since its beginnings to the University of Paris! Almost all the most lively things in the Christendom of that epoch found there either their birth or at least their most immediate impact. Doubtless, the welcome given to all the intellectual novelties—Greek, Arab, and Jewish, so closely mixed with each other—would have helped awaken and keep alive in Thomas intellectual curiosity, openness of spirit, and a positive attitude toward everything valuable in human culture. The clearest sign of the intellectual and spiritual atmosphere of Saint-Jacques, however, would be the striking attention to Sacred Scripture. Though not an exclusively Dominican focus—far from it—we can certainly recognize in this the great labors of Hugh of Saint-Cher and his fellows.

Thomas is highly praised, and rightly, for the luminous clarity of his dogmatic teaching, and we can well identify in him the Dominican mission in the defense of the faith. No doubt, Saint Dominic was the inspiration here.[25] Whatever travesties may later have occurred, what is primary in both figures is attachment to the truth. Has it been sufficiently noted that *ueritas* is the first word in the *Summa contra Gentiles* as well as in the *Summa theologiae?* For both men, the primary attitude then is contemplation of truth—the stories of the witnesses are unequivocal—but the will to communicate that truth is inseparable from the contemplation. For Thomas and Dominic—following Christ in Saint John's Gospel—know that only truth saves and sets free, and that in truth we find the culmination, salvation, and happiness of man. Through his theology and spirituality of the apostolic life, Thomas thus joins Dominic in a common passion for the salvation of others. To announce what one has understood

25. Not to burden this conclusion with references to something supposed to be already known, we refer simply to the foundational work by M.-H. Vicaire, *Saint Dominic and His Times.* Briefer, but very evocative, is G. Bedouelle, *Saint Dominic: The Grace of the Word,* trans. Mary Thomas Noble (San Francisco, 1987).

of the Gospel truth to someone deprived of it is to come to the aid of the worst poverty and to participate in the highest act of divine mercy.

Another aspect that we should not overlook has, perhaps, been less often noted, and we come upon it more and more: the most original contribution of the *Summa* is not its dogmatic side, but its moral teaching, the *Secunda Pars*. Now, this comes precisely from the very fruitful period at Orvieto during which Thomas was responsible for forming the *fratres communes* to preach and hear confessions. He could certainly gauge at that time the limits of current Dominican formation. But it was precisely his faithfulness in carrying out the task he was given by the Order that led him to develop his own genius.[26]

If we turn to more immediately spiritual questions, however, the influences are perhaps less direct, but they can be discovered. Saint Dominic basically left the Friars preachers only his own personal example of poverty, prayer for sinners, voluntary mortification, constant study, tireless preaching, and his concern for a suitable intellectual formation for the friars. That influence was decisive and found institutional form in the Constitution of the Order. But Dominic did not leave a spiritual method like other founders. It has to be admitted, then, that while there are several "Dominican currents" in spirituality, we cannot properly say that there is a "Dominican school of spirituality."[27] We of course see a trace of this in the fact that we do not find a spiritual method in Thomas either. Though we often find allusions and powerful spiritual motivations in him—and these can be highlighted as we have tried to do here—there is no Thomist spirituality given in advance.

We might also note about the founder of the Order of Preachers that Saint Dominic energetically refused to be called "abbé" by his brothers, meaning to show by this that he did not consider himself called to lord it over their consciences, and wanting simply to be their "prior," "brother" Dominic.[28] Thomas's insistence on the virtue of prudence and on conscience as the rule of personal action certainly have theological justification, but may also be read as a translation of the appeal to personal responsibility that Dominic addressed to his brothers. In spiritual theology

26. Cf. my *Saint Thomas Aquinas*, 118–20.
27. See above chapter 14, note 76.
28. His first successor, however, granted him the title "father." Cf. Jordan of Saxony, *Libellus*, n. 109, in M.-H. Vicaire, *Saint Dominique et ses frères, Évangile ou Croisade?* (Paris, 1967), 132.

according to the school of Saint Thomas, the person finds in himself the norm for his action; inhabited by the Spirit, he is a law for himself. He can certainly seek counsel and be better informed, but in the end he decides. If there is a place in Thomist spirituality, then, for a spiritual adviser, there is nothing in it comparable to the role of director of conscience which can have a determining effect in other spiritualities.[29] This may not be the least significant echo of the Dominican heritage in Thomas Aquinas.

At the beginning of this book, we left open the question whether there is a spirituality proper in Saint Thomas. Without joining those simple partisans chastised by Umberto Eco,[30] we believe that the answer is yes. Everyone, of course, can judge for himself. Without claiming to have reproduced here all that ought to have been, we have at least put forward many elements that will allow careful appraisal of Thomas as a spiritual author with his own proper dimensions.

This is not to say that he is everywhere original. Having reviewed, as we have just done, the amplitude of his various debts to others, it would be a disservice to him to claim that he invented everything. On the contrary, we have to recognize that in him, as in numerous authors of the period—Albert or Bonaventure, just to mention his greatest contemporaries—a common fund of Christian thought is practically unchanging. Only ignorance about a large number of the writings of the period made certain judgments possible in the past. Their partiality, not to say their erroneous nature, surprises us today. For us, Thomas is much better situated in his own age and is no less great because we now see him more close-up.

We must not seek Thomas's special character, therefore, in this or that trait, more or less artificially taken out of context, but in the totality of thought that holds various dimensions, easy to sacrifice to one another, in a rarely broken equilibrium.[31] Think, for example, of the way in which he simultaneously maintains man's desire to see God—whom he holds above everything since he cannot conceive of another final happiness for

29. Cf. my entry in *DS*, vol 15, col. 769; once again, I am pleased to emphasize my agreement with W. H. Principe's penetrating book, *Thomas Aquinas's Spirituality*, where he remarks (pp. 24–25) that "self-counselling" is a direct implication of Thomas's teaching on prudence.

30. His characterization is not without some truth: "Thomas Aquinas has the bad luck of being read more by 'fans' than by historians," U. Eco, *Aesthetics of Thomas Aquinas*, trans. Hugh Bredin (Cambridge, Mass., 1988), p. ix.

31. Some readers may recall an earlier remark I made based on a suggestion by S. Pinck-

mankind—and the apophatic dimension of the Eastern Christian tradition, which teaches him an ever greater sense of mystery, in which man loses himself much more than he understands. We might also think of the way he emphasizes, with Augustine, the necessity of grace for full human success, and, at the same time, about the robust intellectual health that inspires his appreciation for the deep goodness of creation. Since the Friars Preachers had to struggle from the start against the Cathars' conception of an evil world, should we not see in this yet another trace of the Dominican?

Among the many things that have found their way into this book, we had to limit ourselves to presenting two main subjects, God and man. That was because we needed to highlight the dialogical nature of the spiritual adventure, which continues today, in our own age of salvation, the Covenant once established between God and his People. But this also throws into greater relief the deep unity that characterizes Thomas's vision of things. God the Trinity, inaccessible in his transcendence, never ceases to be present to this world, which came forth from his creative will, and the Three Persons are also as entirely inseparable in their work in history as they are in the unity of their intimate existence from all eternity. The human race that faces them is not itself a mere collection of more or less disparate individuals, isolated in a world where they exist by chance. Humanity is seen according to God's own view, linked with creation, which we have the mission to humanize, for we are deeply indebted to it, and we are completed without even knowing it by our quest for beatitude, deeply unified (at least beginning to be so) in the Church-Body of Christ, first-fruits of the definitive reunion in heaven. Person and communion all at once, Thomas's human race is indeed made in the image of the Trinitarian communion, and that indelibly marks his approach to spirituality.

---

aers (*Sources of Christian Ethics*, 107–9): "1) If we use the *method of residue* by successively discarding everything found elsewhere in one way or another in order to retain the hard core that resists this process, we doubtless will find nothing original in Thomas. 2) If we use the *method of wholes*, however, we will observe that Thomas puts forward a teaching that simultaneously honors virtually the whole of the Gospel in a dynamic equilibrium. And this is perhaps more rare" (*DS*, vol. 15, col. 772).

Bibliography

1274—Année-charnière—Mutations et continuités. Colloques internationaux du CNRS 558. Paris, 1977.

Actualité de la pensée médiévale. Ed. J. Follon and J. McEvoy. Philosophes médiévaux 31. Louvain-Paris, 1994.

Adriaen, M., ed. See Gregory (Saint), *Moralia in Job libri XI–XXII.*

Aertsen, J. A. "The Circulation-Motive and Man in the Thought of Thomas Aquinas." In *L'homme et son univers au Moyen Age,* pp. 432–39.

———. "Die Transzendentalienlehre bei Thomas von Aquin in ihren historischen Hintergründen und philosophischen Motiven." *MM* 19 (1988): 82–102.

———. *Nature and Creature: Thomas Aquinas's Way of Thought.* STGMA 21. Leiden, 1988.

Aillet, M. *Lire la Bible avec S. Thomas. Le passage de la littera à la res dans la Somme théologique.* Studia Friburgensia n.s. 80. Fribourg, 1993.

Albert the Great (Saint). *Opera omnia ad fidem codicum manuscriptorum edenda. . . .* Ed. Institutum Alberti Magni coloniense. Aschendorff, 1951 ff.

Albert & Thomas Selected Writings. Translated edited and introduced by S. Tugwell, O.P. Preface by L. E. Boyle, O.P. New York-Mahwah, 1988.

Alfaro, J. "Les fonctions salvifiques du Christ comme prophète, roi et prêtre." Mysterium salutis 11, pp. 241–325. Paris, 1975.

Ambrosiaster. *Commentarius in Epistulas paulinas.* CSEL 81. Vindobonae, 1968.

Angelus Silesius. *Cherubinischer Wandersmann.* In Hans Ludwig Held, ed., *Sämtliche Poetische Werke,* vol. 3. Munich, 1952.

———. *The Cherubinic Wanderer.* Translation and foreward by Maria Shrady. Intro. and notes by Josef Schmidt. Preface by E. J. Furcha. New York: Paulist Press, 1986.

Anselm of Canterbury. *Opera omnia.* Ed. F. S. Schmitt. Edinburgh, 1946.

———. *Basic Writings.* Trans. S. N. Deane. 2nd ed. La Salle, Ill.: Open Court Publishing, 1962.

L'anthropologie de saint Thomas. Conférences organisées par la Faculté de théologie et la Société philosophique de Fribourg à l'occasion du 7ᵉ centenaire de la mort de saint Thomas d'Aquin. Ed. N. A. Luyten. Fribourg, 1974.

Aquinas and Problems of his Time. Ed. G. Verbeke and D. Verhelst. Leuven-The Hague, 1976.

Araud, R. "*Quidquid non est ex fide peccatum est.* Quelques interprétations patristiques." In *L'Homme devant Dieu: Mélanges offerts au Père Henri de Lubac,* vol. 1, pp. 127–45. Théologie 56. Paris, 1963.

Aristotle, *Ethique à Nicomaque: Nouvelle traduction, avec introduction, notes and index.* Trans. J. Tricot. Bibliothèque des textes philosophiques. Paris, 1959.

———. *Nicomachean Ethics.* Trans. Hippocrates G. Apostle. Grinnell, Iowa: Peripatetic Press, 1984.

———. *Politics.* Trans. Carnes Lord. Chicago: University of Chicago Press, 1984.

Arnould, J., et al. "Bulletin de théologie. Théologie de la création." *RSPT* 78 (1994): 95–124.

Aubert, J.-M., and S. Pinckaers, eds. See *Loi et Évangile*.

———. "Permanente actualité de l'anthropologie thomiste." *DC* 45 (1992): 244–50.

Augustine (Saint). *Aurelii Augustini opera*. Corpus Christianorum Series Latina. Vol. 27–52. Turnhout.

———. *Christian Instruction*. Trans. John J. Gavigan. Fathers of the Church 2. New York: Cima, 1947.

———. *Confessions*. Trans. Vernon J. Bourke. Fathers of the Church 21. Washington, D.C.: Catholic University of America Press, 1953.

———. *Letters 1–82*. Trans. Sr. Wilfrid Parsons. Fathers of the Church 20. New York: Fathers of the Church Inc., 1953.

———. *On the Literal Meaning of Genesis*. Trans. John Hammond Taylor. Ancient Christian Writers 41. New York: Newman Press, 1982.

———. *Tractates on the First Epistle of John*. Trans. John W. Rettig. Fathers of the Church 92. Washington, D.C.: Catholic University of America Press, 1995.

———. *Tractates on the Gospel of John 1–77*. Trans. John W. Rettig. Fathers of the Church 78–79. Washington, D.C.: Catholic University of America Press, 1988.

———. *Tractates on the Gospel of John 28–54*. Trans. John W. Rettig. Fathers of the Church 88. Washington, D.C.: Catholic University of America Press, 1993.

———. *The Trinity*. Trans. Stephen McKenna. Fathers of the Church 45. Washington, D.C.: Catholic University of America Press, 1963.

Avit (Saint). *Letter 14*. Ed. R. Peiper. MGH, Auctores antiquissimi VI/2. Berlin, 1883.

Bailleux, É. *À l'image du Fils premier-né*.

———. "La création, oeuvre de la Trinité, selon saint Thomas." *RT* 62 (1962): 27–50.

———. "Le cycle des missions trinitaires d'après saint Thomas." *RT* 63 (1963): 166–92.

———. "Le Christ et son Esprit." *RT* 73 (1973): 386–89.

Barzaghi, G. "La nozione di creazione in S. Tommaso d'Aquino." *Divus Thomas* (Bologna) 3 (1992): 62–81.

Bataillon, L.-J. "Un sermon de saint Thomas sur la parabole du festin." *RSPT* 58 (1974): 451–56.

———. "Saint Thomas et les Pères: de la *Catena* à la *Tertia Pars*." In *Ordo sapientiae et amoris*, pp. 15–36.

Bataillon, L.-J., and J.-P. Jossua. "Le mépris du monde. De l'intérêt d'une discussion actuelle." *RSPT* 51 (1967): 23–38.

Bazán, C. B. "Le dialogue philosophique entre Siger de Brabant et Thomas d'Aquin. A propos d'un ouvrage récent de É.-H. Wéber, O.P." *RPL* 72 (1974): 53–155.

Bedouelle, G. *Saint Dominic: The Grace of the Word*. Trans. Mary Thomas Noble. San Francisco: Ignatius Press, 1987.

Belmans, T. G. "Le paradoxe de la conscience erronée d'Abélard à Karl Rahner." *RT* 90 (1990): 570–86.

Bermudez, C. "Hijos de Dios por la gracia en los comentarios de Santo Tomás a las cartas paulinas." *ST* 45 (1992): 78–89.

Bernard, Ch.-A. *Théologie de l'espérance selon saint Thomas d'Aquin*. Bibliothèque thomiste 34. Paris, 1961.

———. "Fruits du Saint-Esprit." *DS*. Vol. 5, col. 1569–1575. 1964.

Bernard, R. *La Vertu*. French translation with notes and appendices of St. Thomas Aquinas, *Summa theologiae* Ia IIae qq. 61–70. Revue des Jeunes. Paris-Tournai-Rome, 1935.

———. *La Foi*. French translation with notes and appendices of St. Thomas Aquinas, *Sum-*

ma theologiae IIa IIae qq. 1–16. Revue des Jeunes. Paris-Tournai-Rome, 1941–42.

Bernath, K. "Thomas von Aquin und die Erde." *MM* 19 (1988): 175–91.

Berrouard, M.-F. "Le Maître intérieur." In S. Augustine, *Homélies sur l'Évangile de saint Jean, BA* 71, pp. 839–40. Paris, 1969.

———. "Saint Augustin et le mystère du Christ Chemin, Vérité et Vie. La méditation théologique du *Tractatus 69 in Iohannis Euangelium* sur Io. 14,6a." In *Collectanea Augustiniana, Mélanges T. J. Van Bavel,* vol. 2, pp. 431–49. Louvain, 1991.

Berteaud, E. "Guides spirituels." *DS.* Vol. 6, col. 1154–69. 1967.

Betz, J., and H. Fries, eds. See *Église et Tradition.*

Beumer, J. B. "Gratia supponit naturam. Zur Geschichte eines theologischen Prinzips." *Gregorianum* 20 (1939): 381–406; 535–52.

Bianchi, L., and E. Randi, *Vérités dissonnantes. Aristote à la fin du Moyen age.* Vestigia 11. Fribourg-Paris, 1993.

Biffi, I. "Per una analisi semantica dei lemmi *theologia, theologus, theologizo,* in San Tommaso: un saggio metodologico nell'uso dell"Index Thomisticus'." *Teologia* 3 (1978): 148–63.

———. *I Misteri di Cristo in Tommaso d'Aquino,* Biblioteca di cultura médiévale 339. Vol. 1. Milan: Jaca Book, 1994.

———. *Teologia, Storia e Contemplazione in Tommaso d' Aquino, Saggi.* La Costruzione della Teologia 3. Milan, 1995.

Bird, Ph.A. In K. E. Børresen, ed., *Image of God and Gender Models in Judaeo-Christian Tradition.* Oslo, 1991.

Blythe, J. M. "The Mixed Constitution and the Distinction Between Regal and Political Power in the Work of Thomas Aquinas." *Journal of the History of Ideas* 47 (1986): 547–65.

Boethius. *The Theological Tractates* and *The Consolation of Philosophy.* With a translation by H. F. Stewart, E. K. Rand, and S. J. Tester. The Loeb Classical Library. Cambridge: Harvard University Press, 1973.

Bonaventure (Saint). *Opera omnia.* Studio et cura PP. Collegii a S. Bonaventura. 10 vols. Quaracchi, 1882–1902.

Bonino, S.-Th. "La place du pape dans l'Église selon saint Thomas d'Aquin." *RT* 86 (1986): 392–422.

———. *Thomas d'Aquin. De la vérité, question 2 (La science en Dieu).* Pensée antique et médiévale. Vestigia 17. Fribourg, 1995.

Bonino, S.-Th., ed. See *Saint Thomas au XXᵉ siècle.*

Borgonovo, G. *Sinderesi e coscienza nel pensiero di san Tommaso d'Aquino.* Studia friburgensia n.s. 81. Fribourg, Suisse, 1996.

Bouëssé, H. "La causalité efficiente instrumentale de l'humanité du Christ et des sacrements chrétiens." *RT* 39 (1934): 370–93.

———. "La causalité efficiente et la causalité méritoire de l'humanité du Christ." *RT* 43 (1938): 265–98.

———. *Le Sauveur du Monde, 1. La place du Christ dans le plan de Dieu.* Chambéry-Leysse, 1951.

———. "De la causalité de l'humanité du Christ." In *Problèmes actuels de christologie,* pp. 147–77.

Bouëssé, H., and J.-J. Latour, eds. See *Problèmes actuels de christologie.*

Bougerol, J.-G. *La théologie de l'espérance au XIIᵉ et XIIIᵉ siècles.* Paris, 1985.

Bouillard, H. *Conversion et grâce chez S. Thomas d'Aquin: Étude historique.* Théologie 1. Paris, 1944.

Boulnois, O. "Puissance neutre et puissance obédientielle. De l'homme à Dieu selon Duns Scot et Cajétan." In *Rationalisme analogique et humanisme théologique*, pp. 31–69.

Bourassa, F. *Questions de théologie trinitaire*. Rome, 1970.

——. "L'Esprit-Saint 'communion' du Père et du Fils." *Science et Esprit* 29 (1977): 251–81; 30 (1978): 5–37.

——. "Dans la communion de l'Esprit-Saint." *Science et Esprit* 34 (1982): 31–56; 135–49; 239–68.

Bourgeois, D. "'Inchoatio vitae eternae.' La dimension eschatologique de la vertu théologale de foi chez saint Thomas d'Aquin." *Sapienza* 27 (1974): 272–314.

Bouthillier, D. "Quand saint Thomas méditait sur le prophète Isaïe." See Torrell, J.-P.

——. "Le Christ en son mystère dans les *collationes* du *super Isaiam* de saint Thomas d'Aquin." In *Ordo sapientiae et amoris*, pp. 37–64.

Boyle, L. E. "The De Regno and the Two Powers." In J. R. O'Donnell, ed., *Essays in Honour of A. C. Pegis*, pp. 237–47. Toronto, 1974. Reprinted in L. E. Boyle, ed., *Pastoral Care, Clerical Education and Canon Law, 1200–1400*. Variorum Reprints. London, 1981.

——. Preface. See *Albert & Thomas selected Writings*.

Bracken, J. "Thomas Aquinas and Anselm's Satisfaction Theory." *Angelicum* 62 (1985): 501–30.

Bréhier, É. *Chrysippe et l'ancien stoïcisme*, Paris, 1951.

Breton, S. "L'idée de transcendantal et la genèse des transcendentaux chez saint Thomas d'Aquin." In *Saint Thomas d'Aquin aujourd'hui*, pp. 45–74.

Bühler, P., ed. See *Humain à l'image de Dieu*.

Bultot, R. "Spirituels et théologiens devant l'homme et devant le monde." *RT* 64 (1964): 517–48.

Buzy, D. "Béatitudes." *DS*. Vol. 1, col. 1306–7. 1937.

Calgary Aquinas Study. Ed. A. Parel. Toronto, 1978.

Callahan, A., ed. See *Spiritualities of the Heart*.

Calvis Ramirez, A. "El Espíritu Santo en la Suma teológica de santo Tomás." In *Tommaso d'Aquino nel suo settimo centenario*, vol. 4, pp. 92–104. Naples, 1976.

Canto-Sperber, M., ed. See *Dictionnaire d'éthique et de philosophie morale*.

Capelle, C. *Thomas d'Aquin féministe?* Bibliothèque thomiste 43. Paris, 1982.

Caquot, A. "Les énigmes d'un texte biblique." In *Dieu et l'être*, pp. 17–26.

Casel, Odo. *The Mystery of Christian Worship, and Other Writings*. Ed. Burkhard Neunheuser. Westminster, Md.: Newman Press, 1962.

——. *Faites ceci en mémoire de moi*. Paris, 1962.

Castaño, S. R. "Legitima potestad de los infieles y autonomia de lo político. Exegesis tomista." *ST* 60 (1995): 266–84.

Catechismus Romanus seu catechismus ex decreto Concilii Tridentini ad parochos Pii quinti pont. max. iussu editus. Ed. P. Rodriguez. Vatican City, 1989.

Catechism of the Catholic Church. Vatican City: Libreria Editrice Vaticana, 1997.

Cazelles, A. "Pour une exégèse de Ex. 3,14." In *Dieu et l'être*, pp. 27–44.

Celui qui est: Interprétations juives et chrétiennes d'Exode 3,14. Ed. A. de Libera and É. Zum Brunn. Paris, 1986.

Cenacchi, G. *Il lavoro nel pensiero di Tommaso d'Aquino*. *ST* 5. Rome, 1977.

Cessario, R. *The Godly Image*. Christ and Salvation in Catholic Thought from St Anselm to Aquinas. Petersham, Mass., 1990.

Chardon, Louis. *La Croix de Jésus où les plus belles vérités de la théologie mystique et la grâce sanctifiante sont établies*. Paris, 1647. New edition with an introduction by F. Florand. Paris, 1937.

———. *The Cross of Jesus*. Trans. Richard T. Murphy. Cross and Crown Series of Spirituality 9. St. Louis, Mo.: Herder, 1957.

Chardonnens, D. "L'espérance de la résurrection selon Thomas d'Aquin, commenteur du Livre de Job." In *Ordo sapientiae et amoris*, pp. 65–83.

———. *L'homme sous le regard de la Providence: Providence de Dieu et condition humaine selon l'Exposition littérale sur le Livre de Job de Thomas d'Aquin*. Bibliothèque thomiste 50. Paris: J. Vrin, 1997.

Chartularium Universitatis Parisiensis. Ed. H. Denifle and E. Chatelain. Vol. 1 and 2. Paris, 1889 and 1891.

Chatelain, E., and H. Denifle, eds. See *Chartularium Universitatis Parisiensis*.

Châtillon, J. "Sacramentalité, beauté et vanité du monde chez saint Bonaventure." In *1274—Année-charnière*, pp. 679–90.

Chenu, M-D. "Évangélisme et théologie au XIIIᵉ siècle." In *Mélanges offerts au R. P. Ferdinand Cavallera*, pp. 339–46. Toulouse, 1948.

———. *Introduction à l'étude de saint Thomas d'Aquin*. Publications de l'Institut d'études médiévales 11. Montreal-Paris, ²1954.

———. *La théologie comme science au XIIIᵉ siècle*. Bibliothèque thomiste 33. Paris, ³1957.

———. *La théologie au douzième siècle*. Etudes de philosophie médiévale 45. Paris, 1957.

———. *Saint Thomas d'Aquin et la théologie*. Maîtres spirituels 17. Paris, 1959.

———. *La Parole de Dieu I: La foi dans l'intelligence; II: L'Évangile dans le temps*. Cogitatio fidei 10 and 11. Paris, 1964.

———. *Théologie de la matière*. Foi vivante. Paris, 1967.

———. "La condition de créature. Sur trois textes de saint Thomas." *AHDLMA* 37 (1970): 9–16.

———. "Les passions vertueuses. L'anthropologie de saint Thomas." *RPL* 72 (1974): 11–18.

———. *Une école de théologie: Le Saulchoir*. Théologies. Paris, 1937 and 1985.

Cicero, *De finibus bonorum et malorum*. With a translation by H. Rackham. The Loeb Classical Library. Cambridge: Harvard University Press, 1961.

———. *De officiis*. With a translation by Walter Miller. The Loeb Classical Library. Cambridge: Harvard University Press, 1968.

Clement of Alexandria. *Paedagogus*. Translated into English as *Christ the Educator*. Trans. Simon P. Wood. Fathers of the Church 23. New York, 1954.

———. *Protreptikos*. With a translation by G.W. Butterworth. The Loeb Classical Library. Cambridge: Harvard University Press, 1939.

Cointet, P. de. "'Attache-toi au Christ!' L'imitation du Christ dans la vie spirituelle selon S. Thomas d'Aquin." *Sources* 12 (1989): 64–74.

Colombo, G., A. Rimoldi, and A. Valsecchi, eds. See *Miscellanea Carlo Figini*.

Combes, A. "Le P. John F. Dedek et la connaissance quasi-expérimentale des Personnes divines selon saint Thomas d'Aquin." *Divinitas* 7 (1963): 3–82.

Vatican Council II: the Conciliar and Post-Conciliar Documents. Rev. ed. Ed. Austin Flannery. New York: Costello, 1992.

Congar, Yves. M.-J. *Divided Christendom; A Catholic Study of the Problem of Reunion*. London: G. Bles, 1939.

———. "The Idea of the Church in St. Thomas Aquinas." *The Thomist* 1 (1939): 331–59.

———. "Théologie." *DTC*. Vol. 15/1, cols. 342–502. 1946.

———. *Lay People in the Church; A Study for a Theology of Laity*. Trans. Donald Attwater. London: Geoffrey Chapman, 1957.

———. "Quod omnes tangit, ab omnibus tractari et approbari debet." *Revue historique de Droit français et étranger.* Series 4, pp. 210–59. 1958.

———. "*Dum visibiliter Deum cognoscimus.* Méditation théologique." *La Maison-Dieu* 59 (1959): 132–61.

———. "Aspects ecclésiologiques de la querelle entre Mendiants et Séculiers dans la deuxième moitié du XIIIᵉ siècle et au début du XIVᵉ siècle." *AHDLMA* 28 (1961): 34–151.

———. *Les voies du Dieu vivant.* Paris, 1962.

———. *The Revelation of God.* Parts 1–2 of *Les voies du Dieu Vivant.* Trans. A. Manson and L. C. Sheppard. New York: Herder and Herder, 1968.

———. *Faith and Spiritual Life.* Parts 3–4 of *Les voies du Dieu Vivant.* Trans. A. Manson and L. C. Sheppard. New York: Herder and Herder, 1969.

———. *Tradition and Traditions; An Historical and a Theological Essay.* New York: Macmillan, 1967.

———. *Sainte Église.* Etudes et approches ecclésiologiques. Unam sanctam 41. Paris, 1963.

———. "Tradition et sacra doctrina chez saint Thomas d'Aquin." In *Église et Tradition*, pp. 157–94.

———. "Avertissement." In Y. Congar and J. Hamer, eds., *La liberté religieuse*, pp. 12. Unam Sanctam 60. Paris, 1967.

———. "La pneumatologie dans la théologie catholique." *RSPT* 51 (1967): 250–58.

———. *L'Église de saint Augustin à l'époque moderne.* Paris, 1970.

———. "Pneumatologie ou 'christomonisme' dans la tradition latine?" In *Ecclesia a Spiritu Sancto edocta*, pp. 42–63.

———. "La personne 'Église'." *RT* 71 (1971): 613–40.

———. "On the *hierarchia veritatum.*" *Orientalia christiana analecta* 195 (1973): 409–20.

———. "'Ecclesia' et 'populus (fidelis)' dans l'ecclésiologie de saint Thomas." In *St. Thomas Aquinas 1274–1974 Commemorative Studies.* Vol. 1, pp. 159–74.

———. "Orientations de Bonaventure et surtout de Thomas d'Aquin dans leur vision de l'Église et celle de l'État." In *1274—Année-charnière*, pp. 691–712.

———. *Une vie pour la vérité: Jean Puyo interroge le Père Congar.* Paris, 1975.

———. "Vision de l'Église chez Thomas d'Aquin." *RSPT* 62 (1978): 523–42.

———. "Saint Augustin et le traité scolastique *De gratia capitis.*" *Augustinianum* 20 (1980): 79–93.

———. *I Believe in the Holy Spirit.* Trans. David Smith. 3 vols. New York: Seabury Press, 1983.

———. "Sur la trilogie Prophète-Roi-Prêtre." *RSPT* 67 (1983): 97–116.

———. *Thomas d'Aquin, Sa vision de la théologie et de l'Église.* London, 1984.

———. *Église et Papauté, Regards historiques.* Cogitatio fidei 184. Paris, 1994.

Conus, H.-T. "Divinisation." *DS.* Vol. 3, col. 1426–1432. 1957.

Corbin, M. "La Parole devenue chair. Lecture de la première question de la *Tertia Pars* de la Somme théologique de Thomas d'Aquin." *RSPT* 67 (1978): 5–40.

Cosmas Indicopleustes. *Topographie chrétienne. SC* 141. Paris, 1968.

Couesnongle, V. de. "La causalité du maximum. L'utilisation par saint Thomas d'un passage d'Aristote." *RSPT* 38 (1954): 433–44.

———. "La causalité du maximum. Pourquoi saint Thomas a-t-il mal cité Aristote?" *RSPT* 38 (1954): 658–80.

Cunningham, F. L. B. *St. Thomas' Doctrine on the Divine Indwelling in the Light of Scholastic Tradition.* Dubuque, Iowa, 1955.

Dachs, H., and G. Putz, eds. See *Politik und christliche Verantwortung.*

Dabin, P. *Le sacerdoce royal des fidèles dans la tradition ancienne et moderne.* Musseum Lessianum 48. Brussels-Paris, 1950.

Dasseleer, P. "Etre et beauté selon saint Thomas d'Aquin." In *Actualité de la pensée médié-vale*, pp. 268–86.

Decker, B. "Schriftprinzip und Ergänzungstradition in der Theologie des hl. Thomas von Aquin." In *Schrift und Tradition: herausgegeben von der deutschen Arbeitsgemeinschaft für Mariologie*, pp. 191–221. Essen, 1962.

Dedek, J. F. *Experimental Knowledge of the Indwelling Trinity: An Historical Study of the Doctrine of S. Thomas.* Mundelein, Ill., 1958.

———. "*Quasi experimentalis cognitio*: a Historical Approach of the Meaning of St. Thomas." *JTS* 22 (1961): 357–90.

De Dignitate hominis: Mélanges offerts à Carlos-Josaphat Pinto de Oliveira. Ed. A. Holderegger, et al. Fribourg, 1987.

Deman, Th. "Accroissement des vertus." *DS.* Vol. 1, cols. 137–66. 1937.

———. "Pour une vie spirituelle 'objective'." *La Vie spirituelle* 71 (1944): 100–122.

———. *La Prudence.* French translation with notes and appendices of St. Thomas Aquinas, *Summa theologiae* IIa IIae qq. 47–56. Revue des Jeunes. Paris-Tournai-Rome, 1949.

Denifle, H., and E. Chatelain, eds. See *Chartularium Universitatis Parisiensis.*

Dictionnaire d'éthique et de philosophie morale. Ed. M. Canto-Sperber. Paris, 1996.

Die Mysterien des Lebens Jesu und die christliche Existenz. Ed. L. Scheffczyk. Aschaffen-burg, 1984.

Dieu et l'être: Exégèses d'Exode 3,14 et de Coran 20,11–24. Études Augustiniennes 8. Paris, 1978.

Dockx, S. "Esprit Saint, âme de l'Église." In *Ecclesia a Spiritu Sancto edocta*, pp. 65–80.

La doctrine de la révélation divine de saint Thomas d'Aquin. Ed. L. Elders. Studi Tomistici 37. Vatican City, 1990.

Dondaine, H.-F. *La Trinité.* French translation with notes and appendices of St. Thomas Aquinas, *Summa theologiae* Ia qq. 27–43. Revue des Jeunes. 2 vols. Paris-Tournai-Rome, 1943, 1946.

———. "Hugues de Saint-Cher et la condamnation de 1241." *RSPT* 33 (1949): 170–74.

———. "L'objet et le 'medium' de la vision béatifique chez les théologiens du XIIIᵉ siècle." *RTAM* 19 (1952): 60–130.

———. "Cognoscere de Deo *quid est*." *RTAM* 22 (1955): 72–78.

Dondaine, H.-F., and B.-G. Guyot. "Guerric de Saint-Quentin et la condamnation de 1241." *RSPT* 44 (1960): 225–42.

Donneaud, H. "La surnaturalité du motif de la foi théologale chez le Père Labourdette." *RT* 92 (1992): 197–238.

D'Onofrio, G., ed. See *Storia della Teologia.*

Downey, M., ed. See *The New Dictionary of Catholic Spirituality.*

Dumont, C. "La réflexion sur la méthode théologique" *NRT* 83 (1961): 1034–50; 84 (1962): 17–35.

Dupuy, M. See Solignac, A., "Spiritualité."

Ecclesia a Spiritu Santo edocta. Lumen Gentium, 53: *Mélanges théologiques offerts à Mgr Gérard Philips.* Gembloux, 1970.

Eco, Umberto. *The Aesthetics of Thomas Aquinas.* Trans. Hugh Bredin. Cambridge: Harvard University Press, 1988.

Église et Tradition. Ed. J. Betz and H. Fries. Le Puy, 1963.

Elders, L. "La doctrine de la conscience de saint Thomas d'Aquin." *RT* 83 (1983): 533–57.

———. "Le Saint-Esprit et la 'Lex Nova' dans les commentaires bibliques de S. Thomas d'Aquin." In *Credo in Spiritum Sanctum*, Atti del Congresso teologico internazionale di Pneumatologia, vol. 2, pp. 1195–1205. Vatican City, 1983.

———. *Autour de saint Thomas d'Aquin: Recueil d'études sur sa pensée philosophique et théologique.* 2 vols. Paris-Bruges, 1987.

Elders, L., ed. See *La doctrine de la révélation divine.*

Elders, L., and K. Hedwig, eds. *Lex et Libertas. Freedom and Law according to St. Thomas Aquinas.* Studi Tomistici 30. Rome, 1987.

Elisondo Aragón, F. "Conocer por experiencia. Un estudio de sus modos y valoración en la *Summa theologica* de Tomás de Aquino." *RET* 52 (1992): 5–50, 189–229.

Elsässer, M. *Das Person-Verständnis des Boethius.* Münster, 1973.

Emery, G. "Le Père et l'oeuvre trinitaire de création selon le Commentaire des Sentences de S. Thomas d'Aquin." In *Ordo sapientiae et amoris*, pp. 85–117.

———. *La Trinité créatrice. Trinité et création dans les commentaires aux Sentences de Thomas d'Aquin et de ses précurseurs Albert le Grand et Bonaventure.* Bibliothèque thomiste 47. Paris, 1995.

———. "Le photinisme et ses précurseurs chez saint Thomas. Cérinthe, les Ebionites, Paul de Samosate et Photin." *RT* 95 (1995): 371–98.

———. "Trinité et Création. Le principe trinitaire de la création dans les Commentaires d'Albert le Grand, de Bonaventure et de Thomas d'Aquin sur les Sentences." *RSPT* 79 (1995): 405–30.

Emonet, P.-M. *L'âme humaine expliquée aux simples*, Chambray-lès-Tours, 1994.

Eschmann, I. T. "A Thomistic Glossary on the Principle of the Preeminence of a Common Good." *MS* 5 (1943): 123–65.

———. "'Bonum commune melius est quam bonum unius'. Eine Studie über den Wertvorrang des Personalen bei Thomas von Aquin." *MS* 6 (1944): 62–120.

———. "St. Thomas Aquinas on the Two Powers." *MS* 20 (1958): 177–205.

Etica et società contemporanea. Ed. A. Lobato. Troisième Congrès de la Société internationale S. Thomas d'Aquin. ST 48–50. Rome, 1992.

Étienne, J. "Loi et grâce. Le concept de loi nouvelle dans la *Somme théologique* de S. Thomas d'Aquin." *RTL* 16 (1985): 5–22.

Ewbank, M. B. "Diverse Orderings of Dionysius's *Triplex Via* by St. Thomas Aquinas." *MS* 52 (1990): 82–109.

Ferraro, G. "Lo Spirito Santo nel commento di San Tommaso ai capitoli XIV–XVI del quarto Vangelo." In *Tommaso d'Aquino nel suo settimo centenario*, vol. 4, pp. 79–91. Naples, 1976.

———. "Il tema dello Spirito Santo nel Commento di San Tommaso d'Aquino all'Epistola agli Ebrei (Annotazioni di dottrina e di esegesi tomista)." *ST* 13 (1981): 172–88.

———. "Aspetti di pneumatologia nell'esegesi di S. Tommaso d'Aquino dell'Epistola ai Romani." *Euntes Docete* 36 (1983): 51–78.

———. "La pneumatologia di San Tommaso d'Aquino nel suo commento al quarto Vangelo." *Angelicum* 66 (1989): 193–263.

———. "Interpretazione dei testi pneumatologici biblici nel trattato trinitario della 'Summa theologiae' di san Tommaso d'Aquino (*1a qq. 27–43*)." *ST* 45 (1992): 53–65.

Filthaut, Th. *La Théologie des Mystères. Exposé de la controverse.* Paris-Tournai, 1954.

Finalité et intentionnalité: Doctrine thomiste et perspectives modernes. Actes du Colloque de Louvain-la-Neuve et Louvain, 21–23 mai 1990. Ed. J. Follon and J. McEvoy. Paris-Leuven, 1992.

Fitzgerald, L. P. "St. Thomas Aquinas and the Two Powers." *Angelicum* 56 (1979): 515–56.

Follon, J., and J. McEvoy, eds. See *Finalité et intentionnalité.*

Fries, H., and J. Betz, eds. See *Église et Tradition.*

Froidure, M. "La théologie protestante de la loi nouvelle peut-elle se réclamer de saint Thomas?" *RSPT* 51 (1967): 53–61.

Gaillard, J. "Chronique de liturgie. La théologie des mystères." *RT* 57 (1957): 510–51.

Gardeil, A. "Fruits du Saint-Esprit." *DTC*.Vol. 6, col. 944–49. 1920.

———. *La structure de l'âme et l'expérience mystique.* Vol. 1. Paris, ³1927.

Gardeil, Henri Dominique. *La charité.* French translation with notes and appendices of St. Thomas Aquinas, *Summa theologiae* IIa IIae qq. 23–46. Vol. 3. Revue des Jeunes. Paris, 1957.

———. *Introduction to the Philosophy of St. Thomas Aquinas.* Vol. 3. Trans. John A. Otto. St. Louis: B. Herder, 1958.

———. "L'image de Dieu." In *Les origines de l'homme* (French translation with notes and appendices of St. Thomas Aquinas, *Summa theologiae* Ia, qq. 90–102), pp. 380–421. Revue des Jeunes. Paris-Tournai-Rome, 1963.

———. "La méthode de la théologie." In *La Théologie* (French translation with notes and appendices of St. Thomas Aquinas, *Summa theologiae* Ia, Prologue and q. 1), pp. 93–140. Revue des Jeunes. Paris-Tournai-Rome, 1968.

Garrigou-Lagrange, Réginald. *The Three Ages of the interior life: Prelude of Life Eternal.* Trans. Sr. M. Timothea Doyle. St. Louis, Mo.: B. Herder, 1947–48.

Gauthier, R.-A. *Magnanimité. L'idéal de la grandeur dans la philosophie païenne et dans la théologie chrétienne.* Bibliothèque thomiste 27. Paris, 1951.

———. *La morale d'Aristote.* Paris, 1958.

Geffré, C. "Théologie naturelle et révélation dans la connaissance du Dieu un." In *L'existence de Dieu,* pp. 297–317. Cahiers de l'actualité religieuse 16. Paris-Tournai, 1961.

Geiger, L.-B. "Saint Thomas d'Aquin et le composé humain." In *L'âme et le corps,* pp. 201–20. Recherches et débats 35. Paris, 1961.

———. "Les idées divines dans l'oeuvre de S. Thomas." In *St. Thomas Aquinas 1274–1974. Commemorative Studies,* vol. 1, pp. 175–209.

———. "L'homme image de Dieu. A propos de *Summa theologiae,* Ia, 93, 4." *RFNS* 66 (1974): 511–32.

Geiselmann, J. R. "Christus und die Kirche nach Thomas von Aquin." *Theologische Quartalschrift* 107 (1926): 198–222; 107 (1927): 233–55.

Gervais, M. "Incarnation et immuabilité divine." *RevSR* 50 (1976): 215–43.

Gerwing, M., and G. Ruppert, eds. See *Renovatio et Reformatio.*

Gillon, L.-B. "Charité, Dominicains." *DS.* Vol. 2, col. 580–84. 1953.

———. "L'imitation du Christ et la moral de saint Thomas." *Angelicum* 36, (1959): 263–86.

———. *Christ and Moral Theology.* Translation of "Charité, Dominicains" and "L'imitation du Christ et la morale de saint Thomas." Staten Island, 1967.

Gilson, É. "Pourquoi saint Thomas a critiqué saint Augustin." *AHDLMA* 1 (1926–1927): 5–127.

———. *The Spirit of Mediaeval Philosophy.* Trans. A. H. C. Downes. New York: Charles Scribner's Sons, 1940.

———. *Les tribulations de Sophie.* Paris, 1967.

———. *Le Thomisme:* Introduction à la philosophie de saint Thomas d'Aquin. Études de philosophie médiévale 1. Paris, ⁶1986.

———. *The Christian Philosophy of St. Thomas Aquinas.* Translation of the fifth edition of *Le Thomisme* by L. K. Shook. New York: Random House, 1956.

Goicoechea, D., ed. See *The Nature and Pursuit of Love.*

Grabmann, M. *Die Lehre des heiligen Thomas von Aquin von der Kirche als Gotteswerk.* Regensburg, 1903.

Gregory (Saint). *Moralia in Job libri XI–XXII.* Ed. M. Adriaen. CCSL 143. Brepols, 1979.

Grillmeier, A. "Généralités historiques sur les mystères de Jésus." Mysterium salutis 11, pp. 333–57. Paris, 1975.

Hamer, J., ed. See Congar, Y. M.-J., "Avertissement."

Hamonic, T.-M. "Dieu peut-il être légitimement convoité? Quelques aspects de la théologie thomiste de l'amour selon le P. Labourdette." *RT* 92 (1992): 239–64.

Hankey, W. J. "'Dionysius dixit, lex divinitatis est ultima per media reducere'. Aquinas, Hierocray and the 'Augustinisme politique'." In *Tommaso d'Aquino: Proposte nuove di lettura*, pp. 119–50.

Harding, A. "Aquinas and the Legislators." In *Théologie et Droit dans la science politique de l'Etat moderne*, pp. 51–61.

Henn, W. *The Hierarchy of Truths according to Yves Congar O.P.* Analecta Gregoriana 246. Rome, 1987.

Héris, Ch.-V. *Le gouvernement divin.* French translation with notes and appendices of St. Thomas Aquinas, *Summa theologiae* Ia, qq. 103–9. Revue des Jeunes. Paris-Tournai-Rome, 1959.

Holderegger, A. ed. See *De Dignitate hominis*.

Holtz, F. "La valeur sotériologique de la résurrection du Christ selon saint Thomas." *ETL* 29 (1953): 609–45.

Hubert, M. "L'humour de S. Thomas en face de la méthode scolastique." In *1274—Année-charnière*, pp. 725–39.

Huerga, A. "La perfección del homo spiritualis." *ST* 42 (1991): 242–49.

Hugueny, E. "Imperfection." *DTC.* Vol. 7, col. 1286–1298. 1923.

Humain à l'image de Dieu. La théologie et les sciences humaines face au problème de l'anthropologie. Travaux de troisième cycle en théologie systématique des Facultés de théologie des Universités romandes, 1985–1986. Ed. P. Bühler. Lieux Théologiques 15. Geneva, 1989.

Humbrecht, T.-D. "La théologie négative chez saint Thomas d'Aquin." *RT* 93 (1993): 535–66; 94 (1994): 71–99.

Hünemörder, C. "Thomas von Aquin und die Tiere." *MM* 19 (1988): 192–210.

Imbach, R. "*Dieu comme artiste.* Méditation historique sur les liens de nos conceptions de Dieu et du Beau." *Les Échos de Saint-Maurice* n.s. 15 (1985): 5–19.

——. "Démocratie ou monarchie? La discussion sur le meilleur régime politique chez quelques interprètes français de Thomas d'Aquin (1893–1928)." In *Saint Thomas au XXe siècle*, pp. 335–50.

Imbach, R. and M.-H. Meleard. *Philosophes médiévaux. Anthologie de textes philosophiques (XIIIe–XIVe siècles).* Paris, 1986.

John Chrysostom (Saint). *Ad Demetrium De compunctione.* PL 47, 406.

John Damascene (Saint). *De fide orthodoxa. Burgundionis versio.* Ed. E. Buytaert. Louvain-Paderborn, 1955.

John of the Cross. *The Collected Works of St. John of the Cross.* Trans. Kieran Kavanaugh and Otilio Rodriguez. Washington, D.C.: ICS Publications, 1979.

John of St. Thomas. *The Gifts of the Holy Ghost.* Trans. Dominic Hughes. New York: Sheed and Ward, 1951.

Jordan, M. D. "Aquinas's Construction of a Moral Account of the Passions." *FZPT* 33 (1986): 71–97.

——. "De Regno and the Place of Political Thinking in Thomas Aquinas." *Medioevo* 18 (1992): 151–68.

——. *The Alleged Aristotelianism of Thomas Aquinas.* The Etienne Gilson Series 15, pp. 32–40. Toronto, 1992.

Journet, Charles. *L'Église du Verbe incarné.* 2 vols. Paris, 1951.

——. *The Church of the Word Incarnate; An Essay in Speculative Theology.* Trans. A. H. C. Downes. New York: Sheed and Ward, 1955.

———. *La Messe, présence du sacrifice de la Croix*. Paris, 1957.
———. "Palamisme et thomisme." *RT* 60 (1960): 429–62.
———. "La sainteté de l'Église. Le livre de Jacques Maritain." *NV* 46 (1971): 1–33.
Käppeli, Th. "Una raccolta di prediche attribuite a S. Tommaso d'Aquino." *AFP* 13 (1943): 59–94.
Kovach, F. J. "Divine Art in Saint Thomas Aquinas." In *Arts libéraux et Philosophie au Moyen Age*, Actes du quatrième Congrès international de philosophie médiévale, Montréal 27 août–2 septembre 1967, pp. 663–71. Montreal-Paris, 1969.
Kühn, U. *Via caritatis. Theologie des Gesetzes bei Thomas von Aquin*. Göttingen, 1965.
Künzle, P. "Thomas von Aquin und die moderne Eschatologie." *FZPT* 8 (1961): 109–20.
Labourdette, M-M. "Connaissance pratique et savoir moral." *RT* 48 (1948): 142–79.
———. "Saint Thomas et la théologie thomiste." In "Dons du Saint-Esprit," *DS*, vol. 3, col. 1610–35. 1957.
———. "La vie théologale selon saint Thomas: L'objet de la foi." *RT* 58 (1958): 597–622.
———. *Cours de théologie morale: La Charité (IIa–IIae, 23–46)*. Toulouse, 1959–1960.
———. "La vie théologale selon saint Thomas: L'affection dans la foi." *RT* 60 (1960): 364–80.
———. "Espérance et histoire." *RT* 72 (1972): 455–74.
———. "La morale chrétienne et ses sources." *RT* 77 (1977): 625–42.
———. "Jacques Maritain nous instruit encore." *RT* 87 (1987): 655–63.
———. *Cours de théologie morale I², La fin dernière de la vie humaine (La Béatitude)*. Rev. ed. Toulouse, 1990.
———. "L'idéal dominicain." *RT* 92 (1992): 344–54.
———. "Qu'est-ce que la théologie spirituelle?" *RT* 92 (1992): 355–72.
Lafont, G. *Structures et méthode dans la Somme théologique de saint Thomas d'Aquin*. Paris, 1961.
Lafontaine, R. *La résurrection et l'exaltation du Christ chez Thomas d'Aquin. Analyse comparative de S. Th. IIIa q.53 à 59*. Excerpta ex Diss. P.U.G. Rome, 1983.
———. "La personne du Père dans la pensée de saint Thomas." In R. Lafontaine et al., eds., *L'Ecriture âme de la théologie*, pp. 81–108. Institut d'études théologiques 9. Brussels, 1990.
Lagarde, G. de. *La naissance de l'esprit laïque au déclin du moyen âge*. Vol. 2. Paris, ²1958.
Lanversin, F. de. See Deman, Th., "Accroissement des vertus."
Laporta, J. *La Destinée de la nature humaine selon saint Thomas d'Aquin*. Etudes de philosophie médiévale 55. Paris, 1965.
La Soujeole, B.-D. de. "'Société' et 'communion' chez saint Thomas d'Aquin. Etude d'ecclésiologie." *RT* 90 (1990): 587–622.
Laugier de Beaurecueil, M.-J. S. de. "L'homme image de Dieu selon saint Thomas d'Aquin." *Études et Recherches* 8 (1952): 45–82; 9 (1955): 37–96.
Lavalette, H. de. *La notion d'appropriation dans la théologie trinitaire de S. Thomas d'Aquin*. Rome, 1959.
Leclercq, J. "Spiritualitas." *Studi medievali* Serie terza 3 (1962): 279–96.
Lécuyer, J. "La pérennité des mystères du Christ." *VS* 87 (1952): 451–64.
———. "La causalité efficiente des mystères du Christ selon saint Thomas." *DC* 6 (1953): 91–120.
Leroy, M.-V. "Chronique d'anthropologie." *RT* 75 (1975): 121–42.
———. "Théologie de la vie religieuse." *RT* 92 (1992): 324–43.
L'homme et son univers au Moyen Age. Actes du septième congrès international de philosophie médiévale (30 août–4 septembre 1982). Ed. C. Wenin. Vol. 1. Louvain-la-Neuve, 1986.

Libera, A. de, and É. Zum Brunn, eds. See *Celui qui est*.

———. Introduction, translation, notes, and index. See Thomas Aquinas, *L'unité de l'intellect contre les Averroïstes*.

———. "Averroisme éthique et philosophie mystique. De la félicité intellectuelle à la vie bienheureuse." In L. Bianchi, ed., *Filosofia e Teologia nel Trecento: Studi in ricordo di Eugenio Randi*, pp. 33–56. Louvain-la-Neuve, 1994.

Livingstone, E. A., ed. See *Studia Patristica*.

Lobato, A., ed. See *Etica et società contemporanea*.

Lohaus, G. *Die Geheimnisse des Lebens Jesu in der Summa Theologiae des hl. Thomas von Aquin*. Freiburg. theol. Studien 131. Freiburg im Breisgau: Herder, 1985.

"La loi dans l'Église." *Communio* (Paris) (1978/3).

Loi et Évangile. Héritage confessionnel et interpellations contemporaines. Actes de troisième cycle d'éthique des Universités de Suisse romande, 1979–1980. Ed. S. Pinckaers and J.-M. Aubert. Geneva, 1981.

Longpré, E. "Bonaventure." *DS*. Vol. 1, col. 1789–1790. 1937.

Lottin, O. "Syndérèse et conscience au XIIᵉ et XIIIᵉ siècles." In *Psychologie et Morale au XIIᵉ et XIIIᵉ siècles*, vol. 2, pp. 103–350. Louvain-Gembloux, 1948.

———. *Morale fondamentale*. Tournai, 1954.

Lubac, Henri de. *Surnaturel: Etudes historiques*. Théologie 8. Paris, 1946.

———. *Augustinianism and Modern Theology*. Trans. Lancelot Sheppard. New York: Herder, 1969.

———. *The Mystery of the Supernatural*. Trans. Rosemary Sheed. New York: Herder and Herder, 1967.

———. *Mémoire sur l'occasion de mes écrits*. Namur, 1989.

Luyten, N. A. "L'homme dans la conception de S. Thomas." In *L'anthropologie de saint Thomas*, pp. 35–53.

Madec, G. *La patrie et la voie: Le Christ dans la vie et la pensée de saint Augustin*. Jésus et Jésus-Christ 36. Paris, 1989.

Maidl, L. *Desiderii Interpres. Genese und Grundstruktur der Gebetstheologie des Thomas von Aquin*. Veröffentlichungen des Grabmann-Institutes 38. Paderborn, 1994.

Mansion, A. "L'immortalité de l'âme et de l'intellect d'après Aristote." *RPL* 51 (1953): 444–72.

Manzanedo, M. F. "El hombre come 'Microcosmos' según santo Tomás." *Angelicum* 56 (1979): 62–92.

———. *Las pasiones o emociones según santo Tomás*. Madrid, 1984.

———. "La amistad según santo Tomás." *Angelicum* 71 (1994): 371–426.

Maritain, J. *Du régime temporel et de la liberté*. Paris, 1933.

———. *De l'Église du Christ*. Paris, 1970.

———. *Integral Humanism* in *Integral Humanism; Freedom in the Modern World; and A Letter on Independence*. Ed. Otto Bird. Trans. Otto Bird, Joseph Evans, and Richard O'Sullivan. Notre Dame, Ind.: University of Notre Dame Press, 1996.

———. *Christianity and Democracy; and The Right of Man and the Natural Law*. Translated by Doris C. Anson. Introduction by Donald A. Gallagher. San Francisco: Ignatius Press, 1986.

———. *Distinguish to Unite, or, The Three Degrees of Knowledge*. Translated under the supervision of Gerard B. Phelan. Notre Dame, Ind.: University of Notre Dame Press, 1995.

———. *Person and the Common Good*. Trans. John J. Fitzgerald. Notre Dame, Ind.: University of Notre Dame Press, 1966.

———. "Réflexions sur le savoir théologique." *RT* 69 (1969): 5–27.

———. *On the Church of Christ; The Person of the Church and Her Personnel.* Trans. Joseph W. Evans. Notre Dame, Ind.: University of Notre Dame Press, 1973.

———. *Approaches to God.* Trans. Peter O'Reilly. London: Allen and Unwin, 1955.

———. *La loi naturelle ou loi non écrite.* Unedited text, prepared by G. Brazzola. Prémices 7. Fribourg, 1987.

Martinez Barrera, J. "Sur la finalité en politique: la question du bien commun selon saint Thomas." In *Finalité et intentionnalité*, pp. 148–61.

———. "De l'ordre politique chez saint Thomas d'Aquin." In *Actualité de la pensée médiévale*, pp. 247–67.

Marty, F. *La perfection de l'homme selon S. Thomas d'Aquin, Ses fondements ontologiques et leur vérification dans l'ordre actuel.* Rome, 1962.

Maurer, Armand. "St. Thomas on the Sacred Name 'Tetragrammaton'." *MS* 34 (1972): 274–86.

———. *Being and Knowing: Studies in Thomas Aquinas and Later Medievals Philosophers.* Toronto, 1990.

Mauro, L. *'Umanità' della passione in S. Tommaso.* Florence, 1974.

McEvoy, J. "Amitié, attirance et amour chez S. Thomas d'Aquin." *RPL* 91 (1993): 383–408.

McEvoy, J., and J. Follon, eds. See *Finalité et intentionnalité.*

Melloni, A. "Christianitas nelli scritti di Tommaso d'Aquino." *Cristianesimo nella storia* 6 (1985): 45–69.

Mennessier, A.-I. *Saint Thomas d'Aquin.* Paris, 1942, ²1957.

———. *Saint Thomas d'Aquin. L'homme chrétien.* 2nd ed. Foi vivante 392. Paris: Cerf, 1998.

Merle, H. "Ars." *BPM* 28 (1986): 95–133.

Merriell, D. J. *To the Image of the Trinity: A Study in the Development of Aquinas's Teaching.* Studies and Texts 96. Toronto, 1990.

Mersch, É. *The Whole Christ: The Historical Development of the Theology of the Mystical Body in Scripture and Tradition.* Translation of the second edition of *Le Corps mystique* (Brussels-Paris, ³1951) by John R. Kelley. Milwaukee, Wisc.: Bruce, 1938.

Meyendorff, J. *Introduction à l'étude de Grégoire Palamas.* Patristica Sorbonensia. Paris, 1959.

Miscellanea Carlo Figini. Ed. G. Colombo, A. Rimoldi, and A. Valsecchi. Venegono Inferiore, 1964.

Mitterer, A. *Geheimnisvoller Leib Christi nach St Thomas von Aquin und nach Papst Pius XII.* Vienna, 1950.

Moltmann, J. *Crucified God: The Cross of Christ as the Foundation and Criticism of Christian Theology.* Trans. R. A. Wilson and John Bowden. New York: Harper and Row, 1974.

———. "Christliche Hoffnung: Messianisch oder tranzendent? Eine theologisches Gespräch mit Joachim von Fiore und Thomas von Aquin." *MThZ* 33 (1982): 241–60.

Mongillo, D. "La Concezione dell'Uomo nel Prologo della Ia IIae." In *De Homine: Studia hodiernae anthropologiae*, Acta VII Congressus thomistici internationalis, vol. 2, pp. 227–31. Rome, 1972.

———. "La fin dernière de la personne humaine." *RT* 92 (1992): 123–40.

———. "Les béatitudes et la béatitude. Le dynamisme de la *Somme de théologie* de Thomas d'Aquin: une lecture de la *Ia–IIae* q.69." *RSPT* 78 (1994): 373–88.

Montagnes, B. "La Parole de Dieu dans la création." *RT* 54 (1954): 213–41.

———. "L'axiome de continuité chez saint Thomas." *RSPT* 52 (1968): 201–21.

———. "Les deux fonctions de la sagesse: ordonner et juger." *RSPT* 53 (1969): 675–86.

———. "L'intention philosophique et la destinée de la personne." *RT* 69 (1969): 181–91.

———. "Les activités séculières et le mépris du monde chez saint Thomas d'Aquin. Les emplois du qualificatif 'saecularis'." *RSPT* 55 (1971): 231–49.

———. "Autonomie et dignité de l'homme." *Angelicum* 51 (1974): 186–211.

Morard, M. "L'eucharistie, clé de voûte de l'organisme sacramentel chez saint Thomas d'Aquin." *RT* 95 (1995): 217–50.

Motte, A. "La définition de la vie religieuse selon saint Thomas d'Aquin." *RT* 87 (1987): 442–53.

Muñoz Cuenca, J. M. "Doctrina de santo Tomás sobre los dones del Espíritu Santo en la Suma teológica." *Ephemerides carmeliticae* 25 (1974): 157–243.

Muralt, A. de. "La toute-puissance divine, le possible et la non-contradiction. Le principe de l'intelligibilité chez Occam." *RPL* 84 (1986): 345–61.

Narcisse, G. "Les enjeux épistémologiques de l'argument de convenance selon saint Thomas d'Aquin." In *Ordo sapientiae et amoris*, pp. 143–67.

———. *Les raisons de Dieu: Argument de convenance et esthétique-théologique selon saint Thomas d'Aquin et Hans Urs von Balthasar*. Studia Friburgensia n.s. 83. Fribourg: Éditions universitaires, 1997.

The Nature and Pursuit of Love: The Philosophy of Irving Singer. Ed. D. Goicoechea. Amherst, N.Y., 1995.

Nautin, P. *Je crois à l'Esprit-Saint dans la sainte Église pour la résurrection de la chair. Étude sur l'histoire et la théologie du Symbole*. Unam sanctam 17. Paris, 1947.

Nédoncelle, M. "Les variations de Boèce sur la personne." *RevSR* 29 (1955): 201–38.

Neels, M. G. *La résurrection de Jésus sacrement de salut. La causalité salvifique de la résurrection du Christ dans la sotériologie de St. Thomas*. Diss. P.U.G. Rome, 1973.

The New Dictionary of Catholic Spirituality. Ed. M. Downey. Collegeville, Minn., 1993.

Nicolas, J.-H. "Réactualisation des mystères rédempteurs dans et par les sacrements." *RT* 58 (1958): 20–54.

———. *Dieu connu comme inconnu*. Paris, 1966.

———. *Les Profondeurs de la grâce*. Beauchesne, Paris, 1969.

———. "Aimante et bienheureuse Trinité." *RT* 78 (1978): 271–92.

———. *Contemplation et vie contemplative en christianisme*. Fribourg-Paris, 1980.

———. "Transcendance et immanence de Dieu." *ST* 10 (1981): 337–49.

———. *Synthèse dogmatique: De la Trinité à la Trinité*. Fribourg-Paris, 1985.

———. *Synthèse dogmatique. Complément: De l'univers à la Trinité*. Fribourg-Paris, 1993.

Nicolas, M.-J. "Les mystères de la vie cachée." In *Problèmes actuels de christologie*, pp. 81–100.

———. "L'idée de nature dans la pensée de saint Thomas d'Aquin." *RT* 74 (1974): 533–90.

———. "La théologie des mystères selon saint Thomas d'Aquin." In *Mens concordet voci (Mélanges A.-G. Martimort)*, pp. 489–96. Paris, 1983.

———. "Les dons du Saint-Esprit." *RT* 92 (1992): 141–52.

Noble, H.-D. *La charité*. French translation with notes and appendices of St. Thomas Aquinas, *Summa theologiae* IIa IIae, qq. 23–46. Vols. 1 and 2. Revue des Jeunes. Paris, ²1950 and 1967.

Novitas et veritas vitae: Aux sources du renouveau de la morale chrétienne. Mélanges offerts au Professeur Servais Pinckaers à l'occasion de son 65ᵉ anniversaire. Ed. C.-J. Pinto de Oliveira. Fribourg, 1991.

O'Donnell, J. R., ed. See Boyle, L. E., "The 'De Regno' and the Two Powers."

O'Meara, T. F. "Virtues in the Theology of Thomas Aquinas." *Theological Studies* 58 (1977): 254–85.

O'Neill, C. E. "L'homme ouvert à Dieu (*Capax Dei*). In *L'anthropologie de saint Thomas*, pp. 54–74. Reprinted in *Humain à l'image de Dieu*, pp. 241–60.

Oeuvres complètes du Pseudo-Denys l'Aréopagite. Trans. M. de Gandillac. Paris, 1943.

Ordo sapientiae et amoris: Image et message de saint Thomas d'Aquin à travers les récentes études historiques, herméneutiques et doctrinales. Hommage au Professeur Jean-Pierre Torrell O.P. à l'occasion de son 65ᵉ anniversaire. Ed. C.-J. Pinto de Oliveira. Fribourg, 1993.

Owens, Joseph. "Aquinas-'Darkness of Ignorance' in the Most Refined Notion of God." *The Southwestern Journal of Philosophy* (Norman, Oklahoma) 5 (1974): 93–110.

Parel, A., ed. See *Calgary Aquinas Study.*

Pascal. *Pensées.* Ed. J. Chevalier. La Pléiade. Paris, 1954.

Patfoort, A. *Thomas d'Aquin. Les clefs d'une théologie,* Paris, 1983.

———. "Cognitio ista est quasi experimentalis (1 Sent., d.14, q.2, a.2, ad 3m)." *Angelicum* 63 (1986): 3–13.

———. "Missions divines et expérience des Personnes divines selon S. Thomas." *Angelicum* 63 (1986): 545–59.

———. "Le vrai visage de la satisfaction du Christ selon St. Thomas. Une étude de la *Somme thélogique.*" In *Ordo sapientiae et amoris,* pp. 247–65.

Paul VI, "Lettre au P. Vincent de Couesnongle, Maître de l'Ordre des Frères Prêcheurs, pour le septième centenaire de la mort de saint Thomas." *RT* 75 (1975): 13–14.

Pedrini, A. *Bibliografia tomistica sulla pneumatologia.* Studi tomistici 54. Rome, 1994.

Pegis, Anton C. "Penitus manet ignotum." *MS* 27 (1965): 212–26.

———. "The Separated Soul and its Nature in St. Thomas." In *St. Thomas Aquinas 1274–1974 Commemorative Studies,* vol. 1, pp. 131–58.

Peiper, R., ed. See Avit (Saint), *Letter 14.*

Pelikan, J. "*Imago Dei.* An Explication of *Summa theologiae,* Part 1, Question 93." In *Calgary Aquinas Study,* pp. 29–48.

Perez Robles, H. R. G. *The Experimental Cognition of the Indwelling Trinity in the Just Soul: The Thought of Fr. Ambroise Gardeil in the Line of Saint Thomas.* Diss. P.U.S.T. Rome, 1987.

Perotto, L. A. "La mistica del dolore nel *Commento* di S. Tommaso al *Libro di Giobbe.*" *ST* 60 (1995): 191–203.

Pesch, O. H. "Die bleibende Bedeutung der thomanischen Tugendlehre. Eine theolo-giegeschichtliche Meditation." *FZPT* 21 (1974): 359–91.

———. "La théologie de la vertu et les vertus théologales." *Concilium* 211 (1987): 105–26.

———. *Christian Existence According to Thomas Aquinas.* Toronto, 1989.

———. *Thomas d'Aquin. Grandeur et limites de la théologie médiévale.* Cogitatio fidei 177. Paris, 1994.

Pius XII, *Litterae encyclicae de mystico Iesu Christi corpore deque nostra in eo cum Christo coniunctione: Mystici Corporis Christi.* June 29, 1943. Ed. S. Tromp. Series theologica 26. Rome, 1963.

Pinchard, B., and S. Ricci, eds. See *Rationalisme analogique et humanisme théologique.*

Pinckaers, Servais. "La nature vertueuse de l'espérance." *RT* 58 (1958): 405–42; 623–42.

———. "Recherche de la signification véritable du terme 'spéculatif.'" *NRT* 81 (1959): 673–95.

———. *Les actes humains.* French translation with notes and appendices of St. Thomas Aquinas, Summa theologiae Ia IIae qq. 18–21. Revue des Jeunes. Paris-Tournai-Rome, 1966.

———. "Le désir naturel de voir Dieu." *NV* 51 (1976): 256–73.

———. "La loi de l'Évangile ou Loi nouvelle selon saint Thomas." In *Loi et Évangile.* pp. 57–80.

———. "Le commentaire du sermon sur la montagne par S. Augustin et la morale de S. Thomas." In *La Teologia morale nella storia e nella problematica attuale: Miscellanea L.-B Gillon*, pp. 105–26. Rome, 1982.

———. "La loi évangélique, vie selon l'Esprit, et le Sermon sur la montagne." *NV* 60 (1985): 217–28.

———. "La dignité de l'homme selon S. Thomas d'Aquin." In *De Dignitate hominis*, pp. 89–106.

———. "Le thème de l'image de Dieu en l'homme et l'anthropologie." In *Humain à l'image de Dieu*, pp. 147–63.

———. "Les passions et la morale." *RSPT* 74 (1990): 379–91.

———. "La conception chrétienne de la conscience morale." *NV* 66 (1991): 688–99.

———. "L'instinct et l'Esprit au coeur de l'éthique chrétienne." In *Novitas et veritas vitae*, pp. 213–23.

———. "La conscience et l'erreur." *Communio* 18 (1993): 23–35.

———. "La voie spirituelle du bonheur selon saint Thomas." In *Ordo sapientiae et amoris*, pp. 267–84.

———. *The Sources of Christian Ethics*. Translated of the third edition of *Les sources de la morale chrétienne: Sa méthode, son contenu, son histoire* (Fribourg-Paris, ³1993) by Sr. Mary Thomas Noble, O.P. Washington: The Catholic University of America Press, 1995.

Pinckaers, Servais, and J.-M. Aubert, eds. See *Loi et Évangile*.

Pinto de Oliveira, C.-J. "Homme et femme dans l'anthropologie de Thomas d'Aquin." In *Humain à l'image de Dieu*, pp. 165–90.

———. "La prudence, concept-clé de la morale du P. Labourdette." *RT* 92 (1992): 267–92.

Pinto de Oliveira, C.-J., ed. See *Novitas et veritas vitae*.

Pinto de Oliveira, C.-J., ed. See *Ordo sapientiae et amoris*.

Plé, A. Notes to *Saint Thomas d'Aquin, Somme théologique*, vol. 2. Paris: Cerf, 1984.

———. *Par devoir ou par plaisir?* Paris, 1980.

Politik und christliche Verantwortung: Festschrift für F.-M. Schmölz. Ed. G. Putz, H. Dachs, et al. Innsbruck-Vienna, 1992.

Porter, L. B. "*Summa Contra Gentiles* III, Chapters 131–35: A Rare Glimpse Into the Heart as well as the Mind of Aquinas." *The Thomist* 58 (1994): 245–64.

Potvin, Th.R. *The Theology of the Primacy of Christ According to St. Thomas Aquinas and its Scriptural Foundations*. Studia Friburgensia n.s. 50. Fribourg, 1973.

Pourrat, P. "Commençants." *DS*. Vol. 2, col. 1143–56. 1953.

"Pour une théologie du Droit canonique." *RSPT* 57 (1973).

Prades, J. "*Deus specialiter est in sanctis per gratiam*". *El misterio de la inhabitación de la Trinidad en los escritos de santo Tomás*." Analecta gregoriana 261. Rome, 1993.

Principe, W. H. "The Dynamism of Augustine's Terms for Describing the Highest Trinitarian Image in the Human Person." In *Studia Patristica*, Vol. 18, no. 3, pp. 1291–99.

———. Review of *La controverse de 1270 à l'université de Paris et son retentissement sur la ;ensée de S. Thomas d'Aquin*, by Édouard-Henri Wéber, O.P. *Speculum* 49 (1974): 163–67.

———. "Toward Defining Spirituality." *Studies in Religion/Sciences religieuses* 12 (1983): 127–41.

———. *Thomas Aquinas' Spirituality*. The Etienne Gilson Series 7. Toronto, 1984.

———. "Affectivity and the Heart in Thomas Aquinas Spirituality." In *Spiritualities of the Heart*, pp. 45–63.

———. "Aquinas' Spirituality for Christ's Faithful Living in the World." *Spirituality Today* 44 (1992): 110–31.

———. "Spirituality, Christian." In *The New Dictionary of Catholic Spirituality*, pp. 931–38.
———. "Western Medieval Spirituality." In *The New Dictionary of Catholic Spirituality*, pp. 1027–39.
———. "Loving Friendship According to Thomas Aquinas." In *The Nature and Pursuit of Love*, pp. 128–41.
Problèmes actuels de christologie. Ed. H. Bouëssé and J.-J. Latour. Paris, 1965.
Putz, G., and H. Dachs, eds. See *Politik und christliche Verantwortung*.
Quelquejeu, B. "'Naturalia manent integra'. Contribution à l'étude de la portée méthodologique et doctrinale de l'axiome théologique 'Gratia praesupponit naturam'." *RSPT* 49 (1965): 640–55.
Rationalisme analogique et humanisme théologique. La culture de Thomas de Vio 'Il Gaetano'. Ed. B. Pinchard and S. Ricci. Naples, 1993.
Re, G. *Il cristocentrismo della vita cristiana*. Brescia, 1968.
The Religious Roles of the Papacy: Ideals and Realities, 1150–1300. Ed. C. Ryan. Papers in Mediaeval Studies 8. Toronto, 1989.
Renovatio et Reformatio wider das Bild vom "finisteren" Mittelalter: Festschrift für Ludwig Hödl zum 60. Ed. M. Gerwing and G. Ruppert. Münster, 1986.
Ricci, S., and B. Pinchard, eds. See *Rationalisme analogique et humanisme théologique*.
Riklin, A. *Die beste politische Ordnung nach Thomas von Aquin*. St. Gallen, 1991. Reprinted under the same name in *Politik und christliche Verantwortung*, pp. 67–90.
Rimoldi, A., G. Colombo, and A. Valsecchi, eds. See *Miscellanea Carlo Figini*.
Rodriguez, Pedro, ed. See *Catechismus Romanus*.
Roguet, A.-M. *Les sacrements*. French translation with notes and appendices of St. Thomas Aquinas, *Summa theologiae* IIIa qq. 60–65. Revue des Jeunes. Paris-Tournai-Rome, ²1951.
———. *L'eucharistie*. French translation with notes and appendices of St. Thomas Aquinas, *Summa theologiae* IIIa qq. 73–83. Revue des Jeunes. Paris-Tournai-Rome, 1960 and 1999.
Ruppert, G, and M. Gerwing, eds. See *Renovatio et Reformatio*.
Ryan, C. "The Theology of Papal Primacy in Thomas Aquinas." In *The Religious Roles of the Papacy*, pp. 193–225.
Sabra, G. *Thomas Aquinas' Vision of the Church. Fundamentals of an Ecumenical Ecclesiology*. Mainz, 1987.
Saffrey, H. D., ed. See Thomas Aquinas (Saint), *Sancti Thomae de Aquino super Librum De Causis Expositio*.
St. Thomas Aquinas 1274–1974. Commemorative Studies. Ed. A. Maurer. 2 Vols. Toronto, 1974.
Saint Thomas au XXᵉ siècle. Actes du colloque du Centenaire de la "Revue thomiste," 25–28 mars 1993-Toulouse. Ed. S.-Th. Bonino. Paris, 1994.
Saint Thomas d'Aquin aujourd'hui. Recherches de Philosophie 6. Paris, 1963.
Saranyana, J. I. "En busca de la ciencia política tomasiana. Sobre el libro IV 'De regimine principum'." *ST* 60 (1995): 256–65.
Scheffczyk, L. "Die Bedeutung der Mysterien des Lebens Jesu für Glauben und Leben des Christen." In *Die Mysterien des Lebens Jesu*, pp. 17–34.
———. "Die Stellung des Thomas von Aquin in der Entwicklung der Lehre von den Mysteria Vitae Christi." In *Renovatio et Reformatio*, pp. 44–70.
Schenk, R. "*Omnis Christi actio nostra est instructio*. The Deeds and Sayings of Jesus as Revelation in the View of Thomas Aquinas." In *La doctrine de la révélation divine de saint Thomas d'Aquin*, pp. 103–31.

———. "Perplexus supposito quodam. Notizen zu einem vergessenen Schlüsselbegriff thomasischer Gewissenslehre." *RTAM* 57 (1990): 62–95.

Schillebeeckx, E. "L'instinct de la foi selon S. Thomas d'Aquin." *RSPT* 48 (1964): 377–408.

———. *Revelation and Theology.* Translated from the Dutch by N. D. Smith. New York: Sheed and Ward, 1967.

Schmitt, F. S., ed. See Anselm of Canterbury, *Opera Omnia.*

Schockenhoff, E. *Bonum hominis. Die anthropologischen und theologischen Grundlagen der Tugendethik des Thomas von Aquin.* Tübinger theologische Studien 28. Mainz, 1987.

Schuhl, P.-M. "Préface." In P.-M. Schuhl, ed., *Les Stoïciens.* La Pléiade. Paris, 1962.

Seckler, M. *Instinkt und Glaubenswille nach Thomas von Aquin.* Mainz, 1961.

———. *Le salut et l'histoire, La pensée de saint Thomas d'Aquin sur la théologie de l'histoire.* Cogitatio fidei 21. Paris, 1967.

Seidl, H. "De l'immutabilité de Dieu dans l'acte de la création et dans la relation avec les hommes." *RT* 87 (1987): 615–29.

———. "The Concept of Person in St. Thomas Aquinas: A Contribution to Recent Discussion." *The Thomist* 51 (1987): 435–60.

Sentis, L. "La lumière dont nous faisons usage. La règle de la raison et la loi divine selon Thomas d'Aquin." *RSPT* 79 (1995): 49–69.

Sertillanges, A. D. *L'idée de la création et ses retentissements en philosophie.* Paris, 1945.

Serverat, V. "L'*irrisio fidei* chez Raymond Lulle et S. Thomas d'Aquin." *RT* 90 (1990): 436–48.

Sieben, H. J. "Mystères de la vie du Christ, I: Etude historique." *DS.* Vol. 10, col. 1874–80. 1980.

Smalley, B. *The Gospels in the Schools c. 1100–c. 1280.* London and Ronceverte, 1985.

Smith, J. C. "Christ as 'Pastor', 'Ostium' et 'Agnus' in St. Thomas Aquinas." *Angelicum* 56 (1979): 93–118.

Solignac, A. "Image et ressemblance." *DS.* Vol. 7, col. 1446–51. 1971.

———. "Imperfection et imperfection morale." *DS.* Vol. 7, col. 1620–30. 1971.

———. "L'apparition du mot *spiritualitas* au moyen âge." *ALMA* 44–45 (1985): 185–206.

———. "Spiritualité." *DS.* Vol. 14, col. 1142–73. 1990.

———. "Syndérèse." *DS.* Vol. 14, col. 1407–12. 1990.

———. "Voies (purgative, illuminative, unitive)." *DS.* Vol. 16, col. 1200–215. 1994.

Somme, L. "L'amour parfait chasse-t-il toute crainte? Le rôle joué par l'expression *Timor filialis* dans l'oeuvre de saint Thomas d'Aquin." In *Ordo sapientiae et amoris,* pp. 303–20.

———. *Fils adoptifs de Dieu par Jésus Christ: La filiation divine par adoption dans la théologie de saint Thomas d'Aquin.* Paris: J. Vrin, 1997.

Spiritualities of the Heart: Approaches to Personal Wholeness in Christian Tradition. Ed. A. Callahan. New York-Mahwah, 1990.

Stoeckle, B. *"Gratia supponit naturam": Geschichte und Analyse eines theologischen Axioms.* Studia Anselmiana 49. Rome, 1962.

Storia della Teologia. Vol. 2. *Medioevo.* Ed. G. d'Onofrio. Casale Monferrato-Piemme, 1995.

Studia Patristica 18, 3. Ed. E. A. Livingstone. Oxford and New York, 1982.

Théologie et Droit dans la science politique de l'Etat moderne. Actes de la Table ronde organisée par l'Ecole française de Rome avec le concours du CNRS, Rome, 12–14 novembre 1987. Collection de l'Ecole française de Rome 147. Rome, 1991.

Thomas Aquinas (Saint). *Sancti Thomae Aquinatis doctoris angelici Opera omnia iussu Leonis XIII. P. M. edita.* Cura et studio fratrum praedicatorum. Romae, 1882 ff.

———. *Liber de Veritate Catholicae Fidei contra errores Infidelium qui dicitur Summa contra Gentiles*. Ed. P. Marc. 3 vols. Paris, 1967.

———. *Super Evangelium S. Matthaei lectura*. Ed. R. Cai. Taurini-Romae, [5]1951.

———. *Super Evangelium S. Ioannis lectura*. Ed. R. Cai. Taurini-Romae, 1952.

———. *Catena aurea in quatuor Evangelia*. Ed. A. Guarienti. 2 vols. Taurini-Romae, 1953.

———. *Super Epistolas S. Pauli lectura*. Ed. R. Cai. 2 vols. Taurini-Romae, [7]1953.

———. *In librum beati Dionysii De divinis nominibus expositio*. Ed. C. Pera. Taurini-Romae, 1950.

———. *Sancti Thomae de Aquino super librum De causis expositio*. Ed. H. D. Saffrey. Textus philosophici Friburgenses 4/5. Fribourg, 1954.

———. *L'unité de l'intellect contre les Averroïstes suivi des Textes contre Averroès antérieurs à 1270*. Latin text, with translation, introduction, bibliography, chronology, notes, and index by A. de Libera. Paris, 1994.

———. *Collationes in decem preceptis*. See Torrell, J.-P.

———. *Summa theologiae*. Latin text and English translation. Blackfriars Edition. New York: McGraw Hill, 1964.

———. *Summa contra Gentiles*. 4 Books. Trans. A. C. Pegis, J. F. Anderson, V. J. Bourke, and C. J. O'Neill. Notre Dame, Ind.: University of Notre Dame Press, 1975.

———. *Commentary on Aristotle's Nicomachean Ethics*. Trans. C. I. Litzinger. 2 vols. Chicago: University of Chicago Press, 1964. Reprint, with a foreword by Ralph McInerny. 2 vols. in 1. Notre Dame, Ind.: Dumb Ox Books, 1993.

———. *Commentary on the Book of Causes*. Translated and annotated by Vincent A. Guagliardo, Charles A. Hess, and Richard C. Taylor. Washington, D.C.: Catholic University of America Press, 1996.

———. *On Kingship, to the King of Cyprus*. Translated by Gerald B. Phelan, revised by I. T. Eschmann. Toronto: Pontifical Institute of Mediaeval Studies, 1982.

———. *Compendium of Theology*. Trans. Cyril Vollert. St. Louis: B. Herder, 1947.

———. *Commentaire de la seconde épître aux Corinthiens*, Introduction, translation and notes by A. Charlier. 2 vols. Paris, 1980.

———. *Commentaire sur l'Évangile de saint Jean*. Preface by M. D. Phillippe O.P.; translation and notes under his direction. 3 volumes published. Versailles-Buxy, 1981, 1982, 1987.

Tillard, J.-M. R. "La communion des saints." *La Vie spirituelle* 113 (1965): 249–74.

Tolomio, I., ed. See *Tommaso d'Aquino*.

Tommaso d'Aquino nel suo settimo centenario. Atti del congresso internazionale (Roma-Napoli, 17/24 aprile 1974). 9 vols. Naples, s. d. (1975–1978).

Tommaso d'Aquino. Proposte nuove di lettura. Ed. I. Tolomio (= *Medioevo* 18 [1992]). Padua, 1992.

Tonneau, J. S. *La loi nouvelle*. French translation with notes and appendices of St. Thomas Aquinas, *Summa theologiae* Ia IIae qq. 106–108. Revue des Jeunes. Paris-Tournai-Rome, 1981.

Torrell, Jean-P. *Inutile sainteté?* Paris, 1971.

———. "Théologie et sainteté."? *RT* 71 (1971): 205–21.

———. *Dieu qui es-tu?* Paris, 1974.

———. "Révélation et expérience (bis)." *FZPT* 27 (1980): 383–400. Reprinted *Recherches sur la théorie de la prophétie*, pp. 101–18.

———. "Dimension ecclésiale de l'expérience chrétienne." *FZPT* 28 (1981): 3–25.

———. "La pratique pastorale d'un théologien du XIIIe siècle: Thomas d'Aquin prédicateur." *RT* 82 (1982): 213–45. Reprinted in *Recherches thomasiennes*, 282–312.

——. "Les *Collationes in decem preceptis* de Saint Thomas d'Aquin. Edition critique avec introduction and notes." *RSPT* 69 (1985): 5–40 and 227–63.

——. "Yves Congar et l'ecclésiologie de saint Thomas d'Aquin." *RSPT* 82 (1988): 201–42.

——. "*Spiritualitas* chez S. Thomas d'Aquin. Contribution à l'histoire d'un mot." *RSPT* 73 (1989): 575–84.

——. "Le traité de la prophétie de S. Thomas d'Aquin et la théologie de la révélation." *ST* 37 (1990): 171–95. Reprinted in *Recherches sur la théorie de la prophétie*, pp. 205–29.

——. "Imiter Dieu comme des enfants bien-aimés. La conformité à Dieu et au Christ dans l'oeuvre de saint Thomas." In *Novitas et veritas vitae*, pp. 53–65.

——. art. "Thomas d'Aquin (Saint)." *DS*. Vol. 15, col. 718–73. 1991.

——. *Recherches sur la théorie de la prophétie au Moyen Age (XIIᵉ–XIVᵉ siècles): Études et textes*. Dokimion 13. Fribourg, 1992.

——. *Initiation à saint Thomas d'Aquin: Sa personne et son oeuvre*. Pensée antique et médiévale. Vestigia 13. Paris-Fribourg: Cerf, 1993.

——. *Saint Thomas Aquinas, vol. 1: The Person and His Work*. Translation of *Initiation à saint Thomas d'Aquin* by Robert Royal. Washington, D.C.: The Catholic University of America Press, 1996.

——. "Le semeur est sorti pour semer. L'image du Christ prêcheur chez frère Thomas d'Aquin." *La Vie spirituelle* 147 (1993): 657–70.

——. *La théologie catholique*. Que sais-je ? 1269. Paris 1994.

——. "Le savoir théologique chez saint Thomas." In *Recherches thomasiennes*, pp. 121–57.

——. "*Adoro te*: La plus belle prière de saint Thomas." In *Recherches thomasiennes*, pp. 367–75.

——. "La philosophie morale de saint Thomas d'Aquin." In *Dictionnaire d'éthique et de philosophie morale*, pp. 1517–23.

——. "La vision de Dieu *per essentiam* selon saint Thomas d'Aquin," *Micrologus* 5 (1997): 43–68. Reprinted in *Recherches thomasiennes*, pp. 177–97.

——. *Recherches thomasiennes: Études revues et augmentées*. Bibliothèque Thomiste 52. Paris: J. Vrin, 2000.

Torrell, Jean-P., and D. Bouthillier. "Quand saint Thomas méditait sur le prophète Isaïe." *RT* 90 (1990): 5–47.

Tricot, J. Introduction, translation, notes, and index, See Aristotle, *Ethique à Nicomaque*.

Tromp, S., ed. See Pius XII, *Litterae encyclicae*.

Trottmann, C. "Psychosomatique de la vision béatifique selon Guerric de Saint-Quentin." *RSPT* 78 (1994): 203–26.

Tschipke, T. *Die Menschheit Christi als Heilsorgan der Gottheit unter besonderer Berücksichtigung der Lehre des hl. Thomas von Aquin*. Freiburg im Breisgau, 1940.

Tshibangu, T. *Théologie positive et théologie spéculative*. Louvain-Paris, 1965.

Tugwell, S., ed. See *Albert & Thomas Selected Writings*.

——. "Editorial." In *Mémoire dominicaine* 2 (Spring, 1993).

——. "La crisi della teologia negativa nel sec. XIII." *Studi* n.s. 1 (1994): 241–42.

Useros Carretero, M. "*Statuta Ecclesiae*" y "*Sacramenta Ecclesiae*" *en la Eclesiologia de Santo Tomás*. Analecta Gregoriana 119. Rome, 1962.

Valsecchi, A. "Gesù Cristo nostra legge." *La Scuola Cattolica* 88 (1960): 81–110; 161–90.

——. "L'imitazione di Cristo in san Tommaso d'Aquino." In *Miscellanea Carlo Figini*, pp. 175–203.

Valsecchi, A., G. Colombo, and A. Rimoldi, eds. See *Miscellanea Carlo Figini*.

Vanni-Rovighi, S. "La vision du monde chez saint Thomas et saint Bonaventure." In *1274 — Année-charnière*, pp. 667–78.

Vannier, M.-A. "Du bonheur à la béatitude d'après S. Augustin et S. Thomas." *La Vie spirituelle* 698 (1992): 45–58.

———. *Saint Augustin et le mystère trinitaire.* Foi Vivante 324. Paris, 1993.

Vauthier, E. "Le Saint-Esprit principe d'unité de l'Église d'après S. Thomas d'Aquin. Corps mystique et inhabitation du Saint-Esprit." *MSR* 5 (1948): 175–96; 6 (1949): 57–80.

Veer, A. C. de. "Rm 14,23b dans l'oeuvre de saint Augustin *(Omne quod non est ex fide peccatum est).* Recherches augustiniennes* 8 (1972): 149–85.

Verbeke, G. "S. Thomas et le stoïcisme." *MM* 1 (1962): 48–68.

———. "Man as Frontier According to Aquinas." In *Aquinas and Problems of his Time,* pp. 195–223.

———. *The Presence of Stoicism in Medieval Thought.* Washington, 1983.

Verbeke, G., and D. Verhelst, eds. See *Aquinas and Problems of his Time.*

Verhelst, D., and G. Verbeke, eds. See *Aquinas and Problems of his Time.*

Vicaire, Marie.-H. *Saint Dominique et ses frères: Évangile ou Croisade?:Textes du XIIIe siècle présentés et annotés.* Paris, 1967.

St. Dominic and His Times. Trans. Kathleen Pond. New York: McGraw Hill, 1964.

———. "Relecture des origines dominicaines." *Mémoire dominicaine* 3 (1993): 159–71.

Villey, M. "La théologie de Thomas d'Aquin et la formation de l'Etat moderne." In *Théologie et Droit dans la science politique de l'Etat moderne,* pp. 31–49.

Viviano, B. T. *Le Royaume de Dieu dans l'histoire.* Lire la Bible 96. Paris, 1992.

Walgrave, J. H. "Instinctus Spiritus Sancti. Een proeve tot Thomas-interpretatie." *ETL* 45 (1969): 417–31.

Walsh, L. G. "Liturgy in the Theology of St. Thomas." *The Thomist* 38 (1974): 557–83.

Wéber, É.-H. *La controverse de 1270 à l'université de Paris et son retentissement sur la pensée de S. Thomas d'Aquin: L'homme en discussion à l'Université de Paris en 1270.* Bibliothèque thomiste 40. Paris, 1970.

———. "L'herméneutique christologique d'Exode 3,14 chez quelques maîtres parisiens du XIIIe siècle." In *Celui qui est,* pp. 47–101.

———. *La personne humaine au XIIIe siècle,* "Bibliothèque thomiste 46," Paris, 1991.

———. Introd., trad., notes and index, See Albert le Grand, *Commentaire de la "Théologie mystique".*

———. "Le bonheur dès à présent, fondement de l'éthique selon Thomas d'Aquin," *RSPT* 78 (1994): 389–413.

Wébert, J. *L'âme humaine.* French translation with notes and appendices of St. Thomas Aquinas, *Summa theologiae* Ia qq. 75–83. Revue des Jeunes. Paris-Tournai-Rome, 1928.

Wenin, C., ed. See *L'homme et son univers au Moyen Age.*

Werner, H. J. "Vom Umgang mit den Geschöpfen—Welches ist die ethische Einschätzung des Tieres bei Thomas von Aquin?" *MM* 19 (1987): 211–32.

Wohlmann, A. *Thomas d'Aquin et Maïmonide. Un dialogue exemplaire.* Paris, 1988.

Zedda, S. "Cristo e lo Spirito Santo nell'adozione a figli secondo il commento di S. Tommaso alla lettera ai Romani." In *Tommaso d'Aquino nel suo settimo centenario,* vol. 4, pp. 105–12. Naples, 1976.

Zomparelli, B. See Solignac, A., "Imperfection et imperfection morale."

Zum Brunn, É. "La 'métaphysique de l'Exode' selon Thomas d'Aquin." In *Dieu et l'être,* pp. 245–69.

Zum Brunn, É., and A. de Libera, eds. See *Celui qui est.*

Index of Scripture

Index of the Works
of Saint Thomas Aquinas

Index of Names

Index of Subjects

Saint Thomas Aquinas, Volume II: Spiritual Master was designed and composed in Electra by Kachergis Book Design of Pittsboro, North Carolina. It was printed on 60-pound Sebago 2000 Eggshell and bound by The Maple-Vail Book Manufacturing Group of York, Pennsylvania.